Taylor's Guide to
Growing
NORTH AMERICA'S
Favorite
Plants

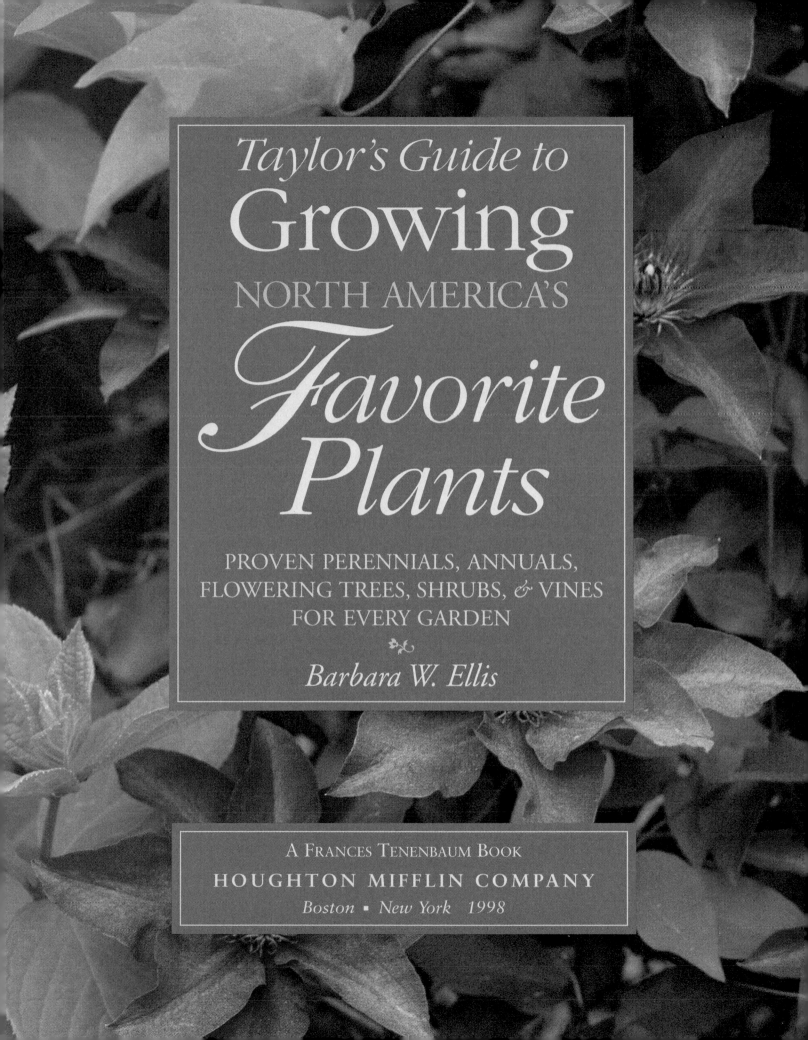

Taylor's Guide to
Growing
NORTH AMERICA'S
Favorite
Plants

PROVEN PERENNIALS, ANNUALS,
FLOWERING TREES, SHRUBS, & VINES
FOR EVERY GARDEN

❧

Barbara W. Ellis

A FRANCES TENENBAUM BOOK
HOUGHTON MIFFLIN COMPANY
Boston • New York   1998

Copyright © 1998 by Houghton Mifflin Company
Text copyright © 1998 by Barbara Ellis
Drawings copyright © 1998 by Steve Buchanan

For information about permission to reproduce selections from this book, write to Permissions, Houghton Mifflin Company, 215 Park Avenue South, New York, New York 10003.

Taylor's Guide and *Taylor's Weekend Gardening Guides* are registered trademarks of Houghton Mifflin Company.

Library of Congress Cataloging-in-Publication Data

Ellis, Barbara W.
    Taylor's guide to growing North America's favorite plants : proven perennials, annuals, flowering trees, shrubs & vines for every garden / Barbara W. Ellis.
        p. cm.
    'A Frances Tenenbaum book.'
    Includes index.
    ISBN 0-395-76535-8
    1. Plants, Ornamental — United States. 2. Plants, Ornamental — Canada. 3. Landscape gardening — United States. 4. Landscape gardening — Canada. I. Title.
    SB407.E67 1998
    635.9'097 — dc21   98-30678
                                                          CIP

Printed in the United States of America.

WCT 10 9 8 7 6 5 4 3 2 1

Book design by Deborah Fillion

*T*o my mother, Jane Ann Ellis, who started me digging in
the dirt and gave me my first garden.

*To my husband, Peter Evans, with thanks for his support
and encouragement during all the long days and lost
weekends it took to write this book.*

*And finally, to my nieces and nephew, who I hope will
become the next generation of Ellis-family gardeners:
Stephanie Liston, Diana Ellis, Jennifer Liston, and Daniel
Hanson.*

*Special thanks to my editor, Frances Tenenbaum,
and to Nancy J. Ondra and Nancy J. Stabile for their
enthusiasm, sharp eyes, and helpful suggestions.
And thanks to Deborah Fillion for her inspired design.*

CONTENTS

What are North America's favorite plants?

■ In the months that this book has consumed my attention, I've had ample opportunity to ponder the question of what makes a plant worthy of being called one of North America's favorites. There are some obvious choices—marigolds and impatiens, for example, as evidenced by the sidewalk sales that pop up at shopping centers everywhere in spring. But I didn't want simply to equate "favorite" with "most commonly planted." Instead, I wanted a book filled with information on proven, versatile plants that experienced gardeners swear by, whether they're valued for their showy flowers, long bloom season, handsome foliage, adaptability, ease of culture, or all of the above. You'll find all the popular favorites here—including irises, chrysanthemums, daylilies, dogwoods, peonies, and roses—plus a host of less well known plants that are well worth getting to know.

Because garden sites, styles, and taste vary so widely, ultimately each gardener needs to make up his or her own list of favorites. Not every plant in this book is suited to every site—or to every gardener. For this reason, I've tried to include as many plants as possible, from adaptable, easy-to-grow species to plants that need careful site selection and extra coddling to look their best. There are also suggestions for a wide range of plants for tough sites, from dry, sunny slopes to sopping wet spots. As you experiment with the plants in this book in your own garden, I hope you'll discover lots of new favorites.

I don't have just one list of favorite plants: my choices vary tremendously. They not only change from season to season and site to site, they also vary as I evaluate different attributes such as flowers, fragrance, foliage, or fruit. Seasonal favorites spring to mind first, and these include plants on nearly every gardener's list. I cherish the daffodils and tulips of spring, and adore the peonies, bearded irises, and astilbes that fill beds and borders in late spring and early summer. To some extent, though, these plants are out of sight and out of mind by summer, although iris and peony foliage provides an attractive foil for summer-blooming perennials. Ask me about favorite plants then, and daylilies, lilies, coneflowers, roses, and sunflowers are on my list. By fall, it's asters, chrysanthemums, and ornamental grasses.

Most of my favorite plants feature more than just showy flowers. Hellebores bear subtle rather than showy blooms, for example, but they come in late winter to early spring at a time when flowers are at a premium in the garden. Add to that their glossy, evergreen foliage that stays handsome all year—plus the fact that hellebores are very easy to grow—and you have a perennial I simply wouldn't want to be without. And what would I do without hostas in my shade gardens? Their flowers are a summer bonus, but their striking leaves are the backbone of the garden.

So, when selecting plants for my garden—and as I did for this book—I look at the flowers but also take into account a variety of other factors. When a plant blooms is one consideration, because flowers either unusually early or late in the season are especially valuable. Length of bloom is another: plants that flower for 8 weeks or more really pull their own weight in the garden. Fragrance—of either flowers or foliage—is another plus. Handsome foliage, attractive habit, and other ornamental attributes such as showy fruit, fall color, or interesting seed heads are also high on my list. In addition, I value plants that are long lived and reliable and look their best with minimal care.

I also have favorite plants for particular sites—diminutive thymes, ground-hugging sedums, and tiny hens-and-chicks (*Sempervivum* spp.) for hot, dry spots at the tops of walls, along pathways, and between steppingstones, for example. Hostas, heucheras, and lungworts (*Pulmonaria* spp.) for shade. Other sites yield other favorite plants.

Sentiment is another reason to add plants to a list of favorites. My mother's shady garden is filled with spring bulbs and woodland wildflowers, which you'll find in my garden today. Plants such as daffodils and Virginia bluebells *(Mertensia virginica)* not only harken back to the garden of my childhood, they symbolize my earliest concept of what a garden is. My early exposure to her woodland garden also fostered a deep interest in native plants, natural areas, and wildlife of all kinds, all of which influence the plants I choose to grow. I likewise value plants that have special meaning—hostas from a friend's garden in Washington, D.C., along with plants I brought from our first house in Virginia to our property here in Pennsylvania, for example. Each spring, peonies that once grew in my great-great-aunt Hattie's garden in Columbus, Ohio, and in my great-grandmother's in Newark, Ohio, flower in my own. Growing plants that remind us of where we came from, or of people who are important to us, adds a whole new layer of meaning to a garden.

How to Use This Book

The entries in this book are arranged in alphabetical order by botanical name. (If you are unfamiliar with botanical names, see "A Word on Nomenclature" below for an explanation of how they work.) The common name of the plant appears in large type at the beginning of each entry. To make it easy for you to acquaint yourself with new and unfamiliar plants, each entry features a pronunciation for the genus name (and species name, if applicable) along with a list summarizing bloom time, the sun or shade exposure that is required, and hardiness. Each entry starts off with a general description of the genus followed by suggestions for selecting plants. Selection criteria vary: In some cases I've organized the species by when they bloom; in others, by what types of sites they grow in. In heavily hybridized genera, such as peonies (*Paeonia* spp.) and daylilies (*Hemerocallis* spp.), I've included guidelines that will help you select from among the hundreds of cultivars currently available.

The "Site and Soil," "Planting," and "Care Through the Season" sections in each entry are designed to answer the questions gardeners always ask about a new plant. Where and when do I plant it? Will it bloom in shade? Survive drought? Do I cut it down at the end of the season? When and how do I divide it? Can I grow it from seeds? "Landscape Uses" includes suggestions for plants that make good planting partners and ideas for how and where to use the plants in the genus.

Don't overlook the general entries — **Annuals & Biennials, Bulbs, Ferns, Ground Covers, Herbs, Ornamental Grasses, Perennials, Shrubs, Vines,** and **Wildflowers.** These feature detailed information about how to select and grow plants in that group. They also include mini-encyclopedias of even more plants and how to grow them.

If you can't find a particular plant on the contents page, don't forget to use the index. All the plants listed in the general entries and anywhere else in the book are listed there by both botanical and common name. At the end of the book, you'll find a Techniques Glossary with instructions on essentials such as propagation methods, planting, and soil preparation. The Problems & Solutions Guide lists some common problems you may encounter and provides safe, organic solutions.

A Word on Nomenclature. Although botanical names may be intimidating at first, it's worth the effort to become familiar with them. While a

plant's botanical (sometimes called Latin) name refers to only that one plant, common names are notorious for being used to refer to more than one plant. In all the better garden centers and nurseries, you'll find botanical names on plant tags and signs, and if you use them, you have the best chance of getting exactly what you want. (Plants sometimes do get misidentified and labels do get switched!)

A plant's botanical name consists of the name of the genus it belongs to along with its species name, or specific epithet; its species is both words together. For example, *Echinacea purpurea* is the botanical name for purple coneflower, with *Echinacea* indicating the genus; *purpurea,* the specific epithet. *Echinacea purpurea* is the species. The genus name with the abbreviation "spp." (as in *Echinacea* spp.) is a reference to all the species belonging to that genus. Botanical names are always typeset in italics, although in many cases the botanical name also serves as the common one — hostas are *Hosta* species, for instance. After the first mention in a given section of text, the genus name is abbreviated: *H. venusta* or *E. purpurea*.

The word "cultivar" (short for "cultivated variety") refers to a hybrid or specially selected form of a species developed by gardeners. (Many gardeners use the words "cultivar" and "variety" interchangeably, but botanists recognize a difference: true varieties are variants that were found first in nature, while cultivars are of garden origin. For example, *Dicentra formosa* var. *alba* is a white-flowered variety of western bleeding heart.) Cultivar names are set off by single quotes. *Echinacea purpurea* 'Magnus' is an outstanding cultivar of purple coneflower with 7-inch-wide flowers. In many cases, the species name of a plant is dropped and the cultivar name is used with just the genus name. Often this is because the plant is the result of crosses between several species, and it's not clear what species it belongs to. Many hostas are listed this way — *Hosta* 'Kabitan' and *H.* 'Paul's Glory', for instance. Daylilies, peonies, roses, and many other popular plants are treated this way.

In order to keep us all on our toes, botanists reclassify plants with some regularity. As a result, plants can be found in books and catalogs under different botanical names. For this reason, I've included former names wherever I think they may be helpful.

Steps to Good Gardening

While much of a gardener's time is spent focused on caring for individual plants, there are a few fundamental principles experienced gardeners rely on, beyond knowing when to cut back a plant or how and when to divide it. They're the secret to successful plantings that look their best, while requiring a minimum of care. Keep them in mind, and you're well on your way to a thriving, glorious garden.

Get to know your soil. Take a trowel out and dig a few test holes. Learn where wet or dry spots are located and which sites have rich or poor soil. Decide what steps you need to take to improve your soil and what plants are suited to the conditions as they exist now.

Study sun and shade patterns. Watch the sun as it travels over your property during the course of the day. Note which spots are in full sun — at least 6 hours per day; 8 is better — and which are shaded for part or all of the day. (Keep in mind that sun and shade patterns vary throughout the year as the sun's position in the sky changes; you may want to take a day to observe sun and shade patterns in spring, midsummer, and fall.) Watch for spots that receive dappled shade or constant shade but good light all day long. Many plants also benefit from a site that receives morning sun and afternoon shade. Plan your garden and select the plants you grow according to the patterns of sun and shade you discover.

Match plants to the site. Use your observations of soil types and sun/shade patterns to help you decide which plants to grow. For best results, fill a site with plants that all thrive in the same or similar conditions. Delphiniums and yarrow (*Achillea* spp.), for instance, may look pretty together, but that doesn't mean the plants will be happy growing side by side. One wants rich, evenly moist soil; the other, dry and well-drained conditions. You're much more likely to have a successful, thriving garden if it is filled with plants that are all happy in the same soil and exposure. For more on matching plants to site, see the **Perennials** entry on page 222.

Care for your soil. Good soil makes a great garden. Get in the habit of adding organic matter to your soil and keeping the soil covered with a protective layer of mulch. In addition, avoid walking on the soil to keep from compacting it, which makes it difficult for water to drain through and for roots to penetrate. See "Soil Building" on page 224 in the **Perennials** entry for more specific suggestions.

Take time to look at your garden. Make a habit of walking through your garden every other day or so to observe the plants and to look for potential problems. Poke a finger in the soil to see if it is dry. Look under leaves and on stem tips to scout out evidence of developing pest populations. Watch for signs that a particular plant needs to be staked or is ready to be cut back. Keep an eye out for great new plant combinations that have popped up or bedmates that need to be separated at the earliest possible opportunity. Regular scouting trips also will keep you abreast of whatever care your garden requires to look its best.

Don't be afraid to experiment. Push the limits: Try a plant in a site where you've never grown it before. Plant something you've never grown. Buy two plants or divide one large clump, put them in different sites, and see where they do best. Combine perennials you've never grown together. While some of your experiments won't work, many will, and most problems can be easily corrected with a spade. The process of experimenting will make you a better gardener.

— Barbara W. Ellis

Achillea

Achillea 'Coronation Gold'

Yarrows

Achillea
■
(ah-KILL-ee-ah)
■
Late-spring to summer bloom
■
Full sun
■
Zones 2 to 9
■

■ Although yarrows have a long, rich history of herbal use — to treat wounds, to reduce fevers, and to control pain — today these easy-to-grow, long-blooming perennials are most likely to be found in flower gardens. Most yarrows produce their tiny flowers in dense, flat-topped or slightly rounded clusters (called corymbs) on tall, stiff stems above the leaves. They bloom from late spring into midsummer, and many bloom intermittently well into fall. Flower colors include pale to deep golden yellow, white, pink, rose-red, and salmon. The fernlike foliage is aromatic and may be green, blue-gray, or gray-green; some people develop a skin rash if they come in contact with it. While the tallest yarrows can reach 4 or even 5 feet in height, most commonly cultivated ones are between 1½ and 3 feet tall.

Yarrows make outstanding cut flowers, and few perennials surpass them as dried flowers — they hold their color exceptionally well. For long-lasting fresh or dried blooms, cut the flowers when about half their buds have opened. They can be dried upside down in bunches in a warm, dry place. Or let them dry upright in a vase with 2 to 3 inches of water in it. Do not replace the water when it is used up, and the flowers will dry in place.

SELECTING YARROWS

The genus *Achillea* contains many weedy species that aren't particularly ornamental. While these are fine for meadow gardens and wild areas, select named cultivars for garden beds and borders. Even the cultivated kinds have characteristics of their wild relatives: yarrows can spread rapidly into broad, dense clumps, and as a result they need dividing frequently.

One of the most popular yarrows is 'Coronation Gold', a hybrid that bears 4- to 5-inch-wide, mustard yellow flowers on 3- to 3½-foot stems all summer long. It tolerates a wide range of conditions, including hot, humid summers, and can be grown in Zones 3 to 9. 'Moonshine', another popular hybrid, has gray-green foliage and bears sulphur yellow blooms all summer on 1- to 2-foot stems. It does not tolerate heat and humidity as well and is best in Zones 3 to 8.

Several cultivars of common yarrow *(A. millefolium)*, a vigorous to invasive native species hardy in Zones 3 to 9, are suitable for the garden and bear flowers in pink, red, and pastel shades. These include 'Cerise Queen', 'Fire King', 'Summer Pastels', and the new Galaxy Series hybrids, all vigorous, mat-forming plants that range from 1½ to 2 feet tall. Woolly yarrow *(A. tomentosa)*, hardy in Zones 3 to 7, bears yellow flowers and remains under 1 foot tall. Because it demands perfect drainage, this species is a good candidate for the rock garden. It does not tolerate heat and humidity well.

Sneezewort *(A. ptarmica)*, which is hardy in Zones 2 to 9, is another tough, long-blooming species that doesn't look like the other commonly grown yarrows. Its leaves are narrow and lance-shaped, and its pure white flowers are borne in loose sprays on 1½- to 2-foot stems. Because it tends to be weedy, stay away from the species and plant only double-flowered cultivars, which have buttonlike, ¾-inch blooms — 'The Pearl' is the most popular.

SITE AND SOIL

Yarrows thrive in full sun and average to poor, well-drained soils — even dry or sandy ones. They also grow in the moister, richer conditions of the average perennial garden, provided the soil is well drained. Soil that is too fertile encourages lush, rank growth, resulting in plants that require staking and spread far too quickly. In heavy clay or where the soil may be too wet, planting in raised beds or on slopes is advisable. Loosening the soil deeply with a garden fork and adding organic matter such as compost before planting will also help improve drainage.

PLANTING

Add yarrows to your garden by purchasing plants or starting seeds, which are fast-growing and rewarding. Keep in mind that seed-grown plants are variable, however, so look for plants propagated by division or cuttings if you want a cultivar such as 'Coronation Gold' or 'Moonshine'. Another

option is to purchase seed-grown plants when they are in flower so you can see the color.

Space most yarrows 2 to 3 feet apart to give them plenty of room to spread. Space *A. tomentosa* considerably closer—8 to 9 inches.

CARE THROUGH THE SEASON

Once established, yarrows require very little care to thrive. They don't need to be fertilized and rarely need watering, since they tolerate considerable drought once established. Poor air circulation can lead to powdery mildew. Stem rot and rust can also affect yarrows. Prune out afflicted plant parts and destroy them, then dust plants with sulfur to help control these fungal diseases.

Tall cultivars and plants growing in rich, moist soil probably will need staking. Stake entire clumps rather than individual bloom stalks, as you would peonies. (See "Staking" in the Techniques Glossary for effective systems.)

Deadheading. Cutting off spent blooms is a worthwhile chore because yarrows rebloom, and plants will flower again in about a month after deadheading, thus lengthening the bloom season. Use pruning shears and cut the stems back to just above a branch—if you see new flower buds arising on the stems near the base of the plant, cut just above these.

Division. Yarrows are vigorous spreaders and will need dividing every 3 to 5 years. Dividing keeps the clumps healthy and dense, as well as in bounds. (Pulling up runners that spread too far is a temporary measure for keeping the plants under control.) To divide, dig plants in spring or early fall. Use a sharp spade to cut off the healthiest-looking portions of the clump, and discard older, less vigorous growth at the center of the clump. Replant the divisions in prepared soil or share them with friends.

Propagation. Yarrows can be propagated by division (see above), seed, or cuttings. Seeds germinate in 10 to 15 days at temperatures between 65° and 70°F. The seedlings grow fast—sow seeds indoors in early winter and the plants may bloom, albeit sporadically, the same year.

Take cuttings from the base of the plant as shoots emerge in early spring and root them in a mix of half vermiculite and half perlite. Cuttings taken in summer after the plants have flowered will also root.

LANDSCAPE USES

Use yarrows in sunny beds and borders with summer-blooming perennials such as coreopsis, daylilies (*Hemerocallis* spp.), and lilies (*Lilium* spp.). Their foliage contrasts nicely with ornamental grasses, yuccas, and bold-leaved perennials and annuals. For a drought-tolerant, lawnlike

ground cover on a dry slope, consider *A. millefolium*, which can be mowed and tolerates foot traffic. Or plant other yarrows in drifts as ground covers (admittedly tall ones), let them flower, then cut them down with hedge shears or a string trimmer. Yarrows offer an added bonus to organic gardeners: they attract a variety of beneficial insects to the garden, such as predatory wasps.

TOP *Achillea millefolium* 'Fire King'

ABOVE *Achillea millefolium* 'Summer Pastels'

Aconitum

Monkshoods

Aconitum
■
(ack-oh-NIE-tum)
■
Summer to fall bloom
■
Partial shade or full sun
■
Zones 3 to 8
■

Common monkshood
(Aconitum napellus)

■ Monkshoods are striking, long-lived perennials invaluable for adding rich blues and purples to the garden from late summer to fall. The common name refers to the hoodlike shape of their individual flowers, which are borne in showy, branched spikes. Another common name, wolfsbane, derives from a more sinister characteristic: the leaves, roots, flowers, and seeds of these plants are all quite poisonous; the roots, where the poison is most concentrated, were once used to poison wolves.

The most commonly grown monkshoods, which are also referred to simply as aconites, are clump-forming perennials grown for their erect, branched spikes of deep blue, purple, or blue-and-white flowers. White- and pale yellow-flowered selections are also available. In addition, monkshoods offer deeply cut foliage that is attractive all season long. (While they make fine cut flowers, monkshoods should be kept out of reach of small children for obvious reasons. Don't include them in arrangements that household pets such as cats might be tempted to sample, either.)

SELECTING MONKSHOODS

Although the most popular monkshoods are similar in appearance, planting more than one species or cultivar is an easy way to extend the bloom season at a time of year when garden color is on the wane in many plantings. Azure monkshood *(Aconitum carmichaelii)* is a popular species that bears its rich blue blooms from late summer through fall (from August or September to October) and averages 2 to 3 feet in height, although plants can exceed 5 feet. Hardy in Zones 3 to 7, it can survive in Zone 2 with protection. Common monkshood *(A. napellus)*, hardy in Zones 3 to 8, is 3 to 4 feet tall and bears blue-violet flowers in mid- to late summer, generally in July and August. *A. × cammarum* (formerly *A. × bicolor*), hardy in Zones 3 to 7, is also 3 to 4 feet tall. It bears blue, violet, purple, or bicolor flowers from mid- to late summer. Several cultivars of this hybrid species are available, including 'Blue Sceptre' and 'Bressingham Spire', which reach only 3 feet and need no staking. Wolfsbane *(A. vulparia)*, hardy in Zones 4 to 8, bears pale yellow flowers on 2- to 6-foot plants from midsummer to early fall (July to September).

SITE AND SOIL

Bloom season and color are reason enough to plant monkshoods, but these plants also relish a site in partial or dappled shade, which makes them even more valuable. They won't tolerate deep shade, but they will grow in full sun. A site that receives afternoon shade is best in southern zones, where monkshoods struggle with summer heat. (They won't grow well in areas where night temperatures do not drop below 70°F.) Rich soil that has plenty of organic matter and remains evenly moist, but not wet, is best. Tall monkshoods have heavy, brittle stems that can break in wind and rain, so choose a protected site.

PLANTING

Plant monkshoods in early spring or early fall. Dig the soil deeply and work in plenty of organic matter. Space them generously—established plants

resent transplanting and can be left in place for many years. For larger species and cultivars (over 3 feet tall), allow 2 feet between plants; smaller types can be spaced slightly closer, between 1 and 1½ feet. Handle the plants carefully: the large, fleshy, tuberlike roots are easily broken. Pot up or plant individual shoots that break off the clump with a piece of root attached. With luck they'll grow into full-size plants. Protect fall-planted clumps with evergreen boughs, cornstalks, or salt hay after the first hard freeze to prevent them from heaving out of the soil during winter.

Since monkshoods emerge late in spring, mark the location of the clumps with a permanent label. Otherwise, it's easy to damage the crowns inadvertently early in the season with a misplaced spade.

CARE THROUGH THE SEASON
In the right site, monkshoods need very little care during the season. Because they require evenly moist soil for best performance, and do not tolerate drought, water deeply during dry spells. Drought-stricken plants look diseased—the leaves turn black and curl, stalks die, and flowers fail to appear. Beyond that, feeding and staking are the two major chores you'll have to attend to. After the foliage has turned brown in fall, cut the plants to the ground.

Fertilizing. Monkshoods benefit from an annual spring feeding with a mix of well-rotted manure and compost. Spread a 1- to 2-inch layer around the plants, keeping it well away from the stems. If you like, top it in late spring or early summer with a layer of shredded bark or other mulch, again kept away from the stems, to help control weeds and retain soil moisture.

Staking. Taller monkshoods, and those growing in very rich soil, need staking to keep them upright and to protect the brittle stems. Arrangements of stakes-and-string or commercial staking systems such as hoops or linking stakes work fine, provided they're sturdy enough for these large plants. (See "Staking" in the Techniques Glossary for illustrations of effective systems.) Install them early in the season, before the plants threaten to flop. Add a second tier of supports, as necessary, for very tall monkshoods.

Division. Although happiest when left undisturbed, monkshoods can be divided in early spring or fall. Divide plants if they become overcrowded or outgrow their space. Since the seeds are difficult to germinate, division also is the best way to propagate these plants so you can share them with friends. Wear rubber gloves when handling the roots (rubbing the plant's sap on skin will cause tingling and numbness), and be sure to keep your hands away from your face, espe-

Azure monkshood
(*Aconitum carmichaelii*)

cially your eyes and mouth. Cut the clumps apart with a sharp spade and replant the divisions in prepared soil at the depth at which they were growing. Water thoroughly. Protect plants divided in fall with a covering of evergreen boughs or other mulch over winter.

Potential Problems. Monkshoods are occasionally attacked by verticillium wilt, a fungal disease that causes leaves and stems to wilt and turn brown quickly. Dig afflicted plants and prune out all diseased growth, and discard—do not compost—it. Replant the clumps in a new site with clean, uninfected soil that is well drained. Poorly drained conditions also can cause crown rot.

LANDSCAPE USES
Because of their height, monkshoods are best grown at the back of the border, although shorter selections can be placed farther forward in plantings. (If small children spend time in your garden, a back-of-the-border site will help keep monkshoods out of their reach.) Never plant monkshoods near the vegetable garden, where their somewhat turniplike roots could be harvested by mistake.

Common monkshood
(*Aconitum napellus*)

Combine monkshoods with other summer- to fall-blooming perennials, including asters, chrysanthemums, fall-blooming anemones (*Anemone × hybrida, A. hupehensis,* and *A. tomentosa),* and sneezeweed (*Helenium autumnale).* Plants that thrive in partial shade such as hostas, hardy begonias (*Begonia grandis),* and snakeroots (*Cimicifuga* spp.) make good companions, too.

Ajuga

Ajugas, Bugleweeds

Ajuga
■
(ah-JEW-gah)
■
Spring bloom
■
Partial shade or full sun
■
Zones 3 to 9
■

Common bugleweed
(*Ajuga reptans* 'Bronze
Beauty')

■ Also called bugleweeds or just plain bugles, ajugas are vigorous, easy-to-grow perennials most often planted as ground covers or edging plants. They bear short, dense spikes of tiny, two-lipped flowers in shades of cobalt blue to blue-purple. Pink- and white-flowered cultivars are available as well. Although the flowers are small, the display is striking for a few weeks in late spring or early summer. Ajugas have spoon-shaped, somewhat spinachlike leaves borne in dense rosettes. While most common ajugas have deep green leaves, variegated cultivars are also available. The foliage is about 6 inches tall; when in bloom, the plants range from 6 to 12 inches in height.

SELECTING AJUGAS
Gardeners treasure these ground-hugging plants more for their foliage and carpeting habit than for their flowers. One important consideration is the speed at which the plants spread. Common bugleweed (*Ajuga reptans*) spreads via fast-growing stolons, which are stems that run along the ground and produce new plants along their length. In the right site, it is a terrific ground cover; in the wrong one, it can be quite invasive, especially in southern gardens. 'Catlin's Giant' and 'Jungle Beauty' are large-leaved, vigorous spreaders that are ideal for covering large areas. Variegated cultivars still spread but are less vigorous than green-leaved selections. These include 'Burgundy Glow' and 'Multicolor', both with white, pink, and green leaves, as well as 'Silver Beauty', with gray-green leaves edged in white.

Both *A. genevensis* and *A. pyramidalis* spread less vigorously than *A. reptans*. *A. pyramidalis* produces stolons, but unlike *A. reptans* it does so only at the end of the season. Its cultivar 'Metallica Crispa' has handsome, crinkled, almost metallic-looking leaves that are dark green with ample amounts of bronze-purple. *A. genevensis*, hardy only to Zone 4, does not produce stolons but does spread slowly by rhizomes.

SITE AND SOIL
Ajugas grow in sun or shade, but a site with light to partial shade is best—a spot in the dappled shade under high trees is ideal, as is a site with morning sun and afternoon shade. Well-drained, average to rich soil that is evenly moist, but not wet, is fine. *A. pyramidalis* will tolerate wetter conditions than the other two species. *A. genevensis* prefers drier conditions, but it tolerates more sun than the other two species if it is in constantly moist soil. *A. reptans* easily spreads into grass, so avoid planting it along a lawn. Installing an edging strip (plastic, metal, or brick) between lawn and bed, along with trimming off wayward stolons, will help contain it.

PLANTING
Plant ajugas in spring or fall—or even in summer provided you keep them well watered. Space spreading types 12 to 15 inches apart; non-spreading selections, about half that distance. Close spacing is also best for variegated cultivars if your objective is a tight mat of plants in short order. Fellow gardeners who have beds of ajuga will surely have plants to spare, so don't hesitate to beg divisions if you want to start a planting.

Mulch to keep down weeds and to keep the soil moist and cool until plantings fill in. Pull weeds regularly so they do not get a foothold in new plantings.

CARE THROUGH THE SEASON
Like other good ground covers, ajugas remain attractive with a minimum of care. Leave the flower spikes on the plants to wither, or remove them if you have the time. In small plantings, pruning shears work fine for this—cut the flower spikes back to the foliage. Large plantings require a more efficient approach. Try hedge shears or a well-aimed string trimmer, or simply mow off the flower stalks with the lawn mower after setting the blade at its highest setting.

In poor soil, feed the plants with a light mulch of well-rotted manure—compost mulch is also a good way to feed the plants and enrich the soil at the same time. Water ajugas in times of drought. In fall, rake fallen leaves off ajugas to prevent the plants from being smothered.

Propagation. Expanding plantings is easy with ajugas, which can be divided at any time during the growing season. Simply dig the clumps, separate the individual rosettes, and replant. Another option is rooting cuttings taken from the stolons. In this case, cut the stolons just below a node and root them in a sterile, moist mix such as half peat moss and half vermiculite. Or simply cut off the small plantlets that arise on the stolons and grow them in potting soil until they are established enough to be moved to the garden. Since cultivars must be propagated by division or cuttings (they do not come true from seed), ajuga is seldom grown from seed.

Common bugleweed *(Ajuga reptans)*

Potential Problems. Crown rot, a fungal disease, can attack ajuga plantings, especially *A. reptans* and especially in the hot, humid conditions of the South. Afflicted plantings develop large dead patches or simply rot entirely. To prevent it, select a site with good air circulation and well-drained soil. If the disease does strike, remove infected plants and either move the healthy ones to a better site or improve conditions on the existing site and dust plants with sulfur to prevent the fungus from spreading.

LANDSCAPE USES
Plant ajugas as a ground cover around shrubs and under trees. They are also quite useful for holding the soil on sloping sites and will tolerate dry shade where lawn grass will not grow. Plant cultivars with ornamental foliage, such as variegated types and 'Metallica Crispa', as edgings or as accents in beds and borders by arranging them in free-form patches. These, along with *A. genevensis* and *A. pyramidalis,* are also attractive plants for shady rock gardens.

The less vigorous ajugas, such as *Ajuga pyramidalis* 'Metallica Crispa Purpurea', can be combined with other ground covers. Here it is growing with *Mazus repens* and white-fruited alpine strawberries (*Fragaria vesca* 'Albacarpa').

Hollyhock

Alcea rosea
■
(AL-see-ah ROSE-ee-ah)
■
Summer to early-fall bloom
■
Full sun or partial shade
■
Zones 3 to 9
■

■ The tall summer spires of hollyhocks are a hallmark of country gardens. Old-fashioned types have single blooms, but there are also semidouble and double-flowered cultivars with blooms that resemble small peonies. Flowers come in white, yellow, pink, red, and even dark maroon and range from 2 to 4 inches wide. The erect spikes bloom from summer into early fall as they grow ever taller: plants that begin blooming at a

Double-flowered hollyhock *(Alcea rosea)*

modest 2 feet may reach 8 or even 10 feet by season's end. Dwarf forms are also available. Large (8- to 12-inch-wide) lobed leaves form a mound of foliage near the base of the plant; smaller leaves are borne up the stems.

Hollyhocks are biennials or short-lived perennials. In the garden, they most often are grown as biennials, in which case the plants produce foliage the first year and flowers the second, after which the plants are pulled up and replaced. When grown as perennials, they are allowed to flower a few more years before being replaced. Hollyhocks typically reseed year after year in sites where they are happy. So-called annual hollyhocks are early-blooming selections (not true annuals) that will flower the first year from seed if started indoors in late winter.

SITE AND SOIL

Hollyhocks will grow in full sun or partial shade, although a site with at least 6 hours of direct sun is best. Average to rich soil is fine as long as it is well drained. Wet soil is fatal. In soil that is either too rich or too moist, plants tend to flop over and will need staking. Planting in a site protected from the wind, such as against a barn or other outbuilding, helps keep these garden giants erect, but good air circulation is also beneficial, so be sure to space plants several inches away from such structures. While they tolerate heat, hollyhocks can have difficulty with the combination of excessive heat and humidity characteristic of Deep South summers. Pale yellow-flowered *Alcea rugosa* is more tolerant of these conditions than is common hollyhock *(A. rosea,* formerly listed as *Althaea rosea)*. Southern and northern gardeners alike may want to try this beauty.

PLANTING

Add hollyhocks to your garden by starting your own from seeds or by buying plants. For the most dramatic show, plan on growing them as biennials, pulling out the plants after they flower the first time (in their second year). Older plants tend to be less vigorous and are more likely to be plagued by diseases such as rust.

Starting from seeds is easy, both indoors and out. However you grow them, barely cover the seeds, as light aids germination, which takes from 10 to 14 days at temperatures between 60° and 70°F. To grow hollyhocks as annuals, start seeds indoors in late winter, 6 to 8 weeks before the last spring frost date. (Outdoor sowing after danger of frost is past may also yield blooms the first year in areas with long growing seasons.) Hollyhocks grown as perennials or biennials can be sown indoors or out. Outdoors, sow seeds in a prepared seedbed in spring or summer up to

2 months before the first fall frost for bloom the following year. Indoors, sow in individual pots 6 to 8 weeks before plants are scheduled to go into the garden. That translates to midsummer sowing for plants that are to be moved to the garden in early fall, winter sowing to produce seedlings for spring planting. If you are growing hollyhocks as biennials or annuals, keep in mind that you'll need to start plants every year to ensure blooms every summer.

Hollyhocks are taller than they are wide and look best with fairly close spacing. Space seedlings or purchased plants 1½ to 3 feet apart. To get them off to a good start, keep the soil evenly moist until they are established.

CARE THROUGH THE SEASON

Once hollyhocks are in the garden, caring for them is an easy matter. Given a sheltered site and not-too-rich soil, they seldom need staking. If plants lean, stake the stems individually, using yarn or soft string to loosely tie the stems to their supports. Or use stakes and string to tie up entire clumps. Hollyhocks appreciate, but do not require, an annual spring feeding — a topdressing of compost, well-rotted manure, or a balanced organic fertilizer will do. Established hollyhocks survive dry conditions quite well, but for top-notch performance, water deeply in dry weather. Mulch helps retain soil moisture and keep down weeds, but keep it away from plant stems.

If you are growing your hollyhocks as biennials, pull up 2-year-old plants after they have flowered and replace them with new seedlings. For plants scheduled to bloom another year, cut the stalks down anytime their ungainliness outweighs the value of their remaining flowers.

To encourage reseeding, crumble a few mature seedpods on the soil surface in midsummer or just before cutting the bloom stalks down in fall. Bear in mind that self-sown seedlings will be variable. If you want a certain cultivar or color, purchase seeds. Self-sown seedlings are easy to move when young — either replant them immediately or pot them up. Avoid moving established, mature plants, which do not transplant well.

Potential Problems. Rust, a fungal disease, causes orange-colored spots on hollyhock leaves. In addition to disfiguring the leaves, it weakens the plants. Growing hollyhocks as biennials helps reduce the impact of this disease, as does a site with good air circulation. Pick off infected leaves and pull up severely infected plants. Discard, do not compost, infected plants. Dust or spray mildly infected plants with sulfur to control the disease.

Japanese beetles, along with various other leaf-feeding beetles, chew holes in hollyhock leaves and eat the flowers. Handpick these pests

Hollyhock *(Alcea rosea)*

Black-flowered hollyhock (*Alcea rosea* 'Nigra')

Musk mallow (*Malva moschata*)

and drop them into a bucket of soapy water. Or spray pyrethrin with 1 tablespoon of isopropyl alcohol added per pint of diluted mixture.

LANDSCAPE USES

Hollyhocks are classic components of cottage and country-style gardens. Plant them along buildings, fences, or walls—for a casual country look, set them against an unpainted outbuilding or board fence. They're especially effective when planted in large clumps that can be seen from a distance, so consider siting a planting that can be enjoyed from the house. Clumps planted along the back of a perennial border or in the center of an island bed are also effective.

Hollyhock Look-Alikes

Mallows (*Malva* spp.) are tough, easy-care perennials that have erect spikes of saucer-shaped flowers in rose, pink, or white. The individual flowers are smaller than those of hollyhocks, but the overall effect is quite similar. Hollyhock mallow *(M. alcea)* has 1½- to 2-inch flowers on 2- to 3-foot plants and is hardy in Zones 4 to 9. Musk mallow *(M. moschata)* has 2- to 2½-inch flowers on 3-foot plants. It is hardy in Zones 3 to 7. Both bloom over a long season, from early summer to fall.

Like hollyhocks, mallows will grow in full sun or partial shade, although full sun is best. Give them average to moderately rich, well-drained soil. Stake the clumps to keep them erect. Although mallows tend to be short lived, they self-sow and are easy to propagate from cuttings. Take cuttings from shoots at the base of the plant in spring, or take tip cuttings in early summer.

Alchemilla

Lady's mantles are grown as much for their handsome foliage as for their flowers. Common lady's mantle *(Alchemilla mollis)*, hardy in Zones 4 to 8, bears 1-foot-tall mounds of pleated, lobed leaves covered with tiny, soft hairs that catch raindrops and dew and hold them like beads of mercury. From late spring to early summer the foliage is topped by frothy, somewhat sprawling clusters of tiny chartreuse flowers. Alpine lady's mantle *(A. alpina),* hardy in Zones 3 to 7, is a ground-hugging, 6- to 8-inch-tall species with deeply lobed leaves edged with silver hairs and loose sprays of yellow-green flowers in summer.

SITE AND SOIL

Grow lady's mantle in evenly moist, well-drained soil rich in organic matter. A site that receives morning sun and afternoon shade is ideal. In the North, lady's mantles can be grown in sun or shade, but in full sun they need even moisture for best growth. Because the plants prefer cool conditions, heat can be a problem in the South

Lady's Mantles

Alchemilla
■
(al-kah-MILL-ah)
■
Late-spring to early-summer bloom
■
Sun or shade
■
Zones 3 to 8
■

Lady's mantles *(Alchemilla mollis)* and yellow-flowered sedums edge a path leading to a stunning specimen of everblooming, large-flowered climbing rose 'New Dawn', which bears fragrant, creamy white flowers.

(Zones 7 and 8), so plant them in partial to full shade—again, afternoon shade is especially helpful—and be sure the soil remains moist.

PLANTING

Plant lady's mantles in spring or fall. Space *A. mollis* 2 to 2½ feet apart; the smaller *A. alpina*, 12 to 15 inches apart. Water thoroughly, and mulch to keep down weeds and to conserve soil moisture. Plants may not bloom well the first year.

CARE THROUGH THE SEASON

Although lady's mantles are drought tolerant once established, watering in dry weather keeps them looking their best. Mulching helps retain soil moisture. If the foliage becomes unsightly by midsummer, simply cut the plants back by gathering the stems in one hand and cutting them to the ground with pruning shears. Then water deeply, and fresh new leaves will appear in fall.

Lady's mantles will self-sow, and seedlings can be left where they sprout or are easy to dig up with a trowel and move wherever you want them. The seeds are produced without pollination, so seedlings are identical to the parent plants. In rich, moist soil, the seedlings can become a problem. If they do, cut back the flower clusters as they fade to prevent self-seeding.

Propagation. Lady's mantles can be propagated by seeds or division. Sow fresh seeds outdoors in summer or early fall, either in containers set in a protected location or a cold frame, or in a shady nursery bed. Divide established clumps if they become too large or die out in the center. Dig plants that need dividing in spring before they flower or in fall, then cut the clumps apart with a sharp spade and replant.

Potential Problems. Slugs and snails can chew holes in the young leaves. See the box on page 166 in the *Hosta* entry for suggestions on dealing with these pests. Plants grown in full sun may wilt on hot afternoons, and within several seasons this may cause the centers of the clumps to die out. Dig and divide afflicted plants, discarding the center of the clump, and move them to a site that receives shade in the afternoon.

LANDSCAPE USES

Lady's mantles are attractive edging plants, especially when the flowers are allowed to spill onto walkways or over walls. They can also be used to edge a perennial border. Combine them with spring-blooming perennials such as astilbes or columbines (*Aquilegia* spp.). For an interesting foliage contrast, plant them with hostas, ferns, or lungworts (*Pulmonaria* spp.). Consider using *A. mollis* as a ground cover and *A. alpina* in a shady rock garden.

Allium

Alliums, Ornamental Onions

Allium 'Purple Sensation'

Allium

(AL-ee-um)

Spring to fall bloom

Full sun

Zones 3 to 9

■ Kin to onions, garlic, leeks, and shallots, ornamental onions are plants for beds and borders, not the vegetable garden. Also called alliums, they produce their small, starry or bell-like flowers in clusters, called umbels, atop hollow, unbranched stems. The clusters can be round and dense or loose and graceful, and they vary from 1-inch pompons to huge 5-inch balls. The grassy or straplike leaves are borne at the base of the plant and are onion scented when bruised, a testament to the plants' culinary relatives. The leaves of most species die back just before or after flowering, leaving a leafless stem and a hole to fill in the garden. Keep this in mind when siting these plants, and combine them with perennials or low-growing shrubs that will hide the yellowing foliage or fill the bare space at the base of the stems.

While many alliums grow from onionlike bulbs (albeit small ones), others produce clusters

Star of Persia (*Allium christophii*)

Lily leek *(Allium moly)*

of poorly developed bulbs that spread by short rhizomes to form small clumps. (For example, dig up a clump of chives, *Allium schoenoprasum,* and you'll find a tight clump of bulbs that really look more like fleshy stems that have hairlike roots attached at the bottom.)

Despite the oniony aroma that is given off when the stems are cut or the foliage is bruised, alliums make handsome cut flowers. Harvest the stems when about half the florets are open. Cutting the flowers the day before you need them and standing them in a tall container of water overnight will allow the odor to dissipate somewhat. The flowers can be dried upright in a vase with 2 to 3 inches of water in it. Do not replace the water when it is used up, and the flowers will dry right in place.

SELECTING ALLIUMS

The genus *Allium* is huge, comprising anywhere from 400 to 700 species, and contains handsome ornamentals as well as weedy species—wild onion or garlic *(A. canadense)* and field garlic *(A. vinale)* are both troublesome weeds. The list below is a guide to some of the more popular ornamental onions. In addition to a brief description, cultural notes worthy of attention and hardiness zones are also included. By selecting species that bloom at different seasons, it is pos-

sible to enjoy these bulbs from spring to fall. You'll find many more species and cultivars to choose from in catalogs of bulbs, unusual perennials, and rock-garden plants.

Spring- to Early-Summer-Blooming Alliums
This group includes the most common and widely planted alliums.

A. aflatunense. Persian onion. Round, 4½-inch-wide, red-violet flower clusters; 2- to 3-foot plants. One of the first alliums to bloom; similar to but much less expensive than *A. giganteum,* and the plants also tend to be longer lasting in the garden. 'Purple Sensation' is a hybrid selection similar to *A. aflatunense* that bears violet flowers on 3-foot plants. Zones 4 to 8.

A. caeruleum. Blue globe onion. Dark blue, 2-inch-wide flower clusters; 1- to 2-foot plants. Requires very well drained soil and a hot site for best results. Zones 3 to 8.

A. christophii. Star of Persia. Huge, starry, silvery purple, ball-like clusters 8 to 12 inches across; 1 to 2 foot plants with broad, strap-shaped leaves and showy seed heads. Good dried flower. Will reseed. Zones 4 to 8.

A. giganteum. Giant onion. Dense, round, 5-inch-wide, rosy purple flower clusters; 3- to 5-foot plants. Expensive and tends to be short lived in the garden. Zones 4 to 8.

A. moly. Lily leek. Loose, 2-inch clusters of golden yellow flowers; 12- to 15-inch plants. Needs very well drained soil that is nearly dry after flowering. Will grow in partial shade. Bulbs produce many offsets in the right conditions, eventually forming attractive clumps. Zones 3 to 9.

A. schoenoprasum. Chives. Rosy pink, 1-inch-wide cloverlike blooms; 1- to 2-foot plants with grassy, edible leaves that remain green all summer and are evergreen in warm climates. Clumps of poorly developed bulbs spread by short rhizomes. Tolerates light shade. Cut plants—foliage and all—to the ground after flowering to encourage reblooming and fresh foliage and to discourage reseeding. Edible flowers. Zones 3 to 9.

Summer-Blooming Alliums
With time, the summer-blooming alliums form broad clumps, and two species have foliage that remains green all season.

A. cernuum. Nodding onion. Nodding rose-purple, pink, or white flowers; 1½- to 2-foot plants. Grows in shade or sun and tolerates heavy (but not wet) soil or dry sandy conditions. Forms large, handsome clumps and naturalizes easily. Zones 4 to 9.

A. senescens. Round, 1-inch-wide clusters of mauve-pink flowers; 10- to 12-inch plants with

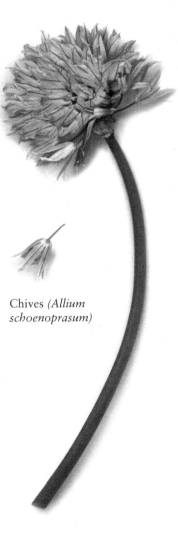

Chives *(Allium schoenoprasum)*

ABOVE *Allium senescens;* BELOW Garlic chives *(Allium tuberosum)*

strap-shaped leaves that are evergreen to 25°F. Spreads slowly into clumps by rhizomes attached to the bulbs. *A. senescens* var. *glaucum* has attractive, twisted, silver-blue leaves. Zones 3 to 9.

A. tanguticum. Lavender-blue, 2-inch-wide flowers; 2-foot plants with foliage that remains attractive all season. Spreads into clumps via rhizomes. Zones 4 to 9.

Late-Summer- to Fall-Blooming Alliums

One relatively common species blooms at this season, along with two relatively rare ones. Garlic chives *(A. tuberosum),* popular in herb and flower gardens alike, bears rounded, 2-inch-wide clusters of starry white flowers on 2-foot plants that have edible leaves. This species is best planted in rich, evenly moist soil. Deadheading prevents excessive self-seeding. The plants spread to form good-size clumps, which have small, poorly developed bulbs. It is hardy in Zones 4 to 8.

Two species, *A. thunbergii* and *A. virgunculae* (which may be the same species listed by two names), are worth searching out for their late-season rose-purple flowers. Both are about 8 inches tall and spread slowly via rhizomes to form small clumps. Their grassy foliage remains green all season. Both are hardy in Zones 4 to 8.

SITE AND SOIL

A site with full sun and well-drained soil is the rule for most alliums. (There are exceptions. See "Selecting Alliums" on page 13 for species that tolerate other conditions.) They will grow well in poor soil or rich and fertile loam, provided it is well drained. They also do nicely in soil that remains on the dry side.

PLANTING

Plant dormant bulbs in fall with the tops at a depth of about three times the diameter of the bulb. (Dormant bulbs are sold and shipped like daffodil or tulip bulbs, with no foliage attached. Plant them pointed end up.) Pot-grown clumps of alliums can be planted in spring or fall. Set the plants at the same depth at which they were growing in the pot.

Spacing varies according to whether the plants spread or not and whether you've purchased dormant bulbs or container-grown plants. Tall, nonspreading species look best when planted in clumps with the bulbs fairly close together—space *A. aflatunense* bulbs about 6 inches apart; *A. giganteum,* 1 foot apart. *A. christophii* is also best spaced 1 foot apart. Space smaller species that do not spread readily or spreading species purchased as dormant bulbs 3 to 6 inches apart. Container-grown plants should be spaced at a distance of about half their height.

CARE THROUGH THE SEASON

Care is minimal, at best. Cut off the blooms of species that self-seed rampantly, such as those of *A. tuberosum*. Chives *(A. schoenoprasum)* respond to an after-flowering haircut by sending up a new flush of blooms. Some alliums—*A. aflatunense* is one—have attractive seed heads that can be left in the garden or harvested for use in dried arrangements.

Resist the temptation to cut the dying foliage back before it yellows completely—it is making food for next year's blooms. With the right planting companions (see "Landscape Uses" below for suggestions), the foliage won't need to be cut off at all—it will just disappear into the emerging leaves of its neighbors.

Alliums occasionally become crowded and need to be divided (crowding reduces bloom) or simply need to be moved to a new location. Spring or fall is the best time for either activity; see "Propagation" below for details.

Propagation. Alliums can be propagated by division—either by dividing the rootstock or by breaking offsets off the parent bulb—as well as by seeds or bulbils. To divide alliums, dig the clumps in fall or in spring just after flowering. Separate the offsets or work the clumps apart with your fingers. Replant in prepared soil. Division is the fastest route to new plants and is the method of choice for cultivars, which may not come true from seed. Some species produce bulbils in the flower heads. These are small bulbs that can be planted like seeds and will yield blooming-size plants sooner. Bulbils are identical to their parents and can be used to propagate cultivars.

Grow alliums from fresh seeds sown outdoors in summer or fall as soon as they are ripe. Either sow in pots and set them in a protected location outdoors, or sow the seeds in a nursery bed. For reseeding types, such as *A. christophii*, simply sprinkle the seeds on the soil where you want plants to grow. Seeds will yield blooming-size plants in about 3 years.

LANDSCAPE USES

Plant combinations are everything when it comes to using alliums effectively. Combine spring and early-summer bloomers with plants that will hide the yellowing foliage yet set off the flowers—intersperse alliums with clumps of low-growing perennials and shrubs, or simply plant the alliums behind their companions. If the two plants bloom at the same time, so much the better, but that isn't necessary for an effective pairing. Alliums with foliage that remains attractive all year can be planted in clumps or drifts along the edges of perennial gardens and are also effective when combined like other alliums.

Giant onion *(Allium giganteum)*

A wide range of plants make good companions, including irises, daylilies (*Hemerocallis* spp.), lavenders (*Lavandula* spp.), thymes, hardy geraniums, catmints (*Nepeta* spp.), pinks (*Dianthus* spp.), and lamb's ears *(Stachys byzantina).* Low-growing shrubs, including *Potentilla* spp. and *Cotoneaster* spp., are also effective with allium flower heads poking up behind them, as are smaller ornamental grasses such as blue fescue *(Festuca glauca).* Alliums can also be allowed to grow up through ground covers. Tall types are dramatic floating a foot or more over surrounding foliage, but combinations where the allium blooms are just above, or mixed into, surrounding foliage and flowers are equally striking.

Anemone

Anemones, Windflowers

Wood anemone *(Anemone nemorosa)*

Anemone

■

(ah-NEM-oh-nee)

■

Spring to fall bloom

■

Full sun or partial shade

■

Zones 3 to 9

■

■ The genus *Anemone* is a charming and diverse group of plants with species that can add color to perennial borders and woodland gardens alike. Also called windflowers, there are anemones that bloom from spring into early summer and others that grace the garden in late summer and fall. Flowers, borne either one per stem or in branched clusters, are generally saucer shaped and have a central boss, or tuft, of showy yellow stamens. Blooms may be single, semidouble, or double and come in white, pastel pinks, rose-red, and scarlet as well as lavender- and violet-blue. (Anemone flowers don't have true petals; instead, the blooms consist of petal-like sepals.) The attractive, deeply cut to almost fernlike leaves are borne at the base of the plant, with some species also producing leaves on the wiry flower stems. Root systems are diverse, too: anemones can have rhizomes, fleshy or fibrous roots, or woody tubers.

SELECTING ANEMONES

Grouping anemones according to bloom season makes selecting, siting, and caring for them easier, because species that bloom at the same time tend to need similar care. As always, there are exceptions, noted below, including the popular florist's anemones along with a couple of the spring-blooming species.

Spring-Blooming Anemones

Plant these species in partial or half-day shade in light, evenly moist soil rich in organic matter (meadow anemone, *A. canadensis*, is an exception). Most are ideal for woodland gardens but will also grow in full sun if the soil remains moist. Since most of these species go dormant after flowering, combine them with other low-growing perennials or bulbs to fill the holes they leave. Once dormant, they tolerate drier conditions.

A. blanda. Grecian windflower. White, pink, or blue, 2-inch-wide daisylike flowers carried just above fernlike leaves; 6- to 8-inch plants. Spreads via woody, knobby tuberous rhizomes and goes dormant after flowering. Zones 4 to 8.

A. canadensis. Meadow anemone. Single, white, 2-inch-wide flowers from late spring to early summer; 6- to 8-inch plants. Vigorous to invasive native wildflower spreading by rhizomes. Good for naturalizing; plant in moist soil in either full sun or partial shade. Zones 3 to 7.

A. nemorosa. Wood anemone. White, pale pink, or lavender-blue, $1/2$- to $3/4$-inch flowers; 4- to 10-inch plants. Spreads by creeping rhizomes and goes dormant after flowering. Zones 4 to 8.

A. sylvestris. Snowdrop anemone. Single, white, 2-inch flowers; 1- to $1^1/2$-foot plants. Has fibrous roots with a woody base and spreads fairly quickly via root suckers. Zones 3 to 8.

Grecian windflower *(Anemone blanda)*

Japanese anemone (*Anemone × hybrida* 'Whirlwind')

Fall-Blooming Anemones

Three species, along with their many cultivars, are often collectively referred to as Japanese anemones—*A. hupehensis*, *A. × hybrida*, and *A. tomentosa* (sometimes sold as *A. vitifolia* 'Robustissima'). From late summer to fall, these bear branched clusters of flowers on wiry stems. The blooms are carried a foot or more above the foliage and wave in the slightest breeze. The showy, 2- to 3-inch flowers, ideal for cutting, can be single, double, or semidouble. Cultivars come in a range of pastels from pale to deep pink and white—all with a showy boss, or cluster, of stamens in the center. Plants grow from 2 to 5 feet tall depending on the species and cultivar. They have fibrous roots with a woody base and slowly spread via creeping rhizomes and suckers to form handsome clumps. Zones 4 to 8; *A. tomentosa* can be grown in Zone 3 with protection.

Plant fall-blooming anemones in partial shade or full sun in a site with evenly moist soil that is well drained and rich in organic matter. Afternoon shade is beneficial, especially in areas with hot summers. A site with good air circulation but some protection from wind is best—planting on the leeward, or sheltered, side of a fence or shrubs is ideal.

ABOVE Japanese anemones *(Anemone hupehensis)* with variegated Russian comfrey (*Symphytum × uplandicum* 'Variegatum')

BELOW Japanese anemone *(Anemone tomentosa)*

Anemone Relatives

Pasqueflower *(Pulsatilla vulgaris*, formerly *Anemone vulgaris)* resembles spring-blooming anemones and has similar cultural needs. Hardy in Zones 5 to 8, the 6- to 10-inch plants bear bell- to cup-shaped flowers in rosy purple, blue-violet, or white in very early spring. The leaves emerge after the flowers have finished blooming and have been transformed into attractive silvery-hairy seed heads. Plant pasqueflowers in full sun in rich, very well drained soil. The plants go dormant in early summer. Divide them only when absolutely necessary, because the roots are easily damaged.

Rue anemone *(Anemonella thalictroides,* formerly *Anemone thalictroides)* is a dainty wildflower native to eastern North America. In spring, it produces white or pale pink, 3⁄4-inch flowers above blue-green, fernlike leaves. Grow it as you would spring-blooming anemones—in rich, moist, well-drained soil in partial shade. Plants reach 6 inches and are hardy in Zones 4 to 7.

Pasqueflower *(Pulsatilla vulgaris)*

Florist's Anemones

Also called poppy anemones, these belong to *A. coronaria* and produce striking 2- to 3-inch blooms with black centers in vivid colors such as scarlet and violet-blue as well as white. The single or double blooms make stunning cut flowers, and the knobby tubers, which look like chunks of bark, are widely available at garden centers and in catalogs. The two most popular groups of florist's anemones are De Caen, which are single-flowered types, and St. Brigid, which are doubles.

Unlike other commonly grown anemones, these are neither hardy nor particularly long lived. In Zones 8 to 10 they can be planted outside in fall in full sun or partial shade in well-drained, somewhat sandy soil rich in organic matter. Add a protective mulch over the beds, but remove it in late winter. In the North, grow these beauties as annuals. They can be planted in spring, but for best flowering, plant several tubers in 6- to 8-inch pots in fall, then overwinter them in a greenhouse, cold frame, sun porch, or other location that remains cool but does not freeze. Water sparingly at planting time and until foliage appears. Once buds develop, water with a liquid fertilizer such as fish emulsion, then keep the soil evenly moist.

PLANTING

Plant the woody tubers for spring-flowering *A. blanda* in fall. Florist's anemones *(A. coronaria)* also are planted outdoors in fall in Zones 8 to 10, but in pots or in the spring in the North. Tubers for both species are sold in catalogs and at garden centers with spring-blooming bulbs such as daffodils and tulips. (Florist's anemones are sold for fall planting even in areas where they are not hardy.) Always soak woody tubers overnight in water before planting (at least 12 hours). Plant tubers of *A. blanda* 2 to 3 inches deep and 3 to 4 inches apart; florist's anemones, 2 inches deep and 8 to 10 inches apart. Set them on their sides, since it's hard to tell top from bottom. Other spring-blooming species—*A. canadensis, A. nemorosa,* and *A. sylvestris*—can be planted in early spring or fall, 2 to 3 inches deep and from 6 to 12 inches apart.

Plant fall-blooming anemones in spring, although pot-grown specimens can also be planted in fall. Select the location carefully—plants will thrive for years in one spot—and dig the soil deeply. Space them 2 or more feet apart, water thoroughly, and mulch to keep the soil moist and cool. Keep newly planted clumps well watered the first season or they can succumb to heat and drought. They will take a season or two to become established and put down enough root growth before they begin blooming in earnest.

CARE THROUGH THE SEASON

Spring-blooming anemones can be planted and left in place without any further care. Don't bother to cut down the dying foliage after plants flower; it will disappear soon enough. Divide clumps that become overcrowded—or that spread beyond where you want them—in late spring or early summer immediately after the foliage has turned yellow but before the plants disappear entirely.

Fall-blooming species require the same care as many other commonly grown perennials. Keep the soil mulched to retain moisture and keep it cool. Cut down the plants after they are killed by frost in fall. (The seed heads are somewhat attractive and can be left until spring, if you like.) Cover clumps with evergreen boughs or other protective mulch in areas with cold, dry winters. Clumps of fall-blooming anemones will need to be dug and divided every 4 to 5 years. Dig the plants in spring and discard the older, woodier portions of the clumps.

Propagation. Anemones are slow from seeds, which can be sown into pots and set outdoors in a cold frame or other protected location. Some types have a woolly coating on the seeds; remove it by gently rubbing the seeds on fine sandpaper. Propagate spring-blooming anemones by dividing the rhizomes or tubers in late spring or early summer, just as the plants go dormant. Fall-blooming types can be divided in spring or immediately after they flower in fall. While division is the easiest way to increase your supply of anemones, fall-blooming species can also be propagated by root cuttings dug in winter or early spring. See "Propagating from Root Cuttings" in the Techniques Glossary for more information on this technique.

LANDSCAPE USES

Plant spring-blooming anemones in shady beds and borders or woodland gardens combined with low-growing woodland wildflowers, bulbs, and ferns. *A. blanda* blooms with early-blooming tulips such as *Tulipa tarda* as well as grape hyacinths (*Muscari* spp.). Many shade-loving perennials make fine companions as well, including the smaller hostas, columbines (*Aquilegia* spp.), fringed bleeding heart *(Dicentra eximia),* lungworts (*Pulmonaria* spp.), and foamflowers (*Tiarella* spp.). Or try them in drifts under shrubs. *Anemone canadensis* and *A. sylvestris* can be used as ground covers.

Use fall-blooming anemones to extend the show in perennial beds and borders, or in the dappled shade at the edge of woodland gardens. Classic planting companions include asters, monkshoods (*Aconitum* spp.), *Boltonia asteroides,* and ornamental grasses.

Annuals & Biennials

■ Without a doubt, annuals are among the plants Americans hold nearest and dearest. Zinnias, geraniums, marigolds, impatiens, and petunias are summertime fixtures in the yards of even nongardeners. Rewarding and easy to grow, annuals add color whether planted in flower beds and borders, as edgings, in foundation plantings, in mixed containers, or in window boxes. Many flower from early summer to frost, while others provide a burst of color at a particular season. Biennials—foxgloves *(Digitalis purpurea)* and Canterbury bells *(Campanula medium)* are two—are less frequently grown than annuals but are almost as easy.

One of the best things about deciding which annuals or biennials to grow is that there's almost no commitment. Whether you start with seeds or purchased plants, the investment is minimal. And since annuals last only a season (biennials, two), it's easy to try new combinations or an entirely new selection each year. With annuals, you can change the color scheme of a garden every year, fill up empty spaces in a perennial bed or border, edge walkways with a ribbon of color, or fill in under shrubs while more-permanent ground covers are getting established. Both annuals and biennials make it a snap to experiment. Even if a particular plant doesn't do well in a given site, you've invested only one growing season, two at the most. Try it again in a different site next year, or never grow it again—it's that simple.

UNDERSTANDING ANNUALS
AND BIENNIALS

True annuals germinate, flower, set seed, and die within a single season, but gardeners use the term in a more general way. For them, annuals are plants that grace the garden for a single season and are killed by frost in fall (whether they set seed or not). A similar broader definition can be applied to biennials. In their first year, true biennials produce foliage and other growth that overwinters, such as thick roots or stems. The second year, they flower, set seed, and die. (Cool-weather annuals, which are sometimes planted in late summer or fall, overwinter as small seedlings or seeds, not nearly full-size plants as do biennials.) Many short-lived perennials are grown as biennials because they flower most abundantly the first

Zonal geranium (*Pelargonium* 'Salmon Queen')

time and peter out in subsequent years. Gardeners thus pull them up and replace them after that first flowering.

Don't confuse what a particular species is described as botanically with how it's grown. For example, botanists classify pansies *(Viola × wittrockiana)* as perennials, but gardeners grow them as annuals or biennials. And wax begonias are perennials, but most gardeners grow them as annuals (they are actually tender perennials grown as annuals and are hardy only in Zones 10 and 11). The discussion in this entry emphasizes how plants are grown, not what they're considered to be botanically.

Once you understand a few common terms, you can figure out how to grow nearly any annual. But while the terms below provide general growing guidelines, the way a particular plant is grown—whether it is grown as an annual or a perennial, when it can be planted, and how well it copes with the local conditions—will vary from region to region.

Cool-Weather Annuals. Sometimes called hardy or half-hardy annuals depending on how many degrees of frost they will tolerate, these are plants that thrive in cool conditions. They are grown for winter or early-spring bloom in the South but die out or stop blooming when the weather gets warm. In areas with cool summers—the Pacific Northwest, New England, mountainous areas, or more northerly areas, such as Zone 4 and north—they can last the entire summer. Pansies, sweet peas *(Lathyrus odoratus),* larkspur *(Consolida ajacis),* and pot marigolds *(Calendula officinalis)* are popular cool-weather annuals.

In warmer zones, plant or sow hardy annuals in fall for bloom in winter or the following spring. Or sow seeds or move transplants in late winter or early spring for bloom from late spring until the plants begin to languish in summer's heat. After that, pull them up and replace them with heat-tolerant plants.

In the North, cool-weather annuals are normally sown in late winter or early spring for spring to summer bloom. Some can be sown as soon as the soil can be worked (meaning it is no longer frozen and is dry enough for you to dig without compacting or otherwise damaging it). Others are best sown just before or on the last frost date (see "Scheduling and Frost Dates" on page 21 for more on these important gardening milestones). They can also be started indoors and moved to the garden as hardened-off transplants on or around the last frost date. If in doubt about whether it's too early to sow or plant, wait a week or two—seeds that sit in soil that is too cold will often rot, and transplants can be damaged or killed by a hard late freeze.

Warm-Weather Annuals. Also called tender annuals, these are the annuals that thrive in summer heat and fill gardens with color from early summer to fall. Seed for warm-weather annuals can be sown outdoors in spring after the last frost date, provided the growing season is long enough. They're also commonly purchased as transplants or started indoors and moved to the garden after the last spring frost date. Moving purchased or homegrown plants to the garden lets you get an early start on the growing season and results in blooms earlier in the season, but not all plants tolerate transplanting well. Zinnias, marigolds, cosmos, and petunias are all warm-weather annuals that do.

Tender Perennials Grown as Annuals. This is another category of annuals that's useful to understand. These are plants that are hardy perennials in southern zones (hardiness varies from plant to plant) but are killed by frost in the North. Tender perennials can be replaced each spring like other types of annuals, but they can also be overwintered indoors. Either take cuttings in late summer to early fall (before cool weather sets in) or dig entire plants and pot them up. A sunny, cool (60° to 65°F) spot is generally best for growing them over the winter months. Wax begonias, coleus, impatiens, salvias, and zonal geraniums *(Pelargonium* spp.) are all tender perennials grown as warm-weather annuals that are frequently overwintered indoors. Snapdragons *(Antirrhinum majus),* too, are tender perennials grown as cool-weather annuals, but they are rarely overwintered indoors. They will overwinter in Zones 8 to 11 and will even survive mild Zone 7 winters.

Biennials. Plants grown as biennials are normally pulled up after they have bloomed to make room for new transplants or self-sown seeds. Biennials can be sown indoors or out. Outdoors, sow seed in a prepared seedbed in spring or summer up to 2 months before the first fall frost for bloom the following year. Indoors, sow in individual pots 6 to 8 weeks before plants are scheduled to go into the garden. That translates to midsummer sowing for plants that are to be moved to the garden in early fall, winter sowing to produce seedlings for spring planting. Keep in mind that you'll need to start new plants every year to ensure blooms every summer.

SITE AND SOIL
For most annuals, cool-weather or warm-weather, along with many biennials, the ideal site is in full sun with well-drained soil rich in organic matter. (This also describes the ideal site for a vegetable garden, but then tomatoes, basil, and peppers are all grown as warm-weather annuals.) There are,

Impatiens
(Impatiens wallerana)

Pot marigold
(Calendula Bon Bon Mix)

however, some annuals and biennials that prefer partial or full shade. Annuals for shade include impatiens, wax begonias, ageratums, pansies, Johnny-jump-ups, coleus, garden balsam *(Impatiens balsamina)*, and sweet alyssum *(Lobularia maritima)*. Money plant *(Lunaria annua)* and Canterbury bells *(Campanula medium)* are two biennials that will grow in partial shade.

SCHEDULING AND FROST DATES

While the growing techniques for cool-weather annuals, warm-weather annuals, and biennials are basically the same, the scheduling changes depending on which type of plant you are growing and where you live. For example, in areas with a long growing season (the number of days from the last spring frost to the first fall frost), marigolds, which are warm-weather annuals, can be sown outdoors where the plants are to grow and still have plenty of time to flower. Farther north, the growing season may be too short for direct-sown plants to bloom adequately, making transplants a better bet. In southern zones, summers are commonly too hot for most cool-weather annuals, and you'll want to plan on late-spring replacements for them.

To determine optimum scheduling and to find out the best way to grow specific annuals in your region, ask your local Cooperative Extension agent or experts at a local public garden or garden center. Neighbors who garden can also advise you, and they may have excess seedlings to share. Watching public plantings sometimes works, too. If gardeners plant out display beds of pansies in fall in your city, for example, it's a good bet you can do likewise. While you're at it, find out the last spring and first fall frost dates for your area, which you'll need to know in order to schedule seed sowing and transplanting. (If you don't know your last spring frost date, it's possible to gauge it: it's about the time neighborhood gardeners set tomato transplants in the garden.)

Most annuals are sown in relation to the date of the average last spring frost. Marigolds are sown indoors 6 to 8 weeks before that date and transplanted outdoors after it, for example. Petunias, which take longer from seed, are sown indoors 10 to 12 weeks before the last frost. Other annuals are sown outdoors on or before that date. To determine the sowing date for a particular annual, count back the required number of weeks from your average last spring frost date.

To keep track of what you want to sow when, jot the information down on a calendar — a list of annuals to be sown on a particular date is really all you need. Also note outdoor sowing dates along with dates when you think plants will be ready for transplanting. Keep track of when

Blocks of annuals—rosy purple ageratum *(Ageratum houstonianum)*, red salvia *(Salvia splendens)*, pink impatiens *(Impatiens wallerana)*, compact white Madagascar periwinkle *(Catharanthus roseus)*, and towering, sweet-scented, white-flowering tobacco *(Nicotiana sylvestris)*—create drifts of color in front of a clump of fragrant, white-flowered *Hosta plantaginea*.

you need to sow biennials on the same calendar as well — late spring and early summer are common times to start the seeds.

The first fall frost date is more important to vegetable gardeners. Use it to find out the length of your growing season (count the days from last spring to first fall frost). Then use the growing-season length to determine if a slow-growing annual will have time to flower before frost. The fall frost date also is helpful for scheduling when to transplant biennial seedlings to their permanent location. They should generally be in place a few weeks before the first frost date to give them time to put down roots before the onset of winter.

PLANTING AND GROWING TECHNIQUES

In sun or shade, before sowing seeds or moving transplants to the garden, prepare the site for planting. Loosen the soil to a depth of 10 to 12 inches to accommodate the roots — most annuals have shallow, fibrous root systems, while biennials tend to have deeper roots. Spread 2 to 3 inches of compost or other organic matter over the site and work it into the soil. If your soil is poor, work a balanced organic fertilizer into the soil before planting as well. Rake the bed smooth and you are ready to plant. If you're planting in an existing bed, simply loosen up the soil surface, add a little organic matter, and rake smooth. For an early start on spring planting (when there are already too many garden chores to keep up with), prepare the soil the previous fall.

Direct Sowing

This technique is used for annuals that grow so quickly that indoor sowing isn't necessary. Sunflowers are a prime example. Direct sowing is also used for annuals that do not transplant well. These either have roots that are easy to damage or are plants that tend to languish in the garden if they are disturbed. Like seeds started indoors, direct-sown seeds are scheduled according to the last spring frost date. Warm-weather annuals are usually sown on or just after the last spring frost date. Cool-weather annuals are sown on or before that date.

Sow annual seeds in the garden where the plants are to grow by sprinkling them thinly over the site. (The thinner you spread them, the less thinning they'll require later on.) Mix a little white sandbox sand in with very fine seeds to make it easier to see where they've already been sown. Keep the seedbed evenly moist until seedlings appear. A daily session with a watering can is about all it takes if spring rains don't water the plants for you.

When seedlings have one or two sets of true leaves (these look like the leaves the plant will have at maturity, only smaller), thin them to the spacing recommended on the seed packet by pulling them up or cutting them off with scissors. Although destroying perfectly healthy seedlings seems like the antithesis of gardening, thinning is necessary to give the remaining plants the room they need to grow.

Starting Seeds Indoors

Sowing seeds indoors offers several advantages, not the least of which is that it gives you a jump on the season over direct-sown seeds. Setting out purchased transplants also gives you an early start, but you'll have a wider choice of annuals if you start from seeds, especially if you order by mail. Indoor sowing also makes it easier to control the environment around the seeds to provide ideal germination conditions such as just the right amount of soil moisture. Using clean containers and a special germination medium reduces pest and disease problems as well.

For indoor sowing, use $2\frac{1}{2}$- to 4-inch plastic pots and/or market packs, depending on the size of the plants you'll be growing. You'll also need flats to carry them in, enough wooden or plastic plant labels to have one for each pot, and a marking pen or pencil. If you are sowing annuals that are difficult to transplant, use individual pots. Many gardeners use peat pots for this

because the transplants can be set in the garden pots and all. Conventional pots work, too, provided the seedlings are handled carefully at transplant time — that is, gently tipped from the container with minimal disturbance to the roots; planted immediately into moistened, prepared soil; and watered in place.

Fill the containers with premoistened seed-starting mix. (To premoisten the mix, pour it into a large bucket and add a quart of warm water. Knead the mix with your hands to help it absorb the water, and keep adding water until the mix is evenly moist. When you squeeze a handful of mix, it should stay in a ball but break apart easily if you tap it lightly. If you add too much water, just add more dry mix.) Press the medium down lightly with your fingers. The final surface of the mix should be $1/2$ to $1/4$ inch below the top of the pot. If you are germinating very small seeds or seeds prone to damping off (a fungal disease that rots the stems right at the soil line and kills the seedlings), sterilize the soil surface before sowing. To do this, pour boiling water over the surface, then let the pots drain and cool before sowing.

To sow, scatter the seeds evenly over the surface of the mix. Handle large- and medium-size seeds with your fingers or tweezers, sowing three or four seeds per pot. For smaller seeds, fold a stiff piece of paper in half, pour the seeds onto the card, and then tap the paper lightly to scatter the seeds. Resist the temptation to sow too thickly, because that results in overcrowded seedlings that are difficult to thin and to transplant. Crowded seedlings are also more likely to be sickly. Either spread the seeds out over several containers or don't sow the entire packet.

The ideal sowing depth for each kind of seed will be listed on the seed packet. Once you've spread out the seeds, cover them with the correct amount of mix. A general guideline is to cover with a layer of mix that's about two to three times the thickness of the seed. Don't cover very small seeds; just press them into the surface.

Label each pot with the plant name and date sown. Using premoistened mix eliminates the need for watering the seeds immediately after sowing. To keep the medium moist and the conditions humid, set the pots in flats and loosely cover them with plastic suspended on a wire frame. (Dry-cleaner's bags suspended on a frame made from coat hangers work well.) Keep the flats out of direct sunlight, because temperatures under the plastic can quickly build up and kill seeds and seedlings. The optimum setup is to place the flats on an old table with fluorescent lights suspended several inches above it.

Caring for Seedlings. Check the mix in the containers daily — ideally more than once a day — and never let it dry out. When you need to water, water from below by setting the pots in a pan filled with an inch or so of room-temperature or warmer water; capillary action will draw the water up through the mix. When the surface of the mix looks moist (usually within 10 to 20 minutes), remove each pot and let it drain. This system also works well for watering seedlings; just allow the top of the mix to dry slightly between soakings. Watering from below takes a little more time than top watering, but it's worth it. You won't have to worry about washing out the seeds or knocking over the seedlings, and the mix will stay evenly moist, promoting good root growth.

Cosmos
(*Cosmos* 'Sonata Pink Blush')

Coleus
(*Coleus* sp.)

Marigold (*Tagetes*
'Safari Yellow')

Watering from below helps prevent damping off and also keeps other diseases from getting started, because the seedlings don't get wet.

Once seedlings appear, begin opening the plastic for a longer period each day, finally removing it entirely. The first leaves the seedlings will produce are the seed leaves, or cotyledons, which are generally oval. Once the first set of true leaves (the ones that look like miniature versions of the leaves the plant will have at maturity) appears, the seedlings are ready for thinning or transplanting. If you have sown only a few seeds per pot, use scissors to remove all but the strongest seedling. (Leave two widely spaced seedlings if you plan on transplanting them into separate pots once they've gotten a little larger. Some gardeners thin to a small clump of two or three seedlings, which they then treat as a single plant.) Once they have been thinned, most annuals can be grown on in the same pots until it's time to move them to the garden. If the seedlings become too crowded before they can be transplanted outdoors, move them to larger pots so their growth won't be checked.

If you want to save a large number of the seedlings that are growing in a single pot, you'll need to transplant them into individual containers. To do this, water the seedlings several hours in advance, and premoisten a light growing (not seed-starting) mix. Fill individual 2- to 4-inch pots or market packs with mix, and gently tamp it down. Next, carefully turn the pot of seedlings on its side and tip them into your hand. Carefully separate individual seedlings, using a pencil or plant label to tease the roots apart. With the pencil or label, make a hole in the medium that's deep enough to accommodate the roots. Then lower the seedling in place so that the point where the roots join the stem is even with the top of the growing mix. *Always* handle seedlings by holding a leaf, because the stem is very easy to crush, and a crushed stem is fatal. Gently push the medium back around the roots. Don't press the soil down around the seedling; just lightly tap the bottom of the pot once or twice on your work surface to settle the mix around the roots. Add a little more mix, if needed, to support the seedling, and label the pot. Water as soon as possible after transplanting. Keep transplanted seedlings out of direct light for a day or so to let them recover, then return them to bright light.

Start fertilizing your seedlings once they've developed their first pair of true leaves. Use a liquid houseplant fertilizer diluted to half its regular strength, or a fertilizer specially blended for seedlings mixed according to the directions on the label. Feed once a week for 3 to 4 weeks. (Supply it from below as you would water.) After that, you can use the fertilizer full strength every 10 to 14 days until the seedlings are ready for transplanting into the garden.

Buying Transplants

Of course, loading up at the local garden center is an easy way to fill your garden with annuals. (Avoid sidewalk displays at grocery stores and home centers, where plants receive minimal care and often are stressed by heat and drought.) Always inspect plants before you buy. Well-grown transplants will be compact and well branched and have healthy-colored leaves. Scorched or brown leaf edges indicate that the plants have dried out in bright sunlight or have been exposed to too much heat. Look for signs of disease such as black or brown spots or moldy or powdery patches. Plants starved for nutrients typically have yellowed lower leaves or yellow patches between veins. Check under the leaves for signs of pests (wear glasses if you need them for reading!) such as aphids, spider mites, or whiteflies. Tip a plant out of its pot to see if the roots are excessively crowded. Plants that are not yet blooming are generally a better buy than ones that are. They recover from transplanting more quickly, because they can direct energy to growing roots rather than to supporting flowers.

Transplanting

Most annuals are moved to the garden on or just after the last frost date. (Some cool-weather annuals, such as pansies and Johnny-jump-ups, go in earlier.) With warm-weather annuals, you generally don't gain much if you move them out too early, especially in a cold, wet spring. Until the soil warms up, they'll often sit and do nothing, and cool weather will check their growth; a late frost can damage or even kill them. Don't worry if you're not the first person on your block to plant; annuals that haven't been stressed by cold weather will catch up quickly to those that have.

Annuals that have been carefully tended indoors aren't ready for the garden: they need to be hardened off before they're transplanted. (Plants on outdoor display in a garden center have already been hardened off.) Hardening off is the process of gradually toughening up seedlings so they will be able to withstand conditions outdoors. About a week before you're ready to transplant, move seedlings outdoors for a few hours every day. Set them in a shaded location that is protected from wind. Leave them out for a few more hours each day, and gradually move them into a more exposed location. Be sure to keep them well watered during this process. The night before you transplant, leave them out all night. (Gardeners who work during the day should start this process on the weekend, and then leave the plants in a very protected location the first full day they'll be away.)

If possible, transplant on a cloudy day—moving plants while it's sprinkling is ideal. To transplant, dig a hole large enough to accommodate the roots, tip the plants out of their pots, set them in place, and firm the soil over the root ball. If the plants have roots that wind around the inside of the pot, use a knife to score the root ball on each side to encourage branching. Water each new transplant with a weak solution of compost or manure tea (see "Making Compost and Manure Teas" in the Techniques Glossary for directions on making a batch) after you've set it in the soil. If the weather promises to be cloudy for a few days, you're all finished. If it's going to be sunny, shade the plants with burlap or bushel baskets propped over the plants for a few days.

Watch the weather for the first week or two after transplanting. If a late frost threatens, cover warm-weather annuals with bushel baskets, sheets, or other coverings in late afternoon and remove the protection the following morning. Cool-weather annuals that have been properly hardened off will generally withstand a light frost, but they may need protection in freezing weather.

CARE THROUGH THE SEASON

Water annuals and biennials regularly to keep the soil evenly moist but not wet. (Most need about 1 inch of water per week—by rainfall or watering—for best growth.) An efficient way to water is to snake a soaker hose through the planting. It can be covered with mulch or just left on the soil surface until the plants fill in.

Weeding and Mulching. Weed annual plantings, especially direct-sown ones, regularly until they fill in. Otherwise weeds will outcompete annuals before they've had a chance to get started for the season. Mulch beds of annuals with shredded bark, chopped leaves, or other organic mulch to retain soil moisture and to control weeds. (Weed before mulching.) Keep the mulch an inch or so away from plant stems. In direct-sown plantings, don't mulch until the plants have produced several sets of true leaves and have been thinned to their final spacing.

Most annuals will grow just fine without supplemental feeding, provided organic matter and a balanced fertilizer were incorporated into the soil at planting time. If your soil is poor, or your annuals aren't growing vigorously, feed monthly with a balanced organic fertilizer.

Succession Planting. To lengthen the bloom season for annuals that flower for a short period of time, consider succession plantings. The easiest way to succession-plant is to sow seed at 2-week intervals where the plants are to grow. You can also start an extra-early crop indoors and follow it with outdoor sowings. This technique is most frequently used with fast-growing, cool-weather annuals such as China asters *(Callistephus chinensis)* and love-in-a-mist *(Nigella damascena)*. In the North, these plants are sown from spring to early summer, and sowing is timed so they will flower before the onset of summer heat. In areas with long, cool falls, try sowing again beginning in late summer for fall bloom. A site with afternoon shade will protect late-summer plantings from heat. In the South, try making succession plantings from late winter to early spring; many cool-weather annuals can also be sown in fall for bloom over winter.

Deadheading. Deadheading is another technique that lengthens bloom, because removing spent blooms before they form seeds encourages many annuals to produce more flower buds. Deadheading also prevents self-sowing, which may or may not be a problem depending on what you are growing. To deadhead, pinch flowers between your thumb and forefinger or snip them off with pruning shears or utility scissors. Never tug at the plant to remove a flower; this damages the roots and checks growth.

Ending the Season. Many annuals—even warm-weather ones—will continue to bloom right up to the first hard frost. If an early frost threatens, cover plants with sheets, bushel baskets, or other coverings in the afternoon and remove the covering the following morning once temperatures have risen. In many years, after protecting plants for a night or two, you will be rewarded by a return of late-summer weather and will be able to enjoy their flowers for several more weeks. When fall sets in for good, pull up annuals and any biennials that have flowered and add them to the compost pile. (First-year biennials don't need any special care to overwinter in areas where they are hardy.) To encourage reseeding, crumble a few seedpods over sites where you'd like the plants to grow next season. To protect the soil over winter, spread a layer of chopped leaves or other organic mulch.

GROWING GUIDE

The following guide to popular annuals and biennials provides germination and basic cultural information. Unless otherwise noted, all of the plants listed will thrive in soil that is well drained and rich in organic matter. Preparing the soil as described earlier in this section will ensure those conditions in most cases. If you have heavy clay soil or are gardening in a low, damp spot, consider installing raised beds to improve drainage. Loosening the soil more deeply and working in

Pansy
(*Viola* × *wittrockiana* 'Arkwright Ruby')

Johnny-jump-up
(*Viola tricolor*)

Wax begonia
(Begonia semperflorens)

more organic matter is also helpful. Unless otherwise noted, seeds will germinate in 1 to 2 weeks. Always harden off seedlings before transplanting outdoors.

Alcea (hollyhocks), *Canna* (cannas), *Dahlia* (dahlias), *Dianthus* (China pink, sweet William), *Digitalis* (foxgloves), and *Gladiolus* (glads; see under **Bulbs** on page 62) have individual entries elsewhere in this book.

Growing-Guide Key

WW. Warm-weather annual

CW. Cool-weather annual

TP. Tender perennial grown as an annual

B. Biennial

Sowing Schedule 1. Sow seeds indoors 6 to 8 weeks before the last spring frost date and germinate at temperatures between 65° and 70°F. Transplant hardened-off seedlings to the garden after the last frost date once the soil has warmed.

Sowing Schedule 2. Sow seeds outdoors in a prepared seedbed where the plants are to grow after danger of frost has passed. Or sow seeds indoors 4 to 6 weeks before the last spring frost date. Germinate at temperatures between 65° and 70°F.

Pot marigold
(Calendula sp.)

Ageratum spp. / **Ageratums, flossflowers**
WW. Full sun or partial shade; partial shade, especially in the afternoon, is best in the South. Sowing Schedule 1, but germinate at 70° to 75°F. Do not cover seeds with soil. Seeds can be sown outdoors where the plants are to grow after the last frost date, but plants are slow growing and frequently overtaken by weeds. Plants will grow taller in partial shade than in full sun. Pinch to encourage branching and a bushy habit. Deadhead. Water during droughts.

Amaranthus spp. / **Love-lies-bleeding, prince's feather, Joseph's coat, summer poinsettias**
WW. Full sun. Sow seeds in individual pots 4 to 6 weeks before the last frost date and germinate at 70° to 75°F. Barely cover seeds with soil. Transplant with care after the last spring frost date. Or sow seeds outdoors after the last spring frost date and after the soil has warmed. Keep soil evenly moist.

Antirrhinum majus / **Snapdragon**
CW, TP. Full sun or light shade. Sow seeds indoors 8 to 10 weeks before the last spring frost date and germinate at temperatures between 65° and 70°F. Do not cover seeds with soil. Germination takes 10 to 20 days. Select heat-tolerant

cultivars for summer bloom. Pinch seedlings to encourage branching and more flowers. Transplant on or before the last frost date in spring, earlier for well-hardened-off seedlings. In Zones 8 to 11, plant out in fall for winter bloom. Deadhead regularly. If plants stop blooming, cut them back hard (by two-thirds or one-half), then water and fertilize to encourage a new flush of flowers. Keep soil evenly moist but not wet.

Begonia semperflorens / **Wax begonia**
WW, TP. Partial shade. Sow seeds indoors 12 to 15 weeks before the last spring frost date and germinate at temperatures between 70° and 75°F. Do not cover the dustlike seeds with soil. See also *Begonia* on page 45.

Brachyscome iberidifolia / **Swan River daisy**
CW. Full sun. Sowing Schedule 2. Make successive sowings every 3 weeks for continuous bloom. Support plants with twiggy brush or let them flop. (Also spelled *Brachycome*.)

Brassica spp. / **Flowering cabbage, flowering kale**
CW. Full sun. Sow seeds indoors in midsummer for transplanting out in late summer to early fall once the weather has cooled off. Germinate at temperatures between 65° and 70°F. Do not cover seeds with soil. Keep soil evenly moist.

Browallia speciosa / **Browallia, bush violet**
WW. Full sun or partial shade. Sowing Schedule 1, but germinate at temperatures between 70° and 75°F. Do not cover seeds with soil, as they require light to germinate. Germination takes 14 to 21 days. Transplant after nighttime temperatures stay above 40°F. Pinch plants to encourage branching. Keep soil evenly moist.

Calendula officinalis / **Pot marigold**
CW. Full sun; partial shade in areas with hot summers. Sow seeds outdoors in spring before the last spring frost date, or sow in fall. Indoors, use Sowing Schedule 1. Cover seeds with soil, as darkness is necessary for germination. Pinch plants to encourage branching, and deadhead regularly. Keep soil evenly moist. Will reseed.

Callistephus chinensis / **China aster**
CW. Full sun or partial shade. Sowing Schedule 1, but sow in individual pots and transplant with care. Or sow outdoors after the last spring frost. Choose disease-resistant cultivars and rotate planting locations annually to avoid problems with soilborne diseases. Stake taller selections. Plant new seeds every 2 weeks for continuous bloom, or plant a combination of early, midseason, and late cultivars to extend flowering.

Campanula medium / Canterbury bells

CW, B. Full sun or partial shade. Sow seeds indoors 6 to 8 weeks before the last spring frost date to grow as a cool-weather annual. Sow seeds outdoors in late spring or early summer to grow as a biennial. See also *C. medium* under *Campanula* on page 64.

Catharanthus roseus / Madagascar periwinkle

WW, TP. Full sun or partial shade. Sow seeds indoors 12 to 16 weeks before the last spring frost date. Germinate at temperatures between 70° and 75°F. Cover seeds with soil, as darkness is necessary for germination, which takes 15 to 20 days. Transplant after the last frost date once the soil has warmed. Perennial in Zones 9 to 11. Cut plants back as necessary to encourage branching, compact growth and more flowers.

Celosia argentea / Cockscomb

WW. Full sun. Sowing Schedule 2, but indoors, germinate between 70° and 75°F. Barely cover seeds with soil. If sowing indoors, transplant with care, because a setback at transplant time leads to small flower heads.

Centaurea spp. / Annual cornflowers

CW. (*C. americana*, basket flower; *C. cyanus*, bachelor's button; *C. moschata*, sweet sultan.) Full sun. Sowing Schedule 2. Cover seeds completely, as darkness is necessary for germination. See also *Centaurea* on page 71.

Chrysanthemum spp. / Annual chrysanthemums

CW. (*C. carinatum*, tricolor chrysanthemum; *C. coronarium*, garland chrysanthemum.) Full sun. Sow seeds outdoors where the plants are to grow in early spring as soon as the soil can be worked. Or use Sowing Schedule 2, but indoors, sow 8 to 10 weeks before the last spring frost date. Sow crops at 3-week intervals for continuous bloom. Can sow outdoors in midsummer for a fall crop of flowers. See also *Chrysanthemum* on page 73.

Cleome hasslerana / Spider flower

WW. Full sun. Sowing Schedule 2, but indoors, germinate between 70° and 75°F. Self-seeds. Pull excess seedlings in spring or cut off seedpods as they form. Tolerates dry conditions.

Coleus spp. / Coleus

WW, TP. Partial or full shade; also tolerates full sun if soil is evenly moist. Sowing Schedule 1. Pinch plants to encourage branching. Remove flowers as they form. Keep evenly moist. Take cuttings in late summer of plants with the most attrctive foliage to overwinter them indoors. (Now listed as *Solenostemon scutellarioides*.)

Swan River daisy
(Brachyscome iberidifolia)

Canterbury bells
(Campanula medium)

ABOVE Cockscomb *(Celosia argentea)*

RIGHT Spider flower *(Cleome hasslerana* 'Violet Queen')

Coleus *(Coleus spp., now Solenostemon scutellarioides)*

Larkspur *(Consolida ajacis)*   Cosmos *(Cosmos bipinnatus)*

Gomphrena
(Gomphrena globosa)
with Japanese
anemones *(Anemone
tomentosa)*

Consolida ajacis / Larkspur, annual delphinium
CW. Full sun. Sowing Schedule 2, or sow seeds outdoors in autumn where hardy (Zone 6 and south). Outdoor sowing is best. Indoors, sow in individual containers and set them in the refrigerator for 2 weeks, then germinate between 50° and 55°F. Cover seeds with soil, as darkness is necessary for germination. Transplant with care. Stake tall plants with twiggy brush. Will self-sow, and seedlings can easily be moved in early spring with a trowel.

Coreopsis tinctoria / Calliopsis
WW. Full sun. Sowing Schedule 2, but indoors, sow seeds 6 to 8 weeks before the last spring frost date. See also *Coreopsis* on page 85.

Cosmos spp. / Cosmos
WW. Full sun. Sowing Schedule 2. If sowing indoors, place pots in the refrigerator for 2 weeks after sowing, then germinate between 70° and 75°F. Best in poor, well-drained to dry soil. Stake with twiggy brush or space plants closely so they will support each other.

Eschscholzia californica / California poppy
CW. Full sun. Sow seeds outdoors on or before the last spring frost date, or sow in autumn south of Zone 7. Can sow indoors 2 to 3 weeks before the last spring frost date, although outdoor sowing is best, since plants do not transplant well. Good in hot, dry sites with poor soil.

Gaillardia pulchella / Blanket flower
WW. Full sun. Sowing Schedule 2, but indoors, germinate at temperatures between 55° and 65°F. Good reliable bloomer for poor, dry soil. See also *Gaillardia* on page 119.

Gomphrena globosa / Gomphrena, globe amaranth
WW. Full sun. Sowing Schedule 2, but indoors, sow seeds 6 to 8 weeks before the last spring frost date. Grows well in moderately fertile to light, dry soil and withstands heat.

Gypsophila elegans / Annual baby's breath
CW. Full sun. Sow seeds outdoors in early spring several weeks before the last spring frost date. Or sow indoors using Sowing Schedule 2, but sow in individual pots and transplant with care, as plants resent being moved. Outdoor sowing is best. Make successive sowings every 2 to 3 weeks through midsummer for continuous bloom. In

mild-winter areas, sow outdoors in fall for winter bloom. Barely cover the seeds with soil. See also *Gypsophila* on page 138.

Helianthus annuus / Sunflower

WW. Full sun. Sowing Schedule 2, but when sowing indoors, use individual pots. Roots give off a chemical that inhibits growth of nearby plants, so best grown away from other annuals. See also *Helianthus* on page 141.

Helichrysum bracteatum / Strawflower

WW. Full sun. Sowing Schedule 1. Transplant with care. Do not cover seeds, as they need light to germinate. Average to dry, well-drained soil. Thrives in areas with long, hot summers.

Iberis spp. / Annual candytuft

CW. (*I. amara*, rocket candytuft; *I. umbellata*, globe candytuft.) Full sun; partial shade in areas with hot summers. Sowing Schedule 2, but indoors, sow seeds 6 to 8 weeks before the last spring frost date. Sow new crops every 2 weeks for continuous bloom. Deadhead to prolong bloom. Self-sows. See also *Iberis* on page 171.

Impatiens balsamina / Garden balsam

WW. Full sun or partial shade. Sowing Schedule 1. Self-sows.

Impatiens wallerana / Impatiens

WW. Partial or full shade. Sow seeds indoors 10 to 12 weeks before the last spring frost date and germinate at temperatures between 70° and 75°F. Do not cover seeds, as they need light to germinate. Transplant after the last frost date once soil has warmed. Pinch plants to keep them bushy. Can be propagated by cuttings.

Kochia scoparia f. *trichophylla* / Burning bush, summer cypress

WW. Full sun. Sowing Schedule 2. Do not cover seeds, as they need light to germinate. Self-sows. (Now listed as *Bassia scoparia* f. *trichophylla*.)

Lantana camara / Lantana

WW, TP. Full sun or partial shade. Sow seeds indoors 12 to 15 weeks before the last spring frost date. Seeds take 8 weeks to germinate at temperatures between 70° and 75°F. Pinch plants to encourage branching. Plant outdoors after the last spring frost. Grown as a perennial in Zones 8 to 11. In the North, root cuttings in late summer to overwinter indoors, or dig individual plants.

Lathyrus odoratus / Sweet pea

CW. Full sun. Sow seeds outdoors in spring as soon as the soil can be worked, or sow indoors 6 to 8 weeks before the last spring frost date. Before sowing, nick the seed coats with a nail file (avoid cutting into the seed or you may damage the embryo) or soak seeds in warm water for 24 hours. Sow ½ inch deep. Water regularly and mulch to keep the soil cool.

Lavatera spp. / Lavateras, tree mallows

WW. Full sun. Sowing Schedule 2, but outdoor sowing is best, since seedlings transplant with difficulty. Germination takes 15 to 20 days. If sowing indoors, sow in individual pots and transplant seedlings with care.

BELOW Impatiens (*Impatiens wallerana* 'Victorian Rose')

BOTTOM Sweet pea (*Lathyrus odoratus*)

TOP Flowering tobacco (*Nicotiana alata* 'Metro Mix')

ABOVE Love-in-a-mist (*Nigella damascena*) with lamb's ears (*Stachys byzantina*)

Limonium sinuatum / **Statice**
WW. Full sun. Sowing Schedule 1, but sow seeds 8 to 10 weeks before the last spring frost date in individual pots. Germination takes 15 to 20 days. Transplant with care. Prefers well-drained, light or sandy soil.

Lobelia erinus / **Edging lobelia**
WW. Partial shade. Sowing Schedule 1, but sow seeds 10 to 12 weeks before the last frost date. Germination takes 15 to 20 days.

Lobularia maritima / **Sweet alyssum**
CW. Full sun. Sow seeds outdoors in spring before the last spring frost date, or sow in fall. Indoors, use Sowing Schedule 1. Outdoor sowing is best, because plants do not transplant readily. Do not cover seeds, since light is necessary for germination. Self-sows, and small plants are easy to transplant.

Lunaria annua / **Money plant, honesty**
B. Full sun or light shade. Sow seeds outdoors in midsummer or in early spring before the last frost date while the soil is still cool. Mature plants do not transplant well. Self-sows. Hardy in Zones 5 to 9.

Matthiola spp. / **Stocks**
CW. Full sun. Sowing Schedule 1, but in the South, sow seeds in midsummer or autumn for late-winter to early-spring bloom. Do not cover seeds with soil. Thrives in cool conditions and is best where nighttime temperatures are in the 60s.

Mirabilis jalapa / **Four-o'clock**
WW, TP. Full sun. Sowing Schedule 2. Tolerates heat and poor soil. Tuberous roots can be dug in fall and overwintered like dahlias. Self-sows.

Moluccella laevis / **Bells-of-Ireland**
CW. Full sun or light shade. Sow seeds outdoors in spring before the last frost date when light frost is still possible. Or sow indoors using Sowing Schedule 1, but germinate at 55° to 65°F. Outdoor sowing is best. Do not cover seeds with soil. Germination takes 25 to 35 days. Self-sows.

Nicotiana spp. / **Flowering tobaccos**
WW. Full sun or light shade. Sowing Schedule 1, or sow seeds outdoors after the last spring frost. Do not cover seeds with soil. Germination takes 10 to 20 days. Self-sows.

Nigella damascena / **Love-in-a-mist**
CW. Full sun. Sow seeds outdoors in early spring. For a continuous supply of flowers, sow new crops every 2 weeks from spring through early summer. Or sow indoors using Sowing Schedule 2, but sow in individual pots and transplant with care, as plants resent being moved. Self-sows.

Papaver spp. / **Annual poppies**
CW. Full sun. Sow seeds outdoors in fall or early spring where the plants are to grow. Or sow indoors using Sowing Schedule 2, but sow in individual pots and transplant with care, as plants resent being moved. Barely cover seeds with soil. Self-sows. See also *Papaver* on page 220.

Pelargonium spp. / **Zonal and scented geraniums**
WW, TP. Full sun; partial shade in areas with very hot summers. Sow seeds indoors 14 to 16 weeks before the last frost date and germinate between 70° and 75°F. Zonal geraniums germinate in 5 to 15 days; scented types, 20 days or more. Pinch plants to encourage branching. Can also be propagated by cuttings. Take 4-inch cuttings in late summer for overwintering, or take cuttings from

Zonal geranium (*Pelargonium* 'Pink Parfait')

Grandiflora petunia (*Petunia* × *hybrida* 'Sugar Daddy')

Phlox drummondii / **Annual phlox, drummond phlox**

CW. Full sun. Sow seeds outdoors in early spring several weeks before the last frost date. Or sow indoors using Sowing Schedule 2, but sow in individual pots and transplant with care, as plants resent being moved. Cover seeds with soil, as they require darkness to germinate. Feed monthly and water regularly. Deadhead to prolong bloom.

Portulaca grandiflora / **Portulaca, rose moss**

WW. Full sun. Sowing Schedule 2, but indoors, sow seeds 6 to 8 weeks before the last spring frost date. Sow seeds in individual pots, and give a 2-week cool treatment in the refrigerator before germinating. Thrives in heat and drought. Best in dry, sandy soil. Self-sows.

overwintered plants in winter or early spring. Remove all but three leaves and let the cuttings dry for about 6 hours to seal the stem ends. Then dust the ends with rooting powder and stick them in pots filled with sterilized sharp sand. (To sterilize, pour boiling water over the sand.) Water thoroughly, then keep the cuttings on the dry side, but do not allow them to wilt. Pot in individual 3-inch pots once they have rooted and move them to a sunny spot. Nighttime temperatures of 50° to 55°F and daytime temperatures that are about 10°F warmer are fine. Transplant seed- or cutting-grown plants after all danger of frost has passed. Deadhead regularly and feed monthly, especially if they are being grown in pots. Take cuttings or dig and pot up plants in late summer or fall for overwintering indoors. Grow plants in a sunny window over winter in a cool (50° to 55°F) room. Keep the soil barely moist. Repot and cut back overwintered plants in late winter, then feed twice a month beginning in early spring once plants are growing actively.

Petunia × *hybrida* / **Petunia**

WW. Full sun or very light shade. Sow seeds indoors 10 to 12 weeks before the last spring frost date and germinate at temperatures between 70° and 80°F. Do not cover seeds with soil, as light is necessary for germination. Pinch plants to encourage branching. Plant outdoors after the last spring frost. Cut back plants that become scraggly in midsummer by one-half, then water and feed, to encourage new growth in fall.

Growing Edible Annuals and Biennials

Add an extra dimension to plantings of annuals and perennials by interplanting herbs such as basil, dill, and curly or flat-leaved parsley. For showy foliage, consider greens such as Swiss chard and even leaf lettuce. All can lend color, texture, fragrance, and flavor to plantings.

Basil *(Ocimum basilicum)* is a warm-weather annual. Grow it using Sowing Schedule 1. Thai basil, with its purple fall flowers, is especially ornamental.

Dill *(Anethum graveolens)* is a cool-weather annual that will reseed. Sow it, along with leaf lettuce (another cool-weather annual), as suggested for love-in-a-mist *(Nigella damascena)*.

Parsley *(Petroselinum crispum)*, a biennial grown as a cool-weather annual, can be sown indoors in late winter or outdoors several weeks before the last spring frost date when the soil is still cool. Soak the seeds for 24 hours in warm water before sowing.

Swiss chard *(Beta vulgaris* ssp. *cicla)* is also a cool-weather annual, but unlike lettuce and dill it tolerates summer heat. Sow it using Sowing Schedule 2, but seeds can be sown outdoors a week or two before the last frost date. Cultivars with red leaves and stems, or with rainbow-colored ones, are especially pretty.

Creeping zinnia *(Sanvitalia procumbens)*

Zinnia (*Zinnia elegans* 'Peter Pan Orange')

French marigolds (*Tagetes* 'Aurora Light Yellow')
with petunia 'Primetime Red Vein'

Narrow-leaved zinnia (*Zinnia haageana*,
formerly Z. *angustifolia)*

Johnny-jump-up *(Viola tricolor)*

Salvia spp. / Salvias, sages
WW. Full sun. Sowing Schedule 1, but germinate
between 70° and 75°F. Sow seed on soil surface.
See also *Salvia* on page 268.

Sanvitalia procumbens / Creeping zinnia
WW. Full sun. Sowing Schedule 2. Do not cover
seeds, as light is necessary for germination. Plants
resent being moved, so transplant with care.

Tagetes spp. / Marigolds
WW. Full sun; afternoon shade in the South. Sowing Schedule 1, but germinate between 70° and
75°F. Or sow all but African marigolds outdoors
on the last spring frost date in Zone 7 and south.
Deadhead to prolong bloom.

Tithonia rotundifolia / Mexican sunflower
WW. Full sun. Sowing Schedule 2, but indoors, sow seeds 6 to 8 weeks before the last spring frost date. Surface-sow, since light aids germination. Tolerates heat and drought.

Tropaeolum majus / Nasturtium
CW. Full sun. Sowing Schedule 2. Outdoor sowing is best, because plants resent transplanting. If sowing indoors, use individual pots and transplant with care. Cover seeds with soil, as they require darkness for germination. Poor, well-drained soil is best. Best in areas with cool summers. Can be propagated by cuttings taken in summer, and some cultivars can only be propagated in this manner. Cuttings also work for overwintering outstanding forms indoors. Climbing types require a trellis.

Verbena spp. / Verbenas
WW. Full sun. Sow seeds indoors 12 to 14 weeks before the last spring frost date and germinate at temperatures between 70° and 75°F. Cover seeds with soil, as darkness is required for germination. See also *Verbena* on page 290.

Viola tricolor / Johnny-jump-up
CW. Partial shade; full sun in areas with cool summers. Sowing Schedule 1, but sow seeds 10 to 12 weeks before the last spring frost date. Or sow outdoors in late summer or fall for bloom the following year. Cover seeds with soil, as they need darkness to germinate. Perennials grown as hardy annuals. Cut back plants in midsummer when they get scraggly; this will also curtail reseeding. Plants die out by midsummer in areas with hot summers. Self-sows.

Viola × wittrockiana / Pansy
CW. Full sun or partial shade. Sowing Schedule 1, but sow seeds 10 to 12 weeks before the last spring frost date. In the South (Zones 7 to 10), seeds can be sown in midsummer and seedlings planted out in early fall for late-winter to early-spring bloom. Cover seeds with soil, as they need darkness to germinate. Perennials grown as hardy annuals. Deadhead (or pick flowers for bouquets) to keep plants blooming. Dies out by midsummer in areas with hot summers.

Zinnia spp. / Zinnias
WW. Full sun. Sowing Schedule 2, but indoors, germinate between 70° and 75°F and transplant with care. Transplanting can cause double-flowered forms to revert to singles, so outdoor sowing is best. Pinch plants to encourage branching and bushy growth. Deadhead regularly to keep them blooming.

Annual Vines

To cover a trellis or fence with color, or to quickly hide an eyesore, consider growing annual vines. The following can be grown on a sturdy trellis or fence but can also be supported on strings or plastic netting hung on a building. Trellises can be erected at the back of a flower border, and vines will also grow up pole tepees or pergolas erected in the center of a bed. Whatever you use, install the support at planting time. In addition to the plants listed below, consider vining forms of nasturtiums *(Tropaeolum majus)* and sweet peas *(Lathyrus odoratus).*

Dolichos lablab / Hyacinth bean
WW, TP vine. Full sun. Sowing Schedule 2, but indoors, sow seeds in individual pots and transplant with care.

Ipomoea spp. / Morning glories
WW, TP vine. Full sun. Sowing Schedule 2. Before sowing, nick the seed coats with a nail file (avoid cutting into the seed or you may damage the embryo) or soak seeds in warm water for 24 hours. Best in average or sandy soil, since plants in rich, fertile conditions produce fewer flowers. Do not fertilize. Popular species include morning glory *(I. tricolor* and *I. purpurea),* cardinal climber *(I. × multifida),* and moonflower *(I. alba,* also listed as *Calonyction aculeatum).*

Phaseolus coccineus / Scarlet runner bean
WW, TP vine. Full sun. Sowing Schedule 2, but indoors, sow seeds in individual pots. Requires a trellis. Beans are edible and best if picked when young. Picking also encourages new flowers.

Thunbergia alata / Black-eyed Susan vine
WW. TP vine. Full sun. Sowing Schedule 2, but indoors, sow seeds 6 to 8 weeks before the last spring frost date.

Morning glories *(Ipomoea tricolor)* with sunflowers *(Helianthus annuus)*

Aquilegia

Columbines

Aquilegia
■
(ack-will-EE-gee-ah)
■
Late-spring to summer
bloom
■
Full sun or partial shade
■
Zones 3 to 9
■

■ Colorful columbines bear their graceful flowers on wiry stems above mounds of attractive, lacy foliage from late spring into summer. They are equally at home in full sun or dappled shade. The blooms come in a wide range of colors, including true blue and violet as well as white, yellow, maroon, pink, lavender, and red. Many selections have bicolor flowers, and there are double-flowered columbines as well.

Over the years, the uniquely shaped blooms have suggested a variety of imaginative common names. The flowers consist of five petals, each forming a cuplike shape below the stamens. The petals narrow further into a hollow spur, which can be long or short, that sticks out behind the bloom. Five petal-like sepals are attached behind the true petals. (In bicolored columbines, petals and sepals are generally different colors.) The word "columbine" is from the Latin *columbinus,* meaning "like a dove," or *columba,* meaning "dove." When looked at from above, the petals of short-spurred types resemble doves with their tails in the air, hence the common names doves-in-a-ring and doves-round-a-dish. A common name for *Aquilegia vulgaris,* granny's bonnet, refers to its flaring, bonnetlike petals. Our native red-and-yellow wild columbine *(A. canadensis)* has been called meetinghouses because the spurs suggest a circle of people with heads bent together in prayer.

While the tallest columbines range from 3 to 4 feet, most are between 1½ and 3 feet in height. Dwarf selections, as small as 6 inches, are also available. The plants are mound shaped, with attractive, one-, two-, or three-part leaves that are often deeply lobed. The foliage ranges from rich green to silver-, gray-, or blue-green and is often silvery underneath. The flowers are borne above the foliage and either dangle or point upward, depending on the plant.

SELECTING COLUMBINES

Both hybrid and species columbines make effective additions to the garden. The best choices ultimately depend on a variety of factors—what colors or bloom shapes appeal to you, the height required for a particular use, or the color scheme of a bed or border, for example.

Of the hybrid columbines, the long-spurred types such as McKana and Music Series hybrids are the most popular. Generally available in mixes of solid colors and bicolors, some are also sold in separate colors, a useful option for gardeners trying to color-coordinate a border. While most hybrids are 2 to 2½ feet tall, earning them a place in mid-border, dwarf hybrids ranging from 15 to as little as 4 inches (Dwarf Fantasy Series) are also available. There are double-flowered, sometimes called carnation-flowered, hybrids, too.

Many columbine species are especially valuable because of their adaptability. All are hardy in Zones 3 to 8 unless otherwise noted. Blue-violet-flowered alpine columbine *(A. alpina)* grows well in shade and blooms in midsummer on 1- to 2-foot plants. Blue-and-white Rocky Mountain columbine *(A. caerulea)* tolerates both heat and drought. Plants range from 1½ to 3 feet in

Columbine (*Aquilegia* Music Series hybrid)

height. Golden columbine (*A. chrysantha*) is another heat-tolerant species and a good choice for gardeners in southern zones. Plants grow from 3 to 4 feet in height and are hardy in Zones 3 to 9. ('Texas Gold' is an especially heat-tolerant selection released by Texas A&M University.) They are also shade tolerant. Wild columbine (*A. canadensis*), native to the eastern United States, bears nodding, red-and-yellow flowers on 1- to 3-foot plants. In the wild, plants grow in relatively dry soil in rocky woods and on ledges — even appearing improbably between rocks where no soil seems to exist. Fortunately, it adapts easily to well-drained garden soil and tolerates shade or sun. Fan columbine (*A. flabellata*) produces long-spurred, lilac-blue flowers with white tips atop dense, compact, 18-inch plants with blue-green foliage and is hardy in Zones 3 to 9.

Keep in mind that columbines are not long-lived plants — 2 to 4 years is about average, although in good conditions plants can last considerably longer. Older plants tend to become woody at the base and will not bloom as well as younger ones, so plan on replacing columbines every few years. Fortunately, they are easy to grow from seed.

SITE AND SOIL

Columbines thrive in a site with average to light soil that is well drained and rich in organic matter and yet remains evenly moist. If you have heavy clay, grow them in raised beds or double-dig and add plenty of organic matter to ensure good drainage. The plants have long, carrotlike taproots that allow them to delve deeply for water during dry spells.

Select a spot in full sun or partial shade. Plants in full sun bloom more and are more robust and more compact than those grown in shade. Flowers last longer in partial shade, however. In southern zones, dappled shade, particularly in the afternoon, is best because of the heat protection it affords. Taller columbines benefit from a site with wind protection provided by a hedge or other barrier.

PLANTING

Add columbines to your garden by starting seeds or by buying plants. One advantage of starting with plants is that you can see the color and shape of the flowers before you buy. For best results, buy small plants that have not yet had a chance to become root bound. (Roots crowding out the hole in the bottom of the pot signal a root-bound plant.) Space most columbines 15 to 18 inches apart. Allow somewhat more distance between taller selections; as little as 8 to 9 inches between dwarf plants.

Wild columbine
(*Aquilegia canadensis*)

CARE THROUGH THE SEASON

Routine care is minimal. Pinching off spent flowers helps prolong bloom and reduces reseeding, but it is entirely optional. (The seed heads are somewhat attractive in their own right.) The plants don't need staking. Cut the foliage back at the end of summer, after it turns yellow. Do this in midsummer in southern zones if plants have been plagued by leaf miners or other pests. New foliage will appear in fall once cool temperatures arrive.

Because of their deep taproots, it's best to avoid transplanting mature clumps of columbines, but seedlings are easy to move, especially in early spring. It is possible to divide columbines. In early spring, carefully dig clumps that need dividing, then use a sharp knife to cut off side plants with a root attached. Plant the divisions in a shady nursery bed in sandy soil until they become established, then move them to their permanent locations.

Any gardener who grows columbines from seed — or finds self-sown seedlings popping up in the garden — will discover that these plants are promiscuous. Nearly any columbine will cross with any other, and seed collected from a plant may not resemble it. (Some beautiful hybrids may result from this process, as well as some downright ugly ones.) If you are growing species and plan on collecting seeds, keep them well away from other columbines. Pull up any plants that do not resemble the species. Rogue out unattractive hybrids as their first flowers open — before they

set seed or cross-pollinate with their neighbors. To maintain hybrid strains, it's best to grow new plants from seed every few years.

Propagation. Columbines are easy from seed, especially if the seed is fresh. Sow them outdoors right where the plants are to grow from early spring up to 2 months before frost. Simply clear a seedbed and loosen the soil, sprinkle the seeds thinly over the site, and pat down to ensure good seed-to-soil contact. If you have collected seed, simply crush the seed capsules over the site. Do not cover the seeds; light speeds germination. Self-sown seedlings are easy to transplant when they are small. Just lift them with a trowel and replant them immediately or pot them up in individual containers. Keep the transplants evenly moist for a week or two.

To sow seeds indoors, sprinkle them over containers filled with moistened soilless medium and cover the pots with plastic to hold in moisture. Then place the covered pots in the refrigerator for a 3- to 4-week cold treatment. After that, germinate the seeds at 70°F. Seedlings should appear in 2 to 3 weeks; some species take up to 2 months or more. Most seedlings will flower the following year; seeds sown indoors in early spring may flower the first year.

Transplant the seedlings into individual pots or a nursery bed when they are large enough to handle. Move them to permanent spots in the garden in early fall. Protect new transplants with bushel baskets or boxes for the first few days.

Potential Problems. Leaf miners are the larvae of tiny flies that chew winding, white tunnels in the leaves. Fortunately, the damage is primarily cosmetic. Since the maggots are between the leaf surfaces, they are protected from sprays. To control them, handpick infested leaves at the first sign of damage and discard them in the trash, not the compost pile. Cut heavily infested plants to the ground and discard the foliage; plants will generally recover from this harsh treatment and sprout new leaves. Aphids also cluster on stem tips, but they do little damage.

Long-spurred columbines, such as this Music Series hybrid, add grace and movement to perennial gardens.

A Flower for Hummingbirds

Columbine flowers are popular with hummingbirds, as well as with butterflies and bees, because of their long, nectar-containing spurs. They are an especially important nectar source for hummingbirds because they bloom early in the season, when other nectar supplies may be scarce.

To roll out the red carpet for hummingbirds, plant red-and-yellow-flowered *A. canadensis* or red-flowered hybrids. *A. formosa* is a native West Coast species that has red flowers. Contrary to popular belief, hummingbirds will visit paler-hued blooms as well, so don't hesitate to include other colors in a planting.

LANDSCAPE USES

Long-spurred hybrids and the taller species of columbines add airy grace to beds and borders in early summer. Plant them in clumps to create drifts of color, interspersed with irises, peonies, hardy geraniums, and other popular perennials. Use dwarf types near the front of plantings. For rock gardens, *A. alpina, A. canadensis,* and dwarf forms of *A. flabellata* are especially effective. In the dappled shade of woodland edges and shade gardens, combine columbines with spring wildflowers, ferns, hostas, heucheras, hellebores, and wild blue phlox *(Phlox divaricata).*

Asters

Aster

■

(AS-ter)

■

Summer to fall bloom

■

Full sun or partial shade

■

Zones 2 to 8

■

ABOVE Frikart's aster
(*Aster × frikartii*)

BELOW Alpine aster
(*Aster alpinus* 'Goliath')

■ Fall would hardly seem complete without the daisylike blooms of asters lining roadsides and filling gardens everywhere. The flowers can be single, semidouble, or double and come in shades of purple, violet, lavender, blue, pink, ruby red, and white. Individual blooms are starry—*aster* is Latin for "star"—and like daisies they consist of ray florets, commonly referred to as petals, surrounding dense buttonlike centers of disk florets, which are usually yellow. While a few species bear solitary flowers (one per stem), most produce their blooms in loose, showy clusters. The plants range from a dainty 6 to 12 inches to a robust 8 feet in height and typically have lance-shaped leaves. Asters form spreading clumps and their flowers are popular with butterflies and bees—as well as with flower arrangers.

SELECTING ASTERS

There are asters for nearly every garden—and gardener. While most asters need full sun and rich, well-drained, evenly moist soil for best performance, there are exceptions. There are asters that will grow well in difficult sites such as dry shade or poor soil. In addition, asters are gener-ally a forgiving lot and will tolerate a range of conditions. (China asters, *Callistephus chinensis*, which are annuals, aren't true asters. For information on growing them, see *Callistephus chinensis* on page 26 in the **Annuals & Biennials** entry.)

Asters for Sun

The most commonly grown asters are plants for sunny beds and borders. Of these, the two most popular species are New England asters (*Aster novae-angliae*) and New York asters (*A. novi-belgii*), both sometimes called Michaelmas daisies. These two species are quite similar and they have been extensively hybridized, both with each other and with other asters. When choosing asters to grow, gardeners commonly make their selections based on a characteristic of a particular cultivar, such as flower color or plant height, because both species require similar culture.

Several other species fall into this grouping as well, including species that stretch the aster blooming season—summer-flowering alpine aster (*A. alpinus*) and Frikart's aster (*A. × frikartii*), along with late-fall-flowering Tartarian aster (*A. tataricus*). While all of these asters grow in full sun, the amount of soil moisture they prefer varies. Plants in soil that is too wet or too dry, depending on the species, tend to lose their lower leaves and flower less.

A. alpinus. Alpine aster. Solitary, 2-inch-wide, violet-purple flowers from early to mid-summer; 6- to 12-inch plants. Requires rich, well-drained soil in full sun. Prefers cool summers and does not tolerate heat or humidity well, but a site with afternoon shade will help plants cope with these conditions. Plants are generally short lived in warmer zones. Good for rock gardens. Zones 2 to 7.

A. × frikartii. Frikart's aster. Loose sprays of lavender-blue flowers over a long season—from midsummer through fall; 2- to 3-foot plants. Requires rich, well-drained soil in full sun. Plants do not tolerate wet soil, especially in winter. Most will need staking to look their best. 'Monch' and 'Wonder of Staffa', both lavender-blue, are the most popular cultivars. Zones 5 to 8.

A. novae-angliae. New England aster. Showy clusters of violet, purple, lavender, rose-red, pink, or white flowers in fall; 3- to 6-foot plants. Individual flowers are 1½ to 2 inches wide; leaves are lance shaped with lobes that clasp the hairy

TOP New England aster (*Aster novae-angliae* 'Purple Dome')

ABOVE New York aster (*Aster novi-belgii* 'Marie Ballard')

ABOVE RIGHT
New England aster (*Aster novae-angliae* 'Alma Potschke')

stem at the base. Rich, evenly moist soil in full sun is best, but plants will bloom in light shade. They will grow in average to dry soil as well. Most require staking to look their best. Rose-pink 'Alma Potschke', royal purple 'Hella Lacy', and light pink 'Harrington's Pink' are fine cultivars. 'Purple Dome' forms dense, compact, 18-inch-tall mounds of deep purple flowers without pinching and does not need staking. Zones 3 to 8.

A. novi-belgii. New York aster. Dense, showy fall clusters of lavender-blue, white, ruby red, pink, or purple flowers; 1- to 4-foot plants, but sometimes taller. Individual flowers are 1 to 1½ inches wide and leaves are much narrower than those of *A. novae-angliae.* Rich, evenly moist soil in full sun or light shade is fine, but plants bloom best in full sun. They will grow in average to dry soil as well. Cultivars over 2½ or 3 feet require staking, but many low-growing selections are available, including 14-inch, lavender-blue 'Professor Anton Kippenburg' and 6- to 10-inch, white-flowered 'Niobe'. Zones 3 to 8.

A. tataricus. Tartarian aster. Large clusters of lavender-blue flowers in mid- to late fall; 5- to 8-foot plants. Full sun or light shade with average to rich soil, either evenly moist or well drained. Plants are strong stemmed and generally do not require staking. 'Jindai' is a comparative dwarf, reaching only 4 to 5 feet. Zones 2 to 8.

Asters for Shade
Shade gardeners can enjoy asters from summer to fall by planting three species native to woodlands and clearings in North America. These species, which are harder to find than more common asters, may be available at local wildflower sales or from catalogs specializing in native plants.

A. cordifolius. Blue wood aster, heart-leaved aster. Pale lavender or white flowers from late summer to fall; 2- to 5-foot plants. Grows in partial shade or full sun in fertile, evenly moist soil. Zones 4 to 8.

A. divaricatus. White wood aster. Loose clusters of small white flowers from midsummer through fall; 1- to 1½-foot plants with black stems. Grows in full shade but blooms best in light to partial shade. Tolerates dry shade once established. Zones 4 to 8.

A. macrophyllus. Large-leaved or bigleaf aster. Flat clusters of white to pale lavender flowers from late summer to fall; 1- to 2½-foot plants. Grows in full shade but blooms best in light to partial shade. Tolerates dry shade once established. Zones 4 to 8.

Asters for Poor Soil
There are even asters for gardeners coping with sunny sites and poor soil. Here again, native asters are the plants to turn to. These species do

not require staking and are worth searching out at local wildflower sales or in catalogs specializing in native plants.

A. ericoides. Heath aster. Loose clusters of white flowers from late summer to fall; 1- to 3-foot plants. In full sun and average garden soil, plants reach 3 feet; in very poor or acid soil, they remain under a foot or so. Zones 3 to 8.

A. lateriflorus. Calico or starved aster. Clouds of starry white to pale lavender flowers from midsummer to fall; 2- to 4-foot plants. Grows in full sun and average to very poor soil; plants growing in poor soil remain more compact than those in richer conditions. Zones 3 to 8.

A. spectabilis. Showy or seaside aster. Violet-purple flowers from late summer to fall; 1½- to 2-foot plants. Grows in full sun. A coastal native ideal for sandy soil. Zones 6 to 8.

PLANTING

Plant asters in spring, taking care to select a site that will provide the sun and soil conditions the species you are planting prefers. A site with good air circulation is a plus, since asters are subject to powdery mildew. Adequate spacing also helps control this fungal disease, and plants perform best when they are not crowded. Plant all but very low-growing cultivars of *A. novae-angliae* and *A. novi-belgii* with at least 2 feet of space on all sides to give them plenty of room. The towering *A. tataricus* needs 3 feet or more. Smaller asters can be planted somewhat closer — try spacing them at about half their height.

CARE THROUGH THE SEASON

To look their best, asters need regular attention, but most will grow satisfactorily with benign neglect. Feed plants in spring with a topdressing of compost, well-rotted manure, or a balanced organic fertilizer spread over the roots (keep it away from the emerging stems). Mulch *A. novae-angliae* and *A. novi-belgii* to help hold moisture in the soil; the other species don't need to be mulched, but it helps control weeds. At the end of the season, rake mulch off species that require well-drained soil to help prevent wet conditions in winter. Deadheading, pinching, staking, and division are other chores to attend to.

Deadheading. Asters will self-sow, and in a wildflower garden or naturalized area planted with native species this isn't a problem. Seedlings from improved cultivars, which are usually the plants grown in beds and borders, won't necessarily resemble their parents, however, and with time will compete with them. For this reason, many gardeners cut back the flowering stems immediately after they fade. Aster seeds help feed birds through the winter, though, so consider

Calico aster
(Aster lateriflorus)

leaving the seed heads in place and then cutting them to the ground in spring. If you choose the latter course, spend some time each spring roguing out the self-sown seedlings.

Pinching. Pinching out the stem tips in spring and again in early summer encourages branching and thus more flowers. It also fosters dense, compact growth and reduces height at blooming time. Some cultivars won't need staking if they are pinched, but pinching makes the flower clusters heavier and staking helps prevent the stems from being broken in heavy rain and wind. To pinch plants, remove 3 to as much as 6 inches of each new stem with pruning shears or your thumb and forefinger. For a faster approach, shear the plants with hedge shears, cutting them back by one-third to one-half.

A. novae-angliae, A. novi-belgii, and *A. tataricus* benefit the most from pinching. For these and other fall-blooming asters, do not pinch after June 15 in the North (from about Zone 6 northward), however, or you may remove the flower buds. In the South, asters can be pinched as late as July 1. Pinch *A.* × *frikartii* once in spring. Do not pinch *A. alpinus.*

Staking. Stake plants in spring or very early summer. Taller asters will need substantial support — ring the clumps with stakes and string or use a commercial system. Smaller asters (2 feet and under) can be staked with similar systems, but pea brush also works. See "Staking" in the Techniques Glossary for more on these methods. Either too much fertilizer or soil that is too rich increases the likelihood that plants will flop and require staking.

Division. Asters produce spreading clumps that tend to become woody and die out near the center after several years. Most asters need to be divided every 2 to 3 years. To divide, dig the clumps in spring (if necessary, they can also be dug in fall). Pull the roots apart and discard the old, woody portion at the center. Replant sections

Aster Companions

Two aster relatives are perfect additions to fall gardens—boltonia (*Boltonia asteroides*) and goldenrods (*Solidago* spp.). Boltonia bears masses of tiny white daisy flowers with yellow centers in fall on 4- to 6-foot plants. (A well-grown clump looks like a giant baby's breath in fall.) The stiff-stemmed plants, which generally stand without staking, are grown just like *A. novae-angliae*—in full sun with rich, evenly moist soil, although they also tolerate drought. They are divided and propagated like asters as well. Compact, white-flowered 'Snowbank' is more often grown than the species. 'Pink Beauty' has pale pink flowers. Boltonias are hardy in Zones 3 to 9.

Classic harbingers of fall, goldenrods are well-known wildflowers that are all too often overlooked by gardeners. Valuable for adding yellow to golden blooms to the fall garden, they are grown much like asters—in full sun with moist, well-drained soil, although they will tolerate more drought. To accompany any of the asters for sun, consider cultivars of European goldenrod (*S. virgaurea*) such as 'Cloth of Gold', 'Goldenmosa', or 'Crown of Rays', all from 2 to 3 feet tall and hardy in Zones 3 to 9. *S. sphacelata* 'Golden Fleece' is a dwarf (1½-foot), very heavy-blooming selection that spreads well, tolerates dry conditions, and is hardy in Zones 4 to 9. For the back of the border, consider 3- to 4-foot *S. rugosa* 'Fireworks', hardy in Zones 4 to 9. Wreath goldenrod (*S. caesia*), hardy in Zones 4 to 8, grows in full sun or partial shade and is suitable for adding color to a woodland site. It also tolerates dry soil. Seaside goldenrod (*S. sempervirens*) is a good choice for a site with poor or sandy soil and is hardy in Zones 4 to 9. Like asters, goldenrods are best divided every 2 to 3 years, in spring or fall, to keep them vigorous and in bounds.

Goldenrod (*Solidago rugosa* 'Fireworks') with feather reed grass (*Calamagrostis* × *acutiflora*)

New England asters (*Aster novae-angliae* 'Hella Lacy') with ornamental grass (*Miscanthus sinensis*)

from the outside of the clump—to make a good-size clump for next season, place three or four pieces in each hole, spacing the pieces several inches apart.

Propagation. Division is the easiest way to propagate asters, but seeds are a good way to add some of the species to your garden. Sow seeds outdoors in fall or early spring. Indoors, sow them in spring in pots and set the pots in the refrigerator for 6 to 8 weeks for a cold, moist period of stratification. Then germinate them at 65° to 70°F. Asters can also be propagated from cuttings taken in spring or early summer and rooted in a mix of half sand and half perlite.

Potential Problems. Asters are prone to powdery mildew, which disfigures the foliage in summer. A site with good air circulation is helpful, as is frequent division to keep the clumps from becoming crowded. Spray sulfur or another organic fungicide beginning in midsummer if mildew is a particular problem. If plants have been plagued with root diseases such as wilt or verticillium, try propagating by cuttings.

LANDSCAPE USES

Sun-loving asters are ideal plants for perennial beds and borders and can also be naturalized in sunny meadows and wildflower gardens. Many asters attain shrublike proportions and will hold their own in a shrub border, where they add valuable fall color. Combine them with ornamental grasses, fall-blooming anemones, *Sedum* 'Autumn Joy', monkshoods (*Aconitum* spp.), and late-blooming perennials such as boltonia and goldenrods—see "Aster Companions" at left for information on these two genera of outstanding fall bloomers. In addition to adding fall color to a wildflower garden, shade-loving asters are attractive with hostas and other foliage plants such as bergenia and lungworts (*Pulmonaria* spp.). *Aster alpinus* and dwarf forms of *A. novi-belgii* are attractive in rock gardens or toward the front of beds and borders.

Astilbe

Astilbes

Astilbe

■

(uh-STILL-bee)

■

Late-spring to summer
bloom

■

Shade to sun

■

Zones 4 to 8

■

Astilbe 'Rheinland'

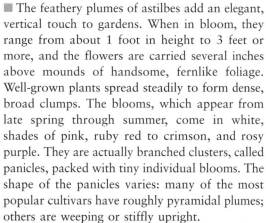

■ The feathery plumes of astilbes add an elegant, vertical touch to gardens. When in bloom, they range from about 1 foot in height to 3 feet or more, and the flowers are carried several inches above mounds of handsome, fernlike foliage. Well-grown plants spread steadily to form dense, broad clumps. The blooms, which appear from late spring through summer, come in white, shades of pink, ruby red to crimson, and rosy purple. They are actually branched clusters, called panicles, packed with tiny individual blooms. The shape of the panicles varies: many of the most popular cultivars have roughly pyramidal plumes; others are weeping or stiffly upright.

Astilbes make attractive, although not long-lived, cut flowers. They dry nicely, too. For fresh use, cut the plumes when about half the individual flowers are open. To increase vase life, split the stems about an inch up from the bottom before plunging them into lukewarm water. For drying, pick when nearly all the flowers are open and hang in a warm, dry, dark place. If left in the garden, the spikes dry to attractive shades of brown and last well into winter.

SELECTING ASTILBES

Plant breeders have introduced many different astilbe cultivars (species astilbes are seldom grown), and choosing among them can be difficult. Instead of selecting by flower color alone, take advantage of the fact that cultivars bloom at slightly different times. Although each cultivar blooms for only a few weeks (the height of bloom falls in June and July), by planting ones described as early, midseason, and late bloomers it's possible to stretch the display for nearly the entire summer. Many also have showy red to bronze foliage in spring, which matures to green. Astilbes are hardy in Zones 4 to 8, but they will survive Zone 3 winters with protection.

Early to midseason cultivars bloom in late spring and early summer. These include white-flowered 'Deutschland'; pink 'Europa', 'Rheinland', and 'Peach Blossom'; and crimson-rose 'Bremen'. Midseason bloomers—and there are many—include blood red 'Fanal', white 'Bridal Veil' and 'Snowdrift', and carmine-rose 'Federsee'. Late-season cultivars include scarlet 'Red Sentinel' and rose-pink 'Cattleya'. All are cultivars of either *Astilbe* × *arendsii* or *A. japonica*.

A. chinensis var. *pumila,* a dwarf variety of Chinese astilbe, makes a good ground cover and bears erect purplish pink plumes over 4 to 6 weeks from mid- to late season. The height varies according to the amount of moisture and shade the plants get. They commonly stay between 10 and 12 inches when in bloom (the foliage is easily half that height), but with abundant moisture and shade they can reach 2 to 2½ feet. *A. chinensis* var. *taquetii,* commonly called fall astilbe, and its cultivar 'Superba' tolerate drier soil and more sun than most astilbes. Both are mid- to late-season bloomers.

A. simplicifolia and its cultivars are also dwarf, late-season bloomers. They have glossy, very fernlike leaves and loose plumes of flowers. Pink-flowered 'Sprite' bears pale pink flowers on 14-inch plants in mid- to late season.

A. thunbergii 'Ostrich Plume' (also sold as 'Straussenfeder') is another late-summer bloomer that reaches 3 to 4 feet and requires ample moisture for best performance.

SITE AND SOIL

The key to growing astilbes successfully is to give them soil that is constantly moist but well drained. Since they are also heavy feeders, a rich complement of organic matter, which also holds moisture, is vital as well. The best exposure is generally a partially shaded one—a site with sun in the morning and shade in the afternoon is ideal. In the North, where summers remain relatively cool, astilbes perform beautifully in full sun provided they receive adequate moisture—from either regular watering or naturally moist conditions. In the South, partial or full shade is essential (plants will bloom less in full shade, however). Wherever they're grown, plants that receive too little moisture and too much sun develop curled leaves with crispy brown leaf edges.

Astilbes are frequently planted along streamsides and ponds, where they benefit from the constant moisture. In such sites, plant them above the water line, however, because constantly wet conditions will lead to root or crown rot. (If you are planting next to a water garden created with a liner, keep in mind that the soil will be no moister there than anywhere else in the garden.)

PLANTING

Plant astilbes in spring or fall. Dig plenty of compost or other organic matter into the soil before setting the plants in place. If growth is just emerging, set the plants with 1/2 inch of loose soil over the buds, or eyes; set fully emerged container-grown plants at the depth at which they were growing in the pots. Preparing the soil in fall for spring planting is an excellent approach, and it

BELOW *Astilbe* 'Peach Blossom'

BOTTOM Astilbes and hostas both thrive in rich, evenly moist soil and partial shade.

BOTTOM RIGHT *Astilbe* 'Bremen'

makes it possible to use coarser organic matter than you can at planting time. In this case, dig in chopped leaves (picked up off the lawn with a bagging lawn mower) or not-quite-finished compost, then mulch the bed to protect the soil until spring. Although astilbes aren't particularly deep rooted, adding organic matter helps keep the soil moist and helps them tolerate drier weather. Space them about 1½ to 2 feet apart. *A. simplicifolia* and its cultivars can be planted somewhat closer, about 1 foot apart.

CARE THROUGH THE SEASON

Once their basic requirements for moist soil are satisfied, astilbes need only a minimum of care. Feed them in spring with a topdressing of compost or a balanced organic fertilizer. They don't require staking. If the woody crowns grow above the soil surface, either top-dress the plants with loose soil to cover the crowns or divide and replant. In fall, cut the foliage to the ground after it is killed by frost (leave the dried flower spikes for winter interest, if you like). This discourages overwintering insects as well as mice and voles that might move in and consume the crowns over winter. (The foliage tends to catch fallen leaves, making a warm, cozy hideout for them.)

Water astilbes regularly in summer if the weather is dry or if your soil tends to dry out. Keep in mind that astilbes are shallow rooted and tend to dry out before the plants around them. Keeping the plants mulched with chopped leaves or compost has a threefold benefit: mulch helps keep the soil moist and cool, it adds essential organic matter to the soil, and it keeps down weeds.

Division. To keep astilbes vigorous, dig and divide them every 3 to 4 years in spring or early fall. The plants form woody crowns, so after lifting the clumps, cut the crowns apart with a sharp spade or saw them apart with a small handsaw or serrated knife. Then pull apart the pieces to divide the fibrous roots. Discard the older, woody portions of the crown and replant or pot up the younger, less woody portions. Division is the best way to propagate astilbes, since cultivars do not come true from seed. Fresh seed can be sown outdoors in summer or early fall, however.

LANDSCAPE USES

Combine astilbes with other perennials that thrive in evenly moist soil, such as hostas, ferns, lady's mantles (*Alchemilla* spp.), lungworts (*Pulmonaria* spp.), and bleeding hearts (*Dicentra* spp.). Shade-loving annuals such as impatiens and wax begonias also make good companions. Or consider interplanting astilbes with tulips or other hardy spring bulbs. Their emerging leaves will hide the fading foliage of the bulbs.

Baptisias

Long lived and easy to grow, baptisias are native North American wildflowers that bear spikes of pea-shaped flowers. The botanical name and the common name "false indigo" both refer to the fact that members of the genus have been used as dye plants, most notably as a substitute for indigo — *bapto* is Greek for "to dye." All are good cut flowers.

Blue false indigo (*Baptisia australis*), hardy in Zones 3 to 9, is the best known and the most ornamental. It produces showy, erect clusters of dark blue flowers in early summer on robust, 3- to 5-foot plants. The foliage, which remains handsome all season, is blue-green. The flowers are followed by spikes of inflated blue-black seed capsules, which can be cut in midsummer for dried arrangements or left to add winter interest in the garden.

Three species are suitable for sites with dry, poor soil. White wild indigo (*B. alba*), hardy in Zones 5 to 8, produces its white flowers on 2- to 3-foot plants. Prairie wild indigo (*B. lactea,* formerly *B. leucantha*), hardy in Zones 4 to 8, is a 3- to 5-foot native with white flowers. Plains wild indigo (*B. bracteata,* formerly *B. leucophaea*), hardy in Zones 3 to 9, is a spreading, 1- to 2-foot-tall plant that bears its creamy yellow flowers in drooping clusters. These species may be available at local wildflower sales or from native-plant specialists.

SITE AND SOIL

Baptisias are best planted in full sun but will also grow in partial shade. Plants in shade will bloom less than those in sun and are more likely to require staking. Grow *B. australis* in rich, evenly moist but well-drained conditions; the other species are suitable for spots with poor, sandy, or dry soil. Owing to their deep taproots, all are drought tolerant once established. Select a site with care, since the plants establish slowly and are also difficult to transplant. The site needs to be large enough to accommodate the plants' eventual spread, because they can be left undisturbed for years. Fill in the gaps around new clumps with annuals.

Baptisia
■
(bap-TEES-ee-ah)
■
Spring to early-summer bloom
■
Full sun or partial shade
■
Zones 3 to 9
■

Blue false indigo
(Baptisia australis)

Blue false indigo
(Baptisia australis)

PLANTING

Plant baptisias in spring or fall, spacing plants 3 feet apart to allow for their spread. It's best to prepare the soil deeply before planting—double digging is ideal. Work plenty of organic matter such as compost into the soil, particularly for *B. australis*.

CARE THROUGH THE SEASON

Once planted, baptisias pretty much take care of themselves. They appreciate, but do not require, an annual spring topdressing with compost, well-rotted manure, or a balanced organic fertilizer. The clumps may need staking, especially in exposed, windy sites or if they are growing in too much shade. Plants in full sun seldom need staking. Deadhead if you don't want seedpods or seeds. Cut the plants to the ground after a hard freeze, and rake any mulch off them after the ground freezes—otherwise mice and voles move in and dine on the crowns and roots over winter.

Division. Baptisias will grow happily for years without being divided, eventually spreading via rhizomes to form broad clumps. (They are not invasive, however.) They can be divided if they outgrow their site or become overcrowded, or for propagation. Dig them in early spring or fall, and dig deeply to get to as many of the roots as possible. Cut the crowns apart with a sharp knife and replant. (If you find that mice or voles have been eating the crowns over winter, in spring lift the remaining portions of the clump, cut out obviously dead or diseased portions, and replant.

Keep the plants evenly moist and mulched through the summer. Although they reestablish slowly, it is possible to save baptisias this way.)

Propagation. Baptisias are relatively easy to grow from seeds, although seedlings take 2 to 3 years to bloom. For best results, sow fresh seeds (those that have just turned black) outdoors in summer immediately after harvesting them. If you don't have access to fresh seeds, scarify the seeds you're using by rubbing the seed coats with a nail file or sandpaper (don't damage the embryo inside the seed, just the hard seed coat) or soak them in hot water overnight. Then sow outdoors or in. Seeds should germinate in about 2 weeks at temperatures of 70°F. Don't allow plants to become potbound, because that can damage the roots. Instead, move them promptly to larger containers. Transplant with care.

LANDSCAPE USES

Use these shrub-sized perennials near the back of the border, in naturalized areas, or even as foundation plants. They are effective when combined with peonies (*Paeonia* spp.), hardy geraniums, columbines (*Aquilegia* spp.), Siberian iris *(Iris sibirica),* and early-blooming salvias such as *Salvia × superba*. Their foliage is an attractive foil for summer-blooming perennials such as daylilies (*Hemerocallis* spp.) and yarrows (*Achillea* spp.) as well as late-blooming plants such as asters and anemones. Even annuals such as spider flower *(Cleome hasslerana)* are more striking against a backdrop of baptisia foliage.

Begonias

Begonia

- (bih-GOAN-yah)
- Summer to fall bloom
- Partial or full shade
- Tender or Zones 6 to 10

Wax begonia
(*Begonia semperflorens*
'Rio Pink')

■ The vast begonia clan is familiar to nearly anyone who has ever put a plant in the soil. Begonias have fleshy leaves and stems and grow from rhizomes, fibrous roots, or tubers. They bear separate male and female flowers, usually on the same plant. (The female flowers have a swollen winged seed capsule, directly behind the petals, that will contain the seeds; males don't.) The flowers are typically carried in clusters of three, with one male flower between two females. The fleshy leaves vary in shape, size, and color. Rounded and wing-shaped foliage is common.

The majority of the more than 1,000 species of begonias are tropical and are grown as houseplants or greenhouse plants in most USDA zones. Three stand out for their popularity in gardens, however: wax begonias, tuberous begonias, and hardy begonias. See "Hardy Begonias" on page 48 for information on growing the latter plants, which are valuable perennials for shady beds and borders that add late-season color.

Ubiquitous wax begonias (*Begonia semperflorens*) need no introduction. Tender perennials grown as annuals, they are undemanding and dependable, rewarding even the most indifferent of gardeners with a colorful summer-long display. Their flowers, borne in abundance from spring to frost, come in pink, red, and white. Most are single, but double-flowered types are available. The rounded, succulent leaves come in green or burgundy, and the plants are compact, ranging from 8 to 15 inches in height.

Tuberous begonias (*B.* Tuberhybrida hybrids) produce showy, exotic-looking flowers in a wide variety of shapes, sizes, and colors. They also are tender perennials, but their tubers make it relatively easy to overwinter the plants to enjoy season after season. Tuberous begonias are divided by flower or plant type into 13 groups. The most popular types all have double flowers, but within the doubles there are crested forms, camellia- and carnation-flowered varieties, picotees, and rosebuds. Colors include pale pink to dark red, yellow, orange, cream, or white. There are also bicolor types—cream with a red edge, or orange with red, for example. Male flowers are larger than females and can be as much as 6 inches across. The plants can reach 2 feet in height, but there are also types with trailing stems, called pendulas, suitable for hanging baskets and window boxes.

SITE AND SOIL

Wax begonias grow in sun or shade, but partial shade is best. Plants grown in full sun must be kept evenly moist, and even then they will struggle in southern zones. Average to rich, well-drained soil is fine.

Tuberous begonias are more demanding, although they're not difficult to grow if you have the right site for them. They grow best in areas with cool (60° to 65°F at night), somewhat humid summers but are disappointing in areas with hot, dry summers. Grow them in partial shade in a spot protected from wind, either in containers or in the ground. Either way, they require loose, well-drained soil rich in organic matter. A location protected from foot traffic is best, since the brittle stems break off easily. (Tail-wagging dogs can present a problem as well.)

PLANTING WAX BEGONIAS

Plant wax begonias outdoors after all danger of frost is past. Although plants are readily available at garden centers, and even grocery stores, it is also possible to start them from seeds sown

Starting Begonia Tubers

To ensure a summer-long display of tuberous begonia flowers, start tubers indoors 8 to 10 weeks before the last spring frost date in flats filled with loose, free-draining potting medium that is barely moist.

If buds are not visible on the tops of the tubers, place the tubers upside down on the surface of the medium. Set them in a warm (70° to 80°F), humid place for about a week. After that, check for buds every few days.

When the tubers have pink buds about 1/2 inch long, plant them with the medium barely covering the tops of the tubers. Water sparingly until the tubers are growing actively—too much moisture can rot them—but after that, water regularly, keeping the soil evenly moist. Keep them in a bright spot, such as a north or east window, but protect them from direct sun.

Move started tubers to individual 4- to 5-inch pots when the shoots are about 1½ inches long. Do not pack the medium into the pots—tuberous begonias require loose, well-drained conditions. To produce the largest blooms, remove all but the strongest bud on each tuber; for more, slightly smaller flowers, remove all but the strongest two buds. If quantity of flowers, not size, is most important, leave all the buds on the tubers.

Top (concave side)

Bottom (convex side)

Sprouts appear from the top, or concave side.

To promote large blooms, thin out weaker stems on the tubers.

in early winter (see "Propagation" on the facing page for germination information). Cuttings are another option, rooted from overwintered plants or a plant or two purchased in late winter. Loosen the soil to a depth of 8 to 10 inches and work in organic matter such as compost at planting time. Space plants 6 to 8 inches apart, closer if they are being grown as an edging or a low hedge.

PLANTING TUBEROUS BEGONIAS

Most gardeners encounter tuberous begonias at garden centers and home stores. There, the dormant tubers are sold packed in plastic bags full of peat moss (or in bins full of it) hanging by a printed card featuring a photo of the enclosed cultivar in full bloom. A wider selection is available through the mail. Buy tubers that are firm and solid, with no soft or moist spots or cuts. They should not be shriveled or deformed. Small pink buds may be evident, but avoid tubers that have already sprouted. Later in spring, pots of started plants are available for sale as well.

Tubers need to be coaxed out of dormancy: if they are simply potted up or planted out in the garden, they will rot rather than grow. See "Start-

ing Begonia Tubers" above for directions on getting dormant tubers up and growing successfully.

Once they have shoots that are several inches tall, they're ready to be moved into the containers where they will bloom or into the garden. Keep plants indoors until all danger of frost has passed and the soil has warmed. Before moving tuberous begonias to garden beds, loosen the soil and add plenty of organic matter such as leaf mold or compost. Fill tubs or large containers with rich potting mixture—8-inch containers are suitable for single tubers; plant 12-inch pots or baskets with three tubers.

Insert stakes right at planting time, to avoid damaging the tubers later. Pencil-thick or slightly smaller stakes are fine. For upright types they need to be about 1½ feet long; for pendulous types, slightly shorter. Carefully tie the brittle stems loosely to the stakes with soft yarn or strips of nylon stocking.

CARE THROUGH THE SEASON

Wax begonias need no care in summer other than watering when the soil gets dry. Tuberous begonias, not surprisingly, need more care, but they

are well worth the extra effort. Water as necessary, letting the soil surface dry out slightly between waterings but keeping the soil farther down
evenly moist. (Soil that remains too wet can lead
to root rot and other diseases.) Mulch plants,
both in the ground and in containers, with
chopped leaves or leaf mold to keep the soil moist
and cool. Feed every 3 weeks with manure tea or
a weak, balanced organic fertilizer. Tie the stems
to the stakes as they grow, making sure they have
adequate support. Disbud plants, if you like, to
encourage the largest flowers by pinching off the
female flowers produced on either side of the
larger male flowers.

Propagation. Begonias can be propagated
from the dustlike seeds in early to midwinter. For
tuberous begonias, purchase seeds of a strain,
such as 'Non Stop', developed for this purpose.
Propagate double-flowered wax begonias from
cuttings only. Sow seeds thinly on the surface of
a moist, sterile seed-starting mix such as two parts
peat moss, one part vermiculite. Do not cover the
seeds with soil, but place a pane of glass or a piece
of plastic wrap over the container to keep the
medium moist. Germination occurs in 15 to 20
days; keep wax begonias at a temperature of 70°F,
tuberous and hardy begonias at 60°F.

Wax and tuberous begonias can also be
propagated from cuttings. For best results with
the latter, take cuttings of young shoots with a
small "heel" of the tuber attached. Root cuttings
in a 50-50 mix of perlite and vermiculite. Wax begonias can also be propagated by digging and dividing the clumps.

Overwintering. Both wax and tuberous begonias are easy to overwinter. Take cuttings of
wax begonias in late summer or dig entire plants.
Pot them in ordinary potting mix and keep them
on a sunny windowsill at temperatures between
60° and 65°F over the winter.

For tuberous begonias, dig the tubers after
the first light frost in fall and spread them out,
tops and all, in a shady, dry, well-ventilated spot
that is protected from further frosts. Let the tops
dry, then shake the soil from the tubers. Store
them at temperatures around 45° to 50°F in shallow trays filled with dry peat moss, or hang them
in net bags or nylon stockings filled with peat.
Check regularly throughout the winter for signs
of rot, and discard rotted tubers. Replant as you
would new tubers in spring.

Potential Problems. Poorly drained, too-wet
soil will cause tuberous begonias to rot, and wet
soil, especially at night, can lead to foliar diseases
such as powdery mildew. Fluctuations in soil
moisture can cause the flower buds to drop—if
the plants are allowed to dry out completely between waterings, for example. Sudden tempera-

Tuberous begonia 'Orange Blaze', a pendulous cultivar

Tuberous begonias growing with Persian violet *(Exacum affine),* an annual

ture fluctuations—from hot to cold or cold to hot—have the same effect. Well-grown plants will recover and produce new buds, however. If plants appear yellowed, stunted, sickly, or wilted despite the amount of moisture in the soil, suspect nematodes. Discarding the tubers and planting new, uninfested ones in sterilized soil or a new location is the easiest course of action.

LANDSCAPE USES

Grow wax begonias as edgings or miniature hedges in flower beds or borders. They are also useful for filling in over spring bulbs such as daffodils or for adding summer color to a shade garden. Use tuberous begonias to add color to shady flower beds or in containers to dress up shaded decks or terraces.

Hardy Begonias

The graceful, arching clusters of hardy begonias (*B. grandis* ssp. *evansiana*, shown below) add an exotic touch to shady gardens in late summer and fall. Borne above large, attractive, wing-shaped leaves, the flowers come in pink or sometimes white. The 2- to 2½-foot plants grow from small tubers and are hardy in Zones 6 to 10; to Zone 5 with winter protection such as mulch and a sheltered site. Plant them in partial or full shade in rich soil that is moist yet evenly drained. They are ideal companions for hostas, ferns, and other woodland plants. There, they will grow without any attention, except for watering during dry spells. Cut plants to the ground after the first hard frost.

Hardy begonias can be propagated from seeds (germinate them as you would seeds of tuberous begonias), but they are easiest from the tiny bulbils produced in the leaf axils. Collect the bulbils in late summer or fall and plant them outdoors where they are to grow. Or plant them indoors in late winter in pots. Either way, plant shallowly, barely covering them with loose soil. The plants can be moved to the garden after the last spring frost.

Bergenias

■ Unlike most perennials, bergenias are grown more for their foliage than for their flowers. The leathery, rounded, cabbagelike leaves are from 8 to 12 inches long and up to 8 inches wide. In fall, they turn from the standard mid-green to bronze-purple or reddish. Although the leaves are often evergreen, they are damaged by harsh winter weather and frequently are not very ornamental by spring. Consistent snow cover or a light covering of a coarse mulch such as oak leaves or evergreen boughs helps moderate fluctuating temperatures and protects leaves from sun, both factors that cause the damage. Even where the leaves are not evergreen, bergenias are still well worth growing, because the plants are attractive from early spring well into fall.

Bergenia plants grow from thick, branching rhizomes that slowly spread into handsome clumps. In early spring (April and May in the North, earlier in the South), dense, 5- to 6-inch clusters of small, bell- or funnel-shaped flowers appear on stems above the foliage. Flowers come in shades of pink, rose-red, or white. Plants are about a foot tall when not in bloom, up to 1½ to 2 feet when they are.

The species most gardeners will encounter is heart-leaved bergenia *(Bergenia cordifolia)*, which has leathery, 10-inch-long leaves and rose-pink flowers. There are also many different hybrids available, derived from heart-leaved bergenia, purple-leaved bergenia *(B. purpurascens)*, and other species. These have been selected for either their flower color or fall foliage color. 'Bressingham White' has white flowers. 'Bressingham Ruby' has maroon-red flowers and leaves that turn maroon in fall. 'Sunningdale' has lilac-magenta flowers and copper-red fall to winter foliage. All are hardy in Zones 3 to 8.

SITE AND SOIL

Bergenias are ideal for a site in partial or dappled shade. In the North, they can be grown in full sun provided the soil remains evenly moist. In southern gardens, shade is preferable, especially in the afternoon. For the largest, most luxuriant leaves, deeply prepared, well-drained, humus-rich soil that remains evenly moist is best. A location

Bergenia
∎
(ber-GYN-ee-ah)
∎
Early-spring bloom
∎
Partial shade or full sun
∎
Zones 3 to 8
∎

RIGHT Heart-leaved bergenia *(Bergenia cordifolia)*

FAR RIGHT Bergenias and foxgloves *(Digitalis purpurea)* growing in the moist but well-drained soil on the bank of a small stream

sheltered from strong winds helps protect the foliage. (Bergenias are ideal for growing along ponds or streams, but they need to be planted high enough above the water line so that they're not sitting in constantly wet soil.) Once established, plants will withstand short periods of drought. They will also grow in slightly acid to slightly alkaline soil.

PLANTING

Plant bergenias in spring, spacing them about 1½ to 2 feet apart to accommodate their spread. For best results, dig the soil deeply and work in plenty of organic matter such as compost. Mulch new plantings to keep the soil moist.

CARE THROUGH THE SEASON

To ensure bold, lush foliage, water bergenias during times of drought. Cut back flower stalks after they fade. Mulch in fall where snow cover is uncertain, and remove damaged foliage in spring. Feed the plants in spring by mulching with compost or spreading a balanced organic fertilizer. Although bergenias spread by rhizomes, they are not invasive and need dividing only when the centers of the clumps become too crowded or die out.

Propagation. Division is the easiest way to propagate bergenias or to rejuvenate clumps that have died out in the center. To divide, dig them in spring after they flower or in fall. Cut the thick rhizomes apart with a knife and discard any old, woody portions. Replant the rest, burying the rhi-

zomes deep enough so the soil will support the heavy leaves. Cuttings are an option if you need lots of plants. Cut pieces of new rhizome that have a rosette of foliage attached in spring and root them in a 50-50 mix of peat moss and perlite.

While division and cuttings are the methods to use for cultivars, bergenias can also be grown from seeds sown anytime. Spread the seeds on the surface of the medium, since light seems to aid germination. Germinate at 70° to 75°F. Fresh seeds are best. A short cold treatment may aid germination for older seeds—set sown pots in the refrigerator for 2 weeks, then germinate as just described. Seed-sown plants will be variable.

Potential Problems. Bergenia flower buds are less hardy than the foliage and may be killed during a harsh winter. A winter mulch helps protect them. The leaves are popular fare for slugs. See the box on page 166 in the *Hosta* entry for suggestions on controlling these pests.

LANDSCAPE USES

Long lived and undemanding, bergenias make excellent ground covers or edging plants. They also tolerate dry shade under trees. Group them in masses of five or more plants for a bold effect, or group them with other plants. Since the flowers are fleeting, the best combinations play off the foliage. Combine them with other shade-loving perennials such as hostas. Ferns and other fine-textured perennials, shrubs, or ground covers make effective companions, too.

Buddleia

Butterfly Bushes

Buddleia
■
(BUD-lee-ah)
■
Summer to fall bloom
■
Full sun
■
Zones 5 to 9
■

Orange-eye butterfly bush *(Buddleia davidii)*

■ Butterfly bushes add summertime color to gardens, because of both the flowers and the fluttering butterflies that are attracted to them like magnets. Hummingbirds also visit these plants.

The most popular species, orange-eye butterfly bush *(Buddleia davidii)*, bears fragrant, 4- to 10-inch-long panicles of ¹/₂-inch-long, trumpet-shaped blooms. While the species has lilac flowers, each with a small orange eye, cultivars with purple, violet, lilac-pink, red-purple, deep pink, purple-blue, and white flowers are available. Also called summer lilac, this long-blooming species produces its lilaclike trusses from midsummer to fall in the North, from early summer onward in the South. The flowers are attractive, but not long lived, in arrangements; to prolong their vase life, remove most of the foliage and plunge the stems in lukewarm water overnight. The leaves are dark green to gray-green, silvery beneath, and 4 to 10 inches long.

Ask gardeners in different parts of the country whether *B. davidii* is a shrub or a perennial, and you'll get different answers. That's because its shoots are killed to the ground from about Zone 6 northward (the roots are hardy throughout Zone 5). For this reason, in the North it is grown as a perennial, albeit a shrub-sized one—its shoots easily reach 5 to 8 feet in a season. In the South, this species is a shrub that can reach 10 to 15 feet. It can be grown in Zones 5 through 9.

Fountain butterfly bush *(B. alternifolia)* is a graceful shrub or small tree with narrow, gray-green leaves and showy clusters of lilac-purple flowers that appear in late spring or early summer along the arching to pendulous branches. It is not killed to the ground in the North and can be grown in Zones 5 to 9.

SITE AND SOIL

Butterfly bushes thrive in full sun in moist, rich, well-drained soil. Established plants tolerate both heat and drought as well as poor soil. Wet soil, especially in winter, is generally fatal. *B. alternifolia* does not bloom as well in very rich soil. It will, however, grow in relatively poor, sandy or gravelly soil.

Butterfly bush *(Buddleia davidii* 'White Profusion')

PLANTING

Plant butterfly bushes in spring, and give plants generous spacing to accommodate the spread of their arching branches. Plants of *B. davidii* can spread from 10 to as much as 15 feet across in the South, between 6 and 10 feet in the North. If space is a problem, consider planting one of the compact cultivars such as 'Nanho Purple' or 'Nanho White', which are between 4 and 5 feet high and wide. Plants of *B. alternifolia* spread to between 10 and 12 feet.

CARE THROUGH THE SEASON

Butterfly bushes need routine spring pruning, and they also benefit from a spring feeding with a balanced organic fertilizer or a topdressing of compost or well-rotted manure. (Vigorous growth encourages the largest blooms in *B. davidii* plants.) Remove the spent blooms of *B. davidii* regularly to prolong flowering. Deadheading *B. alternifolia* does not prolong bloom.

Pruning. Northern gardeners don't need to worry much about pruning *B. davidii,* because freezing winter weather does the pruning for them. Cut off all winterkilled growth in spring. Where they aren't killed to the ground, cut plants that are unkempt or overgrown to within 12 inches of the ground in early spring before they begin growing. Or simply trim wayward growth to shape the bushes and remove some of the older wood each year. Since *B. davidii* blooms on new wood, plants that are pruned in spring will still bloom in summer.

B. alternifolia blooms on old wood (growth from the previous season) and, as mentioned earlier, is not killed to the ground in winter in the North. Although there may be winterkilled growth to remove in spring, save the main pruning for immediately after the plants bloom. As its common name suggests, plants of this species have long, pendulous branches and a fountainlike shape. Trim back branches to shorten overly long growth and to encourage branching. Also remove up to one-third of the older wood and any crossing, rubbing, or weak branches. The next year's flowering wood will be produced in summer.

Propagation. Take cuttings from stem tips in spring or summer and pot up in any suitable cutting mix, such as a 50-50 mix of peat moss and perlite. Dip the base of each cutting in a rooting hormone to speed root formation. Seeds sown anytime, and covered lightly with soil, germinate readily. They will be variable, so use cuttings to propagate improved cultivars.

LANDSCAPE USES

Butterfly bushes are effective additions to plantings of both perennials and shrubs. Use *B. davidii*

Fountain butterfly bush *(Buddleia alternifolia)*

at the back of the border, because the plants are tall and somewhat coarse looking. (For this reason, they are also best used in informal, rather than formal, plantings.) Combine them with summer- and fall-blooming perennials such as asters, sneezeweeds (*Helenium* spp.), purple coneflower *(Echinacea purpurea),* and ornamental grasses. Also pair them with other plants that attract butterflies in informal meadow plantings. Mass plantings of *B. davidii* are most effective in shrub borders. In the North, plant them behind lower-growing shrubs to hide the gap they will leave over winter. While *B. alternifolia* is effective in perennial and shrub plantings, it is also a handsome specimen plant. Use it to anchor a larger perennial border, plant it at the center of a formal or informal bed, or site it alone and underplant with ground covers.

$\mathcal{B}$ulbs

Daffodils (*Narcissus* sp.)

■ Versatile, colorful, easy to plant, and even easier to grow, bulbs belong in every garden. There are bulbs for both sun and shade, and most are as at home in formal perennial borders as they are in casual woodland plantings. Since they come in easy-to-plant packages, bulbs are simple to tuck in between clumps of perennials or the roots of trees. Planted en masse, arranged in either blocks or free-form drifts, they can be used to paint sheets of color over the landscape. It's no wonder bulbs are among America's favorite plants.

Gardeners and botanists differ in their use of the word "bulb." For botanists, "bulb" means a specific botanical structure consisting of a stem surrounded by fleshy, modified leaves. Onions, daffodils, tulips, and lilies all grow from true bulbs. Gardeners refer to plants that grow from a variety of underground structures as bulbs, however, including true bulbs, corms, tubers, tuberous roots, and rhizomes. All are fleshy underground structures that store food.

Gardeners further group bulbs by when they bloom. There are hardy spring bulbs and hardy fall bulbs, along with summer bulbs, which can be either hardy or tender. While the cultural requirements for all the bulbs in each group are not exactly the same (summer bulbs differ the most), there are enough similarities that grouping them in this manner makes it easier to keep track of how to grow them.

HARDY SPRING BULBS

It's hard to imagine a spring garden without the bright colors of hardy bulbs. Of these, daffodils, tulips, crocuses, and hyacinths are best known, but there are many more. The term "little bulbs" refers to a range of small, lesser-known species such as snowdrops (*Galanthus* spp.), squills (*Scilla* spp. and *Puschkinia* spp.), grape hyacinths (*Muscari* spp.), glory-of-the-snow (*Chionodoxa* spp.), and snowflakes (*Leucojum* spp.). Dwarf and species forms of daffodils (*Narcissus* spp.), tulips (*Tulipa* spp.), and crocuses (*Crocus* spp.) are also sometimes considered to be "little bulbs." Hardy spring bulbs require similar conditions and are carefree plants well worth the little bit of effort it takes to plant them.

Site and Soil

Plant hardy spring bulbs in full sun or partial shade. A site shaded by deciduous trees is fine for many of these early-blooming plants. That's because they need full sun in spring, but most will have flowered and died back before the trees leaf out enough to cast substantial shade. Limbing up trees can be a practical solution to a too-dark spot. Soil that is rich in organic matter and well drained but evenly moist is ideal. If the soil has been compacted or isn't loose and free-draining, dig in organic matter to a depth of 1 to 1½ feet for best results. Most hardy spring bulbs will stand drier conditions in summer when they are dormant. They will rot in wet soil.

Planting

For best results, try to get bulbs in the ground as soon as you buy them or receive them in the mail. September is the best time to plant in Zones 2 to 4, October or November in Zones 5 to 7, and November or December in Zones 8 and 9. While earlier planting gives them time to start growing roots before the onset of winter weather, they can be planted up to the time the ground freezes. If you can't plant immediately, store them in a cool, dry place, and after planting, cover the beds with a 1- to 2-inch layer of mulch to delay the onset of frozen soil and give them longer to grow roots. When fall or early-winter planting isn't possible, try holding the bulbs in a cool, dry place and plant in spring. Plants given this treatment will bloom late the first year but generally perform normally thereafter.

Always inspect bulbs before you buy, or examine mail-order shipments as you unpack them. Reject any bulbs that show signs of rot, fungus, or mildew. They should be firm to the touch, never slimy, and be of uniform weight (unusually light bulbs are often afflicted with dry rot). The papery tunic on true bulbs should be intact.

Scheduling Bulb Blooms

The list below is designed to help you select bulbs that bloom at different seasons. By planting a range of bulbs—both different species and various cultivars within a particular genus—it's possible to have bulbs in flower from the beginning of the growing season right up to hard frost. Bear in mind that it's hard to generalize about bloom seasons, especially for spring-blooming hardy bulbs. Not only does the exact time of bloom vary depending on where you live, planting location also affects bloom time. In general, bulbs planted in a south-facing site next to a wall or fence (look for the sites where snow melts first) will bloom first. The same species planted in a protected, north-facing site may be delayed by several weeks. With the highly hybridized genera—most notably *Narcissus* (daffodils) and *Tulipa* (tulips)—there is lots of overlap among the various cultivars. The list that follows includes specific types of daffodils and tulips, but the best approach is to look for cultivars rated "early," "midseason," or "late" and plant some of each.

Grecian windflowers *(Anemone blanda)* with glory-of-the-snow *(Chionodoxa luciliae)* in early spring. The emerging, strap-shaped leaves of *Tulipa tarda* and last year's maplelike leaves of foamflower *(Tiarella cordifolia)* promise blooms later in the season.

Late Winter to Very Early Spring
Chionodoxa. Glory-of-the-snow.
Crocus. C. chrysanthus (snow crocus), *C. angustifolius* (cloth-of-gold crocus), and *C. tommasinianus,* followed by *C. biflorus* (Scotch crocus) and *C. vernus* (Dutch crocus).
Cyclamen coum. Hardy cyclamen.
Eranthis. Winter aconites.
Galanthus. Snowdrops.
Iris reticulata. Reticulated iris.

Early Spring
Anemone. A. blanda (Grecian windflower).
Narcissus. Cyclamineus, Triandrus, and Trumpet daffodils.
Puschkinia scilloides. Striped squill.
Scilla. Squills.
Tulipa. T. kaufmanniana, T. fosteriana, T. greigii, and their cultivars.

Early to Midspring
Hyacinthus. Hyacinths.
Muscari. Grape hyacinths.
Narcissus. Small- and Large-cupped daffodils and Tazetta daffodils.
Tulipa. Single Early, Triumph, Darwin Hybrid, and Double Early tulips. Also *T. clusiana, T. humilis, T. tarda,* and *T. turkestanica.*

Midspring
Anemone. A. nemorosa (wood anemone) and *A. sylvestris* (snowdrop anemone).
Fritillaria. Fritillaries.
Hyacinthoides. Bluebells.
Narcissus. Double, Poeticus, and Jonquilla daffodils.
Tulipa. Lily-flowering tulips. Also *T. bakeri, T. batalinii,* and *T. saxatilis.*

Late Spring to Early Summer
Allium. Ornamental onions:
    A. aflatunense (Persian onion),
    A. caeruleum (blue globe onion),
    A. christophii (star of Persia),
    A. giganteum (giant onion), *A. moly* (lily leek), and *A. schoenoprasum* (chives).
Anemone canadensis. Meadow anemone.
Camassia. Camassias.
Erythronium. Dogtooth violets.
Leucojum. Snowflakes.

Lilium candidum. Madonna lily.
Ornithogalum. Stars-of-Bethlehem.
Tulipa. Darwin, Fringed, Bouquet or Multiflowering, Parrot, and Peony tulips.

Summer
Allium. Ornamental onions:
    A. cernuum (nodding onion),
    A. senescens, and *A. tanguticum.*
Caladium. Caladiums.
Canna. Cannas.
Dahlia. Dahlias.
Gladiolus. Gladioli.
Lilium. Lilies. These bloom in early, mid-, or late summer, depending on the species and cultivar. See *Lilium* on page 187 for details.
Lycoris. Magic lilies.

Late Summer to Fall
Allium. Ornamental onions:
    A. tuberosum (garlic chives),
    A. thunbergii, and *A. virgunculae.*
Colchicum. Autumn crocuses.
Crocus. Autumn-flowering crocuses:
    C. speciosus, C. kotschyanus, C. medius, C. pulchellus, and *C. sativus.*
Cyclamen hederifolium. Hardy cyclamen.
Lilium. L. auratum (goldband lily), *L. formosanum* (Formosa lily), and *L. lancifolium* (tiger lily).
Sternbergia lutea. Winter daffodil.

Buying Bargain Bulbs

While cheap, undersize bulbs are never a good buy, there are ways to stretch your bulb budget and buy top-quality bulbs at the same time. Take advantage of volume discounts offered by suppliers. From one supplier, for example, daffodil bulbs that start at 66¢ each if you buy 6 of one cultivar drop to 56¢ each for 24, and only 47¢ each for 96. While 96 of any one cultivar may seem like a lot, like most spring bulbs, daffodils are best planted en masse, and you can always join forces with fellow gardeners to make bulk orders.

Collections are another great buying opportunity. All manner of collections are offered in catalogs, and they are ideal for adding a wide range of bulbs to your garden. Color is a popular theme—you'll find all-pink collections featuring daffodils, tulips, hyacinths, and glory-of-the-snow (*Chionodoxa* spp.), for example—along with collections of bulbs selected especially for length of bloom or for growing in a lawn, the rock garden, or the woodland garden. Naturalizing mixtures of unnamed bulbs offer lots of color for the money, but if you like to know your bulbs by name and want to plant them in drifts of a single cultivar, look for collections made up of 5 or 10 bulbs each of a set number of cultivars. In general, the bigger the collection, the better the deal per bulb.

White tulips (*Tulipa* sp.) planted with grape hyacinths *(Muscari armeniacum)* and daffodils (*Narcissus* 'Thalia')

When planting, keep in mind that the bulb's roots come out the bottom, and they will grow most vigorously if they are sitting on top of several inches of good soil. This generally isn't a problem if you are planting in an existing bed with improved soil, but if your soil tends to be shallow, work in compost or other organic matter several inches below where the bulbs will sit.

There are three different planting approaches. The first option is to dig a separate hole for each bulb. In this case, a trowel or a trowel-sized bulb planter and a kneeling pad are about all you need to plant the so-called little bulbs. A spade or a long-handled bulb planter should be used for digging the deeper holes required by larger bulbs such as daffodils. If you can requisition a helper, it eliminates excessive bending—one person can dig the holes and the other, on hands and knees, can plant the bulbs. Have the hole digger push the spade forward in each hole and the planter stick the bulb in behind it and then hold it in the ground while the spade is pulled out. Another option is to dig small holes and plant several bulbs in each hole. The third approach is to excavate an entire bed, prepare the soil at the bottom of the excavation (loosen it and work in organic matter such as compost), and then set the bulbs in place and refill. This latter option is used for display beds where the bulbs are meant to bloom all together. See "Landscape Uses" on page 56 for suggestions on planting arrangements.

Set true bulbs pointed end up with the bottom of the bulb about three times as deep as its diameter. (Keep the papery tunic around true bulbs when planting, because it helps protect the bulb.) With some bulb types it can be hard to tell which end is up. If in doubt, plant the bulbs on their sides. Don't add fertilizer to the holes as you plant. Instead, top-dress the planting site with a balanced organic fertilizer. If the soil surface has been compacted during planting, loosen it with a fork to eliminate spots of dense soil that might prevent the bulbs from emerging in spring. Chipmunks sometimes dig up new plantings of bulbs to see (and sample) what is there. Covering the site with a piece of hardware cloth for a few days after planting generally prevents this.

Care Through the Season

Once planted, hardy spring bulbs can be pretty much left to their own devices. An annual fall feeding helps keep them vigorous—top-dress plantings with a balanced organic fertilizer. In good soil, however, most will perform adequately without supplemental feeding. A summertime mulch of chopped leaves, compost, or shredded bark helps keep down weeds and adds organic matter to the soil.

Caring for Ripening Leaves. After spring bulbs flower, their foliage remains green for several weeks, then gradually turns yellow and dies back. It's important to let the leaves ripen naturally, because they need time to manufacture food for next year's flowers. With small bulbs, such as crocuses and snowdrops, the yellowing leaves aren't particularly problematic and will simply disappear under surrounding foliage. While the ripening foliage of larger bulbs such as daffodils can be unattractive, do not cut it back until it has completely yellowed. (Or don't cut it back at all, and just leave it in the garden to rot, where it will add organic matter to the soil.) Resist the temptation to braid, rubber-band, or tie up the leaves, because this reduces their ability to manufacture food—and lumps of tied up foliage aren't all that attractive in their own right. (I've been known to loosely "comb" leaves with my fingers so they are at least not sprawling out in all directions.) See "Landscape Uses" on page 56 for other options for hiding the foliage.

Deadheading. Remove spent flowers of large hybrid bulbs such as daffodils and tulips to direct the plants' energy into producing next year's flowers. Many smaller bulbs self-sow, and if you would like seedlings scattered about, leave the flowers in place. While improved cultivars won't come true from seed, this is an easy way to increase plantings of species bulbs.

Division. When clumps of hardy spring bulbs become too crowded and begin to flower less, they need to be divided. Division is also the easiest way to propagate these plants. Dig the clumps in late spring or early summer, after the leaves turn yellow but before they disappear completely. Or mark the location of plants that need dividing and dig them in fall. (At any season, if you accidentally dig into a clump of bulbs, replant them immediately and they'll probably flower without missing a beat.) To avoid slicing into the bulbs by mistake, start digging a few inches outside of the clump. You'll find that clumps consist of large bulbs and offsets of various sizes. The offsets can be detached and planted individually and will take a year or two to bloom. Replant all of them immediately.

Propagation. Although division is the easiest way to propagate hardy spring bulbs, they can also be grown from seeds collected in mid- to late summer, as soon as they are ripe, and sown right away either in pots set in a cold frame or in a protected location outdoors. Plants will take several years to bloom from seed. Self-sown seedlings are easy to move to a new location in spring.

Potential Problems. You can avoid many common diseases that rot the bulbs if you inspect bulbs before buying them and destroy (or return) diseased bulbs that you find in shipments, before the problem spreads to healthy bulbs. Selecting a site with well-drained soil rich in organic matter is another vital key to keeping bulbs healthy. Wet soil leads to rotted bulbs and roots.

A hard, late freeze can destroy flower buds, but most hardy spring bulbs are quite tough and easily withstand frost, even when in bud or bloom. (The flowering of snowdrops and crocuses isn't hampered by a late snowstorm, but a heavy, wet covering of snow will flatten taller bulbs such as daffodils.)

Animal pests are probably the biggest problem when it comes to growing hardy bulbs. Mice, voles, and chipmunks all relish bulbs—especially tulips and crocuses. (Moles are often blamed for destroying bulb plantings, but they are carnivorous. Mice and voles use mole tunnels to reach bulbs, however.) To protect bulbs from voracious rodents, surround the bulbs with sharp, crushed gravel at planting time. Planting bulbs in hardware-cloth cages is tedious but effective. Daffodils are poisonous and rodents leave their bulbs alone. Snowdrops and other bulbs in the amaryllis family (Amaryllidaceae), to which daffodils belong, may also be rodent resistant because the bulbs are poisonous or at least somewhat so.

Mixed plantings of bulbs add stunning spring color to any garden. Here 'Red Emperor' tulips are planted with grape hyacinths (Muscari armeniacum) and daffodils (Narcissus spp.).

LANDSCAPE USES

Use hardy bulbs in beds and borders, in either sun or shade. They can be planted as edgings or scattered in clumps among early-blooming perennials such as candytuft (*Iberis sempervirens*)—or plant them among perennials that will bloom in summer or fall to stage a season-long display.

Forcing Hardy Spring Bulbs

Forcing bulbs is an easy way to enjoy a dose of spring color in the winter. Forced pots of bulbs also make ideal, relatively inexpensive gifts.

Start with healthy, top-size bulbs—plant pots with all one color or type of bulb, mix colors (combine two different Darwin tulips, for example), or experiment with interplanting different species that bloom at the same time. You can dig bulbs right out of the garden, too. Grape hyacinths indicate their location in fall because that's when their foliage appears. Established plantings of snowdrops often push bulbs to the surface, or you can mark the locations of bulbs that need dividing and dig them in fall, replanting the ones you don't want for forcing. You'll also need a selection of clay bulb pans or azalea pots, both of which are shallower than normal pots.

Cover the hole in the bottom of each pot with a piece of broken pot—it should be a curved piece so that water, but not the planting medium, can drain out of the bottom of the pots. Spread a layer of soilless potting medium in the bottom of the pots and set the bulbs so their tips will be just at or slightly above the surface of the medium. Pack the bulbs closely in next to one another for the best show. You can add a second layer of bulbs by staggering them over the first layer, after sifting in additional potting medium. Place tulips with the flat side of the bulb to the outside of the pot, because the first leaf emerges from that side of the bulb and this creates a pot with an attractive outer ring of leaves. Fill the pots almost to the rim with potting medium and water them thoroughly.

The bulbs then require a period of cold, but above-freezing, temperatures (35° to 40°F) to grow roots. During this period the medium should be kept moist but not wet. Set the pots in a cold frame, an unheated garage, a root cellar, or even a refrigerator for this period. In general bulbs need 3½ to 4 months of cool temperatures to grow roots. After that, they can be brought out for forcing, which takes another 2 to 3 weeks before the plants are in full bloom.

When you bring the pots out of cold storage for forcing, set them for about a week in a dark, cool (55° to 60°F) place. Then force them either under lights or on windowsills in a cool place (65°F days; 60°F nights). Stake tall plants, such as daffodils and tulips, to keep them upright. (Ringing the pots with small stakes connected by string works fine.) If you plan on saving the bulbs, fertilize with a liquid fertilizer such as fish emulsion every other time you water. After the pots have bloomed, set them in a sheltered corner outdoors after the last spring frost date. Keep the pots evenly moist until the foliage has turned yellow. The bulbs can be dumped out of the pots and planted in the garden in spring or fall. Forced bulbs may take a season or two to recover and resume blooming.

Edge a path with bulbs, or plant them along shrub borders or among early-blooming shrubs such as azaleas (*Rhododendron* spp.). Or intersperse bulbs in a bed filled with low-growing ground covers such as periwinkle (*Vinca minor*). Little bulbs, along with species tulips and dwarf daffodils, are excellent rock-garden plants.

In woodland or wild gardens, many bulbs can be naturalized, that is, planted and left to spread without further care. Good subjects for this use include all types of daffodils along with little bulbs such as glory-of-the-snow (*Chionodoxa* spp.), snowdrops (*Galanthus* spp.), winter aconite (*Eranthis hyemalis*), dogtooth violets (*Erythronium* spp.), bluebells (*Hyacinthoides* spp.), grape hyacinths (*Muscari* spp.), and squills (*Puschkinia* spp. and *Scilla* spp.). Camassias (*Camassia* spp.) also are excellent for naturalizing.

To hide ripening bulb foliage, interplant bulbs with perennials that have leaves that will conceal it, such as hostas, fringed bleeding heart (*Dicentra eximia*), or columbines (*Aquilegia* spp.). Overplanting with shallow-rooted annuals such as marigolds or impatiens is another option.

How you arrange the bulbs will depend on the style of your garden. Whether your garden is formal or informal, though, bulbs are most effective planted in groups. Plan on a minimum of three for larger bulbs such as crown imperial (*Fritillaria imperialis*). For daffodils and tulips, six is probably a better minimum. There is no maximum, especially with the little bulbs, which are breathtaking when planted in 50s and 100s. If your bulb budget is limited, buy the most you can afford and divide them regularly to achieve large mass plantings. Many catalogs offer discount prices on quantities of particular species or cultivars—or on collections of bulbs—and these specials are a good way to build a display.

Formal gardens usually call for plants arranged in rows or blocks. Excavating the entire planting area and using string to align the bulbs are the best ways to achieve a formal look. In informal designs, bulbs are typically planted in free-form drifts or clumps. Some gardeners simply toss the bulbs and plant them where they fall for a natural effect. (I always worry about finding all of them, though.) Another approach is to draw a shape on the soil with a stick to indicate a planting area and then distribute the bulbs evenly within it.

When planting bulbs, keep in mind that you don't need to plant only one kind in each hole. Consider layering bulbs in a single spot, for example, by planting daffodils deep, filling the hole partway, and adding snowdrops, grape hyacinths, or crocuses on top. You can combine bulbs that will bloom at the same time, such as contrasting colors of Darwin tulips. Or plan for a succession of bloom by setting early, midseason, and late bloomers in the same spot.

GROWING GUIDE

The following guide to popular hardy spring bulbs provides brief descriptions followed by information on planting, spacing, site selection, and use. Unless otherwise noted, all of the plants listed should be cared for as described earlier. The following hardy spring bulbs are covered in individual entries elsewhere in this book: *Allium* (alliums, ornamental onions), *Anemone* (anemones, windflowers), *Iris* (irises), *Narcissus* (daffodils, narcissus), and *Tulipa* (tulips).

Brimeura amethystina / Brimeura
Graceful, loose racemes of nodding, bell-shaped, pale to dark blue, 1/2-inch flowers in early spring; grassy leaves; 4- to 10-inch plants. Bulb; plant 2 inches deep, 2 to 3 inches apart. (Formerly *Hyacinthus amethystinus*). Zones 5 to 9.

Camassia spp. / Camassias, camass, quamash
Tall spikes of starry, blue or white flowers in late spring; grassy leaves; 1½- to 2-foot plants. Bulb; plant 4 inches deep, 5 to 8 inches apart. Propagate by offsets, although they are not produced in abundance, or from seeds. Camassias seldom need division. They are native North American wildflowers that tolerate damper conditions than most bulbs, especially in spring, when they will survive temporary flooding. Evenly moist soil is best, and essential during the growing season. Plants will tolerate drier conditions when dormant. Wet soil in winter will rot the bulbs. Mass plantings are the most effective. Good cut flowers. Zones 4 to 9.

Chionodoxa luciliae / Glory-of-the-snow
Dainty racemes of clear blue, star-shaped flowers with white eyes in very early spring; grassy leaves; 3- to 8-inch plants. Bulb; plant 3 inches deep, 3 inches apart. Offsets and self-sown seedlings are produced in abundance. Zones 3 to 9.

Crocus spp. / Crocuses
Cup-shaped yellow, white, purple, lavender, or bicolor blooms borne near the ground; grassy leaves; 3- to 5-inch plants. Bloom season varies depending on the species. Snow crocus *(C. chrysanthus),* cloth-of-gold crocus *(C. angustifolius),* and *C. tommasinianus* are among the earliest, blooming from late winter into early spring. Scotch crocus *(C. biflorus)* and Dutch crocus *(C. vernus)* bloom somewhat later, in early to midspring. See "Fall Bulbs" on page 63 for information on fall-blooming crocuses. Corm; plant 3 to

Dutch crocus (*Crocus vernus* 'Vanguard')

4 inches deep, 3 to 4 inches apart. Sandy or gritty, well-drained soil is best; the corms do not do well in clay soils or moist conditions. Dutch crocuses are best for naturalizing in a lawn but will tend to die out after several years unless the turf is sparse. Replace them as necessary. Do not mow the lawn until after the crocus foliage turns yellow and dies back. Zones 3 to 8.

Eranthis hyemalis / Winter aconite
Yellow, cup-shaped flowers with a ruff of green leaves beneath the blooms, which are borne in very early spring; 3- to 8-inch plants. Knobby tuber; plant 2 inches deep and 3 inches apart after soaking the tubers overnight in warm water. Old tubers that have dried out too much may not grow. Propagate by moving self-seeded plants; avoid digging and disturbing the clumps. Requires rich, well-drained soil that remains evenly moist in summer. Zones 4 to 9.

Erythronium spp. / Dogtooth violets, trout lilies
Nodding pink, white, yellow, or cream, lilylike flowers in late spring to early summer; pairs of handsome, broad to oval leaves often mottled with brown or cream; 6- to 14-inch plants. Long, tooth- or fang-shaped bulbs; plant them upright, not lengthwise, 4 to 6 inches deep and 2 to 3 inches apart. Do not let the bulbs dry out before planting; keep them packed in barely damp peat moss or vermiculite. Best in dappled shade and deeply prepared, evenly moist soil rich in organic matter. Mulch plantings with chopped leaves, compost, or shredded bark to keep the soil moist, cool, and rich. Commonly grown species, with

TOP Dogtooth violets
(Erythronium americanum) with mayapples *(Podophyllum peltatum)*

ABOVE Crown imperial *(Fritillaria imperialis)*

ABOVE RIGHT Checkered lily *(Fritillaria meleagris)*

the exception of *E. dens-canis*, are native North American wildflowers. *E. americanum, E. californicum,* and *E. dens-canis* are hardy in Zones 3 to 9; *E. revolutum*, in Zones 5 to 9.

Fritillaria spp. / Fritillaries

Nodding, bell-like flowers, borne singly or in clusters in spring or early summer; lance-shaped or grassy leaves. A large genus containing both easy- and difficult-to-grow species. Crown imperial *(F. imperialis)* is an easy-to-grow, old-fashioned flower with orange, yellow, or red flowers in clusters topped by a sheaf of leaflike bracts. Plants are 2 to 4 feet tall and bloom in early spring. Zones 5 to 9. Checkered lily *(F. meleagris)*, also easy, has solitary red-purple to black

flowers faintly checked with white on 1-foot-tall plants. Zones 3 to 8. *F. persica* produces spikes of mauve-purple flowers on 1- to 3-foot plants. Zones 6 to 8. All three grow in full sun or light shade cast by deciduous trees in rich, well-drained soil. *F. persica* is best in a hot, sun-baked site. *F. michailovskyi*, hardy in Zones 5 to 8, is best reserved for rock gardens, raised beds, and other sites with rich but very well drained soil. There are many other species worth trying, including several native to western North America. These generally require perfect drainage and dry conditions when dormant. If in doubt about whether your garden offers the right conditions, start with a small number of bulbs and experiment to find a suitable site.

Bulbs are fragile and should not be allowed to dry out before planting. (Avoid buying dried-out bulbs at garden centers.) Store them, if you can't plant immediately, in barely moist vermiculite or peat moss. Plant fairly deeply—at least four times their height; plant *F. imperialis* with the tops of the bulbs 5 to 6 inches below the surface. Be sure to prepare the soil several inches *below* where the bulbs will sit, to provide rich and well-drained conditions. Some species, including *F. imperialis,* have open-crowned bulbs that can catch moisture, causing them to rot. To prevent this, place 2 to 3 inches of sharp sand (also called builder's sand) in the bottom of the planting holes and set the bulbs on their sides when planting. Space *F. imperialis* and *F. persica* about 1 foot apart; smaller species, 3 to 4 inches apart. Divide established plantings only when they become too crowded. Dig them after the foliage has ripened. Mulch plantings with compost or feed with very well rotted manure in spring. For species intolerant of moist soil when they are dormant, mulch with granite chips or pea gravel.

Galanthus spp. / Snowdrops

Small, pendent, white or green-and-white flowers with teardroplike petals borne in late winter or very early spring; grassy leaves; 4 to 8 inch plants. Bulb; plant 3 inches deep, 3 inches apart. Produces offsets and self-sown seedlings in abundance. Clumps can be left undisturbed for years and will become quite large. Crowded clumps will push bulbs up to the soil surface. Best in partial shade in rich soil that remains evenly moist but not wet in summer. Common snowdrop *(G. nivalis)* is hardy in Zones 4 to 9; giant snowdrop *(G. elwesii),* Zones 3 to 9.

Hyacinthoides spp. / Bluebells

Erect spikes of bell-shaped blue, white, or pink flowers in midspring; clumps of strap-shaped leaves; 8- to 16-inch plants. Bulb; plant 3 inches deep, 6 inches apart. Self-sows and produces abundant offsets. The plants can be left in place to form large, handsome clumps. Botanists have reclassified plants in this genus numerous times. Spanish bluebell, *H. hispanica,* is also listed as *Endymion hispanicus, Scilla campanulata,* and *S. hispanica.* English bluebell, *H. non-scripta,* is also listed as *E. non-scriptus, S. non-scripta,* and *S. nutans.* Good cut flowers. Some gardeners develop skin allergies to the foliage and flowers. Zones 4 to 9.

Hyacinthus orientalis / Hyacinth

Intensely fragrant, oval trusses of bell-shaped flowers in white, pink, lilac-blue, violet, and yellow borne from early to midspring; strap-shaped leaves; 8- to 12-inch plants. Bulb; plant 4 to 5 inches deep, 3 to 4 inches apart. In the North, cover plantings with evergreen boughs, salt hay, or other loose mulch to protect the shoots when they emerge in spring; remove the mulch after the

Naturalized snowdrops *(Galanthus nivalis)*

Hyacinth *(Hyacinthus orientalis)* with tulips and daffodils

TOP Grape hyacinth
(*Muscari armeniacum*)

ABOVE Siberian squill
(*Scilla siberica*)

4 to 5 inches apart. A site in full sun with well-drained, moderately rich soil is best. Grows well in sandy soils. Clumps can be left undisturbed for years until they become crowded and flowering diminishes. Foliage appears in fall and persists over winter. Can be grown in Zones 6 to 9, but mulch the plants with evergreen boughs or other coarse mulch in fall to protect plants over winter in colder parts of Zone 7 and in Zone 6.

Leucojum spp. / Snowflakes

Nodding, bell-shaped white blooms dotted with green in mid- to late spring; grassy leaves. Bulb; plant 3 inches deep, 3 to 4 inches apart. A site with evenly moist, humus-rich soil is best. Summer snowflake (*L. aestivum*) is 1½ to 2 feet tall and hardy in Zones 4 to 9. Spring snowflake (*L. vernum*) is 8 to 12 inches tall and hardy in Zones 4 to 8.

Muscari spp. / Grape hyacinths

Fragrant, erect, grapelike clusters of tubular or bell-shaped flowers in early to midspring in shades of violet, purplish blue, pale blue, and white; grassy leaves; 6- to 8-inch plants. Bulb; plant 3 inches deep, 3 to 4 inches apart. Produces offsets and self-sown seedlings in abundance. The foliage appears in fall and overwinters. Plant grape hyacinths with tulips, daffodils, and other spring bulbs and their fall foliage will mark the location of the bulbs. *M. armeniacum* and *M. latifolium* are hardy in Zones 4 to 8; *M. botyroides*, Zones 3 to 8.

Ornithogalum spp. / Stars-of-Bethlehem

Erect spikes of starry white flowers, often striped with green on the outside, in late spring; narrow or broad leaves at the base of the plant. The genus includes hardy and tender species. Two hardy species are *O. nutans*, hardy in Zones 6 to 10 and 8 to 18 inches tall, and *O. umbellatum*, hardy in Zones 5 to 9 and 6 to 12 inches tall. Bulb; plant 4 inches deep, 4 to 5 inches apart. Produces offsets in abundance. Both species can become invasive, so they are best restricted to wild gardens or planted along the base of a shrub border where they can spread at will. Can also be naturalized in a lawn, but the grass must be left uncut until the foliage ripens.

Puschkinia scilloides / Striped squill

Small, hyacinth-like clusters of bell-shaped, bluish white flowers with darker blue stripes in early to midspring; straplike leaves; 6- to 8-inch plants. Bulb; plant 3 inches deep, 3 inches apart. Over time, will form good-size clumps, which can be left undisturbed for years. Dig and divide plants if flowering diminishes. Zones 3 to 9.

danger of a hard frost has passed. Plants produce the largest blooms the first spring and smaller, more natural-looking and graceful spikes thereafter. Feeding plants in spring when the leaves emerge with a topdressing of well-rotted manure or a balanced organic fertilizer helps keep the blooms large. For formal plantings with exhibition-size blooms, replace the bulbs annually (bulbs can be moved to less formal areas of the garden, where they'll produce small clumps with time). Good cut flowers. Some gardeners develop a skin allergy to the foliage. Zones 5 to 9.

Ipheion uniflorum / Spring starflower

Star-shaped, lilac-blue, 1-inch flowers in late winter or early spring; grassy, onion-scented leaves; 6- to 8-inch plants. Bulb; plant 3 inches deep,

Scilla spp. / Squills

Erect clusters of bell-shaped or starry rich blue, purple, white or pink flowers, generally in early spring; grassy leaves; common species are 4 to 8 inches tall. Siberian squill *(S. siberica),* with deep blue, nodding, bell-shaped flowers, is the most common. It is hardy in Zones 4 to 8. Twin-leaf squill *(S. bifolia)* bears clusters of purple-blue, starry flowers and is hardy in Zones 3 to 8. There are many other species, both hardy and tender. Bulb; plant 3 inches deep, 3 to 4 inches apart. Over time, will form good-size clumps, which can be left undisturbed for years. Dig and divide plants if flowering diminishes. Most effective planted in large drifts of 100 or more bulbs.

SUMMER BULBS

In terms of cultural needs, summer bulbs are a bit of a mixed bag. There are hardy and tender plants in this category, which are grown differently depending on where you live. Where hardy, they are grown much like any of the other bulbs. In areas where they are not, however, they must be overwintered indoors, a process that sounds difficult but isn't really all that complicated. Whether they are hardy or tender, all of the plants listed below are easy to grow and repay the gardener with abundant color in return for minimal care. The following summer bulbs are covered in individual entries elsewhere in this book: *Begonia* (begonias), *Canna × generalis* (canna), *Dahlia* (dahlias), *Liatris* (gayfeathers), and *Lilium* (lilies).

Agapanthus spp. / African lilies, agapanthus

Rounded clusters, called umbels, of bell- or trumpet-shaped blue, purple, or white flowers borne on stalks well above the foliage; straplike, evergreen or deciduous leaves; 1½- to 3-foot plants. The plants grow from a short, tuberous rhizome and have thick, fleshy roots. Where hardy (Zones 8 to 11), agapanthus are grown outdoors in full sun in deep, rich, well-drained soil that remains evenly moist but never wet. Feed plants grown outdoors in spring when growth begins and remove faded flowers. While some cultivars are hardy to Zone 7, in the North these striking plants are best grown in large containers and overwintered indoors. Use large tubs or plastic pots (the roots of established plants can break terra-cotta pots). Set the tubs on sunny patios or terraces and water regularly to keep the soil evenly moist but not wet. Feed monthly from spring until they begin to flower in summer. Deadhead regularly.

In fall, bring the tubs indoors before frost and store them in a cool (40° to 50°F) bright spot and water sparingly until early summer, when they can be moved back outdoors. Divide plants

grown outdoors or in containers as necessary in spring before new growth begins. Wash soil off the fleshy roots, cut the rhizomes into manageable sections, remove broken roots, and then replant in fresh soil.

Caladium spp. / Caladiums, angel wings

Tender foliage plant grown for its large, arrowhead-shaped leaves that are brightly patterned in greens, pinks, rose-reds, maroon, and white; 1½- to 2-foot plants. Tuber; start tubers indoors 8 to 10 weeks before the last spring frost date (temperatures must remain above 55°F before these tender bulbs can be moved outdoors). Set tubers close together in flats filled with barely moist vermiculite, and cover the tops with 1 inch of vermiculite. Set the flats in a warm (70° to 85°F), humid place until leaves and roots sprout. Then plant the tubers in individual 5- to 6-inch bulb pans (these are shallow pots) filled with potting medium. Water regularly, keeping the soil evenly moist, and set them in a bright spot, such as a north or east window. (Three or more tubers can also be planted in large bulb pans.) In early summer, once soil and air temperatures have moderated, move the plants, still in their containers, to a spot that receives bright, dappled shade but is sheltered from direct sun. Or plant them directly in the garden in a shady spot with evenly moist soil that is rich in organic matter. Water regularly to keep the soil moist. Monthly feedings with a diluted fertilizer will encourage large leaves. Remove the greenish white flowers as they appear. Plants can be grown in containers through the summer.

Although some gardeners grow these plants as annuals and start with new tubers each spring, overwintering them isn't difficult. Let the soil dry gradually in fall, dig the tubers before frost, and set them in a warm, dry spot for several days to dry. Clean off soil and remove roots and tops before storing them in sand or vermiculite in a cool (55° to 60°F) place. Pot-grown plants can be stored under similar conditions—just turn the containers on their sides. To propagate, cut the tubers with a knife in spring, then dust the cut pieces with sulfur before starting the cycle again.

Caladiums are ideal for adding summer-long color to shady beds and borders, or to shady terraces when grown in containers.

Crocosmia spp. / Crocosmias, montbretias

Arching clusters of trumpet-shaped flowers in orange, red-orange, or yellow; sword-shaped leaves; 2- to 3-foot plants. Corm; plant in spring 3 to 4 inches deep, 4 to 5 inches apart. Will form dense, good-size clumps with time. Plant in full sun in a site with evenly moist soil rich in organic matter.

Hardy gladiolus
(Gladiolus communis ssp. *byzantinus)*

TOP *Crocosmia* 'Lucifer'

ABOVE *Crocosmia masoniorum*

ABOVE RIGHT Hardy amaryllis *(Lycoris squamigera)*

Propagate by dividing the clumps in early spring or fall. Crocosmias are hardy in Zones 6 to 9; in Zone 5 and north, dig the clumps in fall, clean the soil off the corms, and overwinter them in a cool, dry place. They may survive outdoors in Zone 5 if given a warm spot against a south-facing wall or if mulched heavily in fall. Use crocosmias in perennial beds and borders with other late-summer- to fall-blooming perennials.

Gladiolus spp. / Gladioli, glads

Flaring, trumpet-shaped spikes in all colors except true blue; sword-shaped leaves; 2- to 4-foot plants. Corm; plant in spring. Corm size determines planting depth: set small corms ($^1/_2$-inch-diameter) 3 inches deep, medium ($^1/_2$- to 1-inch) corms 4 to 5 inches deep, and large corms (over 1-inch-diameter) 6 to 8 inches deep. Space corms from 3 to 6 inches apart depending on their size. Plant in full sun in a site with light, evenly moist soil rich in organic matter. Common gladiolus (*G.* × *hortulanus*) and its many cultivars are reliably hardy in Zones 8 to 10 but will survive outdoors

with a thick winter mulch in Zone 7. Hardy gladiolus (*G. communis* ssp. *byzantinus*) is hardy in Zones 5 to 10 and is planted in spring. With all glads, work a balanced organic fertilizer into the soil at planting time. For best results, plant by digging a shallow trench or hole and filling it gradually with soil as the plants grow. Deep planting helps eliminate the need to stake plants, but stake them if necessary. Interplanting with perennials or annuals also helps support the stems. Plant new corms of common gladiolus at 2- to 3-week intervals from spring to midsummer to prolong the bloom season.

In areas where the plants are not hardy, let the foliage ripen for 6 weeks after flowering. Then dig the corms, cut or twist off the foliage, and set them in a warm, dry place for a few days so they can dry thoroughly before storage. Separate the new corms and small cormels from the old withered one, which will not bloom again. Dust the corms with sulfur or other fungicide and store them in a cool (40°F), dry place over winter.

Use glads as accents in plantings of annuals and perennials. They are most effective when planted in large clumps. They are also excellent cut flowers and can be grown in rows in a cutting garden or even a vegetable garden.

Hymenocallis narcissiflora / Peruvian daffodil, basket flower, spider lily

Very fragrant, spidery, white, daffodil-like trumpets in summer; strap-shaped leaves; 2-foot plants. Bulb; set the bulbs outdoors in spring after the soil has warmed up and temperatures have moderated with the tops 3 to 4 inches below the soil surface, spaced 8 to 10 inches apart. Select a site in full sun or partial shade with deeply prepared soil rich in organic matter. Water deeply in dry weather. Propagate by separating the offsets.

The plants are hardy in Zones 8 to 11; in warm spots in Zone 7 with winter protection. In the North, dig the bulbs in fall before the first frost, leaving as many roots as possible attached. Dry them upside down, with the foliage still attached. When the foliage has dried completely, store them in nearly dry peat moss or vermiculite in a cool (55° to 60°F) place.

Lycoris squamigera / **Hardy amaryllis, magic lily**
Clusters of fragrant, pink, trumpet-shaped blooms in late summer; strap-shaped leaves in spring, long before the flowers; 1½- to 2-foot plants. Bulb; plant in fall with the tops of the bulbs 4 to 6 inches below the soil surface, spaced 9 inches apart. Plant in full sun or partial shade in deeply prepared soil that is well drained and rich in organic matter. Propagate by separating the offsets, but plants are best left undisturbed as long as possible. Disturbing them can prevent flowering for one or two seasons, and undisturbed plants gradually form large clumps. Mark the location of the plants so you don't dig into them by mistake after the foliage dies back in spring. Top-dress with a balanced organic fertilizer before the foliage emerges. Use hardy amaryllis in beds and borders combined with perennials such as hostas or low-growing asters, which will provide a foil for the blooms. Or overplant the bulbs with annuals that will complement the flowers. Zones 6 to 10; to Zone 5 with protection. Red-flowered *L. radiata* is grown in the same manner but is hardy in Zones 8 to 10.

FALL BULBS

Not nearly as well known as the hardy spring bulbs, fall bulbs are a bit harder to find. They're well worth the effort it takes to search them out, though, because of the showy color they add to the garden at the end of the season. Fall bulbs are planted in mid- to late summer instead of fall, but otherwise they are cared for just like hardy spring bulbs. Allow the foliage to ripen naturally before cutting it back. Propagate fall bulbs by separating offsets or by potting up or moving self-sown seedlings.

Colchicum spp. / **Autumn crocuses**
Crocuslike flowers in pink or rose-purple in fall; strap-shaped leaves in spring. *C. autumnale*, 4 to 6 inches tall, and *C. speciosum*, 6 to 7 inches tall, are the most commonly grown. Both are hardy in Zones 4 to 9. A number of excellent cultivars are also available. Corm; plant with 2 to 3 inches of soil over the top of the corm, 6 to 9 inches apart. A site in full sun with rich, well-drained soil that is evenly moist is best. It is important to plant them as soon as they are available in late

summer or very early fall: they'll bloom right on the countertop or in the wheelbarrow if not planted right away. When selecting a site, keep in mind that the ripening foliage, which appears in spring, is unattractive. Choose a site where it won't be too noticeable, perhaps along a shrub border or among perennials such as hostas that will hide it. Although the corms are much more expensive than true crocuses, they are poisonous and not bothered by rodents. With time, they produce showy, large clumps. Propagate by dividing the clumps in summer after the foliage dies back.

Crocus spp. / **Autumn-flowering crocuses**
Cup-shaped rose-purple, purple, or violet blooms in fall; grassy leaves with or just after the flowers; 2- to 4-inch plants. A number of fall-blooming crocuses are available. *C. speciosus*, the first to bloom, has blue-lilac flowers. Other fall species

BELOW Autumn crocus
(*Colchicum speciosum*)

BOTTOM Double autumn crocus
(*Colchicum* 'Waterlily')

Cyclamen for Spring or Fall

Hardy cyclamen, diminutive versions of the showy florist's pot plants, bear small pink or white flowers with reflexed petals. Their round, dark green leaves usually are handsomely marked with silver, and the plants range from 2 to 6 inches in height. *Cyclamen coum* flowers in late winter to very early spring. *C. purpurascens* flowers in late summer, while *C. cilicium* and *C. hederifolium* flower in fall. Plant the tubers 1½ to 2 inches deep and 3 to 4 inches apart. Select a site in partial shade with loose soil that is well drained and rich in organic matter. Mulch plants annually with compost or leaf mold when the leaves fade. All are hardy in Zones 5 to 9 except *C. hederifolium,* which is best grown only to Zone 6. In the North, mulch the plants in late fall with evergreen branches, oak leaves, or other coarse mulch to protect them from winter freezing and thawing cycles. Be sure to uncover *C. coum* in late winter, or you will miss the flowers.

Hardy cyclamen *(Cyclamen coum)*

to look for include *C. kotschyanus, C. medius,* and *C. pulchellus.* All are hardy in Zones 3 to 8. Saffron crocus *(C. sativus)* is hardy in Zones 5 to 8. Corm; plant 3 to 4 inches deep, 3 to 4 inches apart. Select a site in full sun with sandy or poor to average soil that is well drained. Most appreciate dry conditions in summer when they are dormant. Plant the corms as soon as they are available, in late summer or very early fall.

Sternbergia lutea / Winter daffodil, lily-of-the-field

Golden yellow, goblet-shaped flowers; lance-shaped leaves appear with the flowers and persist until spring; 6-inch plants. Bulb; plant 4 to 6 inches deep, 4 inches apart. Plant in midsummer in full sun. Requires very well drained, somewhat fertile soil. Divide plants only if they become overcrowded. Zones 6 to 9.

Campanula

Bellflowers

■ Valued for their flowers in shades of blue, lavender, and purple, bellflowers are easily satisfied plants that add color to the garden over a long season. While the most popular bellflowers are perennials, the genus contains annuals as well as one popular biennial — Canterbury bells *(Campanula medium).* The plants vary in size and shape from mat-forming spreaders to stately, upright perennials for beds and borders. All produce a mound or rosette of lower, or basal, leaves. Flowering stems, which have smaller leaves along their length, rise above the basal leaves from late spring onward.

While the name *Campanula* means "little bell" in Latin, not all bellflowers have bell-shaped flowers. There are bellflowers with narrow, tubular blooms as well as ones with star-shaped or broader, cup- or saucer-shaped ones. The flowers are nodding, outward facing, or upright and typically are carried in branched clusters, called racemes, in shades from white and palest blue to violet-purple. While racemes are most common, some species bear their flowers in rounded heads; others, one per stem (called solitary).

SELECTING BELLFLOWERS

Entire books have been written about the bellflowers — there are about 300 species in all, but the most popular ones are valued because of their reliable bloom and ease of culture. These can be grouped into the taller bellflowers that are appropriate for beds and borders and the low-growing species that are suitable for growing in walls, rock gardens, and similar situations.

One species most gardeners should avoid is creeping bellflower *(C. rapunculoides),* which bears violet-purple bells on 3-foot plants. That's because "creeping" is hardly the right adjective for this fast-spreading, invasive plant that spreads by rhizomes and seeds. Once it is established in a garden, it becomes a weed that is nearly impossible to eradicate.

Bellflowers for Beds and Borders

All of the following species are suitable for planting in either full sun or partial shade and average, well-drained soil. All make handsome cut flowers. The heights given indicate the plants in bloom—the mounds of foliage beneath the flowers are considerably shorter.

C. glomerata. Clustered bellflower. Rounded clusters of violet or white flowers on erect stems from early to midsummer; 1- to 2-foot plants. Vigorous; spreads by underground rhizomes to form broad clumps. Does not need staking. Cut back plants after flowering to encourage repeat bloom. Easy to propagate by division. Tolerates wet soil. Zones 3 to 8.

C. lactiflora. Milky bellflower. Large, branched clusters of white or lavender-blue, 1-inch flowers from early to late summer; 3- to 5-foot plants. Requires well-drained but evenly moist soil for best growth and is a good choice for a site in partial shade, which prolongs flowering. Established plants do not transplant well; best propagated by seeds sown where the plants are to grow. Self-sows. Deadhead plants as the flowers fade and they will rebloom in fall. Requires staking. Zones 3 to 7.

C. medium. Canterbury bells. A biennial with bell-shaped purple, lavender, white, or pink, 1½- to 2-inch-long flowers from late spring to midsummer; 1½- to 3-foot plants. Best in areas with relatively cool summers that are not humid. To grow as a biennial, sow seeda outdoors in late spring or early summer in pots or in a holding bed in a protected site with soil amply amended with compost or other organic matter. Keep seedlings watered and weeded, and thin as necessary. Protect plants over winter with a coarse mulch such as evergreen boughs or salt hay in Zone 7 and north. (The foliage is evergreen and finer materials would hold excess moisture near the crown, leading to rot.) Early the following spring, move plants to the spot where they will flower. To grow them as a cool-weather annual, sow seeds indoors 6 to 8 weeks before the last spring frost date. Either way, pull up plants that have flowered and start new seedlings annually. Taller types may require staking. Zones 5 to 8.

C. persicifolia. Peach-leaved bellflower. Graceful racemes of outward-pointing, bell- to saucer-shaped blooms in pale blue, violet-blue, or white from early to midsummer; 1- to 3-foot-tall bloom stalks over 1-foot-tall mounds of foliage. Evergreen in mild climates. Clump-forming species that spreads gradually but steadily by new shoots that arise at the base of the plant. Also self-sows. Requires staking. Zones 3 to 7.

Campanula
■
(cam-PAN-you-lah)
■
Spring to summer bloom
■
Full sun or partial shade
■
Zones 2 to 8
■

BELOW Clustered bellflower *(Campanula glomerata)*

BELOW RIGHT Peach-leaved bellflower *(Campanula persicifolia)*

Bellflowers for Walls and Rock Gardens

While rock-gardening enthusiasts cultivate some very fussy bellflowers, the species below are just the opposite. All thrive in well-drained, somewhat gritty soil in full sun or partial shade; in the South, afternoon shade is best. Use them in rock gardens, where they add essential color after the main flush of spring color has passed, as well as along pathways, in rock walls, or in raised beds — any site that offers the well-drained conditions they require. They are especially attractive when their sprawling stems are allowed to trail; their creeping roots will also find their way through crevices, and for this reason, plants will pop up in unexpected spots.

C. carpatica. Carpathian harebell. Masses of upward-facing, cup-shaped flowers in blue, violet, or white borne one or two per stem; low,

8- to 12-inch clump-forming plants. Flowers appear over a long season from late spring through summer, with the main bloom from late spring to early summer. Requires well-drained, cool soil (a root-run under rocks is ideal, but mulch also keeps the soil cool) and spreads vigorously in these conditions. Reblooms without deadheading. Can be short lived but self-sows. Zones 3 to 8.

C. cochleariifolia. Spiral bellflower, fairies' thimbles. Nodding, lilac-blue to white flowers in summer, borne one per stem; 3- to 6-inch plants. Creeping, mat-forming plant. Zones 5 to 7.

C. portenschlagiana. Dalmatian bellflower. Bell-shaped, 1-inch-wide, violet-purple flowers borne in panicles from late spring to early summer; 4- to 6-inch plants. A vigorous, mound-forming plant with evergreen to semievergreen leaves that spreads rapidly by underground stems. Sometimes reblooms in fall. More heat tolerant and a better choice for southern gardens than *C. carpatica.* Zones 4 to 8.

C. poscharskyana. Serbian bellflower. Loose, trailing panicles of starry, pale blue flowers in early summer; mounding, 6- to 12-inch plants. A vigorous to invasive bellflower that spreads quickly by underground runners. 'Stella' has violet flowers and is somewhat less invasive. Cut plants back after flowering for repeat bloom in late summer. Zones 3 to 7.

C. rotundifolia. Bluebell, harebell. Dainty, nodding bells on slender stems in summer in pale blue to violet-blue or white; 5- to 12-inch plants. A clump-forming plant that spreads by underground runners. Although sometimes called Scotch bluebell or bluebells of Scotland, this species is also native to Canada south to Missouri and Pennsylvania. The round basal leaves from which the species takes its name die away early in the season. Zones 2 to 7.

SITE AND SOIL

While bellflowers grow in full sun or partial shade, the preferred site depends on where you live and whether you are growing bed-and-border or rock-garden types. Most bellflowers do not tolerate heat well — they grow best in areas where temperatures routinely dip below 70°F at night in summer and languish where daytime temperatures rise above about 90°F. In the South — especially in Zone 8 but also in the hotter portions of Zone 7 — a site with partial shade during the hottest part of the day is ideal. Plants may be short lived in hot climates, but they are still worth the effort of growing them.

Bellflowers grow in slightly acid to slightly alkaline soil. While bed-and-border types are happy in average soil that is moist but well drained, rock-garden species need cool, gritty,

very well drained conditions. They are best tucked between boulders in a rock garden or planted in rock walls where the soil is cool and their roots can run deeply into the crevices. Many also will thrive along pathways, in raised beds, along terraced beds, or at the front of a perennial border, provided the soil is well drained. Self-sown seedlings may appear between paving stones.

PLANTING

Plant bellflowers in early spring or fall, and work plenty of organic matter, such as finished compost, into the soil to encourage good drainage and even moisture. Space plants according to height—rock-garden types can be spaced as close as 9 inches apart, while taller-growing species should be given 1½ feet or more. For best effect, plant in groups of three or more. To start bellflowers in a tight spot in a rock garden or in a rock wall, improve the soil by adding compost and sharp (builder's) sand, then tuck seedlings in with a narrow trowel.

CARE THROUGH THE SEASON

Bellflowers need about the same amount of care as most popular perennials. Feed plants in spring with a topdressing of well-rotted manure or compost, or a balanced organic fertilizer. Water deeply during dry spells, as the plants are not particularly drought tolerant, and remove spent flowers regularly to extend bloom. Mulch plants in summer to control weeds and to keep the soil cool. Divide plants every 3 to 4 years to keep them vigorous and under control. Fast-spreading species may need division every 2 to 3 years. See "Propagation" below for details.

Staking is necessary for taller types, especially those with brittle stems. Stake early in the season: a ring of stakes with string provides good support, but twiggy brush works well for shorter types.

Propagation. Bellflowers can be propagated by division, cuttings, or seeds. Use division or cuttings to propagate named cultivars, unless you don't mind that seedlings will be variable.

Divide plants in early spring or early fall by digging the clumps and cutting them apart with a sharp knife. Discard older, less vigorous portions and replant or give away the rest. To dig individual plants that arise from the runners of some species, use a trowel to sever the runner and dig the new plant.

In spring, take cuttings from the base of the plant before buds or flowers appear. Root them in a 50-50 mix of perlite and vermiculite.

There are several ways to sow the seeds, which are very small. Annual, biennial, and perennial bellflowers can be sown indoors 6 to 8 weeks before the last spring frost date. Move hardened-off seedlings outdoors after the last frost date. After the last frost date in spring and into early summer, perennials can be sown outdoors in a nursery bed or into pots set in a protected location. Or sow them in early spring in pots set in a cold frame. However you sow them, rake the seedbed smooth and sow the seeds on the surface.

Potential Problems. Bellflowers have few problems, but slugs and snails will dine on the flowers and foliage. See the box on page 166 in the *Hosta* entry for control suggestions.

LANDSCAPE USES

Bellflowers are a must for cool-color gardens, which feature blues and purples. Use taller-growing species in the middle of beds and borders, shorter species as edgings. Either way, plant in clumps of three or more for best effect. Combine them with perennials such as astilbes, hardy geraniums, baby's breath *(Gypsophila* spp.), columbines *(Aquilegia* spp.), pinks *(Dianthus* spp.), foxgloves *(Digitalis* spp.), and Siberian iris *(Iris sibirica)*. They are also attractive with hostas and ferns in a semishaded spot. Look for low-growing forms of these plants as companions for the rock-garden types of bellflowers.

TOP Serbian bellflower *(Campanula poscharskyana)*

ABOVE Bluebell *(Campanula rotundifolia)*

Canna × *generalis*

Canna

Canna × *generalis*
■
(CAN-ah jen-er-AL-iss)
■
Summer bloom
■
Full sun
■
Zones 8 to 11; tender perennial grown as an annual
■

RIGHT Canna 'Tropical Rose' (*Canna* × *generalis*)

BELOW Canna (*Canna* × *generalis*)

■ Long grown for their hot-colored flowers in shades of yellow, red-orange, red, and hot pink, cannas add a dramatic, tropical look to gardens. From midsummer to frost, the plants bear showy, 1-foot-tall clusters of 3- to 5-inch flowers. The bold, paddle-shaped leaves—up to 2 feet long and 1 foot wide—typically are green, but in recent years cultivars with handsome bronzed or variegated leaves have become widely available. Cultivars as valuable for their foliage as for their flowers include 'Pretoria', with orange-yellow blooms and yellow-striped leaves; 'Roi Humbert' ('Red King Humbert'), with bronze-purple leaves and red flowers; and 'Durban', with red flowers and leaves striped with orange, yellow, and red.

While most cannas are towering, 5- to 6-foot plants, dwarf cultivars are also available. 'Tropical Rose' bears rose-pink flowers on 2-foot plants. Plants in the Pfitzer Series range from 2½ to 3 feet tall.

Cannas grow from thick, branching rhizomes and are grown outdoors year round from Zone 8 south. In the North, they are replaced annually or dug after the first frost and the roots are overwintered. The plants are so fast-growing and easy to please, they produce a good show even in areas with short growing seasons.

SITE AND SOIL
Cannas thrive in full sun and well-drained, evenly moist soil rich in organic matter. With even moisture, they will withstand the hottest summer weather. The fleshy rhizomes rot in wet soil.

PLANTING
Cannas can be started from seeds (see "Propagation" below), but purchasing rhizomes is faster, easier, and the only way to get most of the improved cultivars. Look for thick, fleshy rhizomes that are firm to the touch and have no soft, rotted-looking spots. Each should have one or two pointed growing tips. Potted plants are also available at many garden centers.

Before planting, dig well-rotted manure and/or compost deeply into the soil. In Zone 7 and south, plant the rhizomes directly outdoors, but north of that, it's best to give them a head start. About 4 to 6 weeks before the last spring frost date, start them indoors by potting the rhizomes in containers or flats filled with fast-draining potting soil (soilless mix and ordinary potting soil to which coarse sand has been added both work). Set the rhizomes with the pointed growing tips up and just deep enough so that they are barely under the soil surface. Place the pots in a warm (75°F) spot out of direct sunlight and keep the soil barely moist. Once they've begun to grow, move them to a sunny spot, keep them evenly

moist, and fertilize weekly with a dilute fertilizer such as fish emulsion.

Move cannas to the garden after the last frost date, when the weather has moderated and the soil has warmed to about 65°F. (About the time tender annuals such as coleus, peppers, and eggplants go into the garden is ideal.) Space dwarf types 1 to 1½ feet apart; full-size cannas, up to 3 feet apart.

CARE THROUGH THE SEASON

For best growth, water regularly: the soil should be evenly moist but not wet. A monthly dose of a balanced organic fertilizer promotes lush growth but isn't required. In spring, control weeds by cultivating the soil surface until the soil has warmed up. After that, mulch to keep down weeds. Remove flowers as they fade to keep the plants neat looking and to encourage new blooms to form. In areas where cannas are grown outdoors year round, they need to be dug and divided every 3 years.

Overwintering. From Zone 7 northward, after the foliage has been blackened by light frost, dig the clumps and cut back the tops to within 6 inches of the soil surface. Leave the soil attached to the roots and set the clumps in boxes or large plastic nursery cans filled with barely damp vermiculite, peat, or sand. Store them in a cool (40° to 50°F), dry place. Sprinkle the soil with water occasionally during winter to keep the roots from shriveling. In spring, about 4 to 6 weeks before

the last frost date, shake the soil from the roots and cut the rhizomes into pieces with no more than two growing points each. Discard pieces of rhizome that are soft or appear rotted. Then start them as you would new rhizomes. Do not divide the rhizomes in fall before storage, because the cut surfaces tend to rot over winter.

Propagation. Dividing the rhizomes is the easiest way to propagate cannas, but some dwarf cultivars, including the Pfitzer Series and 'Tropical Rose', can be grown from seeds started in midwinter. Nick the hard seed coats with a file (take care not to damage the embryo) and soak the seeds in warm water for 48 hours. Then place the seeds in a plastic bag filled with moist peat moss and set it in a warm (75°F) place. Inspect the bag every few days and pot up seedlings as they appear. Seed-grown plants will produce rhizomes that can be overwintered in subsequent years.

LANDSCAPE USES

Unfortunately, cannas have all too often been associated with beds of garish annuals or whitewashed truck tires turned inside out. Use them to add a bold spot of color among annuals and perennials in beds and borders. Mass plantings along foundations, hedges, shrub borders, or walkways are also effective. Cannas make handsome container plants, too, especially the dwarf types. For best results, pot them in large tubs and feed regularly through the summer.

Caryopteris × clandonensis

Bluebeard

Caryopteris × clandonensis

- (care-ee-OP-ter-iss clan-do-NEN-sis)
- Midsummer to fall bloom
- Full sun or very light shade
- Zones 4 to 9

■ The frothy flowers of bluebeard are a welcome sight come midsummer. While the individual flowers are small, only $\frac{1}{2}$ inch long, they are borne in abundance in dense, many-flowered clusters on low, mounding plants that grow from 2 to 3 feet tall and as wide. Also called blue-mist shrub and blue spirea, this species is worth growing for its flower color alone—the flowers are blue to purple-blue—let alone the fact that it blooms from July or August into September, when few other shrubs are in flower. Cultivars with violet and powder blue flowers are available. The flowers are set against handsome, gray-green, fine-textured foliage that emits a pleasant euca-lyptus-like fragrance when rubbed.

Although bluebeard is actually a small shrub, it is grown more like a perennial than a woody plant. While the roots are hardy from Zones 4 to

Bluebeard *(Caryopteris × clandonensis)* with hollyhocks *(Alcea rosea)*

9, the plants seem more herbaceous than shrubby because the shoots are routinely killed to the ground in winter in Zones 4 to 6 and occasionally in Zone 7. Since the flowers are produced on new wood (growth produced in the current year), the plants bloom without interruption.

Inasmuch as bluebeard plants are long lived, consider one of the improved cultivars. 'Blue Mist' bears powder blue flowers, while 'Dark Night' has deep blue-purple ones. 'Longwood Blue' boasts silvery gray-green leaves, lavender-blue flowers, and a compact habit—plants form mounds that are 4 feet tall and as wide.

SITE AND SOIL
Grow bluebeard in full sun in loose, well-drained soil. It will also grow in very light shade. Soil that is too rich results in rampant, lank growth.

PLANTING
Plant bluebeard in spring or fall. Space plants 1 to 1½ feet apart to accommodate their spread. The plants are easy to transplant in spring or fall and can also be dug and divided at that time.

CARE THROUGH THE SEASON
Tough and undemanding, bluebeard needs little care beyond an annual spring haircut. Established plants tolerate dry conditions, but they benefit if watered deeply during droughts. Feed plants in spring with a balanced organic fertilizer, and spread mulch to eliminate competing weeds. After the main flush of bloom, trim off stem tips with spent flower clusters to encourage new shoots and flowers to form.

In the North, cut plants to the ground in spring to remove winterkilled wood. In Zone 7 and south, cut the stems back hard in spring—up to within a few inches of the ground—to encourage dense, shapely growth and more flowers. Early-spring pruning does not interfere with flowering, but pruning later in the season may remove flower buds.

Propagation. Root softwood cuttings taken in late spring, or dig and divide plants in spring or fall.

LANDSCAPE USES
Treat bluebeard as a small shrub or as a perennial. Plant it as a low hedge along a walkway, in front of foundation plants, or in shrub borders. Use it as a filler in perennial gardens, where it is especially attractive with daylilies (*Hemerocallis* spp.), thread-leaved coreopsis *(Coreopsis verticillata)*, and other late-summer-blooming perennials. Bluebeard is also handsome when combined with ornamental grasses. The flowers attract both butterflies and bees.

Centaurea

Cornflowers

■ The thistlelike blooms of cornflowers have an informal, cottage-garden charm. Each bloom is actually a cluster of flowers, or florets, called a head. (Cornflowers, relatives of sunflowers and asters, are in the aster family, Asteraceae). The florets are deeply lobed, giving the blooms a ragged appearance, and the heads have scaly, conelike bases. Colors include deep rich blue, mauve, hot pink, white, pale pink, and yellow.

Centaurea
■
(sen-TOR-ee-ah)
■
Late-spring to summer bloom
■
Full sun or partial shade
■
Zones 3 to 8
■

Bachelor's button *(Centaurea cyanus)*

A Cornflower for Foliage

One member of the cornflower clan, dusty miller *(C. cineraria)*, is grown for its white, woolly, fernlike foliage. Although grown as a warm-weather annual, it is actually a tender, evergreen perennial or subshrub hardy in Zones 7 to 9. To grow it as an annual, sow the seeds indoors 10 to 12 weeks before the last spring frost date. After that date, hardened-off seedlings can be moved to the garden. The plants can be overwintered indoors and propagated by cuttings, like geraniums (see *Pelargonium* spp. on page 30 in the **Annuals & Biennials** entry for details). Plant *C. cineraria* in full sun in well-drained to dry soil. It is also an ideal container plant.

Two other unrelated species, also grown for their ferny white foliage, are called dusty millers: *Tanacetum ptarmiciflorum* (formerly *Pyrethrum ptarmiciflorum* and *Chrysanthemum ptarmiciflorum*) and *Senecio cineraria*. Both are tender perennials grown as warm-weather annuals and are hardy in Zones 8 to 9. They can be grown and propagated just like *Centaurea cineraria*.

Dusty miller *(Centaurea cineraria)*

SELECTING CORNFLOWERS

Both annual and perennial cornflowers are suitable for adding color to sunny garden beds and borders. All make fine cut flowers and can also be dried. For cutting or drying, harvest when the flowers have expanded fully.

Annual Cornflowers

Three annual species are commonly grown. All are easy-to-grow, cool-weather annuals.

Centaurea americana. Basket flower. Pink, rosy lilac, or white flower heads, 4 to 6 inches across, borne throughout summer; 3- to 5-foot plants. A native North American wildflower.

C. cyanus. Bachelor's button. Dark blue, mauve, pink, rosy red, or white flower heads, 1 to 1½ inches across, borne from spring to early summer; ½- to 2½-foot plants. Sow new crops of seeds every 2 to 3 weeks for continuous bloom.

C. moschata. Sweet sultan. Fragrant, fringed, 2-inch-wide flowers in yellow, pink, purple, or white from spring to summer; 1½- to 2-foot plants. Plants generally require staking. (Recently reclassified as *Amberboa moschata*.)

Perennial Cornflowers

Several perennial cornflowers are available, but mountain bluet *(C. montana)* is by far the most popular. A vigorous, even weedy, clump-forming perennial that spreads by rhizomes, it bears rich blue, 2-inch flower heads on 1½- to 2-foot plants in early summer. Hardy in Zones 3 to 8, it prefers cool temperatures and spreads less vigorously in the South than in the North.

Summer-blooming Persian centaurea *(C. dealbata)* bears pink, 1½-inch flowers on 2- to 3-foot plants and is hardy in Zones 4 to 8. *C. hypoleuca*, also hardy in Zones 4 to 8, bears fragrant, 2½-inch flowers in summer on 2-foot plants. Globe centaurea *(C. macrocephala)* produces showy yellow, thistlelike blooms that are 1½ to 2 inches across on 3- to 5-foot plants. It is hardy in Zones 3 to 7.

SITE AND SOIL

All cornflowers thrive in full sun in average to rich, evenly moist soil that is well drained. *C. montana* will grow in partial shade.

PLANTING

Plant perennial cornflowers in spring, spacing the clumps about 1 foot apart. Sow seeds of annual or perennial species outdoors in a prepared seedbed where the plants are to grow on or just before the last spring frost date. In all but the coldest zones, try sowing seeds of annuals outdoors in fall for spring bloom. They can also be sown indoors 4 to 6 weeks before the last spring frost date; hardened-off seedlings can be moved to the garden after that date. Sowing in individual pots is best, because it reduces root disturbance. Indoors or out, cover the seeds with soil, as darkness is required for germination. Cultivate to keep weeds from overcoming the seedlings, and thin direct-sown annual plants to stand 6 to 12 inches apart.

CARE THROUGH THE SEASON
Cornflowers tolerate dry conditions but perform best if watered during dry weather. The plants may or may not need staking. Deadhead regularly to encourage new buds to form. When perennial types stop blooming, cut the plants to within several inches of the ground. This eliminates their unsightly, flopping stems and encourages repeat bloom in fall. Pull up annual species or cut them down after they have finished flowering. Plants will self-sow if you allow a few blooms to mature, however.

Mountain bluet *(Centaurea montana)*

Division. Dig and divide *C. montana* every 2 to 3 years in spring or fall to keep plants contained and vigorous. Or simply dig up portions of the clump that have spread too far. Other perennial species generally need dividing less often, every 3 to 4 years.

Propagation. Propagate perennial cornflowers by division or seed, following the recommendations under "Planting" above.

LANDSCAPE USES
Grow cornflowers in informal or cottage-style gardens and combine them with other early-summer-blooming perennials such as peonies. Sow patches of annual cornflowers in open spaces in between clumps in perennial gardens, and sow rows of them in cutting gardens.

Chrysanthemum

Chrysanthemums

Chrysanthemum
■
(kris-AN-theh-mum)
■
Spring to fall bloom
■
Full sun or partial shade
■
Zones 2 to 10
■

■ From summer daisies to hardy fall mums, chrysanthemums are among our most satisfying and best-loved garden flowers. Although botanists have dismantled this genus, all the popular garden flowers traditionally classified in *Chrysanthemum* are treated here, including Shasta, painted, and oxeye daisies as well as hardy fall mums. (The new botanical names are included in parentheses for reference.) Whatever they are called, all make rewarding, easily cultivated garden plants.

Chrysanthemums bear single, semidouble, or double flowers that are actually a cluster of tiny flowers called florets; the clusters are called heads. (They are relatives of sunflowers and asters, in the aster family, Asteraceae.) The head consists of petal-like ray florets surrounding a densely packed center of disk florets, although double flowers lack dasiylike centers. Flower shape and size vary tremendously, from tiny, dense, and buttonlike blooms or classic white daisies with yellow centers to enormous, fully double, football mums.

SELECTING CHRYSANTHEMUMS
Gardeners and nongardeners alike buy mums for fall color, but chrysanthemums have much more to offer. If you select a few different species, it's not all that difficult to have chrysanthemums in bloom from spring to fall.

Annuals for Spring or Fall
Two cool-weather annual chrysanthemums (still classified as chrysanthemums) are easy to grow in full sun and average to rich, well-drained soil. Tricolor chrysanthemum *(C. carinatum)* bears 2½-inch multicolored blooms in shades of red, orange, yellow, maroon, and white on 2- to 3-foot plants. Garland chrysanthemum or crown daisy *(C. coronarium)* bears yellow, single or double, 1- to 2-inch flowers on 2½- to 4-foot plants. Both are plants for spring or fall bloom except in areas with hot summers—they tend to die out when hot weather arrives. Sow in spring, or in midsummer for fall bloom (see *Chrysanthemum* spp. on page 27 in the **Annuals & Biennials** entry for germination instructions). Space plants 9 to 12 inches apart, stake as necessary, water if the

Feverfew
*(Chrysanthemum
parthenium)*

Painted daisy *(Chrysanthemum coccineum)*

Oxeye daisy *(Chrysanthemum leucanthemum)*

weather is dry, and remove faded flowers promptly to lengthen bloom season. Pull up plants when hot weather arrives and replace with warm-season annuals.

Classic Summer Daisies

Summer-blooming painted, oxeye, and Shasta daisies are long-blooming, easy-care plants suitable for sunny beds and borders. All make outstanding cut flowers.

C. coccineum. Painted daisy. Three-inch flowers with yellow centers and pale to hot pink, red, or white petals on stiff stems from early to midsummer; 1- to 3-foot plants. Attractive fernlike leaves. Blooms in light, part-day shade and tolerates a wide range of soils, from dry and sandy to average or rich garden soil. In the South, where plants may be short lived, a site with afternoon shade is best because it protects them from heat. May need staking. Cut plants back hard after flowering to encourage a second flush of bloom. Propagate by seed, by division in spring, or by cuttings taken from the base of the plant in spring. (Now listed as *Tanacetum coccineum.*) Zones 3 to 7.

C. leucanthemum. Oxeye daisy. White, 2- to 3-inch daisies with yellow centers from late spring to midsummer; 1- to 3-foot plants. A weedy, vigorous plant that spreads by rhizomes. Best for meadow plantings or wild areas. Cut plants to the ground after flowering to encourage repeat bloom and to discourage abundant self-seeding. Propagate by seed sown where the plants are to grow or by division in spring or fall. (Now listed as *Leucanthemum vulgare.*) Zones 3 to 8.

C. parthenium. Feverfew. Tiny, ³/₄-inch-wide, daisy flowers borne in abundance above ferny, aromatic foliage from summer to fall; 1- to 3-foot plants. A short-lived perennial often grown as an annual. Grows in full sun or partial shade in average to sandy, well-drained soil. Single-flowered types reseed with enthusiasm; double-flowered forms do not. Shear plants back after flowering to encourage repeat bloom. Propagate by seed or by cuttings taken in early summer. Seed-grown plants will bloom the first season. (Now listed as *Tanacetum parthenium.*) Zones 4 to 8.

C. × superbum. Shasta daisy. Single, semidouble, or double, 2- to 5-inch white daisies on stiff stems from early summer until early fall; 1- to 4-foot plants. The plants form vigorous clumps and will grow in light shade as well as in full sun. They tolerate somewhat dry, sandy soil and seaside conditions, but they tend to be short lived, especially in hot climates. Dividing plants about every other year helps keep them vigorous. Tall cultivars require staking; short ones, including 8- to 12-inch 'Little Miss Muffet', do not.

ABOVE LEFT Shasta daisy (*Chrysanthemum × superbum* 'Snow Lady')

ABOVE Shasta daisy (*Chrysanthemum × superbum* 'Aglaia')

Deadhead spent flowers to prolong bloom. Propagate by seed or by division in early spring or fall. Most cultivars are hardy in Zones 4 to 8; 'Alaska', hardy to Zone 3, is a good choice for northern gardeners. (Now listed as *Leucanthemum × superbum*.)

Hardy Fall Mums

Chrysanthemums, to most gardeners, are the hardy fall mums *(C. × morifolium,* now *Dendranthema × grandiflorum),* also called garden mums. Backbones of the late-summer to fall garden, they come in an array of showy colors, including bronze, purple, yellow, mauve, red, and white. Flower forms vary as well and include single daisies, tiny buttons, and large doubles. Both buds and flowers withstand light frost, and new buds continue to open long after annuals have been stopped for the season. Plants range from 1-foot cushion types to 2 feet or more.

As often as not, fall mums are grown as annuals. Nothing could be easier: they can be plopped in anywhere for a spot of instant color and be replaced as soon as they stop flowering. (Displays of mums at garden centers and roadside stands were once a sure sign of fall, but these days flowering plants are offered year round.) One reason so many mums are grown as annuals is that cultivar hardiness varies greatly, and many of the plants sold aren't hardy. (Depending on the cultivar, fall mums are hardy in Zones 4 or 5 to 9.) In addition, fall-planted mums frequently aren't well enough established to overwinter successfully in cold climates.

To grow fall mums as the perennials they are, start in spring with rooted cuttings or small, unbloomed plants of hardy cultivars (available from mail-order specialists). Since mums should be divided annually in spring, friends and neighbors who garden may have divisions of hardy cultivars to spare.

Fall mums are short-day plants, which means they need short days and long nights to initiate flower buds. (Actually, it's the long period of darkness at night that's required.) While all mums start forming flower buds in mid- to late July, when days begin to shorten, cultivars take different amounts of time to come into bloom. If you order by mail, you'll find notations in the catalogs about whether cultivars are early-, midseason-, or late-blooming. Early-blooming ones require the fewest number of weeks of short days (long nights) to bloom. They are the best choice in areas with very short seasons, and they generally bloom in September. In areas where a killing frost doesn't come until late October or November, you can lengthen the bloom season by ordering a mix of early, midseason, and late

Hardy fall mums share the spotlight with late-blooming annuals, including dahlias, scarlet sage *(Salvia splendens)*, and marigolds *(Tagetes* spp.).

cultivars. (Midseason types typically bloom in late September through October; late cultivars, after mid-October.) Potted florist mums are often disappointing when moved into the garden, because they usually take longer to come into bloom than cultivars grown for garden use. Although the plants may be perfectly hardy, in the North the late-emerging buds are killed by the first hard freeze.

Prepare the soil before planting as described in "Planting" below, and space plants 1½ to 2 feet apart. (Plant after the last frost date, or harden off plants as you would annuals before moving them outdoors.) At planting time, pinch off any flower buds, and shade cutting-grown plants with bushel baskets or burlap for a day or so after planting. Water whenever the soil becomes dry, and top-dress with a balanced organic fertilizer in early summer and again in midsummer. Cultivate shallowly to control weeds, and mulch plants in early summer. Taller plants may need staking—pea stakes or the type of hoops used for peonies work well.

Pinching the stems of fall mums encourages compact, well-branched plants and an abundance of flowers. To pinch, simply cut the stem just above a leaf with your thumb and a fingernail—

or use pruning shears. Be sure to make a clean cut; tearing or pulling at the shoots weakens growth. Pinch the first time about 2 weeks after planting. Thereafter, pinch each time the shoots and branches are about 6 inches long. To give plants plenty of time to form flower buds, stop pinching in early July in the North, mid-July in the South. If you want large, but fewer, flowers, remove most or all of the side buds that arise on each stem. This shortens bloom time, however, since the main buds open first, followed by the side buds.

Water regularly throughout summer—mums are shallow rooted and shouldn't be allowed to wilt. Once plants come into bloom, deadhead faded flowers to make room for buds that are just opening up. (Deadheading can be tedious, especially in large plantings, and isn't really necessary for a good end-of-season show.) After flowering ceases, cut back plants hard—to 3 to 6 inches. Once the soil has frozen solid, mulch with straw, hay, or evergreen branches. Avoid mulches that would pack down over winter; wet conditions in winter lead to root and crown rot. Mulching isn't necessary in areas where the soil doesn't freeze. In areas where plants are not reliably hardy, clumps can also be cut back and dug in late fall and overwintered in a cold frame. Pot them up in trays or boxes and water a couple of times until freezing weather sets in. Then mulch them with straw and shade the frame over winter. Whether plants are overwintered in the ground or in a cold frame, remove the mulch gradually beginning in early spring. Dig and divide plants as soon as growth appears, discarding any woody portions of the clump. Mums are also easy to root from cuttings taken in early spring, and cuttings will produce good-size blooming plants by fall. Cuttings are the best method to use if nematodes are a problem.

Hardy fall mum (*Chrysanthemum* 'Rose Pink Debonair')

More Fall Mums

Garden or hardy mums *(C. × morifolium)* are so well known that it's easy to overlook the other fall-blooming chrysanthemums. Two other fall-blooming species are worthy of consideration.

C. nipponicum. Nippon daisy. Showy white daisies with yellow centers in fall; shrubby, 2-foot plants. Requires very well-drained soil of average fertility and thrives in sandy conditions. Cut plants back nearly to the ground in spring to maintain an attractive shape. Propagate by seed or division in spring. (Now listed as *Nipponanthemum nipponicum.*) Zones 6 to 10.

C. pacificum. Gold-and-silver chrysanthemum. Branched clusters of golden, buttonlike flower heads; shrubby to mounding, 1-foot plants. Plants spread into broad clumps by runners. May not bloom in the northern part of its range but is still grown for the handsome, silver-edged leaves. Requires poor to average, well-drained soil. Wet soil in winter is fatal. Propagate by seed or division in spring or by cuttings taken from stems at the base of the plant in spring or summer. (Now listed as *Ajania pacifica.*) Zones 6 (5 with protection) to 9.

SITE AND SOIL

All chrysanthemums grow in full sun, although a few tolerate partial shade. In general they grow in average to rich, well-drained soil. Well-drained conditions are especially important in areas with

Gold-and-silver chrysanthemum (*Chrysanthemum pacificum*)

wet winters, since water collecting around the crowns causes the plants to rot. See the individual descriptions in "Selecting Chrysanthemums" on page 73 for specific preferences.

PLANTING

Plant chrysanthemums in spring, and prepare the soil the previous fall or in spring a few weeks before planting. Dig the soil to a depth of 1 foot, and work in compost or other organic matter to improve drainage and to increase fertility. In poorly drained sites, prepare the soil more deeply or grow chrysanthemums in raised beds. Space plants at about half their height.

CARE THROUGH THE SEASON

While hardy mums require regular care to look their best (see "Hardy Fall Mums" on page 75 for details), most chrysanthemums don't need much care other than routine deadheading, which lengthens bloom time, and watering during drought. With all of the perennial species, division is a chore you will have to attend to regularly to keep the plants vigorous.

Division. Chrysanthemums are fast growing and the clumps tend to die out in the center. Digging and dividing frequently, preferably in spring, keeps them vigorous. Discard older woody portions of the clumps and replant only the young, vigorous growth. Fall mums are best divided annually, although, depending on the cultivar and the region, dividing every other year may be sufficient. Divide other species every 2 to 3 years, with the exception of *C. coccineum,* which should be divided every 3 to 4 years.

Propagation. Sow seeds indoors in late winter and germinate at temperatures between 60° and 70°F. Do not cover the seeds with soil, as light aids germination of some species. Many chrysanthemums can also be propagated by basal cuttings, which are cuttings taken from shoots at the bottom of the plant. Take cuttings in spring and root in soilless potting medium. Cover the surface of the medium with clean, dry sand to prevent damping off.

Potential Problems. Use a sharp spray of water to blast aphids and spider mites off plants. These pests can cause twisted, stunted, or yellowed growth, especially on shoot tips. Be sure to blast water under the leaves. Plants that have greenish yellow leaves or distorted growth may be infected with viral diseases; pull them up and destroy, do not compost, them. Foliar nematodes cause yellow-brown spots or blotches on leaves. Destroy infested plants and remove the soil in which they were growing. Propagate new plants from clean cuttings. The nematodes overwinter in the soil, so rotate chrysanthemum plantings.

LANDSCAPE USES

Summer daisies are stunning planted with daylilies (*Hemerocallis* spp.), delphiniums, sneezeweeds (*Helenium* spp.), oxeyes (*Heliopsis* spp.), globe thistle *(Echinops ritro),* and other summer-blooming perennials. Fall-blooming chrysanthemums are ideal for combining with asters, ornamental grasses, monkshoods (*Aconitum* spp.), and other late-blooming perennials. Use fall mums to replace annuals that have stopped blooming, in containers, as edgings, or anywhere that needs a bit of late-season color. Mass plantings are effective for adding bold color in front of hedges or along shrub borders.

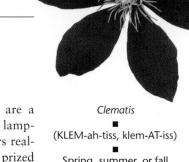

Clematis
Clematis

The large, showy blooms of clematis are a common sight decorating mailboxes and lampposts across the country, but few gardeners realize how diverse and versatile this genus of prized ornamentals really is. The summer-blooming vines with which most gardeners are familiar are large-flowered hybrid clematis. These bear spectacular single, semidouble, or double blooms ranging from 4 to 8 inches across. But there are

Clematis
■
(KLEM-ah-tiss, klem-AT-iss)
■
Spring, summer, or fall bloom
■
Full sun or partial shade
■
Zones 3 to 9
■

also clematis with bell- and tulip-shaped flowers as well as selections with four-petaled blooms that resemble dogwoods and plants with starry flowers. All of these generally have smaller flowers — between 3/4 inch and 2 inches — but they more than make up the difference in the sheer abundance of bloom. There are also spring- and fall-blooming clematis, as well as selections that rebloom and thus contribute color during two seasons. Flowers come in violet, purple-blue, lavender, pink, crimson, mauve, white, and even yellow — plus bicolors. Many bear handsome, fluffy to silky seed heads as well.

Plant size, vigor, and habit likewise vary. While most large-flowered hybrids range from 6 to 12 feet in height, there are clematis that routinely exceed 20 or even 40 feet. And although vines are by far the most common, there are clump-forming herbaceous clematis suitable for growing in perennial beds and borders. (*Clema-*

Clematis 'Nelly Moser'

tis integrifolia, the best known of these, is hardy in Zones 3 to 7 and produces bell-shaped, blue-violet flowers in summer on mounding plants that reach 2 feet and spread as far.)

While you are deciding which clematis to plant, bear in mind that clematis vines need some type of support, to which they attach themselves with twining leafstalks. Unlike vines such as ivy that produce roots along their stems, clematis cannot attach themselves to bare fences or walls. They also cannot wrap around large supports the way wisteria can. Instead, they need strings, lattice, or small supports to cling to. Install trellises or other supports *before* planting, because it's easy to damage the vines if you wait until after. See "Landscape Uses" at the end of this entry for suggestions on trellises and other supports.

SELECTING CLEMATIS

Clematis can be divided by bloom season into three general groups. If you are looking for a vine that blooms at a particular season, this may make the decision of what to buy a little easier, but not much, because there are so many species and cultivars from which to choose. One approach is to select one or more clematis from each group for a long season of bloom.

Pruning is also tied to bloom season. Depending on their origin (clematis hybrids are often the result of complex crosses), clematis bloom on old wood (the previous season's growth) or on new growth produced during the current season. For this reason, the bloom-season group a particular species or cultivar falls into determines how it should be pruned. Pruning guidelines for each group, along with lists of species and cultivars in each, are provided below. If you have a clematis whose name you don't know, the easiest way to figure out how to prune it is to watch it closely to see when it blooms and whether the buds come on old wood or new wood. Then prune according to the category that it fits most closely.

In northern zones, where clematis may be killed to the ground each winter, pruning is a moot point. Don't grow early-blooming clematis, which bloom only on old wood — which will be killed each year — and simply remove deadwood in late winter or early spring each year.

Early-Blooming Clematis

These bloom on old wood in early spring to early summer and typically bear single or bell-shaped flowers. Prune them immediately after flowering by removing dead or damaged growth and cutting back shoots to shape the plants and to keep them in bounds. Plants in this group do not need annual pruning to bloom well.

Clematis integrifolia

Many clematis, including alpine clematis *(Clematis alpina),* have attractive, silky seed heads that follow the flowers.

Clematis montana

Clematis integrifolia

C. alpina. Alpine clematis. Bell-shaped, sky blue and white blooms; 10-foot vines. Handsome silky seed heads. May rebloom in summer or fall. Cultivars include 'Frances Rivis', 'Helsingborg', 'Pamela Jackson', 'Ruby', and 'Willy'. Zones 4 to 9.

C. macropetala. Lavender- to violet-blue, open-bell-shaped flowers; 10-foot vines. May rebloom in summer or fall. Cultivars include 'Bluebird', 'Jan Lindmark', 'Maidwell Hall', and 'Rosy O'Grady'. Zones 4 to 9.

C. montana. Single, white, dogwoodlike flowers; 15- to 45-foot plants. Cultivars include 'Alba', 'Freda', 'Marjorie', 'Mayleen', 'Odorata', and 'Tetrarose'. Zones 5 to 9.

Early Large-Flowered Hybrids

This group of hybrid clematis overlaps in bloom time with the previous one. The plants bloom from late spring into early summer. They also commonly rebloom in mid- to late summer. The first flush of bloom is on old wood. The second flush of flowers is produced on new wood at the tips of the current year's growth. Some cultivars produce double flowers on the old wood and single flowers on new wood. These plants generally do not need heavy annual pruning to bloom well — just a spring shape-up. In spring before growth begins, prune out all dead or damaged growth. Then cut stems back to a strong set of

Clematis 'The President'

buds. These vines can also be cut back fairly hard—from 2 to 4 feet above the ground—and they will produce a single flush of growth later in the season on new wood. Cultivars in this group include 'Barbara Jackman', 'Bee's Jubilee', 'Belle of Woking', 'Blue Ravine', 'Elsa Späth', 'General Sikorski', 'Guernsey Cream', 'Henryi', 'Liberation', 'Marie Boisselot', 'Nelly Moser', 'Niobe', 'Pink Champagne', 'Royalty', 'Royal Velvet', and 'The President'. They are generally hardy from Zones 3 or 4 to 8, but some cultivars are less hardy than others. Summer heat is a problem in Zone 9.

Creamy-white-flowered *C. florida* and its cultivar 'Sieboldii', which bears pink-and-white flowers, fall into this group as well. Both are hardy in Zones 5 or 6 to 9.

Late-Blooming Clematis

This group includes large-flowered hybrids that bloom from summer to early fall, along with several species that bloom from summer into late fall. Prune them hard annually in early spring, before growth begins, by cutting them down to just above a healthy pair of buds 8 to 12 inches above the ground. Prune herbaceous *C. integrifolia* in this manner as well. Large-flowered hybrids in this group include 'Allanah', 'Comtesse de Bouchaud', 'Ernest Markham', 'Gipsy Queen', 'Hagley Hybrid', 'Jackmanii', 'Lady Betty Bal-

four', 'Mrs. Cholmondeley', 'Polish Spirit', 'Star of India', and 'Ville de Lyon'.

C. orientalis. Oriental clematis. Small, bell-shaped yellow flowers in late summer to late fall; 15- to 20-foot vines. Handsome fluffy seed heads follow the flowers in fall. 'Bill MacKenzie' is the most popular. Zones 5 or 6 to 9.

C. terniflora. Sweet autumn clematis. Fragrant, white, star-shaped flowers borne in abundance in fall; vigorous to rampant 15- to 20-foot plants. Attractive seed heads. Reseeds abundantly. (Formerly *C. maximowicziana* and *C. paniculata*.) Zones 4 to 9.

C. texensis. Texas clematis. Bell-shaped, red to red-orange flowers in summer; 6- to 15-foot plants. Native vine. Cultivars include 'Duchess of Albany', 'Etoile Beauty', and 'Gravetye Beauty', all probably of hybrid origin. Zones 3 to 9.

C. viticella. Italian clematis. Bell-shaped 1½-inch flowers from midsummer to fall in purple-blue or rose-red; 6- to 12-foot vines. Cultivars include 'Betty Corning' and 'Etoile Violette', both probably of hybrid origin. Zones 5 to 9.

SITE AND SOIL

Clematis have a reputation for being finicky that isn't necessarily deserved. While they are particular when it comes to site and soil, once established in a suitable site, the plants are long lived and easy to grow.

ABOVE *Clematis* 'Ville de Lyon'

ABOVE RIGHT *Clematis* 'Jackmanii' decorating a cherry tree with northern sea oats *(Chasmanthium latifolium)*

When selecting a site, try to follow the old adage and plant with the "head in the sun and feet in the shade"—plants prefer cool soil conditions (they struggle if soil temperatures exceed about 80°F in summer), and the tops bloom best in full sun or partial shade. Look for a spot where the roots will be shaded by low-growing shrubs or perennials that aren't too aggressive, such as peonies, hostas, or lavenders. A site on the north, or shaded, side of shrubs or even low walls is ideal. Mulch also helps keep the root-run cool. Then provide a trellis or other support so the vines can climb into the sunlight. Clematis are frequently thought of as full-sun plants, but a site with dappled or partial shade, especially during the hottest part of the day, is best. Afternoon shade is essential for good performance in areas with hot summers. Large-flowered hybrids in particular do not tolerate hot, dry summers well, and a bit of shade helps them cope.

It's often been said that clematis require alkaline soil, but they actually will grow in slightly acid to alkaline conditions. They do require well-drained conditions, but they will grow in heavy clay soil, provided it has been worked deeply and has been amended with plenty of organic matter. In sandy soil, replace some of the soil with bagged topsoil and add a generous amount of compost or well-rotted manure to increase fertility and moisture-holding capacity.

If you plan to train clematis over a tree or shrub, plant it away from the main roots of the woody plant to minimize competition. If the site is along a wall or building, plant out from the foundation—1 foot at least, 2 feet is better.

PLANTING

Thorough soil preparation pays off, because clematis vines will be around for many years and good soil encourages deep, widely spreading roots. Ideally, prepare the soil several weeks before planting by loosening it to a depth of 2 feet (1 foot at a minimum). Work in plenty of compost, leaf mold, well-rotted manure, or other organic matter. Mix in a few handfuls of bonemeal as well. And remember to mount your trellis before you plant.

Two kinds of plants are offered: pot-grown ones, which usually are sold as trellised vines, and dormant, bare-root plants. Pot-grown plants are generally the best option, but you may have a better selection if you order bare-root ones through the mail. Early spring is the best time to plant. Water pot-grown plants before planting. For bare-root or pot-grown plants, dig a hole deep enough to accommodate the roots and set the crown (the point where top growth meets the roots) 3 inches below the soil surface. This encourages strong shoots to arise from below the soil and protects the plants against clematis wilt, a fungal disease that can kill top growth. (Afflicted plants normally will resprout from the roots if they are planted deeply, as recommended here, although it may take a year or two for them to reappear.)

Handle the plants very carefully during planting; it's very easy to break the vines off at the soil line — or damage them by twisting or cracking — if the trellis flops one way and the root ball flops the other. Using two hands is safest: hold the root ball in one hand and the vine and trellis in the other.

Firm the soil around the roots and water deeply, soaking the soil to a depth of several inches. Water regularly the first season to encourage the roots to spread into the surrounding soil.

The first spring after planting, prune new clematis vines hard. Cut back to a pair of strong buds about 1 foot above the soil level to encourage branching.

CARE THROUGH THE SEASON

Beyond some annual attention with a pair of pruning shears and training to direct the vines, clematis plants require only a minimum of attention. See "Selecting Clematis" on page 79 for pruning guidelines. When growth begins in spring, watch the plants closely and gently guide the shoots onto the trellis or other support. You may need to tie them in place with soft yarn or strips of nylon stocking to get them started. Some species and cultivars are very fast growing and need checking every other day or so.

Mulch the plants to keep the soil cool and weeds under control. A mix of compost and chopped leaves is ideal because these materials also increase soil fertility. Do not allow mulch to touch the stems, as that leads to rot. Water deeply during dry weather. Feed plants annually in spring by top-dressing with well-rotted manure or a balanced organic fertilizer. (Well-fed, well-watered plants produce the largest flowers.)

Propagation. Layering is the easiest way to propagate clematis vines. In early spring, select a stem and loosen the soil to a depth of 4 to 5 inches along where it will touch the ground. Remove the leaves from the stem you have selected, except at the tip. Cover the stem (leave the tip above ground) with 1 to 2 inches of sandy soil, compost, or mulch and hold it in place with bent pieces of wire. Keep the soil moist all summer. The following spring, check for roots and cut apart and pot up the individual plants, which will appear at the leaf nodes. Clematis can also be propagated by cuttings taken from new shoots at the base of the plant in spring.

While hybrid clematis will not come true from seed, species can be grown by sowing the seeds outdoors in fall or indoors in spring. If sowing indoors, freeze pots of seeds for 3 weeks before germinating them at 70° to 75°F.

Potential Problems. A few insects — including blister beetles, scales, whiteflies, and clematis borers — attack plants, but well-sited, vigorous plants are seldom seriously afflicted. Clematis wilt is best dealt with by deep planting — see "Planting" above for details.

LANDSCAPE USES

Train clematis onto lampposts or mailboxes by affixing strings, wires, monofilament fishing line, or plastic mesh for them to climb. They will climb wooden or metal trellises attached to walls. To add fountains of color in beds and borders, consider pole tepees, wooden pyramids, or metal rose pillars and obelisks. (Use large-flowered climbers or smaller species types for these smaller structures.) Clematis can also be trained over shrubs such as privet (*Ligustrum* spp.) or allowed to sprawl over low walls. Combining them with climbing roses is especially effective, because the rose functions as the trellis. Choose plants that bloom together, or combine plants that flower at different seasons to lengthen the bloom season. Clematis — especially the vigorous, tall species — are stunning when trained up trees. To give them a boost up to the lowest branches, affix string, a trellis, or plastic mesh to the trunk. Surprisingly, three species of clematis make effective ground covers: *C. alpina, C. montana,* and *C. terniflora.* White-flowered *C. recta,* commonly called ground clematis, is also a good ground cover. It bears small starry flowers in summer, followed by silvery seed heads, and is hardy in Zones 3 to 7.

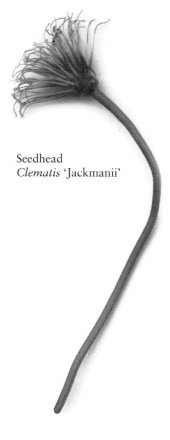

Seedhead
Clematis 'Jackmanii'

Sweet autumn clematis
(Clematis terniflora)

Convallaria majalis

Lily-of-the-Valley

Convallaria majalis
■
(con-vah-LAIR-ee-ah
ma-JAY-liss)
■
Spring bloom
■
Sun or shade
■
Zones 2 to 8
■

Lily-of-the-valley
(*Convallaria majalis*)

■ In the language of flowers, lily-of-the-valley symbolizes the return of happiness — one whiff of the sweetly scented bells explains why. This hard-working ground cover produces oval leaves with pointed tips above a creeping rootstock that branches freely, quickly forming a dense, 8-inch-tall mat. Plants grow fastest in cooler zones; more slowly in hotter ones, especially Zone 8. The ¼-inch, bell-shaped flowers dangle in one-sided racemes and appear in spring from mid-May into June — earlier in the South. The flowers are followed by round, glossy red berries. The foliage turns yellow beginning in late summer and dies back to the ground for winter.

SITE AND SOIL

The ideal site for lily-of-the-valley is one that offers partial shade and has evenly moist soil rich in organic matter. Plants will tolerate a range of conditions, though, from full sun (with adequate moisture) to full shade; established clumps will grow in dry shade. They will not tolerate wet, poorly drained sites, however. For best results in the South, plant in partial to full shade. In cooler zones, plant this fast-spreading ground cover away from other perennials; otherwise, you'll need to divide frequently to keep it in check.

PLANTING

Fall is the best time to plant lily-of-the-valley, which is generally sold as pips — bare-root pieces of the fleshy rhizome that have both growing buds and roots. It can also be planted in late winter or early spring, ideally before the leaves emerge. Potted plants can go into the garden anytime from spring to fall.

To plant, prepare a site by digging the soil deeply and working in plenty of compost or well-rotted manure. Spread out the roots in individual holes, spacing pips 3 to 4 inches apart. The growing buds should be about 1 inch under the soil surface. Plant potted specimens slightly farther apart and set them at the same depth at which they were growing in the pot. Then firm the soil, mulch, and water thoroughly.

Divisions of established plantings are another option, and nearly any gardening friend who has

Forcing Lily-of-the-Valley

Lily-of-the-valley is easy to force for winter bloom. In fall, pot up divisions in a sandy houseplant mix, and set them in a cold frame or protected location outdoors, such as tucked in next to shrubbery along the north side of the house. Cover them with 1 to 2 inches of sawdust, wood chips, or chopped leaves. Bring pots indoors beginning in January. Keep them in the dark for 2 to 3 weeks to encourage long stems, then move them to a sunny windowsill. They'll bloom in 3 to 4 weeks at 65°F. Forced plants can be replanted in the garden in spring.

a bed of this old-fashioned flower will have plants to spare. Dig them in summer or fall, prepare the soil as you would for pips, and space them 6 to 8 inches apart depending on their size. Firm the soil, mulch, and water. If you've moved leafed-out divisions in spring, keep the soil evenly moist all summer.

CARE THROUGH THE SEASON

Lily-of-the-valley requires almost no care, and plantings can thrive with complete neglect for years. Divide them if they encroach on other plantings or if flowering is reduced because of overcrowding. An annual topdressing in late winter or in fall with well-rotted manure or a balanced organic fertilizer helps keep plantings vigorous. Water during excessively dry spells to keep the foliage attractive, or simply let the plants die back. Cut the leaves back when they begin to look unattractive — or leave them to decompose naturally. Water regularly in Zone 8, especially during the hottest times of the year.

Propagation. Dividing the clumps in summer or fall by cutting them up with a sharp knife is the easiest way to propagate. Save the healthiest pips for replanting — look for healthy buds, fat rhizomes, and plenty of roots — and replant as you would new pips, discarding the rest.

LANDSCAPE USES

Use lily-of-the-valley in mass plantings as a ground cover under trees and shrubs. Except in the southern zones, it spreads rapidly and will overtake most other perennials.

Coreopsis

Coreopsis

Also called tickseeds, coreopsis are long-blooming annuals and perennials that bear an abundance of daisylike, single or double flowers. Most blooms are gold to yellow-orange in color, but there are also coreopsis with pale yellow or pink flowers. Both the botanical name *Coreopsis* and the common name "tickseed" refer to the black seeds that follow the flowers. The name *Coreopsis* is from the Greek *koris,* meaning "bug," and *opsis,* "resemblance."

Coreopsis
■
(core-ee-OP-sis)
■
Late-spring to early-fall bloom
■
Full sun or partial shade
■
Zones 3 to 9
■

SELECTING COREOPSIS

The most commonly grown coreopsis are native to North America and are tough, easy-to-grow perennials that thrive in full sun. One common species is a drought-tolerant, warm-weather annual: calliopsis or plains coreopsis *(C. tinctoria)* bears yellow-and-maroon, 1- to 2-inch daisy flowers in summer.

Large-flowered coreopsis *(C. grandiflora)* and lance-leaved coreopsis *(C. lanceolata)* are similar species that bear yellow to yellow-orange, 1- to 2½-inch flowers on 1- to 2-foot plants. Both are good cut flowers and very long blooming—from spring to late summer—if plants are deadheaded regularly. Cut faded flowers to the base of the stalks for best appearance. If the plants become ungainly in late summer, cut them to the ground and fresh foliage will quickly appear. *C. grandiflora* is a short-lived perennial, lasting only 2 to 3 years in the South, slightly longer in the North. *C. lanceolata* tends to be longer lived but blooms somewhat less. Frequent division keeps them vigorous, however, and both are easy from seeds. There are single-, semidouble-, and double-flowered cultivars of *C. grandiflora* that can be grown from seeds (many cultivars are actually crosses between the two species). 'Early Sunrise' will bloom well the first year from seeds sown indoors in midwinter. Both species are hardy in Zones 3 or 4 to 9.

The following three species are popular because of their versatility in the landscape or other ornamental characteristics.

C. auriculata. Mouse-ear coreopsis. Yellow-orange, 2-inch flowers from late spring to summer on 1- to 2-foot plants. It tolerates partial shade—afternoon shade is best—and is often used as a ground cover or edging. Plants spread steadily via stolons but are not invasive. The foliage remains attractive all season if the soil is kept evenly moist. Dwarf, 8-inch-tall 'Nana' is an outstanding cultivar. It is hardy in Zones 4 to 9.

C. rosea. Pink coreopsis. Rosy pink, 1-inch flowers with yellow centers from summer to early fall; mounding, 1- to 2-foot plants with needlelike leaves that cover themselves with tiny flowers. Grows in full sun or partial shade and tolerates moist or dry soil. Can spread vigorously in fertile, moist soil. Zones 4 to 8.

C. verticillata. Thread-leaved coreopsis. Pale to golden yellow 1- to 2-inch daisies in summer; 1- to 3-foot plants. Plants spread slowly via rhizomes. Cut plants back after flowering to encourage a second flush of blooms in fall. 'Moonbeam', with pale yellow flowers, reblooms without deadheading and will flower from early summer to fall. Zones 3 to 9.

Large-flowered coreopsis (*Coreopsis grandiflora* 'Sunburst')

Thread-leaved coreopsis (*Coreopsis verticillata* 'Golden Showers')

Thread-leaved coreopsis (*Coreopsis verticillata* 'Moonbeam')

SITE AND SOIL

Plant coreopsis in full sun in average to rich soil that is well drained. A site with some morning shade and afternoon sun is also fine for these heat-loving plants. *C. auriculata* and *C. rosea* will also grow in partial shade. The plants prefer evenly moist conditions, but once established they will withstand considerable drought. Soil that is too rich causes them to flop.

PLANTING

Add coreopsis to your garden by purchasing plants or by starting seeds, which are fast-growing and rewarding. Cultivars of *C. grandiflora* and *C. tinctoria* that come true from seed are available, and species plants are fine from seed. Cultivars of *C. auriculata* and *C. verticillata* (such as the popular 'Moonbeam') must be propagated by division or cuttings.

Plant in spring and space 1 to 1½ feet apart. Thin direct-sown seedlings of *C. tinctoria* to stand 4 to 6 inches apart.

CARE THROUGH THE SEASON

Removing flowers as they fade is worth the effort, because it lengthens the flowering season for all types of coreopsis. Cut off individual blooms or, for a more efficient approach, use hedge shears and cut back the entire plant by about one-third. Allow some flowers to form seeds if you want plants to self-sow. Divide perennials every 2 to 3 years to keep them vigorous. Discard the older portion of the plant at the center of the clump and replant the rest.

Propagation. Coreopsis can be grown from seeds sown indoors 6 to 8 weeks before the last spring frost date (sow a few weeks earlier if you are growing *C. grandiflora* as an annual). Or sow outdoors in a prepared seedbed or into pots after the last frost date.

Plants can also be propagated by division in early spring or early fall or by cuttings. Take cuttings in spring from the base of the plant or in summer from stem tips. (Tip cuttings are best taken when plants are not in bloom.) Root cuttings in a 50-50 mix of peat moss and perlite. They root quickly and the resulting plants can be moved to the garden by late summer.

LANDSCAPE USES

Plant coreopsis in beds and borders with summer-blooming perennials such as lavenders (*Lavandula* spp.), daylilies (*Hemerocallis* spp.), hardy geraniums, yarrows (*Achillea* spp.), bellflowers (*Campanula* spp.), and purple coneflower (*Echinacea purpurea*). They are most effective when planted in groups of three and allowed to grow together to form drifts.

Cornus

Dogwoods

Cornus

■

(CORE-nuss)

■

Spring to early-summer
bloom

■

Full sun or partial shade

■

Zones 2 to 8

■

A flowering dogwood
(Cornus florida)
underplanted with a
mix of shade-loving
plants

■ Best known for their abundant spring flowers, dogwoods are valuable ornamentals that add interest to gardens all year long. The true flowers are small—the showy white or pink "petals" on flowering dogwood *(Cornus florida)* and other species are actually petal-like bracts. The true flowers are borne in clusters and are white, yellow-green, or yellow. In addition to their spring flowers, most dogwoods boast features that provide year-round interest. Their berries, often brilliantly colored, are attractive to birds and other wildlife, and many have bright fall foliage color as well. In winter, they add colorful stems or attractive bark to the landscape. Several species have exfoliating bark, which shreds or breaks to form patches of subtle color.

SELECTING DOGWOODS

The yellow flowers of cornelian cherry *(Cornus mas)* announce the beginning of the gardening season when they open in late winter to very early spring. Dogwoods continue to flower from that time until early summer, when the showy white flowers of Kousa dogwood *(C. kousa)* open. The three species below are grown primarily for their flowers, although all are attractive year round.

C. florida. Flowering dogwood. Showy, white or pink flowers in mid- to late spring, usually before the leaves unfurl; 20- to 40-foot trees. Showy red fall fruit. Burgundy fall foliage. Handsome gray-textured bark. They require evenly moist, acid to slightly acid soil (pH 4.0 to 6.5) rich in organic matter. Although often planted in full sun, this native species is more suited to a spot in partial or dappled shade—it naturally grows along woodland edges. It is an ideal understory tree on the edge of a shade garden. Specimens grown in shade have a more open habit and fewer blooms than ones in full sun. Grown in ideal conditions, trees are longer lived, healthier, and more resistant to attack by insects and diseases. Ones exposed to sun and drought slowly decline and die. Plants grown in the North tolerate full sun better than those in the South. Susceptible to dogwood an-

TOP Flowering
dogwood blossoms
(*Cornus florida*)

ABOVE Kousa dogwood
fruits (*Cornus kousa*)

thracnose and other diseases and pests (see "Potential Problems" on the facing page for more information). Zones 5 to 8.

C. *kousa*. Kousa dogwood. Creamy white flowers in late spring to early summer with pointed-tipped bracts; 12- to 30-foot trees. Round, pinkish red, raspberry-like fruits ripen in late summer and remain on the tree into fall or early winter. Red-purple to red fall foliage color. Ornamental exfoliating bark in shades of pale to dark gray, and greenish tan on trunk and older branches. Bracts of flowers turn pinkish as they age and last as long as 6 weeks. Blooms appear several weeks after those of C. *florida,* at a time when there is frequently a lull between spring- and summer-blooming flowers. Full sun or partial shade in acid to slightly acid soil (pH 4.0 to 6.5) that is evenly moist but well drained. Grows well in sandy soil rich in organic matter. For best fruit production, plant two trees (if planting a cultivar, plant two different ones). Resistant to dogwood anthracnose and seldom troubled by other diseases or pests. Zones 5 to 8.

C. *mas*. Cornelian cherry. Yellow flowers borne in 3/4-inch-wide clusters open in late winter to early spring, before the leaves unfurl; 15- to 25-foot shrubs. Flowers borne in such abundance that the entire shrub turns golden yellow. Edible red fruits in summer. Purplish red fall color. Attractive, exfoliating, gray to brown bark. Shrubs are rounded (nearly as wide as tall) and densely branched. Good for hedges, screens, or windbreaks. Can be limbed up into a small tree. Produces suckers at base of plant. Best in rich, evenly moist soil in full sun or partial shade but tolerates acid to alkaline pH and clay soils. Zones 4 to 8. Japanese cornel dogwood *(C. officinalis)* produces its yellow flowers even earlier than C. *mas* and has handsome gray, brown, and rust bark. Hardy in Zones 5 to 7, it is rare in the trade but worth searching out.

Dogwoods for Winter Interest

Two dogwoods, both hardy in Zones 2 to 7, are grown for their brightly colored stems, which add interest to the winter landscape. The stems are especially attractive against fresh snow. Tartarian dogwood *(C. alba)* has yellowish white spring flowers, bluish white fruits, red-purple fall leaves, and brilliant blood red stems in winter. The plants reach 8 to 10 feet and spread as far. Red osier dogwood *(C. sericea,* formerly *C. stolonifera)* has dull white spring flowers, white berries, red-purple fall foliage, and purple-red to blood red winter stems. The 7- to 9-foot plants spread quickly to 10 feet or more. Both are easy to transplant, grow in full sun or partial shade, and tolerate a wide range of soils. Moist, well-drained condi-

tions are best; C. *sericea* grows well in wet, swampy sites. Stem color is best on younger stems. Since both species spread vigorously, combine them with other vigorous shrubs.

SITE AND SOIL

Dogwoods will grow in average to rich soil in a site with partial shade or full sun. See "Selecting Dogwoods" at the beginning of this entry for details on the best conditions for each species. Growing C. *florida* as a lawn specimen, with grass growing right up to the trunk, doesn't provide optimum conditions. Lawn mowers banging into the trunk damage the bark around the base of the tree, leaving it open to attack by borers. Replace grass with mulch in a 2-foot or wider circle around the trees to keep lawn mowers at bay. Better yet, remove all grass from under the canopy and replace it with shade-loving ground covers. Mulch the soil to keep it moist and cool, as well as to add organic matter. Pine needles or chopped oak leaves encourage acid conditions. Replacing grass with mulch or ground-cover plants is best for all dogwoods because it protects their trunks. It also makes mowing easier.

PLANTING

C. *florida,* C. *kousa,* and C. *mas* can be difficult to transplant. They are best moved as young trees, either as balled-and-burlapped or container-grown plants. Handle them carefully during transplanting. C. *alba* and C. *sericea* transplant relatively easily. Be sure to plant all species at the same depth at which they were growing in the nursery, and space them generously to accommodate their eventual spread. At maturity, most are as wide as they are tall. Water thoroughly after planting and mulch to keep the soil cool. Water new specimens regularly the first season, keeping the soil out to the edge of the branch spread evenly moist but not wet.

CARE THROUGH THE SEASON

Renew the mulch around dogwoods annually to keep the soil moist and cool. Fertilize annually in spring with a balanced organic fertilizer or a topdressing of well-rotted manure. Do not let fertilizer or mulch touch the trunk or stems of the plant, however. Water deeply during droughts, out to the spread of the branches. Watering, feeding, and mulching are especially important for C. *florida,* because good care helps keep plants vigorous and healthy.

Pruning. Established plants of C. *florida,* C. *kousa,* and C. *mas* need little if any pruning. Remove dead or diseased wood, along with crossing or rubbing branches. Prune C. *alba* and C. *sericea* annually in late winter or early spring to encourage new shoots and to maintain twig color. Annually cut one-half to two-thirds of the older stems to within 6 inches of the ground. Renew overgrown specimens by cutting back all stems to within 6 to 12 inches of the ground.

Propagation. Most gardeners will start with plants, but dogwoods can be propagated by cuttings or from seeds. Take softwood cuttings in spring, dip them in rooting hormone, and root in a 50-50 mix of peat moss and perlite. (Take *C. florida* cuttings immediately after the flowers fall.) Seeds require 3 to 4 months of cool (40°F), moist conditions before germination can occur. Clean off the fleshy berries and place the seeds in plastic bags of moist peat moss in your refrigerator for this period, then pot them up for germination. Cover the seeds with soil and germinate at temperatures between 60° and 65°F. Alternatively, after cleaning the berries, sow outdoors in pots set in a protected location.

Potential Problems. *C. kousa* and *C. mas* have no serious pest or disease problems. *C. alba* and *C. sericea* are attacked by a fungus that causes twig blight or canker, which kills the stems. Prune out diseased-looking stems whenever they appear. Routine pruning to maintain colorful stems often takes care of the problem.

Borers and dogwood anthracnose are serious problems for *C. florida*, which is also attacked by various other pests and diseases. Providing optimum growing conditions (described earlier under "Selecting Dogwoods") is the best defense. Encircling trees with a ring of mulch or groundcover plants as recommended above under "Site and Soil" helps prevent lawn-mower damage, which gives borers easy access. Specimens afflicted with dogwood anthracnose have deformed leaves with purple-edged spots or tan blotches. The disease also kills twigs and causes water sprouts, which are overly vigorous upright shoots, to form. Trees are weakened and often killed. Pruning out afflicted branches and all water sprouts as well as watering regularly is the best way to control the disease's spread. *C. kousa* is immune to dogwood anthracnose (as is *C. mas*), and hybridizers at Rutgers University have introduced crosses between it and *C. florida* that are resistant and have characteristics of both species. These include 'Aurora', 'Celestial', 'Constellation', 'Ruth Ellen', and 'Stellar Pink'.

LANDSCAPE USES

Use *C. florida, C. kousa,* and *C. mas* as specimen plants at the edge of a perennial garden, next to a house, or in a shrub border. Underplant with shade-loving hostas, ferns, wildflowers, or ground covers as well as with spring bulbs. Plant *C. mas* where you can enjoy its early flowers from in-

doors. See "Selecting Dogwoods" on page 87 for more suggestions. *C. alba* and *C. sericea* are best used in mass plantings or in shrub borders. They can also be used to hold soil along banks. All dogwoods make excellent additions to wildlife or bird gardens.

Flowering dogwood (*Cornus florida*)

Cornelian cherry (*Cornus mas*)

$\mathcal{D}$ahlia

Dahlias

Dahlia

■

(DAL-ee-ah)

■

Summer to fall bloom

■

Full sun or light shade

■

Zones 8 to 11;
tender perennials
grown as annuals

■

■ Few plants add as much color to the garden as well-grown dahlias do. In full sun and good soil, the plants bloom in abundance from midsummer to frost. The showy flowers come in an array of shapes and sizes, from enormous doubles 8 inches or more wide to petite daisylike singles, and in all colors except true blue. There are dwarf, 12- to 15-inch-tall dahlias for bedding, but most are tall plants, ranging from 3½ to 6 feet. Although most dahlias have green leaves, some have handsome bronzed or maroon foliage.

Dahlias grow from tuberous roots and can be grown outdoors year round from Zone 8 south. In the North, they can be replaced annually, but the tuberous roots are easy to dig and overwinter. Fast growing and easy to please, the plants produce a good show even in areas with short growing seasons.

SELECTING DAHLIAS

There are literally thousands of dahlia cultivars, with more introduced every year, and deciding which to grow can be as simple or as complicated as you want to make it. First-time growers may be satisfied with the packaged tubers or pot-

Dahlia 'Bishop
of Landaff'

Dahlia 'Orange Julius'

grown plants available at well-stocked garden centers. If you want to choose from a wide range of exhibition-quality plants, plan on ordering by mail or finding a local dahlia enthusiast. For a local source of tubers of good-quality cultivars, find out if the local chapter of the American Dahlia Society has a spring or fall sale. Seeds are a good option if your objective is lots of plants for very little money. Mixes of dwarf dahlias are available from several mail-order companies; a few firms also offer mixes of full-size hybrids. (See "Propagation" on page 92 for more on starting dahlias from seeds.)

Dahlia enthusiasts recognize 16 different flower shapes, including cactus, waterlily, ball, anemone, collarette, and single dahlias. There are size categories to contend with, too, from giant (or AA) blooms that exceed 10 inches to miniatures, which are 2 inches or less across. For dahlias that produce the most blooms per plant, stick to cultivars with flowers less than 6 inches across. If low-growing plants are what you want, look for the word "dwarf" or "bedding" in the description—with dahlias the term "miniature" refers to the flowers only, and the cultivars that produce them are as large as other standard-size plants. Ultimately, the best approach is to grow several shapes and sizes to see which work best in your garden. Another option is to ask for recommendations at a nearby public garden or from a local dahlia enthusiast.

SITE AND SOIL

Dahlias grow and bloom best in full sun. They benefit from good air circulation but need protection from wind. Although they tolerate a site that receives only a half-day of sun, the more hours of sun the better—plants in less than full sun bloom less. In the very hottest climates, a bit of shade during the hottest part of the day provides beneficial protection from excessive heat. The soil should be very rich and well drained yet evenly moist. The fleshy roots rot in wet soil. Slightly acid to neutral pH (6.5 to 7.0) is best. Keep in mind that most blooms will face the sun (south), and place plants accordingly.

PLANTING

While dahlias can be grown from seeds, tubers are easier and faster—and the only way to acquire most of the improved cultivars. Start with thick, fleshy tubers that are firm to the touch and have no soft, rotted-looking spots. You can plant individual tubers or small clumps (four or five tubers), but each must have a piece of stem attached: the eyes, or growing buds, are on the main stem, where it is attached to the tuber, not on the tuber itself.

Dahlias require fertile, well-drained soil for best growth. (The conditions suitable for growing vegetables are ideal.) Prepare the soil a few weeks before it's time to plant by loosening it to a depth of 12 inches and digging in plenty of well-rotted manure or compost amended with a balanced organic fertilizer. If you have sandy or heavy clay soil, add an extra complement of organic matter to improve fertility and water retention in the former, drainage in the latter.

The easiest way to plant is to set the tubers directly in the garden, although starting them indoors is a good way to get a head start in areas with short growing seasons. Tubers can be planted outdoors as early as 2 weeks before the last spring frost date, but it's best to delay plant-

Dahlia 'Alfred Grill'

ing if the weather has been unusually cold or wet. Tubers will rot, not sprout, in cold, wet soil, and plants are very frost tender. Dahlias begin flowering about 2 to 2½ months after planting.

To plant, excavate a 6-inch-deep trench, set the tubers with the eyes pointing up, and cover

---

Pinching and Training Dahlias

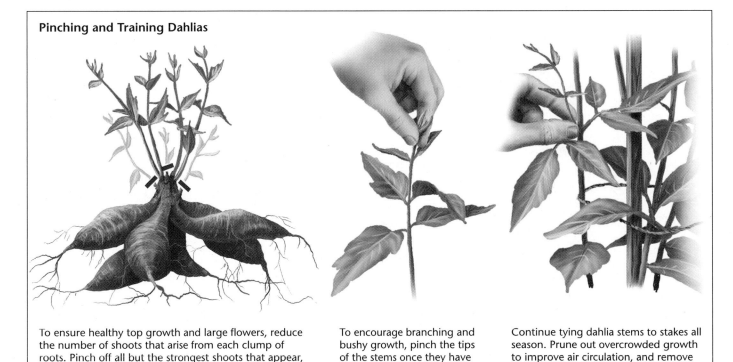

To ensure healthy top growth and large flowers, reduce the number of shoots that arise from each clump of roots. Pinch off all but the strongest shoots that appear, leaving two shoots if you are planting individual tubers, four to eight if you are planting small clumps of tubers.

To encourage branching and bushy growth, pinch the tips of the stems once they have two or three sets of leaves.

Continue tying dahlia stems to stakes all season. Prune out overcrowded growth to improve air circulation, and remove any spindly stems to direct the plant's growth into stronger stems and flowers.

Dahlia Coltness
Hybrids

with about 2 inches of soil (4 inches in hot climates). Gradually fill the trench as the tubers sprout. Space dwarf types 1½ to 2 feet apart; full-size ones, up to 3 feet apart. Cultivars that will exceed about 3 feet in height will require a sturdy stake, which should be installed *before* you plant the tubers. For full-size plants, 6- to 7-foot stakes should suffice. Drive the stakes 1½ feet into the ground so they will be anchored sufficiently to hold plants at maturity. Set each tuber with the eye nearest the stake. Gently firm the soil, water deeply, and label each tuber as you plant. In most areas, spring rains will keep the tubers wet enough until after they have sprouted.

To start dahlias indoors, pot up the dormant tubers in individual pots or deep flats filled with fast-draining potting soil (soilless mix is fine) 4 to 6 weeks before the last spring frost date. Set the buds just above the surface of the soil, and move the containers to a warm (60° to 75°F), bright spot. Keep the soil barely moist. Sprouts will appear in 2 to 4 weeks, and plants can be moved to the garden after the last spring frost date. (If you are unsure about where to divide stored tubers, presprout them using this method to see where the buds are, then divide.) Be sure to harden them off before moving them outdoors. Plant started tubers with the tops of the sprouts at the soil surface. Set pot-grown plants 2 inches deeper than they were growing in the pots.

Once tubers have sprouted, begin pinching back for optimum growth and flower production.

If you are planting individual tubers, pinch off all but two shoots. If you are planting small clumps of tubers, pinch off all but four to eight. (The fewer shoots per plant, the larger the flowers.) When plants have two or three sets of leaves, pinch back the tips of each shoot to encourage branching and bushy growth. After this point, dwarf types can be left to grow pretty much on their own. Begin tying full-size dahlias to their stakes when stems reach 2 feet. Use strips of cloth or nylon stockings and tie loosely, as the stems will continue to enlarge throughout the season. Continue pinching out spindly branches and growth that will overcrowd the center of the plant all season long.

CARE THROUGH THE SEASON

Steady, fast growth is essential for success when growing dahlias. Flowering stops if growth is checked by drought or insufficient nutrients, and it is difficult, if not impossible, to get the plants blooming again. In early summer, after the soil has warmed up, mulch the plants with compost, straw, grass clippings, or other organic mulch. Water deeply every 7 to 10 days in summer. Feed plants with a balanced organic fertilizer when you thin the stems, again when buds first appear, and a third time about a month later. Continue tying tall dahlias to stakes; otherwise their stems are apt to snap.

Deadheading, Disbudding, and Cutting. Deadheading regularly encourages new buds to form. Disbudding (and limiting the number of shoots on each clump) is necessary to produce true dinner-plate-sized blooms. To do this, pinch out the buds that arise on either side of the main flower stalk, and also pinch out the shoots that arise below it. If quantity of bloom, not size, is your objective, don't worry about disbudding.

For arrangements, cut dahlias when the flowers are nearly open but still firm in the center. Cut just above a leaf node, and recut stems under water. For longer-lasting cut flowers, remove all the leaves that will be below the water level and either sear the ends of the stems with a candle flame or plunge them into very hot water for a few seconds. Then condition them overnight in warm (130°F) water.

Propagation. Propagate dahlias by dividing the tuberous roots or from seeds. Cuttings that sprout from the roots in spring also can be rooted. (See "Overwintering" on the facing page for details on dividing.) To grow from seeds, sow indoors 4 to 6 weeks before the last spring frost date. Transplant to individual pots and pinch seedlings back when they have two sets of true leaves. Transplant hardened-off seedlings to the garden after all danger of frost has passed.

Overwintering. Once frost has blackened the plants, cut the stalks back to about 6 inches and carefully dig the roots. Gently shake off the excess soil, and turn the clumps upside down for a few hours to dry. Be sure to attach labels with cultivar names to the clumps of roots as you dig them. Then move the clumps indoors and store them upside down for another week.

For overwinter storage, dahlias require a well-ventilated, relatively dry spot where temperatures remain between 36° and 45°F. High humidity causes the tubers to rot. Experts recommend different storage methods, all aimed at keeping the tubers from either shriveling or rotting, and the best technique may depend on the storage site you have available. A root cellar is ideal, but other options include storing the clumps (whole is best, but if you divide in fall, dust the cuts with sulfur before storage) in boxes of barely moist vermiculite or sand, placing them in paper bags or wrapping them in newspaper, or storing in plastic bags punched with plenty of air holes. Inspect the tubers monthly for signs of rotting. Trim off rotted spots and dust the cuts with sulfur. Barely mist the tubers with water if they begin to shrivel.

In spring, 1 to 2 weeks before it's time to plant dahlias outside, divide the clumps into individual tubers or smaller clumps. Be sure that each piece has a section of the main stem, which is where the buds are. Dust the cuts with sulfur to prevent rotting.

From Zone 8 south, cut back the plants at the end of the season and mulch them over winter. Dig and divide every 2 to 3 years to keep them vigorous.

Potential Problems. Cutworms sometimes cut down new dahlia shoots. If this has been a problem in the past, cultivate shallowly before planting, use cutworm collars, and leave extra stems on the plants. Stalks infested with stalk borers wilt and die. Cut them back to a leaf node below the damaged growth. Blast spider mites and aphids off the plants with a strong spray of water. Good air circulation and thinning out stems helps prevent powdery mildew; spray afflicted plants with a sulfur-based fungicide.

LANDSCAPE USES

Use dwarf dahlias as edging plants and in sunny beds and borders. They are also striking in containers. Taller types can be used at the center of island beds or the back of borders. Cultivars with smaller flowers (less than 6 inches across) generally are most effective when combined with other plants. Grow rows of dahlias for cutting or exhibition in a separate area or in a corner of the vegetable garden.

Delphinium

Delphiniums

■ Few gardeners forget their first encounter with delphiniums. The plants' stately flower spikes would be eye catching in any color, but they are all the more alluring because they come in hard-to-find shades of true blue. Cultivars with sky blue to dark royal blue blooms are available, as well as violet, lavender, pink, mauve, and white. The bloom stalks tower above mounds of maple-like leaves borne from a fleshy crown.

Delphiniums thrive in areas with cool summers and are often grown as biennials or even

Delphinium
■
(del-FIN-ee-um)
■
Late-spring to summer bloom
■
Full sun or partial shade
■
Zones 3 to 7
■

Delphinium 'Butterfly Compacta'

SELECTING DELPHINIUMS

The most popular delphiniums in gardens are hybrids. Elatum Group hybrids (also called *Delphinium × elatum* hybrids) produce dense spikes of single, semidouble, or double flowers on 4- to 6-foot-tall plants. The popular Pacific Hybrids, also sold as Pacific Giants, resemble Elatum Group delphiniums but are shorter lived and are best grown as annuals or biennials. (Pacific Hybrid cultivars often have Arthurian names, including 'King Arthur', 'Guinevere', and 'Galahad'.)

Belladonna Group hybrids (also called *D. × belladonna* hybrids) are shorter than Elatum hybrids—from 3 to 4 feet—and bear loosely branched spikes of flowers. They tend to be more tolerant of hot summer weather and longer lived. The Connecticut Yankee Series cultivar 'Blue Fountains' is more heat tolerant than most and can be grown in Zone 8. While all delphiniums make spectacular cut flowers, the Belladonna Group hybrids are easier to incorporate in smaller, informal arrangements.

SITE AND SOIL

Grow delphiniums in very rich, deeply prepared soil that is well drained. Neutral to alkaline conditions are ideal, but plants will also grow in slightly acid soil. Although delphiniums require regular watering during the summer, constantly wet soil leads to crown rot and death, so avoid locations where water collects: to provide well-drained conditions, plant in a raised mound of soil in an existing bed or border, or in a raised bed.

Delphiniums grow in full sun or partial shade, but where hot summer weather prevails, a site with morning sun and partial or dappled shade during the hottest part of the day is best. North- or east-facing sites afford more heat protection than south- or west-facing ones and tend to yield longer-lived plants. While good air circulation helps prevent disease problems, select a spot sheltered from strong winds.

PLANTING

Add delphiniums to your garden by growing from seed or by starting with purchased plants. Either way, plant in spring after digging in compost, leaf mold, and/or well-rotted manure to a depth of 1½ feet or more. Grade the soil surface with a rake or hoe so water will not collect on the crowns. Handle the plants with care, as the brittle roots are easily broken. Space plants about 2 feet apart; plantings of at least three plants—more is better—are most effective.

CARE THROUGH THE SEASON

Delphiniums require regular attention throughout the growing season: feeding, watering, and stak-

Delphiniums benefit from good air circulation, but a fence can shelter plants from strong winds. A north- or east-facing site affords them protection from heat.

annuals. At best, most are short-lived perennials. Lucky gardeners in the Pacific Northwest and northern and coastal New England, where cool summers prevail, can grow these spectacular plants with relative ease. They can be grown successfully in other parts of the country, given a good site and careful attention to help them cope with summer heat, but are not low-maintenance plants. Because well-grown plants are so breathtaking, many gardeners are more than happy to give delphiniums the extra attention they require. (For delphinium-like flowers with a minimum of effort, consider planting annual larkspur, *Consolida ajacis*. See the description on page 28 in the **Annuals & Biennials** entry for growing information.)

ing are essential tasks for best performance. Gardeners who grow them as biennials or annuals start new plants from seeds each year (see "Propagation" at right for details).

Thinning. For established plants, the growing season starts in spring when the shoots emerge (be sure to cover plants if late frost threatens). Thin the shoots when they are about 3 inches tall by cutting off all but the three strongest ones on 2-year-old plants. Leave five to eight strong shoots on established plants. Thinning directs the plant's energy into producing fewer, larger bloom spikes. It also encourages good air circulation and keeps the plants growing vigorously.

Staking. Delphiniums have hollow, brittle stems that will break off if they are not securely staked. When the stems are about 1 foot tall, provide a stake for each stem. Bamboo poles are traditional, but plastic-dipped steel stakes also are a practical option. Be sure to use stakes that are long enough to be pushed a foot or more into the ground and yet still be tall enough to give the bloom spikes sturdy support. (To avoid a forest of 6-foot-tall stakes dwarfing 1- or 2-foot plants, consider starting with short stakes and adding taller ones as the plants grow.) Use soft yarn, raffia, or strips of nylon stocking to tie the stems to the stakes. Tie firmly, but not tightly, at intervals up the stalks.

Feeding, Watering, and Mulching. Delphiniums are thirsty plants and heavy feeders, so plan on a regular schedule of watering and feeding throughout the season. Water deeply every week, unless a soaking rain does the job for you. Watering right at the soil level, via soaker hoses, helps prevent diseases, as the leaves stay dry. In late spring, spread a layer of mulch around the plants, keeping it away from the stems, to keep the soil moist and cool and to control weeds. About the time you thin the stems, give plants a spring feeding by scratching a balanced organic fertilizer into the soil. Feed again when the first blooms appear.

Encouraging Rebloom and Overwintering. When the main flower stalks fade, cut them off just above the mound of foliage. New flower spikes often will emerge and bloom in late summer or fall. Feed plants that rebloom when the new stalks begin to flower. Allow the foliage to die back naturally, since it produces food for next year's flowers. In the North, once the soil freezes in fall, protect the plants from freeze-thaw cycles over winter with a covering of evergreen boughs, straw, salt hay, or oak leaves. (Do not use other types of leaves, as they will pack down and smother the crowns.) Remove the mulch gradually in spring.

Propagation. Most gardeners start delphiniums from seeds. Since delphinium seeds lose viability quickly, start with fresh ones and store them in the refrigerator until you are ready to sow. For bloom the first season, sow in early to midwinter (December to January). Cover the seeds with coarse vermiculite or the pots with aluminum foil, since darkness is required for germination, which takes 10 to 14 days. Temperatures between 55° and 65°F are best for both germination and growing on. Remove the foil, if used, after seedlings appear, and grow the seedlings in a cool, bright place. Transplant to individual pots when the seedlings have several true leaves. Water regularly and feed weekly with diluted liquid fertilizer. Harden the plants off in early spring, and move them to the garden on or about the last spring frost date. Delphiniums can also be sown in spring, as described above, but plants from late sowings shouldn't be allowed to bloom the first year. (This is the schedule used to grow delphiniums as biennials.) Pick off all the bloom stalks that emerge to encourage vigorous plants for next year.

Delphiniums can also be grown from cuttings taken from the base of the plant in early spring. Using a sharp knife, cut 2- to 4-inch-long, pencil-thick stems that are solid, not hollow. (With experience you'll be able to determine which stems will be hollow — stems thinner than pencil size generally are — but until then you'll need to cut and look.) Each cutting should have a sliver of the crown attached at the base. Wash off the base of the cuttings, dip them in rooting hormone, and root in sand or a 50-50 mix of perlite and vermiculite.

Division in spring is another option, but since the plants resent being moved, they are best left undisturbed.

Potential Problems. Powdery mildew attacks delphiniums, especially in warm climates. Providing good air circulation, planting resistant cultivars, and dusting afflicted plants with sulfur are effective controls. Slugs and snails adore the shoots and foliage; see the box on page 166 in the *Hosta* entry for suggestions on controlling these pests. Planting in well-drained soil and avoiding damage to the crowns are the best ways to prevent crown rot.

LANDSCAPE USES

Plant drifts of taller delphiniums at the back of borders or in the center of island beds to add dramatic vertical accents. Shorter cultivars can be used in mid-border. They are stunning when combined with other summer-blooming perennials such as lilies, columbines (*Aquilegia* spp.), poppies (*Papaver* spp.), peonies, and phlox.

Delphinium 'Bluebird'

Dianthus

Pinks

Dianthus

■

(die-AN-thuss)

■

Spring to summer bloom

■

Full sun or light shade

■

Zones 3 to 9

■

Dianthus
'Telstar Picotee'

■ Charming and old fashioned, pinks are popular garden plants because of their abundant flowers and their basically undemanding nature. Their dainty, often spicy-scented flowers appear over a long season. Pinks come with an impressive pedigree: the name *Dianthus* is from the Greek *dios,* meaning "god," and *anthos,* "flower," and thus is translated as "flower of the gods." Despite the fact that blooms come in all shades of pink, the common name "pinks" comes not from the color of the flowers but from the fringed or ragged edges of the petals, which look as if they've been trimmed with pinking shears. Blooms can also be white, maroon, or ruby red, and many pinks sport blooms in two or more shades, typically with contrasting eyes or other markings. Flowers may be single, semidouble, or fully double. The plants are generally low growing and mound shaped and feature attractive blue- or gray-green, lance-shaped to grasslike leaves that are frequently evergreen.

SELECTING PINKS

Dianthus is a large genus with over 300 species and literally thousands of cultivars. Most of the commonly grown species are hardy perennials that need similar conditions. Sweet William, a biennial, and China pinks, which are grown as annuals, are also popular members of the genus. Most are terrific cut flowers, with the exception of the diminutive dwarf types suitable for rock gardens, which are simply too short to cut. Florist's carnations *(D. caryophyllus)* also fall here, but they are suitable for greenhouse, not garden, culture.

Hardy Pinks

All of the following pinks are easy to grow in full sun and well-drained, slightly acid to alkaline soil. They begin flowering as the main flush of spring perennials and bulbs is waning and so are especially valuable for adding color to the garden from late spring into summer. Most have evergreen leaves. As a general rule, a sunny spot that receives light shade during the hottest part of the day improves the flower display and yields longer-lived plants. (Pinks tend to be short-lived perennials.) Many of these will self-sow if conditions are right.

If you are starting from seeds, keep in mind that pinks are a promiscuous lot that cross indiscriminately with one another. Seed-grown plants often do not resemble their parents, but they may be charming nonetheless. If you want to add a specific species or cultivar to your garden, start with plants propagated asexually — by division, cuttings, or layering.

Alpine pink *(Dianthus alpinus)*

D. alpinus. Alpine pink. Single, 1½-inch flowers in late spring or early summer; mound-forming, 3- to 6-inch-tall plants. Soil rich in organic matter is best. Top-dress the clumps annually in spring with loose soil mixed with compost or leaf mold to help prevent them from dying out in the center. Plants appreciate afternoon shade in all areas with warm summer temperatures and struggle where summer temperatures remain above 85°F. Zones 3 to 8.

D. deltoides. Maiden pink. Single, 1- to 1½-inch blooms in early to midsummer; 6- to 12-inch plants that reach 12 to 20 inches across. Remove spent blooms or shear back plants after the main flush of flowers to encourage plants to rebloom later in summer and in fall. Self-sows enthusiastically. Vigorous, heat tolerant, and relatively long lived. 'Zing Rose' blooms from late spring to fall. Zones 3 to 9.

D. gratianopolitanus. Cheddar pink. Fragrant, single or double, 1-inch flowers in late spring; dense, 4- to 12-inch, mat-forming plants. Remove spent blooms or shear back plants after the main flush of flowers to encourage plants to continue blooming. Heat tolerant and a good choice for southern as well as northern gardens. Zones 3 to 9.

D. plumarius. Cottage pink. Fragrant, 1-inch single, semidouble, or double flowers borne two to five per stem from spring to early summer; mound-forming, 1- to 2-foot plants. Also called border pink. Zones 3 to 9. Allwood pinks (frequently listed as *D. × allwoodii*) are crosses between *D. plumarius* and florist's carnations *(D. caryophyllus)*. They bear 2-inch flowers for up to 8 weeks, but many are not very fragrant. They are also less hardy, from Zones 5 to 8.

Annual and Biennial Pinks

Old-fashioned sweet William *(D. barbatus)* is a short-lived perennial commonly grown as a biennial. The plants are such prolific self-sowers, however, that they often behave more like perennials in the garden. Despite the common name "sweet William," this species' flowers aren't fragrant, but they are borne in showy, flat-topped clusters from late spring into early summer on 1- to 1½-foot plants. Start seeds annually in spring, either indoors or out, to grow sweet William as a biennial. To encourage plants to perform as perennials, remove flowers as they fade and divide them every 2 to 3 years. Zones 3 to 9.

China pink *(D. chinensis)*, a biennial or short-lived perennial, is commonly grown as a cool-weather annual. Also called rainbow pink and Indian pink, this species has scentless flowers with fringed petals that come in a wide variety of colors and patterns. Blooms are borne in

Maiden pink *(Dianthus deltoides)*

Cottage pink *(Dianthus plumarius)*

Sweet William *(Dianthus barbatus)*

Cheddar pink
(*Dianthus gratianopolitanus*)

3-inch-wide clusters from midsummer to fall on 6- to 12-inch plants. Sow seeds outdoors in a prepared seedbed where the plants are to grow after danger of frost has passed. For earlier bloom, sow indoors 6 to 8 weeks before the last spring frost date. Germinate at temperatures between 65° and 70°F. Transplant hardened-off seedlings to the garden after the last frost date. Deadhead regularly to encourage rebloom. China pinks perform best in areas with cool summers.

SITE AND SOIL

Selecting a good site is the key to success with all pinks. They thrive in full sun but are cool-weather-loving plants, so a site with light shade during the hottest part of the day is beneficial because it provides heat protection and helps keep the plants vigorous. Alkaline to neutral soil is best, although plants will tolerate slightly acid soil (to pH 6.5). Pinks will thrive in dry to evenly moist conditions, but the soil must be well drained. (Soil that remains damp, especially in winter, guarantees failure.)

PLANTING

Add pinks to the garden by starting seeds, which are easy to grow, or buying plants in spring. Before planting, test and adjust soil pH as necessary. Work plenty of organic matter, such as finished compost, into the soil to encourage good drainage. Space plants of the tallest species 1½ to 2 feet apart; space others 1 foot apart.

CARE THROUGH THE SEASON

Pinks need very little care to look their best. They appreciate, but do not require, a spring feeding with a fertilizer high in phosphorus—a sprinkling of bonemeal is fine. An annual dose of wood

ashes helps keep soil pH in the right range. Evergreen pinks may need trimming back in spring to remove winter-damaged growth. If necessary, lift up the stems that sprawl out from the crown to remove dead stems and leaves underneath. Top-dress plants with loose soil mixed with compost or leaf mold if the shallow feeder roots are becoming exposed. Don't mulch pinks with organic mulches such as shredded bark, because it tends to keep the soil too damp. Stone chips, especially limestone chips, are an effective mulch.

The plants tend to die out in the center and need dividing every 2 to 3 years to keep them attractive and vigorous.

Cutting off the flowers as they fade helps prolong bloom. Hedge shears make easy work of this task, but you may want to clip individual stems instead to avoid cutting off buds that are yet to open. This is also a good time to trim back scraggly growth. If you want to encourage self-sowing, allow some flowers to set seed.

Propagation. Propagate pinks by growing them from seeds, dividing the plants, or taking cuttings. Long-stemmed types can also be propagated by layering (see the Techniques Glossary for details on this method).

Sow seeds indoors 8 to 10 weeks before the last spring frost date in a fast-draining, soilless medium, and move hardened-off seedlings outdoors after the last frost date. Or sow outdoors in spring just before the last frost date when the soil is still cool in a nursery bed or into pots set in a protected location. Barely cover the seeds with soil. Divide plants in spring by digging the clumps and cutting them apart with a sharp knife. Discard older, less vigorous portions and replant the rest.

Take cuttings in summer from nonflowering shoot tips, cutting just below a leaf node. Cuttings should be 1 to 4 inches long. Remove the lowest leaves and root in coarse sand or a 50-50 mix of vermiculite or perlite and coarse sand. Keep the medium barely moist, as rot is a problem. The cuttings can also be rooted in a protected spot outdoors, again in sand, with a Mason jar placed over them.

LANDSCAPE USES

Pinks are attractive edging plants for beds and borders and can also be used along pathways, walls, and raised beds. The smaller species and cultivars make superb rock-garden plants. Combine pinks with other plants that appreciate well-drained conditions, including thread-leaved coreopsis (*Coreopsis verticillata)*, columbines (*Aquilegia* spp.), bellflowers (*Campanula* spp.), sedums, and thymes. They are attractive combined with dwarf conifers as well.

Dicentra

Bleeding Hearts

Dicentra
∎
(die-CEN-trah)
∎
Spring to summer bloom
∎
Light to full shade
∎
Zones 2 to 9
∎

Fringed bleeding heart
(Dicentra eximia)

∎ Bleeding hearts have a charm that's hard to resist. Common bleeding heart *(Dicentra spectabilis)*, perhaps the best-known species, is an old-fashioned, dependable perennial with arching racemes of dangling, heart-shaped flowers and is hardy in Zones 2 to 9. The striking display — in rosy pink, rose-red, or white — lasts for a few weeks in spring, beginning in March in the South, May in the North. (White-flowered cultivars tend to be less robust than the species. Of the two commonly available white cultivars, 'Pantaloons' is said to be more robust than 'Alba', however.) The bushy, 1½- to 2½-foot-tall plants have brittle, fleshy stems and divided leaves with wedge-shaped leaflets. After blooming, the plants go dormant until the following spring. If the soil is kept evenly moist, the foliage lasts until early summer in the South, midsummer or even early fall in the North.

Fringed bleeding heart *(D. eximia)* and western bleeding heart *(D. formosa)* are both native North American wildflowers. Both are 10- to 18-inch perennials that produce handsome mounds of delicate-looking, blue-green, fernlike leaves. Spikes of pendent, heart-shaped flowers are carried above the foliage from spring to fall, provided the soil is kept evenly moist. (*D. eximia* tends to stop blooming when night temperatures remain above 80°F but resumes when cooler nights return in fall.) A number of cultivars of these two species are available with flowers in shades from pink to maroon, plus white. Both are hardy in Zones 3 to 9.

SITE AND SOIL

Grow bleeding hearts in light to full shade in a site with moist, well-drained soil that is rich in organic matter. Wet, poorly drained soil, especially in winter, leads to root rot and death. For *D. eximia* and *D. formosa,* morning sun and afternoon shade helps encourage summer-long bloom; protection from the hot afternoon sun is essential in the South.

PLANTING

Bleeding hearts can go into the garden in spring or fall. Handle the plants carefully to avoid breaking the brittle roots or rhizomes, and dig a shovelful of compost or other organic matter into

Common bleeding heart *(Dicentra spectabilis)*

White-flowered common bleeding heart (*Dicentra spectabilis* 'Alba')

Fringed bleeding heart (*Dicentra eximia* 'Luxuriant')

the soil at planting time. Space *D. spectabilis* about 3 feet apart and mark the location of the clumps to avoid digging into them accidentally when the plants are dormant. Space *D. eximia* and *D. formosa* 15 to 18 inches apart.

CARE THROUGH THE SEASON

Bleeding hearts need minimal care through the season. Keep the soil evenly moist by watering as necessary and mulching with chopped leaves or shredded bark. The plants are not heavy feeders, but they do appreciate an annual topdressing with compost — simply pull back the mulch in spring, spread a shovelful of compost, then replace the mulch. Remove bloom spikes of *D. eximia* and *D. formosa* as they fade to keep the plants looking neat and to encourage new flowers to form.

When the foliage of *D. spectabilis* turns yellow, cut plants to the ground. Foliage of the other two species can be cut to the ground after a hard freeze or simply left in the garden to decompose.

Division. Once planted, bleeding hearts are best left undisturbed — the fleshy roots of *D. spectabilis* are especially brittle and easily damaged. Divide them in early spring if they outgrow their site, if the clumps become woody and die out in the center, or if blooming decreases. Cut the woody crowns apart with a knife, making sure that each piece has healthy buds and roots. Discard woody portions of the clump. Amend the soil with organic matter before replanting.

Propagation. Division is the easiest way to propagate bleeding hearts, and the best way to propagate all of the cultivars, which do not come true from seed. *D. spectabilis* can also be propagated by root cuttings taken in fall or early winter (see "Propagating from Root Cuttings" in the Techniques Glossary for details) as well as by stem cuttings taken in early spring before plants bloom. When growing any of the bleeding hearts from seed, keep in mind that only very fresh seeds will germinate. Sow in late summer in a peat/vermiculite mix and place pots in a cold frame or other protected location outdoors.

LANDSCAPE USES

Plant bleeding hearts in shade gardens with hostas, ferns, columbines (*Aquilegia* spp.), epimediums, wild blue phlox (*Phlox divaricata*), foamflowers (*Tiarella* spp.), and spring bulbs such as tulips. In areas where *D. spectabilis* dies back early in the season, plant impatiens or begonias near the clumps, but be sure to keep them far enough away to avoid damaging the roots of the bleeding hearts. Or direct-sow annuals such as sweet alyssum (*Lobularia maritima*) around the plants. Both *D. eximia* and *D. formosa* can be used as ground covers in shade plantings.

Dictamnus albus

Gas Plant

Dictamnus albus
■
(dick-TAM-nuss AL-buss)
■
Late-spring to early-summer bloom
■
Full sun or light shade
■
Zones 3 to 8
■

Pink-flowered gas plant (*Dictamnus albus* 'Ruber')

■ Gas plant isn't as widely known as many perennials are, but gardeners who know it wouldn't want to be without it. What's not to love about a plant so fragrant that some people say its volatile oils can actually be ignited? The fact that gas plants are as dependable and long lived as peonies is more important—the shrublike clumps can bloom reliably with little care for decades.

Also called dittany and fraxinella, gas plant produces a stout, handsome clump of glossy, dark green, pinnately compound leaves that are lemon scented when bruised. Sweetly fragrant spikes of flowers appear on 3-foot plants in late spring to early summer—from April into May in the South, May into June from the middle part of the country northward. Individual blooms are 1 inch across with five showy petals and long, curled stamens that give them a spidery appearance. The species has white flowers, but cultivars in various shades of pink are also available. Although the duration of bloom is brief, the foliage remains attractive all season. Furthermore, the flowers yield handsome spikes of star-shaped seedpods.

The characteristic that gave rise to such other common names as burning bush and candle plant is fascinating but not as spectacular as it sounds.

Both leaves and flowers give off a volatile oil that in still, sultry weather *sometimes* can be ignited for a split second with a match. Some sources say the leaves themselves ignite; others, that it's the perfume given off by the older flowers. (Most sources recommend attempting this in the evening, some in the morning.) One thing to keep in mind regarding gas plant's oils is that they will cause a blistering, poison-ivy-like rash in some gardeners, especially in hot weather.

SITE AND SOIL

Gas plants bloom best in full sun, although they also grow in light shade. Well-drained, fertile soil is best. Poorly drained soil leads to root rot. Select a site with care, since the plants establish themselves slowly and should be left undisturbed once planted. Newly planted specimens take 3 to 4 years to begin blooming well.

PLANTING

Purchase pot-grown, 2- to 3-year-old seedlings. Dig the soil deeply and work in compost or well-rotted manure before planting. Space plants 3 to 4 feet apart—they will look puny for a few seasons, but this gives them ample room at maturity. Disturb the roots as little as possible during transplanting. Water thoroughly and mulch.

CARE THROUGH THE SEASON

With the exception of watering during very dry weather, gas plants require very little care. The flowers stand without staking, and plants shouldn't be deadheaded, because the seedpods are ornamental. Feed annually in spring with compost or well-rotted manure if the soil is poor. Gas plants are seldom bothered by pests or diseases.

Gas plants do not transplant well, and disturbing the roots can be fatal. If you *must* divide a clump, do so in spring or fall and use a sharp spade. Dig the clump and cut cleanly through the crown and the roots. Replant immediately.

Propagation. Seeds offer the best propagation method, and starting with fresh seed is the secret to success. To collect it, place a nylon stocking over the ripening spikes—otherwise the spring-loaded capsules scatter seeds everywhere. Sow in pots in late summer or fall and place them in a cold frame or other protected location outdoors. Seedlings should appear in spring, but germination is sporadic. Move 1- to 2-year-old plants to the garden. Plants will bloom in 3 to 4 years.

LANDSCAPE USES

Plant gas plants with other early-summer-blooming perennials such as hardy geraniums, yarrows (*Achillea* spp.), and flax (*Linum* spp.). The foliage is also attractive as a foil for summer- and fall-blooming perennials such as asters.

Digitalis

Foxgloves

Digitalis
■
(dih-jih-TAL-iss)
■
Summer bloom
■
Full sun or partial shade
■
Zones 4 to 8
■

■ Foxgloves are biennials or short-lived perennials that bear erect racemes of tubular to funnel-shaped flowers above a rosette of large, broadly lance-shaped leaves. Blooms come in shades of pink as well as white and creamy yellow and are often spotted inside. The botanical name *Digitalis* is from the Latin for "finger," *digitus,* and refers to the fingerlike shape of the flowers. All parts of the plant are poisonous.

Common foxglove *(D. purpurea)* is an old-fashioned plant that is still popular today. A biennial, it produces a rosette of leaves the first year and flowers the next. Its showy spikes of flowers appear above the mound of foliage in early summer and reach a height of 3 to 5 feet. Plants sometimes bloom for a second or third season as short-lived perennials; they are hardy in Zones 4 to 8. 'Foxy' is a fast-blooming, 2- to 3-foot-tall cultivar that will bloom the first year from seed. It can be grown as an annual if seeds are sown indoors in winter. Yellow foxglove *(D. grandiflora)* is a perennial species that bears pale yellow flowers on 2- to 3-foot plants. Strawberry foxglove *(D. × mertonensis),* another perennial, bears pink or white flowers on 3- to 4-foot plants. Both are hardy in Zones 3 to 8.

SITE AND SOIL
Plant foxgloves in full sun or partial shade—a spot that is shady in the afternoon is beneficial in areas with hot summers. They thrive in evenly moist, well-drained soil that is rich in organic matter. A site protected from winter winds is best.

PLANTING
Foxgloves are easy to grow from seeds, but plants are commonly available as well. For the most dramatic show from *D. purpurea,* grow it as a biennial, pulling out the plants after they flower the

Common foxglove (*Digitalis purpurea* 'Gloxiniiflora')

Common foxglove (*Digitalis purpurea*)

Common foxgloves *(Digitalis purpurea)* with roses, pansies *(Viola* spp.), and rose verbena *(Verbena canadensis)*

first time (in their second year). Keep in mind that you'll need to start plants every year to ensure blooms every summer.

Biennials and perennials are grown in much the same way, and seeds can be sown indoors or out. Outdoors, sow seeds in spring or summer up to 2 months before the first fall frost in a prepared seedbed, a nursery bed, or pots set in a protected location. In early fall or the following spring, transplant seedlings to the spots in the garden where they will bloom. Indoors, sow in individual pots 6 to 8 weeks before plants are scheduled to go into the garden. That translates to midsummer sowing for plants that are to be moved to the garden in early fall, spring sowing to produce seedlings to plant out in late spring or early summer. Germination takes from 15 to 20 days at temperatures between 60° and 70°F. To grow 'Foxy' as an annual, start seeds indoors in midwinter.

Space foxgloves 1 to 1½ feet apart and set them out in drifts of several plants for best effect. Handle the plants carefully when transplanting, and keep them evenly moist until they are established.

CARE THROUGH THE SEASON
Foxgloves need little care once they are moved to the garden. They generally stand without staking and are otherwise trouble free. Water deeply during dry weather. If you are growing foxgloves

as biennials, pull up 2-year-old plants after they have flowered and replace them with new seedlings. For plants scheduled to bloom another year, cut the stalks to just above the foliage after the flowers fade.

Foxgloves self-sow, and to encourage this tendency, allow a flower spike or two to set seed, then crumble the pods over the soil where you want plants to appear. Volunteer seedlings can be moved easily with a trowel once they have produced a small rosette of leaves. Bear in mind that self-sown seedlings will be variable. If you want a certain cultivar or color, purchase seeds.

Propagation. In addition to seeds, foxgloves can be propagated by division. Dig the clumps in early spring or fall and separate and replant them. Even the biennial *D. purpurea* can be propagated in this manner: discard the main rosette that has already bloomed and replant the rosettes that arise around it.

LANDSCAPE USES
Plant foxgloves in beds and borders, and combine them with perennials that bloom in early summer such as bleeding hearts *(Dicentra* spp.) and bellflowers *(Campanula* spp.). They are striking in drifts in the dappled shade of a woodland edge or in a shade garden among hostas, ferns, and spring-blooming phlox such as *Phlox divaricata.* They can also be planted with shrub roses and other old-fashioned plants in a cottage garden.

Echinacea

Purple Coneflowers

Echinacea
■
(eck-in-AY-see-ah)
■
Summer to early-fall bloom
■
Full sun
■
Zones 3 to 9
■

■ Stalwart, sun-loving purple coneflowers are native North American wildflowers that bear an abundance of daisylike blooms in early to midsummer and then bloom sporadically through to early fall. Along with sunflowers and other members of the aster family (Asteraceae), they produce flower heads consisting of ray florets, commonly called petals, surrounding spiny, dense centers of disk florets, which produce the seeds. The petals are purple-pink, rose, or white and droop away from the conelike centers, which are orange-brown to golden brown. The botanical name *Echinacea*, from the Greek *echinos*, meaning "hedgehog," is another reference to the spiny centers. The showy flower heads, from 4 to 6 inches across, make excellent cut flowers.

Purple coneflower *(E. purpurea)*, a 2- to 4-foot plant that occasionally reaches 6 feet, is by far the most commonly grown species. Several cultivars are more compact than the species: 'Bravado', 'Leuchtstern' (also sold as 'Bright Star'), and 'Magnus' have more-horizontal petals than the species and are from 2 to 2½ feet tall. White-flowered cultivars tend to be more compact as well: 'White Swan' is 1 to 2 feet tall, while 'White Lustre' reaches 3 feet. All are hardy in Zones 3 to 9.

Two other species are sometimes grown. Pale coneflower *(E. pallida)* bears pale pink, drooping flower heads on 3- to 4-foot plants and is hardy in Zones 4 to 8. Narrow-leaved coneflower *(E. angustifolia)* is a 1- to 2-foot plant with rose-pink flowers and is hardy in Zones 3 to 8.

Food for Wildlife

Purple coneflowers are popular sources of nectar and pollen for butterflies and bees in summertime and can help feed overwintering birds as well. While removing spent flowers prolongs bloom, you may want to leave some or all of the flower heads intact to provide a natural source of seeds for birds over winter. The standing stalks also add character to the winter landscape. If you do deadhead, cut back to a branch where a new flower bud is visible.

SITE AND SOIL
Plant all coneflowers in full sun in a site with well-drained, average soil. They are native to prairies and open woodlands and will tolerate a range of conditions, including drought and heat. They will bloom in light shade, but the plants tend to get leggy. White-flowered cultivars tend to be more sensitive to poor soil drainage than the pink ones are and can be short lived.

PLANTING
Plant coneflowers in spring or fall. They are easy and reliable from seed, and most of the cultivars come true from seed. Space plants 1 to 2 feet apart, depending on their height at maturity.

CARE THROUGH THE SEASON
Coneflowers can be left pretty much to their own devices once they are planted. Because of their deep taproots, they withstand considerable drought. For best bloom, however, water during dry weather. In average soil, they do not require fertilizing, but mulching with compost in spring

Purple coneflower (*Echinacea purpurea* 'Bright Star')

Purple coneflower *(Echinacea purpurea)*

adds organic matter and some nutrients to the soil. In too-rich soil or not enough sun, they can become lank and floppy; pinching and/or staking helps keep them in line. Cut the plants to the ground in fall, or leave them standing to add winter interest to the garden and cut them down in early spring.

Purple coneflowers can be left for years without needing division, but they can be dug and divided in spring or fall if the plants become crowded or outgrow their space or if the clumps die out in the center.

Propagation. In addition to division, purple coneflowers can be grown from seeds and propagated from basal cuttings (cuttings of shoots from the base of the plant) in spring. Root basal cuttings in sharp sand or a 50-50 mix of vermiculite and perlite.

If you've ever transplanted a purple coneflower, you've probably propagated it using another method: root cuttings. Roots left in the soil often sprout new plants. To take root cuttings, dig pencil-thick roots in fall and root them in sharp sand. (See "Propagating from Root Cuttings" in the Techniques Glossary for details.)

To grow from seeds, sow in a soilless mix and cover the seeds lightly. Placing the moistened, sown pots in the refrigerator for 4 to 6 weeks before germinating at 65° to 70°F helps ensure even germination, although it's not essential to success. Plants self-sow, and seedlings are easy to move with a trowel when they are still small.

LANDSCAPE USES

Purple coneflowers are ideal additions to beds and borders, where they can be combined with other summer-blooming perennials such as daylilies (*Hemerocallis* spp.), yarrows (*Achillea* spp.), gayfeathers (*Liatris* spp.), and Russian sage *(Perovskia atriplicifolia)*. They are tough enough to be combined with ornamental grasses and are suitable for meadow plantings with butterfly weed *(Asclepias tuberosa)*, coneflowers (*Rudbeckia* spp.), and goldenrods (*Solidago* spp.).

Echinops ritro

Globe Thistle

Echinops ritro
■
(ECH-in-ops REE-tro)
■
Summer bloom
■
Full sun
■
Zones 3 to 9
■

Globe thistle (*Echinops ritro* 'Taplow Blue')

■ As their common name suggests, globe thistles are thistlelike, spiny-leaved plants with round flower heads. The 1- to 2-inch flower heads, which are spiny as well, are silvery to metallic blue in color and are carried above the somewhat coarse-looking foliage. (Like *Echinacea*, *Echinops* takes its botanical name from the Greek for "hedgehog," *echinos,* and *opsis,* "appearance," a reference to the spiny blooms.) These clump-forming plants range from 2 to 4 feet in height and have deep taproots.

Although there are about 120 species of globe thistles, *Echinops ritro* is by far the most common. Hardy in Zones 3 to 9, it blooms in mid- to late summer. Plants rebloom, especially if deadheaded. 'Veitch's Blue' bears dark blue flowers on sturdy plants and is a particularly good rebloomer.

The round flower heads are good for both cutting and drying. For fresh use, cut when the florets on top of the flower head open. To dry them, cut the blooms when about one-third of the heads are open.

SITE AND SOIL
Tough, undemanding globe thistles require full sun and a site with poor to average soil that is well drained. Good soil drainage is especially important in winter, because otherwise plants are subject to crown and root rot.

PLANTING
Add globe thistles to your garden by purchasing plants or starting seeds. The cultivars, such as 'Taplow Blue' and 'Veitch's Blue', don't come true from seed, so buy plants propagated by division or root cuttings. Plant in spring, and prepare the soil deeply to ensure good drainage. Space generously, as established plants resent transplanting and can be left in place for many years. Allowing 1½ to 2 feet between plants is adequate.

CARE THROUGH THE SEASON
Established plants are very drought tolerant and need little care. They do not need to be staked, fed, or divided regularly. (In fact, dividing isn't recommended, because it disturbs the deep tap-

Sea Hollies

At first glance, sea hollies (*Eryngium* spp.) look as if they are related to globe thistles. They have rounded flower heads surrounded by stiff bracts, as well as spiny, thistlelike leaves. The colors are similar, too: sea hollies have steely blue-gray to metallic purple blooms. Botanists, however, place them in the parsley family, Apiaceae, while globe thistles reside in the aster family, Asteraceae.

The two plants are grown in a similar fashion, however, and both are suitable for perennial beds and borders. Sea hollies are plants for full sun and average, well-drained soil. They tolerate heat, drought, and poor soil. Good species to look for include amethyst sea holly (*E. amethystinum*), which is hardy in Zones 2 to 8; *E. bourgatii,* hardy in Zones 5 to 8; and *E. planum,* hardy in Zones 5 to 9. *E. giganteum* is a biennial or short-lived perennial that can be grown in Zones 4 to 8.

Like globe thistles, sea hollies seldom need division and actually resent it because of their deep taproots. Separate small plantlets from the base of the clump, as for globe thistles. Plants also self-sow, and seedlings are easily moved. Sea hollies can be hard to grow from seeds, though, because the seeds go dormant quickly. Sow fresh seeds outdoors in fall, or sow indoors in pots and place the moistened, sown pots in the refrigerator for 4 to 6 weeks before germinating at 65° to 70°F.

Globe thistle (*Echinops ritro* 'Taplow Blue')

roots.) Deadheading encourages reblooming and curtails self-seeding. Cut the plants to the ground after the first fall frost.

Propagation. To propagate globe thistles by division without disturbing the entire clump, wash away some soil from around the base of the plant and slice off the small side plants that have arisen there. Pot up the divisions in well-drained, soilless medium and keep them in a protected location until they are established. Another option is to plant them in a nursery bed or a corner of the vegetable garden until they are well established. Take root cuttings in spring or fall. (See "Propagating from Root Cuttings" in the Techniques Glossary for details.)

To grow from seeds, sow on the soil surface (light aids germination) and keep the pots at 65° to 70°F. Plants will bloom the second year from seeds but take up to 3 years to really become established. Cultivars do not come true and are best propagated by division or root cuttings.

LANDSCAPE USES

Plant globe thistles at the back of the border. They are effective when combined with purple coneflower *(Echinacea purpurea)*, coneflowers *(Rudbeckia* spp.), yarrows *(Achillea* spp.), daylilies *(Hemerocallis* spp.), Russian sage *(Perovskia atriplicifolia)*, and ornamental grasses.

Epimedium

Epimediums

■ Epimediums deserve a place in every shade garden. They bear delicate sprays of spring flowers, but their real value lies in their handsome foliage—and their tough, no-nonsense constitution. Epimediums bear early-spring flowers and have attractive, lacy-textured foliage. The plants range from 6 to 15 inches in height and spread steadily, but slowly, to form broad mounds.

Also called barrenwort and bishop's cap (the latter a reference to the flower shape), epimediums start off the spring garden with airy sprays of ½- to 1-inch flowers on wiry stems. Blooms appear with the main flush of spring bulbs such as daffodils and grape hyacinths. The tiny, columbine-like blooms have eight petal-like sepals and four petals that are often spurlike. Flowers come in shades of white, rose, red, or pale to bright yellow; there are also bicolors. Although the individual flowers are small, since they are borne in clusters the overall effect of a well-established clump is showy and effective.

The bright green, wiry-stemmed leaves, sometimes marked with bronze or maroon, emerge with or slightly after the flowers and remain attractive all season. Each leaf consists of several heart-shaped or somewhat triangular leaflets—the size and shape vary depending on the species or cultivar. As the leaves mature, they turn a darker green and become more leathery. Many epimediums also have attractive fall foliage in yellow, bronze, or red.

SELECTING EPIMEDIUMS

All of the commonly available epimediums are undemanding garden plants with reliable spring flowers and handsome, long-lasting foliage. Unless otherwise noted, the following species are all hardy in Zones 5 to 8, and often to Zone 4 with winter protection. Alpine epimedium *(Epimedium alpinum)*, hardy in Zones 3 to 8, bears red flowers on 6- to 9-inch plants. Long-spurred epimedium *(E. grandiflorum)* has large, 1- to 1½-inch flowers; white- and pink-flowered cultivars are available. Red-flowered epimedium *(E. × rubrum)* produces red flowers on 8- to 10-inch plants. Warley epimedium *(E. × warleyense)* has showy, brick red to orange-red flowers on 8- to 12-inch

Epimedium
■
(eh-pih-MEE-dee-um)
■
Spring bloom
■
Partial or full shade
■
Zones 3 to 8
■

Epimedium × youngianum 'Niveum'

Epimedium × youngianum 'Niveum'

Epimedium × perralchicum

plants. Young's epimedium (*E. × youngianum*) is a 6- to 8-inch species with white or rose-pink flowers; it has especially small leaflets that add a delicate fernlike texture to the garden. *E. perralderianum* is a particularly vigorous species that reaches 10 to 12 inches in height and produces yellow flowers. *E. × perralchicum*, another vigorous rhizomatous species, reaches 12 to 16 inches in height and has yellow flowers; its cultivar 'Fröhnleiten' bears 1-inch-wide blooms. Bicolor epimedium (*E. × versicolor*) is another tough, vigorous selection with red-and-yellow flowers on 10- to 12-inch plants.

Epimediums are frequently described as being evergreen, and their leaves certainly are long lasting: they are attractive from early spring all the way into late fall and even early winter. In areas with mild winters, some species are evergreen or at least semievergreen—*E. × perralchicum, E. perralderianum, E. × versicolor,* and *E. × warleyense* are considered to be evergreen species. In the North, however, while the leaves do remain somewhat erect through the winter, sooner or later they turn brown and curl. (At best, the species or cultivars I've grown are semievergreen in my Zone 6 garden, but only during very mild winters. The leaves of the evergreen species listed above last into early winter, longer than those of other species, however.)

SITE AND SOIL

A site in partial shade with rich, evenly moist soil is ideal for epimediums and produces the most luxuriant growth. They can also be planted in full shade as well as in full sun, provided the soil stays moist and is amended with plenty of organic matter. Once established, epimediums perform well in tough conditions such as dry shade. They can even compete with the roots of established trees.

PLANTING

Plant epimediums in spring or fall in soil well enriched with organic matter. Space plants about twice their height apart, closer for nonspreading species or if you are creating a mass planting or using them as ground covers. (*E. grandiflorum* and *E. × youngianum* spread more slowly than species such as *E. alpinum, E. × rubrum, E. × warleyense,* and especially *E. × versicolor.*) Keep the soil evenly moist until plants are established. Mulch around them with chopped leaves or shredded bark to conserve soil moisture and to keep down weeds—replenishing the mulch annually helps add organic matter to the soil.

CARE THROUGH THE SEASON

Once established, epimediums need little care. In late winter, cut back the old foliage so it will not

Epimedium × versicolor 'Sulfureum' with Japanese painted fern *(Athyrium niponicum)* and a variegated vinca *(Vinca minor* 'Argenteovariegata')

interfere with the spring flowers. Even in areas where epimediums are evergreen or semievergreen, this is a worthwhile chore, as the flowers can get lost in last year's leaves. Don't delay this task even into early spring, or you'll have to clip around the emerging flowers, which can be hard to spot among the old foliage. (It's best *not* to get a jump on things and cut back the foliage in early winter in the North, because the foliage helps insulate the plants over winter.)

Propagation. Epimediums are easily propagated by division after flowering in spring or in fall. Simply dig the clumps and cut through the tough, somewhat woody roots with pruning shears. It's also possible to root sections of rhizome. Fill pots with a 50-50 mix of peat moss and vermiculite, lay sections of rhizome on the surface, and keep moist. Epimediums are seldom grown from seeds because only fresh seeds germinate reliably, and most selections are hybrids and do not come true. To grow plants from seeds, sow in late summer in a peat/vermiculite mix and place pots in a cold frame or other protected location outdoors. Seedlings appear in spring.

LANDSCAPE USES

Epimediums are at their glory when allowed to form large clumps, which can produce an impressive display of flowers as well as handsome foliage texture. Established clumps have another advantage: they are dense enough to suppress most weeds. Use epimediums as ground covers for shade, either planted en masse or combined with other shade-loving plants to create a tapestry of color and texture. Use a row of epimediums to edge a bed or walkway; plant specimens in rock gardens, shady beds and borders, and woodland plantings—even among tree roots. Interplant them with spring bulbs such as daffodils, tulips, grape hyacinths (*Muscari* spp.), and Spanish bluebells (*Hyacinthoides hispanica*). They make fine companions for hostas, ferns, hellebores, and all other shade-loving plants.

An Epimedium Relative

If you like epimediums, consider growing their close relative *Vancouveria hexandra*, which is hardy in Zones 5 to 7 and thrives in the same conditions and with the same care. Once listed as *Epimedium hexandra*, this woodland wildflower native to the Pacific Northwest produces white spring flowers and dense, spreading 1½-foot-tall clumps of handsome foliage. The leaves are divided like an epimedium's, but since the leaflets are smaller, the texture is more delicate.

Euphorbia

Euphorbias

Cushion spurge *(Euphorbia polychroma)*

Euphorbia
- (you-FOR-bee-ah)
- Spring to summer bloom
- Full sun or partial shade
- Zones 4 to 10

◼ Without a doubt, the best-known euphorbia is a tropical shrub commonly grown as a Christmas pot plant: the poinsettia. Fortunately for gardeners, this vast and diverse genus contains hardy, easy-to-grow perennials for full sun and partial shade as well. Like poinsettias, hardy euphorbias (or spurges, as they are sometimes called) have insignificant flowers surrounded by showy, petal-like bracts, commonly referred to as the flowers. All euphorbias have milky sap that flows freely when stems or leaves are cut or damaged. The sap may irritate skin.

Most euphorbias make attractive cut flowers. Before adding them to arrangements, sear the stem ends of both perennials and annuals over a candle flame or dip the ends in boiling water to seal in the sap and prolong their vase life.

SELECTING EUPHORBIAS
The hardy perennial euphorbias are grown for their spring to summer flowers, but some also feature handsome foliage color or evergreen leaves. The best site and soil varies from species to species. Most require loose, well-drained soil and can be planted in light to partial shade or full sun. A site with sun in the morning and dappled shade in the afternoon is suitable for many species.

Euphorbia amygdaloides var. *robbiae*. Wood spurge. Greenish yellow flowers from midspring to early summer above shiny, handsome evergreen leaves; 1½- to 2-foot plants. Grows in evenly moist, rich soil in partial to full shade and will also tolerate dry shade once established. Cut off flowers as soon as they fade to encourage new shoots at the base of the plants. Spreads vigorously and can become invasive. A good ground cover. Zones 6 to 9.

E. characias. Clusters of chartreuse flowers from spring to summer above evergreen foliage that is gray-green; 3- to 4-foot plants. Prefers full sun in loose, well-drained soil. The flowering shoots are biennial, so cut them off at the base of the plant after they have bloomed. Zones 7 to 10.

E. dulcis. Greenish yellow flowers in early summer above dark green or bronzed leaves; 12-inch plants. Grows in evenly moist, rich soil in light shade but also tolerates dry shade. Self-sows. 'Chameleon' has colorful purple-maroon foliage. Zones 4 to 9.

E. griffithii. Griffith's spurge. Orange-red flowers in early summer above dark green, lance-shaped leaves; mounding, shrublike, 2- to 3-foot plants. Grows in evenly moist, rich soil in light shade. Tolerates full sun in northern zones but does not tolerate drought. Good red fall foliage color. Zones 4 to 8.

E. myrsinites. Myrtle euphorbia. Yellow spring flowers above evergreen, blue-gray foliage; 6- to 10-inch plants with trailing, prostrate stems. Grows in full sun in loose, well-drained soil and tolerates summer heat well. Select a site protected from winter wind and trim the plants to about 6 inches in spring to shape them. Plants have fragile surface roots and deep taproots that are easily broken, so take care when dividing the clumps. Zones 5 to 9.

E. polychroma. Cushion spurge. Bright yellow-green flowers covering mound-shaped plants in early spring and lasting to late spring if cool weather prevails; compact, 1- to 2-foot plants. Grows in full sun or partial shade, but afternoon shade is beneficial in the North, and essential in the South, because it protects the plants from heat and helps them remain attractive until fall. Can be used as a ground cover. (Also sold as *E. epithymoides*.) Zones 4 to 9.

Annual Euphorbias
Two euphorbias are easy-to-grow, warm-weather annuals. Snow-on-the-mountain *(E. marginata, sometimes sold as E. variegata)* has white-edged bracts, or flowers, and makes an attractive cut flower. Annual poinsettia *(E. cyathophora, sometimes sold as E. heterophylla)* has small red bracts. Both are easy to grow in full sun and well-

drained soil. Sow seeds outdoors where the plants are to grow after danger of frost has passed. Thin seedlings to 1 foot apart.

PLANTING

Plant euphorbias in spring or fall, taking care to select a site that will provide the proper sun and soil conditions for the species you are growing. To ensure good drainage, dig the soil fairly deeply and amend it with plenty of organic matter. Or plant euphorbias in raised beds. Space plants 1 to 2 feet apart, depending on their height.

CARE THROUGH THE SEASON

Established plants need very little care to look their best. Once established, most are quite drought tolerant and do not need supplemental watering. They also do not need staking. Divide the plants if they outgrow their space, if the center of the clump dies out, or for propagation. Removing spent flowers isn't necessary, but it does curtail self-seeding.

Propagation. Propagate euphorbias by digging and dividing the clumps in spring or fall, by cuttings, or from seed. When dividing, pull the clumps apart gently and make sure each section has an adequate number of roots. Discard the central portion of the clump, which can become woody. Take cuttings from shoots that arise at the base of the plant in spring or early summer or from the tips of the stems before flower buds appear or in midsummer, after flowering. Root them in a 50-50 mix of vermiculite and perlite or vermiculite and sharp sand. Fresh seeds germinate in less than 2 weeks at temperatures between 65° and 70°F. Sow on the soil surface or cover lightly. Seeds lose their viability quickly, however. If you want to collect seeds from your own plants, keep in mind that the capsules eject them with some force when they are ripe. Put small paper bags or tie lengths of nylon stocking over the ripening seed heads to catch the seeds.

LANDSCAPE USES

Use euphorbias with other spring- or summer-blooming perennials that thrive in well-drained soil. The species that prefer light shade can be combined with a wide variety of plants, including daylilies (*Hemerocallis* spp.), columbines (*Aquilegia* spp.), lamb's ears *(Stachys byzantina)*, hostas, heucheras, hardy geraniums, and even ornamental onions (*Allium* spp.). *E. polychroma* and *E. myrsinites* are attractive in rock gardens or along rock walls or raised beds and can be combined with spring bulbs. Use *E. amygdaloides* var. *robbiae* as a ground cover in shade, or contrast its foliage with large-leaved hostas, hellebores, and epimediums.

Cushion spurge *(Euphorbia polychroma,* formerly E. *epithymoides)* is vigorous enough to use as a ground cover either alone or combined with other ground covers.

Myrtle euphorbia *(Euphorbia myrsinites)*

$\mathcal{F}$erns

■ Ferns are quintessential plants for shade. Their luxuriant foliage adds lacy texture, elegant form, and rich green color to gardens. Unlike most garden plants, ferns are grown solely for their foliage—they are primitive plants that do not produce flowers or seeds and that reproduce via a two-stage life cycle. (See "Propagation" below for more information on fern reproduction.) Despite their exotic appearance, many ferns are undemanding, easy-to-grow garden plants. Given a suitable site and the right soil conditions, they reward a minimum of care with a lush display.

SITE AND SOIL

Selecting an appropriate site is the key to success with ferns. While there are many ferns with very specific growing requirements, in general they grow in partial or full shade and evenly moist, well-drained soil that is rich in organic matter. An acid pH is usually best. Some species will also grow in sun, others in drier or wetter soil. See "Easy, Hardy Ferns," beginning on page 115, for

Bold clumps of ostrich ferns *(Matteuccia struthiopteris)* and hostas fill a shady garden corner.

more on the requirements of different species. Despite the fact that most ferns will grow in full shade, they require good light for best growth. In the wild, they are commonly found growing on the edges of woods or in clearings, where they receive bright, often indirect light but protection from heat during the day. A site under the high branches of oaks or other deep-rooted trees would provide the dappled sun-and-shade ferns thrive in, whereas one in the dense shade of hemlocks or other evergreens is unsuitable. The dense shade cast by many maples *(Acer* spp., especially Norway maple, *A. platanoides),* coupled with their shallow roots, also creates an unsuitable site for a fern planting. Ferns are obvious choices for shade gardens where hostas and other plants thrive, and they can also be planted where they will receive morning sun and afternoon shade or along the shady, north side of a house.

When assessing the soil on a particular site, be sure to consider root competition from nearby trees and shrubs. Ferns can grow in the pockets of soil between large tree roots if the trees don't have dense, shallow feeder roots, as maples do. Oaks *(Quercus* spp.) are deep rooted and provide plenty of room for ferns to grow. Before planting, use a trowel to dig around in a potential site to see how many surface roots ferns may have to contend with. Trees or shrubs won't gen-

erally suffer if you have to remove a root here or there. If a site has lots of dense and/or heavily branched roots, you're fighting a losing battle trying to plant ferns there.

PLANTING

Prepare the site by digging compost, leaf mold, or other organic matter into the soil before planting ferns, which can go into the garden in spring or fall. Prepare pockets of soil between large tree roots by working organic matter in with a trowel, but take care not to damage the roots. If you remove any roots, cut them off cleanly with a sharp mattock or pruning shears.

Do not dig ferns from the wild yourself, and buy them only from a reputable nursery that sells nursery-propagated, not wild-collected, plants. Also avoid plants described as nursery grown, because these may have been wild collected and then grown at the nursery for a year or two. The end result is the same: individuals who collect wild plants decimate natural areas, and buying collected plants puts money in their pockets. Nursery-propagated plants will look uniform and healthy, while wild-collected ones often have a just-potted-up look, with an off-center crown and broken fronds. Other signs of wild-collected plants include weeds in the pots and unusually cheap prices for the size of the plants offered. If in doubt, ask the owners where the plants came from, and shop elsewhere if you receive an unsatisfactory response. Plant sales run by local native-plant societies, conservation associations, and botanical gardens are other good sources for ferns. They may offer plants rescued from areas that are about to be developed.

Keep ferns moist while they are waiting to be planted by sprinkling with water or covering them with wet burlap. Spacing depends on the size of the plants and how fast they spread. When planting, dig a hole large enough to accommodate the root ball, then tip the plant out of its pot. Score the sides of the root ball with a sharp knife before setting it in the ground. (This seemingly harsh treatment encourages the roots to spread out into the surrounding soil.) Be sure to set the plants at the same depth at which they were growing in the containers; if in doubt about the proper depth, set them slightly higher to avoid burying the crown. After planting, cut off any fronds broken during the process, water deeply, and mulch with chopped leaves. Keep the soil evenly moist until the plants are established.

CARE THROUGH THE SEASON

Once planted in a suitable site, ferns don't require much care and they are seldom troubled by insects or diseases. Mulching in late spring or early summer with chopped leaves (mow them off the lawn with a bagging lawn mower), compost, or shredded bark adds organic matter to the soil and keeps it cool, moist, adequately fertile, and weed free. Ferns don't need supplemental fertilizer beyond this topdressing of organic matter. Water during dry weather.

At season's end, don't cut back the fronds—simply leave them in place and they will rot and add more organic matter to the soil. In late fall or early winter, rake off most, but not all, of the leaves that fall onto fern beds. A thin layer of leaves provides winter protection and will add organic matter to the soil when they begin to rot in spring. Too many leaves will smother the plants. In very early spring, rake off any excess leaves, but be sure to do this before fiddleheads start to emerge; otherwise they'll be damaged.

Dig and divide ferns in spring or early summer when they overgrow their site, if the clumps die out in the center, or for propagation.

Propagation. Digging and dividing the clumps in spring is the easiest and fastest way to propagate ferns. See "Fern Terms" on page 114 for details on the different types of rootstocks you may encounter. Plants with creeping rhizomes can be cut apart with a sharp knife. Be sure that each division has at least one or two growing points. Those with erect rhizomes often produce plantlets around the main crown. These can be cut off with a sharp knife and either planted or potted up. When removing them, cut slightly into the parent plant and be sure each new plant has adequate roots. If the divisions do not, pot them up, set them in a shady, protected spot, and cover them with a Mason jar or a plastic bag to ensure high humidity until they have rooted.

Ferns reproduce sexually from spores, not seeds, and have a life cycle that includes two distinct generations: sporophyte and gametophyte. The ferns grown in gardens are the sporophyte generation. They produce dustlike spores under the fronds in brown dots or patches called sori or on separate fertile fronds. If a spore lands in suitable conditions, it grows into a small, heart-shaped prothallus, which is the gametophyte, or sexual, stage of the life cycle. Once it is fertilized, the prothallus produces a new sporophyte, or full-size garden fern.

There's no getting around it: Growing ferns from spores is challenging and takes patience, but it's not impossible. Fast-growing fungi and mosses are probably the biggest enemies to the tiny germinating spores, which require high humidity to grow. To collect spores, pick a fresh frond that has sori that are still shiny and either black or brown. Late spring or early summer is usually the best time to collect them. Place the frond in an

Fiddleheads, also called crosiers, of cinnamon fern *(Osmunda cinnamomea)*

envelope overnight. The following morning, the envelope should have dustlike spores in it. Tap the frond a few times into the envelope before adding it to the compost pile.

Fill pots to within ½ inch of the rim with a mix of one part loose potting soil, one part coarse sand, and two parts peat moss. But first sterilize the pots by washing them in a 10 percent bleach solution (one part bleach to nine parts water). Sterilize the medium by pouring boiling water over the pots, then cover them loosely with plastic wrap while they cool. To separate the spores from other parts of the sori, tap the contents of the envelope onto a piece of white paper. Then tap the spores and chaff to the edge of the paper: the chaff will fall off first, leaving the spores. Tap the spores onto the sterilized, cooled medium in the pots and set the pots in a clean plastic sweater box (sterilize it if it has been used before) with a lid or in plastic bags to provide high humidity. Place the pots in a bright spot, out of direct sun (a north or east window works well, as do plant lights). Check regularly for signs that the spores are germinating—this takes from 2 to 10 weeks or more. The soil should remain evenly moist but not wet. The spores will grow into heart-shaped prothalli and eventually you'll see tiny fronds that indicate the new sporophytes.

Once small fronds have appeared, thin the plants if necessary, replanting into sterilized pots and medium as before. When the new ferns are 1½ to 2 inches tall, transplant them into 2- to 3-inch pots, again filled with sterilized medium. Use tweezers or a plastic label to handle them. Keep the new plants in their closed box or bag throughout this process. Once they are growing in individual pots, gradually expose them to lower humidity by setting the lid of the sweater box ajar or opening the plastic bag more each day. Keep the soil evenly moist. Once the new

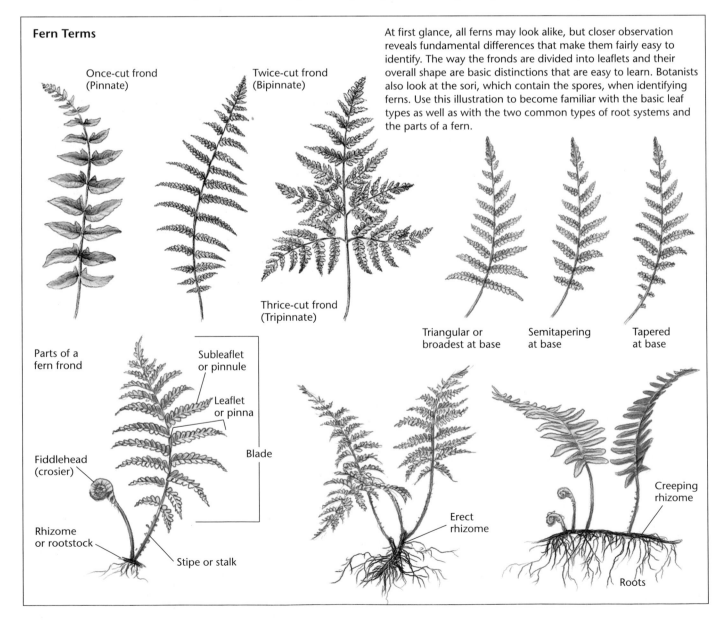

Fern Terms

At first glance, all ferns may look alike, but closer observation reveals fundamental differences that make them fairly easy to identify. The way the fronds are divided into leaflets and their overall shape are basic distinctions that are easy to learn. Botanists also look at the sori, which contain the spores, when identifying ferns. Use this illustration to become familiar with the basic leaf types as well as with the two common types of root systems and the parts of a fern.

Once-cut frond (Pinnate)

Twice-cut frond (Bipinnate)

Thrice-cut frond (Tripinnate)

Triangular or broadest at base

Semitapering at base

Tapered at base

Parts of a fern frond

Subleaflet or pinnule

Leaflet or pinna

Blade

Fiddlehead (crosier)

Rhizome or rootstock

Stipe or stalk

Erect rhizome

Creeping rhizome

Roots

ferns can tolerate average humidity, gradually expose them to the outdoors by setting them in a shaded, protected location for a few hours each day. After a week, plant the ferns in the garden.

LANDSCAPE USES

Plant drifts of ferns in beds and borders as well as in woodland gardens and natural areas, or use them as edgings, foundation plants, ground covers, or specimens. Many can be grown in bog gardens, along ponds or streams, or in other wet sites where few plants will thrive. Ferns are natural companions for shade-loving perennials such as hostas, epimediums, bleeding hearts (*Dicentra* spp.), hellebores, hardy begonia *(Begonia grandis)*, woodland phlox *(Phlox divaricata* and *P. stolonifera)*, and lungworts *(Pulmonaria* spp.). They are also ideal with spring wildflowers such as Virginia bluebells *(Mertensia virginica)* and jack-in-the-pulpits *(Arisaema* spp.) as well as with spring bulbs such as daffodils. All but the most vigorous ferns should be kept away from ground covers that spread aggressively, such as English ivy *(Hedera helix)*, fast-spreading ajugas such as *Ajuga reptans*, pachysandra *(Pachysandra terminalis)*, and vincas *(Vinca* spp.).

EASY, HARDY FERNS

The ferns listed below are but a sampling of the many species available. All are easy to grow in a site with partial shade and evenly moist, well-drained soil that is rich in organic matter. Acid pH is generally best. Many will also grow in other conditions, and exceptions are noted below.

Adiantum spp. / Maidenhair ferns

These moisture-loving ferns have branched, delicate-looking fronds divided into three to five pinnate segments with shiny black stems. The 1- to $2^1/_2$-foot plants spread via creeping rhizomes, and the plants feature pink fiddleheads and new leaves. Maidenhairs require evenly moist, well-drained soil and partial shade, but they will grow in some sun if soil moisture is plentiful. In the right site, they make good ground covers. Northern maidenhair fern *(A. pedatum)* has flat fronds branched in a horseshoelike manner and is native to eastern North America. Western maidenhair *(A. aleuticum,* formerly *A. pedatum* var. *aleuticum)*, native to western North America and eastern Asia, is a similar species. Both are hardy in Zones 2 to 8. Southern gardeners should try southern maidenhair *(A. capillus-veneris)*, a native evergreen species hardy in Zones 7 to 10. In the wild, it is found growing on limestone, and unlike the other two species, which prefer acid soil (pH 5.5 to 6.5), it grows in neutral to alkaline soil (pH 7.0 to 8.0).

Maidenhair fern
(Adiantum pedatum)

Athyrium spp. / Lady ferns

Vigorous and dependable, lady ferns are clump-forming plants with feathery, much-divided fronds. They range from $1^1/_2$ to 3 feet in height and thrive in partial shade and evenly moist soil rich in organic matter. A site protected from traffic is best, because the fronds are brittle and easily broken. European lady fern *(A. filix-femina)*, hardy in Zones 4 to 8, ranges from 2 to 3 or more feet in height and produces thrice-cut fronds that taper slightly at the base. It has erect rhizomes that gradually grow too far out of the soil. To keep the plants vigorous, dig and divide the clumps every few years, and replant the divisions with the crowns at soil level. Lady fern is a good ground cover.

Japanese painted fern *(A. niponicum,* also sold as *A. goeringianum)*, hardy in Zones 4 to 9, has leaves marked with silver or gray and maroon-purple midribs. The variety *A. niponicum* var. *pictum* (also sold as 'Pictum') is more commonly sold than the species and has leaves splashed with burgundy and silver. Plants are about 1 to $1^1/_2$ feet tall and spread vigorously in

Japanese painted fern
(Athyrium niponicum)

moist shade. Unlike many ferns, they produce new fronds all summer long. This species makes a fine ground cover.

Cyrtomium spp. / Holly ferns
These 1- to 2½-foot plants produce handsome clumps of once-cut, semievergreen fronds with leathery pinnae shaped like holly leaves. Japanese holly fern *(C. falcatum)* is hardy in Zones 6 to 10 and has glossy fronds; *C. fortunei* is hardier, to Zone 5, but has dull green ones. Shade and well-drained soil rich in organic matter are essential. The plants rot in wet soil, especially in winter. Both species have escaped gardens and become naturalized in eastern North America.

Cystopteris spp. / Fragile ferns, bladder ferns
Fragile ferns produce clumps of lacy, much-divided fronds that are brittle and easily broken. The plants spread slowly via rhizomes and range from 1 to 1½ feet in height. Bulblet bladder fern

Invasive Ferns

Bracken fern *(Pteridium aquilinum)* is such a notorious spreader that gardeners who have battled it claim that all the bracken in the world is actually a single plant. The plants spread by deep, fast-growing rhizomes and have thrice-cut, roughly triangular leaves on tall stalks, to 18 inches in height. In the wild, it is most often found in poor, infertile soil in full sun or shade.

Hay-scented fern *(Dennstaedtia punctilobula)* is another vigorous spreader that isn't suitable for small gardens. Other species, including ostrich fern *(Matteuccia struthiopteris)*, broad beech fern *(Thelypteris hexagonoptera)*, and New York fern *(T. noveboracensis)*, are also vigorous spreaders but can be contained with regular division.

(C. bulbifera) has thrice-cut fronds that are broadest at the base. It produces tiny bulblets on the fronds that drop to the soil and root or can be potted up in late summer. Hardy in Zones 3 to 8, it is a native species that grows naturally on limestone rocks, but plants will grow in slightly acid to alkaline soil. Partial shade and evenly moist, well-drained conditions are best. Plants growing in moist soil are taller than those growing in drier conditions.

Fragile fern *(C. fragilis)*, another North American native, is hardy in Zones 2 to 9 and has thrice-cut fronds that taper slightly at the base. It prefers neutral to alkaline soil (pH 7.0 to 8.0) and will disappear during dry summer weather, only to reappear in fall. It is suitable for planting in crevices in a shady rock garden.

Dennstaedtia punctilobula / Hay-scented fern
This species is a vigorous to invasive North American native fern suitable only for large, semiwild areas. It has yellow-green, featherlike, thrice-cut fronds that taper slightly at the base and have a haylike fragrance when brushed. The plants are 1½ to 3 feet tall and spread rapidly via branching, underground rhizomes. Also called boulder fern, it is attractive when allowed to grow around rocks or as a ground cover. It will grow in light shade or in full sun, and established plants will tolerate dry conditions and very acid pH. It is hardy in Zones 3 to 8.

Dryopteris spp. / Wood ferns
Wood ferns are handsome, vigorous, easy-to-grow plants that form vase-shaped clumps of fronds with leathery, toothed leaflets. They range from 1 to 4 feet in height. All are plants for evenly moist, well-drained soil that is rich in organic matter. Male fern *(D. filix-mas)*, which is a native species, and golden-scaled male fern *(D. affinis)*, from Europe and Asia, both have twice-cut fronds and grow in shade. A site that is mostly sunny with constantly moist soil is also suitable. Both form handsome clumps, can be used as ground covers, and are hardy in Zones 4 to 8. Divide the plants regularly to keep them vigorous.

Autumn fern *(D. erythrosora)*, hardy in Zones 5 to 8, has shiny, evergreen fronds and bronzy new growth. Evergreen wood fern *(D. intermedia)* is another fine evergreen fern that forms handsome clumps and is native to North America. Hardy in Zones 3 to 8, it prefers shade and evenly moist, well-drained soil with a slightly acid to neutral pH.

Matteuccia struthiopteris / Ostrich fern
One of the largest hardy ferns, this native species produces dramatic, vase-shaped clumps of plume-

like, twice-cut fronds that taper at the base and have smooth stalks. Its spores are produced on separate fertile fronds, which are brown in color and arise at the center of the clumps in summer. The fertile fronds remain erect over winter. Plants range from 2 to 6 feet or more in height. Each clump has an erect rhizome but spreads by underground stolons that give rise to new plants. They make fine, if tall, ground covers. To divide them, or to contain their spread, dig up the new plants that arise from the stolons. This vigorous, easy-to-grow fern thrives in partial shade and marshy or wet soil rich in organic matter but will also grow well in evenly moist, well-drained conditions. (The fronds are largest when the plants are grown in constantly moist soil.) Hardy in Zones 2 to 6, the plants do not tolerate the heat of southern summers well. The smooth, green fiddleheads are edible; harvest in moderation to avoid weakening the plants. Wash the brown scales off the fiddleheads before steaming them.

Onoclea sensibilis / Sensitive fern

Sensitive ferns produce spreading clumps of coarse-looking, long-stalked, once-cut fronds that are roughly triangular in shape and have wavy-edged leaflets. Like ostrich fern, it produces separate dark brown fertile fronds with beadlike leaflets (pinnules) that hold the spores. The plants

are 1 to 3 feet in height. This is a vigorous native fern that grows in a wide range of conditions—in full sun, provided the soil remains moist, or in shade, and in constantly wet, even swampy, soil as well as in dry conditions. It also thrives in the moist, well-drained soil of the average fern garden. The plants spread steadily by branched rhizomes and need dividing every 2 to 3 years. It is a good ground cover and is vigorous enough to compete with other ground covers. The common name "sensitive fern" comes from the fact that the fronds are cut down quickly by the first frost. The fertile fronds remain erect in winter. It is hardy in Zones 2 to 10.

Osmunda spp. / Flowering ferns

These large, stately ferns have featherlike, twice-cut fronds and grow from a thick mat of horse-hairlike roots. Their fiddleheads and leaf stalks are densely covered with hair, and the plants range from 2 to 5 feet or more in height. While all thrive in partial shade, they grow well in constantly moist to wet soil as well as in evenly moist, well-drained conditions. All of the species make good ground covers. Cinnamon fern *(O. cinnamomea)*, a native species hardy in Zones 2 to 10, has twice-cut fronds that taper somewhat at the base and have woolly tufts at the base of the leaflets. It produces tall fertile fronds in late spring that turn cinnamon-brown after the spores are shed. The plants tolerate a little sun but are best in partial shade and prefer slightly acid soil, but they will grow in slightly alkaline soil.

Royal fern *(O. regalis)* has somewhat coarse-looking twice-cut fronds with widely spaced oval leaflets. It produces showy brown clusters of spores at the tips of the fronds. Hardy in

Zones 2 to 10, plants thrive in wet soil, along pond edges, and even in shallow standing water.

Interrupted fern *(O. claytoniana)* resembles cinnamon fern, but the fronds have brown leaflets that bear the spores partway up their length. This "interruption" makes them easy to identify and gave rise to the common name. Hardy in Zones 2 to 8, this species prefers evenly moist acid soil that is well drained, but it will tolerate a wide range of soils, including dry conditions, as well as considerable sun or shade.

Polystichum spp. / Shield ferns

Also called sword ferns, *Polystichum* species bear leathery, often evergreen leaves. Most have erect rhizomes and are 1 to 4 feet or more in height. Christmas fern *(P. acrostichoides)* is an easy-to-grow native evergreen species whose common name derives from the fact that it was once gathered for holiday decorations. Its once-cut fronds have stocking-shaped leaflets, making it easy to identify. The clumps have a branched rhizome as a crown, and the plants can be dug and the branches carefully divided for propagation. A site in partial shade with evenly moist soil rich in organic matter is ideal, but Christmas fern can also be grown in dry soil, on slopes, among rocks, or as a ground cover in the shade garden. It is hardy in Zones 3 to 9. Gardeners in the Northwest should grow western sword fern *(P. munitum)* instead of Christmas fern. Also an evergreen, it ranges from 1$\frac{1}{2}$ to 5 feet in height. It is hardy in Zones 6 to 9 but does not do well in the East.

Soft shield fern *(P. setiferum)* is a European species with shiny, twice-cut fronds. Hardy in Zones 5 to 8, it requires soil that remains evenly moist and will tolerate acid to alkaline soils.

Thelypteris spp. / Maiden ferns

This is a large genus of ferns with twice-cut fronds and creeping rhizomes that thrive in evenly moist, well-drained soil in partial or full shade. Japanese beech fern *(T. decursive-pinnata)*, hardy in Zones 4 to 10, bears erect, bright green fronds that reach 1 to 2 feet in height. Unlike the other species in this genus, it has an erect rhizome, rather than creeping ones, but it bears new plants on short runners around the clumps. To propagate it, dig the clumps and separate the new plants from the main clump.

Two native species that are vigorous spreaders are broad beech fern *(T. hexagonoptera)* and New York fern *(T. noveboracensis)*. Both can be used as ground covers in the shade garden. Broad beech fern reaches about 2 feet in height and has twice-cut fronds on tall stalks that are widest at the base. Plants will grow in somewhat sunny spots and will also tolerate drier soil than many ferns. It is hardy in Zones 5 to 9. New York fern, hardy in Zones 4 to 8, also reaches about 2 feet in height. Its yellowish green fronds taper at the base. Both species are better used in larger gardens and should be dug and divided every few years to contain their spread.

Gaillardia

Blanket Flowers

Gaillardia
∎
(gah-LAIR-dee-ah)
∎
Summer to fall bloom
∎
Full sun
∎
Zones 3 to 8
∎

Blanket flower
(*Gaillardia* × *grandiflora*
'Kobold')

∎ Blanket flowers, or gaillardias as they are also called, are brightly colored annuals or perennials with daisylike flowers. As with other members of the aster family (Asteraceae), their flower heads consist of ray florets, commonly called petals, surrounding rounded, dense centers of disk florets, which produce the seeds. The centers are red-brown, purple-red, red, or yellow, while the petals are bright yellow, orange, red, or maroon and are often bicolored—red with yellow tips, for example. The flowers are produced above a mound of foliage on long stems. They are borne over a long season, especially if the faded flowers are removed promptly, and make outstanding cut flowers.

By far the most popular blanket flower is *Gaillardia* × *grandiflora,* which is a cross between two native North American species—perennial *G. aristata* and annual *G. pulchella. G.* × *grandiflora* is a short-lived perennial hardy in Zones 3 to 8. From early summer to fall, it bears showy, 3- to 5½-inch-wide flower heads. Flowering is heaviest from early to midsummer and somewhat less thereafter. Many cultivars are available, most with brilliant, bicolored flowers in shades of red, maroon, orange, and yellow. The plants are 2 to

Long-blooming blanket flowers *(Gaillardia × grandiflora)* add brilliant summer to fall color even when grown on tough, sunny sites with poor, dry soil.

3 feet tall, but dwarf cultivars are available— 'Baby Cole' reaches 8 inches; 'Kobold', also sold as 'Goblin', grows to 12 inches; and 'Dazzler' reaches 14 to 16 inches. Because of their short stems, dwarf cultivars are not as satisfactory for cut-flower use as full-size ones are.

G. aristata, hardy in Zones 3 to 8, has red-orange centers and yellow petals that are lobed at the tips, giving the flowers a charming ragged appearance. Plants reach 2 to 2½ feet and bloom from summer to fall. *G. pulchella* is a warm-weather annual that also blooms from summer to fall, and plants range from 1 to 1½ feet in height. The 2-inch-wide flowers are single or double and may be red, yellow, or bicolor.

SITE AND SOIL
Grow gaillardias in full sun in average to rich soil that is well drained. They will also tolerate poor, dry soil as well as sandy conditions and are drought- and salt-tolerant enough to grow in seaside gardens. Heavy, wet clay soil spells certain death, however, especially in winter, because it leads to root and crown rot. Plants grown in soil that is too rich and moist tend to be floppy and short lived.

PLANTING
Add perennial gaillardias to your garden by purchasing plants or starting seeds. They can be planted in spring or fall. Space plants 1 to 1½ feet apart depending on their height at maturity.

Sow seeds for perennial and annual gaillardias either outdoors or in. Outdoors, after danger of frost has passed, broadcast seeds for annual *G. pulchella* in a prepared seedbed where the plants are to grow. Outdoors, perennial species are best sown into pots or a nursery bed. Indoors, sow any of the gaillardias 4 to 6 weeks before the last spring frost date and transplant hardened-

off seedlings after danger of frost has passed. Either way, leave the seeds on the soil surface (light aids germination) and thin seedlings sown outdoors to stand about 6 inches apart. When sown outdoors, perennial gaillardias will be large enough to transplant to the garden by early fall and will bloom the following summer. When sown indoors, they may bloom sporadically the first summer but will bloom heavily the second.

CARE THROUGH THE SEASON
Tough, heat-tolerant gaillardias are seldom troubled by insects or diseases and require very little care once they are established. They will tolerate considerable drought but benefit from watering during extremely dry weather. Plants will continue blooming without deadheading, but removing the faded flowers promptly will keep the plants neat looking and encourages them to produce new buds. All but the tallest gaillardias will stand without staking. Divide perennial gaillardias every 2 to 3 years; otherwise they die out in the center of the clumps and lose their vigor. At season's end, after a hard frost, cut the plants to the ground.

Propagation. Gaillardias are easy from seed and can also be propagated by three vegetative methods: division, cuttings, and root cuttings. When deciding how to propagate, keep in mind that while seed-grown strains produce handsome plants, they are somewhat variable. Plan on using one of the vegetative propagation methods to reproduce plants with outstanding flowers or to grow plants with uniform flowers and form. *G. × grandiflora* 'Baby Cole' is always propagated by vegetative means.

Dig gaillardias for division in early spring or early fall. Discard the older portions of the clump and replant the rest.

To propagate by stem cuttings, take cuttings of new shoots in early summer. They root quickly in a 50-50 mix of vermiculite and perlite. To propagate by root cuttings, dig thick roots in winter and pot them in moist sharp sand. Keep them at 40°F until spring, and keep the new plants potted in a protected location over the summer. Plant out in early fall or the following spring. (See "Propagating from Root Cuttings" in the Techniques Glossary for more on this method.)

LANDSCAPE USES
Use gaillardias to add summer color to beds and borders. Combine them with summer-blooming perennials such as coreopsis, daylilies *(Hemerocallis* spp.), yarrows *(Achillea* spp.), red-hot poker *(Kniphofia* spp.), and salvias. Dwarf types make stunning edging plants when planted in masses. All can be combined with annuals and are attractive when added to sunny wildflower gardens.

Geranium

Hardy Geraniums

■ Also commonly called cranesbills, hardy geraniums are versatile, long-lived perennials that feature bountiful flowers and attractive foliage. The mound-shaped plants bear clusters of five-petaled, 1- to 2-inch-wide flowers that are cup- or saucer-shaped. Colors range from shades of pink and magenta to white, purple, and violet-blue, and the main flush of bloom occurs from late spring into early summer. Some geraniums will rebloom into fall, especially if the plants are cut back. The flowers are borne atop dense, spreading mounds of deeply cut, often lacy-looking leaves. Some species feature colorful fall foliage as well. There are also geraniums that are semievergreen to evergreen in mild-winter areas.

Don't confuse these dependable perennials with zonal geraniums or ivy geraniums (both *Pelargonium* spp.), which are popular tender perennials grown as annuals (see *Pelargonium* spp. on page 30 in the **Annuals & Biennials** entry). In fact, hardy geraniums are sometimes dubbed "true" geraniums to distinguish them from their better-known cousins—*Geranium* and *Pelargonium* are both in the geranium family, Geraniaceae. To make matters even more confusing, there are tender members of the genus *Geranium*; this entry is restricted to the hardy species that are commonly used in perennial gardens, however.

SELECTING HARDY GERANIUMS

Deciding which hardy geraniums to grow can be difficult, not because they are hard to grow or finicky about where they are planted but because there are so many species and cultivars to choose from, and they are so versatile. Some of the best species to consider are listed below. Although nearly all of them can be used in a variety of ways in the garden and have similar cultural requirements, the list is divided according to suggested uses in an attempt to make your selection easier.

One geranium to avoid adding to your garden is herb Robert *(G. robertianum)*. An annual or biennial that reseeds with enthusiasm and quickly becomes a hard-to-control weed, it bears $1/2$-inch pink flowers from early summer to late fall. Its leaves are fernlike and aromatic.

Geranium
■
(jer-AY-nee-um)
■
Spring to summer bloom
■
Full sun or partial shade
■
Zones 2 to 8
■

Geranium × 'Johnson's Blue'

Lilac cranesbill
(Geranium himalayense)

Geraniums for Beds and Borders

The following hardy geraniums are suitable for planting near the front of beds and borders. Some of the more vigorous ones can also be used as ground covers. Unless otherwise noted, all thrive in full sun and rich, moist, well-drained soil.

G. clarkei. Clark's geranium. Abundant, $3/4$-inch-wide, violet-purple or white flowers with lilac veins from late spring into early summer; mounding, 15- to 20-inch-tall plants. Spreads quickly by rhizomes and is suitable for large gardens or semiwild plantings. Easy to propagate by division or from seeds. Fast-spreading 'Kashmir Purple' has purple-blue flowers with red veins and comes true from seed. 'Kashmir White', which bears white flowers with lilac-pink veins, can also be grown from seeds, but some seedlings in each batch will be purple flowered. Zones 4 to 8.

G. dalmaticum. Dalmatian cranesbill. Soft pink, 1-inch flowers in late spring and early summer; mounding to trailing, 4- to 6-inch-tall plants. Can be grown in full sun or partial shade in the North but suffers from summer heat in the South, where it should be planted in a site with rich, moist soil and shade during the hottest part of the day. Plants grown in shade flower less and are somewhat taller. An enthusiastic creeper, but not invasive, it spreads by rhizomes. The plants have red-orange fall color and the foliage lasts well into winter; in mild-climate areas it is evergreen. Propagate by division or from seeds. Zones 4 to 8.

G. himalayense. Lilac cranesbill. Violet-blue, 2-inch flowers for several weeks in early summer; clump-forming 12- to 15-inch plants. The plants

ABOVE *Geranium* ×
'Johnson's Blue'

ABOVE RIGHT
Wild cranesbill
(Geranium maculatum)

require evenly moist but well-drained soil for best performance and do not tolerate dry conditions. The stems tend to sprawl, so cut plants to the ground after flowering to encourage new foliage and a tidier-looking plant. Good orange-red fall color. Propagate by division or from seeds. Zones 4 to 8.

G. × 'Johnson's Blue'. Lavender-blue, $1\frac{1}{2}$- to 2-inch flowers in early summer; mounding, 15- to 18-inch plants. A cross between G. *himalayense* and G. *pratense* that spreads via rhizomes. Good in full sun or light shade. The plants get ragged-looking after they flower; cut them to the ground after the main flush of bloom and fresh foliage will appear. Propagate by division. Zones 4 to 8.

G. *maculatum*. Wild cranesbill. Pink $1\frac{1}{4}$-inch flowers from late spring to midsummer; 1- to 2-foot plants. A native wildflower found in woods and shady roadsides in eastern North America. Requires evenly moist, well-drained soil and is best in partial shade. Propagate by division or from seeds. Zones 4 to 8.

G. *phaeum*. Dusky cranesbill. Dark black-purple, maroon, violet, or white 1-inch flowers with reflexed petals; $1\frac{1}{2}$- to $2\frac{1}{2}$-foot plants. A clump-forming species with thick rhizomes. Plants are most attractive in partial shade and evenly moist soil but will tolerate shade and dry soil. Self-sows. Propagate by division or from seeds. Zones 5 to 7.

G. *pratense*. Meadow cranesbill. Blue-violet, $1\frac{1}{2}$-inch flowers in late spring and early summer; 2- to 3-foot plants. Needs full sun and evenly moist soil. Plants usually will flop without staking and self-seed with enthusiasm. Cut them to the ground after flowering to curtail self-seeding and to encourage a new flush of foliage. Or grow them in a semiwild area and let them spread. Propagate by division or from seeds. Zones 2 or 3 to 8.

G. *psilostemon*. Armenian cranesbill. Two-inch-wide magenta flowers with black eyes from early to late summer; mounding, 2- to 4-foot plants. Striking, shrub-sized plants with evergreen foliage. They require staking and are best in rich, evenly moist soil and a site with shade during the hottest part of the day. To maximize the display of red fall foliage, remove spent flowers but do not shear back plants after flowering. Propagate by division or from seeds. Zones 5 to 8.

G. *sanguineum*. Bloody cranesbill. Bright pink, 1- to $1\frac{1}{2}$-inch flowers from spring into summer; spreading, 8- to 12-inch mounds of deeply cut foliage. An adaptable species that grows in sun or shade and also tolerates heat and drought. Plants in shade are slightly taller and flower less than those in sun. Red fall foliage. 'Shepherd's Warning', 4 to 6 inches tall, and G. *sanguineum* var. *striatum*, at 6 to 8 inches, are both small enough for rock gardens or can be used as low edging plants. Self-sows. Propagate cultivars by division or root cuttings; the species can be grown from seeds. Zones 3 to 8.

G. sylvaticum. Wood cranesbill. Violet-blue, 1-inch flowers in early to midspring; bushy, 2½- to 3-foot plants. Best in partial shade and evenly moist soil. Self-sows. Easy from seeds, or propagate by division. Zones 3 to 8.

Geraniums for Ground Covers

The following species and their cultivars are vigorous enough to produce a dense, weed-suppressing mat and generally spread too quickly to be planted in conventional beds and borders. In addition to using them as ground covers, try planting them under shrubs or along a shrub border.

G. endressii. Endres cranesbill. Pale pink, 1-inch flowers in spring; mounding to sprawling, 15- to 18-inch plants. This species is best in areas with cool summers, such as in the Pacific Northwest, where it blooms all season long and can be planted in full sun. In areas with hot summers, give it a spot in afternoon shade; flowering will stop in early summer when hot weather arrives. Plants require well-drained conditions and will tolerate drought. Self-sows. Propagate from seeds or by division or root cuttings. Zones 4 to 8.

G. macrorrhizum. Bigroot geranium. Pink to purplish pink, 1-inch-wide flowers in spring; mounding, 15- to 18-inch plants with aromatic leaves. A vigorous species with fleshy, deep roots that tolerates heat and drought. It grows in full sun or partial shade; in the South, afternoon shade is best. The plants spread by rhizomes, but if given plenty of room they do not need to be divided regularly. The plants send out rhizomes on the soil surface, which can be cut off and re-planted. They can also be propagated by division

Bloody cranesbill *(Geranium sanguineum)*

or root cuttings. Evergreen in mild climates. Zones 3 to 8.

G. × oxonianum. Pink, 1½-inch-wide flowers from spring to fall; 1½- to 3-foot plants. This clump-forming hybrid species (it is a cross between *G. endressii* and *G. versicolor*) is vigorous and long blooming. Full to partial shade is best. Cut plants to the ground when they become unkempt looking in midsummer. This also helps contain self-seeding. 'Claridge Druce' is a vigorous to invasive selection; 'Wargrave Pink' is vigorous but not invasive. Zones 4 to 8.

Geraniums for Rock Gardens

Low-growing hardy geraniums add summer color to rock gardens and can also be planted above walls and along the edges of raised beds. Grayleaf cranesbill *(G. cinereum),* hardy in Zones 5 to 8, bears 1-inch-wide purplish pink flowers on 6- to 12-inch plants. It thrives in the gritty, very well drained soil of the average rock garden and is best

A pale pink bloody cranesbill *(Geranium sanguineum* var. *striatum)*

planted in a spot with afternoon shade. Plants will not tolerate heavy clay or poorly drained sites. 'Ballerina' is an outstanding 4- to 6-inch-tall cultivar that blooms throughout the summer. Propagate the cultivars by division; the species can be grown from seeds.

Two other species are ideal for rock gardens, both of which are listed under "Geraniums for Beds and Borders" above: Dalmatian cranesbill *(G. dalmaticum)* and bloody cranesbill *(G. sanguineum)*, especially low-growing *G. sanguineum* var. *striatum* and 'Shepherd's Warning'.

SITE AND SOIL

Hardy geraniums grow in full sun or partial shade and bloom best in evenly moist soil that is well drained and rich in organic matter. Especially in the South, shade during the hottest part of the day is essential for good performance. See "Selecting Hardy Geraniums" on page 121 for the site and soil preferences of individual species.

PLANTING

Plant hardy geraniums in spring or fall, although in northern zones spring planting is generally best. To ensure good drainage, dig the soil to at least 12 inches and work in plenty of organic matter such as compost or leaf mold.

CARE THROUGH THE SEASON

Once planted, hardy geraniums require only minimal care to look their best. They are seldom troubled by pests or diseases. Feed plants in spring with a topdressing of compost, well-rotted manure, or a balanced organic fertilizer. The taller species are inclined to flop, and there are a couple of ways to deal with this tendency. The

plants can be staked, and in this case pea brush is most effective because of the mounding shape of the plants. (See "Staking" in the Techniques Glossary for details on using pea brush.) Or simply let the plants flop, enjoy their flowers, and then cut them back after most of the flowers have faded. Cut plants to within 1 inch of the ground and a fresh new mound of leaves will arise in a few weeks. Some plants will rebloom sporadically as well. As an end-of-season cleanup, cut plants to the ground after a hard fall frost.

Division. Many hardy geraniums need to be divided regularly to look their best, although if plants are still blooming well and have not outgrown their site, they can be left undisturbed. *G. endressii, G. himalayense, G. sanguineum,* and *G. sylvaticum* tend to need frequent division.

Dig the clumps in spring or fall and gently separate them into new plants. Discard old woody portions at the center of the clumps. Most geraniums have fibrous roots that are easy to separate, but types with thicker rhizomes may need to be cut apart with a sharp knife. Another option for dividing the clumps is to simply cut a portion off the outside edge with a sharp spade without digging the entire plant.

Propagation. Most cultivars are best propagated vegetatively—by division, as described above, or by root cuttings—because they do not come true from seed. Cuttings taken in spring from the base of the plant also root; stick them in a 50-50 mix of vermiculite and perlite. Take root cuttings in fall (see "Propagating from Root Cuttings" in the Techniques Glossary for details).

Sow seeds outdoors in pots in late summer or fall and set them in a protected location. Or sow indoors and place sown pots in the refrigerator for 2 to 3 weeks before germinating at 70° to 75°F. Either way, barely cover the seeds with soil, as light aids germination, and provide high humidity. If you want to collect seeds from your own plants, keep in mind that the capsules eject them with some force when they are ripe. Put small paper bags or tie lengths of nylon stocking over the ripening seed heads to catch the seeds.

LANDSCAPE USES

Use hardy geraniums in beds and borders with other perennials that bloom from late spring into summer, such as bellflowers *(Campanula* spp.), coralbells *(Heuchera* spp.), Siberian iris *(Iris sibirica),* Shasta daisy *(Chrysanthemum* × *superbum),* salvias *(Salvia* spp.), and columbines *(Aquilegia* spp.). The more vigorous species are also attractive when combined with shrubs—consider underplanting shrub roses with hardy geraniums, or combine them with azaleas and rhododendrons *(Rhododendron* spp.) or other shrubs.

Ground Covers

Ground covers are the undisputed workhorses of the garden. Good ones need to look attractive even on tough sites. They should smother weeds with a blanket of foliage and grow vigorously without being too invasive. And they should require a minimum of care—after all, low maintenance is one of the great advantages of ground-cover plantings. Despite this tall order, a wide variety of plants make great ground covers, from flowering perennials to low-growing shrubs. Ferns, ornamental grasses, some herbs, and even prostrate forms of some evergreen trees also can be put into service covering the ground under the right circumstances. While successful ground-cover plantings take time, effort, and a bit of patience to establish, the payoff is well worth it. In addition to providing practical solutions to landscaping problems and problem sites, when compared with lawn grass, ground covers can greatly reduce lawn-care chores such as mowing and trimming. Most will help save water as well. In fact, many ground covers are quite drought tolerant.

Easy-to-grow ground covers create an attractive planting. Here pink-flowered dwarf Chinese astilbe *(Astilbe chinensis* var. *pumila)* shares space with common periwinkle *(Vinca minor)* and junipers.

A mixture of ground covers can be the perfect solution for a site where you want low maintenance and plenty of interest at the same time. Here *Hosta* 'Blue Cadet' and New York ferns *(Thelypteris noveboracensis)* provide outstanding textural contrast.

SELECTING GROUND COVERS

The most successful ground-cover plantings match the sun and soil requirements of the plants to the conditions of the site. If you are starting a new planting, begin with a site assessment. Is the site in full sun, dappled shade, or deep shade? Is the soil dry or wet, acid or alkaline? The best ground-cover choices will thrive in the conditions that already exist on that site. Sure, you will improve the soil before planting and you may limb up trees to let in more light, but if you choose a plant that would thrive there anyway, you're halfway to a successful planting. That's because plants that are matched to the site will need less care to get started, will fill in faster, and ultimately will require less work to maintain.

All too often ground covers are simply seen as a way to fill space with a uniform carpet of green, which puts them only a step above lawn grass: while they require less maintenance than a lawn, when used this way ground covers don't contribute much in the way of color, texture, or year-round interest to the garden. Keep in mind that ground-cover plantings can be ornamental as well as functional. In the lists later in this entry, you'll find suggestions for a wide range of potential ground covers — deciduous and evergreen, flowering and nonflowering. Once you've eliminated plants that won't like your site, choose ones with interesting colors, textures, and habits. Don't limit yourself to plants of a certain height, either. While many homeowners only want ground covers that stay under 6 inches or so, good gardeners know that an effective planting can include plants of various heights, from mat-forming 6-inchers to plants that rise to 3 feet or more.

Frequently the most interesting and ornamental solution is to plant an area with drifts of different plants in harmonious colors and contrasting forms and textures. Mixing up ground covers instead of planting a monoculture makes it possible to plan for a progression of bloom as well as color and interest throughout the year, while still keeping maintenance low. Design mixed plantings in large drifts or blocks, though, because otherwise they will look busy, more like a flower bed. One of the benefits of ground covers from a design standpoint is that large areas planted in a single plant provide visual relief and add a restful quality to the landscape. (Lawn areas have this effect, too.) Keep in mind that ground covers combined in a single planting should have similar cultural preferences and should grow at about the same rate.

PLANTING

Ground covers can be planted in spring or fall, and getting plants off to a good start is essential to success. Thorough soil preparation and keeping the plants weeded, mulched, and watered until they fill in are the keys to a thriving, problem-free planting. If you are installing ground covers in a large area, consider planting in stages to keep maintenance manageable while the plants are becoming established. Weeds can quickly overtake a newly planted area, leaving you with a losing battle to fight. It's far easier and much less aggravating to start off small and convert new manageable-size areas to ground covers gradually as time allows.

For best results, prepare the soil thoroughly before planting by digging or tilling it as deeply as possible — to 12 inches or more is best — and adding plenty of organic matter such as compost or leaf mold. Have the soil tested to determine if any fertilizer amendments are necessary, and add as you dig.

Dig out weed roots and discard them; otherwise the weeds will outgrow the ground covers and overtake the planting. (Chopping up weed rhizomes with a tiller turns one plant into hundreds.) To eliminate weeds or lawn grass on a site without digging it up, and without resorting to herbicides, cut the vegetation back as close to the ground as possible and spread a thick layer of newspaper over the entire area. Use 10 sheets or more, overlapped, and top the newspaper mulch heavily with shredded bark. Cardboard boxes, cut open and spread out, also work under bark mulch. In 2 to 3 months the plants underneath will be killed. To plant, loosen the soil with a digging fork and plant through the mulch and what's left of the newspaper. Woody plants (such as poison ivy) take longer to kill. Cut plants to the ground and cover them with two layers of cardboard plus a thick layer of bark mulch and leave the site covered for a year. Cut back any shoots that manage to emerge during this time. See "Planting Slopes" at right for suggestions on dealing with sites where erosion could become a problem.

Spacing, of course, varies from plant to plant and also depends on the size of the plants you are starting with. You'll find spacing guidelines in the individual listings in this entry, but ask for recommendations when you buy, since plants in 3-inch pots need to be spaced much more closely than ones in quart containers. If budget constraints limit the number of plants you can afford, consider planting a small area at the recommended spacing and propagating the plants by cuttings or division every year or every other year until the desired site is filled. Or space the plants more widely from the outset. Wider spacing means the plants will take longer to fill in, and you'll have to be more careful with weed control for a longer period of time than you would at the closer spacing.

Plant pot-grown ground covers as you would any other plants. If you are starting with bare-root plants, soak them in water for several hours before planting, and carry them to the garden in a bucket of water. Pull them out of the water as you plant, spread their roots over a cone of soil in the hole, and refill the hole with soil. Water each plant deeply as you go, and add more soil as it settles in around the roots. Water the entire planting again when you've finished.

Until the plants fill the space allotted to them, a ground-cover planting will require regular attention. A layer of mulch helps control weeds and protects the soil. Pull weeds weekly at first, and then monthly until the plants fill in. Short, frequent weeding sessions will keep the task manageable. To get plants off to a vigorous start, water regularly so the soil stays evenly moist. Laying soaker hoses on a new planting makes watering easy.

CARE THROUGH THE SEASON
Once established, ground covers need minimal attention. Regular watering for the first two seasons is generally advisable. After that, water during dry weather to keep plants looking their best. Pull weeds as they appear—there will be fewer and fewer each season. It's a good idea to renew the layer of mulch on the soil until the plants are dense enough to outcompete weeds. Many ground covers appreciate a spring topdressing with compost or well-rotted manure.

You can speed up the filling-in process or guide the direction of the growth by moving stems or runners into empty spaces and pegging them down with U-shaped pieces of wire or weighing them down with a shovelful of soil.

Ground-cover beds benefit from being tidied up annually. If leaves smother the plants in fall, rake them off. Leaves that work their way down

Planting Slopes

Since one hard rain can wash away much of the soil on a sloping site, take steps to control erosion at planting time. On a gentle slope, till or dig the soil and amend it with organic matter such as compost. (Another option is to loosen and amend the soil for each plant, and then mulch the entire slope, but plants will not spread as quickly.) Then set the plants at a slightly closer spacing than generally recommended so they'll fill in quickly. Arrange them in rows that go at an angle across the slope, never straight up and down. If possible, as you plant level off small planting areas for each plant that will catch water and pool it around the plant's roots. Mulch after planting.

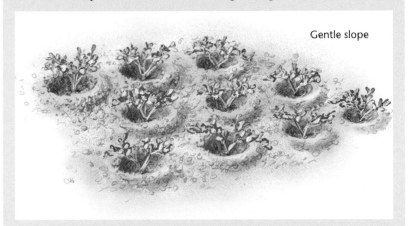

Gentle slope

On steeper slopes, stake burlap over the soil and cut holes in it to insert plants. Another option is to forgo tilling and create planting pockets that will help hold the soil. To do this, level off planting areas, and then stake lengths of old boards below them to create barriers. (Try buying warped or damaged pine boards at a local lumberyard for this purpose; wood shingles also work.) Mulch the site after planting. The boards can be left in place to rot. Terracing a slope with rocks, landscaping stone, or timbers is another good alternative.

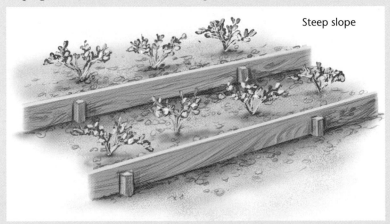

Steep slope

among the plants can be left in place to rot and add organic matter to the soil. In early spring cut back plants that have become ragged looking—on perennials, a lawn mower often works for this, as does a string trimmer. Hedge shears are fine for small plantings. For shrubs, use pruning shears to shape and direct growth. If you have planted drifts of several ground covers, either weed between them to maintain clean edges or let them mingle for a casual, tapestry-like effect.

Once plantings mature, you'll need to dig and divide clumps that outgrow their space or simply pull them up. If clumps die out in the center, dig the plants and discard any old, woody growth at the center of the clumps. Amend the soil with more organic matter such as compost before replanting. If patches of ground covers die out, dig up the afflicted plants and try to determine why they died. Root competition from trees and shrubs, unsuitable soil conditions, and attack by pests or diseases are all possible causes. Reassess your choice of ground cover, amend the soil, and replant.

LANDSCAPE USES

Ground covers can be used nearly anywhere in the landscape to add color and texture and to reduce maintenance. Plant them as edgings along walkways, in front of foundation plantings, or in large beds to replace lawn areas. Eliminate tedious trimming around trees and shrubs—and protect trunks and roots at the same time—by planting ground covers. Underplant one tree or design beds that encompass several trees and shrubs to create an island of greenery. Of course, ground covers are valuable on tough sites where grass doesn't grow or is hard to mow: plant them on slopes, in the shade, or in wet-soil areas.

Unlike lawn grass, ground covers don't work well in areas that receive foot traffic, because most of them can't cope with compacted soil. Install paving stones or walkways through ground-cover beds—or stick with lawn.

A GUIDE TO GROUND COVERS

Many good ground covers are vigorous to invasive plants that need to be used carefully. When selecting ground covers, consider how fast a plant spreads. Plants that are described as vigorous to invasive in the guide that follows can easily overtake a small garden and are best used in large areas where they can spread at will and/or in large gardens. Even the more controlled spreaders will need watching in small gardens or in small areas. Divide plants regularly or pull them up to keep them in bounds.

Many of the plants covered in individual entries elsewhere in this book can be used as ground covers. You'll find references to them in the plant list below. You'll also find more potential ground covers in the following entries: **Perennials,** page 222; **Shrubs,** page 273; **Vines,** page 298; and **Wildflowers,** page 303.

Ground Covers for Shade

Shade-loving ground covers are especially valuable, because they thrive in areas where lawn grass doesn't grow well. They can also be used under trees, along shrub borders, or on shady slopes. To create a large, low-maintenance shade planting, consider combining some of the following in drifts. Keep in mind that some plants listed under "Ground Covers for Sun" on page 133 tolerate shade as well.

Aegopodium podagraria 'Variegata' / Bishop's weed

A vigorous to invasive perennial with white flowers in summer and green-and-white leaves; 1- to 2-foot plants. Grows in shade or sun in any soil and spreads by rhizomes. Useful in dry shade (which helps contain its spread), where few other plants will grow. Space plants 1 foot apart. Do not plant the all-green species, which is even more invasive, and dig out any plants that revert from variegated to all green. Best kept away from other plants and out of good soil but can be used under trees in an area surrounded by lawn. If foliage becomes unsightly, cut or mow plants to the ground in midsummer and they will regrow. Divide in spring or fall to propagate. Zones 4 to 9.

Ajuga reptans / Ajuga

Grow ajuga in sun or shade in well-drained, average to rich soil. See *Ajuga* on page 6 for more information.

Vigorous ground covers such as spotted lamium (*Lamium maculatum* 'White Nancy') are ideal for covering large areas in a hurry.

Anemone spp. / Anemones

Two species of anemones—*A. canadensis* and *A. sylvestris*—can be used as ground covers in partial shade and rich, moist soil. See *Anemone* on page 16 for more information.

Astilbe spp. / Astilbes

A. chinensis var. *pumila* is an attractive ground cover that spreads reliably in partially shaded sites with rich, moist soil. See *Astilbe* on page 41 for more information.

Asarum spp. / Wild gingers

Creeping perennials with heart-shaped leaves and insignificant brown flowers; 3- to 6-inch plants. Handsome evergreen or deciduous plants that spread slowly by rhizomes. Canada wild ginger (*A. canadense*), hardy in Zones 2 to 8, is a deciduous native wildflower. European wild ginger (*A. europaeum*), hardy in Zones 4 to 8, has glossy evergreen leaves and spreads more slowly than *A. canadense*. Partial or full shade and rich, evenly moist soil. Space 6 to 8 inches apart. Plants self-sow and can be divided in early spring.

Bergenia spp. / Bergenias

Grow bergenias in partial or dappled shade in rich, evenly moist soil. They tolerate full sun in the North with abundant moisture. See *Bergenia* on page 48 for more information.

Carex spp. / Sedges

Several handsome grassy-leaved sedges can be used as ground covers, including *C. conica*, *C. elata*, *C. nigra*, and *C. siderosticha* 'Variegata'. See under **Ornamental Grasses** on page 206 for more information on sedges.

Convallaria majalis / Lily-of-the-valley

A site in partial shade with rich, evenly moist soil is best for lily-of-the-valley. Plants tolerate full shade and will also grow in full sun provided they receive adequate moisture. Established plants also grow in dry shade. See *Convallaria majalis* on page 84 for more information.

Dicentra spp. / Bleeding hearts

D. eximia and *D. formosa* both make attractive ground covers for sites in light to full shade with rich, evenly moist soil. See *Dicentra* on page 99 for more information.

Duchesnea indica / Mock strawberry

Low-growing perennial with yellow early- to late-summer flowers, evergreen leaves, and red fruit; 2-inch plants. Spreads by runners that produce small plantlets. Partial or full shade in rich, evenly moist, well-drained soil. Can be used on steep

Heart-leaved bergenia
(*Bergenia cordifolia*)

slopes, and established plants tolerate drought and some foot traffic. The fruit is attractive to birds. Pot up the new plantlets to propagate. Zones 4 to 9.

Epimedium spp. / Epimediums

Epimediums make excellent ground covers for partial or full shade in rich, evenly moist soil. They tolerate full sun in constantly moist soil and will also grow in dry shade and can compete with the roots of established trees. See *Epimedium* on page 107 for more information.

Euphorbia spp. / Euphorbias

Consider *E. amygdaloides* var. *robbiae* for a site in partial or full shade with evenly moist, rich soil. Plants also tolerate dry shade but can be difficult to get established. See *Euphorbia* on page 110 for more information.

Ferns

Many species make valuable ground covers in a wide range of soils and sites, in partial or full shade and rich, evenly moist to constantly wet soils. The following are especially popular: maidenhair ferns (*Adiantum* spp.), lady ferns (*Athyrium filix-femina* and *A. niponicum*), hay-scented fern (*Dennstaedtia punctilobula*), male ferns (*Dryopteris filix-mas* and *D. affinis*), ostrich fern (*Matteuccia struthiopteris*), sensitive fern (*Onoclea sensibilis*), flowering ferns (*Osmunda* spp.), Christmas fern (*Polystichum acrostichoides*), and maiden ferns (*Thelypteris hexagonoptera* and *T. noveboracensis*). See **Ferns** on page 112 for more information.

ABOVE Sweet woodruff
(*Galium odoratum*)

ABOVE RIGHT Hostas,
ferns, and other shade
lovers cover the ground
in a semishaded garden.

RIGHT Purple-leaved
heuchera (*Heuchera
micrantha* var.
diversifolia 'Palace
Purple')

Galium odoratum / Sweet woodruff

Creeping perennial with clusters of tiny, starry, white flowers from late spring to summer and whorls of narrow leaves; 6- to 8-inch plants. Grows in partial to deep shade in rich, well-drained soil but tolerates sandy soil or heavy clay. Spreads at a moderate speed. Space plants 8 to 12 inches apart. Divide in spring or fall to propagate or to keep plants in bounds. Zones 4 to 8.

Gaultheria procumbens / Wintergreen

Slowly creeping shrublet with white or pink summer flowers, aromatic evergreen leaves, and red fall berries; 4- to 6-inch plants. Spreads slowly but steadily via rhizomes. Space plants 1 foot apart. A native wildflower for partial shade and acid, evenly moist soil rich in organic matter. Zones 3 to 8.

Helleborus spp. / Hellebores

Long-lived evergreen perennials, hellebores thrive in light to full shade in rich, evenly moist, well-drained soil. See *Helleborus* on page 143 for more information.

Heuchera spp. / Coralbells

Grow coralbells in shade or sun in rich, evenly moist soil that is well drained. See *Heuchera* on page 157 for more information.

Hosta spp. / Hostas

Hostas produce a weed-smothering blanket of foliage in light to full shade but will tolerate considerable sun with constant soil moisture. Evenly moist, well-drained soil rich in organic matter is best. They can also be grown on sites with constantly damp to wet soil as long as the crowns are planted somewhat above the water line. See *Hosta* on page 160 for more information.

Hydrangea petiolaris / Climbing hydrangea

A vine that makes an excellent ground cover if left to ramble. Plant it in rich, moist, well-drained

soil in full sun or partial shade; afternoon shade is best in the South. See the box on page 168 in the *Hydrangea* entry for more information.

Iris cristata / Crested iris
This native woodland species thrives in rich, well-drained soil in partial or full shade. See *Iris* on page 172 for more information.

Lamium spp. / Lamiums, dead nettles
Yellow archangel *(L. galeobdolon,* formerly *Lamiastrum galeobdolon)* is a fast-spreading perennial grown more for its variegated foliage than for the yellow spring flowers it bears on 8- to 14-inch plants. Spreads vigorously by rhizomes that root wherever they touch the soil. Space plants 1 to 1½ feet apart. Partial or full shade in average to rich, well-drained soil. Tolerates sandy, but not dry, soil. Keep the species and most cultivars away from other plants, which they will overtake. 'Hermann's Pride' is a variegated cultivar that is still vigorous but spreads much less aggressively. Zones 4 to 9.

Spotted lamium *(L. maculatum),* with red-purple or white flowers and silver-marked leaves on 6- to 12-inch plants, is a more moderate spreader. It also spreads by rhizomes. Space plants 8 to 10 inches apart. Partial shade in rich, moist, well-drained soil. In the South, afternoon shade is beneficial, as the plants do not tolerate heat or drought. Cultivars such as 'Beacon Silver' and 'White Nancy' are the most attractive. Plants can be sheared to keep them compact. Zones 3 to 8.

Propagate either species by division in spring or fall or by rooting cuttings taken either in spring or in summer.

Liriope spp. / Lilyturfs
Mounding perennials with spikes of lilac-purple or white flowers and grassy, sometimes variegated leaves; 1- to 1½-foot plants. *L. muscari,* hardy in Zones 6 to 10, forms clumps and has evergreen leaves. *L. spicata,* hardy in Zones 5 to 10, spreads slowly by rhizomes and is semievergreen.

TOP Yellow archangel (*Lamium galeobdolon* 'Hermann's Pride')

ABOVE Lilyturf (*Liriope muscari* 'Big Blue')

Variegated pachysandra
(*Pachysandra terminalis* 'Variegata')

Grow both species in partial or full shade in rich, well-drained soil. Both also grow in full sun and tolerate heat, humidity, drought, and competition from tree roots. Space plants 12 to 14 inches apart.

Pachysandra spp. / Spurges, pachysandras

Allegheny spurge *(P. procumbens)* is a native perennial wildflower with small white flowers in spring and handsome semievergreen leaves on 1-foot-tall plants. Spreads slowly into broad clumps. The old leaves, which are often marked with maroon-brown, become prostrate in fall and fresh green foliage appears at the center of the clumps in spring. Zones 5 to 9.

Japanese spurge *(P. terminalis)* has tiny, creamy white flowers in early summer and evergreen leaves on 6- to 12-inch plants. Spreads steadily by rhizomes to form broad clumps. The cultivar 'Variegata' is slower growing but features handsome cream-edged leaves. Zones 4 to 9.

Plant both species in partial or full shade in a site with average to rich, evenly moist soil. Space plants 8 to 10 inches apart. Propagate by dividing the plants in spring or fall or from cuttings taken in early summer.

Phlox spp. / Phlox

Two species of phlox, *P. divaricata* and *P. stolonifera*, can be used as ground covers in partial or full shade. Both require rich, evenly moist soil that is well drained. See *Phlox* on page 233 for more information.

Pulmonaria spp. / Lungworts

Grow lungworts in partial or full shade and rich, evenly moist soil that is well drained. See *Pulmonaria* on page 244 for more information.

Lungwort
(*Pulmonaria* sp.)

Rhododendron spp. / Rhododendrons and azaleas

Low-growing rhododendrons and azaleas make spectacular ground covers for sites in partial shade with acid soil that is evenly moist but well drained and rich in organic matter. See *Rhododendron* on page 246 for more information.

Sarcococca humilis / Dwarf sweet box

Dwarf shrub with fragrant off-white flowers in spring, dark green evergreen leaves, and black berries; 18- to 24-inch plants. Spreads very slowly by suckers. Space plants 1 foot apart. Partial or full shade in acid, evenly moist soil rich in organic matter. Can be sheared to shape in spring. Propagate by division in spring or early fall. (Also listed as *S. hookeriana* var. *humilis*.) Zones 5 to 8.

Sasa veitchii / Kuma bamboo grass

Fast-spreading bamboo with evergreen leaves edged in white in winter; 3- to 6-foot plants. A vigorous to invasive plant spreading by underground rhizomes. Space plants 3 feet apart. Keep it away from other ground covers and plant only in areas where its spread can be contained—a site that is mowed around regularly or one bounded by concrete, for example. Grows in shade or sun in average soil. Tolerates some drought and temporary flooding. Requires evenly moist soil in full sun. Propagate by division in spring. Zones 6 to 10.

Vinca spp. / Periwinkles, vincas

Trailing perennials (actually subshrubs) with spring flowers and oval evergreen leaves. Greater periwinkle (*V. major*), hardy in Zones 6 to 11, has pale blue flowers and reaches 6 to 10 inches in height. Its green-and-white-leaved cultivar 'Variegata' is often grown as an annual or a container plant. Common periwinkle (*V. minor*), hardy in Zones 4 to 9, reaches 4 to 6 inches and bears lavender-blue or white flowers. It has dark green, oval leaves, but variegated cultivars are also available.

Grow either species in partial or full shade in evenly moist, well-drained soil rich in organic matter. Plants spread steadily and widely by trailing shoots that root where they touch the soil; *V. major* is a more vigorous spreader than *V. minor*. Space plants 1 to 1½ feet apart. Propagate by division in spring or early fall.

Viola spp. / Violets

Grow violets in partial or full shade and evenly moist soil rich in organic matter. Most self-sow abundantly. See *Viola* spp. on page 226 in the **Perennials** entry for more information.

Waldsteinia spp. / Barren strawberries

Mat-forming perennials with yellow flowers from late spring to summer and evergreen strawberry-like foliage. *W. fragarioides*, hardy in Zones 4 to 9, ranges from 4 to 8 inches tall; *W. ternata*, hardy in Zones 3 to 8, is 4 to 6 inches tall. Plant either species in partial or full shade in average to rich, well-drained soil. They will also grow in full sun, but they do not tolerate heat or humidity well.

Xanthorhiza simplicissima / Yellowroot

Clump-forming shrub with tiny brown-purple spring flowers and green leaves that turn bronze, yellow, and red-purple in fall; 2-foot plants. Plants spread steadily by suckers and rhizomes; space them 1½ to 2½ feet apart. Grows in full sun to full shade, although partial shade is best. Best in evenly moist soil rich in organic matter but grows in acid soils that are sandy, loamy, or heavy in clay and tolerates heat and drought. Prune plants as necessary in early spring to shape them. Propagate by severing and replanting the suckers. Zones 3 to 9.

Ground Covers for Sun

Sun-loving ground covers are ideal, low-maintenance replacements for lawn. They also conserve water and can be used to eliminate lawn grass on hard-to-mow slopes. Keep in mind that some plants listed under "Ground Covers for Shade" on page 128 tolerate sun as well.

Achillea spp. / Yarrows

Plant yarrows in full sun and average to poor soil that is well drained. They grow in dry and sandy soils and also tolerate dry slopes. See *Achillea* on page 2 for more information.

Antennaria dioica / Pussytoes

Low-growing perennial with semievergreen, gray-green leaves and fluffy white or pink flowers in early summer; 2-inch plants. Mat-forming plants that spread steadily but slowly by stolons. Average to poor, well-drained soil in full sun or very light shade. Space plants 6 to 8 inches apart. Shear off flower heads after bloom. Propagate by dividing in spring or fall or by potting up plants that arise at the ends of the stolons. Zones 5 to 9.

Arctostaphylos uva-ursi / Bearberry

Shrub with dark green leaves, tiny white spring flowers, red berries, and red fall foliage; 6- to 12-inch plants. Spreading plants forming thick mats 2 to 10 feet or more across. Space plants 1 to 2 feet apart. Full sun or partial shade. Average to poor and infertile, well-drained soil with an acid

pH (4.5 to 5.5). Tolerates salt and sandy soils. Buy container-grown plants, as the species transplants with difficulty. Prune only if necessary to shape plants. Do not feed. Propagate by layering plants in fall or by potting up stems that touch the soil and root at leaf nodes. Zones 2 to 6.

Campanula spp. / Bellflowers

C. portenschlagiana and *C. poscharskyana* make fine ground covers for a site in full sun or partial shade with well-drained soil. See *Campanula* on page 64 for more information.

Cerastium tomentosum / Snow-in-summer

Perennial with small white flowers in late spring and early summer and woolly white leaves; 6- to 10-inch plants. Low, matlike plants that spread fairly quickly. Space plants 1 foot apart. Full sun—light shade in the South—in poor to average, well-drained soil. Will grow on dry slopes and tolerates drought. Propagate by dividing plants in spring or root cuttings of stem tips taken in summer. Can be mowed in early spring if overwintered plants look unkempt. Zones 2 to 7.

Ceratostigma plumbaginoides / Plumbago

Showy blue flowers from summer to fall and orange or red fall foliage; 6- to 12-inch plants. Semiwoody plants that spread fairly quickly by rhizomes. Space plants 1 foot apart. Full sun or partial shade in rich, evenly moist but well-drained soil. Prune out winterkilled growth in spring. Mark the locations of these plants, because they emerge late in spring. Established plants tolerate dry soil. Can be used on banks or rocky slopes. Propagate by dividing plants in spring. Zones 5 to 9.

Yarrow
(*Achillea millefolium*)

Plumbago
(*Ceratostigma plumbaginoides*)

Green-and-gold (*Chrysogonum virginianum*) with *Mazus repens*

Chrysogonum virginianum / Green-and-gold, goldenstar

Native perennial wildflower with starry yellow flowers from spring to early summer; 8- to 10-inch plants. Creeping plants that spread moderately by rhizomes and runners. Space them 6 to 12 inches apart. Full sun or partial shade in rich, moist, well-drained soil. Propagate by dividing in spring or fall. Zones 5 to 8.

Coronilla varia / Crown vetch

Perennial with pink, purple-pink, or white pea-shaped flowers from summer to fall and ferny leaves; 8- to 12-inch plants. Vigorous to invasive plant spreading by roots and self-sown seeds. Space plants 1 to 1½ feet apart. Full sun or light shade and average to poor, well-drained soil. Tolerates sandy soil and drought. Although useful for planting on steep banks to control erosion, keep it well away from other garden plants because of its thuglike character. Plants can be mowed in fall or late winter to keep them neat looking. Propagate by cuttings taken in summer or seeds sown outdoors in fall. Zones 4 to 9.

Dianthus spp. / Pinks

Pinks grow in full sun but benefit from light shade during the hottest part of the day. They prefer well-drained, dry to evenly moist soil and will grow in alkaline to slightly acid soil. See *Dianthus* on page 96 for more information.

Dianthus 'Bath's Pink'

Euonymus fortunei / Wintercreeper

Sprawling or climbing evergreen shrub with all-green or variegated leaves; 1- to 2-foot plants. Full sun or partial shade and average, well-drained soil. Space plants 1½ to 3 feet apart depending on their size. A vigorously spreading species that forms a dense mat of stems that root along their length. Will climb trees or walls. Avoid the all-green species (it is too vigorous for most uses, and variegated cultivars are more interesting) and select one of the improved cultivars with yellow- or white-variegated leaves. Prune plants back anytime to control their spread. Propagate by cuttings taken in summer. Zones 5 to 9.

Fragaria spp. / Strawberries

Perennials with white flowers in spring and edible fruit. Alpine strawberry (*F. vesca*), hardy in Zones 5 to 9, is evergreen to semievergreen, ranges from 6 to 12 inches in height, and has edible fruit. Spreads steadily but slowly via stolons that give rise to new plants. *F.* 'Pink Panda', hardy in Zones 5 to 7, bears pink flowers from spring to fall and seldom sets fruit. It also spreads by stolons but at a faster rate and can become invasive. Both grow in full sun or very light shade and rich, evenly moist, well-drained soil and tolerate acid to alkaline soil. To propagate, sever and transplant the plantlets anytime during the growing season.

Geranium spp. / Hardy geraniums

Use hardy geraniums in full sun or partial shade in rich, evenly moist soil that is well drained. See *Geranium* on page 121 for more information.

Gypsophila repens / Creeping baby's breath

Use this species in full sun or very light shade and rich, moist soil that is neutral to alkaline. See *Gypsophila* on page 138 for more information.

Helianthemum nummularium / Rock rose, sun rose

Dwarf shrub with showy yellow, pink, or white flowers in early to midsummer and evergreen to semievergreen, gray-green leaves; 6- to 12-inch plants. Spreads slowly via trailing stems. Space plants 2 feet apart. Grows in full sun—light shade in the South—and very well drained, average to rich soil that is neutral to alkaline. Tolerates drought. Prune plants after flowering if necessary to shape them or to control their spread. To propagate, root cuttings in late spring or early summer. Zones 6 to 8.

Hemerocallis spp. / Daylilies

Daylilies make an ideal ground cover in full sun or light shade in average to rich soil that is evenly moist but well drained. Plants tolerate drought and poor soil. See *Hemerocallis* on page 146 for more information.

Houttuynia cordata / Houttuynia

Fast-spreading perennial with white, ill-smelling, late-spring flowers and heart-shaped leaves; $1\frac{1}{2}$- to 2-foot plants. 'Chameleon', with leaves edged in pink, cream, and/or red, is more popular than the all-green species, which should be avoided. Both the species and the cultivar are vigorous to invasive plants that spread rapidly and widely via underground rhizomes. Both are difficult to eradicate once established. Space plants 10 to 12 inches apart. Plant in full sun or partial shade in rich, evenly moist soil. Plants will grow in standing water. Select a site where the spread can be controlled, such as in an area bounded by a deep edging strip or concrete. Will also grow in containers, which can be set in a water garden. Propagate by division. Zones 3 to 8.

Iberis spp. / Candytufts

Use candytufts in full sun or very light shade in average to rich soil that is well drained. See *Iberis* on page 171 for more information.

Iris spp. / Irises

Several irises are useful ground covers for moist soil in full sun. *I. pseudacorus* and *I. versicolor* (a native wildflower) can be used in evenly moist soil as well as in constantly wet conditions. Both will also grow in standing water. *I. ensata* is suitable for sites that are wet in spring and summer but dry in fall and winter. See *Iris* on page 172 for more information.

Juniperus spp. / Junipers

Evergreen shrubs and trees with needlelike leaves. Cultivars of several species make excellent, adaptable ground covers for full sun in average, well-drained soil.

Chinese juniper (*J. chinensis*) is a 50- to 60-foot tree, but many low-growing cultivars that stay under 5 feet are available. Green, blue-green, or silvery foliage. Grows in acid to alkaline soils. Hardy in Zones 4 to 9.

Common juniper (*J. communis*) is a 5- to 10-foot shrub, but many low-growing cultivars are available. Gray- to blue-green foliage turns yellowish or brownish in winter. Hardy in Zones 2 to 6, it tolerates extremely poor, dry or sandy soil and acid to alkaline pH. It does not tolerate heat.

Shore juniper (*J. conferta*) is a spreading, 1- to $1\frac{1}{2}$-foot-tall shrub with blue-green needles. Several handsome cultivars with blue to silver-blue foliage are available. Hardy in Zones 5 to 9, it thrives in average, well-drained soil but will also grow in sand and heavy clay, provided it is well drained.

Creeping juniper (*J. horizontalis*) is a spreading, 1- to 2-foot-tall shrub with green, blue-green,

or silvery needles that turn purple in winter. Many improved cultivars are available, from prostrate, 1- to 2-inch-tall types to others selected for foliage color. Grows in hot, dry conditions and heavy clay to sandy or rocky soils. Tolerates exposed sites. Hardy in Zones 3 to 9.

Prune junipers anytime to keep them in bounds. Do not shear them. Instead, prune off individual branches to maintain the plants' natural shape. See "Pruning Shrubs" on page 275 for more information. Propagate junipers by severing and digging up branches that have rooted where they touch the soil.

Lavandula spp. / Lavenders

Lavenders make handsome ground covers in full sun and well-drained soil. Plants grow in very poor to average or rich soil. See *Lavandula* on page 183 for more information.

Lysimachia nummularia / Creeping Jennie

Mat-forming perennial with yellow flowers in summer and evergreen to semievergreen leaves;

Low-growing junipers (*Juniperus* 'Grey Owl') fill in under flame grass (*Miscanthus sinensis* var. *purpurascens*).

Lavandula angustifolia

Rugosa roses
(*Rosa rugosa* 'Pink
Grootendorst'), a gray-
green ornamental grass
(*Leymus arenarius,*
formerly *Elymus
arenarius),* and
Armenian cranesbills
(*Geranium psilostemon*)
form a tall ground
cover.

Sundrop
(*Oenothera* sp.)

2- to 4-inch plants. Fast-growing to invasive plants that spread by stems that root as they touch the soil. (They are fairly easy to pull up, however.) Space plants 1 to 1½ feet apart. Grows in full sun or partial shade and average, well-drained soil but will also grow in constantly wet conditions. Useful for streambanks and other wet spots. 'Aurea' has yellow foliage and spreads somewhat more slowly than the species. Propagate by dividing the plants in spring or fall or by rooting cuttings in spring or summer. Zones 3 to 8.

Nepeta spp. / Catmints
Use catmints in full sun or light shade and average to rich, well-drained soil. See *Nepeta* on page 203 for more information.

Oenothera spp. / Sundrops, evening primroses
Plant sundrops in full sun in poor to average soil that is well drained. Established plants will tolerate drought. See *Oenothera* on page 204 for more information.

Origanum vulgare / Oregano
Woody-based perennial with sprays of white or purplish pink flowers in summer and oval, aromatic leaves; 1- to 3-foot plants. Spreads steadily into broad clumps by creeping stems. Space plants 1 to 2 feet apart. Grows in full sun and poor to average, well-drained soil that contains some organic matter. The plants tolerate drought. Culinary forms of oregano are vigorous enough to be used as ground covers. Dwarf and golden-leaved cultivars are also available. Prune plants hard in spring to shape them. To curtail self-seeding, cut back plants immediately after flowering. Propagate by division in spring or early fall, or take cut-

tings of shoots that appear at the base of the plants in late spring. See also Oregano on page 155 in the **Herbs** entry. Zones 5 to 9.

Ornamental Grasses
A variety of ornamental grasses make fine ground covers for full sun or partial shade in a range of soil types. See **Ornamental Grasses** on page 206 for more information.

Phlox subulata / Moss phlox
Use moss phlox in full sun and average to rich, well-drained soil. See *Phlox* on page 233 for more information.

Persicaria spp. / Snakeweeds, knotweeds
Creeping perennials with showy spikes of pink, petalless flowers and semievergreen leaves. Himalayan knotweed (*P. affinis,* formerly *Polygonum affine),* hardy in Zones 3 to 7, blooms from spring to fall and turns red-brown in fall. It is 6 to 10 inches tall. Snakeweed (*P. bistorta,* formerly *Polygonum bistorta),* hardy in Zones 3 to 8, is 1½ to 2 feet tall and blooms from spring to summer. Both spread vigorously by rhizomes. Space plants 1 to 1½ feet apart. Plant in full sun or partial shade (partial shade is best in southern zones) and rich, moist to wet soil. To propagate plants, divide them in spring or fall.

Potentilla spp. / Cinquefoils
Shrubs or perennials with saucer-shaped white, yellow, orange, pink, or red flowers in summer. Himalayan cinquefoil (*P. atrosanguinea*), hardy in Zones 4 to 8, is a 1- to 2-foot perennial with red flowers. Shrubby cinquefoil (*P. neumanniana,* formerly *P. tabernaemontani* and *P. verna*) is an

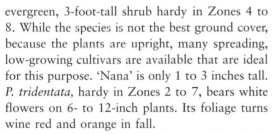

evergreen, 3-foot-tall shrub hardy in Zones 4 to 8. While the species is not the best ground cover, because the plants are upright, many spreading, low-growing cultivars are available that are ideal for this purpose. 'Nana' is only 1 to 3 inches tall. *P. tridentata,* hardy in Zones 2 to 7, bears white flowers on 6- to 12-inch plants. Its foliage turns wine red and orange in fall.

All potentillas thrive in full sun or light shade. They require well-drained, sandy or average soil and do not tolerate heat well. All spread at a moderate pace by creeping stems. Space plants 1 to 1½ feet apart. To propagate, divide plants in spring or fall or take cuttings in early summer.

Rosa spp. / Roses

A surprising variety of roses make excellent ground covers for full sun and average to rich, well-drained soil. See "Landscape Uses" on page 266 in the **Rosa** entry for specific suggestions.

Rudbeckia fulgida / Orange coneflower

Use orange coneflower in full sun or light shade and evenly moist, average to rich soil that is well drained. See **Rudbeckia** on page 267 for more information.

Sedum spp. / Sedums

Sedums are tough ground covers for full sun and average to rich, well-drained soil. They tolerate heat and drought. See **Sedum** on page 271 for more information.

Sempervivum spp. / Hens-and-chicks

Mat-forming perennials with rosettes of succulent, evergreen leaves and panicles of small pink, purplish, or white flowers in summer; 1- to 6-inch plants. Plants spread slowly by runners that give rise to new plants. Space plants 3 to 6 inches apart, depending on the size of the rosettes. Full sun or light shade and poor to average, well-drained soil. Drought tolerant. Mother plants die after they bloom, so pull them up to make room for new plantlets. To propagate, divide the clumps or pick off and plant individual "chicks" anytime during the growing season. Zones 4 to 8.

Stachys byzantina / Lamb's ears

Use lamb's ears in full sun or partial shade in a site with average soil that is well drained. See *Stachys byzantina* on page 231 in the **Perennials** entry for more information.

Thymus spp. / Thymes

Use thymes in full sun or very light shade in a site with average, well-drained soil. Plants tolerate slightly acid conditions but are best in neutral to alkaline soil. See **Thymus** on page 285 for more information.

TOP LEFT Sedums — low-growing *Sedum* 'Ruby Glow' and taller *S. spectabile* — interplanted with blue fescue *(Festuca glauca)* and mugo pines *(Pinus mugo)*

TOP Woolly thyme *(Thymus pseudolanuginosus)*

BOTTOM Hens-and-chicks *(Sempervivum* spp.)

$\mathcal{G}$ ypsophila

Baby's Breaths

Gypsophila
- ■
(jip-SOF-ih-lah)
- ■
Summer bloom
- ■
Full sun or very light shade
- ■
Zones 3 to 9
- ■

Baby's breath *(Gypsophila paniculata)* makes a fine "filler" when planted with other perennials, such as floribunda rose 'Nearly Wild'.

■ Nearly anyone who has ever received a bouquet of flowers is familiar with baby's breath. Despite the small size of their individual blooms, baby's breaths add as much airy elegance to gardens as they do to bouquets. That's because the flowers are produced in such abundance that the plants become cloudlike mounds of bloom in summertime. The flowers, which are borne in loose, branched panicles, are single and star-shaped, in white or pink; some double-flowered cultivars are available. The leaves are blue- to gray-green and narrow to lance-shaped.

SELECTING BABY'S BREATHS
The most popular species by far is common or perennial baby's breath *(Gypsophila paniculata)*, hardy in Zones 3 to 9. When in bloom, plants are 3 to 4 feet tall and wide; dwarf cultivars, which are about 2 feet tall, include 'Bristol Fairy' and 'Pink Fairy'. 'Viette's Dwarf' reaches only 15 inches in height. There are both single- and double-flowered cultivars in white and pink, and plants bloom from mid- to late summer. All rebloom into fall if they are deadheaded regularly. (To do this, remove whole stems.) Baby's breath makes an outstanding fresh or dried flower. To dry it, hang bunches in a warm, dark place.

Creeping baby's breath *(G. repens)*, hardy in Zones 4 to 8, is a 4- to 8-inch perennial that spreads into mats of bluish to gray-green, semi-evergreen leaves. Its loose, broad clusters of 1/2-inch pink or white flowers appear for several weeks from early to midsummer.

Annual baby's breath *(G. elegans)* is easy and fast from seeds sown outdoors where the plants are to grow. Plants range from 1 to 2 feet in height and make good cut flowers, but they do not dry well. Sow new crops every 2 to 3 weeks until midsummer and thin seedlings to 3 to 4 inches apart. See *Gypsophila elegans* on page 28 in the **Annuals & Biennials** entry for more information on growing this species from seeds.

SITE AND SOIL
Baby's breaths need full sun or very light shade in a site with evenly moist yet very well drained soil that is rich in organic matter. Deeply prepared soil is best, because the perennial species have deep, wide-ranging roots and deep digging improves soil drainage. Wet soil in fall and winter leads to crown rot, and plants in poorly drained conditions tend to be short lived. Greek scholars will know that the botanical name of this genus indicates the plants' preference for alkaline soil: *Gypsophila* is from the Greek *gypsos,* meaning "gypsum," and *philos,* "loving." While *G. paniculata* tolerates slightly acid soil (only to pH 6.5), plants tend to be short lived in such conditions. It is best planted in neutral to alkaline soil (pH 7.0 to 7.5). *G. repens* grows well in acid soils as well as in alkaline ones.

PLANTING
It's best to add *G. paniculata* to your garden by purchasing plants, because the best cultivars do not come true from seed. Plants offer a fast way to get plantings of *G. repens* started, but this species is also easy from seeds. Test your soil first and adjust the pH before planting *G. paniculata,* preferably the fall *before* planting.

Plant baby's breaths in spring after digging the soil deeply and adding organic matter to ensure perfect drainage. Well-dug soil also encourages deep roots and improves drought tolerance. Improved cultivars of *G. paniculata* were once frequently sold as grafted plants; now tissue-culture or cutting-grown plants are more common. If you are planting a grafted plant, set the graft union 1 inch below the soil surface to encourage the grafted plant to develop its own roots.

Space *G. paniculata* according to the height of the cultivar you are growing: dwarf cultivars can be spaced 1 foot apart, while full-size ones require a minimum of 2 feet to look their best. Newly planted specimens of *G. paniculata* take

a season or two to become established and produce peak bloom.

CARE THROUGH THE SEASON

Although established plants of baby's breath are drought tolerant, deep watering during dry weather improves the bloom. While full-size plants of *G. paniculata* generally need staking, dwarf cultivars (under 2 feet) don't. 'Bristol Fairy' and 'Pink Fairy' tend to be especially weak stemmed. Pea stakes and stake-and-string supports are both effective methods (see "Staking" in the Techniques Glossary for more on these systems). Cutting bloom stalks to the ground as the flowers fade—or shearing *G. repens* with hedge shears—encourages rebloom. Cut the plants to the ground after the foliage dies back in fall.

Both *G. paniculata* and *G. repens* have deep root systems and are best transplanted when small and left undisturbed. They can be moved if absolutely necessary in spring, but moving them will slow the plants' growth. Be sure to dig deeply to get as many of the roots as possible. Since *G. paniculata* can be short lived, and plants that do survive more than a few years become woody and stop blooming, plan on replacing them—or propagating them—every 2 to 3 years to have vigorous, young plants on hand.

Propagation. Baby's breaths are easy to grow from seeds, but the best forms of *G. paniculata* must be propagated vegetatively, and for home gardeners, that means by cuttings. To grow from seeds, sow outdoors into pots set in a protected location in early spring or early fall. Or sow indoors 8 to 10 weeks before the last spring frost date. Either way, sow in individual pots and barely cover the seeds with soil.

Baby's breaths are difficult to grow from cuttings. Take heel cuttings, which have a piece of the main stem at their base, in early summer, dip them in a rooting hormone, and stick them in a 50-50 mix of vermiculite and perlite or peat and perlite. Set the cuttings in a shaded cold frame in a relatively cool spot (such as a north-facing site), or cover pots with plastic or Mason jars in a similar location.

Divide *G. repens* by digging the clumps in early spring or in midsummer, after flowering. Dig and divide plants for propagation, if the clumps spread too far, or if the plants die out in the center.

LANDSCAPE USES

Plant baby's breaths as fillers in beds and borders. They can be used to fill in the space vacated by spring bulbs or by perennials that disappear in early summer, such as common bleeding heart (*Dicentra spectabilis*) and Oriental poppy (*Pa-*

paver orientalis). The flowers are attractive when combined with taller bellflowers (*Campanula* spp.), purple coneflower *(Echinacea purpurea)*, lilies (*Lilium* spp.), and gayfeathers (*Liatris* spp.). *G. repens* makes an excellent rock-garden plant and can be planted between paving stones or used as a ground cover or edging.

Baby's Breath Look-Alikes

Like baby's breaths, sea kales (*Crambe* spp.) produce mounds of white flowers that are ideal when used as fillers in beds and borders. The two plants are grown in similar sites and soils and can be used in much the same manner in the landscape. They aren't at all related, however: baby's breaths are in the pink family, Caryophyllaceae, while sea kales are in the brassica family, Brassicaceae, making them close kin to broccoli and cabbage. *C. cordifolia* produces its tiny white flowers in airy mounds that can reach 5 feet across and 8 feet in height. *C. maritima* bears its flowers in denser clusters that can be 2 feet across and 2½ feet tall. Both species are hardy in Zones 6 to 9 and prefer much the same conditions as baby's breaths: full sun or very light shade and rich, moist, well-drained soil that has been deeply prepared. Both tolerate poor soil and can be grown in seaside gardens, although they are best planted in protected sites out of strong wind. They prefer neutral soil and don't grow well in acid conditions.

Sea kales are deep rooted and best left undisturbed once they are planted. They are easy to grow from seeds sown as recommended for baby's breaths and can also be propagated by root cuttings taken in fall (see "Propagating from Root Cuttings" in the Techniques Glossary).

Sea lavender *(Limonium latifolium)* is another baby's breath look-alike that has airy clusters of pale pink flowers. It grows in average to rich, moist, well-drained soil in full sun or partial shade. Like sea kales, it tolerates seaside conditions and is best left undisturbed once planted. Germinate the seeds as recommended for baby's breaths, but be aware that plants are slow to bloom from seeds. For faster propagation, cut new crowns from the outside of the clumps in spring (be sure to get some roots). Sea lavender is hardy in Zones 3 to 9.

Sea kale *(Crambe cordifolia)* with white foxgloves *(Digitalis purpurea)*

Helenium

Sneezeweeds

Helenium

■

(hell-EE-nee-um)

■

Early summer to fall bloom

■

Full sun

■

Zones 3 to 8

■

■ Despite its unattractive common name, "sneezeweed," the genus *Helenium* contains some spectacular perennials that add glowing color to the garden over a very long season. These easy-to-grow plants are related to sunflowers and belong to the aster family, Asteraceae. They bear yellow, orange, bronze, or red daisylike flower heads consisting of ray florets, commonly called petals, surrounding dense, buttonlike centers of disk florets that produce the seeds. The petals are wedge-shaped and toothed at the ends, giving the flowers a lacy appearance. As it turns out, the common name is more apropos than the botanical one. The plants do not cause sneezing, but contact with the foliage can cause an allergic skin reaction and all parts of the plants are poisonous if eaten. The name *Helenium*, in honor of Helen of Troy, is a questionable choice for a genus of plants native only to North and Central America.

SELECTING SNEEZEWEEDS
Common sneezeweed *(H. autumnale)* is far and above the most popular species. Native to North America, it is a clump-forming perennial that grows wild in moist soils and produces its yellow flowers with brown centers from late summer to fall. Plants range from 2 to 5 feet in height. In gardens, cultivars of *H. autumnale* are more often grown than the species. (Many are actually hybrids of mixed parentage.) Cultivars that stay under 3 feet in height include 'Butterpat', with yellow flowers; 'Crimson Beauty', with bronze-red flowers; and early-blooming 'Moerheim Beauty', which bears coppery red blooms from early to late summer. 'Kugelsonne' is a strong-stemmed, 5-foot cultivar with yellow flowers. 'Wyndley' bears yellow flowers striped with dark orange from midsummer to early fall on 2½- to 3-foot plants. Another early-blooming selection is 'Zimbelstern', which bears yellow-brown flowers on 4-foot plants from mid- to late summer. All are hardy in Zones 3 to 8.

Orange sneezeweed *(H. hoopesii)*, native to the western United States, bears yellow to orange, 3-inch-wide flowers in early to midsummer on 2- to 3-foot plants. Unlike *H. autumnale*, *H. hoopesii* tolerates dry soil. It is hardy in Zones 3 to 7.

SITE AND SOIL
Sneezeweeds, also called heleniums, need a site in full sun. Fertile soil that is rich in organic matter and evenly moist yet well drained is best. *H. autumnale* will also grow in constantly moist to wet conditions.

PLANTING
Plant sneezeweeds in spring or early fall after digging plenty of compost, leaf mold, or well-rotted manure deeply into the soil. While the species can be grown from seeds, the cultivars do not come true, so buy vegetatively propagated plants to add them to your garden. Space plants 1 to 1½ feet apart.

Sneezeweed (*Helenium* 'Wyndley')

CARE THROUGH THE SEASON

Feed sneezeweeds in spring with a balanced organic fertilizer. A topdressing of compost or well-rotted manure is another feeding option. If a clump produces too many stems that are too close together, thin them out to leave from 3 to 5 inches between the remaining stems, leaving only the strongest ones. Taller-growing cultivars frequently require staking, although the plants can be left to sprawl over onto their neighbors. (Plants tend to be taller and rangier — and need staking more often — in the South where nights are hot.) If you decide to stake, install stakes in spring or early summer when the new growth is still only 1 to 2 feet tall. Water deeply during dry weather. Pinching in midsummer (July) reduces the ultimate height of the plants and makes them more compact.

If the plants look too unattractive after they finish blooming, cut them back by half; otherwise, leave the seed heads for fall interest. Cut them to the ground anytime from late fall to late winter before growth resumes in spring.

Sneezeweeds grow best when divided frequently. Dig the clumps every 3 or 4 years in spring, discard the older central portion, and replant the rest.

Propagation. Species sneezeweeds are easy to grow from seeds. Sow outdoors in pots or a nursery bed in early spring or fall, or sow indoors 8 to 10 weeks before the last spring frost date. Barely cover the seeds with soil.

Propagate the cultivars vegetatively — by cuttings or division — because they do not come true when grown from seed. Digging the clumps and dividing them in early spring yields large plants quickly. Take cuttings from shoots at the base of the plant in spring or early summer and root them in a 50-50 mix of vermiculite and perlite or peat and perlite.

LANDSCAPE USES

Because of their size, most sneezeweeds are best used at the back of borders or near the center of island beds. The shorter species can be used in mid-border. Plant a mix of early- and late-blooming cultivars for a long-lasting show, or concentrate on late-blooming ones to create a crescendo of color at season's end. Combine them with other late-blooming perennials such as asters, goldenrods (*Solidago* spp.), and boltonia (*Boltonia asteroides*). They can add valuable color when planted near spring- and early-summer-blooming perennials that have finished for the year, and they are attractive in combination with ornamental grasses as well. Also consider *H. autumnale* for the moist soil around ponds or in low-lying, sunny wildflower plantings.

Helianthus

Sunflowers

■ While annual sunflowers are popular with gardeners and nongardeners alike, the robust, perennial sunflowers are less well known. All are sturdy, easy-to-grow plants with showy daisylike flowers in yellow and gold. Like other members of the aster family, Asteraceae, sunflowers have flower heads consisting of ray florets, commonly called petals, surrounding dense, rounded centers of disk florets, which produce the seeds. Sunflowers have large, coarse leaves that are oval-, lance-, or heart-shaped.

Not surprisingly, the majority of sunflowers are plants for full sun. Even the botanical name

Helianthus
■
(hee-lee-AN-thuss)
■
Summer to fall bloom
■
Full sun or partial shade
■
Zones 3 to 9
■

Annual sunflower *(Helianthus annuus)*

Maximillian sunflower
(Helianthus maximilliani)

commemorates this preference: *Helianthus* is from the Greek *helios,* meaning "sun," and *anthos,* "flower." Both the botanical name and the common name could just as easily refer to the sunny colors of the flowers themselves, however. The flowers make attractive additions to fresh bouquets and can also be dried. Pick the flowers just as the ray florets unfurl. Hang blooms destined for drying in a dark, warm place. Sunflowers attract beneficial insects to the garden and their seeds provide winter food for a wide variety of songbirds.

A Sunflower Relative

Called oxeye, false sunflower, and sunflower heliopsis, *Heliopsis helianthoides* is a native wildflower that bears sunflower-like golden yellow flowers with darker yellow centers. The 3- to 6-foot plants bloom from midsummer to early fall. *H. helianthoides* ssp. *scabra* is more compact than the species—to about 3 feet—and a better garden plant. Its cultivars 'Gold Greenheart' (also sold as 'Goldgrünherz'), 'Light of Loddon', and 'Summersonne' (also sold as 'Summer Sun') are all good choices with semidouble or double flowers.

Like sunflowers, oxeyes prefer a place in full sun but grow in partial shade as well. Give them a site with average to rich soil. Plants perform best in evenly moist, well-drained soil, but they tolerate dry conditions, too.

Care for and propagate oxeyes just as you would sunflowers. Plants growing in rich, moist soil may need dividing more frequently, about every 2 to 3 years.

SELECTING SUNFLOWERS

Several sunflowers warrant consideration for use in beds, borders, or wild gardens. All of the following thrive in full sun and, unless otherwise noted, average to rich soil that is evenly moist yet well drained. Because of their deep roots, all are drought tolerant once established. See *Helianthus annuus* on page 29 in **Annuals & Biennials** for information on growing annual sunflower.

H. angustifolius. Swamp sunflower. Branched clusters of yellow, 3-inch-wide flowers with purple to brown centers from early to midfall; 4- to 8-foot plants. Also tolerates partial shade and grows in wet soil. Plants in shaded sites bloom less than those in sun and are taller. Zones 6 to 9.

H. maximilliani. Maximillian sunflower. Clusters of 2- to 3-inch-wide yellow flowers with brown centers from late summer to fall; 4- to 10-foot plants. Also grows in wet soil. Zones 3 to 8.

H. × multiflorus. Many-flowered sunflower. Showy golden yellow flowers, to 5 inches across, from late summer to midfall; 3- to 5-foot plants. A cross between *H. annuus* and *H. decapetalus.* Double-flowered cultivars, including 'Loddon Gold' and 'Flore Pleno', are available. Grows best in moist, rich soil. Zones 5 to 9.

H. salicifolius. Willow-leaved sunflower. Clusters of golden yellow 2- to 3-inch-wide flowers from early to midfall; 3- to 7-foot plants. Zones 3 or 4 to 8.

Sunflowers for Shade

While the full-sun species listed above are showier, the native sunflowers described below can add valuable late-season color to a spot that receives shade for part of the day or high, dappled shade (but good light) all day. Unless otherwise noted, they require average to rich soil that is evenly moist yet well drained. These species may be available at local wildflower sales or from catalogs specializing in native plants.

H. decapetalus. Thin-leaved sunflower. Yellow, 2- to 3-inch-wide flowers with yellow centers from late summer to midfall; 4- to 5-foot plants. Also grows in wet soil and can be planted near ponds and streambanks. Zones 4 to 8.

H. divaricatus. Woodland sunflower. Yellow, 2-inch-wide flowers with yellow centers from midsummer to midfall; 2- to 6-foot plants. Also grows well in dry soil. Zones 3 to 8.

H. strumosus. Pale-leaved wood sunflower. Yellow, 4 1/2-inch-wide flowers with yellow centers from midsummer to early fall; 3- to 6-foot plants. Also tolerates dry soil. Zones 4 to 9.

PLANTING

Add sunflowers to your garden by starting seeds or buying plants. Cultivars are best purchased as plants, however. Plant in either spring or fall, taking care to select a site that will provide the sun and soil conditions the species you are planting prefers. For all sunflowers, a site with some wind protection is best, because plants growing in windy spots generally need staking. Give them plenty of room—2 feet or more between plants—as all are large and vigorous.

CARE THROUGH THE SEASON

Sunflowers are tough plants that thrive with a minimum of care. They benefit from an annual early-spring feeding with compost or well-rotted manure. Pinching the stem tips once in early summer or midsummer—or pinching both times—encourages dense growth and helps curtail height, but it isn't absolutely necessary. (Plants growing in shade benefit the most from pinching.) While sunflowers usually stand without staking, those growing in shady spots or windy ones may need support, which should be installed by midsummer. Water sunflowers that require moist soil regularly during dry weather, especially in the South. Deadheading—or cutting blooms for bouquets—extends the flowering season. Cut the plants to the ground in fall after the flowers have faded, or wait until spring, to leave the seed heads as winter fare for birds.

Regular division keeps plants looking their best and prevents them from overtaking the garden. Every 3 to 4 years, dig sunflowers in early spring or fall, after they bloom, and divide them. Discard the older, central portion of the clumps; then cut the remainder into manageable chunks and replant.

Propagation. Sunflowers are easy to propagate by division (see above), seeds, and cuttings. Sow seeds outdoors in pots or a nursery bed after danger of frost has passed. Or sow indoors in individual pots 4 to 6 weeks before the last spring frost date.

Take cuttings from stems at the base of the plant in spring and root them in a 50-50 mix of perlite and vermiculite. Some sunflowers also produce small plantlets along the outside of the clumps, which can be dug with a sharp spade and potted up or moved to a new location without disturbing the rest of the clump.

LANDSCAPE USES

Perennial sunflowers are big, vigorous plants best used in large gardens. Combine them with other summer- to fall-blooming perennials such as asters, monkshoods (*Aconitum* spp.), boltonia, goldenrods (*Solidago* spp.), and Joe-Pye weed (*Eupatorium* spp.). They are ideal for meadow and semiwild plantings and are also effective when combined with ornamental grasses.

*H*elleborus

Hellebores

Helleborus
■
(hell-eh-BORE-us)
■
Winter to early-spring bloom
■
Light to full shade
■
Zones 4 to 9
■

■ Early-season bloom is enough reason to add hellebores to any shade garden, but consider that these long-lived perennials feature evergreen foliage, require almost no maintenance, and have an amazingly long bloom season, and you have a plant no shade gardener should be without. Hellebores bloom in winter and early spring, at a time when any signs of life in the garden are welcome indeed. Their blooms, borne singly or in small clusters, come in subtle shades of cream, purple, dusty mauve, cream-pink, and green. (The flowers may not sound showy when compared with the colorful flowers of summer, but a clump of hellebores in full bloom on a wintry morning is incomparable.) The plants tend to be low in

Lenten rose
(*Helleborus* × *hybridus*)

stature—generally under 2 feet—and the leathery, dark green leaves are divided into lobes or leaflets and are often toothed.

Although sometimes called Christmas or Lenten roses, hellebores are no kin to true roses. They're actually members of the buttercup family, Ranunculaceae. The showy parts of the flowers are not true petals but petal-like sepals, which remain attractive for literally 2 to as many as 4 months in spring as seed capsules form. All parts of the plants are poisonous if ingested, and the sap from bruised leaves can cause a skin rash in some people.

Stinking hellebore *(Helleborus foetidus)*

White-flowered Lenten rose *(Helleborus × hybridus)*

SELECTING HELLEBORES

The two most popular, and hardiest, species of hellebores are Christmas rose *(Helleborus niger)* and Lenten rose *(H. × hybridus,* often sold as *H. orientalis).* Several other species and hybrids are worth searching out, however, and all of the ones listed below feature evergreen foliage. Hellebores exhibit two general growth patterns. Some are clump forming and produce leaves only at the base of the plant. The leaves, which last a year and are typically flattened to the ground by late winter, die as new shoots and flowers appear in the center of the clumps in winter or early spring. Other hellebores are shrublike, producing leafy stems that are biennial—they remain standing over winter provided heavy snowfalls don't pack them down—and flower buds form at the top of the stems. After flowering, the stems die back to make room for new ones for the following year's flowers.

Unless otherwise noted, all thrive in light to full shade and a site with rich, well-drained, evenly moist soil.

H. argutifolius. Corsican hellebore. Clusters of nodding, pale green, 1- to 2-inch flowers from late winter to early spring; 1½- to 2-foot plants. Shrubby type with biennial stems. Zones 7 to 8; to Zone 6 with winter protection.

H. foetidus. Stinking hellebore. Large, showy clusters of nodding, ½- to 1-inch green flowers from midwinter to early spring; 1½- to 2-foot plants. The narrow, deeply cut, spidery leaves have an unpleasant scent when crushed, but the flowers sometimes have a pleasant fragrance. Shrubby type with biennial stems. In Zones 8 and 9, provide a site with shade during the hottest part of the day, as the plants do not tolerate heat well. Zones 6 to 9; to Zone 5 with winter protection.

H. × hybridus. Lenten rose. Clusters of outward-facing, 2- to 3-inch flowers in cream, greenish white, white, purple, or mauve from late winter to early spring; 12- to 18-inch, clump-forming plants. Easy to grow and tolerant of slightly acid to slightly alkaline conditions and dry to evenly moist, well-drained soils. Zones 4 to 9.

H. niger. Christmas rose. Saucer-shaped, white or pink-flushed, 2- to 3-inch flowers from early winter to early spring; 12- to 15-inch plants. Flowers are borne one per stem or occasionally in clusters of two or three. Despite the common name, these clump-forming plants generally bloom in early spring. For bloom in winter, provide a protected location. More difficult to grow than *H. × hybridus,* it requires evenly moist soil that is neutral to slightly alkaline. Zones 4 to 8.

SITE AND SOIL

Plant hellebores in light to full shade and evenly moist, well-drained soil that is rich in organic matter. A neutral to slightly alkaline pH is best, although *H. × hybridus* tolerates slightly acid soil. Avoid sites in deep year-round shade such as under evergreens. Sites under deciduous trees provide ideal conditions: essentially full sun over the winter months and shade (or bright, indirect light) with protection from heat during the day from midspring to fall.

A sheltered site, important if your heart is set on winter bloom, also helps keep the evergreen foliage at its best. Look for a spot shielded from winter winds — buildings, hedges, fences, or large shrubs offer good protection. To encourage early flowers, try plants on a south-facing slope or along the base of a south-facing wall (but shaded from summertime sun).

PLANTING

Add hellebores to your garden by purchasing plants. (They can also be grown from seeds, but the seeds must be fresh and the gardener patient. See "Propagation" at right for more information.) Once planted, hellebores can remain undisturbed for years, so prepare the site thoroughly by digging organic matter such as leaf mold or compost deeply into the soil. Test your soil and adjust the pH (preferably the fall before planting) if it is very acid.

CARE THROUGH THE SEASON

Once planted, hellebores don't need any regular care. They appreciate, but do not require, a spring feeding to add organic matter to the soil. Use compost or leaf mold. The leaves that fall onto the beds from overhead trees break down and eventually add plenty of organic matter. In fall, if the plants below are in danger of being smothered, rake off excess leaves. In areas where plants are marginally hardy, after the soil freezes cover them with evergreen boughs, salt hay, or coarse leaves that will not mat down over winter, such as oak leaves. Remove the covering in late winter or early spring.

The leaves of clump-forming species may be tattered looking by late winter or early spring, and you can cut them off if you like. An easier option is to leave them in place: new foliage will cover them up quickly, and the old leaves will function as mulch and return organic matter to the soil. On shrubby species, cut back the stems that have already bloomed to make room for new growth, unless you want seedlings, in which case leave the stems to allow the seeds to ripen.

Once planted, hellebores are best left undisturbed. If you must move them, or want to di-

Hellebores Indoors

One way to enjoy hellebores is to bring the flowers indoors for fresh use. The blooms can be cut with short stems ($\frac{1}{2}$ to 1 inch long) and floated in water. If you want to cut longer stems and arrange them, the blooms require special handling to last. Before setting the flowers in cold water for an overnight drink, make a cut partway up through the base of the stems. *H. × hybridus* is particularly finicky and wilts promptly and permanently if not conditioned before use. For it, make a shallow slit on the side of the stems, all along their length. In either case, plunge the blooms into cold water up to the base of the flowers overnight.

vide the clumps, dig them in spring after flowering. Handle the plants carefully, as the roots are brittle and easily broken. Do not divide *H. argutifolius* or *H. foetidus*. The rhizomes of these shrubby species are very short, and division is nearly always fatal, because you end up cutting off either the roots or the growing points.

Propagation. Some hellebores can be propagated by division, but the clumps are showiest (and happiest) if allowed to grow undisturbed. By far the easiest way to propagate them is to move self-sown seedlings, which are generously produced. Dig the small seedlings in spring or summer and replant them. (My clumps produce an abundance of seedlings right around the base, actually under the old leaves, where they will be smothered if they are not moved. If the soil is moist, I can dig up all I need with my fingers or a trowel.) Named cultivars do not come true from seed, but seedlings are generally very attractive and resemble their parents.

To grow hellebores from seeds, sow seeds as soon as they are ripe in summer. Sowing into pots set in a cold frame or a protected location outdoors is best. Plants take 3 or more years to bloom from seeds.

LANDSCAPE USES

Plant hellebores in shade gardens and woodland plantings. Large drifts or clumps are most effective. Be sure to site them where they can be enjoyed from indoors — outside a window or along a patio, for example — or along pathways that are used in winter and spring. *H. × hybridus* is an especially valuable ground cover, but other species can be used for this purpose as well. Combine them with spring bulbs, early-flowering wildflowers, ferns, and other shade-loving perennials. For a season-long show, try planting hellebores with Virginia bluebells *(Mertensia virginica)* and tulips or daffodils for winter to late-spring color, then add hardy amaryllis *(Lycoris squamigera)* and hardy begonias *(Begonia grandis)* for color in summer and fall.

$\mathcal{H}$emerocallis

Daylilies

Hemerocallis 'Golden Prize'   *Hemerocallis* 'Silent Entry'

Hemerocallis

■

(hem-er-oh-CAL-iss)

■

Late-spring to early-fall
bloom

■

Full sun or light shade

■

Zones 3 to 9

■

■ Showy, versatile, long lived, and easy to grow, daylilies deserve a place on America's Top-Ten List of favorite plants. Their abundant, colorful flowers belie a rugged, undemanding nature: daylilies perform beautifully in the toughest of conditions. They tolerate drought, survive extremes of heat and cold, and grow well in a wide range of soils. Use them for everything from solving difficult landscape problems to adding long-lasting color to a shrub border or perennial planting.

The name *Hemerocallis* describes the fleeting nature of the blooms; it's from the Greek *hemera,* meaning "day," and *kallos,* "beauty." Although most individual flowers last for only a day, selections worth their salt produce a wealth of buds over a period of 3 to 4 weeks; a good-size clump can produce well over 300 flowers in a single season. By selecting daylilies with different bloom seasons, you can enjoy flowers for as many as 3 to 4 months—which is far more than a day of beauty.

Daylilies produce 1- to 2-foot-tall clumps of long, arching, sword-shaped or grassy leaves that are arranged in fans. Colorful, trumpet-shaped flowers are borne on erect stalks, called scapes, ranging from 1 to as much as 7 feet in height. The flowers of single daylilies have six petals, which are more correctly called tepals because three are

true petals and three are sepals. Well-formed clumps of standard-size plants spread 2 to 4 feet; small plants, 1 to 2 feet. The plants have thick, fibrous roots with fleshy, white, tuberlike swellings on them.

SELECTING DAYLILIES

Buying daylilies can be overwhelming. Not only are there hundreds to choose from—and breeders introduce new cultivars every year—but the terminology can be daunting as well. One of the best ways to select daylilies is to visit local displays. You'll find them at garden centers that have display gardens as well as at botanical gardens. One advantage of this approach is that you're likely to find locally adapted cultivars—the daylilies suitable for gardens in northern Florida are different than the ones recommended for northern Minnesota.

When you are looking at display plantings, start by identifying colors and bloom shapes that appeal, but don't be swept away by the blooms alone. Look closely at the plants, too. Are they vigorous? Is the foliage attractive? Also examine the bloom scapes. Well-branched scapes with lots of buds of various sizes indicate a long bloom season; poorly branched scapes with buds that are all of a similar size indicate a short one.

If you are just starting out, bypass the newest cultivars, which can be expensive, and look for tried-and-true selections or ones that have received awards. Fragrant, yellow-flowered 'Hyperion', introduced in 1925, is still a classic that quickly forms impressive clumps, for example. 'Ed Murray', introduced in 1970, is a fine deep red daylily that received the Stout Silver Medal from the American Hemerocallis Society.

Of course, daylilies are available by mail as well. Since the hardiness and heat tolerance of cultivars vary, it's a good idea to buy from a grower located in a climate similar to your own. Gardeners in the Deep South are likely to find more-heat-tolerant selections from companies in Louisiana or Georgia, while those in Zone 3 will find hardier selections from growers in the Upper Midwest or New England states. See "Foliage Types" on page 148 for more on hardiness.

Collections, often offered in mail-order catalogs, are another option for getting good daylilies at a reasonable price. For top-quality plants, however, stick to collections with labeled plants rather than inexpensive "hybridizers' mixes." Hybridizers' mixes contain seedlings from top-quality hybrids, and can contain some fine-looking plants, but keep in mind that they generally consist of the *rejected* seedlings. You'll need to be prepared to rogue out plants with unremarkable or unattractive flowers or habit. Named, labeled plants are your best bet, especially if garden space is limited. If you can visit a local breeder, you may find that they have divisions of established clumps or nice-looking seedlings for sale at bargain prices.

Species Selections

Although the rusty orange trumpets of tawny daylily *(H. fulva)* are a familiar sight along roadsides in early summer, daylilies are not native wildflowers. Originally from eastern Asia, China, and Japan, tawny daylily—along with fragrant, yellow-flowered lemon lily *(H. lilio-asphodelus)*—was brought to North America by early European settlers. Because of their tough constitution, both have escaped cultivation. Tawny daylily earned the name "homestead lily" because it was carried across the country by homesteaders. Clumps of both species still thrive on old farms and along roadsides despite years of neglect.

Species daylilies have enjoyed renewed popularity in recent years. There are about 15 species, the most widely offered being *H. lilio-asphodelus* (also listed as *H. flava*). An early-season bloomer, it bears clear yellow flowers that last from 1 to 2 days and is hardy in Zones 3 to 9. The late-spring-blooming *H. aurantiaca* bears fragrant orange-yellow flowers with cinnamon-colored buds. It is hardy in Zones 3 to 10. Citron daylily *(H. citrina)* produces fragrant, lemon yellow trumpets on 3-foot stalks that open toward evening and remain open until about noon the following day. Vigorous and heavy blooming, it is hardy in Zones 5 to 9. Middendorff daylily *(H. middendorffii)* bears yellow-orange flowers and reblooms throughout the summer. It is hardy in Zones 3 to 9.

Hybrid Types and Terms

Today hybrid daylilies are far more popular than the species. While the best-known daylilies bear orange or yellow trumpets, hybridizers have introduced cultivars in an array of colors, shapes, and sizes. Colors include peach, apricot, yellow-orange, maroon, orange-red, buffy orange, pinkish lavender, and plum. Pale yellow or pink blooms that are nearly white are also available. True blue, white, and black flowers have eluded breeders thus far. (Cultivars described as purple or lavender tend to be on the red-purple end of the spectrum rather than violet-purple.) Blooms may be a single color or feature shades of a single color or two contrasting colors.

TOP Species daylilies, such as *Hemerocallis aurantiaca*, have a special charm.

ABOVE *Hemerocallis* 'Savannah Lover'

TOP *Hemerocallis*
'Stella de Oro'

ABOVE *Hemerocallis*
'When I Dream'

size affects garden use, for obvious reasons. For example, 'Peach Fairy' bears 2½-inch flowers on 26-inch plants, while 'Mini Pearl' bears 3-inch flowers on 16-inch plants. Both are miniatures.

Bloom Season

Daylilies are classified by bloom season, too, a fact that can be used to advantage when planning. For an extended season of flowers, select cultivars in several of the following standard categories: extra early (EE), early (E), early midseason (EM), midseason (M), late midseason (LM), late (L), and very late (VL). Bloom season depends on where you live. Early cultivars begin blooming in late May or June in Zones 6 and 7, as early as March in Zone 9, and as late as the end of June in Zones 3 and 4. Midseason means July flowering in Zones 6 and 7, and late cultivars bloom in about August in those zones.

Keep in mind that you can plan a progression of color as well as of bloom. For best results, select a variety of harmonious colors for different seasons—the bloom times will overlap, and otherwise you're likely to end up with screaming orange next to delicate pink.

Reblooming daylilies offer another way to maximize flowering. They produce a main flush of bloom followed by additional spikes later in the season. They're a good choice for getting the most color in a limited amount of space. Everbloomers, such as well-known 'Stella de Oro' (also a miniature), flower continuously through the season after a first main flush of bloom. 'Happy Returns', 'Pardon Me', 'Little Grapette', and 'Eenie Weenie' are other popular rebloomers.

Foliage Types

Daylilies may be deciduous (also called dormant), semievergreen, or evergreen. Evergreen types remain green all winter in the South; they benefit from a protective layer of mulch in winter in Zone 6 and the northern part of Zone 7. Semievergreens are deciduous in the North, but in the South they generally stay green on the lower parts of the leaves but turn brown or yellow on the tops. Deciduous types go dormant in fall and return in spring wherever they are grown.

To some extent, foliage type affects hardiness, and for this reason, too, it's best to buy plants from a nursery located in a climate similar to your own. Deciduous cultivars usually are the best choices for the northernmost zones, although there are evergreens that are hardy to Zone 3 (their foliage will go dormant in the North). In general, evergreens are the best choices for southern gardens. Semievergreens vary widely in hardiness; they'll be found in both northern and southern gardens.

Shapes vary, too. Trumpets are classic lily-shaped flowers, while recurved blooms have petals that curve back to form an almost flat face. Spider- and star-shaped blooms have narrow, widely spaced petals. Petal edges can be ruffled as well.

"Diploid" and "tetraploid" are terms that classify hybrids according to their chromosome count. Diploid daylilies have two sets of chromosomes; tetraploids, four—twice the normal number. Tetraploid plants are usually larger than diploids and produce larger, more brightly colored flowers. Tetraploids also often have ruffled or frilled petal edges.

"Miniature" becomes a somewhat confusing term when applied to daylilies, because it doesn't mean the plants are small, it means the flowers are—under 3 inches across. The plants themselves may or may not be miniature (the term "dwarf" is sometimes used to indicate small plants). Plant

SITE AND SOIL

For best bloom, plant daylilies in full sun or light shade—a site that receives a half day of full sun and dappled sun thereafter is fine. For modern hybrids, 8 hours of full sun produces the best bloom.

Plants thrive in average to rich soil that is well drained and evenly moist. While they tolerate poor soil and drought, they do not bloom as abundantly in tough conditions. Too-rich soil (as well as overfertilizing) can lead to the production of foliage at the expense of flowers. Avoid sites where they will have excessive competition from shallow-rooted trees and shrubs.

PLANTING

Both container-grown and bare-root plants are available. Good-quality plants should have at least two fans (a fan consists of one set of leaves with attached roots), although new cultivars are sometimes shipped in one-fan divisions.

Container-grown plants and large field divisions can be set in the garden almost anytime the ground isn't frozen, but it's best to plant in cool, damp weather. Avoid planting in the heat of summer, if possible, or keep plants well watered for several weeks if you do. Bare-root daylilies are best planted in spring or fall. Plant at least a month before the first fall frost date, especially in Zones 3 and 4, so they can begin growing roots before the ground freezes.

Prepare the soil before planting, either by digging organic matter into the entire bed or by digging a shallow, wide hole for each plant and mixing in a shovelful of compost or humus. Soak bare-root plants in water for 1 to 2 hours before planting. Set plants with the crown (the point where the roots meet the leaves) at the soil surface. Spread the roots out evenly in the hole. Space standard-size plants about 2 feet apart; vigorous cultivars, 3 feet; and dwarf plants, 1½ feet. (To create drifts of color from large clumps, divide them at planting time into two- or three-fan divisions. Then space them as above.) Water thoroughly after planting. Keep the soil evenly moist until plants become established.

CARE THROUGH THE SEASON

Once established, daylilies require a minimum of care and are seldom troubled by pests or diseases. An annual spring topdressing with well-rotted manure or a balanced organic fertilizer is all the feeding they need. Clean up old foliage in spring or fall and compost it—or simply leave it in place to mulch the plants. To retain soil moisture and to keep down weeds, mulch with chopped leaves or shredded bark; keep the mulch an inch or so away from the crowns of the plants.

Hemerocallis 'Whooperee'

In many parts of the country, average summer rainfall will provide all the water daylilies need, especially if the soil is mulched—1 inch of rain a week is ideal. Plants bloom best when the soil remains evenly moist, and moist soil is particularly important when buds are forming and plants are flowering. If you can't water during dry periods, don't worry; plants tolerate considerable drought, although they'll bloom less.

Deadheading. Faded blooms look like damp tissue paper, so remove them regularly to keep plants attractive and to prevent the limp, old flowers from interfering with new ones that are opening. (Tetraploids are especially notorious for needing regular deadheading.) However, deadheading often isn't practical in naturalized or mass plantings. Some plants drop spent blooms naturally, or "self-shed," a characteristic to look for when evaluating plants. Be sure to pick off any seedpods that begin to form—hybrids do not come true from seed and producing seeds saps energy from the plants. Remove bloom stalks after the last flowers fade.

Dividing. Although some gardeners divide plants every 3 years like clockwork, daylilies can go 10 or more years without being divided. When plants become crowded, begin to bloom less, or

A driveway edged with hot-colored hybrid daylilies (*Hemerocallis* spp.) with a few true lilies (*Lilium* spp.) mixed in

outgrow their space in the garden, it's time to divide. Daylilies can be divided anytime the ground isn't frozen, but early spring and early fall are best. Cut back the foliage to 2 to 3 inches, then dig the clumps and shake off excess soil or wash it off with a hose. Once you can see individual fans, begin to divide the clump into pieces — force the clumps apart with two garden forks placed back to back, work them apart with your fingers, or simply cut through them with a large serrated knife. Three- or four-fan divisions are ideal; you can make one- or two-fan divisions if you need lots of plants, but these will take longer to make a nice clump. Replant the divisions immediately in prepared soil and water well. Pot up the extras for friends. Be sure to label plants if you know the cultivar name. If you can't replant immediately, keep the roots moist by heeling in the divisions: set them in a cool, shady spot and cover the roots with moist soil or compost.

Propagation. Division is by far the easiest way to propagate daylilies, but they can also be grown from seeds. Starting from seeds is a good way to add species daylilies to your garden; cultivars do not come true. Indoors, mix seeds with moistened growing medium and place them in a plastic bag in the refrigerator for 6 to 8 weeks, then sow in pots and germinate at 65° to 70°F. Outdoors, sow in pots in early spring several weeks before the last frost date and set them in a cold frame or a protected location outdoors.

LANDSCAPE USES

Daylilies are among the most versatile perennials in the landscape. Mass plantings are an effective way to add a ribbon of summer color along the front of hedges or shrub borders. Or use them as ground covers, to plant a bank that's hard to mow, in front of foundation plantings, along a walkway, or in the strip of land between the sidewalk and street. They can be combined with ornamental grasses and meadow plants, and they are also attractive along a stream or pond — take care to plant them high enough above the water line to ensure moist but well-drained soil. (The plants will survive periodic spring floods, however.) For mass plantings, choose vigorous plants or ones described as "landscaping" cultivars.

Daylilies are perfect for beds and borders. Standard-size plants are fine for positions in the center of plantings; dwarf types make good edgings or front-of-the-border accents. There are tall back-of-the-border candidates with bloom stalks that reach 6 to 7 feet — 'Autumn Minaret' is one. Daylilies make fine container plants as well. To ensure good bloom from a container-grown plant, water regularly and feed with manure tea or other organic fertilizer monthly.

Dividing Daylilies

To make good-size clumps of daylilies in short order, divide established plants into divisions with three or four fans each, as shown here. These will establish quickly and take about a year to reach peak bloom.

Fans

Three-fan division

Herbs

Rich in legend and lore, herbs are plants grown for a purpose. Today the best-known herbs are the culinary ones such as basil, oregano, parsley, rosemary, sage, and thyme. Medicinal herbs, used to treat all manner of ailments, once figured much more prominently in gardens than they do today. While some of these are still used, including chamomile and feverfew, now they are more commonly grown as ornamentals. Some herbs, including lavender, are grown purely for the fragrance of their foliage and/or flowers. All manner of fragrant herbs can be added to wreaths, potpourris, lotions, and oils.

Most gardeners include a few herbs in their gardens for cooking, crafts, or ornament, while herb enthusiasts turn all their space over to these fascinating plants. One of the best things about herbs is that most are very easy to grow and require a minimum of maintenance. They are adaptable to a wide variety of sites, from tiny courtyard gardens or raised beds to large sunny borders. Most thrive in similar conditions as well: grow them in full sun and average to somewhat fertile soil that is evenly moist yet well drained. Herbs grown in soil that is too rich tend to become lanky and often are inferior in flavor and color to those grown in leaner soil.

SELECTING HERBS

There are any number of ways to include herbs in a garden. Traditionally, they are grown in a plot all their own, devoted to plants currently used as herbs as well as ones with a history of herbal use. But there's no reason herbs can't be planted elsewhere in the garden. Curly parsley or chives make handsome edging plants, lavenders are ideal for adding color and fragrance to sunny perennial plantings, and thymes make excellent additions to rock gardens. Some herbs, including oregano and thyme, make fine ground covers. See "Culinary Herb Growing Guide" on page 153 for information on the most popular herbs used in cooking, all of which can be grown in beds and borders or a proper herb garden.

SITE AND SOIL

Select a site in full sun for herbs. While well-drained soil is essential for most, rich, fertile soil isn't. Most herbs have the best flavor and fragrance when grown in average to poor or even

sandy soil. Neutral to slightly alkaline pH is generally best, although most will grow in slightly acid soil. If your soil is heavy clay or the site is not well drained, dig the soil deeply—to at least 1½ feet—before planting. Work leaf mold or compost into the soil to add organic matter and to improve drainage, but do not add manure or other nutrient-rich organic matter. Test the pH and adjust it to between 6.5 and 7.5. Planting in raised beds is another good option for providing herbs with well-drained soil.

PLANTING

Most gardeners start their herb plantings with a mix of seeds and plants. Buying plants is usually the easiest route with perennials, because one or two plants of each is generally sufficient. Be sure to smell and taste the foliage of culinary herbs such as oregano and tarragon before you buy. Seed-grown plants of some herbs, especially of oregano and tarragon, often have no flavor or fragrance, and no amount of coddling will produce it. (Divisions of flavorless herbs are no bet-

Consider mixing herbs into perennial plantings. Here chives (*Allium schoenoprasum*) are planted with hostas, forget-me-nots (*Myosotis* spp.), and Oriental poppies (*Papaver orientale*).

ter.) Although hardy perennial herbs can be planted in fall, spring is the best time to plant because both annuals and hardy and tender perennials can be put out then. If possible, prepare the soil and adjust the pH the fall before planting.

CARE THROUGH THE SEASON

Herbs are tough, low-maintenance plants that require a minimum of care once they are planted. Most herbs, including lavender, sage, thyme, lemon verbena, and rosemary (when grown in the ground, not in pots), will tolerate very dry soil and need watering only during extended droughts. Basil, parsley, and mints are best kept evenly moist. A layer of mulch helps control weeds and keeps the soil moist and cool, but it isn't essential. Granite chips or cocoa hulls are good mulch choices for herb plantings. Keep mulch well away from the stems of herbs that prefer dry conditions, such as those just listed.

Pot-grown herbs require special attention. Since the soil dries out quickly in containers, monitor it regularly and water frequently. Burying the pots to the rim in the garden helps reduce the need to monitor soil moisture, since the soil stays cooler and doesn't dry out as quickly. (This works best for plants in clay pots; water won't

move through plastic ones!) Plants in containers also deplete the available nutrients quickly, so feed monthly with compost tea or a weak solution of fish emulsion.

Overwintering. Overwinter tender herbs indoors, either by bringing in an entire container-grown plant or by taking cuttings. To minimize the annual upheaval, larger shrubs such as sweet bay and rosemary are best kept in containers year round in areas where they are not hardy. (Rosemary still tends to be fussy about being moved.) Bring plants indoors in late summer or fall, before they are set back by cold weather or frost. A bright, cool spot is best for overwintering: temperatures from about 40° to 60°F are fine for most tender perennials over winter. Be careful not to overwater: the plants are dormant, or nearly so, when kept at these temperatures, so for best results, keep the soil barely moist, never too dry or too wet.

Taking cuttings and rooting them is a good option, especially if space is at a premium. Stick the tips of the cuttings in a rooting hormone, and root them in a 50-50 mix of vermiculite and perlite. Once the cuttings have rooted, pot them on in regular potting soil, and keep them in a cool, bright place.

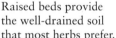

Raised beds provide the well-drained soil that most herbs prefer.

In spring, harden off plants gradually (as you would seedlings) before moving them outdoors for the summer. Set them in a shady protected spot for an hour or so, and gradually move them to more sun and for longer periods each day before leaving them out altogether.

Division. Spreading herbs such as mints and oregano should be divided regularly to keep them in bounds. Dig and divide the clumps every 2 to 3 years; watch mints very closely and pull up their wandering rhizomes several times a year to keep them in bounds. Even plants grown in containers sunk in the soil can spread: the rhizomes can hop the rim of the pot and spread at will if not monitored. Clumping herbs such as chives also benefit from division every 2 to 3 years to keep them healthy and vigorous, as do herbs that tend to become woody, such as winter savory and tarragon. Dig the clumps, discard older woody portions, and replant the rest.

Propagation. See "Culinary Herb Growing Guide" at right for propagation suggestions for individual species.

Harvesting. Herbs are at peak flavor and fragrance just before the flowers open, and this is the best time to harvest for drying, freezing, or other uses. To dry herbs, pick them in late morning after the dew has dried and bundle five or six stems with a rubber band. Hang them in a warm, dry, dark place to dry. Flower heads and/or foliage can also be spread on screens in a warm, dry place. For culinary herbs, freezing is another option. Spread whole leaves on cookie sheets and then move them to plastic bags after they are frozen. Or chop leaves in a food processor (I generally add olive oil while chopping when I do this) and pack the resulting mixture in ice cube trays. The frozen cubes can be transferred to plastic bags when they are thoroughly frozen.

Don't think that harvesting has to stop when flowers appear, however. For fresh use (or dried or frozen, for that matter), harvest perennial herbs as needed until late summer; annuals can be harvested until frost. Keep in mind that thoughtful harvesting can take care of most of the pruning and shaping herbs need. When picking leaves or flowers, try to make cuts that will improve the shape of the plants.

Potential Problems. In the right site, herbs are seldom troubled by pests and diseases. Cutworms, damping off, and aphids can attack seedlings. In poorly drained soil or unusually wet years, root rot and other soilborne diseases can take their toll on established plants. The best defense is good site selection and care.

CULINARY HERB GROWING GUIDE

Store-bought herbs don't hold a candle to fresh, homegrown ones, and in addition to being useful, many culinary herbs are handsome in the garden as well. Try to find a convenient spot for growing culinary herbs, so it is easy to step out the door and clip a few leaves to add to the soup pot. All of the following can be planted in a separate herb garden or mixed into beds and borders. If you combine culinary herbs with other ornamen-

A mix of thymes, chives *(Allium schoenoprasum)*, bleeding hearts *(Dicentra spectabilis* and *D. eximia)*, and *Sedum* 'Autumn Joy' cover a raised bed edged with rocks.

Lemon balm
(Melissa officinalis)

tals, be sure to use only organic pest controls, and avoid applying even organic sprays and dusts a few weeks before harvest.

Basil, dill, and parsley are all culinary herbs grown as annuals. See the box "Growing Edible Annuals and Biennials" on page 31 in the **Annuals & Biennials** entry for information about growing them from seeds. Cilantro, called coriander when grown for its seeds, is another easy-to-grow annual herb. Grow it as you would dill.

Chives / *Allium schoenoprasum*
See *Allium* on page 12.

Fennel / *Foeniculum vulgare*
Feathery foliage and yellow, flat-topped flowers; 4- to 6-foot plants. Sow seeds outdoors where the plants are to grow in spring or start them indoors in individual pots 6 to 8 weeks before the last spring frost date. Space plants 1 foot apart. Plants will self-sow; remove spent flowers to reduce the number of volunteer seedlings. Cut plants to the

Tea Herbs

Many different herbs can be blended together to create teas. Culinary herbs such as mint, sage, and thyme are frequently used in tea blends. Bee balm *(Monarda didyma)* and the hips and petals of roses *(Rosa* spp.) make tasty tea additions. Foliage of scented geraniums *(Pelargonium* spp.) can also be added to teas (see under **Annuals & Biennials** on page 30 for information about growing them). Lemon verbena and chamomile are two classic tea herbs worth adding to any garden.

Lemon verbena *(Aloysia triphylla)* is a tender perennial with lance-shaped leaves that have a lemon fragrance and flavor that can be used in teas, cooking, and potpourri. It bears sprays of tiny white or lilac flowers in late summer. Perennial in Zones 9 to 11, in the North it can be grown as an annual or kept in a pot and overwintered indoors. Plants can reach 10 feet in areas where they are hardy but are considerably shorter when grown as annuals. Grow lemon verbena in full sun and average, well-drained soil that is on the dry side. Propagate it by cuttings taken in summer. To overwinter, trim the plants back and bring them indoors in early fall, and keep them in a cool, bright place (above 45°F). Water sparingly, keeping the soil barely moist. Plants are deciduous and will lose their leaves over winter. Prune and repot in spring before moving the plants back outside.

Chamomile *(Chamaemelum nobile)* bears fragrant, fernlike leaves and yellowish white, daisylike flower heads on 8- to 9-inch plants. The foliage has an applelike scent when crushed and can be dried and added to potpourri. The flowers can be used fresh or dried in tea or potpourri. Grow chamomile in full sun or partial shade in loose, well-drained soil that is on the dry side. It can be used as a ground cover and will tolerate some foot traffic. Plants are hardy in Zones 4 to 8. Propagate by division in spring or early fall or by seeds sown in spring.

ground after frost in fall. 'Purpureum' has handsome bronze-purple foliage, comes true from seed, and is especially effective when planted in perennial gardens. Zones 4 to 9.

Garlic / *Allium sativum*
Narrow, grassy leaves and insignificant flowers; 2½- to 3-foot plants. Plant cloves outdoors in early fall for harvest in mid- to late summer the following year. Spring planting also works but yields smaller cloves. Do not plant cloves from the grocery store, which are treated to prevent sprouting. Loose, deeply dug soil that is evenly moist and well drained is best. Cut off flowers and their stems as they appear in summer; they are edible and can be chopped like chives, as can the foliage. Harvest leaves in moderation, however, if you want large cloves. Dig the cloves in mid- to late summer once the foliage turns yellow. Garlic can be left in the soil from year to year to form large clumps used for foliage and occasional bulb harvest. Zones 2 to 10.

Garlic chives / *Allium tuberosum*
See *Allium* on page 12.

Lemon balm / *Melissa officinalis*
Wrinkled, oval leaves with lemon fragrance and flavor and spikes of small pale yellow to white flowers in summer; 2- to 4-foot plants. Grows in average well-drained soil in full sun and also tolerates partial shade. Does not tolerate heat well; a site with shade during the hottest part of the day is best in Zone 7 and south. Sow seeds outdoors in fall or early spring, or sow indoors 6 to 8 weeks before the last spring frost date. Either way, do not cover the seeds with soil. Cut plants to the ground after frost in fall. Can be propagated by division in spring or by cuttings taken in spring or summer. Zones 4 to 10.

Marjoram / *Origanum majorana*
Tender perennial often grown as an annual, with oval, gray-green leaves and sprays of tiny white or pinkish flowers in summer; 1- to 3-foot plants. Grows in average to rich, well-drained soil in full sun. Sow seeds outdoors where the plants are to grow after the last spring frost date, or start them indoors 6 to 8 weeks before that date and transplant after danger of frost has passed. Propagate plants with the best flavor by cuttings or division only. In Zones 9 to 11, marjoram can be grown outdoors year round as a perennial, and it is evergreen. In the North, take cuttings or pot up entire plants or divisions in fall to overwinter indoors. Propagate by division in spring or early fall, or take cuttings of shoots that appear at the base of the plants in late spring.

Mints / *Mentha* spp.

Rounded, glossy or hairy leaves with strong flavor and fragrance and dense clusters of small white or lilac flowers in summer; 1- to 3-foot plants. Grows in full sun and rich, evenly moist soil. Vigorous to invasive perennials best planted in large containers sunk to the rim in the soil. Also can be planted in semi-wild areas. Cut plants to the ground in late fall or early spring. Propagate by division in spring or fall or by cuttings taken in late spring or summer. Most mints—including peppermint *(M. × piperita)* and spearmint *(M. spicata)*—are hardy in Zones 3 to 9; apple mint *(M. suaveolens)* and pineapple mint *(M. suaveolens* 'Variegata') are hardy in Zones 6 to 9. Corsican mint *(M. requienii)*, which prefers shade and reaches a height of only ¹/₂ inch, is also hardy in Zones 6 to 9.

Oregano / *Origanum vulgare*

Oval, gray-green leaves and sprays of tiny white or purplish pink flowers in summer; 1- to 3-foot plants. Grows in poor to somewhat fertile, well-drained soil; wet soil, especially in winter, can be fatal. Look for *O. vulgare* ssp. *hirtum* or *O. heracleoticum* and taste a leaf before you buy, as flavor and fragrance vary from plant to plant. Since seed-grown plants often have no flavor, purchase only vegetatively propagated plants and propagate only by cuttings or division. Cut back plants after flowering to curtail self-sowing. Propagate by division in spring or early fall, or take cuttings of shoots that appear at the base of the plants in late spring. See also *Origanum vulgare* on page 136 in the **Ground Covers** entry. Zones 5 to 9.

Rosemary / *Rosmarinus officinalis*

Tender evergreen shrub with aromatic, needle-like, gray-green leaves and lavender to white summer flowers; 1- to 5-foot plants. Requires full sun, good air circulation, and poor to average soil that is evenly moist yet well drained. Plants resent disturbance and are best not moved after planting. Hardy in Zones 8 to 10; the cultivar 'Arp' is hardy to Zone 7. In the North, try growing rosemary in a container year round. Start with a large clay pot (12 inches in diameter at least) that has adequate drainage holes. Fill with light, fast-draining soil mix—standard soilless medium or a cactus blend is fine. Set the plants outdoors in spring after the weather warms up and danger of frost has passed. Choose a sunny spot and keep the soil evenly moist but never wet. Sinking the pots to the rim in the garden helps keep the soil moist and reduces the need for constant monitoring. (Plants can dry out very quickly on a sunny patio.) Water monthly with compost tea from spring to midsummer. (See "Making Compost and Manure Teas" in the Techniques Glossary for directions on making this inexpensive fertilizer.) Bring the plants indoors in late summer and overwinter them in a sunny, cool spot (above 45°F). Water sparingly and do not fertilize. Propagate by cuttings dipped in rooting hormone and stuck in a 50-50 mix of vermiculite and perlite. Pinch and prune plants as necessary to shape them, immediately after the flowers fade.

Sage / *Salvia officinalis*
See *Salvia* on page 268.

LEFT Purple-leaved sage (*Salvia officinalis* 'Purpurascens') with littleleaf lilac (*Syringa pubescens* ssp. *microphylla)* and comfrey (*Symphytum officinale)*

ABOVE Variegated sage (*Salvia officinalis* 'Icterina') with golden oregano (*Origanum vulgare* 'Aureum')

Rosemary
(*Rosmarinus officinalis*)

A practical yet handsome herb garden with rows of chives *(Allium schoenoprasum)*, rosemary *(Rosmarinus officinalis)*, archangel *(Angelica archangelica)*, and gray-leaved cardoon *(Cynara cardunculus)*

Savories / *Satureja* spp.

Fragrant, narrow leaves and white, pink, or pinkish lavender flowers in summer. Summer savory *(S. hortensis)* is a 10-inch-tall annual. Grow it from seeds sown outdoors after the last spring frost date where the plants are to grow. (Seedlings do not transplant well.) Do not cover the seeds, which require light to germinate. Sow new crops of seeds every 3 to 4 weeks for a continuous supply of leaves. Winter savory *(S. montana)*, which reaches about 16 inches in height, is a shrubby perennial hardy in Zones 5 to 8. Grow it from seeds sown as you would summer savory, or start with plants. Plants become woody and need to be renewed every 2 to 3 years. To do this, take cuttings in summer and root them in a 50-50 mix of vermiculite and perlite or divide the plants in early spring.

Sweet bay / *Laurus nobilis*

Tender tree or shrub with leathery, dark green leaves and greenish yellow spring flowers; to 40 feet where hardy. Grows in rich, evenly moist soil in full sun or partial shade. Best planted in a spot protected from wind. Hardy in Zones 8 to 11, plants can be grown in pots year round and brought indoors for overwintering. Plant in a large pot filled with average potting soil. Move plants outdoors to a sheltered spot in spring after danger of frost has passed. To keep the soil moist and cool, sink the pots to the rim in the garden, or keep them above ground and water regularly to keep the soil evenly moist. Fertilize monthly with compost or manure tea from spring through midsummer. (See "Making Compost and Manure Teas" in the Techniques Glossary for directions on making both types of fertilizers.) Bring the pots indoors in early fall and overwinter in a bright, cool place (above 45°F). Plants can be propagated by cuttings of new, semiripe shoots taken in summer. Dip the stem tips in a rooting hormone and stick them in a 50-50 mix of vermiculite and perlite.

Tarragon / *Artemisia dracunculus* var. *sativa*

Shrubby perennial with narrow leaves and yellowish white flowers in late summer; 2- to 4-foot plants. Grows in full sun in well-drained or even dry soil. A somewhat weedy-looking plant. In late summer, cut back the plants and remove the flowers to encourage bushy growth and more foliage. Taste and smell the foliage of plants before you buy: French tarragon *(A. dracunculus* var. *sativa)* has a subtle licorice fragrance and flavor, while Russian tarragon *(A. dracunculus* var. *dracunculoides)* is more vigorous and has a more pungent, less pleasing flavor. French tarragon is propagated only vegetatively, primarily from cuttings. Russian tarragon is grown from seeds. Take cuttings of stem tips or heel cuttings of side shoots in early summer. Or propagate by division in early spring or fall. After a few years, the plants gradually become woody and less productive, so grow new plants from cuttings or dig and divide them every 3 to 4 years.

Thyme / *Thymus* spp.
See *Thymus* on page 285.

Heuchera

Heucheras

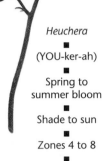

Once grown solely for their airy sprays of tiny, colorful flowers, today's hybrids of these native North American wildflowers are as likely to be planted for their ornamental foliage as for their flowers. Whether grown for flowers or foliage, all heucheras are mound-shaped perennials with low, semievergreen to evergreen leaves. The delicate-looking panicles of tiny flowers are carried on erect stems above the foliage. Some heucheras boast colorful bell- or funnel-shaped flowers; others have inconspicuous blooms. Common names reflect this distinction: heucheras grown for their flowers are commonly called coralbells, while those grown for their foliage are typically referred to as alumroots or simply heucheras.

Heuchera
- (YOU-ker-ah)
- Spring to summer bloom
- Shade to sun
- Zones 4 to 8

SELECTING HEUCHERAS
Hybrid heucheras have all but replaced the species in cultivation, and as with any genus that has been heavily hybridized, plant names can be a bit confusing. Expect to find cultivars listed under different species in different sources or to see them listed without any species name at all. The best approach is not to worry too much about the nomenclature and to look for cultivar names you recognize or that have been recommended to you — or read the descriptions to find plants with characteristics that appeal.

Coralbells
Coralbells have tiny flowers — they are only about $3/8$ to $1/2$ inch long — but these are borne on erect spikes in such abundance that the plants create quite a show when in bloom. The overall effect is airy and delicate looking — like a lace curtain suspended above a mound of foliage. Flowers appear from late spring into early summer in shades of pink, coral, red, rose-red, and white. Coralbells remain attractive even when they're not in bloom, because the plants have evergreen foliage as well. The dark green, 3- to 4-inch-long leaves, which form a low mound that stays under about 6 inches in height, are rounded and scalloped into five to seven lobes.

Expect to find coralbells listed under two different species: *Heuchera sanguinea* and *H. × brizoides*. They were once all listed as belonging to *H. sanguinea*, a showy wildflower native to the southwestern United States, but many of the most popular cultivars have been moved to *H. × brizoides* to reflect their hybrid origin. (The name *H. × brizoides* indicates cultivars that are crosses between *H. sanguinea*, *H. americana*, and *H. micrantha*.) Still, experts disagree on what cultivars belong where.

When in bloom, hybrid coralbells *(H. × brizoides)* are from $1 1/2$ to as much as $2 1/2$ feet in height. They have slightly larger leaves than *H. sanguinea* cultivars and also tend to be more heat tolerant, which makes them better choices for southern gardens. Cultivars currently thought to belong to *H. × brizoides* include 'Chatterbox', 'Firefly', 'June Bride', 'Mt. St. Helens', 'Raspberry Regal', and 'Rosamundi'. Cultivars of *H. sanguinea* are shorter — from 1 to about $1 1/2$ feet — and include 'Cherry Splash', 'Coral Cloud', 'Pluie de Feu', 'Splendens', and 'White Cloud'. Members of both species are hardy in Zones 4 to 8; to Zone 3 with winter protection.

Coralbells *(Heuchera sanguinea)*

TOP Heuchera
'Palace Purple'

ABOVE Heuchera
'Chocolate Ruffles'

Heucheras for Foliage

You'll find foliage heucheras listed under their cultivar names alone, or under two species — American alumroot *(H. americana)* and small-flowered alumroot *(H. micrantha)*. Regardless of their parentage, these feature showy leaves that can resemble maple leaves or be lobed and ruffled. The leaves are 3 to 6 inches long and form 1- to 1½-foot-tall mounds of foliage. A wonderful and confusing array of color combinations is available, including green with gray and silver overtones and veins, purple-brown with metallic mottling, rose-burgundy with silver overtones and purple veins, and green with purple-red mottling. New leaves are produced all season long, and although the color may wash out during the hottest part of the summer, rich colors return when cool fall temperatures spark a new flush of foliage. Sprays of white, greenish white, or pinkish flowers appear in early summer above the foliage. Some gardeners remove the flowers when they appear; others enjoy their subtle appeal. Foliage heucheras are hardy in Zones 4 to 8.

'Palace Purple' *(H. micrantha* var. *diversifolia* 'Palace Purple') is probably the best known of the foliage heucheras. It has metallic bronze-red leaves and greenish white flowers. Other good cultivars to look for (and new ones are being released every year) include 'Chocolate Ruffles', 'Chocolate Veil', 'Dale's Strain', 'Garnet', 'Persian Carpet', 'Pewter Veil', 'Ruby Ruffles', and 'Velvet Knight'.

SITE AND SOIL

Plant heucheras in evenly moist soil that is well drained and rich in organic matter. While they can be grown in full sun to full shade, a site with morning sun and afternoon shade is often the best choice. Coralbells *(H.* × *brizoides* and *H. sanguinea)* grow well in full sun in areas with cool summers, but benefit from the heat protection afternoon shade provides in warmer zones. They will survive in full shade but will not flower well. Foliage heucheras are more shade tolerant, and a site that is shady in the afternoon is especially beneficial because it helps keep the leaves from bleaching out. They will grow in full shade, but their foliage will not be as brightly colored and the plants will tend to be taller and leggier.

PLANTING

Spring is the best time to plant heucheras, although they can be planted in early fall as well. Prepare the soil before planting by digging in plenty of compost or other organic matter. This is particularly important in sites with heavy clay soil, because it improves drainage, as well as in droughty, sandy conditions, because it increases soil water retention. Plant the crowns about 1 inch below the soil surface. Water thoroughly and mulch to keep the soil cool, moist, and weed free. Space plants 10 to 12 inches apart. Heucheras take a season or two to settle in after planting, so don't expect a spectacular show until the plants are well established.

CARE THROUGH THE SEASON

Heucheras need only minimal care to look their best. In spring, feed them with a topdressing of compost mixed with well-rotted manure or a balanced organic fertilizer. Renew the mulch layer in early summer; compost or chopped leaves are good choices and add plenty of organic matter to the soil as they decompose. Water regularly during dry weather.

Deadheading coralbells *(H. sanguinea* and *H. × brizoides)* encourages new flowers to form. Cut off the stems just below the foliage as the flowers fade. To speed the task, gather a handful of spent stems and cut them all off at once. Some foliage heucheras, including 'Palace Purple', self-sow, something you may or may not want to discourage by deadheading.

Heucheras form clumps of shallow, woody roots and are frequently heaved out of the soil in winter by alternating cycles of freezing and thawing. Check plants during mild spells in winter and reset them if necessary or cover the crowns with a bit of mulch. In areas where snow cover is uncertain, protect the plants in fall after the soil freezes with a loose mulch such as evergreen branches, oak leaves (large ones that will not pack down), or salt hay. Remove any mulch in spring and push plants back into the soil as necessary.

Division. Heucheras need to be divided regularly for best garden performance — division in spring about every 4 or 5 years is best, although some gardeners divide every 3 years and others leave plants in place for 8 or 9 years at a stretch. To determine if your plants need dividing, look closely at the crowns. Plants with congested, woody crowns that have risen above the soil surface should be divided. Leaves that are smaller than they should be or sparser blooms and shorter bloom stalks are other signs that plants need dividing. Dig the clumps in spring, discard the oldest and woodiest parts of the plants, and replant the rest, setting the roots back about 1 inch below the soil surface.

If you need lots of plants, try cutting off and planting individual "branches," or sections of the woody roots. Select branches with at least one rosette of foliage and remove the foliage from the bottom half before planting them either back in the garden or in pots set in a shady, protected location. Although spring is the best time to divide plants, sections can be removed and planted almost anytime the soil can be worked. Keep them evenly moist while they form roots.

Propagation. Most heuchera cultivars need to be propagated by division, because they don't come true from seed. 'Palace Purple' is an exception, although self-sown seedlings will be variable, and some may be entirely green leaved. (For uniform plants, propagate by division.) Self-sown seedlings may or may not be attractive, so rogue out those that don't measure up and move any that you want to save to suitable locations. If you

want to try heucheras from seeds, sow them indoors or out. Outdoors, sow in pots set in a cold frame or a protected, north-facing location. The seeds are tiny, so cover them only lightly with soil.

LANDSCAPE USES

Heucheras make attractive edging plants when planted along a path or formal walkway. The delicate blooms of coralbells are especially effective when the plants are arranged in large drifts or clumps. Try them along the front edge of a bed or border. Although they are fairly tall when in bloom, the flowers don't block out plants growing behind them. Use foliage heucheras to add color and interest to shade gardens. They are effective when combined with ferns, hostas, spring bulbs, lungworts (*Pulmonaria* spp.), and bleeding hearts (*Dicentra* spp.).

Coralbells
(Heuchera sanguinea)

*H*osta

Hostas

Hosta
■
(HOSS-tah)
■
Late-spring to late-summer bloom
■
Light to full shade
■
Zones 3 to 7
■

ABOVE *Hosta* 'Gold Edger'

ABOVE RIGHT A mixed planting of hostas in a moist woodland garden with maidenhair ferns (*Adiantum* spp.), violets, and rhododendrons

■ There's little argument that hostas are among the top plants for a shade garden. Not only are these long-lived, easy-to-grow perennials adaptable to a wide range of sites and soils, they are very versatile in terms of landscape use as well. Hostas are grown primarily for their lush mounds of foliage, which range from as little as 2 inches to more than 3 feet in height on well-grown specimens. The leaves are amazingly variable and can be as little as 1 inch long to 12 inches or more. The colors and patterns they come in are diverse, to say the least: Leaves can be solid dark green to mid-green, chartreuse, blue-green, or blue-gray in color. Variegated leaves in a wonderful array of patterns are available, too, including combinations of green leaves with white or yellow-green margins; chartreuse leaves with dark green edges; and leaves irregularly blotched with white, cream, or dark green. The shape and texture of the leaves also vary dramatically, offering gardeners another way to add contrast to a planting of hostas.

Leaves can be heart shaped, nearly round, or lance shaped. Texture varies from smooth or ribbed to deeply corrugated.

Hostas contribute flowers to the garden as well. They bear white, pale lavender, or deep purple trumpet-shaped flowers. (Despite the descriptions in catalogs and books, hostas with true blue flowers don't exist; those described as being blue or lavender-blue are actually in shades of purple and lavender.) The 1- to 2-inch-long flowers are borne on erect spikes that rise above the mounds of leaves. Some cultivars carry their flowers just at the top of the foliage, but on most hostas the blooms are carried a foot or more above the leaves. Flowering time is variable — from late spring to late summer — and depends on the parentage of the particular cultivar. Hostas, members of the lily family, Liliaceae, were once commonly called plantain lilies, a reference to the lilylike flowers. Funkia, another common name, is a former botanical name.

A HOSTA BUYER'S GUIDE

Hostas can be expensive, and a basic under-standing of how they are priced can help you get the most for your money. Fortunately, it isn't very difficult to fill your garden with great plants at good prices.

Don't be afraid to pay a little more for good-size, high-quality specimens. They'll fill in faster and look attractive much more quickly than sickly, bargain-basement ones. Also remember that hostas are long-lived plants and are good long-term garden investments. It's worth spending a little extra to buy topnotch cultivars—all hostas will multiply over the years, and the extra investment up front will leave you with more plants of a great-looking cultivar rather than more of an ordinary-looking one.

Several factors affect the price of hostas. Choice, newly introduced hostas are notoriously expensive simply because propagators haven't had time to produce enough plants to go around yet. (Hosta cultivars have to be propagated asex-ually, by division or tissue culture.) Don't buy a hosta cultivar just because it is new or rare. For one thing, the price tends to come down after a year or two as more plants become available. Also, new cultivars aren't necessarily the best performers. For the best value and garden per-formance, concentrate on classic older culti-vars—the best selections remain available for years. Add choice new ones to your garden after they've been offered for a few seasons and the price comes down.

Plant vigor also plays a role in pricing: fast-growing cultivars that produce large clumps in a few seasons (or quickly fill out pots in nurseries) tend to be cheaper than slower-growing ones. These same cultivars will grow vigorously and can be divided more frequently in your garden, something to keep in mind if you are looking for ground covers or plants to form large drifts.

Finally, when comparing prices, pay atten-tion to the size of plant you are buying. Pot size is an obvious place to start comparing prices, but also look at the size of the plant in the pot. (Read the ordering information in catalogs to determine and compare plant size.) Turn a pot on its side and you'll see that the leaves are arranged in one or more roughly vase-shaped clumps. A pot that contains two or more clumps is generally more vigorous and further along than one with only a single clump. (I actually look for overcrowded pots at nurseries and divide them with a sharp knife as I plant. Getting three or four plants from a single overcrowded container isn't unusual, and I have managed to separate over a dozen indi-vidual plants from some cram-packed pots—all for the price of one hosta.)

Hosta 'Wide Brim' with other shade-loving perennials, including purple-flowered *Mazus repens*, alpine strawberries *(Fragaria vesca)*, and Spanish bluebells *(Hyacinthoides hispanica)*

Bear in mind that hostas growing in con-tainers in a nursery are rarely as good looking—or as large—as they will be after a few years in your garden. Read descriptions on plant labels, which should include indicated size at maturity. The largest cultivars are especially notorious for looking puny in containers—container culture tends to dwarf the leaves and the size of the clumps. It also adversely affects the color and pat-terning of the leaves. With good soil and room to spread, the plants will be transformed after a few seasons in the garden.

SELECTING HOSTAS

There are literally hundreds of hostas from which to choose, and plant breeders introduce new ones each year. As a result, it can be hard to make choices in a well-stocked nursery, and looking through the pages of a catalog specializing in hostas can be downright intimidating. (There are about 70 species of hostas, and hundreds of cul-

Hostas for Fragrance

All of the following plants produce fragrant flowers, which makes them especially appealing as cut flowers. All are outstanding garden plants.

H. plantaginea and its cultivars 'Aphrodite' and 'Royal Standard' bear very fragrant white flowers in late summer. The flowers, which can reach 6 inches in length, are borne on 30-inch stalks that rise well above the 2- to 2½-foot-tall mounds of foliage. *H. plantaginea* and its cultivars will grow in full sun or partial shade and require good light for best bloom.

Other fragrant hostas include:

'Fragrant Bouquet'. White flowers in midsummer above 16-inch-tall mounds of green-and-cream leaves. Fast growing.

'Honeybells'. Pale lavender flowers in late summer above 20-inch-tall mounds of green leaves. Fast growing.

'Invincible'. Lavender flowers in late summer above 20-inch-tall mounds of glossy green leaves. Fast growing.

'So Sweet'. White flowers in late summer above 15-inch-tall mounds of green leaves with gold margins that turn creamy white. Fast growing.

'Summer Fragrance'. Lavender flowers in midsummer above 2- to 2½-foot mounds of green leaves edged in white. Medium to fast grower.

'Sweetie'. White flowers in midsummer above 30-inch-tall mounds of chartreuse leaves edged in white.

Fragrant-flowered *Hosta plantaginea,* sometimes called August lily

tivars, which are more commonly grown than the species. Because of the extensive hybridization in the genus, most are listed with cultivar names only.) All require basically the same growing conditions and care. They are best for Zones 3 to 7 but will also grow in Zones 8 and 9 if given adequate shade and plenty of water in the summer.

One good way to choose among them is to consider how large your garden is and how you want to use the plants in the landscape. In a small garden, there may be room for only one or two clumps of the truly large hostas but space for plenty of medium and small ones. When selecting hostas, think about foliage color and contrast. Pair a cultivar with dark green, white-edged leaves with one that combines chartreuse with dark green edges, for example. Don't make the mistake of buying all variegated cultivars — solid blue-leaved or green-leaved cultivars are handsome companions that can be used to set off the variegated types. Interspersing large-leaved hostas with pockets of brightly colored small-leaved ones (set near pathways where they can be appreciated up close) is also effective, as is planting a range of leaf shapes and textures.

The following lists include many of the best cultivars. Heights given are for the foliage mounds only; the flowers can rise as much as 1½ feet above the leaves. Unless otherwise noted, plants have pale lavender flowers in midsummer.

Large Hostas

These giants of the hosta world add a bold, tropical look to shade gardens. Variegated cultivars make striking specimen plants, and clumps of large blue-leaved hostas are handsome backdrops for variegated foliage, when contrasted with fine-textured ferns, or even when used to set off the flowers of brightly colored annuals. Established clumps are easily one and a half to two times as wide as they are tall, and in rich, evenly moist soil they will exceed the heights listed.

'Black Hills'. Corrugated, very dark green leaves in 30-inch-tall clumps. Pale lavender flowers in late spring to early summer. Medium to fast growing.

'Blue Angel'. Blue-gray, corrugated, heart-shaped leaves in 30-inch-tall clumps. Handsome, tall stalks of white flowers in midsummer. Thick leaves have good slug resistance.

'Blue Mammoth'. Corrugated, oval, blue-green leaves in 36-inch-tall clumps. Pale lavender flowers in late spring to early summer. Medium to slow growing. Good slug resistance.

'Blue Umbrellas'. Heart-shaped, puckered blue to blue-green leaves in 36-inch-tall clumps. Pale lavender flowers in early summer. Leaves turn green by midsummer.

'Krossa Regal'. Ribbed, powdery blue-gray to gray-green leaves in 36-inch-tall, vase-shaped clumps. Leaves turn green by midsummer. The lavender mid- to late-summer flowers are carried on 5- to 6-foot-tall stalks if the plants receive adequate moisture. Slow growing.

'Regal Splendor'. Ribbed, blue-gray to gray-green leaves variegated with creamy white and yellow in 30-inch-tall clumps. A sport of 'Krossa Regal'. Slow growing.

'Sagae' (formerly *Hosta fluctuans* 'Variegata'). Blue-gray, smooth-textured leaves with creamy edges and wavy margins in 30-inch-tall, vase-shaped clumps. White flowers in mid- to late summer. Slow growing. Good slug resistance.

H. sieboldiana 'Elegans'. Heart-shaped, puckered and corrugated, blue-gray-green leaves in 30-inch-tall clumps. White flowers in early summer. Slow growing. Good slug resistance.

'Sum and Substance'. Heart-shaped, yellow-green to yellow leaves in 30-inch-tall clumps. Tolerates considerable sun. Medium to fast growing. Slug resistant.

Medium Hostas

The following hostas range from 1 to 2 feet in height and can be used as specimens, ground covers, or edgings. Variegated and golden-leaved cultivars are especially valuable for adding color to a shady garden from spring to fall. These plants will spread one and a half to two times as wide as they are tall.

'Abba Dabba Do'. Green leaves edged in yellow in 2-foot-tall clumps. Tolerates considerable sun.

'Big Daddy'. Puckered, heart-shaped, blue-green leaves in 2-foot-tall clumps. White flowers in early summer. Medium to slow growing.

'Birchwood Parky's Gold'. Green-gold, heart-shaped leaves in dense, 15-inch-tall clumps. Foliage color is best in brighter sites. Fast growing.

'Blue Cadet'. Heart-shaped, blue-green leaves in dense, 12-inch-tall clumps. Fast growing.

'Blue Wedgwood'. Blue-gray-green, wedge-shaped leaves in 12-inch-tall clumps. Thick leaves have good slug resistance.

'Brim Cup'. Puckered, cupped, dark green leaves with white margins in 15-inch-tall clumps. Medium to fast growing.

H. fortunei 'Aureomarginata'. Dark green leaves with yellow margins in 20-inch-tall clumps. 'Albomarginata' has white margins.

'Francee'. Dark green, heart-shaped leaves with white margins in 20-inch-tall clumps. Handsome, funnel-shaped lavender flowers in summer. Medium to fast growing.

'Frances Williams'. Blue-green, heart-shaped, corrugated leaves with golden edges in 2-foot-tall clumps. The leaf edges tend to scorch if plants are exposed to low humidity or in too much sun. White flowers in early summer. Slow growing.

Hosta sieboldiana 'Elegans' with spiny bear's breech *(Acanthus spinosus)*

Hostas and astilbes make great planting partners because they thrive in similar conditions. Here *Astilbe* 'Rheinland' and 'Peach Blossom' are combined with white-edged *Hosta* 'Francee', blue-green 'Love Pat', and chartreuse 'Solar Flare'.

Variegated hostas add season-long color to the garden. Here chartreuse-and-green-leaved *Hosta* 'Golden Tiara' is combined with white-edged 'Heartsong' and lime green 'Abiqua Recluse'.

'Golden Tiara'. Small, round to heart-shaped green leaves with irregular golden margins in 12-inch-tall clumps. Abundant purple flowers in summer. Other excellent "Tiara" cultivars include 'Diamond Tiara', 'Emerald Tiara', and 'Grand Tiara'. Handsome, vigorous, and medium to fast growing.

'Gold Standard'. Golden leaves with green margins in 2-foot-tall clumps.

'Great Expectations'. Yellow leaves with blue-green edges in 20-inch-tall clumps. Gold centers turn creamy white by midsummer. White flowers in early summer. Slow growing.

'Halcyon'. Rounded blue leaves in dense, 15-inch-tall clumps. Vigorous and tough, and holds its color well through the summer. Thick leaves with good slug resistance.

'Love Pat'. Blue-green, corrugated leaves in 20-inch-tall clumps. White flowers in early summer. Slow growing. Thick leaves with good slug resistance.

H. montana 'Aureomarginata'. Ribbed, dark green leaves with irregular yellow margins in 2-foot-tall clumps. 'Mountain Snow' has white margins. Medium to slow growing. Plants are late to emerge in spring.

'Sun Power'. Yellow-green leaves in vase-shaped, 20-inch-tall clumps.

H. tokudama. Heart-shaped, heavily puckered leaves in 15-inch-tall clumps. White flowers in summer. 'Aureonebulosa' has yellow-green leaves with irregular blotches and margins of blue-green. 'Flavocircinalis' has blue-green leaves with irregular yellow-green margins. Slow growing and late to emerge in spring. Slug-resistant leaves.

H. ventricosa. Dark, glossy green leaves in 20-inch-tall clumps. Handsome dark purple flowers in late summer. 'Aureomarginata' has leaves variegated with yellow and cream.

'Wide Brim'. Green leaves with wide creamy white margins in 18-inch-tall clumps.

'Zounds'. Puckered golden yellow leaves in 2-foot-tall clumps. White flowers in early summer.

Small Hostas

Low-growing hostas—all of these are under 1 foot in height—are handsome when used in small drifts along pathways, as edgings in shade gardens, or as accent plants. They are also quite at home in shady rock gardens. Small hostas spread two to three times as wide as they are tall.

'Chartreuse Wiggles'. Lance-shaped, yellow-green leaves with wavy margins in 6-inch-tall clumps. Lavender flowers in late summer. Foliage has best color in bright light. Medium to fast growing.

'Ginko Craig'. Lance-shaped, dark green leaves with white margins in 8-inch-tall clumps. Lavender flowers in late summer. Fast growing.

'Gold Edger'. Heart-shaped chartreuse leaves in dense, 7-inch-tall clumps. 'Radiant Edger' has chartreuse leaves with dark green centers and is less vigorous. Fast growing.

'Just So'. Round, corrugated, yellow-green leaves with green margins in 6-inch-tall clumps. Medium to slow growing.

Hosta montana 'Aureomarginata'

'Kabitan'. Lance-shaped yellow leaves with dark green margins in 10-inch-tall clumps.

'Little Aurora'. Round gold leaves in 10-inch-tall clumps.

'Tiny Tears'. Green, heart-shaped leaves in dense, 2-inch-tall clumps. Dark lavender flowers in midsummer.

H. venusta. Green, heart-shaped leaves in broad, 4-inch-tall clumps. Pretty lavender flowers in midsummer.

SITE AND SOIL

While hostas will tolerate a wide range of conditions, they grow best in light to full shade in evenly moist soil that is rich in organic matter. A site with a few hours of morning sun and shade for the rest of the day is fine. In the South, shade during the hottest part of the day is essential for success. Blue-leaved cultivars generally keep their color best if planted in cool, shady spots that receive good light but no direct sun, and a spot in bright but dappled shade brings out the best color in variegated cultivars. (Too much sun tends to cause the yellow- or white-colored areas of the leaves to bleach out or turn brown.) Golden-leaved cultivars such as 'Sum and Substance' tolerate considerable sun but still benefit from shade during the hottest part of the day in all but the coolest zones.

Although hostas are fairly drought tolerant (especially cultivars with thick leaves), they will not attain full size without even moisture and will not survive constantly dry soil. They will grow in heavy clay as well as constantly moist conditions, and they can be planted along streambanks, bogs, and ponds, provided the crowns are set above the water line where the soil has adequate drainage.

Try to plant hostas in a site protected from wind, but if that's not possible, water frequently during windy weather because the plants can lose moisture quickly through their large leaves.

PLANTING

Hostas can be moved into the garden nearly anytime the ground can be worked, but early-spring or fall planting is generally best. Before planting, dig the soil deeply and amend it with plenty of organic matter such as compost. Deep digging encourages deep, wide-spreading roots, which in turn improves drought tolerance. Space plants as far apart as their height at maturity. If you are planting in drifts, divide larger clumps at planting time and space them out as you would individual plants.

Mark the location of the clumps, since hostas emerge late in spring (some are later than others) and it's easy to dig into a clump by accident. After planting, hostas take at least two to four seasons to become established and to reach their full size; large hostas can take longer.

CARE THROUGH THE SEASON

Once planted, hostas need only minimal care to look their best. Mulch the plants in spring with

Dealing with Slugs and Snails

Hostas are caviar to slugs and snails, which chew large, irregular holes in the leaves and leave behind shiny, slimy trails. Handpicking and trapping are effective if practiced regularly. Handpick at night about 2 hours after sunset and drop the pests in a jar of water. (Adding a dash of rubbing alcohol to the water will anesthetize your captures and keep them from climbing out of the jar.) Overturned flowerpots, boards, cabbage leaves, and the rinds of grapefruits can all be set out as traps in shady spots. Scrape out slugs and snails that hide there to escape the heat and crush them or gather them in your collection jar. To make pot- or board-traps more attractive to your prey, crush some of the pests on the trap itself. To make beer traps, cut a hole in the top of a plastic butter tub, fill the tub two-thirds full of beer, and replace the lid, which helps keep the beer from evaporating (or being drunk by a beer-loving dog). Sink the plastic tub to the rim in the soil. Empty the contents periodically and replace the beer.

chopped leaves or shredded bark to control weeds and to keep the soil moist and cool. Keep the mulch away from the leaf stalks to minimize problems with rotting. (If slugs are a problem, you may want to dispense with a permanent mulch layer.) Feed annually in spring with compost mixed with well-rotted manure to add nutrients and organic matter to the soil. Established plants will tolerate drought, but watering as needed to keep the soil evenly moist promotes the best growth.

As the flowers fade, cut the bloom stalks back to below the foliage. Cut the leaves to the ground after frost kills them in fall. (Some hostas have attractive yellow fall foliage.) Or leave them in the garden, where they will rot and add organic matter to the soil.

Division. Hostas are easy to divide, but they can grow well for years without needing it. The crowns don't become woody, clumps don't die out in the center, and they rarely become too crowded. Leaving the clumps undisturbed is best if you want them to achieve maximum size. If you need to divide or move a clump, digging in spring before the leaves unfurl or in early fall is best. Dig up as many of the fleshy, white, rope-like roots as possible, and cut through the thick rhizome with a sharp knife. Then replant the divisions. If you need a plant or two from an existing clump to propagate it, leave it in the ground and use a sharp spade to cut off the plants you need from the outside of the clump (make sure you get some roots, too). Gently digging some of the soil away from the plant may help you determine where to cut: get down on your hands and knees to look under the foliage to locate the small suckers or crowns that arise around the outside of the clump. It's also possible to cut a pie-shaped wedge out of the center of the clump to make a relatively large division. Fill the resulting hole with topsoil. If any pieces come off with part of the crown but no roots, pot them up in soilless mix and hold them in a shady, protected place. Keep them evenly moist and they will grow roots.

Propagation. Hosta cultivars are propagated asexually by division or tissue culture. Species hostas can be grown from seed. (Plants will self-sow if the flower stalks aren't cut back as they fade.) Sow seeds indoors or out in spring, and lightly cover them with soil. Germination takes 3 to 4 weeks.

Potential Problems. Slugs and snails chew holes in hosta leaves. There are slug-resistant hostas available; see "Dealing with Slugs and Snails" at left for other control suggestions. Deer love hostas as well; see the Problems & Solutions Guide for suggestions on controlling them. Voles, chipmunks, and other rodents relish the fleshy crowns and roots of hostas and can do considerable damage over winter. If they have been a problem in your garden, raking mulch off the beds in fall and removing faded hosta foliage can help discourage them from moving in. A resident cat can help with control, but encouraging a diverse community of predators is more natural and probably more effective. Hawks, snakes, and owls are all effective mouse predators. Pressing down or refilling holes that appear in the garden may help. (I divide my best hostas and grow the divisions in two different locations as insurance against rodents.) It's possible to save partially gnawed crowns. Trim the gnawed edges with a sharp knife, then dust them with sulfur to protect against rot. Pot the crowns up or move them to a nursery bed until they recover.

LANDSCAPE USES

Combine hostas with other shade-loving plants such as ferns, bleeding hearts (*Dicentra* spp.), hellebores, lungworts (*Pulmonaria* spp.), epimediums, and woodland phlox (*Phlox divaricata* and *P. stolonifera*). Underplant them with daffodils and other hardy spring bulbs; their emerging foliage will hide the bulb foliage as it ripens. Woodland wildflowers such as Jacob's ladder (*Polemonium* spp.), Virginia bluebells (*Mertensia virginica*), and bloodroot (*Sanguinaria canadensis*) are also natural companions. Hostas are most striking when they are allowed to form large clumps or are planted in large drifts. Fast-growing cultivars are the best choices for use as ground covers and edgings. Hostas also make fine container plants.

Hydrangea

Hydrangeas

Hydrangea
■
(hi-DRAN-jee-ah)
■
Early-summer to fall bloom
■
Full sun or partial shade
■
Zones 3 to 9
■

■ Hydrangeas are easy-to-grow ornamentals that add color to the garden from early summer into fall, at a time when few other shrubs are in bloom. Although their individual flowers are small, they are borne in showy clusters consisting of tiny fertile flowers and larger sterile flowers with petal-like sepals. While most hydrangeas are large shrubs, one species is sometimes trained as a small tree and another species is an outstanding ornamental vine.

Hydrangea blooms make fine additions to large fresh arrangements and are excellent dried flowers if picked at the right time. For fresh use, pick the blooms when the florets are fully mature. Flowers in fresh bouquets can be left to dry upright in a vase with 2 to 3 inches of water in it. Do not replace the water when it is used up and the flowers will dry in place. To collect flowers for drying, wait until they are just past mature. White flowers that have begun to fade to cream, green, or pink are ready for harvest, as are blue flowers that have turned lavender, greenish, or maroon. Bundle the stems with rubber bands and hang them upside down in bunches in a warm, dry place. Flowers left on the plants will eventually turn tan to beige in color and are attractive in dried arrangements in their natural hue. They can also be spray painted.

SELECTING HYDRANGEAS

Like many popular shrubs, hydrangeas have been heavily hybridized, and improved cultivars are much more likely to be found in gardens than the species. Florist's, or bigleaf, hydrangeas *(Hydrangea macrophylla)* are probably the best known of the bunch. They are less hardy than some of the other species listed below and are covered separately.

H. arborescens. Smooth hydrangea. Rounded or flattened, 6-inch-wide flower clusters in early summer and again in late summer to fall; rounded, 3- to 5-foot shrubs with large, oval, deciduous leaves. Grows in acid to slightly alkaline soil that is rich and evenly moist. Wilts dramatically and requires regular watering in dry spots or during dry summers. Best in partial shade, especially in the South, but in northern zones tolerates full sun if given evenly moist soil. Stems are killed to the ground in the North, where plants are treated as shrub-sized perennials. Since they bloom on new wood (growth of the current season), this doesn't interrupt flowering the following year. Where plants aren't killed back in winter, cut them to within several inches of the ground in late fall or early spring to promote an attractive, rounded shape and to ensure stems strong enough to hold up the heavy flowers. Thinning out stems in spring (where they aren't killed to the ground) promotes a more attractive shape and larger flowers. 'Grandiflora', with 6- to 8-inch-wide blooms, is the most commonly available and is frequently referred to as hills-of-snow hydrangea. 'Annabelle' blooms 2 weeks later than 'Grandiflora' and has larger, more numerous flowers. Deadheading encourages repeat bloom from late summer into fall, especially with the cultivar 'Annabelle'. Propagate by cuttings or division. Zones 3 to 9.

Panicle hydrangea *(Hydrangea paniculata)*

LEFT Slightly acid to slightly alkaline soils (pH 6.0 to 7.5) yield pink flowers on florist's hydrangeas *(Hydrangea macrophylla)*, while acid soil (pH 5.5 to 5.0) yields blue to purple ones.

RIGHT Hortensia-type florist's, or bigleaf, hydrangea *(Hydrangea macrophylla* 'Nikko Blue')

Climbing Hydrangea

One of the most ornamental vines available is climbing hydrangea *(H. petiolaris,* formerly *H. anomala* ssp. *petiolaris* but recently restored to *H. petiolaris)*. Hardy in Zones 5 to 7 or 8, it bears flat-topped clusters of white flowers in early to midsummer set against glossy green leaves. The trunk of this vigorous vine—it can reach 60 to 80 feet with support—has cinnamon-brown exfoliating bark that is very attractive. Plant it in full sun or partial shade in rich, evenly moist soil that is well drained. A cool site (perhaps north facing) with afternoon shade is best in the South, where growth is less vigorous. The plants climb by root-like holdfasts and can be trained up trees or up and over brick or stone walls; sturdy support is essential. (Do not train them onto walls that will require periodic painting.) Climbing hydrangea can also be left to sprawl on the ground, where it forms a dense, effective ground cover. The plants are notoriously slow to establish after transplanting and grow very slowly for the first 2 to 3 years. Prune plants only if necessary in late winter or early spring to redirect wayward growth. To propagate, take cuttings in late spring or early summer and root as you would other hydrangeas.

H. paniculata. Panicle hydrangea. Pyramidal clusters of white flowers in mid- to late summer that age to mauve-pink; 10- to 25-foot shrub or small tree. *H. paniculata* 'Grandiflora', commonly called peegee hydrangea, is the most frequently grown. When trained to a single trunk as a small tree, it is sometimes called tree hydrangea. 'Grandiflora' has enormous clusters of sterile flowers that range from 6 to 12 inches long and wide. 'Tardiva' blooms from early to late fall and has smaller, more graceful flower clusters. Both the species and the cultivars are tough and tolerant. Plant in full sun or partial shade, although shade during the hottest part of the day is best in the South. Keep the soil evenly moist for best growth, but plants will grow well in drier soil than *H. arborescens* or *H. macrophylla* will tolerate. Flowers are borne on new wood and plants can be pruned in late winter or early spring. Remove old, nonflowering, or dead wood. Cut back plants grown as shrubs to keep them in bounds. For the largest flowers on 'Grandiflora', thin out the stems when pruning, leaving only 5 to 10 per plant. Zones 3 to 9.

H. quercifolia. Oakleaf hydrangea. Pyramidal, 4- to 12-inch-long clusters of white flowers in early to midsummer that age to purple-pink; somewhat rangy 4- to 6-foot shrubs. Handsome dark green, glossy foliage shaped like oak leaves that turns brilliant red and orange-brown in fall. Attractive cinnamon-colored exfoliating bark. Tolerates full sun but is best in partial shade in a site with evenly moist, cool soil that is well drained. Tolerates drier soil than *H. arborescens* or *H. macrophylla* does. Several improved cultivars with flowers larger than those of the species are available, including 'Snowflake', which has double flowers, and 'Snow Queen', which has strong stems that hold the flower clusters erect and stunning bronze-red fall color. Plants may be killed to the ground in winter in Zone 5, in which case they will produce foliage but no flowers the following season. Even in areas where it is killed to the ground, it is worth growing for the handsome foliage. Plants bloom on old wood (growth from the previous season) and can be pruned if necessary immediately after they flower. Or simply remove spindly or winterkilled growth, along with crossing and rubbing branches, in early spring, leaving the main shoots, which bear the flower buds. Zones 5 to 9.

A lacecap-type florist's hydrangea (*Hydrangea macrophylla*)

Florist's Hydrangea

Also called bigleaf hydrangea, *H. macrophylla* is a 3- to 6-foot-tall shrub with blue or pink flowers in midsummer and large, oval leaves. Cultivars are divided into two groups in this heavily hybridized genus: hortensias and lacecaps. Hortensias, sometimes called mopheads, have large, nearly round flower clusters with all sterile flowers. Lacecaps have flattened, disk-shaped clusters with small fertile flowers in the centers and large sterile ones around the edges. A vast number of cultivars are available, not all of which are suitable for planting outdoors—many were developed as pot plants for the florist trade and either aren't hardy or have blooms that are so large that they flop over when exposed to wind and rain. Hortensia types suitable for the garden include 'All Summer Beauty', 'Ami Pasquier', 'Nikko Blue', and 'Otaksa'. 'Forever Pink' and 'Pia' are dwarf hortensias that reach about 2 feet in height. Lacecaps include 'Blue Billow', 'Blue Wave', 'Mariesii', and 'White Wave'. Variegated-leaved lacecaps—'Quadricolor' and 'Variegata'—make attractive foliage plants in partial shade.

Flower color depends to a large extent on soil pH. Acid soils (pH 5.0 to 5.5) yield blue to purple flowers, while more slightly acid to slightly alkaline soils (pH 6.0 to 7.5) yield pink to red ones. Growth is best below pH 6.5, and above 7.5 the leaves become chlorotic, or yellowed. (Some cultivars are more affected by pH than others, and white-flowered cultivars are not affected by pH at all.) If the soil pH is between those ranges, flowers tend to turn intermediate and often unattractive shades of mauve. Lime is used to raise soil pH (make it less acid) and sulfur is used to lower it (make it more acid). Wood ashes also raise soil pH; working peat moss into the soil at planting time lowers it. The quantity required varies according to the existing pH and the soil type, however. It takes more lime or sulfur to adjust the pH in clay soil than it does in sandy soil, for example. The best approach is to have the soil tested and follow the soil-test lab's recommendations. It's not practical to adjust soil pH more than a point or so to affect flower color and any changes you do make should be done gradually over several seasons. If you have strongly acid soil and want to grow pink hydrangeas, growing them in containers is the best option.

Plant bigleaf hydrangeas in full sun or partial shade in a spot with moist, well-drained soil that has been amended with compost, leaf mold, or other organic matter. In the South, they are best located in areas with shade during the hottest part of the day. The plants are ideal for coastal gardens, as they thrive in seaside conditions. Water regularly to keep the soil moist or the plants will be constantly wilted.

Hardiness plays a factor in whether plants will bloom successfully or not. Although bigleaf hydrangeas are root hardy into Zone 5, they bloom on old wood and are normally killed to the ground in Zone 5 and even in Zone 6 in severe winters. They can be grown as far south as Zone 9. Plants that are killed to the ground will produce foliage but no flowers the following sum-

Oakleaf hydrangea
'Snow Queen'
(Hydrangea quercifolia)

mer. A hard late-spring frost can also kill the flower buds once they begin to emerge, so protect plants if a cold snap threatens in spring. In areas where they are not killed back, prune bigleaf hydrangeas immediately after they bloom by removing spindly growth and cutting back some of the oldest stems. Leave the strong new stems that begin to appear after the flowers fade, as they produce good blooming wood for the following summer.

SITE AND SOIL
Hydrangeas grow in full sun or partial shade and prefer evenly moist soil that is well drained and rich in organic matter. A site protected from cold winter winds is best. See "Selecting Hydrangeas" at the beginning of this entry for more details on the preferences of individual species.

PLANTING
Plant hydrangeas in spring or early fall. For best results, loosen the soil over a wide, fairly shallow planting area. Ideally, the site should be large enough to encompass the eventual spread of the plants' branches. Do not amend the soil with compost or other organic matter unless you do it over a large planting area. See "Planting Shrubs" on page 274 in the **Shrubs** entry for details on getting plants settled successfully and off to a good start.

CARE THROUGH THE SEASON
Beyond some annual attention with pruning shears, hydrangeas really need very little care to look their best. Pruning specifics are covered under "Selecting Hydrangeas" above. When pruning, remove deadwood and growth that is more than about 3 years old, which does not bloom as well as younger wood. Thinning out up to one-third of the oldest canes each year is a good approach. Some gardeners prune off the brown flower clusters in fall or winter to spruce up the plants for spring. Hydrangeas (except climbing hydrangea) can be rejuvenated by cutting all of the stems to within a few inches of the ground in late winter or early spring.

    Propagation. Propagate hydrangeas by taking cuttings in early summer. Dip them in a rooting hormone and root them in a 50-50 mix of perlite and vermiculite. *H. arborescens* can be propagated by division. Don't dig up the entire plant, though; simply slice off a section from the outside of the clump with a sharp spade.

LANDSCAPE USES
Plant hydrangeas in shrub borders and hedges. They are also attractive additions to woodland gardens and sunny to partially shaded flower beds—combine with rhododendrons and azaleas as well as with large hostas, ferns, and other bold perennials that thrive in similar conditions.

Iberis

Candytufts

■ The flat-topped, icy white blooms of perennial candytuft *(Iberis sempervirens)* are as sure a sign of spring as daffodils and tulips. Also called evergreen candytuft, this species blooms in late winter in southern gardens — from February into March; later in spring in the North — from April into May or as late as early June. A close look at the flowers reveals that each bloom is a cluster of diminutive, four-petaled flowers, a characteristic that marks candytuft as a member of the mustard family, Brassicaceae. The white blooms stand out starkly against narrow, evergreen, 1 to 1½-inch-long leaves that are very dark green. The plants are actually woody-stemmed perennials, sometimes referred to as subshrubs. They range from 6 to 12 inches tall and form neat mounds that spread from 12 to 15 inches across. 'Little Gem' is a dwarf cultivar that ranges from 5 to 8 inches tall. 'Autumn Beauty' and 'Autumn Snow' bloom in spring and again in fall on 8- to 10-inch plants. All are hardy in Zones 3 to 9.

Rock candytuft *(I. saxatilis)*, which also is evergreen, bears similar flowers on smaller plants — from 3 to 6 inches in height. It is hardy in Zones 2 to 7.

There are also annual candytufts that are very easy to grow. See *Iberis* spp. on page 29 in the **Annuals & Biennials** entry for information about growing them.

SITE AND SOIL
Plant candytufts in a site with full sun or very light shade. They grow in any average, well-drained soil. Although candytufts are unaffected by pests and diseases, wet soil, especially in winter, can lead to root rot and death.

PLANTING
Set plants out in spring or early fall. Space them 1 to 1½ feet apart to accommodate their spread.

CARE THROUGH THE SEASON
Immediately after flowering, cut plants back by one-third to remove spent blooms and to encourage branching. (Hedge shears accomplish this task with a few quick cuts.) Every 2 to 3 years, cut plants back hard — by about two-thirds — to

Iberis
■
(eye-BEER-iss)
■
Spring bloom
■
Full sun or very light shade
■
Zones 2 to 9
■

Perennial candytuft *(Iberis sempervirens)*

keep growth compact and dense. Plants seldom need dividing, provided they're given enough space to spread at planting time. If necessary, divide plants immediately after they bloom.

Propagation. Dividing the clumps is an easy way to propagate candytufts; in addition, the stems often root where they touch the ground, and these rooted pieces can be cut from the parent plant and potted up or transplanted to a new spot. Tip cuttings taken in late spring or early summer root quickly and easily. Pot them up in a 50-50 mix of perlite and vermiculite. Seed for perennial candytufts germinates in 2 to 3 weeks at 60°F; most cultivars are propagated by division, however, and seed-grown plants will be variable.

LANDSCAPE USES
Grow candytufts as edging plants at the front of beds and borders, along walkways, or as ground covers. Both *I. sempervirens* and *I. saxatilis* are classic rock-garden plants and look especially attractive cascading over rocks, low walls, or the edges of raised beds — particularly with other trailing plants such as basket-of-gold *(Aurinia saxatilis)* and moss phlox *(Phlox subulata)*. Candytufts combine well with other spring-blooming perennials and bulbs such as tulips, daffodils, bleeding hearts *(Dicentra* spp.), peonies *(Paeonia* spp.), baptisias, and columbines *(Aquilegia* spp.). Repeat-blooming candytufts add a touch of icy white to the fall garden, and the handsome foliage contributes winter color.

Irises

Iris
■
(EYE-riss)
■
Spring to midsummer
bloom, fall rebloom
■
Sun to shade
■
Zones 2 to 11
■

■ Irises are irresistible perennials that have a place in every garden. The botanical name given to these versatile beauties is right on target: the name *Iris* is in honor of the mythological Greek goddess Iris, messenger to Juno, who rode to Earth on a rainbow. Bearded irises come in the widest range of colors, but these plants, which thrive in full sun and well-drained soil, are just the beginning of the story. There are other species of iris for sunny beds and borders, as well as ones suitable for shady woodlands, rock gardens, bog plantings, and even standing water.

Although each species blooms for a relatively short time, with careful selection it's possible to extend the display for several months. The earliest of the irises start blooming in February to mid-March in the South, from March into mid-April in more northern zones. Bearded irises, by far the best known, grace the garden from late spring into early summer, and the show continues through early and midsummer (June to July) when Japanese irises reach their peak. There are even irises that rebloom in late summer and fall.

Iris is a vast genus containing about 300 species and literally thousands of cultivars. (Entire books have been written on the progeny of a single species.) All bear flowers with six petals,

or segments. Of these, three point up or out and are called standards, and three point out or down and are called falls. (See "Iris Terms" on the facing page for more information on the words used to describe irises.) Generally the flowers are borne in small clusters and the buds open in succession, a convenient characteristic that lengthens the display from each flower stalk. All of the taller irises make spectacular cut flowers, and new buds will continue to open on cut stems, just as they would in the garden. The foliage is sword shaped, strap shaped, or grassy. Plants grow from spreading rhizomes or bulbs; the rhizomes of some species spread widely and others form dense, grasslike clumps. Botanists have divided the species and cultivars into sections or groups, of which the bearded irises are one.

SELECTING IRISES

There are irises for nearly every garden situation — sun to shade, dry soil to standing water. For best results, look at the site and soil conditions your garden has to offer and match those conditions to irises that will naturally thrive there.

Bearded Irises

The showiest members of the genus, bearded irises are sometimes listed as *I. germanica,* although they actually are hybrids between that species and several others. (*I. pumila,* a 4- to 8-inch-tall species with violet-blue and purple flowers, is an important parent of the dwarf bearded hybrid cultivars.) All have fuzzy beards at the top of each fall and are plants for full sun and well-drained soil. Most gardeners aren't aware that the bearded irises are divided by height and flower size into six groups. Tall bearded irises, which bear 4- to 8-inch-wide blooms atop plants that are 27 inches tall or more, are by far the most popular, and their colorful flowers are a common sight in beds and borders in spring. Although cultivars in the other groups are harder to find, it pays to search them out because the groups bloom at slightly different times, and planting a selection of them extends the bearded iris display for a couple of weeks in spring. First to bloom are the miniature dwarf beardeds, which are under 8 inches tall and have 1- to 3-inch-wide flowers. Standard dwarf bearded cultivars (8 to 16 inches in height) bloom next, followed by intermediate bearded irises (16 to 27 inches), which have 4- to 5-inch-wide blooms. The last three groups — miniature tall bearded, border bearded, and tall bearded irises — bloom together in late spring to early summer. (Miniature tall beardeds and border beardeds are both 16 to 27 inches tall, and these two types are distinguished by the slightly smaller flowers of the miniatures.)

Reblooming Irises

Irises are renowned spring-blooming perennials, but all too few gardeners are familiar with the reblooming, or remontant, irises. These flower in spring or early summer, slightly before the tall bearded irises, and again periodically from early to late fall. In areas with warm, dry summers, they may also bloom in summer. (Rebloomers don't rebloom in areas with humid, wet summers, such as Florida and the Gulf Coast.)

Many rebloomers bear fragrant flowers, and most are tall beardeds, but there are also intermediate and dwarf bearded cultivars that rebloom. Reblooming irises may not be available at local nurseries but are well worth searching for. Cultivars to look for include fragrant purple 'Autumn Bugler', yellow 'Baby Blessed', yellow 'Corn Harvest', fragrant white 'Immortality', wine-purple 'Mulberry', and light blue 'Sugar Blues'.

Grow reblooming irises as you would bearded irises, but water them deeply and regularly in mid- to late summer if the weather is dry. They should also be fed twice a year — in spring and again in midsummer. If a hard frost threatens before plants are finished blooming in fall, cut the flower stalks and bring them indoors to enjoy.

Iris Terms

Irises come in a remarkable array of flower types and plant forms. There are three basic flower types, however: bearded, beardless, and crested. The plants can grow from widely spreading rhizomes or short rhizomes that produce grasslike clumps. Some irises also grow from bulbs.

Standards. The inner three petals of the flower. These usually point up or out and are quite showy.

Falls. The outer three petals of the flower. These usually spread out or hang down and feature a beard, crest, or signal near the base.

Beard. Bearded irises have a chenille-like strip of hairs at the top of the falls, running down the center. The beard can be the same color as the falls or a contrasting color. Bearded irises spread by thick, fleshy rhizomes that run near the soil surface.

Crest. Crested Irises have a crest or ridge at the base of each fall, running down the center. They spread by rhizomes.

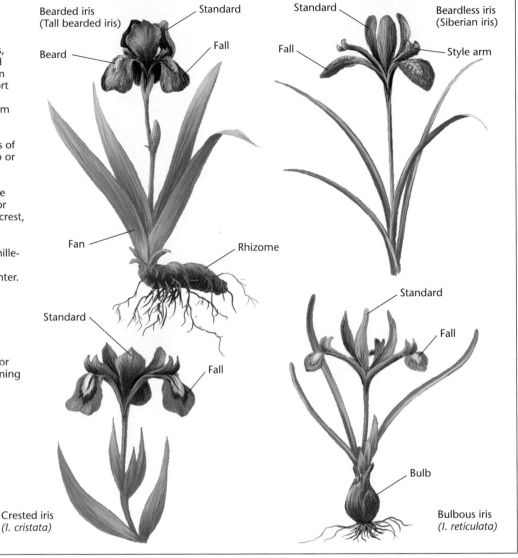

Bearded iris (Tall bearded iris) — Standard — Fall — Beard — Fan — Rhizome

Standard — Beardless iris (Siberian iris) — Fall — Style arm

Crested iris (*I. cristata*) — Standard — Fall

Bulbous iris (*I. reticulata*) — Standard — Fall — Bulb

There are hundreds of cultivars from which to choose, especially of tall bearded irises, and more are introduced every year. Flowers come in colors from white and pale yellow, through peach, pink, raspberry, bronze-red, lilac, purple, and violet-blue, to chocolate brown and red-black. The falls and standards may be the same color or contrasting solid colors, or they may have margins or mottling in contrasting colors — in purple and white, for example. The beards can be the same color as the falls or a contrasting hue. Many cultivars are fragrant. Obviously, deciding among them can be a wonderfully frustrating task. Select colors you like, or look for award-winning cultivars to try. Winners of the American Iris Society's Dykes Medal are all good cultivars, including 'Beverly Sills', 'Bride's Halo', 'Dusky Challenger', 'Edith Wolford', 'Honky Tonk Blues', 'Jessy's Song', 'Silverado', and 'Victoria Falls'. Since the plants need to be divided regularly, gardening friends and neighbors will likely have pieces to share, too.

Planting and Care. All the bearded irises require similar growing conditions. When planting them, select a site in full sun and average to rich, well-drained soil with a slightly acid to slightly alkaline pH. They have thick, fleshy rhizomes that grow on or near the soil surface and fibrous roots that descend into the soil below the rhizomes. They are hardy in Zones 3 to 9.

Plant bearded irises from midsummer to early fall. Loosen the soil before planting and amend it with organic matter such as compost. If the soil is especially poor, work in some well-rotted manure (dig it deeply into the soil, well away from the rhizomes) or a balanced organic fertilizer. Avoid using too much manure or high-nitrogen fertilizers, both of which promote foliage growth at the expense of flowers. Prepare a wide, 1- to 1½-foot-deep planting bed. For each rhizome, form a cone of soil in the bottom of the bed that reaches to the soil surface. Set the rhizome on top of the cone with its roots spread out on either side. The top of the rhizome should be just above

Bearded irises, such as this unnamed yellow-and-maroon-flowered beauty, can often be found at abandoned farmsteads.

Tall bearded iris 'Pale Yellow'

Dividing Iris Rhizomes

To divide irises with spreading rhizomes, such as bearded irises, use a sharp knife to cut the rhizomes into pieces with at least one fan of leaves. Destroy old, diseased, and borer-infested portions of the rhizomes. Replant with the tops of the rhizomes just above the soil surface.

the soil surface. Rhizomes planted too deeply are susceptible to rot. To create good-size, attractive-looking clumps quickly, arrange the rhizomes in groups of three or five, spacing the individual pieces 1 to 1½ feet apart (slightly closer for miniature and dwarf bearded types). Water plants regularly until they become established. Once established, the plants are quite drought tolerant.

Avoid mulching bearded irises, because mulch keeps the soil too damp around the rhizomes and can cause them to rot. The shallow rhizomes are easy to damage with weeding tools such as hoes, so hand weeding is best. Tall bearded cultivars may need staking. An annual fall cleanup helps control iris borers. Cut back the old foliage and destroy it. Also rake up any debris around the plants that may harbor the overwintering pupae.

Bearded irises spread vigorously by rhizomes and require regular division to perform at their

Tall bearded iris 'Cherry Sundae'

peak. Dig the clumps in midsummer or early fall—early fall is best in warmer zones. Dividing at least 2 months before the first fall frost date is advisable because it gives the divisions time to put down new roots before cold weather arrives. Poorly rooted divisions will heave out of the soil over winter. Inspect the clumps carefully for signs of iris borers (see "Potential Problems" on page 181 for information on dealing with these pests). Divide the rhizomes with a sharp knife, discarding spongy, old portions along with any rhizomes infested with fat, fleshy iris borer larvae (squash the larvae) or any that smell or are slimy, both signs of bacterial soft rot. Save plump, young sections of rhizome, each with at least one fan of leaves, for replanting. Cut the leaves back by two-thirds, then replant as you would new rhizomes. Water deeply to settle the plants in the soil and again every 10 to 14 days if the weather is dry. Shade them with upturned bushel baskets or

Tall bearded iris 'Keskimaki'

ABOVE Irises can also bring variegated foliage to the garden. This is *Iris pallida* 'Variegata', a bearded iris hardy in Zones 5 to 9. It is grown like other tall bearded irises.

RIGHT Japanese irises *(Iris ensata)* require plenty of moisture during the growing season but drier conditions over winter.

Japanese iris (*Iris ensata* 'Caprican Butterfly')

burlap for a few days if the weather is hot and sunny. To help keep newly transplanted irises from heaving out of the soil over winter, cover them with evergreen boughs, salt hay, or other loose mulch after the ground freezes in late fall. Newly divided clumps bloom sparingly the first year.

Irises for Sunny Beds and Borders

Bearded irises are obvious choices for sunny beds and borders, but several other easy-to-grow irises belong there as well. All of the species listed here thrive in full sun or light to partial shade and rich, well-drained soil that remains evenly moist. Several plants listed under "Irises for Moist to Wet Soil" below also can be grown in the rich, moist,

well-drained conditions of the average perennial bed or border, including *I. pseudacorus, I. versicolor,* and the Louisiana irises.

I. ensata. Japanese iris. Beardless, round, flat, 4- to 8-inch-wide flowers in early to midsummer; 2- to 2½-foot clump-forming plants with short rhizomes and grasslike leaves. The flowers can be single or double and have large, showy falls, with standards that point downward and come in violet-blue, purple, lavender-blue, white, rose-pink, and wine red. Grows in full sun or partial shade and very rich, acid soil—pH 5.5 to 6.5. (If you are growing Japanese irises near a lawn, keep lime, which is commonly spread on lawns to raise the soil pH, well away from the plants.) Requires constantly moist to even boggy soil in spring and summer when in active growth but needs drier conditions in winter. Space plants 9 to 12 inches apart. Divide clumps in early spring or early fall every 3 to 4 years. Mulch to keep the soil moist and cool, but do not pile mulch over the crowns of the plants. Disease and pest resistant. (Formerly *I. kaempferi*.) Zones 4 to 9.

I. sibirica. Siberian iris. Beardless, violet-blue, white, purple, or yellow, 3-inch-wide flowers in

early summer; 1- to 3-foot clump-forming plants with attractive grassy leaves. Many cultivars are available, including ones with bicolor blooms. Grows in full sun or light shade, although the foliage may be floppy in shade. Plants tolerate a wide range of soils and grow in poor, dry soil, but they are taller and more robust in evenly moist, well-drained or constantly wet conditions. They can be grown along the edges of a water garden with up to 2 inches of standing water over the crown of the plant. Space plants 9 to 12 inches apart. The clumps of grassy leaves have fibrous roots with very short rhizomes and resent being disturbed. Divide them in early spring or early fall, but only when they become so crowded that blooming is reduced or if the clumps die out in the center. Newly planted or divided clumps take a season or two to become established. Mulch the plants to keep the soil moist and cool, and feed annually in spring. Disease and pest resistant. Zones 2 to 9.

I. tectorum. Roof iris. Crested, 2- to 5-inch-wide flowers in lavender or white borne in late spring or early summer; 10- to 16-inch-tall plants. Full sun or partial shade in rich, evenly moist but well-drained soil. Also tolerates dry soil in shade. Spreads into broad clumps by fleshy rhizomes. Divide immediately after flowering every 3 to 5 years when clumps become overcrowded. Set the rhizomes so the tops just show above the soil surface, spacing them 6 to 12 inches apart. A good ground cover. Zones 5 to 9.

Irises for Moist to Wet Soil

All of the irises below can be grown in full sun in constantly moist soil or in standing water. Consider them for planting along a stream or water garden or in a low, boggy section of the lawn or a garden bed. In addition to these irises, *I. sibirica* and *I. ensata* can be grown in moist to wet sites.

Louisiana irises. These are hybrids derived from several native species that bloom from late spring to early summer and range in height from 1½ or 2 feet up to 5 feet. Flowers come in purple to blue-black, sky blue, vermilion red, and violet. Plants are grown much like Japanese irises (*I. ensata*) and require full sun or partial shade and very rich, constantly moist to wet soil with an acid pH. Unlike Japanese irises, which are clump formers, Louisianas have widely spreading rhizomes and need to be divided in late summer or early fall every few years to keep them in bounds. Their spreading habit makes them suitable tall ground covers for a wet site. Plant the rhizomes about 1 to 2 inches under the soil surface, spacing them 1 to 1½ feet apart. Never let the roots dry out during planting or transplanting. Louisianas are typically hardy in Zones 6 to 11, but hardiness varies depending on the cultivar, and some can be grown as far north as Zone 4 with winter protection.

I. pseudacorus. Yellow flag. Bright yellow, 2½-inch-wide flowers in early summer; 3- to 4-foot plants with sword-shaped leaves. Flowers have large falls and small standards. Plants spread

ABOVE Roof iris
(*Iris tectorum*) with
wild blue phlox
(*Phlox divaricata*)

RIGHT Yellow flag
(*Iris pseudacorus*)

steadily into broad clumps by creeping rhizomes but do not spread as fast as bearded irises. Grows in full sun or light shade in a wide range of soils, from evenly moist and well drained to constantly wet or boggy. Will grow with up to 10 inches of water over the crown. Space clumps 1 to 1½ feet apart and divide when they overgrow their space. Also tolerates drought, but plants are stunted in drier soil. Long lived and vigorous. Zones 4 to 9.

I. versicolor. Blue flag. Blue-violet or purple, 2- to 3-inch-wide flowers in early to midsummer; 2- to 2½-foot plants. Flowers have narrow falls and small standards. A native North American wildflower that requires acid soil. Zones 2 to 9. Southern blue flag (*I. virginica*) is a similar native species hardy in Zones 7 to 11. Space and divide both species as you would *I. pseudacorus*.

Bulbous Irises

Iris bulbs are commonly offered in fall alongside daffodils and tulips, and most are as easy to grow as other spring bulbs. Suppliers offer a mix of species, plus Dutch, English, and Spanish irises, which are groups of hybrids. All are grown in average to rich, well-drained soil in full sun or in a site that is sunny in spring but shaded in summer by deciduous trees. Like other spring bulbs, they bloom and then die back after flowering. Most require a warm spot with dry soil during their summer dormancy. Bulbous irises are frequently grown as annuals or short-lived perennials, especially in regions with wet summers, because they do not bloom reliably after the first year in many areas. Without their dry summer dormant period, the bulbs tend to produce many small, nonflowering-size bulblets. In good sites, though, these bulblets eventually reach flowering size.

Plant iris bulbs in late summer to early fall. Combine them with perennials that do not need watering in summer; a site along the top of a wall, in a raised bed, or in a rock garden also helps provide the hot, dry soil they require in summer. Another option is to lift the bulbs after the foliage ripens and store them in paper bags in a warm, dry, dark place over summer to give them the hot, dry ripening period characteristic of their native habitats. Or try potting the bulbs in sand and setting the pots in a hot place protected from rain (a cold frame works well). Sprinkle them with water once a month and replant in fall.

After they flower, feed them with a fertilizer high in phosphorus, such as bonemeal. The foliage remains green for several weeks, then gradually turns yellow and dies back. Let the leaves ripen naturally, because they need time to manufacture food for next year's flowers. Bulbs can be

Iris reticulata

tops a full 4 inches below the soil surface to discourage them from breaking into many bulblets that are too small to flower. They require warm, dry soil during summer when they are dormant. Zones 5 to 8.

I. histrioides. Violet-blue, 2½- to 3-inch-wide flowers in early spring; 4- to 6-inch plants. Classified as a reticulated iris because of the brown netlike covering on the bulbs. Best in rich, well-drained soil. Good for naturalizing but may break up into many small bulbs that take several years to achieve flowering size. Zones 4 to 9.

I. reticulata. Fragrant, 2-inch-wide flowers in late winter to early spring; 4- to 6-inch plants. Flowers come in shades from sky blue and violet-blue to red-purple. Grasslike, four-sided leaves. Good for naturalizing but may not return reliably in areas with hot, wet summers. Zones 3 to 8.

Dutch, English, and Spanish irises all belong to a group called the xiphium irises. All are hybrids, but English irises are thought to be hybrids of primarily *I. latifolia* (formerly *I. xiphioides*). *I. xiphium* played a major role in the development of Spanish and Dutch irises. Gardeners who want reliable bloom each year often grow these irises as annuals. All make excellent cut flowers, although cutting generally removes so much foliage that the plants won't return the following year.

Dutch and Spanish irises are similar, producing white, yellow, or violet flowers on 15- to 30-inch plants. They bloom from late spring to early summer; Spanish irises bloom about 3 weeks after Dutch cultivars. Give them full sun and a site with warm, dry soil during summer; they do not rebloom reliably in areas where they do not receive these conditions. To provide dry summer dormancy, cultivars of both groups can be dug after the foliage ripens and be replanted in fall. Zones 6 to 9.

dug in fall as necessary for transplanting or to divide the clumps.

Plant the species listed below 3 to 4 inches deep and 4 to 5 inches apart.

I. bucharica. Creamy white and yellow, 2- to 2½-inch-wide flowers in spring; 8- to 16-inch plants. This species belongs to a group called Juno irises, because it has bulbs with fleshy roots attached; handle them carefully at planting time (and when transplanting) to avoid breaking the brittle roots. Best for dry, well-drained spots in full sun and good for rock gardens. Zones 5 to 9.

I. danfordiae. Danford iris. Fragrant, yellow, 2-inch-wide flowers with brown spots in late winter or early spring; 3- to 6-inch plants. Classified as a reticulated iris because of the brown netlike covering on the bulbs. Plant the bulbs with the

ABOVE Crested iris
(Iris cristata)

RIGHT Pacific Coast iris
'Ami Royale'

English irises bear their 4- to 5-inch-wide flowers on 20-inch plants in midsummer in shades of violet-blue, purple, white, and lilac-rose. Grow them in full sun or partial shade with rich, well-drained soil that is constantly moist. They are difficult to accommodate in much of North America but are relatively easy in the Pacific Northwest and the Northeast. Where conditions suit them, they are longer lived than Dutch and Spanish irises. Zones 5 to 8.

Irises for Shade

Several species of iris can be used to add color to shady sites. Japanese iris *(I. ensata)* and roof iris *(I. tectorum)* are two species that can be grown in full sun or partial shade. Several species of bulbous iris can be grown in gardens that receive shade in summer but are in full sun in spring.

I. cristata. Crested iris. Pale to lavender-blue or white, $1\frac{1}{2}$- to 2-inch-wide flowers; spreading clumps of 4- to 8-inch-long straplike leaves. Grows in partial or full shade in evenly moist, well-drained soil rich in organic matter. Slightly acid soil pH is best. Spreads into broad mats by fleshy rhizomes near the soil surface. Early-spring planting is best. Space plants 4 to 6 inches apart with the tops of the rhizomes just showing above the soil surface. Divide the clumps in early spring if they become overcrowded or die out in the center. Good for rock gardens, woodland gardens, and wildflower gardens (it is a native species) or as a ground cover in shade. Zones 3 to 9.

I. foetidissima. Stinking iris. Grown for its showy fall seed heads, which have scarlet seeds, rather than for its dull purple flowers, which appear in early summer; 1- to 3-foot plants. Grows in partial or full shade in evenly moist, well-drained soil rich in organic matter. Space 1 foot

apart. Plants take two or more seasons to become established and form good-size clumps. Zones 7 to 9; to Zone 6 with winter protection.

Pacific Coast irises. These hybrids, developed from crosses with *I. douglasiana* and other West Coast natives, bear showy flowers in spring that resemble Siberian irises. The blooms have wide, ruffled falls, and standards come in an array of patterns and colors, including purple, violet-blue, white, yellow, and pink. The clump-forming plants range from $1\frac{1}{2}$ to 2 feet tall and have evergreen leaves that are strap shaped or grassy. Grow Pacific Coast irises in partial shade; in areas with cool summer temperatures they can be grown in full sun. They prefer rich, slightly acid soil that is well drained and require evenly moist soil in fall, winter, and spring, before blooms appear, followed by dry soil in summer, when many, but not all, cultivars appreciate a dry, dormant rest period. The cool Pacific Northwest is ideal for growing these irises, but they can be grown in other parts of the country, although they aren't suitable for areas with hot, wet summers. The rhizomes don't ship well and may be difficult to obtain in the East, where many gardeners resort to growing them from seeds. Plant in fall with the rhizomes about 1 inch below the soil surface, 6 to 10 inches apart. Feed them annually in spring with a balanced organic fertilizer. Water only every 2 to 3 weeks during summer if the weather is dry. Dig and divide the clumps in fall every 3 to 4 years. Pacific coast irises are hardy in Zones 7 to 9; to Zone 6 with winter protection.

PLANTING

The best time to plant, as well as the best site, is determined by the type of iris you are growing. All irises appreciate soil amended with organic matter, but too much manure or other fertilizer will yield irises that produce plenty of foliage but few flowers. See "Selecting Irises" on page 172 for specifics on the individual groups.

CARE THROUGH THE SEASON

Irises range from low- to high-maintenance plants. See "Bearded Irises" on page 172 for information on caring for these plants and the descriptions of the other irises in "Selecting Irises" for specifics on special care.

The herbaceous perennial irises benefit from at least one feeding a year in early spring as growth begins. Siberian and Japanese irises appreciate a second feeding just as the flowers fade. Beardeds do best with a second feeding in late summer. Feed bulbous species once a year as the flowers fade. Do not use a high-nitrogen fertilizer.

Deadheading faded flowers keeps the plants from spending energy on seed production but does not cause plants to rebloom. (Do not deadhead *I. foetidissima,* which is grown primarily for its showy seeds.)

Division. Most irises require regular division to look their best. See "Selecting Irises" for specifics on when plants need dividing. To divide plants that form clumps or that spread moderately by underground rhizomes — including Siberians, Japanese, and Louisianas — cut the foliage back by half to give a clear view of the crowns, and dig the clumps. Sever the crowns with a knife or sharp spade into sections with four to six fans each. Do not let the roots dry out before replanting, and set the rhizomes about 1 inch below the soil surface.

Propagation. Division is the easiest way to propagate most irises. Propagate bulbous species by separating and replanting the small bulblets. Iris species can be grown from seeds, but cultivars do not come true. To sow in fall, soak seeds in water for 24 hours and plant in pots set outdoors in a shady, protected location. To sow in spring, mix seeds with moistened peat moss in plastic bags. Store the bags in the refrigerator for 3 weeks to provide a moist, cool stratification period. Then sow in pots set outdoors in a protected location and keep them evenly moist.

Potential Problems. Borers and bacterial soft rot go hand in hand and are the biggest problems encountered by anyone who grows bearded irises.

The other irises are relatively problem free if grown in suitable sites, although they can be infested by borers as well. Good site selection — full sun and well-drained soil — and shallow rhizome planting help prevent problems with bearded types as well, as does an annual fall cleanup.

Borers are moth larvae that hatch on the leaves in spring and tunnel down through the fans to the rhizomes, where they grow into fat, pinkish, 2-inch-long larvae. The larvae eat out the centers of the rhizomes and leave wounds that commonly become infected with bacterial soft rot, which is characterized by smelly, slimy, rotted rhizomes. Watch iris leaves in spring for signs of tunneling borers and squash the larvae in the leaves between your thumb and forefinger. Dusting the rhizomes in spring with pyrethrin kills emerging larvae. Ragged, water-soaked leaves that fall at odd angles are signs of borer/rot problems. Dig the clumps and inspect the rhizomes. (Do this every time you divide irises as well, even if they do not show signs of disease.) Kill larvae you find, and discard diseased-looking rhizomes. It's best to replant only healthy, disease- and insect-free rhizomes, but if healthy rhizomes are at a premium, cut away all diseased growth and soak the pieces you can salvage in a 10 percent bleach solution (one part bleach to nine parts water) for half an hour, then dust the cut ends with sulfur before replanting.

LANDSCAPE USES

Irises are classic plants for beds and borders, where they will bloom with hardy geraniums, peonies (*Paeonia* spp.), bellflowers (*Campanula* spp.), and columbines (*Aquilegia* spp.). See "Selecting Irises" for other suggestions on where they can be incorporated in the garden.

Siberian iris
(*Iris sibirica* 'White Swirl')

Stinking iris
(*Iris foetidissima*) is grown for its showy fall fruit. It is named for its foliage, which has a fetid odor if crushed.

Kniphofia uvaria

Torch Lily

Kniphofia uvaria
■
(nih-FOE-fee-ah
you-VAIR-ee-ah)
■
Summer bloom
■
Full sun
■
Zones 5 to 9
■

■ The common names of _Kniphofia_—known as torch lily, red-hot poker, and poker plant—serve as a description of the flowers. The bold, tropical-looking flower clusters consist of densely packed, 1- to 2-inch-long, tubular flowers in fiery colors. Unopened buds at the tops of the clusters are darker in color—generally orange or orange-red—while open flowers turn yellow, giving the flowers a two-toned, hot-poker effect. Blooms are borne on erect spikes above clumps of grassy evergreen or deciduous leaves.

Common torch lily _(K. uvaria),_ hardy in Zones 5 to 9, is by far the most readily available, although there are some 70 species and many cultivars, some of which are becoming available in North America. It bears red-orange and yellow spikes atop 1- to 4-foot stalks. Although the leaves are evergreen, they aren't particularly showy in winter.

ABOVE Torch lily
(_Kniphofia uvaria_
'Robin Hood')

ABOVE RIGHT Torch lily
(_Kniphofia uvaria_)

SITE AND SOIL
Torch lilies require full sun for best bloom. Plant them in average to rich soil that is evenly moist but well drained. Well-drained conditions are especially important in winter. Plants do well in sandy soil.

PLANTING
Plant torch lilies in spring after loosening the soil to a depth of 1 to 2 feet and working in plenty of organic matter to ensure good soil drainage. The plants have thick rhizomes and fleshy roots, and the rhizomes should be set at a depth of no more than 2 to 3 inches. Space plants 2 feet apart.

CARE THROUGH THE SEASON
Torch lilies are easy to grow, provided they receive full sun and are planted in well-drained soil. Feed them with a balanced organic fertilizer in spring. Spread a layer of mulch around the plants to keep the soil evenly moist, but do not let it touch the clumps. To keep the plants neat looking, cut the flower stalks to the ground after the blooms fade. If the foliage becomes too unkempt looking, it can be cut back by half in late summer with no harm to the plants.

The plants can be marginally hardy in the colder portions of Zone 5 and may benefit from winter protection. (Experts differ on hardiness recommendations, and hardiness can vary depending on the conditions in a particular season. A wet fall followed by cold winter weather can kill plants any given year.) Try tying up the leaves over the crowns in late fall. Some gardeners mulch with salt hay or straw in addition to—or instead of—tying up the leaves. The roots can be lifted in fall and overwintered in damp sand, as dahlias are, but torch lilies perform best when left in the ground.

Division. Torch lilies can be left for years without needing division. The plants resent being disturbed, but they can be dug and divided in spring if they become crowded or outgrow their space. To make divisions without disturbing the plants, try severing offsets from the outside of the clumps in spring. Do not let the roots of divisions or offsets dry out before replanting them.

Propagation. Named cultivars do not come true from seed and should be propagated by division, but the species can be grown from seeds and even seeds from cultivars can yield plants with attractive flowers. Sow seeds in pots in early spring or fall and set them in a cold frame or a protected location outdoors. To sow indoors in winter, plant seeds in a soilless mix. Place the moistened, sown pots in the refrigerator for 6 weeks to help ensure even germination, although this treatment is not essential to success. Then germinate at 65° to 70°F.

LANDSCAPE USES
Use torch lilies as vertical accents among other summer-blooming perennials. Combine them with yarrows (_Achillea_ spp.), common sneezeweed _(Helenium autumnale),_ daylilies (_Hemerocallis_ spp.), and coneflowers (_Rudbeckia_ spp.).

Lavenders

Lavandula
- (lah-VAN-due-lah)
- Early- to midsummer bloom
- Full sun
- Zones 5 to 9

■ Common, or English, lavender *(Lavandula angustifolia)* is a favorite of herb and perennial gardeners alike. Not only are both flowers and foliage fragrant, the plants are attractive all year long. Lavenders are also fairly easy to please in the garden. In summer, the plants are covered with erect spikes of tiny lavender-purple flowers that are set off handsomely by the dense mounds of silver- to gray-green, needlelike leaves, which are evergreen. The main flush of bloom generally occurs in early to midsummer—from June into July—but plants often bloom intermittently thereafter. While lavender-purple is the most common flower color, blue-violet, pale pink, and white cultivars are also available.

Gardeners who haven't grown lavenders before may be surprised to find that the plants are actually shrubs or subshrubs rather than herbaceous perennials. Like other subshrubs, lavenders have a woody base and soft upper shoots. Common lavender, hardy in Zones 5 to 9, grows from 2 to 3 feet in height. Low-growing selections are also available—'Hidcote' and 'Munstead' both grow to only 1½ feet.

Spanish lavender *(L. stoechas)* is another popular species with flower spikes topped by showy, purple, petal-like bracts that resemble rabbit ears. It is grown like common lavender, but it is less hardy, from Zones 8 to 9. Lavandin *(L. ×*

Lavender (*Lavandula angustifolia* 'Old English')

intermedia) is a hybrid species resulting from a cross between common lavender and spike lavender *(L. latifolia)*. It is also grown like common lavender and is hardy in Zones 5 to 9.

SITE AND SOIL

Lavenders thrive in full sun—at least 6 hours per day is best. Although plants tolerate very light shade, they will be leggier and will bloom less than those grown in full sun. A south-facing site is ideal, and while good air circulation is beneficial (it helps prevent fungal diseases that mar the foliage), look for a spot protected from winter winds, especially in Zone 5 and the colder parts of Zone 6.

A site with well-drained soil is a must: wet soil is fatal. Given well-drained conditions, plants tolerate a range of soils from very poor, even gravelly, to humus rich. Moderately fertile soil is best. Lavenders are also flexible about soil pH, growing in slightly acid to alkaline conditions (pH 6.0 to 8.0). In areas with severe or wet winters, or in gardens with clay soils, plant lavenders in raised beds or along terraces built into a slope to ensure a well-drained root zone. Another option is to build low mounds of light, fast-draining soil right in a bed or border.

Lavenders in Containers

Lavenders make handsome container plants for a sunny deck or patio, and container culture is an ideal way to grow tender species, such as the striking *L. stoechas*. Use large pots (12-inch-diameter or more) or tubs that have plenty of holes for drainage. Fill with a coarse, fast-draining potting mix and keep the soil moist but not wet. Water monthly with a weak fertilizer such as fish emulsion.

Depending on where you live, container-grown plants can be overwintered outdoors or must be brought indoors in fall. In Zones 5 and 6, overwinter pots of common lavender indoors; in the coldest parts of Zone 7, insulate the pots with bags of leaves or bales of hay and leave them outdoors. Indoors, keep overwintered plants in a sunny, cool (40° to 50°F) spot.

Lavender (*Lavandula angustifolia* 'Munstead') with thrift (*Armeria maritima*)

PLANTING

Plant lavenders in spring or early fall; spring planting is advisable in the northern limits of the plants' hardiness. It's best to start with purchased plants rather than trying to grow lavenders from seeds. Space plants according to their height: full-size cultivars need 2½- to 3-foot spacing; dwarf types, considerably less, from 10 to 15 inches. Water plants thoroughly at planting time and keep the soil evenly moist, but not wet, until plants are established and growing well.

CARE THROUGH THE SEASON

Given full sun and well-drained soil, lavenders require only a minimum of care to keep them looking their best. Despite the common name "English lavender," *L. angustifolia* is native to the rocky, dry slopes of the Mediterranean region and thrives in heat and sun. Established plants don't need watering except during severe droughts. In the right site, lavenders are seldom troubled by pests or diseases. Leaf spot may disfigure the foliage in areas with humid summers or during especially rainy weather; adequate spacing and a site with good air circulation helps prevent this. In poorly drained soil, root rot is a problem.

Lavenders don't need annual fertilizing, but if plants aren't growing as vigorously as they should, spread a layer of compost or a balanced organic fertilizer around them in spring, keeping the compost or fertilizer away from plant stems. Avoid mulching lavenders unless your soil is very well drained. (If the rest of the garden is mulched, extend a light covering of mulch just inside the drip line for aesthetic purposes.) In the North, mulch around the plants to protect the roots after the soil freezes in fall, keeping the mulch away from plant stems. Also consider protecting plants from cold damage by covering them with cut evergreen boughs or even cornstalks in late fall. Remove the mulch in spring.

Many gardeners cut off spent flower spikes after the main flush of bloom in summer, but clipping individual spikes can be a tedious task. Using hedge shears is an efficient method of accomplishing this task, but that means sacrificing spikes that haven't yet bloomed. (Use a rake to remove sheared blooms.) Another approach is to gather a handful of spent blooms in one hand and clip them off all at once with pruning shears. Still another option is to simply leave the spent blooms on the plant.

Pruning. Without regular pruning, lavender plants become leggy and sprawl out from the center as they mature. Annual pruning prevents this, but pruning hard every few years works as well. Since light and air can penetrate the clumps, pruning encourages new, dense growth. Prune plants in spring, just as the new growth begins, or wait and prune in summer, either as part of the harvesting process or immediately after the main flush of bloom.

To prune plants that have sprawled (in this case the topmost branches cover up and eventually smother those buried beneath), shorten the center/topmost branches by cutting them back to just above new, upright shoots that arise near the center of the plant. Cut back all of the branches in graduated layers, shortening the center branches the most and the outer branches the least, and always cutting just above a new branch. (I always think of it as giving the plant a shag haircut as I do this.) The result is an even, layered mound of branches. For leggy plants that are still upright, shorten all the branches equally to maintain an even mound of foliage. For large plantings of lavender, hedge shears are the tool of choice for pruning—don't worry about making neat cuts above a branch; simply shear as you would a hedge. Gently rake off fallen branches.

Harvesting. For greatest fragrance, harvest the flower spikes just before the buds begin to open. (Cutting off the flowers encourages the plants to rebloom.) Cut spikes individually, bundle them in small bunches with a rubber band, and hang in a warm, dark place to dry. If you have large plants, combine harvesting with a mid-summer haircut by trimming off entire branches—flowers and all—and hanging them to dry. (See "Pruning" on the facing page for more on this technique.)

Propagation. Lavenders are easiest to propagate from cuttings taken in mid- to late summer, after the new shoots have stopped growing for the season and are firm but not hard or brittle. To make cuttings, break off 2- to 3-inch-long side shoots by pulling them downward so they come off with a small section of the parent branch, or heel, at the base. (Cuttings without a heel will also root, however.) Root them in damp sand in a shady spot—a shady cold frame is ideal.

Plants can also be propagated by division in spring or fall, but established plants resent disturbance and it's best to avoid dividing them. If you do divide, cut off divisions cleanly with pruning shears, handle them carefully, and replant them as soon as possible. Lavenders are slow and difficult from seeds, and cultivars do not come true, so propagation by cuttings or division is most common. If you do want to try growing lavenders from seeds, sow seeds in a moist, sterile medium and refrigerate the containers for 4 to 6 weeks for cold stratification. Then germinate them at 70°F, which takes 2 to 3 weeks.

LANDSCAPE USES

Lavenders are as at home in the herb garden as they are in the perennial border. Combine them with other summer-blooming perennials such as daylilies (*Hemerocallis* spp.), yarrows (*Achillea* spp.), and globe thistle (*Echinops ritro*). Shrub roses are also stunning combined with lavenders. For an effective textural contrast, pair lavenders with gray-leaved lamb's ears (*Stachys byzantina*) or with woolly thyme (*Thymus pseudolanuginosus*). Dwarf types make good edging plants and can also be used in traditional knot gardens or rock gardens. Both dwarf and full-size cultivars make attractive low hedges as well. Dwarf cultivars are especially effective as ground covers.

Liatris

Gayfeathers

Liatris
■
(lie-AH-triss)
■
Summer to early-fall bloom
■
Full sun
■
Zones 2 to 9
■

Gayfeathers bear tall, feather- or wandlike spikes of flowers that belie their membership in the aster family, Asteraceae. Gayfeathers don't have daisylike flowers with ray florets, or petals, like sunflowers and other aster-family plants do. Instead, their erect spikes are densely covered with buttonlike flower heads of disk florets, which produce the seeds. Despite the lack of petals, the spikes are quite showy: they have a fuzzy or feathery texture and come in pinkish purple, purple, mauve-purple, or white. An unusual characteristic of the spikes is that they open from the top down. The plants grow from corms or thick tuberous roots and have grasslike leaves at the base and up the stems. Unless otherwise noted, all of the species described below are hardy in Zones 3 to 9.

Also commonly called blazing stars or simply liatris, these easy-to-grow plants are native North American wildflowers. They are popular with birds, butterflies, and bees, and they make outstanding cut flowers as well. To use them this way, make a cut up through the base of the stem, remove any leaves that will be under the water, and condition them overnight before arranging. The blooms hold their color well when dried, too. Cut them when most of the flowers on the stalk have opened and hang them in a warm, dry, dark place.

Spike gayfeather (*Liatris spicata*) is the most commonly grown of the approximately 40 species in the genus. It bears erect spikes of pink-purple flowers from mid- to late summer. The plants are 2 to 5 feet tall, normally stand without staking, and bear 1- to 2½-foot-long flower spikes. Compact, mauve-violet-flowered 'Kobold', which is 2 to 2½ feet tall, is the best-known and most widely available cultivar.

Three species, all with pink-purple flowers from midsummer to early fall, are suitable for sites with dry, well-drained soil. Rough blazing star (*L. aspera*) reaches 3 to 6 feet and has 1-inch-wide flower clusters in spikes that can be 3 feet long. Dotted blazing star (*L. punctata*), hardy in Zones 2 to 8, is a compact 6- to 14-inch plant with small, ⅛-inch-wide flower heads in 6-inch-long spikes. Cylindrical blazing star

Spike gayfeather (*Liatris spicata*) with *Achillea* 'Coronation Gold'

Spike gayfeather
(Liatris spicata) with
pot marigolds
(Calendula officinalis)

(L. cylindracea) grows naturally in dry, alkaline soils. It ranges from 6 inches to 2 feet in height and bears 1-foot-long spikes of $^1/_8$-inch-wide flower heads.

Kansas gayfeather or prairie blazing star *(L. pycnostachya)* is a 3- to 5-foot plant with densely packed, 1- to $2^1/_2$-foot-long, mauve-purple flower spikes in midsummer. Tall gayfeather *(L. scariosa)* is a similar but shorter species that ranges from $2^1/_2$ to 3 feet in height. It produces pale purple, 1- to $1^1/_2$-foot-long spikes in late summer and early fall and is hardy in Zones 4 to 9.

SITE AND SOIL
Grow gayfeathers in full sun in average to rich soil that is well drained. If a full-sun site isn't available, try them in a spot that receives an hour or two of dappled shade in the morning or afternoon. Unlike the other species, *L. spicata* will grow well in evenly moist soil. In soil that is too damp, most other species will succumb to crown rot; well-drained conditions are especially important in winter. Established plants are quite drought tolerant.

PLANTING
Add gayfeathers to your garden by buying plants, starting seeds, or growing from the corms or tuberous roots. Plant in spring or early fall, setting corms $2^1/_2$ inches deep and tuberous roots 4 to 6 inches deep; set container-grown plants at the same depth at which they were growing in the nursery. Space plants 1 foot apart. Since gayfeathers can remain undisturbed for years, prepare the soil deeply and thoroughly at planting time. Dig in plenty of organic matter to ensure well-drained soil conditions.

CARE THROUGH THE SEASON
Gayfeathers are tough plants that require little maintenance. Mulch the plants with chopped leaves or compost to add organic matter to the soil and to control weeds. They don't need an annual spring feeding. Plants growing in soil that is too rich will require staking. Cut plants to the ground in fall, or leave them until early spring to give birds time to feed on the seeds. Divide clumps in early spring or fall only if they outgrow their space or die out in the center.

With gayfeathers, deadheading takes an unusual turn because the tops of the flower spikes can be cut off to remove the spent flower heads, leaving the fresh ones beneath them. (This sort of cleanup also makes cut blooms look more attractive in arrangements.) Deadheading is optional, though, and it doesn't encourage rebloom. One reason to avoid deadheading is that birds relish the seeds into winter.

Propagation. Propagate gayfeathers by dividing the clumps of corms or tuberous roots in early spring or fall or from seeds. Separate the corms with your fingers or cut apart the roots with a knife. Make sure each section has roots and at least one bud. Several cultivars, including 'Kobold' and those of the *L. spicata* Floristan Series, can be grown from seeds. (Plants propagated vegetatively, by division or corms, are more uniform.) Sow seeds in pots in fall or early spring and set the pots in a cold frame or a protected location outdoors. To sow indoors in winter, plant seeds in a soilless mix and place the moistened, sown pots in the refrigerator for 6 weeks to help ensure even germination, although this treatment is not essential to success. Then germinate at 65° to 70°F.

LANDSCAPE USES
Use gayfeathers in sunny beds and borders as well as in sunny meadows and wildflower plantings. They are most effective when planted in large clumps or drifts and add handsome vertical accents to many combinations. Try them with ornamental grasses, purple coneflower *(Echinacea purpurea)*, Russian sage *(Perovskia atriplicifolia)*, globe thistle *(Echinops ritro)*, and Shasta daisy *(Chrysanthemum × superbum)*.

Lilium

Lilies

■ Showy, exotic-looking lilies are among the most dramatic flowers grown in gardens. They bear blooms in a rainbow of colors, from fiery hues such as orange, red, hot pink, and yellow to pastel shades of pink, rose-red, cream, and

Lilium
■
(LIL-ee-um)
■
Summer to fall bloom
■
Full sun or partial shade
■
Zones 3 to 9
■

white. The flowers, which are usually borne in branched clusters, are carried on erect unbranched stems that arise from a bulb. They have six petals (correctly called tepals) and may point upward, outward, or down. Flower shapes vary as well: lily flowers can be flaring trumpets, star-shaped, cup- or bowl-shaped, or funnel- or bell-shaped. Recurved or reflexed blooms have petals that curve back from the center of the flower toward the stem. The leaves are narrow and lance-shaped or grassy and are borne up the stems. Lilies, which belong to the genus *Lilium*, are sometimes referred to as true lilies. That's because literally hundreds of plants share the common name, including daylilies (*Hemerocallis* spp.), lily-of-the-valley (*Convallaria majalis*), magic lilies (*Lycoris squamigera*), and trout lilies (*Erythronium* spp.).

Lilies make spectacular cut flowers. When cutting, select stems that have at least two buds that are opening and cut as short a stem as possible, to leave adequate foliage on the plants to support next year's flowers. Recut the stems under water. Lily flowers have six anthers that dangle on the ends of threadlike filaments. Some gardeners remove the anthers before bringing the flowers indoors, because they contain pollen that stains fabric. The anthers add considerable charm to the flowers, however, so instead of removing them, consider placing arrangements on washable surfaces, such as glass. Brush pollen off fabric or other surfaces with a dry sponge.

Lily bulbs differ in several respects from the bulbs of daffodils, tulips, and other spring bulbs. Daffodil and tulip bulbs are tunicate, meaning they are hard, onionlike bulbs with tightly packed layers of scales covering one another and a papery covering over the whole bulb. Lily bulbs consist of fleshy, overlapping scales that are attached at the base of the bulb but are loose at the top. They are more easily bruised or damaged by rough handling than tunicate bulbs. They also dry out easily and don't undergo the summer dormant period that makes daffodil and tulip bulbs so easy to ship and stock in garden centers in fall.

SELECTING LILIES
With a little planning, it's possible to fill the garden with a parade of lilies from early summer (mid- to late June) right through fall (October). Bloom peaks in midsummer, from July to August, in most areas. Today hybrids are grown more commonly than the species, although species lilies are still popular. Hybrid lilies are showy, vigorous, easy to grow, and resistant to common lily diseases, including the viruses that made garden lilies the sickly, problem-prone plants they were 50 years ago.

Asiatic Hybrid lilies line a walkway with bachelor's buttons and snapdragons.

ABOVE Asiatic lily 'Enchantment'

RIGHT Asiatic Hybrid lily 'Montreux' with *Astilbe* 'Montgomery', goldflame honeysuckle *(Lonicera heckrottii),* and smoke tree *(Cotinus coggygria* 'Purple Cloak')

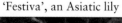
'Festiva', an Asiatic lily

As with any other large, heavily hybridized genus (*Iris* is another example), selecting among the different offerings and wading through the terminology can be confusing. There are about 100 species of lilies, numerous hybrid groups, and countless cultivars within those groups. The North American Lily Society has divided the hybrids into nine divisions based on the origin of the plants and the shape and position of the flowers. The divisions are often referred to in descriptions in catalogs and at garden centers.

Seven of the divisions plus some of the more popular species lilies are grouped below by bloom time. (Division VIII is reserved for hybrids between different divisions, and Division IX comprises all the true species lilies.) Note that, when possible, hybrid divisions are combined with the species from which they take their name. (*L. candidum* includes Candidum Hybrids, Division III, for example.) Expect bloom times to overlap — early-summer-blooming lilies won't be finished when the earliest midsummer bloomers begin. In addition, cultivars in each division can bloom at different times. Early- to midseason-blooming Asiatic lilies can flower in mid-June, late June, or July. That's all the better for gardeners, though, since planting three lilies that bloom at slightly different times in early summer adds color to the garden just as effectively as planting three that bloom at completely different seasons does. Catalogs or garden center displays should specify bloom time for individual cultivars.

Lilies for Early- to Midsummer Bloom
The following lilies generally bloom from mid-June to mid-July, but some cultivars can last as

late as August. Of the early-blooming lilies, the Asiatics are by far the most numerous and most commonly planted.

Asiatic Hybrids (Division I). These bear 4- to 6-inch-wide flowers on 2- to 5-foot-tall plants and are hybrids of several Asian species. Flowers can point upward, outward, or down and come in a wide range of colors, including orange, yellow, red, pink, purple, cream, and white. Blooms, which are not fragrant, can be a solid color or two-tone, and many have spots in contrasting colors. Asiatics seldom need staking and are vigorous, long-lived plants that form clumps in the right site — well-drained soil in full sun. Cultivars include 'Citronella', 'Connecticut King', 'Côte d'Azur', 'Enchantment', 'Fire King', 'Mont Blanc', and 'Montreux'. Mid-century and Harlequin hybrid lilies are Asiatics. Zones 3 to 8.

L. candidum. Madonna lily. Fragrant, waxy white, 2- to 3-inch-long flowers in clusters of 5 to 20 blooms; 3- to 6-foot plants. Candidum Hybrids (Division III) have 4- to 5-inch flowers in erect clusters on 3- to 4-foot plants. Blooms come in deep red, yellow-orange, and pale yellow to tan. Candidum Hybrids are not as common as Asiatics and Orientals; cultivars include 'Ares', 'Cascade', 'Prelude', and 'Zeus'. Nankeen lily (*L. × testaceum*), which has yellow-orange flowers, is also a Candidum. Unlike most lilies, *L. candidum* and Candidum Hybrids should be planted with no more than 1 inch of soil over the tops of the bulbs. When planted in fall, they will produce a low clump of evergreen leaves before winter. Grow in neutral to slightly alkaline soil. Long lived and easy to grow. Zones 4 to 9.

L. martagon. Turk's-cap lily. Nodding, purple-pink, 2-inch-wide flowers with recurved petals and dark spots; 3- to 6-foot plants. *L. martagon* var. *album* has white flowers. Martagon Hybrids (Division II) are also called Turk's-cap hybrids. These bear racemes of nodding, 3- to 4-inch recurved flowers on 3- to 6-foot plants. The species and many of the cultivars have an unpleasant scent. Martagon lilies include the Backhouse hybrids, among them 'Mrs. R.O. Backhouse', and the Paisley and Marhan hybrids. Grow *L. martagon* and the Martagon Hybrids in full sun or partial shade. They tolerate a wide range of well-drained soils, from acid to slightly alkaline. Zones 3 to 8.

American Hybrids (Division IV). A less well known group of early-season bloomers, these were developed by crossing a variety of native North American species, including the well-known Canada lily (*L. canadense*) as well as a number of West Coast natives. They bear clusters of 4- to 6-inch flowers that are recurved or sometimes funnel shaped. The 4- to 8-foot plants require acid soil rich in organic matter. Partial shade is best, especially during the hottest part of the day. The Bellingham hybrids, including yellow-orange 'Shuksan' and 'Buttercup', a yellow spotted with maroon, are examples. American Hybrids are hardy in Zones 5 to 8.

L. longiflorum. Easter lily. Fragrant, white, 7-inch-long trumpets; 1^1/$_2$- to 3^1/$_2$-foot plants. This species gave rise to the Longiflorum Hybrids (Division V). Although the species is not usually considered a garden plant—it is normally hardy only in Zones 7 to 9 and is grown primarily in pots—the cultivar 'Mount Everest' can be grown in Zones 5 to 8 and blooms early in the season. Grow in partial shade. Tolerates alkaline soil.

L. pumilum. Coral lily. Fragrant, recurved, 2-inch-wide, scarlet flowers; 1- to 2-foot plants. Full sun or partial shade. Requires acid soil. Bulbs are short lived, lasting only 2 to 4 years, but plants will self-sow. Deadheading prolongs the life of the bulbs, but leave some flowers to form seedpods. (Formerly *L. tenuifolium.*) Zones 3 to 7.

Turk's-cap lily
(*Lilium martagon*)

Lilies for Mid- to Late-Summer Bloom

The following lilies bloom during the peak of the lily season—from July into August.

Oriental Hybrids (Division VII). The Orientals are popular, showy, late-blooming hybrids with fragrant flowers that can reach 10 inches across. The blooms are typically bowl shaped, flat faced, or recurved, but trumpet-shaped Orientals have also been developed. White, pink, rose-red, and dark maroon-red are common colors; many cultivars feature flowers striped with yellow or spotted with red. Plants range from 2 to 8 feet tall, and the taller-growing ones generally require staking. Cultivars include 'Black Beauty', 'Casa Blanca', and 'Early Rose'. Zones 3 or 4 to 8.

ABOVE 'Imperial Pink', an Oriental Hybrid lily

ABOVE RIGHT 'Imperial Silver', an Oriental Hybrid lily

'African Queen', a Trumpet or Aurelian Hybrid lily

Trumpet and Aurelian Hybrids (Division VI). Many of the lilies in this division have classic trumpet-shaped blooms, but cultivars with bowl-shaped, flat-faced, or recurved blooms are also included in this division. The flowers, borne in clusters, are usually fragrant and generally face outward or are nodding. Colors include red, pink, gold, yellow, orange, and white; the flowers of some cultivars are purple-red, brown, or green on the back or outside. Plants range from 4 to 8 feet tall and nearly always require staking. Cultivars include 'African Queen', 'Black Dragon', 'Copper King', and the Golden Splendor Group. Zones 4 to 8.

L. canadense. Canada or meadow lily. Yellow-orange, 3-inch-wide flowers with slightly recurved petals and dark spots; 3- to 6-foot plants. A native North American wildflower. Grow in damp to evenly moist, acid soil in full sun or partial shade. Spreads to form broad clumps via rhizomatous bulbs. Zones 3 to 7.

L. henryi. Henry lily. Recurved, 2½- to 3-inch-wide, orange flowers in clusters; 3- to 10-foot plants. Grow in partial shade in neutral to alkaline soil. Plants require staking. Self-sows, and seedlings bloom in about 3 years. A parent of the Trumpet and Aurelian Hybrids (Division VI). Zones 4 to 8.

L. regale. Regal lily. Fragrant, 6-inch-long, trumpet-shaped flowers that are white inside and purple- to wine-colored on the outside; 2- to 6-foot plants. Vigorous and easy in a wide range of well-drained soils but will not grow in very alkaline conditions. Plants emerge early in spring and can be killed by late frosts. Cover emerging plants with bushel baskets or burlap if a late frost threatens. Overplanting with shallow-rooted perennials such as bellflowers (*Campanula* spp.), hardy geraniums (*Geranium* spp.), or catmint (*Nepeta* spp.) can also help. Self-sows, and seedlings begin blooming in about 2 years, so do not deadhead all the flowers to allow seeds to form. A parent of the Trumpet and Aurelian Hybrids (Division VI). Zones 3 to 8.

L. speciosum. Japanese lily. Fragrant, 7-inch-wide, pink or white flowers; 3- to 5½-foot plants. *L. speciosum* var. *rubrum* has deep pink flowers. A vigorous species requiring evenly moist but very well drained, acid soil that is rich in organic matter. Wet soil in winter leads to rot and death of the bulbs. Will grow in full sun or partial shade. One of the parents of the Oriental Hybrids. Susceptible to viral diseases, and has been largely replaced by the Oriental Hybrids. Zones 4 to 8.

L. superbum. American Turk's-cap lily. Orange-red, 3-inch-wide flowers with slightly recurved petals and dark spots; 4- to 8-foot plants. A native North American wildflower. Grow in damp to evenly moist, acid soil in full

LEFT 'Black Dragon', a Trumpet or Aurelian Hybrid lily

ABOVE A yellow Aurelian Hybrid lily

sun or partial shade. Established plants will tolerate drought. Spreads via rhizomatous bulbs. Zones 4 to 9.

Lilies for Late-Summer to Fall Bloom

Although the main display of lilies comes to a close in late summer, three species are worth considering because of their late-season bloom.

L. auratum. Goldband lily. Fragrant, white, 12-inch-wide, bowl-shaped flowers with a yellow stripe on each recurved petal; 2- to 5-foot plants. Blooms borne in clusters of a dozen or more beginning in mid- to late summer, generally August and September. Susceptible to various viral diseases. Requires well-drained, acid soil; wet soil in winter is fatal. A parent of the Oriental Hybrids. Zones 5 to 8.

L. formosanum. Formosa lily. White, 3- to 8-inch-long, trumpet-shaped flowers in late summer to midfall, generally late August or early September to October; 4- to 7-foot plants. Susceptible to viral diseases. Requires evenly moist, acid soil and spreads via rhizomatous bulbs. Plants are easy and fast from seeds sown indoors in midwinter; seedlings can begin blooming the first year from seed. Zones 5 to 9.

L. lancifolium. Tiger lily. Orange-red, 5- to 9-inch-wide flowers with dark purple-black spots; 3- to 5-foot plants. Grow in evenly moist, acid to slightly alkaline soil. Plants can be infected

Tiger lily *(Lilium lancifolium)*

with viral diseases without showing symptoms. To avoid spreading viral diseases to other lilies, buy certified virus-free bulbs. (Formerly *L. tigrinum*.) Zones 3 to 9.

SITE AND SOIL

In general, lilies require rich, evenly moist soil that is well drained to thrive. Soil pH tolerance varies; see "Selecting Lilies" on page 187 for preferences. While the plants need plenty of soil moisture during the growing season, they will rot if the soil remains too wet. Well-drained soil is essential in winter when the bulbs are dormant.

Like *Clematis* species, lilies like their heads in the sun and their feet in the shade. Plant them where the bulbs will be shaded by nearby, shallow-rooted perennials. While most lilies grow best in full sun, colors remain brightest and flowers last longest in a spot with shade during the hottest part of the day. Many lilies thrive in partial shade as well—see "Selecting Lilies" for individual preferences. Lilies that tolerate partial shade still need good light to bloom well: a site with morning sun and afternoon shade is ideal, but they can also be grown in bright dappled all-day shade.

Plant lilies in a site sheltered from strong winds. The plants are top heavy when in bloom and can be blown over or can break off at the base. For best results, prepare the soil before buying bulbs so you will be ready to plant them as soon as possible. Amend the soil with compost, leaf mold, or other organic matter over a wide area, to accommodate clumps of bulbs, and dig in amendments to a depth of 2 feet. Work in some very well rotted manure as you prepare the soil, but avoid using fresh manure. Or fertilize at planting time by incorporating a balanced organic fertilizer into the soil below the bulbs.

PLANTING

Lilies can be planted in early spring or fall. If you are ordering bulbs through the mail for fall planting, have them arrive about a month before the last fall frost date. That way the bulbs will have time to put down roots before the ground freezes.

Inspect lily bulbs carefully before you buy or before you accept a mail-order shipment. The bulbs should have plump, fleshy scales. Ideally, they should have fleshy roots attached to the bottom of the bulb, although some dealers cut off the roots before shipment. (Bulbs with roots generally recover from shipping and transplanting more quickly.) Reject bulbs that have dry, withered scales or roots, as well as any that show signs of rot or mold. Some garden centers offer clumps of potted lilies. Although you may have a more limited choice and potted plants are usually more

expensive than bulbs, potted lilies will get off to a fast start in the garden.

It's important to plant lily bulbs as soon as possible after they arrive or you bring them home from the garden center. Unlike hardy spring bulbs such as daffodils, lily bulbs are not completely dormant when they are shipped. The bulbs come packed in moist peat moss or other material; do not allow them to dry out before planting. If you can't plant right away, store the bulbs in the refrigerator or a dark, cool (40°F) place.

Planting depth varies depending on the size of the bulb and the type of bulb you are planting. In general, plant lily bulbs with the tops at a depth of two to three times the height of the bulb. That typically translates to a depth of 6 to 9 inches. Plant smaller bulbs slightly closer to the surface. Many lilies produce roots along the stem *above* the bulb, which help anchor the plant, and deep planting encourages this. (The soil in the bed is prepared much more deeply—to 2 feet—because lilies have roots below the bulbs as well, and deep digging encourages rich, well-drained soil.) *L. candidum* and *L. × testaceum* are the exceptions to this rule; plant them with only 1 inch of soil over the noses of the bulbs. Space bulbs 1 to 1½ feet apart and, for best effect, plant them in clumps of at least three to five. Mark the locations of the bulbs to avoid digging into them by accident.

CARE THROUGH THE SEASON

Once planted, many lilies thrive for years with only minimal care. Feed the plants with well-rotted manure or a balanced organic fertilizer in spring when new growth emerges. If you have access to fresh or only partially rotted manure, it can be applied in late fall, after the plants are dormant. (Keep fresh manure away from lily bulbs.) Taller lilies will require staking. Insert stakes in spring when the new growth is about 1 foot tall. Be careful not to pierce the bulbs when driving in the stakes. Tie the stems to the stakes loosely with soft yarn or strips of nylon stocking. Mulch the plants to control weeds and to keep the soil cool, but keep mulch away from the stems to prevent rotting. When plants are actively growing, water them deeply whenever the weather is dry.

Deadhead flowers as they fade. Letting the plants set seeds takes energy away from the bulbs and next year's flower display. Let species lilies set some seeds if you want to save the seeds or to let plants self-sow; hybrids generally don't come true from seed and can be propagated much more quickly by one of the vegetative techniques described below. Cut lily stalks to the ground in fall.

While some lilies are vigorous and long lived, others may persist for only a few years. Because

Asiatic lily 'Dreamland'

they are so showy, many gardeners happily replace short-lived selections. Vigorous lilies can be divided if the clumps outgrow their space or become overcrowded, a condition signaled by lots of stems but relatively few flowers. To divide lilies, dig the clumps in early spring or late summer to early fall. Be sure to dig very deeply around the edges of the clump to avoid slicing into the bulbs by mistake. Separate the bulbs and replant them as you would new bulbs. If you can't replant immediately, pack them in moist (not wet) peat moss and store them in a cool spot.

Propagation. Some lilies produce pea-sized, purple-black bulbils in the leaf axils; others produce small bulblets near the base of the stems, under the soil just above the bulbs. Both bulbils and bulblets offer an easy way to propagate lilies. Plant them in pots or in a nursery bed at a depth of two to three times their height. Lilies can also be propagated by division, as described above.

Scaling is another method used to propagate lilies. Dig up a bulb immediately after the flowers fade and pull off a few of the thick scales on the outside, near the base of the bulb. Replant the parent bulb. (You can also pull a scale or two off a newly purchased bulb.) Dust the scales with sulfur and plant them right away in a flat filled with moist, soilless mix. Plant the scales pointed end up. Cover the flat with a plastic bag suspended on a wire frame and set it in a shady, protected spot outdoors or a warm, bright place indoors out of direct light. Keep the medium moist but

not wet. In 6 to 8 weeks the scales should produce small bulblets at their bases, which can be potted up.

To grow lilies from seeds, plant seeds in pots in late summer or fall and set them in a protected place outdoors. Or sow indoors in midwinter; if no top growth appears within 4 weeks of sowing, place the pots in your refrigerator for 6 to 8 weeks. Then set them in a warm place. Most lilies take 3 to 6 years to reach flowering size when grown from seed.

Potential Problems. Stunted plants or leaves that are mottled with yellow indicate plants that are infected with viral diseases, which are spread by aphids. Dig and destroy infected plants. Control aphids with insecticidal soap. Providing good cultural conditions is the best way to prevent other problems.

LANDSCAPE USES

Lilies are perfect for planting in perennial beds and borders. Although their flowers are showy, when out of bloom the plants are not particularly attractive. They are effective when combined with other sun-loving perennials such as daylilies (*Hemerocallis* spp.), Siberian iris (*Iris sibirica*), bellflowers (*Campanula* spp.), and Shasta daisy (*Chrysanthemum* × *superbum*). In shadier sites, they are stunning with ferns, hostas, and lady's mantles (*Alchemilla* spp.) as well as with shrubs such as rhododendrons and azaleas. They can be combined with annuals in sun or in shade.

Asiatic lily 'Enchantment' adds brilliant orange color to this fiery-hued planting, which also features yellow goldenrod (*Solidago* spp.), scarlet bee balm *(Monarda didyma)*, orange butterfly weed *(Asclepias tuberosa)*, and yellow whorled loosestrife *(Lysimachia punctata)*.

_M_agnolia

Magnolias

Magnolia

■

(mag-NOLE-ee-ah)

■

Spring to early-summer bloom

■

Full sun or partial shade

■

Zones 4 to 9

■

■ Magnolias are shrubs or trees grown for their showy, often fragrant flowers. The first species to bloom grace gardens in early to midspring and open their flowers before or just as the new leaves appear — from February into March in the South, in April farther north. Later-blooming magnolias flower after the oval leaves emerge. Blooms can be saucer-, cup-, goblet-, or star-shaped and come in shades of pink, purple-pink, white, and creamy yellow. Although magnolias don't have attractive fall foliage, the flowers are followed in late summer by interesting conelike fruits with red berries. The leaves are oval and are often large and somewhat coarse looking.

If spring-flowering magnolias have one drawback, it's that their flowers open very early in the season and are frequently killed by late frosts. (The overwintering buds are hardy, but once they begin to show color, they can be killed by temperatures of 25° to 30°F.) On average, the flowers will be killed 1 year out of every 3 or 4, leaving a tree filled with limp, brown petals. Gardeners who love magnolias are willing to put up with this record, because the trees are truly spectacular the years they do bloom successfully.

SELECTING MAGNOLIAS

Several species of magnolia are small enough to accommodate in a garden or large shrub border. Others, including southern magnolia _(Magnolia grandiflora)_, which can reach 60 feet, are generally best used as a lawn specimen. Hardy in Zones 7 to 9, southern magnolia has evergreen leaves and bears large, fragrant, waxy white flowers intermittently from late spring to fall. The cultivar 'Little Gem' stays under 20 feet in height and can be used effectively for screen plantings and in shrub borders.

All of the species below except _M. virginiana_ bloom in early to midspring before the leaves emerge. Unless otherwise noted, they are hardy in Zones 5 to 9.

M. × loebneri. Loebner magnolia. Fragrant, star-shaped, 3- to 5-inch-wide flowers in white

or sometimes pink; 20- to 30-foot trees or large shrubs spreading to 20 feet. Several cultivars are outstanding. 'Ballerina', 15 to 20 feet tall, bears very fragrant white flowers with up to 30 petals that open slightly later than those of other selections and tend to escape late spring frosts. 'Leonard Messel' bears pink flowers. 'Merrill' has white flowers and has grown successfully in Zone 3. 'Spring Snow' bears white flowers slightly later than most and tends to escape late-spring frosts.

M. × *soulangiana.* Saucer magnolia. Fragrant, purple-pink or white, 3- to 6-inch, goblet- or tulip-shaped flowers; 20- to 30-foot trees or large shrubs spreading to 30 feet. Requires plenty of room. Begins blooming when plants are quite small. Many cultivars are available with pure white, pale pink, purple-pink, or rose-red blooms. Occasionally reblooms in late summer or fall after a wet summer. The silver-gray bark is attractive in winter.

M. stellata. Star magnolia. Fragrant, white, star-shaped, 3- to 4-inch flowers; 3- to 10-foot shrubs or small trees spreading 10 to 12 feet. Blooms of the species have 12 to 18 petals, but the cultivars 'Centennial' and 'Royal Star' have showier flowers with up to 30. Easy, versatile, and trouble free. Zones 4 to 8.

M. virginiana. Sweet bay. Lemon-scented, 2½-inch-wide, cup-shaped white flowers with yellow stamens from late spring to early summer; 10- to 60-foot multistemmed shrubs or trees spreading to 20 feet. Blooms in spring and early summer and often intermittently to fall. Attractive, silver-backed leaves. Plants are deciduous and only 10 to 20 feet tall in the North, evergreen to semievergreen and to 60 feet in the South. Grow in rich, acid, evenly moist soil in full sun or shade; this native North American species also thrives in wet or even swampy conditions. May be damaged during cold winters in the northern part of Zone 5.

SITE AND SOIL

Grow magnolias in full sun in rich, evenly moist, slightly acid to neutral soil. Most will tolerate partial shade; *M. virginiana* grows well in shade. For best results with early-spring-blooming species, select a protected site that will discourage the buds from opening too soon: a north-facing spot is ideal; a south-facing site encourages buds to open early. Since the large leaves can tear in heavy wind, a protected site is again best.

PLANTING

Magnolias have wide-ranging, fleshy roots with few lateral roots and no root hairs (most plants use root hairs to absorb minerals in the soil; magnolias depend on soil fungi for this process). For

ABOVE Star magnolia
(Magnolia stellata)

LEFT Sweet bay
(Magnolia virginiana)

this reason, they can be tricky to transplant and need special care for the first year or two afterward. Before planting, loosen the soil over a wide, deep planting area. Balled-and-burlapped (B&B) magnolias should be planted in early spring, before the leaves emerge; container-grown specimens can be planted in spring or summer. (In areas with mild winters, B&B magnolias can be planted in early fall as well.) Handle the plants carefully to avoid breaking any of the roots (B&B plants lose a substantial portion of their root system when they are dug). On container-grown plants, clip back any roots that have begun to circle around the bottom of the pot. Set the plants at the depth at which they were growing in the nursery or the pots and water thoroughly. Water newly transplanted specimens regularly for the first two growing seasons while they reestablish their root system. Plants that dry out, especially during the first summer, frequently die. Mulch the plants with compost, chopped leaves, or other organic matter to keep the soil moist and cool and to control weeds.

CARE THROUGH THE SEASON

Once they are established, magnolias need minimal care to look their best. Keep the area around the root zone mulched. It's best to keep lawn grass away from the base of the plants, since magnolias have thin bark and are easily damaged by lawn mowers and string trimmers.

Magnolias set their buds in summer for bloom the following season, so prune plants, if necessary, in summer immediately after they flower. (The large, often fuzzy flower buds are easy to spot at the tips of the branches in winter. If you pruned in spring, you would cut off the flower buds.) Generally magnolias require little pruning; just remove crossing and rubbing branches and any other wayward growth.

Propagation. While most gardeners buy trees and shrubs, magnolias are fairly easy to propagate. Take cuttings in early summer once the new flower buds have formed, and make a shallow, 1-inch-long slice with a sharp knife through the bark and into the wood at the base of each cutting. Dip the cuttings in a rooting hormone and stick them in a 50-50 mix of peat moss and perlite. *M.* × *loebneri* and *M. stellata* are easiest to root from cuttings. Magnolias can also be layered in early spring; see "Layering" in the Techniques Glossary for instructions. If the plant doesn't have a flexible stem that can be bent to the ground, cut the smallest stem available to the base of the plant in spring, and layer one of the stems that arise from the cut the following spring. Layers take a year to root. To grow magnolias from seeds, clean off the fleshy berry and plant the seeds in fall in pots set in a protected location outdoors. (Cultivars don't come true from seed.)

LANDSCAPE USES

Plant magnolias as specimens or accents, or use them in mixed plantings of shrubs and perennials. Spring-blooming species are attractive with azaleas and rhododendrons and can be underplanted with spring bulbs. Plant them along the edges of woodland gardens; they are especially stunning when in bloom if they are planted in front of evergreens. *M. virginiana* can be combined with ferns and hostas in shade gardens.

Crab Apples

Malus
■
(MAL-us)
■
Spring bloom
■
Full sun
■
Zones 4 or 5 to 8
■

■ Beloved for their abundant spring flowers, crab apples add color to the landscape during fall and winter as well, when the foliage drops and the showy fall fruit is revealed. The cup-shaped flowers, which are often fragrant, are borne in clusters and may be white or pale to deep pink. The flowers may be single, semidouble, or double. The plants have a two-tone effect when the flowers are opening, because the buds are one color and the flowers another — red or pink buds with white flowers is most common. From late summer onward, crab apples are covered with round red, orange-red, or yellow edible fruit that can range from $3/8$ to $1^1/2$ inches in diameter.

Birds and other wildlife relish crab apple fruits. If you want to feed birds, look for cultivars that feature small fruit — under $1/2$ inch in diameter at least, but $1/4$ to $1/3$ inch is better still be-

Crab apple 'Donald Wyman'

cause even small birds can fit the fruit in their mouths. Small-fruited crab apples may be hard to find, because most homeowners request large-fruited ones, but songbirds will appreciate the time you spend looking for them!

Crab apples are small trees—20 to 25 feet is about the average height at maturity, although some are hardly larger than shrubs and grow to only 10 to 12 feet tall. Most spread about as wide as they are tall and have a rounded habit. There are also weeping crab apples.

SELECTING CRAB APPLES

Like many popular plants, crab apples have been heavily hybridized, and improved cultivars are much more likely to be found in gardens than the species. In addition to looking for showy flowers, colorful fruit, and attractive habits, hybridizers have selected for disease resistance, and today a host of disease-resistant crab apples are available. These are your best bet for overall performance and low maintenance. (Crab apples are related to apples and are susceptible to several serious apple diseases, including fire blight, cedar-apple rust, and apple scab. See "Potential Problems" on page 198 for more on these diseases, as well as simple cultural controls.)

Before selecting a crab apple, it's a good idea to talk to your local Cooperative Extension Service or consult with experts at nearby nurseries or botanical gardens. New disease-resistant selections are being introduced annually. Local recommendations also are valuable because some diseases are more serious than others in different parts of North America.

The following are some of the disease-resistant crab apples available. Unless otherwise noted, all have persistent fruit that holds on the trees well into winter. All are hardy in Zones 5 to 8, and most will grow in the warmer portions of Zone 4 as well. Although older crab apple selections sometimes flower every other year, these all provide reliable annual bloom.

'Adams'. Red buds, deep pink flowers; red, $1/2$- to $5/8$-inch fruit; 25-foot tree.

'Adirondack'. Red buds, white flowers; red to orange-red, $1/2$-inch fruit; 12-foot tree.

'Angel Choir'. Pale pink buds, double white flowers; red, $3/8$-inch fruit; 12-foot tree.

'Autumn Glory'. Red buds, white flowers; orange-red, $1/4$-inch fruit; 12-foot tree.

'Baskatong'. Purple-red buds and flowers, which fade to pink; 1-inch, red-purple fruit that falls early; 25- to 30-foot tree. Hardy to Zone 3; a good choice for northern gardens.

'Callaway'. Pink buds, white flowers; persistent, maroon-red, $3/4$- to $11/4$-inch fruit; 15- to 25-foot tree. A good choice for southern gardens.

Flowering crab apples are small to medium-size trees with spring flowers and handsome fall fruit.

'Centurion' ('Centzam'). Red buds, rose-red flowers; $5/8$-inch, bright red fruit; columnar, 25-foot tree.

'Color Parade'. Red buds, white flowers; red, $1/2$-inch fruit; 10- to 12-foot tree with semiweeping habit.

'Coral Cascade'. Coral-red buds, white flowers; coral-orange, $3/8$-inch fruit; 15-foot tree with semiweeping habit.

'Donald Wyman'. Red to pink buds, white flowers; $3/8$-inch, red fruit; 20- to 25-foot tree.

'Firebrand'. Red buds, white flowers; brilliant red, $1/4$-inch fruit; 14-foot tree.

'Golden Dream'. Red buds, white flowers; yellow-gold, $1/4$- to $1/3$-inch fruit; 12-foot tree.

'Harvest Gold' ('Hargozam'). Pink buds, white flowers; $3/8$-inch golden fruit; 20-foot tree.

'Little Troll'. Red buds, white flowers; orange-red, $1/3$-inch fruit; 16-foot tree with weeping habit.

'Molten Lava' ('Molazam'). Red buds, white flowers; red-orange, $3/8$-inch fruit; 15-foot tree with weeping, spreading habit.

'Peter Pan'. Red buds, white flowers; red, $1/4$-inch fruit; 14-foot tree.

'Prairifire'. Red buds, pinkish red flowers; red-purple, $3/8$-inch fruit; 20-foot tree.

'Professor Sprenger'. Pink buds, white flowers; red-orange, $1/2$-inch fruit; 25-foot tree.

'Sugar Tyme' ('Sutyzam'). Pink buds, white flowers; red, $1/2$-inch fruit; 18-foot tree.

SITE AND SOIL

Plant crab apples in full sun to ensure a good display of flowers and fruit. Soil should be average to rich and well drained yet evenly moist: crab apples will not tolerate wet soil. Although slightly acid pH is best, they tolerate a wide range, from quite acid to slightly alkaline (pH 4.0 to 7.5).

Crab apple leaves and fruit (*Malus* 'Profusion')

PLANTING

Plant container-grown or balled-and-burlapped crab apples in spring or early fall. Plant bare-root specimens in early spring while they are still dormant. To prepare a site for planting, loosen the soil over a wide, fairly shallow planting area. Ideally, the site should be large enough to encompass the eventual spread of the plant's branches. Do not amend the soil with compost or other organic matter unless you do it over a large planting area—see "Planting" on page 274 in the **Shrubs** entry for details. When planting bare-root trees, soak the roots in a bucket of water for about 2 hours before planting. Then spread the roots over a cone of soil in the hole, fill, and flood the site with water to eliminate any air pockets. Be sure to plant any crab apple at the same depth at which the tree was growing in the nursery. Mulch the area—it's best to keep lawn grass away from the tree to reduce competition and to protect the trunk from mower damage. Water regularly during the first season.

CARE THROUGH THE SEASON

Crab apples need minimal pruning or other care to look their best. Established plants are quite drought tolerant.

Pruning. Prune plants, if necessary, in late winter or early spring. Because crab apple trees don't need to bear the heavy fruit load that full-size apple trees do, they don't require the extensive pruning and training that makes an apple tree capable of bearing several tons of fruit. Remove rubbing and crossing branches along with any deadwood. Also prune out any new growth that is growing in the wrong direction—toward a branch that it will rub against or toward an overly congested part of the center of the tree. Remove water sprouts, which are overly vigorous shoots that grow straight up and seldom bloom. Also remove suckers that arise around the trunk. (Crab apples are frequently grafted onto a rootstock, and suckers that arise below the graft union will not resemble the tree and likely will overtake it. They are also unattractive.)

Old, overgrown crab apples can tolerate fairly severe pruning to rejuvenate them or to reduce their size. Remove all deadwood and water sprouts first, then cut back some of the older branches just above a side branch that points to the outside of the plant. If the tree needs more growth in the center, prune above an inward-pointing branch. Also remove some branches by cutting them off at the base where they arise from a larger branch or the trunk of the tree. Be sure to make a proper pruning cut—see "Pruning" in the Techniques Glossary for instructions. Feed rejuvenated plants with a balanced organic fertilizer and water them during dry weather for the first season.

Propagation. Crab apples generally are not propagated from seeds, because many do not produce viable seeds and hybrids do not come true. Most hybrids are grafted or budded, but they can be propagated by cuttings. See "Rooting Cuttings" in the Techniques Glossary for details on how to do this. Seed for the species can be sown outdoors in fall.

Potential Problems. Crab apples do not require the elaborate spray schedules that apples do, because their fruit does not have to be edible. When planting a new crab apple, the best thing to do to prevent problems is to select a disease-resistant one. Good culture helps control problems on even disease-susceptible crabs. Vigorous plants resist most pest problems. Mulch around the trunks to keep the soil moist, and keep lawn mowers at bay, as fungi that cause cankers can enter wounds in the trunk. If scale or aphids have been a problem, spray with dormant oil in late winter as the buds begin to swell.

Here are suggestions on controlling the three major diseases that may attack crab apples.

Shoots that die suddenly and have blackened leaves that hang on the tree are a sign of fire blight. Prune off afflicted shoots 6 inches below the point where signs of the disease appear. Destroy or discard the prunings and sterilize saws or pruners with alcohol between cuts to avoid spreading the disease.

Plants that have leaves and fruit with dark spots and cracked fruit are infected with apple scab, a fungal disease that overwinters on the leaves. An annual fall cleanup to remove leaves and dropped fruit helps control the disease. Compost the leaves away from the trees or bury them.

Crab apples growing near junipers (*Juniperus virginiana, J. horizontalis,* or *J. scopulorum*) can develop cedar-apple rust, which causes orange galls on the junipers and yellow to orange spots on crab apple leaves and fruits. Afflicted leaves and fruit drop prematurely. Keeping junipers at least 500 feet away from crab apples and planting resistant crab apples are the best controls.

LANDSCAPE USES

Although commonly planted as lawn or street trees, crab apples are frequently overlooked when it comes to planning a perennial or shrub border. Smaller crab apples are attractive large plants for the back of a perennial border and add two seasons of color to shrub borders. Or consider planting a pair of crab apples in a formal arrangement or a specimen to anchor one end of a perennial border. Underplant crab apples with spring bulbs, wildflowers, or ground covers.

Monarda

Bee Balms

Monarda
■
(moe-NAR-dah)
■
Summer bloom
■
Full sun or light shade
■
Zones 3 to 9
■

■ Also called bergamots and horsemints, bee balms feature fragrant foliage and showy, ragged-looking clusters of two-lipped, tube-shaped flowers. The flowers, particularly the red forms, are popular with hummingbirds. All bee balms are native North American wildflowers. Like many members of the mint family (Lamiaceae), they have square stems and spread by fast-creeping rhizomes to form broad clumps.

The flowers are attractive in fresh arrangements and also hold their color fairly well when dried. For fresh or dry use, cut the flowers when they have just opened. To dry, hang them in a warm, dark place.

Monarda didyma, also called Oswego tea, is by far the most popular species. Hardy in Zones 4 to 8, it bears scarlet, maroon, red-violet, or pink flowers. While plants are generally about 3 feet tall, they can range from 2 to 4 feet, with rich, moist soils yielding the tallest plants. One drawback of this species is its susceptibility to powdery mildew, which destroys the appearance of the plants but seldom kills them. (Afflicted plants have large white blotches on the leaves and eventually drop their leaves.) Hybridizers have developed several mildew-resistant cultivars, including red-flowered 'Jacob Cline', pink 'Marshall's Delight', and lilac-purple 'Prairie Night' ('Prärienacht'). 'Petite Delight' is mildew resistant and reaches only 12 to 15 inches in height. Popular 'Cambridge Scarlet' is quite vigorous but is not mildew resistant.

Wild bergamot *(M. fistulosa),* hardy in Zones 3 to 9, is a 3- to 5-foot species with lavender-

ABOVE Bee balm (*Monarda didyma* 'Cambridge Scarlet')

RIGHT Bee balm (*Monarda didyma* Panorama hybrid)

pink flowers that is less susceptible to mildew. Although best used in wild gardens, this species has been crossed with *M. didyma* to produce mildew-resistant cultivars.

SITE AND SOIL

Bee balms thrive in full sun but tolerate light shade. *M. didyma* requires evenly moist, well-drained soil that is rich in organic matter. Plants should never be allowed to dry out during the growing season if they are to look their best. *M. fistulosa* tolerates drier conditions and grows in average to rich soil. To help combat powdery mildew, select a site with good air circulation.

PLANTING

Plant bee balms in either spring or early fall. Space plants 1 to 2 feet apart to accommodate their spread. Planting in a bucket with the bottom removed and sunk to the rim in the soil can help contain spreading.

CARE THROUGH THE SEASON

Bee balms are easy to grow and require very little care to look their best. The plants seldom need staking, unless they are growing in very rich soil. Removing spent flower heads regularly encourages plants to rebloom. A look down the stems will reveal new stems and flowers forming in the leaf nodes; cut just above the nodes.

Dividing the clumps to control their spread is the most crucial task that growers of bee balms face. The plants can be aggressive spreaders, especially in rich, moist soil. Regular division also keeps the plants growing and blooming vigorously. Dig the clumps in spring or early fall every 2 to 3 years to keep them in bounds. Discard the older portions of the clump and replant or give away the rest.

Propagation. Division is the easiest way to propagate bee balms, but they can also be grown from cuttings taken in spring from stems that arise at the base of the plant. Root them in a 50-50 mix of perlite and vermiculite. Most cultivars do not come true from seed, but Panorama Mix is an exception. Sow its seeds in pots in spring or fall, and set the pots in a protected location or in a cold frame.

LANDSCAPE USES

Grow bee balms in sunny beds and borders, and combine them with other summer-blooming plants such as lilies (*Lilium* spp.), hardy geraniums, and summer daisies (*Chrysanthemum* spp.). Bee balms are also traditionally included in herb gardens: the dried leaves can be used to make a citrusy-tasting tea. The flowers are edible and are pretty when added fresh to salads.

Narcissus

Daffodils

Narcissus
■
(nar-SIS-us)
■
Spring bloom
■
Full sun or partial shade
■
Zones 4 to 9
■

■ Daffodils mark the coming of spring long before their blooms decorate the garden. The tips of their strap-shaped leaves poke above the soil surface in winter, generally after a spell of mild weather. The flowers are not far behind. The earliest daffodils begin blooming in late winter, especially in protected sites; blooming commences in late January or early February in the South, about a month later in the North. The flowers consist of a central corona (which is called a trumpet if it is long and a cup if it is short) surrounded by six petals (more properly called perianth segments) that are collectively called the perianth. Flowers can be single or double and are borne one per stem or in clusters of up to 20.

Daffodil 'Fortissimo'

While all *Narcissus* species are commonly called daffodils, dwarf daffodils with small cups are sometimes referred to as jonquils.

Although nearly everyone is familiar with golden yellow trumpet daffodils, the wide range of daffodil shapes, sizes, and even colors comes as something of a surprise to many gardeners. Yellow, orange, and white are the most common colors, but there are also pink daffodils. (These generally emerge yellow and turn pink as they mature.) Many offerings feature bicolor blooms—a yellow perianth with an orange cup or trumpet, for example. Bloom season varies, too, and cultivars are generally rated as early-, midseason-, or late-blooming. By planting some that fall into each category, it's possible to have daffodils in bloom for 3 months or more in spring.

It goes without saying that daffodils make fine cut flowers. For best performance, pick the blooms when they are about half open. (Picking is better than cutting the stems.) Make a slit an inch or two up the stems and run them under warm water for a few minutes. This reduces the amount of sticky sap that flows out. Then put them in water up to their necks for several hours for conditioning before arranging them. Always condition daffodils separately from other flowers, because the thick sap can clog stems.

SELECTING DAFFODILS

There are about 50 species of daffodils and thousands of cultivars, which are much more commonly grown in gardens today than the species. Daffodils have been divided into 12 divisions based on flower shape and origin, and catalogs and well-labeled nursery displays refer to these divisions when describing their offerings. (Mail-order catalogs offer the widest variety of choices.) While you don't need to know the names of the divisions, knowing they exist will help you make good choices. If you select cultivars from several different divisions, you'll be assured of an interesting variety of flower shapes and sizes, for example. Most full-size daffodils are 3½ to 4½ inches across, but there are tiny 1½-inch-wide selections. Plant size varies, too. Full-size daffodils are usually 18 inches tall, but there are tiny miniatures that range from 4 to 6 inches in height.

In addition, cultivars in the different divisions tend to bloom at similar times, so varying your selections also helps to extend the bloom season. (Keep in mind that bloom season should be indicated for each cultivar offered in a catalog or at a nursery, because it is variable.) While most daffodils are hardy from Zones 4 to 8 (Zone 3 with protection), hardiness varies from cultivar to cultivar, too. Reputable firms will indicate the hardiness of their offerings; be suspicious of any that

Daffodils for Early Bloom

If you are in the race to have early color in the garden, buy Trumpet Daffodils (Division I) and Cyclamineus Daffodils (Division VI). Cultivars such as 'February Gold', 'February Silver', 'Jetfire', 'Jumblie', 'Minnow', and 'Tête-à-Tête' are also early blooming. A warm, south-facing site (where the snow melts first) will yield the earliest flowers.

say they're all the same. (Paperwhites, *N. papyraceus*, commonly sold for forcing, are hardy only in Zones 8 and 9. They can be forced into bloom in trays of pebbles and water, but if you live in the South and want to plant the bulbs outdoors after forcing, pot them in soil. See "Forcing Hardy Spring Bulbs" on page 56 for details.)

When you buy bulbs, avoid bargain-basement offers. Cheap usually means cheap. Landscape-size or "round" bulbs are 3 years old and produce one or more flower stems the first year. They are the least expensive and generally are a good buy. Double-nose or bedding-size bulbs are 4 years old and typically will produce two flower stems the first year. Exhibition-size or triple-nose bulbs are 5 years old and produce three or more

Daffodil 'Thalia'

Daffodils for Fragrance

Many daffodils feature delicious fragrance as a bonus. All of the following bloom in mid- to late season. Triandrus Daffodils (Division V), hardy in Zones 4 to 9, bear two or more nodding flowers per stem with reflexed (backward-pointing) petals. They generally have a fruity fragrance. Jonquilla Daffodils (Division VII) and Tazetta Daffodils (Division VIII) also bear several flowers per stem. Jonquillas have a sweet fragrance; Tazettas are musky sweet. Both groups can be grown in Zones 5 to 9. Poeticus Daffodils (Division IX) bear one flower per stem and feature a spicy-sweet fragrance. The flowers look something like dogwood flowers and have very small cups.

Daffodil 'Salomé', which has a cup that opens apricot-yellow and matures to pale pink, with Lenten roses (*Helleborus × hybridus*)

flower stems. (I ususally break apart double- and triple-nose bulbs and space them out when I plant, because it delays the time when they'll need dividing. Although this yields larger drifts, expect a somewhat sparser display for a season or two until the bulbs are established.) One way you can really save money on daffodils is by buying in bulk or by buying collections. See "Buying Bargain Bulbs" on page 54 for suggestions on filling your garden at great prices.

SITE AND SOIL
Plant daffodils in full sun or partial shade. A site shaded by deciduous trees is fine because it provides spring sunshine while the leaves are ripening, and shade isn't a problem once the plants are dormant. Well-drained soil is essential: the bulbs

of nearly all daffodils rot in damp soil. (Unlike other daffodils, *N. poeticus* and its cultivars tolerate moist to wet soil in winter and spring and fairly damp conditions in summer. Try them in waterside sites, but keep the bulbs well above the water line.) Beyond that, though, daffodils aren't particular. They'll grow in sandy to loamy soil and tolerate acid to alkaline conditions (pH 5.0 to 8.0), although slightly acid soil is best. Ideally, the soil should be evenly moist from fall to spring and drier during summer, but plants generally bloom well despite dry soil in spring.

If you have heavy, wet soil, dig in lots of organic matter such as compost or leaf mold to improve drainage. In this case, planting on the shallow side is best. Planting in raised beds filled with improved soil is another option for dealing with heavy clay and poorly drained sites.

One thing to keep in mind when siting daffodils is that the trumpets will face toward where they receive the most sun. That's generally south or west. (Daffodils outside my kitchen window generally face east, because they receive morning sun and are shaded by the house in the afternoon.) Although it's not always possible, try to plant so the fronts of the flowers will be facing the house or pathways you frequent in spring.

PLANTING
Plant daffodil bulbs in fall. Early planting is best, because it gives the bulbs time to grow roots before cold weather arrives. Adjust planting depth according to the size of the bulbs, which varies among species and cultivars. Plant two to three times as deep as the bulbs are tall, generally with the shoulder of the bulb (the point where it swells out from the nose, or top) 4 to 6 inches below the soil surface. The bulbs of full-size species and cultivars are larger and need to be set more deeply than miniatures, which can have very small bulbs. Space large hybrids 6 to 10 inches apart; miniatures, slightly closer. Bulbs planted at the wider spacing will look sparse at first, but they will fill in and will need dividing less frequently. See "Planting" on page 52 of the **Bulbs** entry for more information.

CARE THROUGH THE SEASON
Like other spring bulbs, daffodils need minimal care once they are planted. The plants will survive just fine without watering, but if the weather is unusually dry in spring or fall, weekly watering ($1/2$ inch per week) is beneficial. Let the leaves ripen for 6 to 8 weeks after the flowers fade so they can make food to support next year's flowers. For complete information on caring for daffodils and other spring bulbs, as well as on using them in the landscape, see **Bulbs** on page 52.

Nepeta

Catmints

- *Nepeta*
- (NEP-uh-tah)
- Spring to fall bloom
- Full sun or light shade
- Zones 3 to 9

Tough and easy to grow, catmints are mounding perennials with aromatic, gray-green leaves and showy spikes of small, two-lipped lavender, purple, violet, or white flowers. Catnip *(Nepeta cataria)* is the member of the clan that has an intoxicating effect on cats. Commonly grown in herb gardens, it has a long history as a medicinal and tea herb but is not especially ornamental. Plants reach 3 feet in height and bear dense spikes of whitish flowers. Catmints, which are popular in flower gardens, have less effect on cats.

N. × *faassenii* is a 1½-foot-tall hybrid with lavender-blue flowers. White-flowered cultivars are also available. It begins blooming in early summer — spring in the South. If the plants are cut back hard after the first flush of flowers, they will rebloom until early fall. The plants grown in gardens as *N. mussinii,* sometimes called Persian catmint, are now thought to belong to *N.* × *faassenii.* 'Six Hills Giant' reaches 3 feet in height and bears showy spikes of violet-purple flowers. All are hardy in Zones 4 to 8; to Zone 3 with winter protection. *N. sibirica* is a 3-foot-tall species with lavender-blue flowers in summer and is hardy in Zones 3 to 9.

Catmint
(Nepeta × *faassenii)*

SITE AND SOIL

Grow catmints in full sun or light shade. They require well-drained average soil and thrive in drier sites than many commonly grown perennials will tolerate. Damp soil leads to crown rot and death.

PLANTING

Plant catmints in either spring or fall. Since they grow best in sites with average soil that is well drained but not too rich in nutrients, do not work manure into the soil before planting. Incorporating compost or leaf mold will add organic matter and improve soil drainage without adding an abundance of nutrients.

CARE THROUGH THE SEASON

Once planted, catmints are easy to satisfy. They do not require watering or an annual feeding, although a spring topdressing of compost or chopped leaves adds organic matter and some nutrients to the soil. Taller-growing selections may need staking — pea brush is effective (see "Staking" in the Techniques Glossary for details). The plants can also be allowed to flop. Shear the plants back hard — by one-third to two-thirds — after the main flush of flowers fade. (I generally wait until after dark to do this, because the flowers are very popular with bees, and the bees will have gone to bed by that time.) Sheared plants will produce fresh new foliage and rebloom until frost. Catmints don't need dividing regularly. Dig the clumps for propagation, if they outgrow their site, or if they begin to look less vigorous. They can be short lived in the South.

Propagation. Propagate catmints by digging the clumps in early spring or fall and dividing them. Or take cuttings in summer and root them in a 50-50 mix of vermiculite and perlite. Stem tips also root and can be potted up or moved to a new site. *N. cataria* can be grown from seeds, and it self-sows with abandon unless deadheaded, but none of the commonly grown ornamentals come true from seed, so propagate them vegetatively by cuttings or division.

LANDSCAPE USES

Catmints make stunning edging plants along beds and borders or walkways. (Since they are attractive to bees, set them back from the path a bit so you can walk past them without brushing the blooms.) They make attractive ground covers, too, and are especially effective when planted under roses. The taller types can be planted in mid-border and combined with other perennials that thrive in dry soil such as yarrows *(Achillea* spp.), sundrops *(Oenothera* spp.), and sea hollies *(Eryngium* spp.).

Oenothera

Sundrops

Oenothera
∎
(ee-no-THEER-ah)
∎
Spring to fall bloom
∎
Full sun
∎
Zones 4 to 8
∎

∎ As their common name suggests, sundrops bear showy yellow flowers that add a touch of sunny color to the garden. "Suncups" and "golden eggs" are two other names used to describe the flowers, but the plants are also commonly called evening primroses. There's no relation to true primroses (*Primula* spp.); the name refers to the fact that several species feature flowers that open in the late afternoon or evening. Sundrops bear saucer- or cup-shaped flowers that have four petals; yellow is the most common flower color, at least for the garden-grown species, but there are also white- and pink-flowered species.

SELECTING SUNDROPS

Most sundrops are native to North America and, unless otherwise noted below, are hardy in Zones 4 to 8. The species below are the most popular garden plants. One species, *Oenothera biennis,* is a common roadside weed not generally grown as a garden plant. It bears yellow flowers that open in the evening, stands 3 to 5 feet tall, and is suitable for wild areas. It has one benefit, though, that gardeners may want to consider: the plants are extremely attractive to Japanese beetles. Try growing it as a trap crop, well away from more cultivated plantings. Handpick beetles drawn to the plants (early morning is the best time for this), or just let it lure them away from other parts of the garden.

    O. fruticosa. Common sundrops. Clusters of deep yellow, 1- to 3-inch-wide flowers from late spring through summer; 1- to 3-foot clump-forming plants. The most frequently grown and

An Evening Primrose

While day-blooming sundrops are most commonly grown in gardens, if you want night-blooming plants, try tufted evening primrose (*O. caespitosa*). It features richly fragrant, white, 4-inch-wide flowers that open at sunset on 4- to 8-inch-tall plants. The following morning the flowers fade to pink and die. Plants bloom in summer for 4 to 6 weeks and are suitable for rock gardens or along rock walls.

Common sundrops (*Oenothera fruticosa* ssp. *glauca*)

showiest species. Plants sold as *O. tetragona* have recently been moved here and botanists currently list them as *O. fruticosa* ssp. *glauca.* Best in average to rich, well-drained soil. A variety of compact cultivars are available that range from 1½ to 2 feet tall and make outstanding garden plants. 'Summer Solstice' ('Sonnenwende') blooms from early summer to fall on 12- to 16-inch plants and features maroon fall foliage. 'Youngii' blooms from early to midsummer on 1½-foot plants and has scarlet autumn leaves.

    O. macrocarpa. Ozark sundrops, Missouri evening primrose. Solitary, yellow, 5-inch-wide flowers from late spring to fall; spreading, 6-inch-tall plants. Grows in full sun or partial shade and requires average, well-drained or dry soil; tends to be short lived in the rich, evenly moist but well-drained conditions of the average perennial border. Allow plants to dry out between waterings. Planting in rock gardens or raised beds helps provide the drainage they need to thrive. Self-sows. Can be invasive in suitable sites. (Formerly *O. missouriensis.*)

    O. speciosa. Solitary, 1- to 2½-inch-wide flowers; spreading, 1-foot-tall plants. While the species bears white flowers, pink-flowered forms such as 'Rosea' are most often grown in gardens.

Stunning but
fast-spreading
Oenothera speciosa

Shear plants after the main flush of bloom in early summer to encourage repeat bloom. Plants spread vigorously by thin, underground rhizomes and can be difficult to eradicate once established. (I spent four years trying to eradicate a clump after seeing that a relatively small plant had managed to spread nearly 3 feet in all directions in little more than a year. I now grow *O. speciosa* 'Siskiyou Pink', formerly *O. berlandieri* 'Siskiyou Pink', as a ground cover around shrubs where it is free to spread at will. It is supposed to be less invasive and is quite pretty.) Zones 5 to 8.

SITE AND SOIL

Grow sundrops in full sun (*O. macrocarpa* will grow in partial shade) and poor to average, well-drained soil. Established plants tolerate drought. They resent wet soil, especially in winter. Planting in rock gardens or raised beds ensures adequate drainage. *O. fruticosa* and its cultivars tolerate richer soil and are suitable for planting in beds and borders with well-drained, evenly moist conditions.

PLANTING

Plant sundrops in early spring. Loosen the soil to a depth of $1^{1}/_{2}$ to 2 feet and amend it with compost or other organic matter to improve drainage.

CARE THROUGH THE SEASON

Sundrops are carefree plants once established. They are drought tolerant enough to rarely need watering and don't require annual feeding to grow well. If you mulch to control weeds, keep the mulch several inches away from the crowns of the plants. Divide the plants as necessary in early spring or late summer if they outgrow their space or begin to lose vigor.

Propagation. Propagate improved cultivars by division (either dig and divide the entire plant or use a trowel to remove offsets from the outside of the clumps) or by shoot or root cuttings. Take cuttings in spring or early summer from shoots at the base of the plant and root them in a 50-50 mix of perlite and vermiculite. Take root cuttings from roots that run along the soil surface. (See "Propagating from Root Cuttings" in the Techniques Glossary for details.)

LANDSCAPE USES

Combine *O. fruticosa* and its cultivars with other summer-blooming perennials, including daylilies (*Hemerocallis* spp.), yarrows (*Achillea* spp.), lavenders (*Lavandula* spp.), catmints (*Nepeta* spp.), and yuccas (*Yucca* spp.). Consider low-growing *O. macrocarpa* for a spot in the rock garden, along a rock wall, or in a raised bed.

Ornamental Grasses

Few plants add as much appeal to a garden, and ask as little in return, as ornamental grasses do. They are truly four-season plants, contributing color, texture, and form to the landscape every month of the year. Unlike many perennials, they also add movement and sound to a garden: clumps of grasses rustling in the breeze lend a magical element to any planting. Consider that ornamental grasses are versatile, easy to please, and nearly carefree, and it isn't any wonder that they are so popular.

Ornamental grasses do have a subtle beauty that can take time to appreciate. They produce clumps of narrow, fine-textured leaves that range from neat mounds a few inches tall to dramatic fountains of foliage several feet tall. Most feature foliage in shades of green, silver, or blue-green from spring through summer, but there are variegated grasses with leaves that are banded or striped with white or yellow. One selection, Japanese blood grass (*Imperata cylindrica*

'Rubra'), is grown for its stunning leaves that are tipped in red at the beginning of the season and turn scarlet by fall. Depending on the species, ornamental grasses may have erect or broadly arching leaves. Some are clump forming; others, spreading. In summer and fall, the plants are topped by clusters of tiny flowers that sway in the slightest breeze. The flowers are arranged in spikes, racemes, or panicles and can be green, pink, purple-red, silver, white, or bronze in color.

Ornamental grasses add structure, color, and interest to the fall and winter landscape, too. The flowers turn tan, brown, or fluffy white as seeds form in summer and fall, and the foliage follows suit. Several grasses exhibit spectacular fall color before ripening to the tawny shades of winter—flame grass *(Miscanthus sinensis* var. *purpurascens)* is one. Many have foliage and seed heads that remain standing through winter; others contribute evergreen foliage to the winter landscape.

Sedum 'Autumn Joy' makes a stunning companion for ornamental grasses in fall.

SELECTING ORNAMENTAL GRASSES

There are grasses for nearly every part of the garden—for sun or shade, poor soil or rich. While all require similar care, grasses are divided into two general types—warm season and cool season—and this classification determines optimal timing of some cultural activities such as when to plant or to divide. Warm-season grasses grow actively when most other perennials do—from spring, once the soil has warmed up, through summer—at temperatures between 80° and 95°F and are dormant from fall through winter. Over winter, most have tan, brown, or white leaves and flowers, which add color to the landscape. Some remain standing until spring; others are gradually beaten down by snow and rain.

Cool-season grasses grow actively when temperatures are between 60° and 75°F. They begin active growth in late summer or fall, when daytime temperatures are cooler, and resume growing in early spring once the weather warms up but before hot summer temperatures arrive. Many have evergreen leaves, although grasses that are evergreen in the South may be killed to the ground in northern gardens.

When adding grasses to your garden, two other factors are important to keep in mind: habit and size. Grasses can be clump-forming or running. Clump formers gradually form large, dense clumps or mounds but stay put in the garden. Running grasses spread by creeping stems or rhizomes, and the speed at which they spread can vary: some are slow, steady spreaders; others race through the garden and can become extremely invasive. It's not surprising that clump-forming grasses are the best choices for most garden situations. (Before accepting a gift grass from a fellow gardener, ask how fast it spreads—anyone who has any of the invasive species will have plenty to share.)

Finally, size is a key consideration, since many popular ornamental grasses are shrub-sized plants. When acquiring a new grass, bear in mind that even clump-forming types will be nearly as wide as they are tall once they are established. That means a clump of *Miscanthus sinensis* 'Gracillimus', which ranges from 5 to 6 feet in height, will form a clump 5 to 6 feet across. Given adequate space and the right site, the big grasses are absolutely stunning, but they literally can overwhelm a small garden.

The following lists provide a sampling of some of the best ornamental grasses for gardens. Unless otherwise noted, all require full sun and grow in average, evenly moist but well-drained soil. The descriptions specify whether each is a

Drifts of tough perennials such as orange coneflowers *(Rudbeckia fulgida)* or annuals such as flowering tobacco *(Nicotiana* spp.) add color to a grass garden from summer into fall.

warm- or cool-season grass; see "Care Through the Season" on page 212 for specifics on how growing techniques differ for the two types.

Large Grasses for Full Sun

The following are some of the best shrub-sized grasses. Use them as backdrops in beds and borders, as specimens, and in shrub borders and foundation plantings.

Calamagrostis × *acutiflora* / **Feather reed grass**
Clump-forming, cool-season grass with upright to arching, 2- to 3-foot-tall mounds of leaves and narrow, erect, 5- to 6-foot-tall, golden tan flower spikes in midsummer. Flowers stand through winter. Will grow in heavy clay and tolerates heat with adequate soil moisture. It is evergreen in warm climates and deciduous in the North. 'Karl Foerster' is an early-blooming cultivar that is more compact and earlier blooming in northern gardens than 'Stricta', the other commonly avail-

Eulalia or Japanese silver grass *(Miscanthus sinensis)*

able cultivar. In hot climates, the two are virtually identical. Plants may not bloom well in warm climates. Zones 5 to 9.

Cortaderia selloana / **Pampas grass**
Clump-forming, warm-season grass with 5- to 12-foot-tall clumps of narrow leaves topped with 8- to 12-foot-tall, featherlike flower heads from summer to fall. Individual plumes can be 1 to 3 feet long. Leaf edges are sharp — wear gloves and a long-sleeved shirt when working around plants. Tolerates light shade and dry soil but is best with adequate moisture. For the best-quality plants, buy named cultivars. Evergreen foliage. Cut plants to the ground annually or every other year in early spring. 'Pumila' is only 5 feet tall and can be grown in a container and overwintered indoors in a cool, frost-free place. Zones 8 to 11; to Zone 7 with winter protection.

Miscanthus sinensis / **Eulalia, Japanese silver grass**
Clump-forming, warm-season grass with 3- to 5-foot-tall, vase-shaped mounds of foliage and purplish, plumelike flowers from summer to fall that reach from 6 to 10 feet tall. Flowers turn fluffy and light tan and stand through winter. Silvery summer leaves turn yellow to tan in fall. *M. sinensis* var. *purpurascens* (frequently sold as 'Purpurascens') reaches 3 to 4 feet — 4 to 6 feet in flower — and has red-orange fall foliage. Variegated cultivars, including 'Variegatus', which is striped white, and 'Zebrinus', which has pale yellow bands, are available. These generally require staking to prevent them from flopping, especially in large, established clumps or if plants are not grown in full sun. (They tolerate some light shade.) 'Gracillimus' and 'Morning Light' are two cultivars with narrow, silvery leaves that stand without staking, as does *M. sinensis* var. *purpurascens*. Zones 4 to 9.

Molinia caerulea / **Purple moor grass**
Clump-forming, warm-season grass with 1- to 2-foot-tall mounds of leaves and airy spikes of flowers in early to midsummer that fade to yellow-brown and reach a height of 2 to 4 feet. Flowers are showy through fall. In late fall or early winter, flowers and foliage break off, so plants do not need to be cut back in spring. *M. caerulea* ssp. *aurundinacea*, commonly called tall moor grass, produces 2- to 3-foot-tall clumps of leaves topped by flowers that reach 3 to 4 feet. Zones 5 to 9; to Zone 4 with winter protection.

Panicum virgatum / **Switch grass**
Clump-forming, warm-season grass, native to North American prairies, with 3-foot-tall mounds

of leaves and 4- to 8-foot-tall, silvery or pinkish flowers that reach from 4 to 8 feet. Flowers turn whitish or buff-brown toward fall, and foliage turns yellow, then brown in fall. Prefers rich, evenly moist soil in full sun but tolerates dry, sandy conditions and boggy soil. Will also grow in light shade. 'Haense Herms' turns orange-red in fall. 'Heavy Metal' has metallic blue-green leaves and good yellow fall color. Zones 5 to 9.

Medium to Small Grasses for Full Sun

Use the following grasses as accents or edgings in beds and borders. Several are also effective ground covers.

Festuca glauca / **Blue fescue**

Clump-forming, cool-season grass with rounded, 6- to 12-inch-tall mounds of blue- or silver-green leaves topped in summer by tan seed heads that are not particularly ornamental. Foliage is evergreen. Requires well-drained soil in areas with wet summers and does not grow well where summers are hot and humid. Will grow in light shade, and part-day shade is best in southern zones. Cut plants back in spring or fall, not during summer, to keep the clumps neat. Self-sows, but seedlings may not have blue leaves. Some gardeners clip off the seed heads because these can detract from the foliage. Can be used as a ground cover. For best color, buy named cultivars—'Elijah Blue' and 'Sea Urchin' are two good selections. (Formerly *F. cinerea* and *F. ovina* 'Glauca'.) Zones 4 to 9.

Helictotrichon sempervirens / **Blue oat grass**

Clump-forming, cool-season grass with 2-foot-tall clumps of erect, evergreen to semievergreen, gray-blue leaves. In early summer, 3- to 4-foot spikes of yellow, oatlike seed heads appear. Requires well-drained soil and may succumb to root rot in heavy clay. Does not grow well in areas with hot, humid summers. Tolerates light shade. Cut back plants in early spring. Zones 4 to 9.

Imperata cylindrica 'Rubra' / **'Rubra' blood grass**

Slow-spreading, warm-season grass with erect, 1½-foot leaves that are green at the base and scarlet at the tops. Insignificant flowers. Foliage turns all red in fall and brown in winter. The plants have a spreading habit but are not invasive. Best in moist soil but does not grow well in heavy clay. Does not tolerate drought. In areas with hot summers, plant it in a spot with shade during the hottest part of the day. Rogue out any portions of the clumps that revert to all-green foliage. (Sometimes listed as 'Red Baron'.) Zones 4 to 9, but mulch plants with evergreen boughs or salt hay in Zone 4.

Silvery leaved blue fescue *(Festuca glauca)* with blood grass (*Imperata cylindrica* 'Rubra')

The foliage of blood grass (*Imperata cylindrica* 'Rubra') turns scarlet in fall.

ABOVE Flame grass *(Miscanthus sinensis* var. *purpurascens)* with Japanese anemones *(Anemone tomentosa)*

RIGHT Northern sea oats *(Chasmanthium latifolium)*

Pennisetum alopecuroides / Fountain grass

Clump-forming, warm-season grass with rounded, 2- to 3-foot-tall mounds of narrow leaves topped by bottlebrush-like, pinkish to white flowers in midsummer. Flowering stems stick out on all sides, and clumps are 3 to 4 feet tall when in bloom. Tolerates light shade. Self-sows prolifically; pull up seedlings as they appear or cut off seed heads in midfall to curtail this tendency. Can be used as a ground cover. 'Hameln' is a compact cultivar that is 2 to 3 feet tall when in bloom. 'Little Bunny' reaches only 10 to 11 inches. Zones 5 to 9. *P. setaceum* and its purple-leaved cultivars 'Burgundy Giant' and 'Rubrum' are handsome, fast-growing tender perennials (hardy in Zones 9 to 11) grown as annuals in the North.

Phalaris arundinacea var. *picta* / White-striped ribbon grass

Running, warm-season grass with showy green-and-white-striped leaves in 2- to 3-foot-tall clumps. White, spike-shaped flower heads in early summer on stems that reach 4 feet. Spreads by underground runners and can be very invasive; divide plants regularly to control their spread. In midsummer, if foliage turns brown or plants become unkempt looking, cut them to the ground to initiate a fresh flush of leaves. Rogue out any all-green growth. Can be used as a ground cover. Tolerates partial shade and wet soil (where it spreads especially quickly). Will also grow in standing water. Zones 4 to 9.

Grasses for Partial Shade

While ornamental grasses typically are plants for full sun, there are a few for shade gardeners, too. The species below will grow in bright, dappled all-day shade or a half day of sun and a half day of shade. Unless otherwise noted, all are best in rich, evenly moist soil that is well drained. In addition, some of the plants listed above for full sun will also grow in light shade. *Miscanthus sinensis* var. *purpurascens* tolerates partial shade but is somewhat less brilliant in fall.

Chasmanthium latifolium / Northern sea oats

Clump-forming, warm-season North American native grass with 2- to 3-foot-tall bamboolike leaves and showy, drooping seed heads in midsummer. Seed heads emerge green and change to warm brown as they ripen. The foliage also turns rich brown in fall. Self-sows with enthusiasm. Cut back plants in fall before the seed heads shatter, or weed out seedlings in spring. Will also grow in full sun. Zones 5 to 9.

Hakonechloa macra 'Aureola' / Variegated hakone grass

Slow-spreading, warm-season grass with 1½- to 2-foot mounds of bamboolike, green-and-yellow-striped leaves. Flowers are insignificant. The plants have a spreading habit but are not invasive—most gardeners never have enough of this striking plant. Requires rich, evenly moist soil for best growth. Zones 5 to 9.

Sedges for Partial Shade

Sedges (*Carex* spp.) aren't true grasses, but they are some of the best grasslike plants for shady beds and borders and produce clumps or spreading mounds of grasslike leaves. They are grown primarily as foliage plants, although they do bear small clusters of flowers. Many variegated forms are available. Unless otherwise noted, the following sedges grow in partial shade in evenly moist, well-drained soil. They will tolerate sun with consistent soil moisture. Treat them as you would cool-season grasses.

C. conica 'Marginata', a clump-forming, 6-inch-tall, evergreen sedge with narrow, $1/8$-inch-wide, dark green leaves edged in white, is hardy in Zones 5 to 9. *C. morrowii* 'Variegata' is a clump former with evergreen, silver-edged, $1/4$- to $1/2$-inch-wide leaves in $11/2$- to 2-foot-tall mounds. It is hardy in Zones 5 to 9. (Other cultivars of *C. morrowii* are hardy only to Zone 7.) *C. siderosticha* 'Variegata' is a handsome, spreading sedge with deciduous green-and-white-striped leaves that are broader — to $3/4$ inch wide. It appreciates constantly moist to wet soil and spreads with time to make an attractive ground cover. It is hardy in Zones 6 to 9; to Zone 5 with winter protection.

SITE AND SOIL

Plant ornamental grasses in full sun or partial shade. They thrive in average to rich soil that is evenly moist and well drained but will also tolerate adverse conditions such as dry soil. Soil that is too rich can cause the larger grasses to flop over. See "Selecting Ornamental Grasses" earlier in this entry for specific preferences. Most grasses are stunning when lit from behind by the late-afternoon sun, a feature to keep in mind when siting plants and designing plantings.

PLANTING

While some species grasses, including *Chasmanthium latifolium*, are easy to grow from seeds, you'll need to buy plants (which are sold either in containers or bare-root) to add most cultivars to your garden, because they don't come true from seed. (Some species, including *Helictotrichon sempervirens*, can be grown from seeds but are very slow to establish.) Plant both warm- and cool-season grasses in spring so that they have plenty of time to become established before summer. Cool-season grasses can also be planted in fall. Container-grown plants can be moved to the garden in summer, but be sure to water regularly until they are established. In most gardens, the only soil preparation necessary is loosening the planting site with a fork. Amending the soil with organic matter is beneficial, though, and is especially helpful in improving drainage if the soil is high in clay. Adding organic matter also improves the fertility of poor, sandy soil.

Container-grown plants establish quickly and are available from neighborhood garden centers or by mail. Tip the plants out of their pots and examine the root ball. If roots are densely packed around the outside of the root ball or winding

Grasses for Meadow and Prairie Plantings

A wildflower meadow or prairie planting isn't complete without grasses, and native species are your best choices. To find grasses that will thrive with little care in your garden, consult field guides or your local conservation district office for advice on what species grow naturally in your area. All of the following thrive in full sun and average to rich, evenly moist but well-drained soil. Propagate by germinating seeds or by division.

Andropogon spp. Bluestems. Clumping, warm season.

Bouteloua spp. Grama grasses. Clumping, warm season.

Elymus canadensis. Canada wild rye. Clumping, cool season.

Panicum virgatum. Switch grass. Clumping, warm season.

Schizachyrium scoparium. Little bluestem. Clumping, warm season.

Sorghastrum nutans. Indian grass. Clumping, warm season.

Spartina pectinata. Prairie cord grass. Running, warm season.

Sporobolus heterolepis. Prairie dropseed. Clumping, warm to cool season.

Tridens flavus. Purple-top. Clumping, warm-season.

around in circles, score the roots on three or four sides with a sharp knife. This harsh treatment encourages the roots to extend out into the surrounding soil. Set the plants so the crowns are at the same depth at which they were growing in the pot. In newly dug soil, set them slightly higher — 1 to 2 inches above the soil line — because they will settle. Then refill the hole, and water.

Bare-root plants are also available by mail. Examine them carefully when they arrive. Each plant should have a minimum of two or three growing points — more is better — and healthy-looking, abundant roots. Scratch a root and look at it closely: it should be whitish, not black, where you have scratched. Plant bare-root plants as soon as possible, and don't let them dry out during the process. If you can't get them into the garden within a day or two, pot them up and set them in a shady, protected location. When planting, spread the roots over a cone of soil and set the crowns slightly above the soil surface.

In general, space grasses as far apart as they are tall. That means, for example, two clumps of 5- to 6-foot *Miscanthus sinensis* 'Gracillimus' should be spaced with that distance between them. If you are massing plants as ground covers, covering a slope, or combining them with other perennials, think of the height as the spacing on center; that is, a 4-foot-tall plant should be allowed 2 feet of space on all sides. Don't scrimp on spacing, particularly with the warm-season grasses, which can grow for years without needing division. If you are growing one of the invasive running grasses and want to contain its spread, consider planting in a container sunk to the rim in the soil.

CARE THROUGH THE SEASON

Once planted, ornamental grasses are truly low-maintenance plants that are rarely troubled by pests or diseases. Mulch them to control weeds — it's best to keep mulch away from the crowns of the plants, however, especially with cool-season grasses, which tend to be fussier about soil drainage. Most grasses are quite drought tolerant once established and do not require regular watering. (Water specimens that do need evenly moist soil as necessary.) They also don't require annual feeding, although an annual topdressing with compost adds organic matter and some nutrients to the soil.

Some larger grasses need staking. Install sturdy stakes early in the season before the new growth is more than a few feet tall. Metal pipes driven into the ground around the clump and connected by heavy twine are usually sufficient. Another option is to use a large tomato cage made of steel reinforcing wire and attach it to sturdy poles driven into the ground.

Spring Cleanup for Warm-Season Grasses. Leave grasses standing over the winter to enjoy the color and texture they add to the landscape. In late winter or early spring, cut the stems of warm-season grasses to within a few inches of the ground. Ideally, give plants their annual "haircut" before new growth emerges in spring, but if you are late getting to it, cutting off some of the new growth won't permanently hurt the plants. (Actually, cutting back the plants is optional, but most gardeners prefer to see the fresh green leaves, which would be partially obscured by the old foliage.) Wear a long-sleeved shirt, long pants, and gloves for the task, since many grasses have tiny, sharp barbs on their leaves. Pruning shears are perfect for cutting back the smaller grasses, but the larger plants can be hard to cut back without larger equipment. Short-handled loppers allow you to jam the blades into the clumps to cut. Chain saws and string trimmers make the task fast and easy, but you'll need a string trimmer with a sawblade attachment for the larger perennial grasses. (Before cutting down large clumps, tie up the leaves with string so they are easy to carry away.) Cut just above the densest, woodiest part of the crown — you'll end up with a low, bowl-shaped mound of brown stems, which will be obscured by new growth within a few weeks.

Chop up the dried grass stems and add them to the compost pile. (A thick layer of unchopped *Miscanthus* stems can be laid down under a new compost pile, but this works only if you are making cool compost and plan on leaving the pile for a year.) But don't add the remains of reseeding grasses such as *Pennisetum* to the compost pile, or you'll spread seeds everywhere with the compost.

Variegated eulalia
(Miscanthus sinensis)
with tender perennial
Pentas lanceolata
'Ruby Glow Red' and
white-flowered,
narrow-leaved zinnias
(*Zinnia angustifolia*
'Whitestar')

If you don't want to discard them with the trash, try piling them in a mound with a little soil over them and keeping them very wet for a few weeks until the seeds and stems rot. Covering the mound with plastic will speed the process. The rotting process will destroy most or all of the seeds, and the remains of the pile can be composted.

Spring or Fall Cleanup for Cool-Season Grasses. These grasses generally resent the harsh buzz cut that keeps warm-season types looking their best, but most still benefit from an annual trim. Cut back cool-season grasses in fall or early spring, before new growth emerges, but trim them back only to about two-thirds of their full height. Fescues (*Festuca* spp.) can be cut back to a height of about 3 to 4 inches. Trim sedges (*Carex* spp.) in spring, also before new leaves emerge.

Division. Divide warm-season grasses if they outgrow their space, die out in the center of the clump, or begin to flop. Otherwise they can be left for years without dividing. Cool-season grasses tend to need dividing more frequently, because the clumps die out in the center.

Divide warm-season grasses in spring, just as new leaves are beginning to emerge. With established clumps of large grasses such as *Miscanthus,* you'll need an ax or a mattock for the task — as well as a strong back. Get someone to help you, as dividing big grasses isn't easy. First, dig around the clump with a sharp spade. If the clump is small enough, haul it out of the hole to divide it.

If it isn't, chop it into manageable sections while it is still in the hole and then move the divisions. Divide smaller grasses as you would any other perennial: dig the clumps; break or cut them into sections; discard any old, woody portions; and re-plant. Whether you are dividing large grasses or small ones, do not allow the pieces to dry out during the process.

Propagation. Propagate named cultivars by division. You can propagate grasses that spread by rhizomes by digging up plants on the outside of the clumps. To grow species from seeds, sow in pots in spring and set them outdoors in a protected location.

LANDSCAPE USES

Larger grasses make handsome backdrops for borders or centerpieces for island beds. Smaller grasses can be used in mid-border or as edgings. Combine them with summer-blooming perennials such as coreopsis, sneezeweeds (*Helenium* spp.), purple coneflower *(Echinacea purpurea),* cone-flowers (*Rudbeckia* spp.), and sedums. They are also ideal for meadow plantings with sun-loving wildflowers. Combine shade-loving grasses and sedges (*Carex* spp.) with ferns, hostas, lungworts (*Pulmonaria* spp.), and shade-loving wildflowers. When planting grasses, consider how their fine-textured foliage will contrast with surrounding plants. They are especially effective with bold-leaved plants.

Peonies

Paeonia
■
(pay-OH-nee-ah)
■
Spring to early-summer
bloom
■
Full sun or light shade
■
Herbaceous,
Zones 2 to 7 or 8;
tree, Zones 3 to 9
■

■ Peonies may look delicate, but actually they are as tough as nails. The lavish blooms of these old-fashioned plants reappear annually with even minimal care. In fact, plants in abandoned gardens can bloom reliably for years despite complete neglect. With a good site and a bit of regular attention, though, they are simply spectacular—the glory of the garden in spring to early summer.

There are two general types of peonies: herbaceous peonies and tree peonies. Herbaceous peonies, which die to the ground each year, are the best known and most popular. For more on their woody cousins, which will grow in more shade and warmer temperatures than herbaceous types will, see "Tree Peonies" on page 219.

Herbaceous peonies bloom from late May to early June in the central zones and as early as April in the South. The showy flowers, borne on 1½- to 3-foot plants, are often very fragrant and range from 5 to 8 inches or more across. They are unparalleled as cut flowers and come in a range of colors from white to red, including pure white, ivory, cream, pale yellow, pale pink, rose-pink, crimson, and maroon. The plants have handsome, dark to bright green leaves that remain attractive all season. In spring, the emerging stems are ferny and maroon-red to purple-mauve and make an attractive complement to spring bulbs such as daffodils and grape hyacinths (*Muscari* spp.).

Peonies, of course, make stunning additions to fresh arrangements. The flowers last longest if cut when the buds are about half open and the first petals are beginning to unfurl. Leave two strong sets of leaves on the plant. Make a 1- to 2-inch slit up the base of the stem and place the flowers in a deep container of water overnight until you are ready to arrange them. The buds can also be stored dry in the refrigerator for 3 to 6 weeks. (Cut off the foliage and wrap them in paper.) A few days before you want flowers, take them out, recut the stems, and place them in a deep container of warm water.

SELECTING PEONIES

To explore the full range of peony cultivars available, plan on ordering them by mail. Lucky gardeners will have a local nursery with a good selection, but most nurseries carry only a few choices. Hybridizers have introduced hundreds of cultivars, so be prepared for pleasant frustration when making selections. Because plants are so long lived, it's worth hunting out top-quality cultivars. See "Peony Classics" on the facing page for a selection of cultivars to consider.

Bloom Season. Although each peony blooms for only a few weeks in spring, it's possible to extend the season by planting cultivars with different bloom seasons. Select a mix of early-, midseason-, and late-flowering cultivars. In warmer zones, early-blooming peonies are the best choices.

Flower Form. Once you start reading catalog descriptions, you'll discover that peonies come in an array of flower forms. Planting a mix of forms adds variety to plantings and lets you enjoy the full range of selections available. Single-flowered plants have a central cluster of showy, golden yellow stamens surrounded by a single row of petals. Semidoubles have two or more rows of petals surrounding a central boss of stamens. Double flowers have one or more rings of full-size petals surrounding a central cluster of smaller petaloids, which are modified stamens and carpels that look like petals. Japanese-type blooms have a ring or two of petals around a cluster of petaloids that are narrow and flat. Peonies that have flowers with a dense, rounded center are called "bombs" by some growers and "anemones" by others.

Peonies are long lived, even with minimal care, but given a good site and rich soil they are absolutely spectacular. This is an old-fashioned, fragrant, double peony passed down in the author's family.

Peony Classics

The list below includes classic, old peony cultivars along with some newer selections.

'America'. Early single with fiery red flowers and golden stamens. Mild fragrance. Strong stems.

'Bowl of Beauty'. Early Japanese type with rose-pink outer petals and creamy white centers. Strong stems.

'Bowl of Cream'. Midseason double with bowl-shaped, 8-inch, pure white flowers.

'Do Tell'. Midseason Japanese type with pale shell pink outer petals and cream, pink, and rose-red centers.

'Fairy's Petticoat'. Early double with ruffled pink flowers. Delicate fragrance.

'Festiva Maxima'. Early double with white flowers flecked occasionally with red. Very fragrant. Good for southern gardens. An old cultivar, introduced in 1851.

'Gold Rush'. Midseason to late Japanese type with ruffled white outer petals surrounding a cluster of gold stamens with white petals.

'Kansas'. Midseason double with large, red flowers that do not fade. Introduced 1940.

'Krinkled White'. Early single with pure white flowers with a crepe-paper-like texture and showy yellow stamens. Introduced 1928.

'Miss America'. Early semidouble with white petals and gold stamens. American Peony Society Gold Medal Winner.

'Monsieur Jules Elie'. Early double with rose-pink flowers composed of large outer petals and denser centers. Fragrant. Good for southern gardens. Introduced 1888.

'Mrs. F.D. Roosevelt'. Midseason double in shell pink. Fragrant. Introduced 1932.

'Nippon Beauty'. Late Japanese type with dark red outer petals and red inner petaloids edged with yellow.

'Pink Lemonade'. Midseason anemone or bomb type with pink outer petals surrounding a dense cluster of pink, cream, and yellow petals. Fragrant.

'Raspberry Sundae'. Midseason anemone- or bomb-type blooms with pale pink outer petals and a dense central cluster of darker pink petals rimmed with creamy white petals. Mild fragrance.

'Sarah Bernhardt'. Late double with shell pink blooms flecked occasionally with red. Fragrant. Introduced 1906.

'Scarlett O'Hara'. Early single with vibrant red flowers and yellow centers. Strong stems. Introduced 1958.

'Seashell'. Midseason single with shell pink flowers. Strong stems. Introduced 1937.

Species Selections. While most peonies grown today are hybrids, species peonies are sometimes available.

Paeonia lactiflora is perhaps the most important parent of hybrid herbaceous peonies. It usually bears single white flowers, but some specimens have pink or red ones. Zones 2 to 8.

P. officinalis, one of the parents of today's hybrids, bears red flowers on 2-foot plants. Its cultivar 'Rubra Plena', a double red, is an old-fashioned plant once commonly called piney. Both 'Rubra Plena' and double pink-flowered 'Rosea Superba' were also commonly called Memorial Day peonies because they bloom in late May. Zones 3 to 8.

The most commonly available species is fernleaf peony *(P. tenuifolia).* It has finely divided, fernlike leaves and single, ruby red flowers that are about 3 inches across. 'Rubra Plena' is a double cultivar. Zones 3 to 8.

Semidouble peonies have two or more rows of outer petals around a central cluster, or boss, of petal-like stamens.

Peony Hedges

Traditionally, peonies have been planted in a row along driveways and walkways, creating a glorious late-spring "hedge." Although this is a convenient arrangement in winter, because the plants disappear and the site can be piled high with shoveled snow, in summer, cutting the lawn around the plants isn't easy. Converting a peony hedge into a low summer border makes sense from a maintenance standpoint and also makes it easier to provide plants with good care. Remove the grass around the plants for at least a foot on each side. To keep the grass from reinvading the site, install an edging strip all around the planting. In spring, amend the soil with well-rotted manure and then mulch.

In summer, fill in between the clumps of peonies with low-growing annuals such as petunias and marigolds. You can also consider adding low perennials such as catmints (*Nepeta* spp.). In fall, plant bulbs such as daffodils, grape hyacinths (*Muscari* spp.), and crocuses. Keep the plantings about 6 inches *inside* the edging strip so you can run one wheel of the lawn mower inside the bed and mow and trim in one easy step without damaging anything.

Peonies are commonly grown with lawn grass running right up to the base of the plants. Clumps are striking, and easier to trim around, if the grass is removed and they are underplanted with low-growing perennials or annuals.

SITE AND SOIL

Select a site with care, because peonies grow best if planted in a permanent location. They are deep-rooted plants with thick, fleshy roots and almost woody crowns. Plants will thrive for years without needing to be divided—20 years is not unusual, and there are plants that have bloomed in the same site for a century. That said, however, early pioneers carried the roots of these tough perennials across the continent when they headed westward, so don't turn down divisions from a favorite aunt's garden or hesitate to take a piece of a cherished plant with you when you move.

Peonies tolerate a wide range of soils as long as the soil is well drained. (For poorly drained sites, two possible solutions are double digging, which loosens the soil and improves drainage, and planting in raised beds.) The plants are fairly adaptable when it comes to pH, although slightly acid to slightly alkaline soil is best. Adjust the pH if your soil is very acid or very alkaline. Add plenty of organic matter to the soil at planting time to loosen clay soils and to increase the water- and nutrient-holding capacity of sandy ones.

Peonies bloom best in full sun but will also flower, although less abundantly, in a site with light shade for part of the day. A site with good air circulation is preferable, but look for a spot that is protected from wind, as strong wind damages the heavy blooms. Keep plants away from trees and shrubs, which will compete with the roots. (If necessary, peonies can also be put "on hold" in a less-than-ideal site. In the years when I didn't have a permanent garden, my mother held plants from my Great Aunt Hattie's garden on the edge of her shady woodland. There, they bloomed sporadically for 20 years, producing fewer flowers each year as the site got shadier. They began blooming abundantly about 3 years after I moved them to my full-sun borders.)

Gardeners in Zone 7, and especially those trying peonies in Zone 8, where summer heat and humidity take their toll, should look for a cool site with afternoon shade. (Plants still may be short lived or fail to bloom in the warmer parts of Zone 8.) In northern areas with late-spring frosts, look for a site that receives some morning shade, which will help protect the buds on frosty mornings.

PLANTING

Peonies are commonly sold as bare-root plants, with three- to five-eye divisions ("eye" is the industry term for "bud"). Fall is the best time to plant peonies, which are generally shipped from September to November. Good mail-order suppliers will ship at the proper planting time for your zone. Container-grown peonies can be planted in early spring as well.

Inspect the roots carefully when they arrive. They should not be broken or diseased-looking. Look for the small, red buds that indicate the top of the clump. There should be at least three healthy-looking buds. If the roots look dried out, soak them in water for a few hours before planting. If you can't plant right away, repack the roots in moistened packing material (sawdust is commonly used). The plants can be held for up to a week in a dark, cool place. If you can't plant within a week, dig a trench in a shady spot and heel them in.

To plant in an existing garden, dig a hole that will accommodate the roots—at least 12 to 18 inches deep. In a new garden or if your soil is poor, double-dig at least 2 weeks before your peonies are scheduled to arrive and thoroughly soak the soil to settle it before planting. (Preparing the soil the spring before is better.) Either way, incorporate organic matter such as compost as you dig. It's a good idea to work a handful or two of bonemeal into the planting site as well.

Space plants from 3 to 4 feet apart to accommodate their spread at maturity. Set the roots with the buds facing upward and *no more than* 2 inches below the soil surface—if planted too deeply, peonies will fail to bloom. In northern zones, planting a full 2 inches deep protects the buds in winter. In central portions of the United States, a planting depth of 1 inch is a good goal. Farther south, shallower planting ensures that the buds will feel the slightest essential nip of winter cold. In a newly prepared site, the soil and the roots will tend to settle, so when in doubt, plant more shallowly.

After planting, water thoroughly and mulch with evergreen branches, loose straw, or even dried cornstalks to prevent frost heaving over the first winter.

CARE THROUGH THE SEASON

Peonies are heavy feeders, so each spring work well-rotted manure, compost, or a balanced organic plant food into the soil around plants. Keep the fertilizer away from the stems. (I also like to weed around the emerging stems in early spring, because invading grass and weeds are easiest to see then. Take care not to damage the emerging stems, though, and don't dig deeper than about 1 inch, to avoid disturbing the roots.) Mulch the plants to control weeds and to retain soil moisture, but keep mulch away from plant stems. Plants need to be watered in dry regions.

Staking. Most peonies will need staking to keep the flowers from bending over to the ground, especially in rainy, windy weather. Single-flowered cultivars, especially those described as "strong stemmed," often stand up just fine on their own, however. The secret to natural-looking staked plants is to get the stakes in place early in the season—when the emerging stems are 1 to 2 feet tall or so is best, although they can be staked effectively when buds are still marble sized. Early staking allows the foliage to grow up and through the supports, eventually concealing them. Tying up a clump of peonies after the flowers have begun to open—or worse yet, after the blooms have fallen over—generally results in plants with a hog-tied look that is more unattractive than the flopped-over posture. Fortu-

nately, flopping doesn't cause permanent damage—you can still try to tie the plants up or simply leave them in place and vow to do better next year. See "Staking" in the Techniques Glossary for specific techniques.

Disbudding—or Not. Peonies produce a central bud and two smaller side buds. Some gardeners remove the side buds to direct the plants' energy into the main flower. To lengthen the bloom season from each clump, however, leave all the buds in place. Clip off the central flower immediately after it fades. The side buds will open after the main one and provide an extra week or two of bloom. After flowering, cut off spent blooms to keep the plants from expending energy on seed production.

TOP Japanese-type peony 'Bowl of Beauty' with tall bearded irises

ABOVE Tree peonies reach 3 to 5 feet in height and bear their enormous flowers about 2 weeks before herbaceous peonies, which are more commonly grown.

Fall Cleanup. In late fall, cut peony stems to the ground. Compost the foliage if fungal diseases such as botrytis and leaf spot haven't been a problem. If they have, discard or burn the foliage.

Division. Sparse flowers indicate that plants may be overcrowded or the soil depleted. Division may also be necessary if a clump has simply grown too large. Divide in late summer or early fall, digging deeply to get as many roots as possible. Wash the soil off the clumps with a hose and use a sharp knife to divide them into pieces with about five eyes each. Discard old, woody portions of the crown that don't have healthy buds. Replant in a prepared site as you would a new plant.

Division is also the method of choice for propagating all but species peonies, since the seed of cultivars does not come true. To germinate seeds, sow outdoors in fall or very early spring when they will still be exposed to cool temperatures. Or prechill seeds in the refrigerator for 3 weeks before sowing indoors. Plants will take several years to reach blooming size.

Potential Problems. Peonies are troubled by few diseases. Botrytis is a fungal disease that can rot the buds or shoots. Infected buds turn brown and fail to open; shoots appear burned. Promptly remove any infected plant parts and remove and destroy the foliage in fall. Clear away and dispose of mulch and the top $\frac{1}{2}$ inch of soil around in-

fected clumps as well. A site with good air circulation helps prevent the disease. An annual fall cleanup also helps control fungal leaf spot diseases, which disfigure the foliage.

Peony flowers invariably have ants in them, which visit the buds and flowers for their sweet nectar. They generally do no harm and are best ignored.

Failure to bloom can be caused by a variety of factors. Plants may be planted too deeply—dig and replant if the buds are more than 2 inches below the soil surface. Plants may also be too small to bloom: peonies can take 2 or more years to bloom after being planted. Established clumps may stop blooming because of overcrowding, in which case division is the remedy, or because the soil is depleted. In the latter case, amend the soil with compost or well-rotted manure in spring. Thrips, tiny insects that feed by rasping buds and new stems, can cause buds to abort. Distorted stems are another sign of infestation. Spray infested plants every 3 days for 2 weeks with insecticidal soap.

LANDSCAPE USES

Peonies are classic plants for perennial beds and borders. Combine them with other late-spring to early-summer bloomers such as bleeding hearts *(Dicentra* spp.), Siberian iris *(Iris sibirica)*, blue false indigo *(Baptisia australis)*, early-blooming salvias such as *Salvia* 'East Friesland', and candytuft *(Iberis sempervirens)*. They're large enough plants to hold their own when planted along the front of a shrub border, but be sure to locate them far enough away from the shrubs so they don't suffer from root competition. Peony foliage is good for setting off summer- to fall-blooming perennials as well as annuals.

Tree Peonies

Despite their name, tree peonies are actually shrubby plants that range from 3 to 5 feet or more in height and spread. About 2 weeks before herbaceous peonies bloom in spring, tree peonies bear breathtaking flowers, from 6 to 10 inches or more across, with a texture best described as a cross between crepe paper and silk. Blooms come in a range of colors from pastel pinks, corals, and creams to maroon, magenta, and pale to golden yellow. They may be single, semidouble, or double. Many are fragrant. Individual plants bloom for about 10 days, but planting early-, midseason-, and late-blooming cultivars will extend the flowering season to about a month. Tree peonies can be grown in Zones 3 to 9; unlike herbaceous types, they will bloom well with only a cool rest period in winter. The plants are deciduous, and their deeply cut, grayish green leaves are attractive all season long.

Selecting Tree Peonies. Choosing which ones to plant can be a challenge, but since the plants are very long lived, it's worth seeking out good-quality cultivars rather than just buying the first plant you come across. As with herbaceous types, mail order is generally the way to go. For bloom within a season or two of planting, buy 3-year-old plants. There are Japanese, Chinese, European, and American tree peonies to choose from (they are commonly listed as cultivars of *P. suffruticosa* and *P. lutea*).

Planting Tree Peonies. Plant tree peonies in fall about 6 weeks before the ground freezes. Select a permanent site; they do not transplant well. Avoid sites where the plants will need to compete with tree or shrub roots. Like herbaceous peonies, they like well-drained soil amended with plenty of organic matter. Tree peonies will grow in full sun but are best planted in a partially shaded site—with 3 to 4 hours of direct sun, preferably in the morning. Shade is especially valuable during midday and afternoon because it protects the flowers during the hottest part of the day, making them last longer. (You can also use well-placed umbrellas to shade flowers of plants growing in sun.) *Unlike* herbaceous peonies, tree peonies are planted deeply—with the buds between 4 and 5 inches below the soil level. (Tree peony cultivars are actually budgrafted onto herbaceous peony roots. Deep planting encourages the cultivar to root on its own and discourages the herbaceous rootstock from sprouting.) Space plants from 5 to 6 feet

ABOVE Tree peony 'Golden Mandarin'

LEFT Tree peony 'Amber Moon'

apart to accommodate their spread at maturity. Mulch plants as you would herbaceous types the first winter. Newly planted specimens will take a season or two to bloom.

Care Through the Season. Feed plants each spring with a topdressing of compost and bonemeal. Mulch with chopped leaves to keep down weeds. In areas where rainfall is scarce, you'll also need to water. Prune away deadwood and stems that show signs of borer infestation whenever you spot them. You can also prune to remove congested growth, to encourage bushy growth, or to shape the plants. Tree peonies bloom on new wood, so prune them immediately after they flower.

In Zone 5 and north, provide winter protection to prevent stem damage. Stake the main stems and surround the plants with chicken wire frames, then fill the frames with oak leaves or other coarse mulch that will not pack down. Snow will also insulate the plants, but exposed stems may be damaged.

Corn poppy *(Papaver rhoeas)* is an easy-to-grow annual. Plants reach 3 feet and will self-sow. The popular Shirley poppies are a selection of this species.

$\mathcal{P}$*apaver*

Poppies

Papaver
■
(pa-PAH-ver)
■
Spring to midsummer
bloom
■
Full sun
■
Zones 2 to 8
■

■ Poppies have large, silky, crepe-paper-textured blooms in showy colors that make unforgettable residents in any garden. The blooms are bowl- or cup-shaped and range from 1 to 8 inches or more across. Hot colors predominate — orange, orange-red, scarlet, hot pink, and yellow blooms are common — but there are also soft pink, pale yellow, and white poppies. The flowers are followed by distinctive, rounded seed capsules. Poppies generally have toothed or deeply divided, almost fernlike leaves that disappear in midsummer.

Most poppies make stunning additions to fresh arrangements. Cut them when the buds begin to open. The stems secrete latex and need to be seared to prolong their vase life. Bring the flowers into the house, recut the stems, and dip the tips into an inch or two of boiling water for a few seconds or sear the ends with a match or the flame of a gas stove. Stand the flowers in cold water for several hours before arranging them. Sear the stems again if you cut them while arranging the flowers.

SELECTING POPPIES

The commonly grown poppies are perennials or annuals. By far the best known and longest lived of the perennials is Oriental poppy *(Papaver orientale)*. Other species tend to be short-lived perennials. The most frequently grown annual poppy is corn poppy *(P. rhoeas)*, which reaches 3 feet in height and has 3-inch-wide red, orange, yellow, pink, or white blooms. See "Planting" below for information on growing it from seeds.

P. alpinum. Alpine poppy. Cup-shaped, 1½-inch-wide flowers in early to midsummer on 6- to 10-inch-tall stems above a tuft of fernlike leaves. A short-lived perennial that reseeds abundantly.

Does not tolerate the heat and humidity of southern summers. Requires well-drained soil; good for rock gardens or along the tops of walls where it gets the drainage it needs to thrive. Zones 4 to 7.

P. croceum (formerly *P. nudicaule*). Iceland poppy. Showy, 3- to 5-inch-wide flowers on 1- to 2-foot-tall stems in spring and early summer in the full range of poppy colors. This short-lived perennial self-sows abundantly if a few seedpods are allowed to ripen, so it returns year after year in sites where it is happy. Plants grow best in areas with cool nights and warm days and tend to melt in midsummer in areas with hot, humid summers. Fortunately, they can be grown as annuals, since they bloom the first year from seeds. Even in areas where plants return for a few years, many gardeners pull them up after the second year of bloom to make room for younger, more vigorous plants. Zones 2 to 8.

P. orientale. Oriental poppy. Brilliant red-orange flowers with purple-black centers on 2- to 4-foot-tall stems above low, deeply divided, coarse-looking foliage. The flowers appear for a few weeks in early summer and are usually 4 to 6 inches wide, but improved forms bear flowers that can reach 8 inches or more across in a range of colors, including red, pale salmon, pink, white, and scarlet-orange. The leaves disappear by mid- to late summer, when the plants go dormant, and reappear about 6 weeks later in fall. Plants spread by runners to form broad clumps; cultivars tend to spread more slowly than the species. Zones 3 to 7.

SITE AND SOIL

Plant poppies in full sun. In areas with hot summers, however, a site with morning sun and afternoon shade is best. *P. orientale* thrives in average to rich, well-drained soil; be sure to combine it with plants that will cover the space it leaves in the garden in midsummer — see "Landscape Uses" on page 222 for suggestions. *P. croceum* prefers rich, evenly moist conditions, while *P. alpinum* requires very well drained soil. Since poppies have large, delicate flowers, a site protected from wind is best.

PLANTING

Add *P. orientale* to your garden by purchasing vegetatively propagated plants, as the improved

TOP LEFT Oriental poppy (*Papaver orientale* 'Carnival')

LEFT Oriental poppy (*Papaver orientale* 'Raspberry Queen')

ABOVE Oriental poppies (*Papaver orientale*) with white-flowered gas plant (*Dictamnus albus*)

cultivars do not come true from seed. Gardeners growing the orange-flowered species or the cultivars may have divisions to share, since the plants spread. The best time to plant is in fall. Container-grown plants are available at nurseries and can be planted in spring. Space plants 2 feet apart and mulch them over the first winter with straw or evergreen boughs to discourage frost heaving. They are generally not planted in drifts because of the space they leave in the garden during their summer dormancy. Plants typically take a season to become established and begin blooming well.

Start short-lived perennial and annual poppies from seeds. A variety of improved strains of seeds are available. For best results, sow the seeds outdoors where the plants are to grow in fall or in early spring as soon as the soil can be worked. Rake up the soil to prepare a seedbed, sprinkle the seeds, and cover them lightly with a handful of loose soil.

CARE THROUGH THE SEASON

Poppies don't require any special care to thrive. With short-lived perennial species, let some seedpods ripen to ensure self-sowing. Don't let *P. orientale* self-sow if you are growing one of the cultivars: the seedlings will have the typical orange flowers of the species.

Division. Clumps of *P. orientale* have deep roots and are happiest if left undisturbed, but in most gardens they spread enough to need dividing every 5 years or so. Late summer to early fall, just as the new leaves are beginning to emerge from summer dormancy, is the best time to divide. Dig deeply to get as many of the roots as possible, and replant the most vigorous portions of the clumps. This is also the best time to transplant; to do so successfully, take a large ball of soil when you are moving a clump.

Propagation. Seed and division are the most frequently used propagation methods. *P. orientale* can also be propagated by root cuttings. To take root cuttings, dig pencil-thick roots in fall and root them in sharp sand. See "Propagating from Root Cuttings" in the Techniques Glossary for more information.

LANDSCAPE USES

Combine poppies with irises, bellflowers (*Campanula* spp.), and other spring-blooming perennials. Be sure to include some summer- to fall-blooming perennials that will fill in after Oriental poppies go dormant in summer, such as Russian sage *(Perovskia atriplicifolia)*, baby's breath *(Gypsophila paniculata)*, asters, boltonia, Shasta daisy *(Chrysanthemum × superbum)*, and Oriental Hybrid lilies.

Perennials

■ Perennials mark the progress of the gardening season. They contribute some of the first blooms of spring, a crescendo of color from early to midsummer, and an abundance of flowers from late summer right up to the first killing frost of fall. Some add color beyond the end of the growing season in the form of stray flowers that appear after frost and seed heads that stand through winter. Evergreen perennials add green or sometimes burgundy or purple to the winter landscape. There are perennials for every part of the garden—sun or shade, rich soil or poor. You'll find an abundance of choices whether you want plants for a bed or border, rock garden, woodland planting, ground cover, edging, or specimen. There are so many to choose from, settling on a manageable number to grow can be a monumental task.

When deciding which perennials to grow (or selecting any plants, for that matter), keep the following rule in mind: Match the plant to the site. In other words, select plants that will grow well in the sun, soil, and weather conditions you have

Coneflowers
(Rudbeckia fulgida)

Lupine
(Lupinus polyphyllus)

available in your garden. Plants that are chosen because they will thrive in the conditions available in your yard inevitably look better, bloom better, and have fewer problems with pests and diseases than ones that have to struggle to survive. In addition, a garden full of plants matched to their site will look great with a minimum of care. So, before picking out that first perennial, take time to learn more about the site where you want to grow it.

Start by looking at the sun and shade pattern in your yard on a typical day. Does the site offer all-day sun—8 hours or more—or sun for a few hours in the morning or afternoon and dappled shade the rest of the day? Or perhaps deciduous trees cast day-long shade all summer but leave the site sunny in spring and fall. It's tempting to plant for the amount of sun you wish you had, but the results generally are disappointing, so stick to plants that will thrive in the amount of sun available. You'll find descriptions of the exposure plants prefer throughout this book under the heading "Site and Soil." If you want to experiment, plant the majority of the garden with perennials that prefer the sun and/or shade conditions available, but leave some room for plants that only tolerate them. For example, fill a shady site with hostas, ferns, epimediums, and shade-loving wildflowers. Then experiment with perennials that prefer brighter conditions— astilbes, columbines (*Aquilegia* spp.), and hardy geraniums. Plant them in the brightest spots and see how they do. Even if they don't quite perform up to expectations, the garden will still look fine because most of it is planted with shade-loving selections.

Also dig a few test holes to find out about the soil. Is it damp, heavy clay? Rich and loamy? Sandy? You can improve any soil by adding organic matter and using some of the techniques mentioned in "Planting" below, but starting out with perennials that will thrive in the conditions that already exist is almost always the best course of action. For example, yarrows (*Achillea* spp.) will grow well right from the start in a site with poor, dry soil, and they'll perform even better if the soil is amended with organic matter. Delphiniums planted in the same site will fail without herculean soil-building efforts and extensive care through the season. That said, keep in mind that the longer you tend a garden and care for the soil in it, the richer it gets and the wider the variety of plants you can grow in it becomes. Loose, well-drained soil that remains evenly moist, is rich in organic matter, and has a slightly acid to neutral pH will satisfy the widest variety of perennials. See "Care Through the Season" on page 224 for tips on building great soil for perennials.

Lamb's ears
(*Stachys byzantina*)

Take the "match the plant to the site" rule one step further, and it isn't hard to see why the best gardens are made up of plants that all thrive in similar conditions. Preparing the soil in an entire bed and then filling it with plants that will be happy there is a much more practical approach than trying to satisfy each plant individually—especially if their needs are diverse. So, once you know what kind of site you have to work with, start a list of perennials that will thrive there as it is. Include plants that will grow there with some site modification—such as double digging to provide deeper, richer, better-drained soil than you currently have, or removing a branch to let in a little more light. You'll find ideas for perennials to grow on most of the pages of this book. Asking neighborhood gardeners and looking at public plantings in your area will give you more ideas. In addition to the perennials covered in individual entries in this book, you'll find lists and descriptions of even more perennials to consider at the end of this entry.

PLANTING

Whether you are starting a new perennial garden or reworking an existing one, devote some time to improving your soil. In an existing garden, get in the habit of improving the soil by working in organic matter in the form of compost or leaf mold every time you add or move a plant. You may want to work in a balanced organic fertil-

Lady's mantle
(*Alchemilla mollis*)

Violet (*Viola odorata*)

Coralbells
(*Heuchera sanguinea*)

izer at the same time—having a soil test done will tell you whether your soil lacks fertility or if you should be routinely taking steps to adjust pH. If you are starting a new garden, see "Soil Preparation" in the Techniques Glossary for details on soil-improvement methods such as double and single digging, which are excellent ways to get a site ready for perennials. If possible, prepare the soil the season *before* you plan to plant, then mulch it. The waiting period allows the soil to settle before planting. Late fall, when the air is cool and crisp, is a great time to prepare new garden beds for spring planting. (Knowing that you have space ready to fill makes ordering plants from catalogs in winter that much more enjoyable, too.) You'll find specific recommendations for planting times in every entry in this book. See "Planting" in the Techniques Glossary for details on planting container-grown and bare-root perennials.

CARE THROUGH THE SEASON

Spring is probably the busiest time in the garden—and the most fun—as plants reemerge from their winter dormancy. Planting, dividing, weeding, and fertilizing are among the most important activities. Also remove any winter protection covering less-than-hardy perennials. From late spring into summer other tasks take over, including mulching, staking, deadheading, cutting back, watering, and pest control—along with the ever present job of keeping weeds at bay. (Don't forget to cut flowers to bring indoors and to just take time to stand back and enjoy the show!) Late summer and fall usher in another round of planting and dividing, plus cutting back plants when they stop blooming, watering if the weather is dry, and more weeding. In late fall, cut plants back for the winter, and after the soil freezes, provide protection for those that may not be hardy by covering them with evergreen boughs, salt hay, or straw. From fall through winter, also keep an eye out for winter weeds, which germinate in fall and set seed by spring. Pulling them up on warm winter days gives you a reason to be out in the garden as well as prevents them from getting a foothold.

Soil Building. Improving the soil is an ongoing process, not a once-and-done affair. The best way to keep garden soil fertile, and the plants in it healthy and thriving, is to add organic matter regularly. Organic matter improves soil drainage and also holds nutrients in the soil for plants to use. Spreading a layer of compost over the garden (or at least around the plants, if you don't have enough compost) is a great way to get organic matter into the soil. Organic mulches such as shredded bark and chopped leaves (pick them up off the lawn with a bagging lawn mower or chop them in a shredder) likewise add vital or-

ganic matter, albeit more slowly than compost does. Mulch also protects the soil from erosion by wind or water and compaction by rain (raindrops pounding down on bare soil exert considerable force). Although many perennials don't need to be fertilized regularly throughout the growing season as vegetables do, most benefit from an annual feeding. In spring, use very well rotted manure or a balanced organic fertilizer. If you have fresh manure available, use it in late fall so there is plenty of time for it to rot over winter.

In addition, avoid working soil when it is either too wet or too dry. Before digging or cultivating, squeeze a handful of your soil to test its moisture content. If it stays in a lump when you open your hand but breaks apart when you tap it lightly, it's at the ideal stage for digging. If it stays in a claylike lump, wait a few days to let it dry out, then test it again. If it is dusty dry, water thoroughly, then wait a day and test again. After digging, stay off the bed as much as possible. Half of the volume of good garden soil is pore space—about half of this consists of small pores that hold water and about half comprises larger pores that hold air once the soil drains after a rain. Walking, sitting, kneeling, or standing on soil compresses soil pores, thus reducing the amount of large pores that hold air, which plant roots need to grow, and impeding soil drainage. Compacting the soil also simply makes it more difficult for roots to penetrate. Walk around garden beds or lay down steppingstones if you are inclined to cut through the beds. For more detailed information on building and caring for soil, see *Taylor's Weekend Gardening Guides: Soil & Composting* (Houghton Mifflin 1998).

Potential Problems. Matching each plant to an appropriate site and building healthy soil will allow you to circumvent most problems with pests and diseases. Get in the habit of watching plants closely for signs of problems. Look under leaves for evidence of infestations, and know which plants need regular watering or feeding to keep them healthy. Keep in mind that plants that need periodic dividing may exhibit signs that can be mistaken for a disease, such as weak, spindly growth. See the Problems and Solutions Guide for help with identifying and dealing with pests and diseases.

PERENNIALS FOR SHADE

All of the following perennials thrive in partial or full shade in evenly moist, well-drained soil that is rich in organic matter. For more plants that flourish in these conditions, see **Ground Covers** on page 125 and **Wildflowers** on page 303. Many bulbs also thrive in shade—see **Bulbs** on page 52 for ideas. There also are individual entries on many shade-loving plants throughout this book, including *Ajuga*, *Alchemilla*, *Astilbe*, *Bergenia*, *Dicentra*, *Epimedium*, Ferns, *Helleborus*, *Heuchera*, *Hosta*, and *Pulmonaria*.

Brunnera macrophylla / Siberian bugloss
Clusters of tiny, 1/4-inch-wide blue flowers in mid- to late spring; 1- to 1 1/2-foot mounds of large, heart-shaped leaves. Self-sows. Divide in spring or fall if plants outgrow their space or for propagation. Or take root cuttings in late winter or early spring. Zones 3 to 8.

Corydalis lutea / Yellow corydalis
Clusters of golden yellow, 1/2-inch-long, tubular flowers from spring to fall; 12- to 16-inch mounds of fernlike, evergreen or semievergreen leaves. Self-sows. Established plants are best not disturbed, but seedlings are easy to move. Sow fresh seeds outdoors in fall. Zones 5 to 8.

Ligularia spp. / Ligularias
Erect spikes or rounded clusters of golden yellow flowers in summer over mounds of bold, rounded or lobed foliage; 3- to 6-foot plants. *L. dentata* reaches 3 to 5 feet tall and bears flattened clusters of daisylike flowers over mounds of heart-shaped, 12-inch-long leaves. *L. przewalskii* has deeply cut leaves, while *L. stenocephala* has triangular, toothed ones. Both species bear spikes of flowers that reach 5 to 6 feet in height. All ligularias require very rich, constantly moist soil and light to partial shade, preferably during the afternoon. They wilt dramatically (and quite unattractively) with inadequate soil moisture. A site protected from wind is best. Propagate by division in spring or fall if necessary. The species can be grown from seeds sown in spring or fall in pots set in a protected location outdoors, but cultivars should be propagated by division. All are hardy in Zones 4 to 8.

Myosotis sylvatica / Forget-me-not
Clusters of tiny, 3/8-inch-wide blue, white, or pink flowers with yellow eyes in spring and early summer; 5- to 12-inch plants with gray-green leaves. A biennial or short-lived perennial frequently grown as a biennial. Self-sows abundantly. Will grow in full sun and is best in poor to average soil. To propagate, sow seeds in pots in spring and set them outdoors in a protected location. Zones 5 to 9.

Polygonatum odoratum 'Variegatum' / Variegated Solomon's seal
Foliage plant grown for its arching, 2- to 3-foot-tall stems with oval leaves with irregular white margins. Bell-shaped, 1 1/4-inch-long, white flow-

Siberian bugloss *(Brunnera macrophylla)*

Forget-me-not *(Myosotis sylvatica)*

Variegated Solomon's seal *(Polygonatum odoratum* 'Variegatum') with foamflower *(Tiarella cordifolia* 'Echo Red Heart')

Meadow rue (*Thalictrum aquilegiifolium*)

Spiderwort (*Tradescantia* spp.)

ers are borne under the stems in late spring. Spreads steadily by rhizomes. Yellow fall foliage color. Divide clumps in spring or fall to propagate. Zones 4 to 8.

Thalictrum spp. / Meadow rues
Rounded, fuzzy-looking clusters of tiny, petalless flowers in early to midsummer; mounds of blue-green, lobed leaves. *T. aquilegiifolium* has purple or white, 6- to 8-inch-wide flower clusters and ranges from 2 to 3 feet tall. It is hardy in Zones 4 to 8. *T. rochebrunianum* has loose clusters of lilac-pink or white flowers on 3-foot plants and is hardy in Zones 4 to 7. Meadow rues tolerate full sun with adequate soil moisture. Plants may need staking. They can be divided, if necessary, in early spring or fall for propagation. Sow seeds in fall or early spring into pots and set them in a protected location outdoors.

Tradescantia spp. / Spiderworts
Saucer-shaped, 1-inch-wide flowers with three petals in violet, lavender-blue, pink, rose-red, or white from early to midsummer; $1\frac{1}{2}$- to 2-foot plants with long, lance-shaped leaves. Cut back plants after the main flush of flowers to discourage reseeding, to encourage rebloom, and to keep the plants neat. Divide clumps in spring or fall for propagation. Zones 4 to 9; to Zone 3 with winter protection.

Tricyrtis hirta / Toad lily
Clusters of white, purple-spotted flowers in late summer and fall in the leaf axils along the stems; lance-shaped leaves along upright, 2- to 3-foot-tall stems. Plants spread by rhizomes, and clumps can be divided in spring for propagation. Zones 4 to 9.

Viola spp. / Violets
Purple, lilac, white, or yellow flowers in spring; mounds of heart- or lance-shaped leaves. Plants spread by creeping rhizomes and also self-sow; they can become quite weedy and invasive, but they make a dense, weed-smothering ground cover in the right site. Pull up unwanted seedlings wherever they appear. There are some 500 species, many of which are native wildflowers. Hardiness varies from Zones 3 to 9, depending on the species.

PERENNIALS FOR SUN
Gardeners with full sun have a wealth of perennials from which to choose. Page through the other entries in this book for some of the most popular choices — from *Achillea* to *Yucca*. The plants listed below also make attractive additions to perennial gardens. You'll find more plants for

full sun in **Wildflowers** on page 303 and **Ground Covers** on page 125.

Acanthus spinosus / Spiny bear's breech

Erect spikes, to 3 feet long, of showy, 1-inch-long, white-and-purple flowers from late spring to early summer; mounds of spiny, thistlelike, evergreen leaves. Grows in full sun or partial shade. Best in rich, deep, well-drained soil. Divide in spring or fall if necessary or for propagation. Or propagate by root cuttings in fall or early winter. Cut winter-damaged leaves off in early spring to make room for new growth. Zones 5 to 9.

Amsonia tabernaemontana / Willow blue star

Clusters of pale blue, $1/2$-inch-wide, star-shaped flowers in spring and early summer; 1- to 2-foot plants. Grows in full sun or partial shade. Cut plants that are growing in shade back after flowering to keep them neat looking. Divide plants in spring or fall to propagate, or take stem cuttings in early summer. Zones 3 to 9.

Anchusa azurea / Italian bugloss

Loose clusters of $1/2$-inch-wide, rich blue flowers in early summer; 2- to 5-foot plants with hairy leaves. Best in average, well-drained soil that is evenly moist; soil that is too rich causes rank growth. Wet soil in winter will kill the plants. Short-lived perennial; divide plants every 2 to 3 years to keep them vigorous. Self-sows with enthusiasm. Cut back plants hard after flowering to encourage rebloom. Can also be propagated by root cuttings taken in early spring. Named cultivars such as 'Loddon Royalist' are the best choices for the garden. Zones 3 to 8.

Armeria maritima / Thrift, sea pink

Round, 1- to $1^1/2$-inch-wide clusters of pink, rose, or white flowers in spring and early summer; low, 2- to 3-inch mounds of grasslike, evergreen leaves. Requires very well drained, poor to average soil. Plants dislike heat and humidity; in areas with hot summers, select a site with afternoon shade to keep them as cool as possible. Good for rock gardens and grows well in seaside gardens. Divide plants in early spring or fall for propagation or if the clumps die out in the center. Sow seeds in pots in spring and set them in a protected location outdoors. Zones 3 to 8.

Artemisia spp. / Artemisias, wormwoods

Shrublike perennials grown for their finely cut, aromatic, silver or gray-green leaves. The flowers are insignificant. Grow them in average, well-drained soil. Wormwood *(A. absinthium)* is a clump-forming species that reaches 2 to 3 feet in height and is hardy in Zones 3 to 9. White sage

TOP Thrift *(Armeria maritima)*

ABOVE Silvermound artemisia *(Artemisia schmidtiana)*

(A. ludoviciana) is 2 to 4 feet tall; both it and its popular cultivars 'Silver King', 'Silver Queen', and 'Valerie Finnis' spread quickly by creeping rhizomes and need to be divided every 2 to 3 years. They are hardy in Zones 3 to 9. *A.* × 'Powis Castle' forms compact, 2- to 3-foot-tall clumps of silver-white leaves and is hardy in Zones 5 to 8. Silvermound artemisia *(A. schmidtiana)* forms soft, round, 1- to 2-foot mounds of foliage and spreads slowly by rhizomes; 'Nana' is a compact cultivar. Both are hardy in Zones 3 to 7. In areas with hot, humid summers, clumps of silvermound artemisia tend to fall open in the middle; cut the plants back hard (by half to two-thirds) if they flop, or grow clump-forming species in areas with hot summers. Dig clumps of spreading species in spring or fall to propagate them. For shrubby, clump-forming species, take

Butterfly weed
(*Asclepias tuberosa*)

Valerian
(*Centranthus ruber*)

cuttings in early summer and root them in a 50-50 mix of sand and perlite.

Asclepias tuberosa / Butterfly weed
Rounded, horizontal clusters of bright orange or orange-red flowers in midsummer; 1- to 3-foot plants. Native perennial wildflower for full sun and average, well-drained soil in full sun. Plants have deep, fleshy taproots, which make them quite drought tolerant once established. Propagate them by cuttings in late spring or early summer or by root cuttings in fall. Or sow fresh seeds in fall outdoors in pots set in a protected location or in a nursery bed. Transplant seedlings as soon as they have two sets of true leaves, because they develop taproots early and can be difficult to move after that. Zones 3 to 9.

Aurinia saxatilis / Basket-of-gold
Dense clusters of tiny, 1/2-inch-wide, golden yellow flowers in spring; 10- to 12-inch plants with gray-green, evergreen leaves. Requires well-drained soil that is not too rich. Plants resent rich, moist conditions and do not grow well in areas with hot, humid summers. Cut them back by one-third after flowering to keep them compact. Propagate by division in fall, or take stem cuttings in spring and root them in a 50-50 mix of peat and perlite. Zones 3 to 7.

Calamintha nepeta / Lesser calamint
Clouds of dainty, 1/4-inch, pale mauve-pink flowers from midsummer to fall; mounding, 18-inch-tall plants with aromatic leaves. Grows in most well-drained soils and tolerates heat and drought. Also grows in light shade. Divide plants in spring to propagate, or sow seeds in pots in spring and set them in a protected location outdoors. Good edging or rock-garden plant. Zones 5 to 9.

Centranthus ruber / Valerian, Jupiter's beard
Rounded clusters of fragrant, funnel-shaped, pinkish red or white flowers through summer; 1- to 3-foot plants with blue-green leaves. Easy to grow in poor to average, well-drained soil with a slightly acid to alkaline pH. Cut plants back by half after flowering if they become floppy or unattractive. Will self-sow, and seedlings are easy to move. Divide plants in spring to propagate. Easy from seeds sown in spring in pots set outdoors in a protected location. Zones 4 to 8.

Eupatorium spp. / Bonesets, Joe-Pye weeds
Native wildflowers grown for their showy, rounded clusters of small fuzzy flowers in summer and fall. Hardy ageratum (*E. coelestinum*), hardy in Zones 6 to 10, bears fluffy clusters of lilac-blue flowers that resemble annual ageratum in late summer to fall on 2- to 3-foot plants. *E. fistulosum*, hardy in Zones 3 to 8, ranges from 5 to 10 feet or more in height, depending on how rich and moist the soil is. It bears mauve-pink, 6- to 10-inch-wide flower clusters in midsummer and tolerates partial shade. *E. purpureum*, also hardy in Zones 3 to 8, bears pale rose-pink or purplish flowers on 3- to 6-foot plants. A variety of cultivars of the latter two species are available that bear large, showy blooms that make them ideal for adding late-season color to the back of beds and borders. They are also appropriate for wildflower plantings. Grow all of the species in full sun and average to rich soil. Evenly moist to wet conditions are ideal, although they will also grow in the rich, well-drained conditions of the average perennial border. Dig plants in spring or fall if they outgrow their space or for propagation; *E. coelestinum* benefits from being divided every 3 to 4 years, while the other species can thrive for years untouched. Or propagate by cuttings taken in early summer. Most species will self-sow, but named cultivars should be propagated by cuttings or division.

Gaura lindheimeri / White gaura
Airy spires of small white or pink flowers from early summer to fall; 3- to 4-foot plants. A native perennial that thrives in moist, well-drained soil and full sun. Good drainage is essential to

success, and plants form deep taproots and are quite drought tolerant (and difficult to dig) once established. Tolerates heat and humidity. Take cuttings from shoots that arise at the base of the plant or from stem tips in spring or early summer. Or sow seeds outdoors in fall in pots set in a protected location. Zones 5 to 9.

Geum spp. / Avens
Orange, red, or yellow, 1½-inch-wide flowers in late spring and summer; 1- to 2-foot plants with deeply divided leaves. Two species are commonly grown: *G. chiloense* (formerly *G. quellyon*), hardy in Zones 5 to 9, and *G. coccineum* (formerly *G. × borisii*), hardy in Zones 4 to 9. Both grow in full sun but benefit from a site with afternoon shade south of Zone 6. They require evenly moist but well-drained soil, and good drainage is especially important in winter. Plants can be short lived; divide them in spring or fall every 2 to 3 years to keep them vigorous. Propagate named cultivars by division. (Although seed-grown plants aren't identical to asexually propagated ones, 'Lady Stratheden' and 'Mrs. Bradshaw' can be grown from seeds sown in spring and set in a protected location outdoors.)

Hibiscus moscheutos / Rose mallow
Giant, 6- to 10-inch-wide, disk-shaped flowers in summer in white, pink, or red on shrubby, 4- to 8-foot plants. Flowers last only a day but are borne in abundance. Remove spent blooms regularly, because they look like limp tissue paper and are unattractive. Easy to grow in moist, rich soil in full sun or partial shade. The plants are late to emerge in spring, so mark the location of the clumps to avoid digging into them accidentally. Sow seeds indoors in winter; seedlings may start blooming the same year. Many popular cultivars come true from seed, including the Disco Belle Series, 'Lady Baltimore', and 'Lord Baltimore'. Clumps can be divided in spring if they outgrow their space or for propagation, but the woody clumps can be hard to divide. Zones 5 to 10.

Linum spp. / Flax
Loose clusters of saucer-shaped, clear blue flowers from early to midsummer; 1- to 1½-foot plants with blue-green, needlelike leaves. Perennial flax *(L. perenne),* hardy in Zones 4 to 9, bears 1-inch-wide flowers, while narbonne flax *(L. narbonense),* hardy in Zones 5 to 9, bears 2-inch-wide blue flowers with white eyes. Grow both species in full sun or light shade in average soil that is very well drained. Good drainage is especially important in winter. Plants tend to rot out in heavier soil but should be long lived if given a well-drained site that is not soggy in winter. Cut back plants after they flower to keep them neat looking. Plants will self-sow, so allow some flowers to set seed if you want new plants. They seldom need division. Propagate by stem cuttings taken in early summer and rooted in a 50-50 mix of perlite and vermiculite. Or sow seeds outdoors in spring or fall; they require cool (50° to 60°F) soil to germinate.

Lupine
(Lupinus polyphyllus)

Lychnis spp. / Campions, catchflies

Orange, red, rose, or white flowers in spring or summer; 2- to 3-foot plants. Maltese cross *(L. chalcedonica)* bears rounded clusters of ½-inch-wide, star-shaped, scarlet flowers from early to midsummer. Rose campion *(L. coronaria)* produces broad clusters of 1-inch-wide, rose-pink flowers above rosettes of silver-gray leaves. Both species are short-lived perennials but self-sow abundantly to replace themselves. Grow them in full sun or light shade and average to rich, moist but well-drained soil. Afternoon shade is beneficial in the South. Treat them as biennials or pull up older plants after 2 years' bloom to make room for seedlings. Or dig and divide clumps every 2 to 3 years, discarding the oldest portions, to keep them vigorous. Deadheading prolongs bloom, but allow some flowers to set seed to ensure new plants. Zones 4 to 8.

Penstemon spp. / Penstemons, beardtongues

Spikes of tubular flowers with two upper and three lower lips in spring and summer. Native North American wildflowers. Common beardtongue *(P. barbatus)* bears 1- to 1½-inch-long, pink to red flowers on 1½- to 3-foot plants in early summer. It tolerates heat and is hardy in Zones 3 to 8. Foxglove penstemon *(P. digitalis)* bears white flowers in late spring on 2- to 4-foot plants, is also hardy in Zones 3 to 8, and tolerates southern heat and humidity. Its cultivar 'Huskers Red' has red foliage and white flowers. Hairy beardtongue *(P. hirsutus),* hardy in Zones 3 to 9, has pale to rich purple, 1-inch-long flowers in summer on 2- to 3-foot plants. Its cultivar 'Pygmaeus' is only 8 inches tall. Grow penstemons in full sun in very well drained, average to somewhat fertile soil. Most are good candidates for rock gardens. Well-drained soil is essential for most species, especially in winter, although *P. digitalis* will tolerate moist conditions. To keep the clumps vigorous, divide them every 4 to 6 years, discarding the oldest portions. Sow seeds outdoors in fall. Indoors, sow seeds in winter in pots and store them in the refrigerator for 4 to 6 weeks before germinating them in a cool (55° to 65°F), bright place.

Physostegia virginiana / Obedient plant

Dense, erect spikes of two-lipped, 1-inch-long, rose-pink or white flowers from midsummer to early fall; 3- to 4-foot plants. A vigorous, fast-spreading perennial native to eastern North America. Slower growing 'Variegata' has cream-edged leaves. Grow in full sun or partial shade in average, evenly moist soil. Plants tolerate wet conditions but will flop over in very fertile soil. Compact cultivars ranging from 2 to 3 feet in

Lupinus spp. / Lupines

Erect spikes of densely packed, pealike flowers in purple, violet, yellow, pink, red, or white in spring and summer; 3- to 5-foot plants. Hybrid lupines, including the 2½- to 3-foot-tall Russell hybrids, are the most popular and are hardy in Zones 3 or 4 to 8, but they do not grow well in areas with hot, humid summers, and south of Zone 6 they are best grown as annuals in the eastern and central states. They thrive in the cool, moist summers of the Pacific Northwest and in coastal New England. Grow them in full sun or light shade in rich, evenly moist, well-drained soil that is slightly acid.

height are available and tend not to flop. Divide the clumps every 2 to 3 years to keep them in bounds or for propagation. Or propagate by stem cuttings — take in early summer and root in a 50-50 mix of perlite and vermiculite. Zones 3 to 9.

Scabiosa spp. / Pincushion flowers

Rounded, pincushion-like flower clusters in lavender, white, yellow, or rose-purple from summer to early fall; 2-foot plants. Grow in full sun or partial shade in a spot with well-drained, average to rich soil that is neutral to slightly alkaline. Plants do not tolerate soil that is too moist, especially in winter. In the South, plant them in a site that receives afternoon shade. Deadhead regularly to prolong bloom. Divide clumps in spring if they outgrow their space or become crowded or for propagation. Or propagate by taking cuttings from shoots that arise at the base of the plant in spring and root them in a 50-50 mix of perlite and vermiculite. 'Butterfly Blue' and 'Pink Mist' (also sold as 'Butterfly Pink') are outstanding, long-blooming cultivars. Zones 4 to 9.

Pincushion flower (*Scabiosa* spp.)

Stachys byzantina / Lamb's ears

Perennial grown primarily for its mounds of woolly-white, feltlike leaves and stems, although spikes of tiny purple flowers appear in spring and summer; 1½-foot plants. Grow in very well drained, average soil in full sun or partial shade. Grows well in sandy soil. Does not do well in areas with hot, humid, rainy summers, where plants are frequently subject to crown rot. Many gardeners remove the flowers as they appear; the cultivar 'Silver Carpet' does not flower. If the foliage looks diseased or the stems appear to be rotting, cut plants back in midsummer. They will recover in fall when cooler weather arrives. Cut plants to the ground in fall or early spring; fall is best if you live in an area with wet winters, because cutting down then prevents the leaves from smothering the crowns. Divide plants in spring if they outgrow their space or for propagation. Zones 4 to 8.

Stokesia laevis / Stoke's aster

Violet-blue, pink, or white, 4-inch-wide, cornflower- or asterlike flowers from midsummer to early fall; 1- to 2-foot plants. A native North American wildflower. Plant in full sun or light shade in rich, evenly moist, well-drained soil. Poorly drained soil leads to crown rot and death. Generally requires staking. Deadheading encourages plants to rebloom. Propagate by dividing the clumps in spring or fall, by root cuttings taken in late winter or early spring, or by sowing seeds in fall and setting the pots in a protected location over winter. Zones 5 to 9.

Lamb's ears (*Stachys byzantina*)

$\mathcal{P}$erovskia atriplicifolia

Russian Sage

Russian sage (*Perovskia atriplicifolia*)

Perovskia atriplicifolia

■

(per-OFF-ski-ah
ah-trih-plih-cih-FOE-lee-ah)

■

Mid- to late-summer
bloom

■

Full sun

■

Zones 5 to 9

■

■ Russian sage, also simply called perovskia, is a striking sight come midsummer. The plants produce airy spikes of tiny, lavender-blue flowers that create a cloudlike haze of color above silver- to gray-green, deeply cut leaves and silvery stems. Although the individual tubular flowers are tiny, the overall effect is quite showy, because they are carried in 12- to 15-inch-long panicles that last from mid- to late summer. Russian sage is a shrubby, and shrub-sized, perennial: plants range from 3 to 5 feet in height, although they rarely exceed 3 feet in Zone 5. The silvery foliage, handsome in its own right, is aromatic when brushed.

SITE AND SOIL
Grow Russian sage in full sun in very well drained, poor to average, sandy or loamy soil. The plants grow well in dry as well as alkaline soil and are good choices for seaside gardens.

Well-drained soil is especially important in winter, when plants are dormant. To improve drainage, dig the soil deeply and work in organic matter such as compost or chopped leaves before planting. Or plant Russian sage in raised beds or even mounds of soil built up in a bed or border to ensure that the crowns do not stay wet in winter.

PLANTING
Plant Russian sage in spring or fall. Space plants 2 feet apart. Although the plants do not spread, they form substantial clumps with time. Newly planted specimens take a year or two to become established.

CARE THROUGH THE SEASON
Russian sage plants require very little care to look their best. Mulching and feeding are optional. If you do feed, do so sparingly — a spring topdressing with compost will suffice. After the first hard frost in fall, cut plants back to within 1 foot of the ground. In the colder portions of Zone 5 (and some gardeners grow this plant in Zone 4), plants are killed to the ground over winter but resprout in spring. In northern zones, cover the plants with evergreen boughs or straw over winter. A rainy fall or wet winter increases the chances that plants will not return in spring. For best results, do not divide Russian sage, because the woody crowns are hard to separate successfully.

Propagation. Propagate Russian sage by taking cuttings from shoots that emerge from the base of the plants in spring or early summer. Dip the stem tips in a rooting hormone and root them in a 50-50 mix of sand and perlite. Small offsets also appear on the outside of established clumps, and these can be used for propagation. Gently remove some soil around the offset, then carefully sever it from the main clump with a sharp trowel and dig it up. Seeds of Russian sage are seldom available, and improved cultivars do not come true from seed.

LANDSCAPE USES
Russian sage makes a stunning addition to sunny, late-summer beds and borders. Combine it with ornamental grasses, boltonia, globe thistle *(Echinops ritro),* sea hollies *(Eryngium* spp.), purple coneflower *(Echinacea purpurea),* and gayfeathers *(Liatris* spp.).

Phlox

Phlox
■
(FLOCKS)
■
Midspring to early-fall bloom
■
Sun to shade
■
Zones 2 to 9
■

■ Gardeners with either sun or shade can enjoy the cheerful sight of phlox flowers. The earliest phlox to bloom are ground-hugging species that thrive in full sun and blanket themselves in color from midspring to early summer. Phlox light up shade gardens in spring and early summer as well, when foot-tall woodland species come into bloom. The season culminates when the stately summer-blooming species come into their own, including popular garden phlox *(Phlox paniculata)*, which has been a classic much-loved perennial for beds and borders for many years. While most phlox are perennials, one highly valued species is an annual: *P. drummondii.* See the description on page 31 in the **Annuals & Biennials** entry for details on growing it.

Moss phlox *(Phlox subulata)*

Pale pink moss phlox *(Phlox subulata)* with rosy purple *Aubrieta × cultorum*

The name *Phlox* is taken from the Greek word for "flame," a reference to the fact that many of these charming beauties come in hot colors such as crimson and magenta-pink. There are also phlox with softer colors, including white, pale pink, lavender, lavender blue, and purple. Most phlox are native North American wildflowers (one of the 70 or so species in the genus is from Siberia), but some of the most popular species—especially *P. paniculata* and moss phlox *(P. subulata)*—have been extensively hybridized. Most produce their showy flowers in rounded clusters. Low-growing types hold their flowers so close to the ground that it's hard to see the clusters at all, and the plants look as if they have a mat of flowers directly above the foliage. Each flower has a tubular base and five petals, more accurately called petal lobes, and the petals may have a notch in the tip.

SELECTING PHLOX

Where not to plant phlox is more a question than where to plant them, for there are species for every part of the garden. Plant a selection of the following and you'll not only enjoy the various shapes, sizes, and colors, you'll stretch out the bloom season as well.

Low-Growing Phlox for Sun

These ground-hugging species are stunning additions to rock gardens and can also be used as ground covers and edgings. All are best grown in full sun in average to rich, well-drained soil and require very little care to thrive. In areas with hot, dry summers, dappled afternoon shade is beneficial. Space *P. bifida* 6 to 8 inches apart; *P. douglasii* and *P. subulata,* 10 to 12 inches apart. Space slightly closer if you are planting either of the latter species as a ground cover. Cut back or shear the plants after they bloom to keep them neat looking. To encourage the stems to root, and to allow water to seep down into the soil rather than run off of it, gently lift up the edges of the clumps in late winter and remove any dead leaves, then carefully loosen the soil under the plants.

These species can be grown for years without being divided. Dig and divide them in fall if they outgrow their space, die out in the centers of the clumps, or appear to be growing less vigorously, or to propagate the clumps. It's also possible to propagate by cuttings taken in early to midsummer of new shoots that arise near the base of the plants. (Do not try to root older shoots, which become woody.) Root them in coarse sand or a 50-50 mix of sand and perlite.

P. bifida. Cleft phlox, sand phlox. Fragrant, star-shaped, ³/₄-inch-wide, lavender to white flowers with deeply cleft petal ends in spring;

mounding, 6- to 8-inch plants with needlelike, evergreen leaves. Will grow in poor, very well drained soil. Zones 4 to 8.

P. douglasii. Douglas's phlox. White, lavender, or pink, 1/2-inch-wide flowers borne singly or in very small clusters from late spring to early summer; mounding, 3- to 8-inch plants with narrow, lance-shaped leaves. White-, magenta-, red-, and violet-pink-flowered cultivars are available. Zones 4 to 8.

P. subulata. Moss phlox, creeping phlox, moss pink. Lavender, purple, pink, or white, 1/2- to 1-inch flowers that blanket the plants in mid- to late spring; mat-forming, 2- to 6-inch plants with dense, needlelike leaves that are evergreen. A good ground cover. Tolerates dry soil and is a good choice for slopes or above rock walls. Many cultivars with solid and bicolor blooms are available. Zones 2 to 9.

Phlox for Shade

Shade-loving phlox are easy to grow and undemanding. Plant them in light to full shade in a site with evenly moist soil that is well drained and rich in organic matter. Both of the following species spread into broad clumps via creeping stems that root where they touch the soil; *P. stolonifera* spreads more quickly and widely than *P. divaricata.* The clumps need to be divided only if they outgrow their space.

Propagate both species by digging and dividing them in spring after the flowers fade. Digging up rooted plantlets that appear is another easy option. You can also propagate by taking cuttings

in spring or early summer from shoots that arise near the base of the plants. Root them in a 50-50 mix of vermiculite and perlite.

P. divaricata. Wild blue phlox, woodland phlox. Clusters of fragrant lavender, pale violet, or white flowers in spring; 10- to 14-inch plants with semievergreen leaves. Self-sows, yielding attractive lavender-flowered seedlings. Cut back spent flower stalks after they fade to keep plants neat looking. May be disfigured by powdery mildew; keeping the soil evenly moist and thinning out the stems helps prevent the disease. Space plants 10 to 12 inches apart. Zones 3 to 9.

P. stolonifera. Creeping phlox. Loose clusters of pink, lilac-blue, or white flowers in spring; 4- to 6-inch-tall plants. Space plants 1 1/2 to 2 feet apart. Zones 3 to 8.

Phlox for Sunny Beds and Borders

Garden phlox *(P. paniculata)* is a classic perennial for beds and borders, and is far and away the most popular species, but it is also the most demanding of the taller phlox to grow. In recent years, gardeners have rediscovered the benefits of disease-resistant Carolina phlox *(P. carolina)* and wild sweet William *(P. maculata).* Both begin blooming before *P. paniculata.*

Grow all of the following species in full sun or partial shade and rich, deeply prepared soil that remains evenly moist. All are best in areas with relatively cool summers, and none tolerate drought. In southern zones, a site with light shade during the hottest part of the day is best. Space plants 1 to 1 1/2 feet apart. Deadheading will prolong bloom and also prevents self-sowing. Named cultivars do not come true from seed, and seedlings, which generally have unattractive, magenta-pink flowers, will be more vigorous and will overwhelm the cultivars you are growing. Rogue out seedlings that do appear.

Tall phlox, especially *P. paniculata,* frequently require staking. Surrounding the clumps with stakes and string in early summer before the stems get more than a foot or so tall is an effective method. See "Staking" in the Techniques Glossary for details.

Ideally, dig and divide all of the following species every 2 or 3 years in fall to keep them vigorous and healthy. They can also be divided in spring. Split the clumps into sections of three to five stems each, and discard the older, woodier portions of the clumps. Dig compost or well-rotted manure deeply into the soil before replanting. For best effect, arrange the plants in drifts of three to five.

Dividing is the easiest way to propagate these species, but new plants can also be grown from

ABOVE Creeping phlox *(Phlox stolonifera)* with foamflowers *(Tiarella cordifolia)*

BELOW Wild blue phlox *(Phlox divaricata)* with hostas

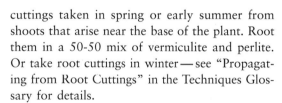

cuttings taken in spring or early summer from shoots that arise near the base of the plant. Root them in a 50-50 mix of vermiculite and perlite. Or take root cuttings in winter — see "Propagating from Root Cuttings" in the Techniques Glossary for details.

P. carolina. Carolina phlox, thick-leaved phlox. Clusters of purple to pink, 3/4-inch-wide flowers in summer; 3- to 4-foot plants with glossy, oval leaves. Resistant to powdery mildew. Zones 4 to 9.

P. maculata. Wild sweet William, meadow phlox. Elongated clusters of fragrant, 3/4- to 1-inch-wide, mauve-pink flowers in early to mid-summer; 2- to 3-foot plants with narrow, glossy leaves. Cultivars offer the best colors: 'Miss Lingard' (sometimes listed under *P. carolina*) has white flowers, 'Omega' is white with a lilac eye, and 'Rosalinde' is rose-pink. Resistant to powdery mildew. Zones 4 to 8.

P. paniculata. Garden phlox. Rounded clusters of fragrant, 1/2- to 1-inch-wide flowers in summer to early fall; thin, 2- to 5-inch-long leaves

on 3- to 4-foot plants. This is a heavily hybridized species, and many cultivars are available with pale to rose-pink, orange-red, crimson, purple, lilac, or white flowers. Bicolor blooms are also available. Gardeners who grow this species will have to contend with powdery mildew, which destroys the appearance of the plants. For more on dealing with powdery mildew, see "Potential Problems" on page 236. Several mildew-resistant cultivars have been developed, including 'David', which has white flowers, and 'Katherine', 'Pax', and 'Sandra'. 'Bright Eyes' is a compact selection that grows from 2 to 2 1/2 feet tall and bears pink flowers. Zones 3 to 8.

PLANTING

Plant phlox in spring or fall, taking care to select a site that will provide the sun and soil conditions the species you are planting prefers. A site with good air circulation is a plus with phlox that are subject to powdery mildew. Adequate spacing also helps control this fungal disease, and plants perform best when they are not crowded.

TOP LEFT
Wild sweet William
(*Phlox maculata* 'Miss Lingard')

TOP RIGHT
Garden phlox (*Phlox paniculata* 'Starfire')

BOTTOM LEFT
Garden phlox
(*Phlox paniculata*)

BOTTOM RIGHT
Garden phlox (*Phlox paniculata* 'Norah Leigh') offers striking variegated foliage.

It's easy to mistake dame's rocket or sweet rocket *(Hesperis matronalis)* for one of the taller species of phlox such as wild sweet William *(P. maculata)* or garden phlox *(P. paniculata).* Both dame's rocket and the phlox bear rounded clusters of flowers, but phlox blooms have five petals, while those of dame's rocket have only four. Dame's rocket is a native wildflower, hardy in Zones 3 to 8, that produces its sweet-smelling, pink or white flowers from late spring to midsummer. It is lovely in wildflower gardens and along the edges of shady woodlands, and it thrives in full sun or partial shade in average to rich soil that is evenly moist. Although individual plants are short lived, they self-sow prolifically, so plantings return year after year. The plants go dormant in midsummer; cut them down after the foliage turns yellow. Combine them with other moisture-loving perennials that will fill the space they leave. Be sure to allow some flowers to set seed each year to ensure a new crop of seedlings in spring. Dame's rocket is easy to grow by sowing seeds outdoors in early spring where the plants are to grow.

Garden phlox
(*Phlox paniculata*
'Bright Eyes')

CARE THROUGH THE SEASON

Low-growing phlox—*P. bifida, P. douglasii,* and *P. subulata*—along with shade-loving *P. divaricata* and *P. stolonifera* will thrive for years with little care. They don't require annual feeding, staking, or regular dividing. Water the two shade-loving species as necessary (neither tolerates drought) to keep the soil evenly moist. Mulching annually in spring also helps to keep the soil rich, cool, and moist.

Feed *P. carolina, P. maculata,* and *P. paniculata* in spring with a topdressing of compost or well-rotted manure. Thin out the stems in spring by removing the smallest ones if the clumps look too crowded. Leave about 3 inches between stems to increase air circulation. To produce extra-large bloom trusses, remove all but four or five of the strongest stems from each clump. Water the plants deeply and regularly if the weather is dry. Watering from below, using soaker hoses, is best because it keeps the leaves dry and helps prevent foliar diseases. If you would like to delay bloom and to keep the plants more compact (thus eliminating the need to stake), pinch out the tips of the stems once or twice from late spring to early summer. This reduces the size of the individual flower clusters but increases the number each clump produces. Remember to deadhead plants through the season and to rogue out self-sown seedlings. (Plantings that have "reverted" actually have been overtaken by seedlings.)

Propagation. While the species can be grown from seeds sown outdoors in fall (sow in pots and set them in a protected location), most phlox are propagated asexually by cuttings or division because the cultivars do not come true from seed. Dividing plants in spring or fall is the easiest way to propagate all phlox. Summer-blooming species (listed under "Phlox for Sunny Beds and Borders" beginning on page 234) can also be grown from cuttings. Take them either in spring from new shoots that arise at the base of the plant or in early summer from more mature shoots. They can also be propagated by root cuttings taken in late summer or fall (see the Techniques Glossary for more on propagating from root cuttings).

Potential Problems. Spider mites cause leaves to curl under and to develop rusty-looking patches, especially on *P. paniculata.* Blast them off the plants with a steady stream of water from the hose. Powdery mildew causes large white blotches on the leaves, which eventually drop off. To prevent it, select a site with good air circulation, plant resistant cultivars, thin stems in spring so air can circulate through the clumps, and keep plants well watered (from below, to keep foliage dry) during dry spells. To check the disease, spray wettable sulfur on the foliage weekly once the first patch of white appears. Clean up and destroy all mildew-infected plant debris in late summer.

LANDSCAPE USES

Combine shade-loving phlox with hostas, ferns, spring bulbs, lungworts (*Pulmonaria* spp.), bleeding hearts (*Dicentra* spp.), and shade-loving wildflowers. The low-growing species that thrive in sun can be used in rock gardens or other areas with well-drained soil. Pair them with plants such as basket-of-gold (*Aurinia saxatilis),* perennial candytuft (*Iberis sempervirens),* lavenders (*Lavandula* spp.), and thymes. Combine the species for sunny beds and borders with hardy geraniums, Shasta daisy (*Chrysanthemum × superbum),* and balloon flower (*Platycodon grandiflorus).*

Platycodon grandiflorus

Balloon Flower

Platycodon grandiflorus

■

(plat-ee-KOE-don
gran-dih-FLOR-us)

■

Summer bloom

■

Full sun or light shade

■

Zones 3 to 8

■

Balloon flower
*(Platycodon
grandiflorus)*

■ Dependable, old-fashioned balloon flowers bear inflated flower buds that split open into broad, shallow, bell-shaped flowers. The common name refers to the balloonlike buds, while the botanical name refers to the 3-inch-wide flowers: *Platycodon* is from the Greek *platys,* meaning "broad," and *kodon,* "bell." The genus contains only *P. grandiflorus,* a stunning, clump-forming perennial that bears purple, blue-violet, lilac-blue, pink, or white flowers from early to midsummer. The plants have blue-green, oval- to lance-shaped leaves and are hardy in Zones 3 to 8.

Compare balloon flowers with bellflowers (*Campanula* spp.) and it will come as no surprise that they are related: both belong to the bellflower family, Campanulaceae. *P. grandiflorus* ssp. *mariesii* (also sold as 'Mariesii') bears purple-blue flowers on 1- to 1½-foot plants. 'Sentimental Blue' is a dwarf type with lilac-blue flowers on 10- to 14-inch plants. 'Shell Pink' has pale pink flowers on 2-foot plants. Fuji Series is a seed-grown strain of white-, pink-, and purple-blue-flowered plants that range from 2 to 3 feet tall. 'Double Blue' bears double lilac-blue flowers on 1½- to 2-foot plants.

The flowers are attractive in arrangements. Pick stems when at least two buds have opened. The stems exude white, milky latex, so sear the cut stem ends with a lighted match before conditioning them overnight in warm water.

SITE AND SOIL

Balloon flowers thrive in full sun or light shade and average to rich, well-drained soil. In the South, a spot that receives afternoon shade is best. Plants in rich soil and partial shade are more likely to need staking.

PLANTING

Plant balloon flowers in spring or early fall. Dig the soil deeply and work in plenty of organic matter at planting time, since the clumps will grow happily in one place for many years. Space plants about 1 foot apart and handle them carefully, as their long, fleshy roots are easily broken. Balloon flowers are late to emerge in spring, so mark the location of the clumps to avoid digging into them accidentally with a misplaced spade.

CARE THROUGH THE SEASON

Balloon flowers need very little care to look their best and are rarely troubled by pests or diseases. They seldom need staking, but if they do, pea stakes or a ring of stakes and string will hold them up. The plants bloom well without annual feeding, although a spring topdressing with compost or a balanced organic fertilizer is beneficial and helps improve the soil. Mulch to control weeds, but be sure to keep the mulch a few inches away from the crowns of the plants.

Although removing spent flowers is a tedious job, it does pay off, because deadheading lengthens the bloom season. The plants have good yellow fall foliage. Cut them to the ground after a hard frost in fall, or wait until the stems emerge in spring to remove the previous season's debris. (I follow the latter schedule as added insurance against digging into the dormant crowns by mistake in spring.)

Established clumps seldom need dividing, but they can be dug in spring or early fall for propagation or transplanting. Dig deeply and handle the clumps carefully to avoid damaging the fleshy roots. Use a sharp knife to cut the crowns into sections.

Propagation. Propagate balloon flowers by division, or look for rooted shoots that sometimes appear at the base of the clump. Dig some soil away from the side of the clump and sever them carefully to be sure you take roots with the shoots. (If you get a shoot with very few roots attached, pot it up and treat it like a cutting.)

Most cultivars also come true from seed. Sow seeds in fall in pots set in a protected location outdoors, or sow indoors in winter and germinate at temperatures between 60° and 70°F. Seedlings take 2 years to bloom. Balloon flowers also self-sow, and seedlings are easy to move to new locations.

LANDSCAPE USES

Combine balloon flowers with catmints (*Nepeta* spp.), daylilies (*Hemerocallis* spp.), thread-leaved coreopsis (*Coreopsis verticillata,* especially 'Moonbeam'), phlox *(Phlox maculata* and *P. paniculata),* lamb's ears *(Stachys byzantina),* and ornamental grasses.

Primroses

Primula
■
(PRIM-you-lah)
■
Early-spring to
early-summer bloom
■
Partial shade
■
Zones 3 to 8
■

■ Primroses, or primulas as they are also called, belong to a vast clan that contains many appealing perennials for the garden. While there are finicky primroses best left to specialists, there are a number of easy-to-grow species that thrive with little care in a variety of sites, including rich, moist woodlands or lightly shaded borders, bog and waterside gardens, and rock gardens.

The name *Primula* alludes to the early-blooming nature of many primroses—it is taken from the Latin *primus,* meaning "first." The bell-, funnel-, or tube-shaped flowers are borne in clusters and often feature spreading petals. The plants produce low clumps of narrow or oval leaves, and the flowers are carried on stalks either among the leaves or above them.

SELECTING PRIMROSES

There are over 400 species of primroses, and botanists have divided the genus into more than 35 sections. Not only have entire books been written about these appealing plants, primrose enthusiasts have been known to turn over their entire gardens to them. With this vast bounty of plants to try, it's hard for the average gardener to know where to start. The best approach is to select primroses that will thrive in the sites you already have available in your garden. If you get bitten by the bug, you can always install special beds for the finickier species later.

While the widest assortment of primroses grow best in areas with cool, moist summers—the Pacific Northwest is ideal primrose-growing territory—fortunately there are species that will thrive in almost any part of the country. Unless otherwise noted, the primroses listed below grow in rich, evenly moist soil that is well drained. A steady supply of moisture is particularly important when they are actively growing in spring. Although they can be planted in full sun if the soil remains evenly moist, a site with partial shade

Japanese primrose *(Primula japonica)*

A Primrose for Bogs and Watersides

Japanese primroses *(P. japonica)* add spectacular midspring to early-summer color to sites with constantly wet soil such as along streams and ponds and in bog gardens. They are classified as candelabra primroses, because the 3/4-inch-wide flowers are borne in one to six tiers along erect stems that can reach 1 1/2 to 2 feet. Flowers come in red, white, and shades of pink. Japanese primroses require partial or full shade (but good light) and constantly moist to wet soil, but they will not grow in stagnant conditions—plant them where there is at least gentle water movement. Set them slightly above the water line, so the crowns are above it and the roots can delve down for as much moisture as the plants desire. Plants self-sow and are hardy in Zones 5 to 8.

(but good light) is best. Especially in areas with warm summers, look for a spot that is shaded during the hottest part of the day.

P. denticulata. Drumstick primrose. Round clusters of bell- or trumpet-shaped, 3/4-inch-wide, lavender-purple or white flowers in early spring on thick, 8- to 12-inch stalks; rosettes of 10-inch-long leaves. Flowers have yellow eyes. Thrives in rich, constantly moist soil and also grows well in soil that is wet to boggy in spring and summer. Plants require better drainage in winter, however, when wet conditions can rot them. Self-sows. Zones 3 to 8.

P. elatior. Oxlip primrose. Dainty clusters of tubular, 1-inch-long flowers on 10- to 12-inch stems in early to midspring; evergreen to semievergreen rosettes of puckered, 8-inch-long leaves. Zones 4 to 8; to Zone 3 with winter protection.

P. juliae. Magenta-pink, 1-inch-wide flowers with yellow eyes borne one per stem in early spring; 2- to 3-inch-tall rosettes of leaves. Spreads slowly to form 10- to 12-inch-wide clumps. Robust, red-purple-flowered 'Wanda' is said to be easier to grow than the species. Zones 3 to 8.

P. Polyanthus Group. Polyanthus primroses. Clusters of showy, 1- to 2-inch-wide flowers on 6-inch-tall stems in early to midspring; rosettes of evergreen to semievergreen, rough-textured, 6- to 7-inch-long leaves. Flowers come in a wide range of colors, including pale to deep yellow, red, orange, violet-blue, white, and pink, and often have yellow eyes. Bicolor blooms are also available. Best in evenly moist conditions but will tolerate soil that is occasionally on the dry side. Frequently sold as florist's pot plants, which can be hardened off and planted in the garden. These hybrids are also listed as *P. × polyanthus* and are crosses of *P. elatior, P. juliae, P. veris,* and *P. vulgaris*. Zones 3 to 8.

P. sieboldii. Siebold primrose. Clusters of delicate, lacy-looking, 1-inch-wide flowers in early spring; rosettes of 8-inch-long leaves. Flowers come in pale pink, rose, white, pale purple, and purple-red. Plants go dormant in midsummer. Zones 3 to 8.

P. veris. Cowslip primrose. Clusters of fragrant, nodding, 1-inch-wide yellow flowers in early to midspring on 10-inch stalks; rosettes of evergreen to semievergreen, 8-inch-long leaves. Zones 4 to 8.

P. vulgaris. English primrose. Clusters of pale yellow, 1- to 1½-inch-wide flowers in early spring; rosettes of evergreen to semievergreen, 9- to 10-inch-long leaves. Many cultivars are available, with both single and double flowers, in white, orange, magenta, purple, pink, lavender, and yellow. Some are fragrant. (Formerly *P. acaulis*.) Zones 4 to 8.

English primrose
(*Primula vulgaris*
'Black Auslese')

CARE THROUGH THE SEASON

Primroses benefit from an annual spring mulch of chopped leaves or shredded bark, which serves to control weeds and to keep the soil moist and cool. Spreading some well-rotted manure in spring also helps maintain soil fertility. Water as necessary to keep the soil evenly moist, especially during spring and early summer when the plants are blooming and actively growing. In most areas, they will look bedraggled by midsummer because of the heat and humidity.

Division. Primroses seldom need to be divided, but if they become overcrowded and begin to lose vigor, divide them in spring or early summer, just after the flowers fade. Some of the faster-growing Polyanthus Group primroses benefit from being divided every 3 to 4 years. Dig the clumps and tease apart the individual plants with your fingers. Divisions with several crowns reestablish most quickly in the garden, but if you want lots of plants, separate each crown, which is a growing point with its own tuft of leaves. If you divide down to individual crowns, cut the leaves back by half and shade the plants with a bushel basket or a piece of lattice for a few weeks. Either way, amend the soil with organic matter before replanting the divisions, and water regularly for several weeks to ensure that they become well established.

Propagation. Division is the easiest and quickest method for propagating primroses. Individual offsets, or crowns, also can be severed from the outside of the clumps with a trowel without disturbing the entire clump.

To grow primroses from seeds, sow them in pots in fall or early spring and set the pots in a cold frame or a protected location outdoors. Or sow indoors in winter, again in pots, and place the pots in the refrigerator for 3 to 4 weeks before germinating them at 60° to 65°F, which takes 1 to 2 months. Either way, cover the seeds with a dusting of moist vermiculite and keep the soil evenly moist. Transplant to the garden in fall or the following spring.

Potential Problems. Slugs like to dine on primrose leaves—see "Dealing with Slugs and Snails" on page 166 in the *Hosta* entry for suggestions on combating these notorious shade-garden pests. In hot, dry summer weather, spider mites can infest the foliage. Control them with a stiff spray of water from the hose.

LANDSCAPE USES

Combine primroses with shade- and moisture-loving perennials such as ferns, hostas, bleeding hearts (*Dicentra* spp.), lungworts (*Pulmonaria* spp.), and wildflowers. They also make fine companions for early-spring bulbs.

SITE AND SOIL

Grow primroses in partial shade and evenly moist soil that is rich in organic matter. A site protected from wind is best. Although primroses are low growing and make delightful plants for edging pathways, keep them away from concrete walkways and other surfaces that might reflect heat. Before planting, work plenty of compost into the soil. Incorporating very well rotted manure is beneficial as well.

PLANTING

Plant primroses in spring. While most gardeners get started with primroses by purchasing plants, they are fairly easy to grow from seeds, and starting with seeds is often the best way to acquire some of the more unusual species. Many strains come true from seed, or at least yield attractive plants, even if they aren't identical to their parents. Space plants 5 to 6 inches apart, then water deeply and spread a layer of mulch to keep the soil moist and cool.

Prunus

Cherries

Prunus
■
(PRUE-nuss)
■
Spring bloom
■
Full sun
■
Zones 2 to 8
■

■ Cherries, peaches, plums, almonds, and a variety of other outstanding ornamental trees and shrubs all belong to the genus *Prunus*. Their spring clusters of flowers are fleeting, but when the plants are in bloom they add a delicate beauty to the garden that few other plants can match. Flowers come in white to pale or deep pink and can be single or double. Double-flowered selections generally are ornamental for a longer period of time in spring than single-flowered ones.

It comes as no surprise that many *Prunus* species feature tasty, edible fruit that birds and other wildlife relish as much as gardeners do. Species that bear fruit too small for people to bother with make fine additions to wildlife gardens. In addition to beautiful flowers and flavorful fruit, some cherries contribute good fall foliage color. Many also have handsome bark, which is commonly marked with raised, corky, horizontal ridges called lenticels.

SELECTING CHERRIES

Gardeners have a wealth of *Prunus* species, both shrubs and trees, from which to choose. Some are especially valuable because of their adaptability — western sand cherry (*P. besseyi*), for example, tol-

erates the heat and drought of the Great Plains without complaint. Others feature weeping habits or ornamental bark — Sargent cherry *(P. sargentii)* has shiny red-brown bark that makes it a standout in the winter landscape. Gardeners looking for handsome, low-maintenance landscape plants should stay away from peaches and other *Prunus* species grown primarily for their fruit. Most are prone to a variety of diseases and insects and require specialized care to produce a crop of fruit.

Shrubs

Use the following cherries to add spring color to shrub borders. Several also make attractive additions to wild areas or bird gardens.

P. besseyi. Western sand cherry. Clouds of 1/2-inch-wide white flowers in mid- to late spring; 4- to 6-foot suckering shrubs spreading to 6 feet or more. Edible, purple-black, 3/4-inch fruit in summer. Tolerates heat and drought and requires well-drained soil. Spreads by underground roots that produce suckers, which can be severed and dug up to propagate it. Good low-maintenance cherry substitute, but fruit is generally made into jam or jelly rather than eaten fresh. Zones 3 to 6.

P. × cistena. Purple-leaved sand cherry. Fragrant, pinkish white flowers in spring; 7- to 10-foot shrubs spreading from 5 to 7 feet. Attractive red-purple leaves all summer and blackish purple fruit. Cut the plants to the ground in spring if they become overgrown or unshapely, or remove one-third of the oldest branches each year. Plants may be killed back in Zone 3 and even after harsh winters in the northern parts of Zone 4 but will regrow from the roots. Zones 3 to 8.

P. glandulosa. Dwarf flowering almond. Pink or white, single or double, 1/2-inch-wide flowers along the branches in midspring; 4- to 5-foot shrubs spreading 3 to 4 feet. Occasionally bears red fruit. Commonly sold but is attractive only in spring and unattractive the rest of the year. There are better choices for the garden. Plants can be cut to the ground in spring if they become overgrown or unattractive, but they will not flower the following spring. Zones 4 to 8.

P. 'Hally Jolivette'. Double, 11/4-inch white flowers with pink centers that open over several weeks from mid- to late spring; 15-foot shrubs or small trees. Plants are as wide as they are tall. They bloom for 10 to 20 days in spring and begin flowering when very small. Handsome cherry for small yards or for use in shrub or perennial borders. Zones 5 to 8.

P. maritima. Beach plum. Single or double, 1/2-inch-wide white flowers in mid- to late spring; 5- to 6-foot suckering shrubs that will spread widely, to 6 feet or more. Purple, 1/2- to 1-inch,

Double-flowered cherry (*Prunus* 'Kanzan', commonly sold as 'Kwanzan')

Prunus 'Hally Jolivette'

Sargent cherry *(Prunus sargentii)*

edible (in jams and jellies) fruit in late summer. Tolerates salt and sandy soil and is a good choice for seaside gardens. Spreads by underground roots that produce suckers, which can be severed and dug up to propagate it. Zones 3 to 6.

P. tomentosa. Manchu cherry, Nanking cherry. Fragrant, white, 3/4-inch-wide flowers in early to midspring; 6- to 10-foot shrubs spreading to 15 feet. Small (1/3-inch), red, edible fruit in early to midsummer. Attractive exfoliating, red-brown bark. Valued for its early flowers and showy fruit and can be used for hedges. Good low-maintenance cherry substitute for edible landscapes, and fruit can be eaten fresh or made into jam and jelly. Zones 2 to 7.

Trees

The genus *Prunus* abounds in small ornamental trees. Any of the following can be used as specimens or lawn trees, and they make attractive additions to shrub borders, too. Also consider using them to anchor a planting of perennials — perhaps mixed with shrubs. All of the species listed here have attractive spring flowers and at least one other ornamental feature — interesting habit, attractive bark, or good fall color.

P. cerasifera. Cherry plum, purple plum. Fragrant, white, 3/4- to 1-inch flowers that open before the leaves emerge; rounded, 15- to 30-foot trees that spread to 25 feet wide. Edible, 1-inch fruit. Purple-leaved cultivars are the most popular and the most frequently planted. They have the best foliage color in full sun. 'Atropurpurea', sometimes called Pissard plum, bears pink flowers and red-purple leaves. It can be grown to Zone 4 but can be killed back somewhat after a hard winter. 'Newport', with pink flowers and dark purple foliage, is reliably hardy to Zone 4. 'Thundercloud' bears pink flowers and deep purple leaves but is reliably hardy only in Zone 5, and it may be subject to dieback in the coldest portions of that zone after a hard winter. All can be grown through Zone 8.

P. × incam 'Okame'. Okame cherry. Rich pink, 3/4- to 1-inch-wide flowers in early spring before the leaves emerge; vase-shaped to rounded, 25- to 30-foot trees spreading to 25 feet. Attractive red-brown bark with long, horizontal lenticels and attractive branching habit. Rich yellow-orange fall color. Flower buds resist late frost in spring. Plants are heat and cold tolerant. Zones 5 to 8.

P. sargentii. Sargent cherry. Single, pink, 1 1/4- to 1 1/2-inch flowers in midspring before the leaves emerge; 20- to 30-foot trees that spread as wide. Attractive, polished red-brown bark, red-tinged leaves in spring, and excellent bronze- to orange-red fall foliage. Purple-black fruit in sum-

mer. Longer lived than most cherries. Seldom troubled by pests or diseases. Zones 4 to 7.

P. serrulata. Japanese flowering cherry. Clusters of single or double, ¹/₂- to 2¹/₂-inch, pink or white flowers in mid- to late spring before or as the leaves unfurl; the species reaches 75 feet, but popular cultivars are rounded-headed or vase-shaped, 20- to 35-foot trees. Plants seldom set fruit. Foliage often has a red tint in spring and turns bronze, red, or orange-red in fall. Trees tend to be short lived, lasting only an average of 15 to 20 years. Many cultivars are available. Zones 5 to 8.

P. × subhirtella. Higan cherry. Clusters of white or pink, ³/₄-inch-wide flowers in spring before the leaves unfurl; 20- to 40-foot trees that spread from 15 to 30 feet. Yellow fall foliage and attractive winter form. Red fruit appears occasionally. The species is seldom grown, but weeping Higan cherries are popular for their graceful form; 'Pendula', 'Pendula Rosea', and 'Pendula Rosea Plena' are three. 'Autumnalis' is an erect selection that bears white flowers with a pink tinge that open sporadically in fall during mild weather and in spring. All are long-lived trees that tolerate heat and cold and are seldom troubled by diseases or pests. Zones 5 to 8.

TOP Weeping cherry (*Prunus × subhirtella* 'Pendula')

ABOVE *Prunus × subhirtella* 'Stellata'

SITE AND SOIL
Grow *Prunus* species in full sun and average to rich soil that is well drained and evenly moist. They will grow in light shade but tend to flower less. Slightly acid to slightly alkaline soil is fine.

PLANTING
Plant *Prunus* species in spring. You'll find bare-root, balled-and-burlapped, and container-grown

specimens offered at garden centers and nurseries. All are fine. To prepare a site for planting, loosen the soil over a wide, fairly shallow planting area. Ideally, the site should be large enough to encompass the eventual spread of the plants' branches. Do not amend the soil with compost or other organic matter unless you do it over the entire planting area. When planting bare-root trees, soak the roots in a bucket of water for about 2 hours before planting. Then spread the roots over a cone of soil in the hole, fill halfway with soil, and flood the site with water. Finish filling with soil and water deeply. Be sure to plant at the same depth at which the trees or shrubs were growing in the nursery. Mulch the area — it's best to keep lawn grass away from the trees to reduce competition and to protect the trunks from mower damage. Water regularly during the first season.

CARE THROUGH THE SEASON

Prunus species tend to be short-lived plants, but good care lessens the chances that they will be plagued with problems and can extend their life. Mulch the plants to keep the soil moist, cool, and rich in organic matter, as well as to keep lawn mowers away from the trunks. Feed plants in fall or spring with a topdressing of compost or a balanced organic fertilizer, but don't overdo it — overfeeding causes rank growth that is more susceptible to pests and diseases. If your soil is very acid, adjust the soil pH upward by spreading lime so that it is closer to neutral.

Pruning. Pruning is best kept to a minimum, since removing large branches opens the plants to diseases and insects. Prune, as necessary, in late winter or early spring, and try to remove problem growth when it is still small to minimize the size of the wounds. Remove rubbing and crossing branches, deadwood, and any new growth that is growing in the wrong direction — toward a branch that it will rub against or toward a congested part of the center of the tree.

Propagation. While cherries can be grown from seeds sown outdoors in fall, most cultivars do not come true from seed. Try rooting cuttings taken in early summer; some selections root easily, others do not. Dip the bases of the cuttings in rooting hormone and root in a 50-50 mix of perlite and vermiculite.

LANDSCAPE USES

Use *Prunus* species as lawn specimens and plant them in shrub borders. The spring flowers are especially attractive when the plants are sited in front of evergreens, which will act as a backdrop. Cherries are stunning when underplanted with a mix of hardy spring bulbs.

Lungworts

Pulmonaria
■
(pull-mon-AIR-ee-ah)
■
Late-winter to spring bloom
■
Partial or full shade
■
Zones 3 to 8
■

■ Lungworts are underappreciated perennials that add season-long interest to the garden. Also called pulmonarias and Bethlehem sage, they are among the earliest perennials to bloom. Their small clusters of dainty, bell-shaped flowers appear from late winter to late spring in shades of lavender- or violet-blue as well as white, pink, and red. Lungworts frequently have buds that turn purple-blue as they age. For most of the season, though, gardeners treasure lungworts for their foliage. Most of the cultivated kinds produce mounds of broadly oval green leaves splashed with white or silver — a few selections have so much white on them that very little green is left. The largest leaves are produced in a low rosette at the base of the plant, and smaller leaves are borne on the flower stems as well. The leaves are still quite small when the plants start flowering in late winter and may not extend fully until after the plants have stopped blooming for the year. The foliage remains attractive all through the season until early winter, and in mild-climate areas, some lungworts are evergreen.

Bethlehem sage
(Pulmonaria saccharata)

Bethlehem sage *(Pulmonaria saccharata)* is the most commonly grown species and produces pink buds that open to purple-blue or red-violet flowers and mounds of 10- to 11-inch-long, silver-spotted leaves. The mounds of foliage are from 8 to 10 inches tall, and plants are 4 to 5 inches taller when in bloom. Plants are evergreen in areas with mild winters and are hardy in Zones 3 to 8. 'Mrs. Moon', with pink buds and bluish lilac flowers, is the most commonly available cultivar. 'Pierre's Pure Pink' has shell pink flowers and silver-spotted leaves.

Longleaf lungwort *(P. longifolia)* forms broad clumps of lance-shaped, 18-inch-long leaves with silver spots. It bears purple-blue flowers and is hardy in Zones 4 to 8. Red lungwort *(P. rubra)*, which has solid-green leaves, is one of the earliest to bloom, producing reddish pink flowers from late winter to midspring. It is hardy in Zones 5 to 8.

Many hybrid lungworts are now available and feature outstanding foliage or flowers. Keep in mind that hardiness varies. 'Janet Fisk', with white-marbled leaves, is hardy in Zones 3 to 8. 'Roy Davidson', hardy in Zones 5 to 8, produces narrow mid-green leaves evenly blotched with silver. 'Sissinghurst White', hardy in Zones 4 or 5 to 8, bears white flowers and spotted leaves. 'Spilled Milk', hardy in Zones 5 to 8, has attractive, broad leaves that are mostly silver-white.

SITE AND SOIL

Grow lungworts in partial or full shade in a site with evenly moist soil that is rich in organic matter. A site with morning sun and afternoon shade is also suitable.

PLANTING

Plant lungworts in spring or fall. Space them according to the length of their leaves: most can be planted 10 to 12 inches apart, but *P. longifolia* should be spaced 1½ to 2 feet apart because of its unusually long leaves.

CARE THROUGH THE SEASON

Lungworts require very little care to look their best in the garden. They don't need staking and have few problems with pests and diseases. (In areas with humid summers, the fungal disease powdery mildew can be a problem.) Deadheading after the flowers fade is optional. To deadhead, clip off the flowering stems just below the foliage. Don't deadhead if you'd like the plants to self-sow. (Lungworts hybridize freely, so the seedlings will not be identical to the parents, but you may find some very attractive new plants nonetheless.) Remove old leaves in spring, after the plants flower, or leave them to decompose.

Established lungworts *(Pulmonaria* spp.) form broad clumps that offer spectacular spring bloom.

Established plants tolerate drought, but the foliage becomes tattered and unattractive if the soil gets too dry in summer, so watering during dry weather is beneficial. Keeping the soil evenly moist prevents drought stress and thus the onset of powdery mildew. Mulch with chopped leaves or shredded bark in spring to keep the soil moist and cool, keeping the mulch away from the crowns of the plants. A spring feeding with compost or a balanced organic fertilizer is beneficial but optional. Lungworts don't need regular division, but some gardeners dig and divide the clumps every 3 to 4 years.

Propagation. Division is the best way to propagate lungworts. Dig the clumps in spring after they have flowered or in early fall. For best results, separate them into fairly good-size clumps. Newly divided plants will wilt dramatically, but don't give up on them. Mulch and water the new divisions, and shade them with an upside-down bushel basket for a week or so until they recover. Self-sown seedlings are easy to dig and move to new locations.

LANDSCAPE USES

Use lungworts in shady beds and borders as well as in woodland gardens. They can be planted along shrub borders and also make fine ground covers. They are effective when combined with ferns, hostas, bleeding hearts *(Dicentra* spp.), epimediums, and hellebores *(Helleborus* spp.). Also interplant the clumps with spring bulbs.

Rhododendron

Rhododendrons and Azaleas

Rhododendron

■

(roe-doe-DEN-dron)

■

Spring to summer bloom

■

Shade to sun

■

Zones 3 to 9

■

A Northern Lights hybrid azalea, one of a group of especially hardy deciduous azaleas, with tall bearded irises, forget-me-nots (*Mysotis* spp.), and bugleweed (*Ajuga reptans*)

■ Rhododendrons and azaleas are spectacular shrubs that bear clusters of showy flowers, known as trusses. These come in an astounding array of colors, from white and pale pink to rose-pink and salmon, through lavender and violet-blue, to yellow, brilliant orange, brick red, and scarlet. Many varieties feature bicolor blooms — commonly with a blotch of a contrasting color at the throat. In a sense, the derivation of the name *Rhododendron* sums up why these shrubs are so popular: the name is taken from the Greek words *rhodon,* meaning "rose," and *dendron,* "tree." Few plants surpass the sight of a rhododendron or azalea in full bloom.

While gardeners recognize a distinction between rhododendrons and azaleas, botanists don't: both currently belong to the genus *Rhododendron* (azaleas were once classified separately, in *Azalea*). The distinctions between the two groups are subtle. Rhododendrons have 10 or more stamens, whereas azaleas generally have 5. Most rhododendrons are evergreen; most azaleas, deciduous. Most rhododendrons have bell-shaped flowers, while azalea flowers are funnel shaped.

The genus contains an incredibly diverse group of plants, including dwarf shrubs that remain under a few inches tall to trees that exceed 50 feet. (Most garden types range from 1 to about 20 feet tall.) Leaves can be deciduous or evergreen and range from $1/2$ inch long to 1 foot or more. Deciduous species can bear their blooms before, as, or after the leaves emerge. While there

are tropical species that can be grown in green-houses, this discussion covers hardy selections suitable for a wide range of North American gardens. Even with that restriction, it would be easy to fill a whole book with suggestions of species and cultivars to try—indeed, entire books have been devoted to azaleas or rhododendrons alone. There are from 500 to 900 species, along with literally thousands of cultivars, and breeders are continually introducing new ones. Gardeners in the Pacific Northwest have the widest choice, because their cool, moist summers and mild winters are ideal for growing rhododendrons and azaleas. In the central states, alkaline soils, winter cold, and summer heat and drought make growing these plants difficult, if not impossible.

SELECTING RHODODENDRONS AND AZALEAS

Gardens planted with large drifts of only one or two kinds of azaleas or rhododendrons are a common sight in spring, but this approach to planting is the horticultural equivalent of putting all your eggs in one basket. While in a good year they may all bloom together in a blaze of glory, if the weather is bad—too hot, too cold, or too rainy—or if a late freeze occurs, the entire season's bloom can be over in a matter of days. With careful selection and the right site, it's possible to have plants in bloom from early spring to early summer and beyond. Not only does planting a variety of species and cultivars extend the bloom season, it also provides insurance against unseasonable weather that can destroy the flowers.

When deciding which azaleas and rhododendrons to grow, one good place to start is to visit a local botanical garden or arboretum—or a well-stocked garden center—to find out which ones grow best in your area. Adaptability and hardiness vary depending on the parentage of each particular cultivar. The plants frequently survive colder winter temperatures than the flower buds do, so it's particularly important to select plants with flower buds that will survive the minimum winter low temperatures in your area. In many cases, hardiness for the hybrids is indicated by the lowest temperature the buds will survive.

The main bloom season comes from mid- to late spring—generally from late March or early April into May in the South, from May to early June in the North.

Hybrid Azaleas

A vast number of hybrid azaleas are available, both deciduous and evergreen. These are grouped according to their origin or parentage, and many different groups exist. Ask for local recommendations of groups or cultivars that are adapted to

Exbury azalea
'Gold Dust'

your area. Hardiness varies from cultivar to cultivar even within groups. (The azaleas sold in spring by florists typically are not hardy: most can be grown outdoors only in Zone 8 and south.)

The Exbury and Knap Hill azaleas are among the most common deciduous azaleas available. These 8- to 12-foot plants produce clusters of large, 2- to 3-inch-wide flowers in midspring. Flowers tend toward hot colors, including orange, red, and yellow, although there are cream and pink varieties. The shrubs also exhibit good red, orange, or yellow fall foliage color. They do not tolerate heat well and can be prone to mildew. Most are hardy to –20°F, making them suitable for Zones 5 to 8.

The Gable hybrids are some of the hardiest evergreen azaleas. They bear 2-inch-wide flowers in clusters from early to midspring and have 1-inch-long leaves. Colors include rose- to lavender-pink, red to red-orange, and white. Flowers can be single or double. Plants are hardy in Zones 5 or 6 to 8. Two other popular groups of hybrids

Evergreen Gable hybrid
azalea 'Cadis'

to look for are the Girard hybrids, which can be deciduous or evergreen and are suitable for Zones 5 or 6 to 8, and the Glenn Dale azaleas, which are also evergreen but are less hardy—to –10°F, but more commonly to 0°F.

Gardeners looking for ground covers may want to try Gumpo hybrid azaleas or North Tisbury hybrids. Gumpo azaleas, such as 'Gumpo Pink' and 'Gumpo Red', bear 2-inch-wide flowers on foot-tall plants that are hardy to –10°F. The North Tisbury azaleas were developed on Martha's Vineyard specifically for use as ground covers and have especially wide-spreading habits. Most bloom in early summer, stay under 12 to 15 inches, and are hardy to –10° or –15°F. Cultivars include 'Joseph Hill', 'Late Love', 'Marlee', 'Pink Pancake', and 'Susannah Hill'.

Gardeners living in Zones 3 and 4 who want reliably hardy azaleas should consider some of the Northern Lights cultivars, which were developed by the University of Minnesota and are generally hardy to –40°F. They bear clusters of fragrant, 1½-inch-wide flowers on 6- to 7-foot plants. Cultivars include 'Apricot Surprise', 'Golden Lights', 'Rosy Lights', and 'Spicy Lights'.

Species Azaleas

Species azaleas are often overlooked in favor of their showier hybrid cousins, but they have a simple charm that hybrids often lack and that adds a graceful touch to the garden. The hardiness zones listed here are conservative. If you have a protected location, try growing these species one zone north. All are native to North America.

R. arborescens. Sweet azalea. Small clusters of fragrant, white to pale pink, 1½- to 2-inch

flowers in late spring to early summer; 8- to 20-foot plants. Zones 5 to 9.

R. calendulaceum. Flame azalea. Showy clusters of yellow, orange, or red, 2-inch-wide flowers in mid- to late spring as the leaves emerge; 4- to 8-foot plants. Zones 6 to 8.

R. periclymenoides. Pinxterbloom azalea. Clusters of mildly fragrant, 1½-inch-wide, pale pink, white, or violet-purple flowers in early to midspring before the leaves emerge; 4- to 6-foot plants that spread steadily by stolons. Tolerates shade and relatively dry soil. Good for naturalizing. Zones 4 to 9.

R. prinophyllum. Roseshell azalea. Clusters of very fragrant, pink, 1½-inch flowers in late spring; 2- to 8-foot plants. Zones 4 to 8.

R. schlippenbachii. Royal azalea. Fragrant, rose-pink flowers in 2- to 3-inch clusters in midspring just as the leaves appear; 6- to 8-foot plants. Good yellow to red fall color. Prefers acid soil but will grow in soil with a neutral pH as well. Zones 5 to 8.

R. vaseyi. Pinkshell azalea. Pale pink to rose, 1½-inch-wide flowers in midspring before the leaves emerge; 5- to 10-foot plants. Red fall foliage. Zones 5 to 8.

Hybrid Rhododendrons

While there are many hybrid rhododendrons, there are far fewer groups of them than of hybrid azaleas. Again, start your search by talking to local rhododendron enthusiasts. Specialty catalogs are also a good source of information, and the best ones will point you toward cultivars that have the characteristics you're looking for. In the South, heat tolerance is an important consideration, while in the North hardiness is. Lucky gardeners in the Pacific Northwest, where mild winters and cool summers are the rule, can grow most hybrids. Here, too, hardiness varies from cultivar to cultivar and is generally given as a minimum low temperature rather than a zone. Red-flowered 'Nova Zembla', for example, is a heat-resistant cultivar that tolerates temperatures to –25°F. It is a good choice for the Midwest.

Of the hybrid groups, the evergreen Dexter hybrids are the best known and the most widely available. These are hardy to about –10°F and include fragrant pink 'Dexter's Peppermint', pink-flowered 'Scintillation', and mauve-pink 'Tom Everett'. 'PJM' is a popular, lavender-pink-flowered cultivar hardy to Zone 4. It has been used extensively in breeding hardy evergreen rhododendrons. Another name to look for in catalog descriptions is David Leach, a renowned expert on rhododendrons who has released a number of outstanding hybrids, including 'Bali', 'Hong Kong', and 'Nepal'.

Species Rhododendrons

As is true with azaleas, species rhododendrons are often overlooked in favor of hybrids. The following are some of the best, most widely adapted species. Plant them in partial shade in the North; full shade is best in the South.

R. carolinianum. Carolina rhododendron. Pale rose-purple, pale pink, or white, 1¼-inch flowers in handsome trusses in late spring; 3- to 5-foot plants. Rounded, 2- to 3-inch-long, evergreen leaves. A native North American shrub. Zones 5 to 8.

R. catawbiense. Catawba rhododendron. Trusses of lilac-purple to pinkish, 1½- to 2½-inch-wide flowers with spotted throats in mid- to late spring; usually 6- to 10-foot plants but can reach 15 feet or more. Rounded, dark green, 3- to 6-inch-long, evergreen leaves. This native plant is a key parent of most of the hardy rhododendron hybrids grown today. Zones 5 to 8; to Zone 4 in a protected location.

R. mucronulatum. Korean rhododendron. Small clusters of rose-purple 1½-inch-wide flowers in early to midspring; 4- to 8-foot plants. Leathery, 1- to 4-inch-long, deciduous leaves. Good yellow, bronze, or red fall foliage color. Very early flowers bloom before the leaves emerge, but the buds are susceptible to late-spring freezes. Zones 4 to 7.

R. yakushimanum. Yakushimina rhododendron. Trusses of rose-colored buds and white, 1½- to 2-inch-wide flowers in midspring; compact, 3- to 5-foot plants. Dark green, evergreen leaves with dense, woolly hairs on the undersides. Very compact grower and good for small gardens. Cultivars include 'Mist Maiden', 'Pink Parasol', 'Yaku Prince', and 'Yaku Princess'. Zones 5 to 9.

SITE AND SOIL

In the right site, rhododendrons and azaleas are easy to grow. In the wrong one, though, they sulk, are continually plagued with pests and diseases, or fail altogether. They require acid soil (pH 4.5 to 6.5) that is cool, evenly moist, well drained, and well aerated. A rich complement of organic matter is essential to success because it holds moisture, provides nutrients the plants need to grow, and keeps the soil loose and well aerated. Both rhododendrons and azaleas have very fine, shallow roots that usually lack root hairs, and soil that is too wet, poorly aerated, or compacted will cause them to grow poorly or rot altogether.

A site in partial shade is best for rhododendrons and azaleas in most parts of the country. In northern zones (Zone 5 and north) and in the Pacific Northwest where summers are relatively cool, they do fine in full sun. The farther south

Rhododendron 'PJM'

you live, the more shade they should have. (Plants need good light to bloom well, so even in the South high shade is best.) Shade is especially important during the hottest part of the day. Plants subjected to the heat and stress of full sun in areas with hot summers will be prone to a host of pests and diseases.

If you are testing the limits of hardiness of a particular plant, select a protected site. Careful siting helps prevent damage to the buds of the very early blooming species and keeps evergreen species from becoming sun scalded in winter. Look for a spot that faces north or northeast to shield the plants from the winter sun coming from the south or southwest. (Although it would seem

Yakushimina rhododendron *(Rhododendron yakushimanum)*

Summer-Blooming Azaleas

Surprise your friends and astound your neighbors with a planting of azaleas that bloom long after most gardens have settled into summer garb. Swamp azalea *(R. viscosum),* hardy in Zones 4 to 9, produces clusters of very fragrant, white to pale pink, 1-inch-wide flowers from early to midsummer. As the common name suggests, these 3- to 8-foot plants tolerate wet to boggy soil that is high in organic matter. (They will not grow in heavy, wet clay, however.)

Plumleaf azalea *(R. prunifolium)* bears red- to red-orange flowers in midsummer on 8- to 20-foot plants. It requires shade, especially during the hottest part of the day. Although established plants will tolerate some drought, for best results keep plants mulched and water regularly to keep the soil evenly moist. Zones 6 to 9; to Zone 5 in a protected location.

that south-facing sites would be best, that isn't true. On warm winter days, south-facing sites heat up, but the soil doesn't necessarily thaw out enough for water to be available to plant roots. Evergreen leaves and emerging buds can become desiccated because they begin to give off water through their pores but can't take up any to replace it from their roots.) It's also possible to erect screens of burlap or of evergreen boughs stuck in the ground around plants in fall to protect them from wind, but these techniques make for plants that are unattractive to look at all winter long.

Because of their requirement for acid soil, keep plants away from cement foundations, which tend to release lime into the soil. If in doubt about the soil's pH, take a soil test before you plant. Also keep these plants away from walnut trees *(Juglans* spp.). Walnuts release a substance called juglone into the soil that is toxic to many plants, including *Rhododendron* species.

You have a couple of options if your soil is unsuitable for growing rhododendrons and azaleas. If poor drainage, clay, or compaction is the problem, consider creating large, deeply dug beds with amended soil that is rich in organic matter and has the proper pH. Raised beds filled with rich soil are appropriate for poorly drained sites, too. Digging a hole and amending the soil in that hole alone simply won't work—you need to improve the soil over a wide area to encourage roots to spread out and to provide the conditions rhododendrons and azaleas thrive in. In sandy soil, adding lots of compost and leaf mold—up to one-third of the soil volume—is in order. Plan on renewing the soil's supply of organic matter annually. While it's possible to lower the pH of neutral soil enough to keep rhododendrons and azaleas happy, if your soil is alkaline, consider growing other shrubs: lowering the pH and keeping it low will be a yearly struggle for as long as the plants live.

PLANTING

You can plant container-grown azaleas and rhododendrons anytime during the growing season, although spring or early fall is generally best. Plant balled-and-burlapped plants in late summer after the new growth has matured. When planting, loosen the soil to at least 1 foot and prepare a wide, relatively shallow planting site. Amend the soil over the entire area with plenty of compost or leaf mold. With container-grown plants, loosen the roots on the outside of the soil ball so they are sticking out into the surrounding soil. (Don't let them dry out during planting.) Otherwise the roots have a tendency to stay in the soil that was once contained in the pot rather than grow out into new soil.

If you are planting native species of azaleas or rhododendrons, do not buy wild-collected plants and never collect from the wild yourself. Patronize only reputable nurseries that sell nursery-grown plants. Individuals who collect and sell wild plants decimate natural areas, and buying collected plants from them simply puts money in their pockets. Nursery-grown plants will look uniform and healthy, while wild-collected ones often have a just-dug look, with a cluster of unpruned stems at the base, broken or recently pruned growth, and weeds growing around the base of the plant. A cheap price for the size of the plants offered is another tip-off. If in doubt, ask the owners where the plants came from, and shop elsewhere if you receive a vague or otherwise unsatisfactory response. Plant sales conducted by local native-plant societies, conservation associations, and botanical gardens are other good sources for native azaleas and rhododendrons. Such organizations may offer plants rescued from areas that are about to be developed.

It is important not to plant azaleas and rhododendrons too deeply. When planting, set them slightly higher than the surrounding soil— 1 to 2 inches higher—and then mulch the roots with shredded bark or chopped leaves. (Look for the soil mark on the trunk that indicates the depth at which they were planted.) The plants will settle down into the soil after a season or two. Most azaleas and rhododendrons spread as wide as they are tall, so space them accordingly. A plant that matures at 6 to 8 feet, for example, should be planted with 3 to 4 feet of space on all sides.

Water newly planted specimens deeply and then mulch them with a 2- to 3-inch layer of chopped leaves or shredded bark. This adds organic matter to the soil and keeps it moist and cool. Water regularly, about every 10 to 14 days, for at least the first season if the weather is dry.

CARE THROUGH THE SEASON

Once a site is selected and the plants are in the ground, the major work of growing rhododendrons and azaleas is over. Renew the 2- to 3-inch layer of chopped leaves or shredded bark mulch annually. Mulch is especially important because the plants are very shallow rooted, and it's crucial that the soil remain cool near the surface. Mulching also eliminates the need to cultivate the soil to control weeds, which disturbs the roots.

If you can, remove the spent flowers on rhododendrons to direct the plants' energy to flowers for the following year. Cut just below each flower, and take care not to damage the shoots that will give rise to the season's new leaves that arise just below it.

Rhododendrons and azaleas don't need to be fed regularly—mixing some compost in with their mulch every year is sufficient. If the plants begin to bloom poorly or to grow more slowly, feed them in spring with well-rotted manure or a balanced organic fertilizer. (If the leaves begin to turn yellow, take a soil test to see if the soil pH is too high, a condition that causes nutrients in the soil to be unavailable to the plants.)

Pruning. Rhododendrons and azaleas do not need regular pruning. Remove damaged, diseased, or dead growth anytime. Always cut above a bud or a strong side branch when you prune them—stumps generally won't resprout.

If you are faced with huge, overgrown plants, it is possible to rejuvenate them by renewal pruning in early spring. In areas with cool, humid summers, plants can be cut back to about 1 foot tall and most will regrow. (Keep the plants well watered during the summer following this harsh treatment.) If you don't want to gamble at losing the entire plant, first look for small shoots that have arisen near its base on old wood. Plants that have new growth near the base will usually survive severe pruning. If you don't see any, try cutting back a branch or two without cutting down the entire plant. This may encourage new shoots to form, and if they do, you can safely renewal-prune the following spring.

Propagation. Rhododendrons and azaleas can be propagated by layering or seeds. Layering is slow but effective—plants may take two seasons to grow roots. See "Layering" in the Techniques Glossary for details. *Rhododendron* species can be grown from seeds sown in a soilless potting mix or a 50-50 mix of peat moss and vermiculite. Barely cover the seeds with soil and set the pots in a cold frame or outdoors in a protected location. Indoors, germinate them where temperatures remain around 50°F. Seeds from cultivars can be germinated this way, too, and although they will not come true, they may yield some interesting seedlings. Rhododendrons can also be propagated from cuttings, although this method tends to be difficult. Take cuttings of evergreen types in late summer, cut the leaves in half to reduce water transpiration, and wound the base of the cuttings by making a shallow, 1½-inch-long cut in the base of the stems. Take cuttings of deciduous types in late spring. Root either type by dipping the cuttings in rooting hormone and sticking them in a 50-50 mix of peat moss and coarse sand. Cover the pots with plastic to maintain high humidity.

Potential Problems. Good culture will eliminate most disease and insect problems. Lace bugs cause mottled leaves with black flecks, but they are most problematic on plants growing in full sun in the South—especially along cement walkways, where reflected heat adds even more stress. The best control is to move the plants to a suitable site. (Because they are shallow rooted, azaleas and rhododendrons are fairly easy to move. Dig them in spring or fall.) Insecticidal soap and horticultural oil (be sure to use the

Both azaleas and rhododendrons thrive in rich, acid soil and partial shade. They are ideal for adding color to woodland edges and shade gardens.

growing-season dilution) are effective controls. Rhododendrons with notched leaves are probably infested with black vine weevils. The adults eat the leaf edges, while the larvae feed on the roots. Spray weekly with pyrethrin several times to control the adults. Drenching the soil with a solution of parasitic nematodes is a good way to control the larvae.

Yellow leaves generally indicate chlorosis, a condition brought on by soil that is not acid enough. Spread sulfur to lower pH (get a soil test and follow the recommendations). Mulching with chopped oak leaves or pine needles also helps lower soil pH. If leaves turn yellow or brown and wilt, and the tips of the branches die, either borers or dieback is the culprit. Prune out and destroy

Summersweet *(Clethra alnifolia)*

Mountain laurel *(Kalmia latifolia* 'Carousel')

Rhododendron Companions

Instead of designing a planting composed entirely of rhododendrons and azaleas, consider combining them with other trees and shrubs that thrive in similar conditions—partial shade and rich, well-drained, acid soil. A mixed planting offers contrasting flowers as well as foliage color and texture and also extends bloom season. Flowering dogwood *(Cornus florida)*, oakleaf hydrangea *(Hydrangea quercifolia)*, and sweet bay *(Magnolia virginiana)* make fine companions and are covered in individual entries in this book. The plants listed below are all easy to grow and require care similar to that given to rhododendrons and azaleas once they're established in the right site. With the exception of *Enkianthus campanulatus* and *Pieris japonica*, all are native to North America.

Aesculus parviflora. Bottlebrush buckeye. Showy, 8- to 12-inch-long, plumelike clusters of white flowers from early to midsummer; 8- to 12-foot, multistemmed plants with large, compound leaves. Yellow fall foliage. Plants spread by suckering. Also tolerates neutral to slightly alkaline soil and will grow in full sun. Plants may establish slowly. Zones 5 to 9.

Clethra alnifolia. Summersweet, sweet pepperbush. Fragrant, white flowers in feathery, 2- to 6-inch-long clusters from mid- to late summer; 3- to 8-foot plants. Yellow fall foliage. Plants spread by suckers and are largest in moist soil. Grows well in deep shade and wet soil. Zones 3 to 9.

Enkianthus campanulatus. Pendulous clusters of bell-shaped, 1/2-inch-long flowers in spring to early summer as the leaves emerge; 6- to 8-foot plants, but can exceed 15 feet in ideal conditions. Flowers are creamy yellow, white, red, pink, or pale orange, depending on the cultivar. Good yellow to orange-red fall color. Zones 5 to 8; to Zone 4 in a protected location.

Fothergilla gardenii. Dwarf fothergilla. Bottlebrush-like, 1- to 2-inch-long spikes of fragrant white flowers in spring; 2- to 3-foot plants. Large fothergilla *(F. major)* bears similar flowers in mid- to late spring on 6- to 10-foot plants. Both have outstanding yellow, orange, and scarlet fall foliage. *F. gardenii* is hardy in Zones 5 to 9;

afflicted growth, cutting back to healthy wood. Seal all pruning cuts with fingernail polish, white glue, wood glue, or a tree-wound compound.

LANDSCAPE USES

Rhododendrons and azaleas can be underplanted with a variety of perennials. Combine them with shade-loving phlox *(Phlox divaricata* and *P.* *stolonifera)*, lungworts *(Pulmonaria* spp.), bleeding hearts *(Dicentra* spp.), hostas, and gingers *(Asarum* spp.). Ferns and shade-loving wildflowers also make good companions, as do dogwoods *(Cornus* spp.). A variety of popular shrubs make ideal additions to a planting of rhododendrons and azaleas. See "Rhododendron Companions" below for suggestions.

F. major, Zones 5 to 8, but to Zone 4 with winter protection.

Itea virginica. Virginia sweetspire. Dense, narrow, 2- to 6-inch-long spikes of small, fragrant, creamy white flowers in midspring; 3- to 5-foot plants. Spreads to form broad clumps that can be divided in fall. Excellent bronze to red fall foliage. 'Henry's Garnet' is compact, from 3 to 4 feet in height, and has showier flowers and fall foliage than the species. Also thrives in moist to wet soil and will grow in slightly alkaline conditions. Zones 6 to 9.

Kalmia latifolia. Mountain laurel. Clusters of cup-shaped, intricately marked white, pink, rose-red, or red flowers from late spring to early summer; 4- to 15-foot plants with shiny evergreen leaves. Many cultivars with outstanding flowers are now available. Tolerates full shade but blooms best with some sun. Is especially intolerant of heavy, wet soil and poor drainage. Zones 5 to 9.

Leucothoe fontanesiana. Drooping leucothoe. Pendulous clusters of small, fragrant, urn-shaped white flowers in midspring; 3- to 6-foot plants with evergreen leaves. Does not tolerate drought. A site protected from winter winds is best. Zones 5 to 8.

Mahonia aquifolium. Oregon holly-grape. Yellow flowers in early to midspring followed by clusters of blue-black berries in late summer to fall; 3- to 6-foot plants with shiny, compound, evergreen leaves. Plants spread by stolons. A number of cultivars with improved flowers or form are available. Tolerates full sun but not hot, dry soil. A site protected from winter winds is best. Creeping mahonia *(M. repens)* is a good 10-inch-tall evergreen ground cover with yellow spring flowers and blue summer fruit. Both are hardy in Zones 5 to 8.

Pieris japonica. Japanese pieris. Arching, 3- to 6-inch-long sprays of small white flowers in early spring; 9- to 12-foot evergreen shrubs. New growth is red. Many cultivars are available, some selected for flowers and others for showy new growth. Select a site protected from winter winds. Hardy in Zones 6 to 8. Mountain andromeda *(P. floribunda)* is a similar, but native, species that is hardy in Zones 5 to 8.

Oregon holly-grape *(Mahonia aquifolium)*

Japanese pieris *(Pieris japonica)*

Roses

Rosa
■
(ROE-sah)
■
Late-spring to fall bloom
■
Full sun
■
Zones 2 to 9
■

■ There's little argument that roses top the list of North America's favorite plants. Christened the "queen of flowers" by the Greek poet Sappho some 2,000 years ago, roses enjoy a popularity that hasn't wavered much since. They are vigorous shrubs with thick, often thorny stems, usually called canes. The flowers, which are borne singly or in few- to many-flowered clusters, are single, semidouble, or double. They come in a rainbow of colors, including shades of red, ma-

Large-flowered climbing rose 'America'

roon, deep rose-pink or salmon, pale pink, white, yellow, orange, and gold. (Flowers described as lavender or purple are typically pinkish lavender or mauve-purple; so-called black roses are deep maroon.) Many roses feature bicolor flowers. Single and semidouble blooms open to reveal a showy boss of yellow stamens; double flowers don't generally reveal their stamens until the flowers are past their prime. The fragrance of roses is legendary, but not all roses are fragrant. Most roses bloom in late spring to early summer, although some bloom closer to midsummer. Reblooming, or remontant, roses produce a main flush of flowers early in the season and one or more, usually smaller, flushes of bloom from midsummer to fall. Many roses develop showy fruit, called hips, beginning in late summer to fall. The hips last well into winter, when hungry birds and other wildlife descend upon them.

SELECTING ROSES

Take one look around a garden center in early spring, when dormant rosebushes with colorful printed tags are piled everywhere, and it's easy to see there's no shortage of beautiful-looking roses. Instead of being wooed by the first pretty picture or two you see, however, take time to make careful choices. Most gardeners have room for only a few bushes, not to mention limited time available to care for them. Hardy, disease-resistant roses are a valuable investment that will pay off for years to come in the form of vigorous, heavy-blooming bushes that will be a joy to tend.

The performance of different types and cultivars of roses varies from one part of the continent to another. Plants that thrive in the Pacific Northwest can't necessarily tolerate hot, humid southeastern summers or cold midwestern winters, for example. (All-America Rose Selections winners have been tested in gardens across the United States and are proven performers, although disease resistance varies.) Before you buy, talk to gardeners who grow roses in your area, along with rosarians at botanical gardens and public plantings, to get some local recommendations. Ask for hardy roses that are also disease resistant. If you are visiting a local rose garden, find out whether the plants you are looking at survive without special winter protection. (See "Winterizing" on page 265 for information on what it takes to overwinter roses that are not hardy.) Also find out what type of spray program is being used—it's not unusual to find rose gardens that are sprayed with chemical pesticides and fungicides on a biweekly basis all summer long. Whether you want low-maintenance roses or don't mind plants that need occasional spraying, it's best to steer toward selections that show

at least some disease resistance. Not only are the chemicals used to keep disease-prone plants healthy bad for the environment, but spraying isn't a fun chore, and the planting inevitably ends up smelling like chemicals instead of roses anyway. (For information on organic controls for rose pests and diseases, see "Potential Problems" on page 266.)

Experts divide roses into two general groups: old garden roses, which were introduced before 1867, and modern roses. The plants are further divided into groups based on parentage, habit, and bloom type—hybrid teas, grandifloras, rugosas, floribundas, and polyanthas, for example. To help you determine which roses will best fit your garden and your lifestyle, the list below is divided by maintenance requirements rather than by the traditional old-versus-modern system. (Climbing roses are dealt with separately, because their care is somewhat different from that needed by shrub-type roses.) In addition, some of the new groups of roses that have been bred for hardiness and disease resistance (usually lumped together as shrub or modern shrub roses) have been called out separately, so you'll recognize them when you see them in catalogs or at garden centers.

The category "High-Maintenance Roses" isn't meant to be disparaging, it's merely stating a fact. If you want to grow good hybrid teas or grandifloras—and many gardeners wouldn't dream of being without them—be prepared to tackle major annual spring pruning and a summer-long program of pest and disease control. Fortunately, hybridizers are introducing new disease-resistant cultivars every year, making common rose diseases such as black spot, mildew, and rust easier to cope with. Keep in mind that "disease resistant" doesn't mean "disease free." Plants described as disease resistant may still show signs of disease, but they generally won't be devastated by these afflictions. Catalogs usually rate disease resistance informally, by adding adjectives such as "good," "some," or "excellent." If disease resistance isn't mentioned at all, the plant probably isn't resistant. The same is true for other desirable characteristics: if a description doesn't mention fragrance, rebloom, or ornamental hips, the plant probably doesn't exhibit those characteristics.

Low-Maintenance Roses

Although the roses listed below require considerably less care than hybrid tea roses, don't mistake the term "*low*-maintenance" for "*no*-maintenance." For best performance, all roses still benefit from annual pruning, feeding, and a basic pest and disease control program. See "Care Through the Season," beginning on page 265, for details. There also are some floribunda roses that deserve low-maintenance status—see "Floribunda Roses" on page 259 for a list.

English Roses. Developed by English hybridizer David Austin, these very popular new roses combine the fragrance and form of classic old roses with the reblooming character of modern ones. (English roses are now being introduced by other hybridizers as well.) Performance varies across North America because of our hot summer weather, and which cultivars will do best in your garden will depend on where you live. (English roses were bred and selected in the United Kingdom, where cool summers are the rule, and tend to stay smaller and rebloom more consistently there than they do here.) Here, the main flush of bloom comes in late spring to early summer, and some cultivars rebloom throughout the season. Others put on a lush display of flowers for about

ABOVE Canadian rose 'William Baffin'

ABOVE RIGHT Shrub rose 'Carefree Beauty' planted with lavender

6 weeks in late spring to early summer, but when grown in areas with hot summers, they respond to the heat by producing extremely tall, vigorous canes (to 8 feet or more) topped by occasional flowers for the rest of the season.

English roses are vigorous growers that need to be pruned hard in spring, much like hybrid tea roses. Cut the larger plants—such as 'Gertrude Jekyll' and 'Graham Thomas'—back hard after each flush of bloom to encourage new flowers and strong, thick canes. Compact selections that stay between 3 and 4 feet tall—such as 'Belle Story', 'Fair Bianca', 'Heritage', and 'Lilac Rose'—need less-severe pruning and probably are the best choices for North America. Because of their pruning requirements and the fact that plants perform best with regular spraying (disease resistance varies from moderate to good or excellent), English roses are somewhere in the middle as far as low versus high maintenance is concerned. They are hardy in Zones 5 to 9.

Hardy Canadian Roses. Northern gardeners should thank their lucky stars for Canadian breeding programs that have produced outstanding, superhardy landscape roses with good to excellent disease resistance. Most, but not all, are modern shrub roses. The Prairie Series roses, produced in Morden, Manitoba, include 'Prairie Dawn' and 'Prairie Youth'; both are reblooming types hardy to Zone 3 without winter protection. Parkland Series roses, including 'Cuthbert Grant', 'Morden Blush', and 'Morden Fireglow', are

killed to the ground in Zone 3, but since they bloom on new wood, they flower annually. In Zone 2, try them with winter protection; the canes are hardy to Zone 4. Geographers and history buffs will have no problem identifying Explorer Series roses—they're named for early Canadian explorers—but gardeners will want them for their high disease resistance, their hardiness, and their abundant, recurrent, fragrant flowers. Explorer Series roses include rugosa cultivars ('Charles Albanel', 'David Thompson', and 'Henry Hudson') and hardy climbing roses ('John Cabot', 'Max Graf', and 'William Baffin') as well as floribunda- or grandiflora-like shrub roses ('Alexander Mackenzie', 'Champlain', and 'John Franklin'). Most are hardy to Zone 3; some, to Zone 2.

Modern Shrub Roses. This is a catchall category that includes many of the hardy Canadian roses described above, along with Meidiland roses, English roses, and the products of other breeding programs. In general, shrub roses are tough plants with abundant flowers and a pleasing shape (they even look fairly attractive out of bloom) and range from as little as 1 foot in height to 10 to 12 feet. One group to watch for are the roses developed by the late Dr. Griffith Buck, a horticulture professor from Iowa State University. 'Prairie Princess', a semidouble with coral-pink flowers, was used in the Canadian breeding programs. 'Carefree Beauty' and 'Hawkeye Belle' both produce double fragrant pink flowers all

Hybrid musk rose 'Buff Beauty'

summer, are disease resistant, and are hardy to Zone 4. ('Hawkeye Belle' is crown hardy to Zone 4, meaning it is killed to the ground there, but it grows back from the roots each year.) The Meidiland shrub roses—including 'Bonica', 'Scarlet Meidiland', and 'Sevillana'—are also popular. These are disease-resistant shrubs with abundant showy clusters of small flowers. They need minimal pruning and are hardy in Zones 4 to 9.

Old Roses. Although most old roses bloom only once a year, they are still very popular because the best ones feature lovely, often fragrant blooms and good disease resistance. They also thrive with a minimum of care. Alba roses *(R. alba)*, including the popular 'Semi Plena', bear fragrant, semidouble or double, white or blush pink flowers in late spring or early summer. The plants have handsome gray-green leaves and attractive red hips in fall. They are very disease resistant and are hardy in Zones 3 to 8. Gallica roses, including 'Complicata' and apothecary's rose *(R. gallica* var. *officinalis)*, thrive in full sun but will also bloom in partial shade (but good light). Most show good disease resistance and are hardy in Zones 4 to 8. Hybrid musk roses, hardy in Zones 5 or 6 to 9, feature disease resistance and repeat bloom. 'Ballerina' and 'Buff Beauty' are two examples.

Polyantha Roses. Polyanthas are tough, easy-to-grow roses with large clusters of small flowers borne in late spring to early summer and then in nearly continuous flushes through fall. They are

Hybrid musk rose 'Ballerina' with *Clematis* 'Jackmanii'

ABOVE Rugosa rose
'Will Alderman'

RIGHT Floribunda rose
'Betty Prior'

disease-resistant, compact (2½- to 3-foot) plants that bloom abundantly with little care. Popular pink-flowered 'The Fairy' is the best known of the polyantha roses. They are hardy in Zones 4 to 9.

Rugosa Roses. Tough, rugged, disease-resistant rugosa roses feature showy, fragrant flowers that are single or double and come in white, pink, or rose-red. They also bear tomato red hips, attractive dark green wrinkled foliage, and stunning yellow, orange, red, and purple fall foliage — along with very thorny canes. While the species and many of the cultivars easily reach 5 to 8 feet tall, dwarf cultivars are also available that stay under about 3 feet and are good for low hedges or ground covers. (Pavement Series roses range from 2 to 3 feet and spread to 3 feet.) Rugosa roses are ideal plants for seaside gardens, because they tolerate salt and poor, dry soil. Most are hardy in Zones 3 to 8.

Species Roses. Species roses generally fall into the low-maintenance category as well. Consider eglantine rose or sweetbrier *(R. eglanteria,* formerly *R. rubiginosa),* which has single pink flowers in late spring to early summer, showy red hips, and apple-scented foliage on 8-foot plants. It is very disease resistant and hardy in Zones 4 to 9. Red-leaved rose *(R. glauca,* formerly *R. rubrifolia)* has single pink flowers, showy gray-purple leaves, and orange-red hips. It is hardy in Zones 2 to 8. Scotch brier *(R. pimpinellifolia,* formerly *R. spinosissima)* produces single, creamy white flowers on dense, 2- to 3-foot, suckering plants with fernlike leaves and purple-black hips. It is a good disease-resistant ground cover hardy in Zones 3 to 9. Moyes rose *(R. moyesii),* hardy in Zones 5 to 8, has single red flowers and flask-shaped, red-orange hips in fall. Memorial rose *(R. wichuraiana)* bears fragrant white flowers and orange-red hips on sprawling stems. It can reach a few feet in height but spreads to 20 feet with time and makes a good ground cover. It prefers full sun but will tolerate light shade and is hardy in Zones 5 to 9.

High-Maintenance Roses

Despite the increasing popularity of modern shrub roses, the hybrid teas, grandifloras, and floribundas remain the most popular garden roses. All are reblooming, or remontant (sometimes described as everblooming), plants that produce their showy flowers in flushes from late spring through fall. To look their best, they require rigorous annual pruning and careful attention to pest and disease control. Hardiness varies from cultivar to cultivar with all floribundas, grandifloras, and hybrid teas. Most cultivars will withstand −10°F, or Zone 6, but require winter protection north of that zone.

Floribunda Roses. Floribundas are crosses between hybrid tea roses and polyanthas, and they bear clusters of flowers, some fragrant, all summer long. The blooms may be single, semi-double, or fully double. The plants range from 2 to about 4 feet in height. Floribunda roses require less-severe pruning than hybrid tea and grandiflora roses. Floribundas with excellent disease resistance deserve to be on the list of low-maintenance roses. These include 'Betty Prior' (hardy to Zone 5), 'Class Act' (Zone 6), 'Es-

Hybrid tea rose
'Voodoo'

capade' (Zone 6), and 'Nearly Wild' (Zone 5; to Zone 4 with winter protection).

Grandiflora Roses. These roses, the result of crosses between hybrid teas and floribundas, bear large flowers in showy clusters from late spring through fall. The flowers are usually semidouble or double and may or may not be fragrant. The plants are large and vigorous, ranging from 4 to 6 feet or more in height.

Hybrid Tea Roses. Hybrid tea roses bear classic, narrow buds, generally one per stem, from late spring to fall. Although the flowers typically are double or semidouble, there are also single-flowered hybrid tea roses. Fragrance varies: the blooms may be very fragrant or completely scentless. The plants are tall and upright—from 3 to 5 feet or more—and tend to lose their leaves at the bottom. Although traditionally grown in beds devoted to roses alone, hybrid tea roses are more attractive when combined with lower-growing perennials that will hide their bare "ankles."

Climbing Roses

While climbing roses don't actually climb (they lack tendrils or twining stems that true vines use to attach themselves to structures), they do produce long, supple canes that can be tied to trellises (either freestanding or mounted on walls), arbors, pergolas, and other structures. They are also attractive when trained along fences, or up posts or pillars to add height and color to the garden. The largest climbers can be trained to grow up trees or allowed to engulf entire structures, such as sheds, making them useful for hiding unattractive landscape elements. (For more on support systems, see "How Vines Climb" on page 299 in the Vines entry.)

Climbing roses have a varied heritage, and several different groups are available. (There is even some overlap with shrub roses, as some of the shorter, sturdier climbers can be grown as large shrub roses.) Here's a rundown of the groups you are most likely to encounter.

Rambling vs. Climbing Roses. The distinction between rambling and climbing roses is an artificial, often arbitrary one based on the general growth habits of different plants, the ways they are used, and the pruning they require, rather than any clear-cut botanical distinction. In general, rambling roses have thin, lax, flexible canes that are easier to wrap around supports than is the stiffer growth of climbing roses. Nearly all ramblers bloom once in early to midsummer, and they bear large clusters of smallish (under 2 inches) flowers on short side shoots on 1-year-old canes. After flowering, they send up long (often very long) canes from the base of the plant. Climbing roses usually have stiffer and woodier canes, tend to be somewhat smaller, and generally produce a first flush of bloom in early summer followed by repeated flushes of flowers throughout the season. Like ramblers, they produce vigorous canes from the base of the plant, but they also tend to send up canes from older wood.

Because of their vigorous growth, ramblers can be difficult to keep in bounds—prune annually if this is your goal. They can also be allowed to scramble where they will with minimal pruning and training. Kordesii and wichuraiana climbers can be grown this way. *R. multiflora* hybrids, including 'Seagull', 'Seven Sisters', and 'Tausendschon', can also be grown as ramblers.

Two large-flowered climbing roses decorate the fence around a vegetable garden. Both fragrant, pink-flowered 'America' and scarlet 'Dublin Bay' bloom from spring to fall.

Large-Flowered Climbers. As their name suggests, these bear large blooms, generally in clusters. Some flower only once, but many are remontant. Most produce their new canes on old wood, so it's important not to remove too much older wood when pruning. For this reason, it's also important to plant cultivars that are hardy in your area, since if the plants are killed back too far, they won't bloom. (The canes can be protected in winter — see "Winterizing" on page 265 for details.) Most show good to excellent disease resistance. The following exhibit excellent disease resistance: 'Altissimo', 'America', 'City of York', 'Dublin Bay', 'Eden Climber', and 'New Dawn'. Most are hardy in Zones 5 to 9.

There are also large-flowered climbing roses that are actually sports, or mutations, of hybrid tea roses, grandifloras, floribundas, or polyanthas. For example, 'Climbing Iceberg' is derived from the floribunda rose 'Iceberg'. Both have white flowers and show some disease resistance. Hardiness varies — most can be grown in Zones 6 or 7 to 9. Again, if the plants are to flower, the canes must be hardy enough to survive the winter. When pruning these sports, remove as little of the previous season's wood as possible.

Kordesii Climbers. Although they are not generally called out separately in catalogs, it pays to be familiar with kordesiis. They are tough, medium-size climbers with dark green leaves and excellent disease resistance. Red-flowered 'Dortmund' blooms once if not deadheaded and has handsome red hips in fall. It will produce several flushes of flowers (but no hips) if deadheaded. Canadian Explorer Series hybrid 'William Baffin', hardy to Zone 3 (or to Zone 2 with winter protection), also has kordesii "blood." Most other kordesii climbers are hardy in Zones 5 to 9.

Hybrid Wichuraiana Climbers. These are vigorous, large rambling or climbing roses that owe their sprawling canes to memorial rose *(R. wichuraiana)*. They have dark green, very disease resistant foliage. They bloom once in early to midsummer and produce handsome hips in fall. 'American Pillar', 'Dorothy Perkins', and 'White Dorothy Perkins' are three excellent wichuraiana climbers. Most are hardy in Zones 5 to 9.

SITE AND SOIL

Roses require full sun — at least 6 hours a day — to bloom well. If you don't have a spot with all-day sun, look for one with morning sun and afternoon shade (but good light). Morning sun dries off the leaves and helps prevent black spot, mildew, and other rose diseases. Light shade in the afternoon helps protect the plants from heat.

Well-drained soil that is loose, well aerated, and rich in organic matter is ideal for roses. The plants limp along or fail altogether in soil with poor drainage, but they will grow in well-drained heavy clay or in sandy conditions. (If you have heavy clay, be sure to dig deeply and to add plenty of organic matter to ensure good drainage. Add organic matter to sandy soil, too, to ensure that it is rich enough and retains enough moisture.) Raised beds provide the best conditions for roses, and many experts use them to grow all their roses. Slightly acid pH (6.5 to 6.8) is ideal, but roses also grow in acid soil (to about pH 5.5) as well as in slightly alkaline conditions (to pH 7.5).

A spot with good air circulation is important because it helps cut down on foliar diseases, but at the same time a site sheltered from cold, northwest winds is also advisable. That's because wind can desiccate the canes over winter. A warm, south- or east-facing site is a good location for a rose — especially a climber — that is near the limits of its hardiness.

PLANTING

Most roses are sold as bare-root plants, but container-grown specimens are frequently available at garden centers as well. For best results, invest in premium, Number 1 grade plants, which will have three or four thick, healthy, well-spaced canes and a root system that looks vigorous and well branched. (The size of healthy canes will vary considerably, depending on the type of rose you are planting. Canes on a healthy hybrid tea rose are thicker than those on a miniature rose or some shrub roses, for example.) The canes should be smooth and greenish or reddish in color. Reject plants with broken, shriveled, or spindly canes or with canes that are crowded together to form a lopsided-looking plant. Also reject plants with a root system that looks shriveled or otherwise damaged. Bare-root plants should be completely dormant, with buds that have not yet begun to open.

Roses generally are budded onto a vigorous rootstock, but plants grown on their own roots are becoming more common. (Species and some of the modern shrub roses are typically grown on their own roots.) If you are growing roses at the limits of their hardiness, own-root roses are a good choice because even if they are killed to the ground during a harsh winter, they will come back from the crown.

Roses are normally planted in early spring, but they can be planted in mid- to late fall as well, before the soil freezes. While container-grown roses can be planted nearly anytime the soil can be worked, it's crucial to get bare-root plants in the ground while they are dormant, so the roots can begin growing before the plants leaf out. Whenever you plant, prepare the soil before bringing roses home — this is especially important for bare-root roses, which should be planted as promptly as possible. If you can't plant bare-root roses immediately, inspect them as soon as you receive the plants, spray the roots with water, and repack them in the material in which they were shipped. Then set them in a cool, but not freezing, place. Heel them in if you can't plant within 10 days — see "Heeling In" in the Techniques Glossary for details.

Digging beds in fall for planting the following spring is ideal. To prepare an entire bed for planting roses, have the soil tested and adjust the pH if necessary. Then loosen and amend the soil with plenty of compost, leaf mold, or well-rotted manure to a depth of about 20 inches. (If you have heavy clay soil, consider double-digging to improve drainage and work in organic matter to an even greater depth.) To plant a rose in an existing garden, dig a hole that is at least 2 feet deep

Miniature Roses

It may come as a surprise that miniature roses are hardy plants that can be grown outdoors year round. (Most will survive in Zones 5 to 9 without winter protection.) Miniatures are everblooming plants that are especially effective when combined with low-growing perennials, used as edgings, or planted in front of foundation shrubs. Although they are susceptible to standard rose diseases and require regular spraying, pruning is fairly easy. They bloom on the current season's wood and benefit from hard pruning in late winter to early spring to encourage new canes and an abundance of flowers. Remove one or more of the older canes each year to encourage new ones to form, and cut back remaining growth by one-third. In summer, shear plants after the main flush of bloom to remove faded flowers. A spray program to control foliar diseases is in order. Also watch for the telltale webs and yellow-spotted leaves caused by mites on the buds and stems when the weather gets hot in summer.

Miniature roses make fine container plants. Here pink-flowered 'Nostalgia' shares space with white 'Ice Queen', trained as a standard.

Canadian rose
'John Cabot'

and 1½ feet across. The larger the hole, the more vigorous the plant will be. Amend the backfill with compost and some well-rotted manure as well as a generous handful of rock phosphate or three generous handfuls of bonemeal.

Since plant size varies so widely, the best guideline to use for spacing is to set plants as far apart as their spread at maturity. Ask at the nursery when you buy the plants or check plant tags for more specific recommendations.

Other than removing dead, damaged, or spindly canes, don't prune newly planted bushes. Most bare-root roses are pruned before they are packaged and shipped (or will come with pruning recommendations provided by the grower). Resist the temptation to shorten roots that won't fit in the hole you have prepared — dig a bigger hole to accommodate them. For pot-grown roses, cut off broken or damaged roots before planting and loosen any that circle around the root ball. Plant a container-grown rose as you would any shrub: dig a wide, shallow hole and set the plant at the same depth at which it was growing in the pot.

Before planting bare-root roses, soak them overnight in water, then carry them to the garden still in their buckets of water to make sure the roots don't dry out. If the roots on your plants all radiate out from roughly the same point, build a cone of soil in the bottom of each planting hole, set the shrub on top of the cone, and spread the roots out in all directions. If the rose you are planting has a more irregular root system, a cone of soil will just get in the way, in which case the easiest approach is to hold the plant in place and spread the roots as you fill. In the North (Zone 6 and colder), set the plants so the knobby-looking bud union (also referred to as the graft union) will be 3 inches *below* the soil surface. Planting at this depth encourages the grafted rose to form its own roots. In the South, set the bud union 1½ inches above the soil line. Set own-root roses with the crown about 1 inch below the soil surface. Fill the hole, stopping several times to gently firm the soil around the roots. When the hole is half full, flood it with water and let the water drain away. Then continue filling and tamping down. (The filling, tamping, and flooding process is important because it eliminates air pockets in the soil.) When the hole is full, form a wide saucer of soil around the plant and water thoroughly.

To keep the plants from becoming desiccated, mound moist, loose soil or compost as high as you can over the canes for the first few weeks. When you see the leaf buds beginning to swell, gently remove the mounded soil (down to the saucer of soil). Water plants deeply and thoroughly every 3 to 5 days the entire first season to keep the soil moist and the roots actively growing. Regular watering is essential for good long-term performance, because the roots have trouble keeping the top growth supplied with adequate moisture until they are well established. Be sure to continue watering in fall so the plants do not go into winter with dry soil.

Remove at least the first flower buds that form on newly planted bushes, allowing only the second cycle of bloom to develop to maturity. Doing this encourages new canes and stronger growth for the summer as well as for the remainder of the year.

PRUNING ROSES

All roses benefit from basic pruning to keep them healthy and vigorous and to promote an ongoing supply of new canes from the base of the plant. In the early years, the goal of pruning is to establish a well-spaced framework. Shrub roses are usually vase- to mound-shaped and should have canes that radiate out in all directions. This minimizes rubbing and crossing branches and allows air and light into the center of the plant to help reduce disease problems. To prune roses, you'll need a good pair of bypass pruning shears along with a pair of long-handled pruners or loppers, again with bypass blades, or a small pruning saw. A pair of heavy-duty gloves, a long-sleeved shirt, and long pants are also in order.

Timing. The best timing and techniques depend on the type of roses you are pruning. Reblooming roses — including hybrid teas, grandifloras, floribundas, polyanthas, rugosas, and many shrub roses — bloom on new wood, or growth of the current season. Prune them in late winter or early spring, just as some of the buds on the largest canes are beginning to swell but before the plants are actively growing. (In most parts of North America, this is 4 to 6 weeks before the last hard spring frost date.) Roses that bloom once in late spring to summer — including many old roses and some shrub roses — produce their flowers on year-old or older wood. Prune them immediately after they finish blooming. Pruning in spring would cut off many of the current season's flower buds.

Basic Pruning for All Roses. The first steps in any pruning operation are the same whatever type of rose you are pruning. When making any pruning cuts, always cut just above an outward-facing bud. (See "Pruning" in the Techniques Glossary for directions on making a proper pruning cut.)

First, remove dead and damaged wood, which will be black or dark brown and may look shriveled or dried out. If the entire cane is dead, cut back to the base of the plant or to the bud union. If the entire cane isn't dead, make the first cut as high as possible above an outside or outward-facing bud. Examine the color of the center of the cane, which is called the pith. If the pith is white, you have cut back to live wood. If it is brown, cut a little more off the top of the cane until white pith appears. If by now you have cut the cane to the desired height, go on to the next one. In northern zones, you may find that once you have removed winterkilled wood, you don't need to cut the canes back any farther to reach the ideal height. After a severe winter, if your plants seem very damaged, cut back to where the pith is slightly colored or is a very light tan.

Next, remove canes or branches that cross the center of the plant, along with branches that rub one another. For the latter, remove the smaller of the two or select the one that is growing in the best direction. Finally, cut off spindly or weak branches, including shoots that did not terminate in a flower. For large roses such as hybrid teas, removing shoots thinner than a pencil is a good guideline. For smaller roses, use the main flowering canes as a guide and remove shoots that are decidedly smaller than average. (Thick wood always produces more-vigorous growth than thin wood does. In addition, new stems will be no larger than the cane from which they have arisen; usually they are smaller. Keep this principle in mind whenever you are cutting back canes of any size rose—the farther down you prune a stem, the thicker the new growth will be.)

Established roses also need annual renewal pruning to encourage new, vigorous canes to form. To do this, remove a few of the oldest canes each year. The number you remove will depend on the type of rose, the bush's vigor, and the number of healthy canes.

To prevent borers from drilling into the cut cane ends, seal all pruning cuts with fingernail polish, white glue, wood glue, or a tree-wound compound.

Late frost sometimes damages new growth after you prune, causing blackened or yellow shoots or leaves. If this happens, after danger of freezing weather has passed cut the shoots back again to healthy wood as you did in early spring.

Rose pruning isn't a once-and-done affair. Deadheading and cutting roses for bouquets also are pruning operations and offer you a chance to shape the bushes. See "Care Through the Season" on page 265 for details.

Pruning Once-Blooming Roses. In early to midsummer, immediately after once-blooming roses have finished for the season, cut back canes by one-third and cut back side shoots that have already flowered by up to two-thirds. (If the rose you are pruning produces attractive hips, you

Rose Hips for Fall

Roses that feature showy red hips add color to the fall garden as well as providing a feast for overwintering birds. Rugosa roses *(R. rugosa)*, albas *(R. alba)*, eglantine rose *(R. eglanteria,* formerly *R. rubiginosa)*, red-leaved rose *(R. glauca,* formerly *R. rubrifolia)*, Scotch brier *(R. pimpinellifolia,* formerly *R. spinosissima)*, and Moyes rose *(R. moyesii)* all produce showy hips. Many modern shrub roses also have attractive hips, including some of Meidiland Series shrub roses such as 'Sevillana'. Some climbers, including 'Dortmund', feature showy hips as well. To encourage maximum bloom but still be able to enjoy the hips on reblooming roses (rugosas, modern shrubs, and 'Dortmund'), deadhead the first bloom cycle, then let hips form from the second and subsequent flushes of flowers.

Rugosa roses *(Rosa rugosa)* feature showy flowers, handsome foliage, and colorful red hips.

Hips of red-leaved rose *(Rosa glauca)*

Hybrid tea rose
'Perfect Moment'

may want to skip cutting back side shoots, which removes them. Deadhead the hips in late winter or early spring instead.) On established plants, also remove one or two of the older canes to encourage new ones to form. In fall, if a plant has produced any extremely vigorous new canes from its base, you may want to trim them back by one-third to prevent winter winds from damaging them. Do this about 5 weeks before the first frost date in your area. Most once-blooming roses can also be pruned lightly in early spring to improve their shape and to remove wayward growth.

Pruning Reblooming Roses. Some reblooming roses require more attention than others. All are pruned in late winter to early spring. Always start by removing dead, diseased, and crossing or rubbing wood as well as spindly or weak stems.

Hybrid tea and grandiflora roses require hard pruning every year to encourage thick, vigorous new wood, which will produce the most abundant flowers. To ensure a continuing supply of thick, new canes, remove all but three to six of the youngest, most robust canes. In the North, cut these canes back to 12 to 14 inches or less, depending on the amount of winter damage. In the South, the plants are left higher—18 to 24 inches. Where winter damage has been severe, you will be in good shape if you are able to keep at least three canes with three or four buds each.

Floribunda roses need only moderate pruning. To encourage new canes and an abundance

of flowers, remove the oldest canes at the base of the plant, leaving six to eight canes per plant. Cut back all of the remaining branches and canes by about one-fourth.

Polyanthas benefit from a light annual pruning. Cut back all growth by no more than one-quarter to one-third, and remove the oldest canes, leaving from six to eight main, well-spaced ones.

Rugosa roses and reblooming shrub roses can be pruned to fit the space to some extent. Prune hard if you want a small plant; leave the canes taller if you want a tall shrub for the back of a border. For a middle-of-the-road approach, remove one-third of the oldest canes, then cut back the remaining canes by one-third to one-half. For light pruning, simply prune to shape the plants.

Pruning and Training Climbing Roses. Like other roses, climbing roses are pruned based on when they bloom. Prune reblooming climbers in late winter or early spring. Prune once-blooming climbers in summer, after they have finished blooming. While climbing and rambling roses grow well with a minimum of pruning, they benefit from regular training. The canes bloom best if they are trained horizontally, so plan on tying them to wires or a fence, or spread them out over the face of a broad trellis. Tie the canes loosely to the supports with soft string. In general, do not prune climbing or rambling roses until they are 2 years old. Be especially cautious about pruning climbing forms of hybrid teas, floribundas, and grandifloras when they are young, because hard pruning can cause these plants to revert to a shrub habit.

Most climbing roses bloom on side branches produced by old wood; wood that is between 2 and 3 years old blooms the best. Climbing forms of reblooming roses such as hybrid teas, floribundas, and grandifloras bloom on new wood. To prune these reblooming types, remove up to one-third of the oldest canes, then shorten the branches that have already flowered to leave only three or four buds.

Rambling roses bloom once during the season and bear their flowers only on year-old or older wood. After they flower, they produce new canes from the base of the plant that yield next season's flowers. Prune them in summer after they have finished flowering by cutting off one-third of the oldest canes at the base of the plant or just above a vigorous branch. Then cut back all side branches, leaving four buds. Also remove weak, twiggy growth. Some rose growers untie rambling roses and lay the canes on the ground to prune them. Another option for pruning very vigorous ramblers that produce an abundance of new canes each year is simply to treat the canes as biennials and cut all of the canes that have bloomed in the current year to the ground or to another vigorous cane or branch. (Do this in summer, when you would normally prune a rambler.)

Some climbers and many ramblers will also grow satisfactorily with a minimum of pruning. Simply remove dead and diseased wood and occasionally remove the oldest canes at the base of the plant. This is generally the best system for roses that have been trained up trees, where pruning can be nearly impossible. It also works well in large gardens, where space is not a problem.

CARE THROUGH THE SEASON

In addition to annual pruning, roses need regular attention to look their best. Pruning continues to some extent all season long: remove shoots that have terminated without a flower bud throughout the season. In addition, hybrid teas are typically disbudded to encourage large, single-stemmed flowers. To disbud, remove side buds on flowering shoots, leaving only the main terminal bud.

Mulching and Watering. Mulch roses with shredded bark, chopped leaves, or other organic mulch to keep the soil moist and cool and to control weeds. Renew the mulch annually in spring. Water weekly if the plants do not receive 1 inch of rainfall per week. To prevent foliar diseases, water early in the day so the leaves have time to dry out completely by nightfall. Installing soaker hoses makes watering easy and efficient, but overhead watering helps keep mite populations under control. Be sure to continue watering right through fall until the plants enter dormancy.

Fertilizing. Feed all roses in spring with a balanced organic fertilizer mixed with compost or a mix of well-rotted manure and compost. You can fertilize in fall instead by giving each bush two shovelfuls of well-rotted manure after they are dormant and the ground has frozen. Reblooming roses need regular boosts to fuel their flower production: water them monthly with 1 to 2 gallons of fish emulsion or manure tea (for instructions on "brewing" the latter, see "Making Compost and Manure Teas" in the Techniques Glossary).

Deadheading. Regular deadheading encourages reblooming roses to produce new flowers. To deadhead, cut ¼ inch above the second five-leaflet leaf (counting from the tip of the stem down), preferably above an outward-facing leaf. Prune tall roses that have several sets of five-leaflet leaves much harder if you want to control their height. To deadhead reblooming climbers, cut back branches either to the first five-leaflet leaf or to leave only three or four buds on the branch. On newly planted bushes, cut about ¼ inch above the only first five-leaflet leaf, in order to retain as much foliage as possible on the plant. To improve the appearance of cluster-flowering roses such as grandifloras, snip off the central flower, which fades first. Once the entire cluster has flowered, prune it off as you would any rose. Do not deadhead roses that produce showy hips in fall.

Cutting Roses. It goes without saying that roses make great cut flowers. Using sharp pruning shears, cut ¼ inch above the second five-leaflet leaf (counting from the tip of the stem down) on established plants. Cut above an outward-facing leaf whenever possible. For longer stems, especially on hybrid teas and grandifloras, cut farther down, above the third or fourth five-leaflet leaf. On newly planted bushes, cut ¼ inch above the *first* five-leaflet leaf. This retains foliage on the plant to encourage strong growth.

Winterizing. To encourage plants to enter dormancy and the wood to harden off before cold temperatures arrive, stop deadheading roses in late summer or early fall, 3 to 5 weeks before the first frost date in your area. (Even though roses in the Deep South may not go dormant, leaving the spent blooms on beginning in November gives the plants a rest from blooming. In January, you can begin pruning for the coming year.) In the North, where plants may be buffeted by winter winds, cut back the canes by one-third in late fall, after the plants are dormant. This prevents the canes from whipping around in winter winds and being damaged.

Many roses require winter protection to survive in the North, including hybrid teas, grandifloras, floribundas, and most English roses. If you are growing roses in zones where winter temperatures routinely dip below 0°F (Zone 6 and north), winter protection is in order for roses that are not reliably hardy. After the plants are completely dormant, mound shredded bark, soil, or compost over the plants, forming an 8- to 12-inch-tall mound. Gently remove it in early spring if it hasn't washed away.

Removing Root Suckers. Canes that arise from the more vigorous rootstock of a budded plant are called root suckers. These will outcompete the rose you planted if they are not removed. Root suckers typically have leaves that look different from those of the budded plant, canes that are slenderer and more arching, and thorns that look different as well. (Roses that spread naturally by suckers, including many species and shrub roses, will send up canes near the main crown even if they are budded plants. In this case, the foliage and flowers will resemble those of the main plant, and these suckers shouldn't be removed.) To remove unwanted suckers, dig down into the soil to where they are attached to the plant to confirm that they arose below the bud union, which looks like a gnarled or swollen place

Grandiflora rose
'Candelabra'

Floribunda rose
'Escapade'

Rugosa rose
(*Rosa rugosa* var. *alba*)

Hybrid tea rose
'Radiance'

Grandiflora rose
'Sonia'

on the trunk, then pull them off or snap them off with a trowel. If you can't find the point where the sucker is attached because digging down farther would damage the plant, cut the sucker off as deeply as possible. Never cut off root suckers at the soil line, as this simply encourages them to grow back.

Propagation. Roses with flexible stems, including old roses, climbers, and species roses, are easy to propagate by layering. Bend the stems to the ground after the first flush of bloom in early summer, and you'll have plants with enough roots to pot up in 10 to 12 weeks. See "Layering" in the Techniques Glossary for complete directions.

Roses can also be propagated by cuttings. Fill pots with a 50-50 mix of peat moss and perlite or perlite and vermiculite and moisten it before taking cuttings. Cut 1- to 2-foot-long stems that are firm and green. Remove flower buds and side shoots, and cut the stems into 4-inch lengths with at least two leaf nodes, making cuts just below a leaf node. Strip all but the top set of leaves off each cutting. Dip the stem tips in rooting hormone and stick them in the pots. Label the pots with the name of the plant, cover them with plastic, and set them in a warm, bright place, but out of direct light. Cuttings will root in 6 to 8 weeks. (See "Rooting Cuttings" in the Techniques Glossary for more information.) Or try the old-fashioned yet effective method your grandmother may have used. Take cuttings as above, but loosen a patch of soil right in the garden in the shade of the parent plant, stick in a cutting, and place a quart-size Mason jar firmly over it. The cutting will root in place and can be potted up or moved to a new location in about 8 weeks.

Potential Problems. Roses are subject to a variety of fungal diseases, including black spot. Afflicted leaves develop black spots, turn yellow, and fall. Powdery mildew causes gray patches on the leaves, especially in the South where humidity is high in the summertime. In the West, rust causes red patches on the undersides of the leaves. The easiest way to control these diseases is by good culture: plant disease-resistant roses and provide full sun and good air circulation. If only a few leaves show signs of these diseases, pick them off and destroy them. A couple of organic controls are effective for controlling fungal diseases. Fungicidal soap is available at garden centers. Sulfur—sold as wettable or flowable sulfur—is also good. Apply it according to label directions. Combining sulfur with an antitranspirant prolongs its effectiveness because this helps spread the sulfur out on the leaves. (Sold in garden centers, antitranspirants are sprays that reduce moisture loss from plant foliage. They are most commonly used on broad-leaved evergreens

to protect them from wind damage over winter.) Spray in the early morning, and do not apply sulfur when the weather is hot and dry, because it will burn the foliage. Instead, spray an antitranspirant alone or mixed with 3 teaspoons of baking soda per gallon of liquid. Still another option is horticultural oil mixed at a growing-season dilution, again with 3 teaspoons of baking soda per gallon of water. (Dilute the oil even more than normal if the weather is hot and dry.) If you have planted disease-resistant roses, wait to see if foliar diseases crop up before spraying. If you know they are a problem on your plants, spray in spring as soon as the foliage has emerged. Susceptible plants will need to be sprayed every 2 weeks to keep them free of disease.

Cankers are brown, dead patches that sometimes appear on rose canes. Caused by a fungus, they eventually girdle the stem and kill it. Prune off infected stems and discard or destroy them.

Aphids cluster on stem tips and flower buds. Control them with a strong spray of water or, for serious infestations, use insecticidal soap or neem (a commercially available organic insecticide derived from the seeds of the neem tree). Mites cause yellow-spotted growth and webbing near the stem tips beginning in summer when the weather is hot and dry. Blast them off the plants with water from the hose or use insecticidal soap. Handpick Japanese beetles or spray plants with neem as a repellent.

LANDSCAPE USES

Add roses to perennial gardens and shrub borders. They are especially attractive when underplanted with low-growing perennials such as lavenders (*Lavandula* spp.), catmints (*Nepeta* spp.), sages (*Salvia* spp.), sundrops (*Oenothera* spp.), feverfew (*Chrysanthemum parthenium*, now listed as *Tanacetum parthenium*), and sea kale (*Crambe cordifolia*). Clematis and roses make delightful companions. Plant them together and let the clematis climb up the sturdier roses. (Use smaller clematis for this, as some of the more vigorous selections will overwhelm the roses.) Pair clematis and roses that bloom either together or, to extend bloom time, at different times.

Many roses adapt quite well to use as ground covers. Because of their dense foliage, low-growing forms of rugosa roses are ideal for this purpose. (The 2- to 3-foot-tall cultivars in the Pavement Series are especially suitable.) Roses with long, flexible canes such as wichuraiana climbers can be left to trail over the ground as ground covers. 'Max Graf', the result of a cross between *R. rugosa* and *R. wichuraiana,* and 'White Max Graf', both hardy in Zones 4 to 8, make excellent ground covers.

$\mathcal{R}$udbeckia

Coneflowers

Tough, easy-to-grow coneflowers are summer-blooming perennials that bear an abundance of orangy yellow, daisy-shaped flowers. Because the best-known coneflowers have dark brown centers, *Rudbeckia* species are also called black-eyed Susans. Like sunflowers and other members of the aster family (Asteraceae), coneflowers produce flower heads consisting of ray florets, commonly called petals, surrounding spiny centers of disk florets, which produce the seeds. All the coneflowers listed below are native North American wildflowers hardy in Zones 3 to 9.

Orange coneflower (*R. fulgida*), the best known of the bunch, is a 1½- to 3-foot-tall perennial with 2- to 2½-inch daisies that have orange-yellow petals and chocolate brown cen-

Rudbeckia
■
(rude-BECK-ee-ah)
■
Summer to fall bloom
■
Full sun or light shade
■
Zones 3 to 9
■

BELOW LEFT Orange coneflower (*Rudbeckia fulgida* var. *sullivantii* 'Goldsturm')

BELOW RIGHT Double-flowered black-eyed Susan (*Rudbeckia hirta* 'Goldilocks')

ters. These long-blooming plants have hairy, dark green, oval- to lance-shaped leaves and bloom from midsummer to early fall. The popular, widely planted cultivar 'Goldsturm' (*R. fulgida* var. *sullivantii* 'Goldsturm') bears 3- to 4-inch flowers on 2-foot plants.

Ragged or green-headed coneflower (*R. laciniata*) bears 3- to 6-inch flowers with yellow petals and green centers from midsummer to fall. Plants range from 3 to 6 feet or more in height. Showy, double-flowered forms, including 'Golden Glow' and 'Goldquelle', are also available. *R. maxima* is a towering 5- to 9-foot species that bears 3- to 5-inch-wide flowers in late summer that have orange-yellow petals and cone-shaped, 1½-inch-tall brown centers.

One popular coneflower, *R. hirta*, is a biennial or short-lived perennial commonly grown as an annual. While the species has orange-yellow petals and dark brown centers, many seed-grown cultivars are available that feature petals marked with combinations of gold, yellow, mahogany, and bronze. Old-fashioned gloriosa daisies fall here, with their 3- to 6-inch-wide, single or double flowers from midsummer to fall. Dwarf forms are also available, including 10-inch-tall 'Becky'.

SITE AND SOIL
Plant coneflowers in full sun or light shade in a site with average to rich soil. While plants thrive in evenly moist soil, they are drought tolerant once established.

PLANTING
Add coneflowers to your garden by starting seeds or buying plants. Plant *R. hirta* in spring; perennial species can be planted in spring or fall. Space lower-growing species 1 to 1½ feet apart and taller ones 2 feet apart. Set dwarf forms of *R. hirta* about 6 inches apart. Plan on replacing *R. hirta* annually, although the plants sometimes survive for a second summer.

CARE THROUGH THE SEASON
Once established, perennial coneflowers take care of themselves. They don't need regular feeding or watering and are not troubled by pests or diseases. While *R. fulgida* and shorter cultivars of *R. hirta* don't need staking, *R. laciniata* may need some support. Surprisingly, giant *R. maxima* also stands without staking. Plants that flop can be cut to the ground after they finish flowering if they look unattractive. Most gardeners leave them standing until spring because the cones add winter interest and the seeds are popular with birds.

Coneflowers also don't need dividing regularly. Dig them in spring or fall if they outgrow their space or die out in the centers of the clumps, or for propagation.

Propagation. Propagate coneflowers by division or seeds. Sow *R. hirta* indoors 6 to 8 weeks before the last spring frost date, or sow outdoors in a prepared seedbed where the plants are to grow 2 weeks before the last spring frost date. Seeds germinate in less than 2 weeks. Sow seeds for perennial species outdoors in early spring or fall and set the pots in a cold frame or a protected spot. To sow them indoors, sow the pots and set them in the refrigerator for a month, then germinate them at about 70°F. While seeds of the popular cultivar 'Goldsturm' are available, plants propagated by division are more uniform and many gardeners prefer them.

LANDSCAPE USES
Add coneflowers to sunny beds and borders as well as meadow plantings. *R. fulgida* can be planted en masse and used as a low-maintenance ground cover. All manner of sun-loving perennials make fine companions, including ornamental grasses, purple coneflower (*Echinacea purpurea*), daylilies (*Hemerocallis* spp.), yarrows (*Achillea* spp.), Russian sage (*Perovskia atriplicifolia*), butterfly weed (*Asclepias tuberosa*), and goldenrods (*Solidago* spp.).

Salvia

Salvias, Sages

Salvia
■
(SAL-vee-ah)
■
Summer to fall bloom
■
Full sun or very light shade
■
Zones 3 to 10
■

■ The diverse salvia clan contains popular annuals, tried-and-true hardy perennials, savory herbs, and half-hardy or tender shrubs, many of which are grown as tender perennials in the North. Most are prized for their showy, erect spikes of two-lipped flowers in shades of red, pink, white, yellow, violet, or true blue. Many also feature aromatic leaves, including well-known culinary or

Salvia × superba 'May Night' ('Mainacht')

common sage *(Salvia officinalis)*. The square stems of most salvias mark them as members of the mint family, Lamiaceae.

SELECTING SALVIAS

The most widely grown of the hardy sages is violet sage *(S. × superba)*, hardy in Zones 4 to 7. From early to midsummer, it bears an abundance of erect spikes of violet flowers on 1½- to 3½-foot plants. 'East Friesland' is a compact, 1½-foot-tall selection with violet-purple flowers. 'May Night' ('Mainacht'), which may be listed as a cultivar of *S. × sylvestris*, bears indigo flowers on 1½-foot plants. Meadow sage *(S. pratensis)*, hardy in Zones 3 to 9, is another popular salvia that bears violet spikes from early to midsummer on 1- to 3-foot plants.

Common sage *(S. officinalis)* is another perennial species, hardy in Zones 5 to 8. Unlike most salvias, it is grown for its fragrant, flavorful leaves rather than its spikes of lilac summer flowers. Plants are semiwoody, are generally 1 to 2 feet tall, and have hairy, evergreen leaves. Handsome variegated cultivars, including 'Icterina' and 'Tricolor', can be used for cooking or as ornamentals.

The flaming red blooms of scarlet sage *(S. splendens)*, a tender perennial grown as an annual, are a common sight in summer. The 1- to 1½-foot plants produce dense spikes of flowers from summer to fall. While scarlet is the most common color, and is especially popular with hummingbirds, pinkish purple, white, and pink cultivars are available. Mealycup sage *(S. farinacea)* is another tender perennial grown as an annual. It bears dense spikes of small violet or white flowers from summer to fall on 2-foot plants. The plants are hardy from Zone 8 south and can be overwintered indoors in a frost-free place if desired. Texas sage *(S. coccinea)* is an annual that produces graceful spikes of red, pink, or white flowers from summer to fall on 2- to 2½-foot plants.

Enthusiasts have devoted entire gardens to the tender perennial sages, most of which can be grown as perennials in Zone 8 and south. Pineapple sage *(S. elegans)* bears pineapple-scented leaves and spikes of scarlet flowers on 4- to 6-foot plants in fall. 'Scarlet Pineapple' has more strongly scented leaves than the species and reaches about 3 feet in height. Cleveland sage *(S. clevelandii)* produces spikes of violet-blue or white flowers in summer on 1½- to 2-foot plants that have very aromatic foliage. Gregg sage *(S. greggii)*, which withstands Zone 7 winters, is especially variable. It bears red, pink, yellow, purple, or violet flowers from late summer to fall on 1- to 2-foot plants.

Scarlet sage (*Salvia splendens* 'Flare')

Texas sage (*Salvia coccinea* 'Lady in Red')

Mealycup sage
(*Salvia farinacea*)

SITE AND SOIL
Plant salvias in full sun or very light shade in well-drained, evenly moist soil that is not too rich. Very rich soil causes plants to flop. Most are tough and drought tolerant once established.

PLANTING
Plant hardy perennial salvias in spring or early fall, annuals and tender perennials in spring. Since the perennial types form broad mounds, space them as far apart as their height at maturity. Space annuals and tender perennials somewhat closer — at about half their height.

CARE THROUGH THE SEASON
Perennial and annual salvias are easy-to-grow plants that require very little care to look their best. Feed perennials in spring with a topdressing of compost or a balanced organic fertilizer. Annuals and tender perennials are satisfied for the season if you amend the soil before planting them out. Mulch to keep weeds under control and to retain soil moisture. Watering is seldom required once plants are established. Although in most cases the plants do not need staking, they will tend to need some help remaining erect if they are growing either in too much shade or in soil that is too rich.

Remove flower spikes as they fade to keep the plants neat looking and to encourage them to send up new flowers. Cut perennial species to the ground in late fall or early spring.

Tender perennials can be replaced each spring like annuals or be overwintered indoors. To overwinter them, either take cuttings in late summer to early fall, before cool weather sets in, or dig entire plants and pot them up. Grow them in a sunny, cool (60° to 65°F) spot for the winter, then harden them off and return them to the garden after danger of frost has passed the following spring.

Division. Hardy perennial salvias seldom need to be divided. Dig and divide clumps in spring or early fall if they outgrow their space or for propagation. To keep *S. officinalis* vigorous, every 3 to 4 years replace plants or propagate them by division or cuttings. Otherwise the plants become woody and less productive.

Propagation. Salvia species and many cultivars come true from seed, especially those typically grown as annuals, such as cultivars of *S. splendens*. Use asexual propagation — division or cuttings — for cultivars of perennials and tender perennials. Divide in spring or early fall, or in spring or early summer take cuttings either from shoot tips or from shoots that arise at the base of the plant. Root them in a 50-50 mix of perlite and vermiculite.

Salvias are easy to grow from seeds sown indoors 6 to 8 weeks before the last frost date; sow *S. farinacea* 10 to 12 weeks before the last frost date. Germinate at temperatures between 65° and 70°F, and transplant hardened-off seedlings to the garden after the last frost date once the soil has warmed and all danger of frost has passed.

LANDSCAPE USES
Salvias add bright color to sunny beds and borders. Combine them with coneflowers (*Rudbeckia* spp.), daylilies (*Hemerocallis* spp.), yarrows (*Achillea* spp.), and other perennials that thrive in well-drained conditions.

Sedum

■ Tough, drought-tolerant sedums belong on every list of low-maintenance perennials. Fortunately, these hardworking garden residents are as pretty as they are practical. Most produce their tiny, star-shaped flowers in dense, showy clusters that can be from $\frac{1}{2}$ to 8 inches or more across. The plants range from 1-inch-tall ground covers to 2-foot mound formers. Sedums, also called stonecrops, have fleshy leaves that are oval and somewhat flattened or are rounded and borne in dense rosettes. Some species are evergreen; others, deciduous. Many feature ornamental foliage.

SELECTING SEDUMS
Sedums can be roughly divided into mat-forming plants and clump forming or mounding ones. The low-growing mat formers are ideal ground covers, while the clump-forming species are commonly used in beds and borders.

Mat-Forming Sedums
Low-growing sedums range from well-behaved plants that spread modestly to fast-spreading species that can become quite invasive. Use the modest spreaders in rock gardens or as edgings, or combine them with other low-growing perennials that thrive in dry soil. Fast-spreading sedums

Sedums

Sedum
■
(SEE-dum)
■
Summer to fall bloom
■
Full sun
■
Zones 3 to 9
■

are best used alone as ground covers where they can spread as they will. Or plant several of them together and let them fight it out. Both types are great plants for filling in between steppingstones.

S. acre. Gold moss sedum. Small, $\frac{1}{2}$-inch-wide clusters of starry yellow-green flowers in summer; 2-inch plants with evergreen leaves. A fast-spreading type; 'Aureum', which has yellow leaves, is a more modest spreader. Zones 4 to 9.

S. kamtschaticum. Golden yellow flowers in 1- to 2-inch-wide clusters in late summer; flat, oval leaves on 4-inch plants with thick rhizomes. Modest spreader. 'Variegatum' has white-edged leaves. Zones 4 to 9.

S. spathulifolium. Starry yellow flowers in $\frac{1}{2}$-inch-wide clusters borne just above the foliage in summer; 4-inch-tall plants with tiny, fleshy, evergreen leaves. A modest spreader that tolerates light shade. 'Cape Blanco' has silver-blue leaves; 'Purpureum' has red-purple and silver ones. Zones 5 to 9.

ABOVE Low-growing sedums, such as *Sedum kamtschaticum*, make fine, vigorous ground covers.

RIGHT Gold moss sedum *(Sedum acre)* filling the cracks between steps backed by iris foliage

Sedum 'Autumn Joy'

Sedum 'Ruby Glow' with hardy prickly pear cactus *(Opuntia humifusa)*

Evergreen *Sedum spathulifolium* hugs a rock wall with purple-flowered *Aubrieta × cultorum.*

Showy stonecrop *(Sedum spectabile)*

S. spurium. Two-row sedum. Pinkish purple or white, star-shaped flowers in loose clusters in late summer; fleshy, 1-inch-long, evergreen leaves. Vigorous spreader. 'Dragon's Blood', the most commonly grown cultivar, has purple-tinted leaves and dark pink flowers. 'Elizabeth' has bronze and maroon leaves. 'Tricolor' produces pink-, white-, and green-striped ones. Zones 4 to 9.

Sedums for Beds and Borders

By far the best-known sedum for beds and borders is 'Autumn Joy', a hybrid also sold as 'Herbstfreude', the name given to it by its German hybridizers. The plants add nearly three seasons of interest to the garden. In summer, the 2-foot-tall, 2-foot-wide clumps produce broccoli-like clusters of flower buds that open in early fall into rounded, 8-inch-wide heads of densely packed flowers. The flowers start out as pale green buds, open to dark pink, and gradually age to bronze. The red-brown heads stand through winter. Plants are hardy in Zones 3 to 9.

Several other popular sedums for beds and borders are hybrids. 'Ruby Glow' bears loose, 2½-inch-wide clusters of pinkish red flowers from midsummer to early fall on 10-inch plants.

The plants have oval, purplish green leaves borne on arching stems and are hardy in Zones 5 to 9. 'Vera Jameson' is similar but has rose-pink flowers and purplish to burgundy leaves. It is hardy in Zones 4 to 9.

As its common name suggests, October daphne (*S. sieboldii*) bears its 2½-inch clusters of pink flowers in fall. Hardy in Zones 3 to 8, the plants have fleshy blue-green leaves edged in pink. Showy stonecrop (*S. spectabile*) resembles 'Autumn Joy'. Hardy in Zones 3 to 9, it blooms slightly earlier, in late summer, and self-sows to some extent. Hot-pink-flowered 'Brilliant' is its best-known cultivar.

SITE AND SOIL

Grow sedums in full sun in well-drained, average to rich soil. They will also grow in poor, dry soil. Wet soil leads to root or crown rot and death.

PLANTING

The best time to plant sedums is in spring or early fall, although they can be set into the ground anytime in summer provided they are watered regularly until established. Space clump- or mound-forming types 2 feet apart—slightly closer if you are planting them in drifts and want them to fill in quickly. Space the vigorous, mat-forming species 12 inches apart; the more modest spreaders, 6 to 8 inches.

CARE THROUGH THE SEASON

Sedums need next to no care to thrive. They don't require annual feeding, staking, or regular watering and are not troubled by pests or diseases. Mulch them with shredded bark or other organic mulch to control weeds, although mulching isn't essential either. Cut clump-forming sedums such as 'Autumn Joy' to the ground in late winter or early spring. Dig and divide the clumps if they outgrow their space, but otherwise they don't need regular division.

Propagation. Sedums are easy to propagate by division or cuttings. Divide the clumps in spring or fall, or take cuttings anytime the plants are not in flower and root them in a 50-50 mix of perlite and vermiculite.

LANDSCAPE USES

Use low-growing sedums as edgings, in rock gardens, along paths, or as ground covers. The most vigorous types will easily carpet a hot, sunny bank. Combine clump-forming sedums with late-summer- to fall-blooming perennials such as asters, coneflowers (*Rudbeckia* spp.), daylilies (*Hemerocallis* spp.), and ornamental grasses. Because of their basically undemanding nature, they are ideal for low-maintenance landscapes.

$\mathscr{S}$hrubs

■ Flowering shrubs add color to the landscape wherever they are used—in foundation plantings; as hedges, screens, or ground covers; or in beds and borders. While there are many popular old-fashioned shrubs legendary for their spectacular spring bloom, it pays to consider what they add to the landscape the rest of the year. In many cases the answer is "Not much." Because of their size, it is especially important that shrubs be hard-working plants. In other words, they should add color, texture, or interest to the landscape for more than a single, fleeting season. For a garden that is interesting all year long, plant a mix of shrubs that feature flowers as well as colorful berries, variegated or evergreen leaves, attractive branching habits, interesting bark, and/or fall foliage color. The fewer shrubs you have room for, the more judicious you should be about your choices.

Successful shrub plantings start the same way successful perennial gardens do—by matching plants to the site you have available. Look for shrubs that grow well in your soil and the amount of sun or shade you have available. Amending soil or adjusting pH on a case-by-case basis just doesn't yield a healthy, vigorous plant-

There are many cultivars of Japanese barberry (*Berberis thunbergii*). Here purple-leaved 'Atropurpurea' highlights the yellow foliage of 'Aurea'.

Use shrubs such as oakleaf hydrangea (*Hydrangea quercifolia*) as specimens, hedges, or foundation plants or in a border combined with other shrubs, small trees, and perennials.

Butterfly bush
'Petit Indigo'
(Buddleia davidii)

ing, but matching plant to site does. Also consider the local climate and weather you deal with. If you are a gambler, you may want to experiment with shrubs that are only marginally hardy in your zone or whose flower buds will be killed by late-spring frosts 3 years out of 4. For the main plants in your landscape, however, stick to shrubs that are solid performers and perfectly hardy in your area. Depending on where you live, either winter cold or summer heat may be the deciding factor. Get ideas from gardeners in your neighborhood, or visit local botanical gardens or arboretums to find shrubs that are stellar performers. See **Perennials** on page 222 for more on site evaluation and matching plants to a particular site.

When choosing shrubs, also consider plant height and spread *at maturity* before you buy. (You'll find this information on the plant tag or in the catalog description. If you don't find it in either place, and nursery personnel can't tell you size at maturity, shop elsewhere.) Matching the mature size of a shrub to the site where you want to plant it has a tremendous effect on the long-term maintenance it will require, and well-chosen shrubs generally need only minimal attention to keep them healthy and attractive. Shrubs that require constant pruning to reduce their size are in the wrong place; removal and replacement is the best option. Not only does this reduce maintenance, but plants that need constant hacking back to keep them "in bounds" are rarely very attractive anyway.

PLANTING

Most common landscape shrubs are available as balled-and-burlapped or container-grown specimens, either of which can be planted in spring or fall. Gardeners once dug deep holes for shrubs and amended the soil with peat moss, compost, and fertilizer in each hole as they planted. Studies of long-term performance have shown that this is not a good practice. Shrubs and trees planted in this manner rarely send their roots out beyond the confines of the original hole. Instead, they wind them around and around in the amended soil as if it were a container. Eventually the roots become as potbound as they would be if they really were growing in a pot, and growth suffers. (Trees planted this way actually can blow over because the top growth isn't supported by wide-spreading roots.)

When you plant, the object is to encourage roots to extend out into the surrounding soil, and there are two ways to accomplish this. The first is to dig a shallow hole that is two to three times as wide as the root ball. Loosen the soil on the sides of the hole, then set the plant in place and

check to make sure it is positioned at the same depth at which it was growing in the nursery. (Lay a straight board across the hole from rim to rim to gauge this.) Refill the hole without amending the soil.

The second method, which is one of the best approaches to planting shrubs, is to prepare planting sites that accommodate groups of plants. Mark off an area where you want to plant a mix of shrubs, trees, and even perennials and ground covers, then remove the grass and work compost, well-rotted manure, or other organic matter as deeply into the soil as you can manage — 12 inches is fine. Then plant the entire area, mulch, and water deeply. Since the whole site has amended soil, roots are encouraged to spread as they will. Although this approach requires more work up front, it's great from a maintenance standpoint because you end up with large plantings that you don't need to trim around.

With either planting method, take a good look at the roots before you set each shrub in the soil. Sever roots that wind around the bottom of the container. If there is a solid mass of roots around the outside of the root ball, score the sides in three or four places with a sharp knife. Then tease some of the roots out to encourage them to spread into the surrounding soil before refilling the hole (don't let them dry out before you finish planting). If you are planting a balled-and-burlapped plant, set the plant in the hole and remove any staples or ties holding the burlap in place. Then cut off as much of the fabric as you can easily manage without disturbing the root ball and push the rest down into the bottom of the hole before filling over it with soil.

Again with either planting method, form a broad saucer of soil around each plant that will collect and direct water. Then flood the soil around newly planted shrubs to settle it and eliminate air pockets. Finally, mulch with shredded bark or other organic matter, keeping it an inch or two away from the stems of the plants. Then water again, and continue watering regularly — providing 1 inch of water every 10 to 14 days if nature doesn't do so — for the first season to give them a good start and to encourage a vigorous, wide-spreading root system.

A few shrubs are available bare-root, and these should be planted in spring while they are still dormant. Before planting, soak them overnight in a bucket of water, and carry them to the garden still in their buckets to make sure the roots don't dry out. Dig a hole for each the way you would for a balled-and-burlapped or container-grown plant. If the roots on your plants all radiate out from roughly the same point, build a cone of soil in the bottom of each hole, set the shrub on top of the cone, and spread the roots out in all directions. If the plant has a more irregular root system, a cone of soil will just get in the way, in which case the easiest approach is to hold the plant in place and spread the roots as you fill. Refill the hole, stopping several times to gently firm the soil around the roots. When the hole is half full, flood it with water and let the water drain away. Then continue filling and tamping down. (The filling, tamping, and flooding process is important because it eliminates air pockets in the soil.) When the hole is full, form a wide saucer of soil around the plant and water thoroughly. Water bare-root plants deeply and thoroughly every week for the entire first season to encourage a vigorous root system.

CARE THROUGH THE SEASON

Established, well-chosen shrubs are usually low-maintenance plants. Renew the mulch around them annually, and if you want to give them an extra boost, feed in spring with a topdressing of compost mixed with well-rotted manure or with a balanced organic fertilizer. Pruning is the only regular attention shrubs need, and the best shrubs won't need much care in this area, either.

Propagation. Propagation methods vary from plant to plant, but shrubs are commonly propagated by cuttings or layering as well as from seeds. See the descriptions of individual shrubs for recommendations on the techniques to try. Since shrub cuttings are generally more difficult to root than cuttings from perennials, they take a bit more preparation. Wounding cuttings and dipping them in a rooting hormone helps ensure success. To wound a cutting, make a shallow, 1½-inch-long cut in the base of the stem before dipping it in rooting hormone. Stick cuttings in a 50-50 mix of peat moss and coarse sand or perlite and vermiculite, or in coarse sand alone. Cover the pots with plastic to maintain high humidity. You may have to experiment to determine which technique works best for each plant. Some shrub cuttings root easily, others are more difficult. See "Rooting Cuttings" in the Techniques Glossary for more information.

Shrubs that produce suckers are typically easy to propagate. Dig gently around the sucker to see if it has adequate roots, then sever the root that joins the new plant to the parent. Dig the new plant and pot it up or move it to a new location. For details on specific propagation methods, see the Techniques Glossary.

Germination requirements vary for shrubs, but if you want to try growing from seeds, sow them in individual pots set outdoors in a cold frame or a protected location either in late summer or fall, or in very early spring, when the seeds will still be exposed to frost. Mulch the soil with very small pea gravel (the kind sold for aquariums), and cover the pots with hardware cloth to protect the seeds from rodents.

PRUNING SHRUBS

The best way to start any pruning operation is to step back and decide what you want to accomplish. Most shrubs look best if allowed to retain their natural shape. Opting for a natural look instead of creating sheared cubes and gumballs not only reduces pruning chores to a large extent, it

Effective Pruning

After removing dead, damaged, or diseased growth on a shrub, use thinning cuts to eliminate rubbing branches and growth that crowds the center of the plant. Then thin out a few of the oldest stems to encourage new, vigorous growth, which will bear the most flowers. Finally, use heading cuts to shape the plant and to shorten branches that have grown too long.

also yields more flowers. Always remove dead, damaged, or diseased growth first, using thinning cuts and cutting back to healthy wood. Then eliminate crossing and rubbing branches as well as wayward growth with thinning cuts. (See "Pruning" in the Techniques Glossary for illustrations and explanations of proper heading and thinning cuts.) Also remove water sprouts, which are vigorous erect shoots that seldom bloom, and reverted growth—a branch that has all-green leaves on an otherwise variegated shrub, for example. While you do this, consider the overall balance of the branching: shrubs should have well-spaced branches radiating in all directions, with no congested or lopsided growth. Use thinning cuts to eliminate lopsided or congested growth and encourage a balanced, attractive shape. Finally, shorten branches that have grown too long, using heading cuts to shape the plant.

Deciding When to Prune. The best time to prune flowering shrubs depends on whether blooms are produced on new wood (the current season's growth) or on old wood (growth formed the previous year). (You actually can safely prune any flowering shrub in late winter or early spring, regardless of what wood it blooms on; you simply may sacrifice bloom for a season.) Most spring-flowering plants bloom on old wood and should be pruned immediately after they've flowered. Pruning any other time of year would cut off most of the flower buds.

Plants that bloom in summer usually do so on new wood. Prune them in late fall (after the plants are dormant) or in winter or very early spring. This encourages the formation of flowering wood that will bloom during the growing season. Prune plants that bloom twice or throughout the growing season at the same time.

Rejuvenating Shrubs. Sometimes called renovation or renewal pruning, rejuvenation is a technique that promotes new, vigorous growth, which produces more flowers. It can be done radically or gradually, but it can only be used on shrubs that sprout readily from old wood. If you aren't sure whether a given plant will withstand rejuvenation, look among the older stems for suckers or new shoots near the base of the plant, which are a good indication that it will resprout. (The entries that follow indicate which plants can be rejuvenated, but if you are pruning a shrub that isn't covered here, it's best to ask an expert at a nursery or botanical garden.) For radical rejuvenation, simply cut the entire shrub to within a few inches or a foot of the ground in late winter or early spring. Rejuvenate suckering plants by removing the old growth and encouraging selected suckers.

If you are concerned that the total removal of all growth may be too much of a shock (for the plant or for you), rejuvenate gradually. Remove a portion of the oldest stems or canes each year for 2 to 3 years. You can remove up to one-third of the oldest stems on vigorous plants; remove only a stem or two on less vigorous specimens. Once a rejuvenated shrub has begun to thrive again, continue thinning out a few of the oldest stems annually to keep it growing and looking its best.

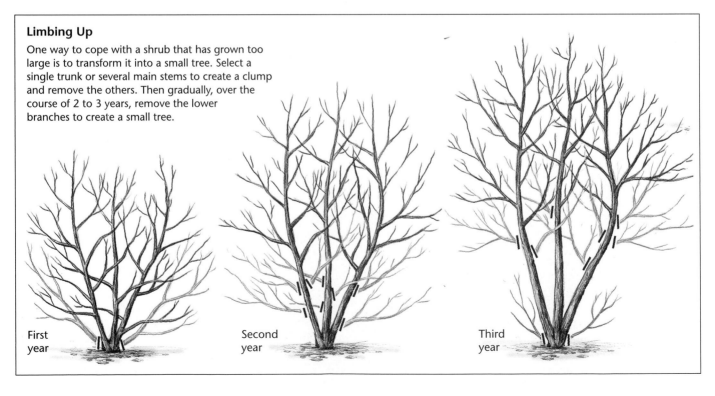

Limbing Up

One way to cope with a shrub that has grown too large is to transform it into a small tree. Select a single trunk or several main stems to create a clump and remove the others. Then gradually, over the course of 2 to 3 years, remove the lower branches to create a small tree.

First year

Second year

Third year

POPULAR FLOWERING SHRUBS

In addition to the shrubs listed below, many of the most popular flowering shrubs and small trees are covered in individual entries in this book. These include butterfly bush (*Buddleia* spp., page 50), bluebeard or blue-mist shrub (*Caryopteris* × *clandonensis,* page 70), dogwoods (*Cornus* spp., page 87), hydrangeas (*Hydrangea* spp., page 167), lavenders (*Lavandula* spp., page 183), magnolias (*Magnolia* spp., page 194), tree peonies (*Paeonia* spp., page 214), cherries (*Prunus* spp., page 241), roses (*Rosa* spp., page 254), lilacs (*Syringa* spp., page 282), and viburnums (*Viburnum* spp., page 294). The popular rhododendrons and azaleas (*Rhododendron* spp.) likewise are covered in a separate entry, beginning on page 246. There you'll also find information on other shrubs that thrive in partial shade in acid, evenly moist, well-drained soil—see "Rhododendron Companions" on page 252. Several of the ground covers covered in the entry that begins on page 125 also are shrubs.

Abelia × *grandiflora* / Glossy abelia

Funnel-shaped, 3/4-inch white flowers flushed with pink from early summer through fall; spreading, 3- to 6-foot plants with evergreen or semievergreen leaves. Grow in full sun or partial shade and rich, evenly moist, slightly acid soil. Plants flower on the current season's growth. To prune, thin out approximately one-third of the oldest stems in late winter or early spring to encourage vigorous plants and abundant flowers. Overgrown plants can be rejuvenated if cut to within 3 inches of the ground. Propagate from cuttings taken in early or midsummer, dipped in rooting hormone, and rooted in a 50-50 mix of peat and perlite. Zones 6 to 9; will grow in Zone 5 but is killed to the ground if temperatures drop below –10°F.

Berberis spp. / Barberries

Barberries are deciduous or evergreen shrubs grown for their spring flowers, handsome foliage, and attractive fall fruit. The plants typically are thorny and make good hedges, barriers, ground covers, or additions to shrub borders. The best known is Japanese barberry *(B. thunbergii),* a 3- to 6-foot shrub hardy in Zones 4 to 8 that spreads somewhat wider than its height. It produces tiny yellow spring flowers under the leaves, bright red fall fruit, and good orange, red, and red-purple fall foliage. Plants tolerate dry soil. 'Crimson Pygmy' is a low, dense cultivar with red-purple leaves that ranges from 1¹/₂ to 2 feet in height and spreads to 4 feet. Paleleaf barberry *(B. candidula),* hardy in Zones 5 to 8, forms 2- to 4-foot mounds of shiny, evergreen leaves that can spread to 5 feet, making it a good ground cover. It bears yellow spring flowers under the foliage and is deciduous in cold Zone 5 winters. Korean barberry *(B. koreana),* hardy in Zones 3 to 7, bears clusters of showy yellow spring flowers and bright red berries. The 4- to 6-foot plants are deciduous and have good red-purple fall color. Barberries have an attractive natural shape and don't need much pruning to look their best. Thin out crowded growth in late winter or early spring as necessary by removing several of the oldest stems. Or prune after plants flower. When used as hedges they should not be sheared—they are more attractive if allowed to retain their natural shape. Propagate by cuttings taken in spring or early summer.

ABOVE LEFT Purple-leaved Japanese barberry (*Berberis thunbergii* 'Crimson Pygmy')

ABOVE Yellow-leaved Japanese barberry (*Berberis thunbergii* 'Aurea')

Calycanthus floridus / Sweet shrub, Carolina allspice

Red-brown, 2-inch flowers in late spring and early to midsummer with a rich, fruity fragrance; 6- to 9-foot plants in height and spread. Flower fragrance varies from plant to plant. Grow in sun or shade in rich, evenly moist soil. Tolerates acid or alkaline conditions. Flowers appear on old wood, so prune if necessary immediately after flowering. Propagate by cuttings taken in midsummer, or dig up and replant suckers that appear in spring. Zones 4 to 9.

Camellia spp. / Camellias

These fall-, winter-, or spring-blooming evergreen shrubs are grown for their showy flowers borne in white, red, and all shades of pink. Japanese camellia *(C. japonica)* reaches 10 to 15 feet tall, spreads to about 10 feet, and bears 3- to 5-inch-wide flowers. Sasanqua camellia *(C. sasanqua)* is smaller — from 6 to 10 feet tall and about 4 to 5 feet wide — and bears 2- to 3-inch flowers in fall or winter. Grow camellias in partial shade and moist, acid soil that is well drained. A protected site is best. Prune immediately after flowering. Propagate by cuttings taken in spring or early summer. Both species generally are hardy in Zones 7 to 9 but will be killed or damaged in severe winters in Zones 7 and 8.

BELOW Bearberry cotoneaster *(Cotoneaster dammeri)*

BELOW RIGHT Fall foliage of rockspray cotoneaster *(Cotoneaster horizontalis)*

Chaenomeles speciosa / Flowering quince

Clusters of pink, red, white, salmon, or orange, single or double, 1- to 2-inch flowers in early spring; 3- to 8-foot shrubs with spiny branches that spread into broad clumps to 15 feet wide. Flowers appear on old wood before or as the leaves appear. Plants are spectacular in spring but frequently are defoliated because of disease by late summer. Grows in full sun or partial shade and tolerates dry soil. Requires acid to neutral pH. Remove two or three of the oldest, most crowded stems to open up the center of the plant. Plants can also be rejuvenated if cut back to within 2 to 3 inches of the ground. The plants are generally unattractive when out of bloom, and other shrubs, especially *Viburnum* species, are better choices. Propagate by cuttings taken in summer. Zones 4 to 8.

Corylopsis spp. / Winter hazels

Although not too commonly grown, these shrubs or small trees are valued for their pendulous clusters of fragrant yellow flowers, which are borne in early spring before the leaves emerge. Fragrant winter hazel *(C. glabrescens)*, hardy in Zones 5 to 8, reaches 8 to 15 feet tall and spreads as far. It grows in full sun or light shade. Buttercup winter hazel *(C. pauciflora)*, hardy in Zones 6 to 8, reaches 4 to 6 feet in height and spreads as far. It is best in shade. Spike winter hazel *(C. spicata)*, also 4 to 6 feet high and wide, is hardy in Zones 5 to 8 and grows in full sun or partial shade. All winter hazels prefer evenly moist, well-drained soil with an acid pH. A sheltered site is best because the flowers and flower buds can be damaged by prevailing winter winds and late-spring frosts. Prune plants if necessary to shape them immediately after they flower. Propagate by cuttings taken in early to midsummer.

Cotoneaster spp. / Cotoneasters

A large genus of handsome spreading shrubs grown for their spring to early-summer flowers, red fall fruit, glossy evergreen or deciduous leaves, and attractive branching habits. Cranberry cotoneaster *(C. apiculatus)*, hardy in Zones 4 to 7, reaches 3 feet tall and spreads twice as far. It is deciduous and features bronze- or purple-red fall foliage and especially attractive bright red fruit. Bearberry cotoneaster *(C. dammeri)*, hardy in Zones 5 to 8, is evergreen to semievergreen and ranges from 1 to 1½ feet in height but spreads to 6 feet. It makes a good, dense ground cover. Rockspray cotoneaster *(C. horizontalis)*, hardy in Zones 5 to 7, is deciduous or semievergreen and has an attractive fish-bone-like branching habit. Plants reach 2 to 3 feet in height and spread easily twice as far. Although they do not tolerate

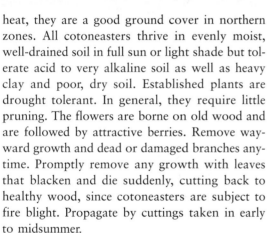

heat, they are a good ground cover in northern zones. All cotoneasters thrive in evenly moist, well-drained soil in full sun or light shade but tolerate acid to very alkaline soil as well as heavy clay and poor, dry soil. Established plants are drought tolerant. In general, they require little pruning. The flowers are borne on old wood and are followed by attractive berries. Remove wayward growth and dead or damaged branches anytime. Promptly remove any growth with leaves that blacken and die suddenly, cutting back to healthy wood, since cotoneasters are subject to fire blight. Propagate by cuttings taken in early to midsummer.

Deutzia gracilis / Slender deutzia
Old-fashioned plant grown for its clusters of ½- to ¾-inch white flowers borne in midspring; 2- to 4-foot plants that spread as far. Tolerant of acid to alkaline soils and easy to grow, but not particularly attractive when out of bloom. Plants bloom on old wood, so prune in spring or early summer, as soon as possible after they flower. Thin out up to one-third of the oldest or weakest stems to reduce crowding. Propagate by cuttings taken in early summer. Zones 5 to 8.

Forsythia spp. / Forsythias
These popular shrubs are a sure sign of spring. All bear quantities of small, yellow, four-petaled flowers in late winter or early spring before the leaves emerge. Border forsythia (*F.* × *intermedia*)

reaches 8 to 10 feet tall and can easily spread to 12 feet. While the stems are hardy in Zones 4 to 8, the flower buds are killed over winter in Zone 4 and frequently in Zone 5, making this plant a poor choice north of Zone 6. *F. mandschurica* 'Vermont Sun' has flower buds hardy to Zone 4. *F. viridissima* 'Bronxensis', a cultivar of greenstem forsythia, is hardy in Zones 5 to 8 and makes a good ground cover because plants grow only 1 foot tall and can spread to 3 feet. Grow forsythias in full sun for best flowering. Plants thrive in rich, well-drained soil but tolerate poor soil and can be grown in acid to alkaline pH. Prune in spring or early summer, immediately after flowering. Thin out up to one-third of the oldest or weakest stems. If spreading is a problem, dig up suckers and cut back arching stems, which root when they touch the ground. Otherwise, let the plants grow in a naturally arching shape. Avoid shearing, which destroys the natural shape and cuts off flower buds. To rejuvenate sheared, overgrown, or badly shaped plants, cut all stems to within a few inches of the ground. Propagate by potting up rooted suckers or taking cuttings in early summer.

Hamamelis × *intermedia* / Witch hazel
Yellow, orange, or red, ribbonlike flowers borne in late winter to early spring before the leaves emerge; 12- to 15-foot plants that spread as far. Oval leaves turn yellow in fall. Grow in full sun or partial shade in average to rich soil that is

St. Johnswort
(*Hypericum* 'Hidcote')

promotes rampant growth at the expense of flowers. Prune immediately after flowering in late spring or early summer, since blooms are borne on old wood. Remove up to one-third of the oldest stems, or rejuvenate overgrown plants by cutting all stems back to within a few inches of the ground. Propagate by dividing clumps or slicing off suckers, or by cuttings taken in summer. Zones 4 to 9.

Kolkwitzia amabilis / Beautybush
Pink, bell-shaped flowers in late spring to early summer; 6- to 10-foot plants that spread nearly as far. An old-fashioned shrub that is very pretty in bloom but rather unattractive the rest of the year. Other shrubs are better choices for year-round appeal. Grow in full sun and any well-drained soil. Plants bloom on old wood, so prune immediately after flowering by thinning out up to one-third of the oldest stems. Plants will also withstand rejuvenation pruning; cut all stems to the ground after flowering. Propagate by cuttings taken in early summer. Zones 4 to 8.

Philadelphus spp. / Mock oranges
Old-fashioned shrubs grown for their fragrant, white, early-summer flowers that can be single or double; 10- to 12-foot plants that spread as far. Hybrids are grown more often than the species, and fragrance varies considerably. Fragrant-flowered cultivars include 'Belle Etoile', 'Innocence', 'Lemoinei', 'Perle Blanche', and 'Virginal'. Flowers are borne on old wood, so prune in late spring or early summer, immediately after the plants bloom. Remove up to one-third of the oldest stems each year, or rejuvenate overgrown plants by cutting all of the stems to within a few inches of the ground. Propagate by cuttings taken in early summer. Zones 5 to 8.

moist but not wet. Grows in acid to slightly alkaline soil. Prune in spring, immediately after plants flower, if necessary to shape the plants or to remove wayward growth. Propagate by cuttings taken in early summer. Zones 5 to 9.

Hypericum spp. / St. Johnsworts
These spreading, evergreen or semievergreen shrubs are grown for their yellow summer flowers. Aaron's-beard St. Johnswort *(H. calycinum),* hardy in Zones 5 to 8, bears bright yellow, 3-inch-wide flowers from early summer through early fall on 1- to 1½-foot plants. The plants spread by stolons to 2 feet or more, making this a good ground cover. In mild-winter areas, they are evergreen to semievergreen but can be killed to the ground in severe winters, just as they are annually in northern zones. (Since they bloom on new wood, their flowering is uninterrupted.) Plants grow in full sun or partial shade and tolerate poor, dry soil and alkaline conditions. *H.* 'Hidcote', hardy in Zones 6 to 9, is an outstanding hybrid with fragrant, 2½-inch, golden yellow flowers from midsummer to fall on 3-foot plants. Grow in full sun or partial shade and well-drained soil. Cut both types to the ground in late winter or early spring. Propagate by cuttings taken in early summer or by division.

Kerria japonica / Japanese kerria
Yellow, 1¼- to 2-inch-wide flowers in mid- to late spring; 3- to 6-foot plants that spread by suckers to form broad clumps. Has green stems that are attractive in winter. Double-flowered and variegated forms are available. Grow in partial or full shade; will grow in full sun, too, but the flowers fade more rapidly than in shade. Best in average, well-drained soil; soil that is too rich

Shrubby cinquefoil
(*Potentilla fruticosa*)

Potentilla fruticosa / Shrubby cinquefoil
Yellow, 1-inch-wide flowers from early summer to fall; 1- to 4-foot plants that spread as far. Many cultivars are available and are better choices than the species. Grow in full sun or partial shade. Thrives in evenly moist, rich soil but tolerates poor, dry conditions. The plants bloom on new wood, so prune them in late winter or early spring by removing up to one-third of the oldest stems. Head back taller branches to encourage branching and dense growth. Propagate by cuttings taken in early summer. Zones 2 to 7.

Pyracantha coccinea / Scarlet firethorn
Clusters of small white flowers in early summer followed by orange-red berries in late summer to fall; evergreen, 10- to 12-foot plants that spread as far. Grow in full sun and average, well-drained

soil. Tolerates acid to slightly alkaline conditions. Can be difficult to transplant; container-grown plants are best. Improved cultivars are worth looking for, as they feature showier, more abundant fruit or compact growth habits. Hardiness varies from Zones 5 or 6 to 9, depending on the cultivar. Prune as necessary immediately after flowering, removing crossing, rubbing, and crowded growth along with water sprouts and suckers. Keep in mind that excessive pruning will reduce the berry display. Propagate by cuttings taken in early summer.

Spiraea spp. / Spireas

These are deciduous or evergreen shrubs grown for their showy clusters of tiny flowers in spring or summer. Japanese spirea *(S. japonica),* hardy in Zones 3 to 8, bears rounded clusters of rose-pink or white flowers in mid- to late summer. Plants range from 3 to 6 feet in height and spread as far. The many improved cultivars are the best choices, including ones formerly listed as *S. × bumalda* such as 'Anthony Waterer', which has dark pink flowers on wide-spreading, 3- to 4-foot plants. 'Goldflame' is 2½ feet tall and has pink flowers; its leaves emerge orange or bronzy in spring, turn yellow-green in summer, and shade to scarlet, orange, and yellow in fall. These and other spreading cultivars can be used as ground covers as well as in borders. Bridalwreath spirea *(S. prunifolia),* hardy in Zones 4 to 8, is an old-fashioned, 4- to 9-foot shrub with arching branches that spread as far. While the branches are covered with clusters of white flowers in spring, the plants are unremarkable for the rest of the year. Vanhoutte spirea *(S. × vanhouttei),* hardy in Zones 3 to 8, is another large, wide-spreading, old-fashioned shrub. It reaches 6 to 8 feet in height, spreads to 10 to 12 feet, and bears white spring flowers, but it is not particularly attractive when out of bloom. Spring-blooming spirea species bloom on old wood and should be pruned immediately after they flower. *S. japonica* and its cultivars bloom on new wood; prune them in late winter or very early spring. To prune all spireas, thin out up to one-third of the oldest stems each year as well as overcrowded growth. Spireas will withstand rejuvenation pruning and can be cut to within a few inches of the ground if necessary. Propagate by cuttings taken in early to midsummer.

Vaccinium spp. / Blueberries

Blueberries offer white spring flowers, tasty blue berries, and showy yellow, orange, or red fall foliage. Highbush blueberry *(V. corymbosum)* is hardy in Zones 3 to 7 and ranges from 6 to 12

Highbush blueberry *(Vaccinium corymbosum)*

Old-fashioned weigela *(Weigela florida)*

Syringa vulgaris

Common Lilac

Syringa vulgaris

■
(sih-RING-gah
vul-GAIR-iss)

■
Late-spring to
early-summer bloom

■
Full sun or light shade

■
Zones 3 to 7

■

French hybrid lilac
(Syringa vulgaris
'Boule Azure')

■ Adaptable, easy-to-grow common lilac *(Syringa vulgaris)* was one of the first plants early settlers brought to North America, and it is still popular today. Its showy, 4- to 8-inch-long panicles of small, very fragrant flowers appear in late spring to early summer, just after flowering dogwoods *(Cornus florida)* begin to bloom. The species bears single, pale lilac flowers, but cultivars with single or double flowers are available in white, pink, purple, magenta, violet, and lavender-blue. There are literally hundreds from which to choose, all showier than the species. (Cultivars are sometimes referred to as French lilacs because the first improved lilacs were developed by French hybridizer Victor Lemoine and his son. Many of Lemoine's cultivars are still available and are some of the best lilacs on the market.)

Common lilacs are large shrubs or small trees, ranging from 8 to 15 feet in height. The plants spread by suckers and if left unchecked will produce broad clumps 15 feet or more across.

feet high and wide. Rabbiteye blueberry *(V. ashei),* hardy in Zones 8 to 10, ranges from 3 to 15 feet in height and spreads as far. Lowbush blueberry *(V. angustifolium),* hardy in Zones 2 to 8, can be used as a ground cover because plants range from 1 to 2 feet tall and spread as far. All blueberries thrive in moist, acid (pH 4.5 to 5.5) soil in full sun or partial shade. Mulch the plants to keep the soil moist and cool and to protect the shallow roots. Propagate by cuttings taken in early summer.

Weigela florida / Old-fashioned weigela
Clusters of funnel-shaped, 1- to 1½-inch-long, pink, red, or white flowers in spring or early summer; 6- to 9-foot plants that spread from 9 to 12 feet wide. Many new cultivars are available with richly colored flowers that are more attractive than those of the species, including 'Red Prince', which has red flowers, and 'Polka', which bears pink flowers from early summer intermittently to fall. 'Wine & Roses' has burgundy foliage and pink flowers. Dwarf cultivars are also available, including 'Minuet', which grows to 3 feet and has pink flowers, and 'Rumba', also to 3 feet, which bears pinkish red flowers from early summer to fall. Grow all in full sun and average, well-drained soil. The plants bloom on old wood, so prune immediately after flowering. Thin out up to one-third of the oldest stems. Dieback can be a problem after severe winters, and this will kill the season's flowers. Propagate by cuttings taken in early to midsummer. Zones 5 to 8.

While common lilacs are spectacular in bloom, they don't add much to the landscape after the flowers fade. They lack fall foliage color, and their heart-shaped, blue-green leaves are typically marred by powdery mildew by late summer. Still, many gardeners wouldn't want to be without them. The plants are hardy in Zones 3 to 7; most cultivars languish in the summer heat and humidity of Zone 8 in the Southeast. A few cultivars developed in southern California also may be suitable for the Southeast, including 'Blue Boy' and 'Lavender Lady'.

A bouquet of cut lilacs is one of the pleasures of growing these old-fashioned plants. Cut them when about half the flowers have opened and either slice up through the stem bases with a sharp knife or smash them with a hammer. Then let them sit overnight in a deep bucket of hot water.

SITE AND SOIL

Lilacs bloom best in full sun. They will flower, although somewhat less, in a site that receives only 6 hours of direct sun a day. They need average to rich soil that is loose and well drained. Soil pH between 6.5 and neutral is ideal, but lilacs will grow in acid to slightly alkaline soil. Look for a spot with good air circulation, as air movement helps reduce powdery mildew.

PLANTING

Plant container-grown or balled-and-burlapped lilacs in spring or early fall. Plant bare-root specimens in early spring while they are still dormant. Lilacs growing on their own roots are a better buy than grafted plants. (Ask whether plants are grafted when you buy at the garden center or nursery or look for this notation in catalog descriptions.) That's because the common lilac or privet rootstocks of grafted plants tend to produce suckers that must be rigorously controlled or they will outgrow the grafted plant. Own-root plants will also produce suckers that should be controlled, but they will be identical to their parent and offer a handy way to propagate.

See "Planting" on page 274 in the **Shrubs** entry for directions on planting container-grown, balled-and-burlapped, or bare-root plants. Be sure to set the shrub at the same depth at which it was growing in the nursery. Mulch the area to keep the soil moist and cool, keeping the mulch an inch or so away from the base of the plant. Water deeply every week during the first season, and water during dry weather for at least another season or two until plants are established. Lilacs take a few years to become established and to start producing full-size blooms, so coddle newly planted specimens a bit, and don't worry if they flower sparsely at first.

Common lilac (*Syringa vulgaris* 'Sensation')

CARE THROUGH THE SEASON

Lilacs need annual feeding, regular pruning, and other minimal care to look their best. Feed plants in spring with compost mixed with well-rotted manure or a balanced organic fertilizer. If your soil tends to be either too acid or too alkaline, test and adjust pH every other year. Remove flowers after they fade — you can snap them off between your thumb and index finger or clip them with pruning shears. (This keeps the plant from spending energy setting seed, which can cause some cultivars to bloom in alternate years.) Be careful not to remove the new buds at the base of each bloom, because they represent next year's flowers. For the same reason, don't shear plants in an effort to remove spent flowers quickly.

Pruning. Lilacs bloom on old wood, so prune them as necessary in late spring or early summer immediately after they flower. To rejuvenate older plants, remove one or two of the oldest stems each year to ensure a steady supply of healthy new wood. You can also rejuvenate lilacs radically by cutting the entire plant to within about 1 foot of the ground. As part of the pruning process, pull up suckers regularly, but leave the strongest sucker or two on own-root plants if you need new blooming wood as part of the rejuvenation process. (Remove all suckers on grafted plants.) Plants that are left to produce suckers at will become overcrowded, do not bloom as well, and spread into broad, unmanageable clumps.

Propagation. The easiest way to propagate ungrafted lilacs is to pot up the suckers. Sever the roots that connect them to the main plant with a sharp spade.

Potential Problems. Powdery mildew disfigures lilac foliage in hot, humid summer weather but doesn't really cause permanent harm to the plants. A site with good air circulation helps prevent it. Borers tunnel through trunks and branches, leaving small holes and piles of sawdust as evidence of their entry. They most often enter through wounds in the trunk, so avoid damaging it with lawn mowers or string trimmers. Prune out borer-infested wood promptly. Scale, which are sucking insects that look like clusters of bumps on twigs, can also be a problem on lilacs. To control them, use a dormant oil spray in late winter or early spring before growth starts.

LANDSCAPE USES

Lilacs are most effective when combined with other shrubs that will provide landscape interest after their flowers have faded in early summer. Use them in shrub borders or hedges and informal screen plantings, ideally with lower-growing shrubs or perennials in front of them.

The Other Lilacs

While nearly everyone can recognize common lilac, many gardeners are unfamiliar with some of the other lilacs that are available. The plants below are grown the same way common lilacs are. Unless otherwise noted, all are hardy in Zones 3 to 8 and bloom in late spring to early summer.

S. meyeri. Meyer lilac. Fragrant, purple-pink flowers in 4-inch-long panicles; 5- to 6-foot plants. Compact, mounding plants with abundant showy blooms. Is not troubled by powdery mildew and seldom needs pruning. 'Palibin', a 4- to 5-foot plant with pink flowers, is the best-known cultivar.

S. pubescens ssp. *patula.* Fragrant, 5-inch-long panicles of lilac-purple flowers; 9- to 12-foot plants. The dwarf cultivar 'Miss Kim', which ranges from 4 to 8 feet in height and spreads nearly as far, is the most popular. It has very pale pinkish lilac flowers and purple autumn foliage. (Formerly *S. patula*.)

S. reticulata. Japanese tree lilac. Fragrant, creamy white flowers in 6- to 12-inch-long panicles that are nearly as wide; 20- to 30-foot trees. Blooms in early summer after other lilacs are finished. Hardy in Zones 3 to 7.

S. villosa. Late lilac. Somewhat fragrant, pinkish purple or white flowers in 3- to 7-inch-long panicles; 6- to 10-foot plants. Blooms in early summer and is hardy in Zones 2 to 7. This is one parent of Preston lilac *(S. × prestoniae)* and its cultivars, which are also hardy to Zone 2. Seldom requires pruning and does not produce suckers.

Syringa pubescens ssp. *patula* 'Miss Kim' edged with snow-in-summer *(Cerastium tomentosum)*

Thymus

Thymes

Thymus
■
(TIE-muss)
■
Late-spring to summer bloom
■
Full sun or light shade
■
Zones 4 to 9
■

■ Handsome, useful thymes are valued as cooking herbs, ground covers, and ornamentals as well as for their tough, no-nonsense constitution. Rounded, lacy-looking clusters of pink, rose-purple, or white flowers cover the plants in late spring or summer. Take a close look at the tiny flowers and you'll see the two-lipped structure that marks thymes as members of the mint family, Lamiaceae. The plants are shrubby or mat-forming and have small (½ inch or less), very aromatic, evergreen leaves. Not only can you choose fragrances from classic thyme to lemon or caraway, but handsome variegated cultivars are available, too. The mat-forming thymes make

especially good ground covers, and shrubby species that are essential culinary herbs are also attractive landscape plants. All are quite drought tolerant and about as low maintenance as any plant can get.

Of the culinary thymes, common or garden thyme *(Thymus vulgaris),* hardy in Zones 4 to 8, is the best known and the one most often used in cooking. It is a 6- to 12-inch subshrub (a low-growing, shrubby perennial with a woody base) that forms a spreading, 16-inch-wide mound of twiggy branches covered with gray-green, aromatic leaves. White or rose-purple flowers appear from late spring to early summer. Lemon thyme *(T. × citriodorus),* hardy in Zones 5 to 9, has lemon-scented leaves and also is an attractive landscape plant and culinary herb. The plants form shrubby, 10- to 12-inch-tall mounds that spread to about 2 feet and are topped by clusters of pale lilac flowers in summer. Cultivars with leaf margins edged in gold ('Aureus') or silver ('Argenteus') are available, as are yellow-leaved cultivars. Caraway thyme *(T. herba-barona),* hardy in Zones 6 to 8, has caraway-scented leaves on shrubby 2- to 4-inch-tall plants that spread to 2 feet across. Pink to mauve flower clusters appear in summer.

Several ground-hugging thymes make ideal carpetlike ground covers. All have aromatic leaves that release their fragrance when they are walked on or brushed. (While they tolerate being stepped on occasionally, none will withstand regular foot traffic.) Woolly thyme *(T. pseudolanuginosus),* hardy in Zones 6 to 8, has silvery-hairy leaves and sparse pale pink flowers. Plants are 1 to 3 inches tall and can spread to 3 feet. Mother-of-thyme *(T. pulegioides),* hardy in Zones 4 to 9, is about 3 inches tall and spreads to a foot or more. It bears mauve-pink flowers and has lemon-scented leaves. Wild or creeping thyme *(T. serpyllum),* which is also called mother-of-thyme and is hardy in Zones 4 to 9, bears purple flowers in summer on plants that reach 10 inches tall and spread to about 1½ feet. Dwarf cultivars, such as 1-inch-tall 'Pink Chintz', are especially handsome as ground covers. *T. serpyllum* var. *coccineus* (formerly *T. praecox* 'Coccineus') is a 3-inch-tall creeper that has bright purple-red flowers.

SITE AND SOIL

Thymes thrive in full sun, although most will tolerate a few hours of light shade per day. They are at their best in warm, dry soil that is sandy or gravelly, but they also grow in soil that is rich in organic matter or even in heavy clay provided it is very well drained. Slightly acid to slightly alkaline pH (pH 6.0 to 8.0) is best. Moist soil or poorly drained clay leads to fungal diseases and

Lemon thyme *(Thymus × citriodorus)*

A mix of thymes can be used as ground covers or as a low-maintenance substitute for lawn grass.

rot, while soil that is too rich causes rampant growth and foliage that has less fragrance and flavor. If your soil drainage isn't perfect, consider planting in raised beds. Other suitable sites include along the top of a rock wall, on a rocky slope, between paving stones, or in a rock garden. A spot with good air circulation is beneficial, especially for *T. pseudolanuginosus,* which can be troubled by mildew in humid weather.

PLANTING

Plant thymes in spring or early fall, spacing them from 6 to 12 inches apart, depending on their ultimate spread. If drainage is questionable, work coarse sand or gravel into the soil. Mulching with gravel or coarse sand keeps the crowns dry and deters weeds. Avoid organic mulches such as shredded bark, which tend to hold too much moisture near the plants.

To plant thymes between paving stones or rocks, start with small plants that have fairly well developed roots. Excavate a site with a narrow trowel or a pointed object such as a screwdriver. Dig as large an area as you can, then mix some of the soil with coarse sand. Spread the roots out as you set the plants in place, and fill in around them with the sand/soil mix. Water thoroughly.

CARE THROUGH THE SEASON

Thymes can pretty much be left to their own devices once they are established. They don't need regular watering or feeding. Promptly remove leaves and other debris that fall on them, and be sure to rake out tree leaves that can become caught in the shrubby types in fall. Otherwise they are more likely to rot over winter. Toward the northern part of their range, shrubby thymes appreciate a winter covering of evergreen boughs; cover the plants after the ground freezes in late fall and remove the branches in spring. For max-

imum flavor, harvest thyme for drying just before the flowers open; otherwise, trim off stem tips whenever you need them. Keep in mind that harvesting is a pruning process, and try to shape the plants as you cut.

Pruning. Mat-forming thymes seldom need any pruning, although some gardeners shear the plants after they bloom. The flowers will dry up and gradually disappear if they are left in place. Trim shrubby thymes in mid- to late summer after they flower to keep them neat looking. Shrubby thymes that become old and woody generally do not resprout well from old growth, although you can try cutting them back hard. (Take steps to propagate them before cutting them back hard in case they don't respond. That way, you'll have plants on hand to replace them.) On variegated- or golden-leaved forms, promptly prune off or dig out any growth that reverts to all green.

Division. Divide (or propagate and replace) shrubby thymes every 3 to 4 years, since they tend to become woody and less productive. Mat-forming thymes need dividing only if they die out in the centers of the clumps or for propagation. With either type, divide in spring or early fall, and dig deeply (roots can extend as far as 2 feet down) and handle the plants carefully. Gently separate the clumps with your fingers and a pair of pruning shears, replant, and water generously.

Propagation. Thymes can be grown from seeds, but cuttings, division, and mound layering are faster methods and ensure plants that are true to type. (Thymes hybridize easily and seedlings seldom resemble their parents. It also takes up to 3 years for plants to bloom from seeds.) Shrubby thymes are easiest to propagate by cuttings or layering; mat-forming ones, by division. Take cuttings in spring or summer when the plants are not in bloom, strip off the lower leaves, and root the cuttings in moist, sharp sand.

Mound layering is a very easy way to propagate the shrubby thymes. See the Techniques Glossary for details.

LANDSCAPE USES

Thymes make attractive edging and ground-cover plants in herb gardens, along pathways, and in flower beds that have the well-drained soil they prefer. Combine them with pinks (*Dianthus* spp.), sedums, hens-and-chicks (*Sempervivum* spp.), rock rose *(Helianthemum nummularium),* and other herbs such as lavenders (*Lavandula* spp.). Thymes can be underplanted with hardy bulbs such as ornamental onions (*Allium* spp.), grape hyacinths (*Muscari* spp.), and crocuses and will cover the ground year round without competing with the bulbs. Mat-forming types are best for this purpose.

Tulipa

There's little doubt that tulips are beloved signs of spring. Gardeners and nongardeners alike look forward to their showy flowers, which come in soft pastels as well as the boldest hues of spring. Colors include deep red, violet-purple, golden yellow, orange, mauve, pale pink, and white—everything except true blue. Many varieties feature bicolor blooms—with red-and-white or red-and-yellow stripes, for example. The most familiar tulips have cup-shaped blooms, but bowl-shaped, double-flowered cultivars are available along with goblet- and star-shaped ones. There are also tulips with fringed petal edges, ruffled petals (called parrot tulips), and ones that bear several blooms per stem. (Tulip "petals" are more correctly called tepals.)

Tulip bulbs are somewhat teardrop shaped and are covered with a brown skin, called a tunic. Popular hybrids have broadly oval, bluish or gray-green leaves, but some have strap-shaped or long, very narrow leaves. The leaves are borne near the base of the plant.

Tulips make outstanding cut flowers. Cut them just above the foliage with a sharp knife as the buds begin to open. Leave as much foliage as possible on the plant so it will be able to manufacture food for next year's flowers. The stems often bend while they are being conditioned. To prevent this, wrap bunches of cut budded stems in damp newspaper before standing them in cold water overnight.

SELECTING TULIPS

There are about 100 species of tulips and hundreds of named cultivars, which have been organized into 15 divisions based on flower shape and origin. While you don't need to know the names of the divisions, knowing that they exist will help you choose which tulips to grow. Catalogs and well-labeled nursery displays often use them to organize their offerings. Planting tulips from several divisions ensures that you will have a variety of shapes and sizes of flowers to enjoy. In addition, cultivars in the different divisions tend to bloom at different times. See "Scheduling Bulb Blooms" on page 53 for a guide to bloom time for the major divisions. Keep in mind that the time a particular plant flowers will vary depending on where you live, the weather, the cultivar (all cultivars in a division don't necessarily bloom at the same time), and the site where it is growing. With care-

Tulips

Tulipa
■
(TOO-lip-ah)
■
Spring bloom
■
Full sun or light shade
■
Zones 3 to 8
■

ful selection, it's possible to plan a parade of tulips that lasts for 8 weeks or more in spring.

Most tulips can be grown in Zones 3 to 8 but actually perform best in Zones 4 to 6. They require a cool, moist winter and a warm, dry summer for optimum growth. In the South, summer heat and rain tend to diminish their performance. Some cultivars are better performers in the South than others; a reputable garden center will stock good selections for your area. If you are ordering by mail, look for recommendations that are called out for your region, or don't hesitate to ask for suggestions. In Zones 9 to 11, the bulbs aren't exposed to cold enough temperatures in winter to bloom. Gardeners in these zones should buy precooled bulbs and treat them as annuals. (To precool your own bulbs, store them in the refrigerator at temperatures between 40° and 45°F for 8 to 10 weeks.)

Darwin Hybrid tulips 'Apeldoorn Elite' (ABOVE) and 'Pink Impression' (BELOW)

Perennial Tulips

Typically, tulips are "one-hit wonders" in the garden. They bloom spectacularly the first year and peter out thereafter. For this reason, many gardeners treat them as annuals, or at best biennials, and replace them each fall. (Because of their sensational bloom, they are well worth the minimal investment in time and money it takes to replace them.) Perennial plantings of tulips are possible in Zones 3 to 7, however, provided you select and plant carefully.

Although species tulips are best known for behaving as perennials, there are also hybrids that can be depended on for repeat performance. Kaufmanniana tulips, including *Tulipa kaufmanniana* (sometimes sold as waterlily tulip or 'Waterlily') and its cultivars such as 'Johann Strauss' and 'Stressa', are good perennializers, as are Fosteriana tulips. These include *T. fosteriana* and its cultivars such as the popular 'Orange Emperor' and 'Red Emperor'. Greigii tulips, including *T. greigii* and cultivars such as 'Czar Peter', 'Red Riding Hood', and 'Sweet Lady', likewise perennialize. Greigiis also feature handsome mottled or striped foliage that is attractive even after the flowers fade.

Two other species that behave as perennials are *T. saxatilis* (formerly *T. bakeri*) and its cultivar 'Lilac Wonder' and *T. batalinii* and cultivars such as 'Bright Gem', 'Red Gem', and 'Yellow Jewel'. *T. humilis* and *T. tarda* also perform as perennials.

Some hybrid tulips perennialize as well. Darwin Hybrid and Triumph tulips are the best choices, but it pays to experiment with different cultivars and various sites to find out what works best in your garden. (I have a clump of golden yellow Darwin Hybrid tulips above a rock wall on a terraced slope. The 10 bulbs I originally planted produced 50 flowers last spring, when the planting was in its eighth year. The tulips are combined with drought-tolerant lavender and other herbs, so I don't water the bed during the season for the most part. As a result, they receive the dry summer conditions they prefer. I let the foliage ripen completely each year, but I don't fertilize at all.)

Good site selection, thorough soil preparation, and deep planting (with the base of the bulbs 8 to 10 inches below the soil surface) are the secrets to perennial plantings of tulips. Letting the foliage ripen and feeding the bulbs annually are also important. Follow the recommendations in "Site and Soil," "Planting," and "Care Through the Season" to encourage your plants to perennialize.

When buying tulips, look for fat, fleshy bulbs with no signs of mold or black, rotted blotches. The brown tunic should be present and intact. Avoid buying cheap bulbs, which may not have been stored or handled properly. This is especially important because the bulbs resent being exposed to temperatures above 70°F either in the ground or anytime they are stored. Storage at high temperatures reduces or destroys the quality of the bulbs and the flowers they will produce. (When you buy tulips, the flower buds are already formed inside the bulbs.) If you are looking for ways to stretch your bulb-buying dollar, pay attention to featured cultivars or collections in catalogs. Most companies also discount bulk purchases. See "Buying Bargain Bulbs" on page 54 for more information.

SITE AND SOIL

Plant tulips where they will receive at least 5 hours of full sun daily and light shade for the rest of the day. (Morning sun and afternoon shade is beneficial in the South, because it protects the flowers from hot temperatures.) Well-drained soil rich in organic matter is best, although plants will bloom satisfactorily for a year or two in a wide range of soils, provided they are well drained.

PLANTING

Plant tulips in fall as soon as they are available—early fall in northern zones, toward early winter in the South. If you can't plant right away, be sure to store them in a dry place where temperatures stay between 60° and 70°F. Either spread the bulbs on trays or store them in mesh bags or paper bags with holes punched in them to ensure good air circulation.

To provide the rich, well-drained conditions tulips prefer, dig the soil deeply and work in plenty of organic matter such as compost or leaf mold before planting. Also incorporate a balanced organic fertilizer into the soil as you dig. It's best to avoid using manure unless it is very well rotted and you can incorporate it into the soil several inches away from where the bulbs will be.

Deep soil preparation is important, because the soil several inches *below* the bulbs needs to be improved and well drained. (Improving the soil around the bulbs doesn't benefit the roots, which emerge from the base of the bulbs.) Set the bulbs with their bases at least 8 inches below the soil surface—10 inches is better. This keeps them cool in summertime and discourages them from breaking up into lots of smaller, nonflowering bulbs after the first year. (If you are growing the bulbs as annuals, a depth of 5 to 6 inches is fine.) Deep planting also makes it easy to fill in on top of the bulbs either with annuals or with shallow-rooted perennials.

If you are aiming for a planting that blooms all together at one time and at one height, be sure to plant all the bulbs at the same depth. Otherwise they will bloom unevenly. The easiest way to do this is to excavate the bed to 8 inches, improve the soil below that, set the bulbs in place, and then refill. Space bulbs 2 to 6 inches apart, depending on their size. If you are growing tulips as annuals and plan to pull them up after they bloom, you can set them considerably closer—even bulb to bulb.

ABOVE LEFT Fosteriana tulip 'Purissima', also sold as 'White Emperor'

ABOVE Kaufmanniana tulip 'Showwinner'

Rodents such as chipmunks adore tulip bulbs, and you may want to take steps to keep them at bay. As you plant, fill in around each bulb on all sides with sharp, crushed gravel. (This also helps improve drainage around the bulb.) Working blood meal into the soil likewise helps discourage rodents. A more aggressive tactic involves excavating the bed and lining the bottom and sides with ½-inch hardware cloth, then setting the bulbs in place and refilling. Cover the top of the bed with mesh as well, removing it in late winter. You can also plant groups of bulbs in mesh baskets.

CARE THROUGH THE SEASON

Tulips will bloom come spring without any further care. Since they need evenly moist soil when they are actively growing and blooming, water if the weather is dry in spring. See **Bulbs** on page 52 for details on deadheading, feeding, propagation, and potential problems you may encounter, along with suggestions for using tulips in the landscape. As with other bulbs, tulip foliage remains green for several weeks, then gradually turns yellow and dies back. The leaves need to ripen naturally if the bulbs are to flower the following year. Remove the leaves after they have turned yellow—or nearly so. Another option is to dig the bulbs carefully after the flowers fade, retaining as many roots as possible. Plant the bulbs temporarily in a nursery bed to allow the foliage to ripen fully. Space the bulbs fairly closely together, setting the tops at a 45° angle to the soil surface and the bulbs at a depth of 2 to 3 inches. Water as necessary to keep the soil evenly moist but not wet. When the leaves have turned completely yellow, dig the bulbs and store them in a dry spot with good air circulation and temperatures no higher than 70°F. (Be sure to select a rodent-proof location.)

Greigii tulip 'Plaisir'

Verbena

Verbenas

Verbena
■
(ver-BEAN-ah)
■
Summer to fall bloom
■
Full sun or light shade
■
Zones 3 to 10
■

Purple-flowered *Verbena bonariensis* with daylilies (*Hemerocallis* spp.) and *Achillea* 'The Pearl'

■ By far the best-known verbena is a tender perennial commonly grown as an annual—garden verbena (*Verbena* × *hybrida*). It produces rounded, 3-inch-wide clusters of small, brilliantly colored flowers from summer to frost. The flowers—in violet-purple, hot pink, magenta, scarlet, white, and soft pink—are borne above mounds of dark green leaves on 10- to 18-inch-tall plants. Many named cultivars that come true from seed are available.

V. bonariensis (formerly *V. patagonica*) is a tender perennial grown for its airy clusters of rosy purple flowers that grace the garden from midsummer to frost. Hardy in Zones 7 to 9, *V. bonariensis* can attain shrublike proportions in the South, where plants range from 4 to 6 feet tall. (Cut them back as necessary in spring to encourage branching and to keep them compact.) They easily reach a height of 2 to 4 feet in the North and are best used in the middle or back of the border, making fine airy-textured fillers.

There also are hardy verbenas for the perennial garden. Blue vervain *(V. hastata),* hardy in Zones 3 to 7, bears stiff, branched, 2- to 4-inch-wide clusters of flowers from early summer to early fall on 3- to 5-foot plants. Rose verbena *(V. canadensis),* hardy in Zones 4 to 10, is a perennial native to North America that frequently is grown as an annual. It produces a main flush of 2½-inch-wide, rose-pink flower clusters in early summer, then blooms sporadically until fall if spent flowers are removed. The mounding, 1½- to 3-foot plants have stems that root where they touch the soil and are attractive ground covers for poor, well-drained, sandy soil. Cut plants back hard if the spreading stems extend too far or lose their leaves. 'Homestead Purple' is a mildew-resistant, purple-flowered cultivar that reaches 1½ feet in height.

SITE AND SOIL

Verbenas thrive in full sun and tolerate light shade. They are especially valuable because they succeed in poor to average, well-drained soil; grow well in sandy conditions; and also endure heat and drought. While *V. hastata* will tolerate evenly moist, well-drained soil, the other species will languish in the moist conditions of the average perennial garden.

PLANTING

Plant verbenas in spring, taking care to move tender species to the garden after the last spring frost date. Space them 8 to 12 inches apart.

CARE THROUGH THE SEASON

Once in the garden, verbenas will grow without much additional care. Mulch them to keep weeds down, and water if the weather is dry until the plants are well established. Trim back creeping species to control their spread and to keep them bushy. Deadhead or shear the plants after the main flush of flowers to encourage rebloom. *V. bonariensis* and *V. × hybrida* will bloom until frost without deadheading, but the latter will branch and bloom more abundantly with deadheading. Pinch or cut back *V. bonariensis* seedlings in spring to encourage branching. Divide perennial species in spring if they outgrow their space or die out in the centers of the clumps, or for propagation.

Propagation. Sow *V. × hybrida* indoors 12 to 14 weeks before the last spring frost date and germinate at temperatures between 70° and 75°F. Cover the seeds with soil, as darkness is required for germination. Start 4 weeks earlier for *V. bonariensis*, *V. hastata*, and *V. canadensis*. Sow the pots and place them in the refrigerator for 2 weeks, then germinate as above. Verbenas are also easy to grow from cuttings taken in spring (to grow extra plants from purchased ones) or late summer to overwinter the plants indoors where they are not hardy.

LANDSCAPE USES

Combine verbenas with other perennials that thrive in dry, well-drained soil, such as lavenders (*Lavandula* spp.), yarrows (*Achillea* spp.), sedums, purple coneflower (*Echinacea purpurea*), globe thistle *(Echinops ritro)*, and yuccas.

ABOVE LEFT
Rose verbena
(Verbena canadensis)

ABOVE Garden verbena
(*Verbena × hybrida*
'Sissinghurst')

Veronica

Speedwells

Veronica
∎
(ver-ON-ih-kah)
∎
Midspring to fall bloom
∎
Full sun or partial shade
∎
Zones 3 to 8
∎

∎ Vigorous, easy-to-grow speedwells offer flowers in a rich palette of colors that includes glorious true blue, violet-blue, pink, and white. The individual blooms are tiny, but they are borne in dense, showy, bottlebrush-like spikes that stand out above the lance-shaped or rounded, deep green leaves. While the most popular speedwells are upright, there are also low-growing, mat-forming species that can be used as ground covers or in rock gardens. Although the vigor of most species is a blessing, gardeners should avoid creeping speedwell *(Veronica filiformis)*, a mat-forming, 2-inch-tall species with pale blue flowers that becomes a serious weed in gardens and lawns.

The taller species of speedwell can be used as cut flowers. Pick the spikes when the flowers at the very base begin to show color. Condition them overnight in water before arranging.

Speedwells for Beds and Borders

Upright speedwells are perfect for adding rich color and spiky accents to perennial beds and borders. They range from about 1 to 3 feet in height when in bloom, but out of flower they are somewhat shorter. All spread to form broad mounds and can be used as tall ground covers. This group includes species along with hybrids of uncertain parentage.

V. austriaca ssp. *teucrium*. Hungarian speedwell. Rich, deep blue flowers in 4- to 6-inch-long spikes in late spring and early summer; 6- to 24-inch-tall plants. Plants may rebloom if cut back after flowering. They may flop and can be left that way, or to keep them erect, stake them in early spring with pea brush. 'Crater Lake Blue', from 12 to 18 inches tall, is the best-known selection. (Formerly *V. teucrium* and *V. latifolia*.) Zones 3 to 8.

V. gentianoides. Gentian speedwell. Loose, 10-inch-long spikes of pale blue to white (*not* gentian blue, as the species name might suggest) flowers in late spring to early summer; 6- to 20-inch plants that form dense mats of foliage. Unlike most speedwells, this species prefers evenly moist soil and should not be allowed to dry out. Zones 4 to 8.

V. spicata. Spike speedwell. Dense, foot-long spikes of flowers from early to late summer;

ABOVE *Veronica* 'Sunny Border Blue'

RIGHT Spike speedwell (*Veronica spicata* 'Goodness Grows')

1- to 2-foot plants. Blue, violet-blue, pink, and white cultivars are available. A long-blooming plant that is easy and trouble free in well-drained soil. Woolly speedwell *(V. spicata* ssp. *incana,* formerly *V. incana)* features spikelike flowers borne over densely hairy, gray-green leaves. Woolly speedwell does not do well in areas with hot, wet summers; give it especially well drained conditions and avoid getting the leaves wet when watering. Zones 3 to 8.

V. 'Sunny Border Blue'. Violet-blue, 7-inch-long spikes of flowers from early summer to late fall; 18- to 20-inch plants with handsome, glossy leaves. An outstanding, vigorous, long-blooming hybrid. Zones 4 to 8.

Low-Growing Speedwells

Harebell speedwell *(V. prostrata)* is the most widely available of the low-growing species. Ranging from 3 to 6 inches in height and spreading to 1½ feet, it produces short spikes of starry blue flowers in late spring or early summer and is hardy in Zones 5 to 8. The foliage of creeping speedwell *(V. repens),* which is also hardy in Zones 5 to 8, reaches only 1½ inches in height but spreads to 1½ feet at least. When in bloom in mid- to late spring, the plants reach 3 to 4 inches tall. This species requires richer soil and is less drought tolerant than *V. prostrata.* For a hot, dry spot, consider Turkish speedwell *(V. liwanensis).* Hardy in Zones 4 to 9, it produces dense mats of thymelike leaves and blue flowers in spring. The plants grow about 2 inches tall and spread to 1½ feet.

SITE AND SOIL

Speedwells thrive in full sun or partial shade and average to rich soil that is very well drained. They will not tolerate constantly moist conditions, especially in winter. Since they are fairly shallow rooted, they also are not particularly drought tolerant.

PLANTING

Plant speedwells in spring or fall, after loosening the soil and working in compost or leaf mold to ensure rich, evenly moist but well-drained conditions. Space upright species about 1 foot apart and low-growing speedwells 16 to 18 inches apart to accommodate their spread.

CARE THROUGH THE SEASON

Speedwells are easy-care plants in the landscape. They do not need annual fertilizing, but they do need to be watered in dry weather. The taller-growing cultivars may need staking—very rich soil increases the likelihood that they will flop. Install stakes or pea brush in spring before plants

get too tall. Most speedwells benefit from being divided regularly—about every 3 to 4 years—in either spring or fall.

Propagation. Propagate species speedwells by digging the clumps and dividing them, by cuttings, or from seeds. Take cuttings from stem tips in late spring or early summer. Sow seeds indoors 8 to 10 weeks before the last spring frost date. Do not cover the seeds, as light aids germination. Propagate cultivars by cuttings or division, because they do not come true from seed.

LANDSCAPE USES

Plant taller speedwells in beds and borders with other plants that thrive in well-drained soil. Consider combining them with daylilies (*Hemerocallis* spp.), pinks (*Dianthus* spp.), hardy geraniums, coreopsis, balloon flower *(Platycodon grandiflorus),* and ornamental grasses. Depending on their height, they can be used in mid-border or as edging plants.

Mat-forming speedwells make attractive edgings as well. They can also be used as ground covers or allowed to trail over rocks. Underplant them with small spring bulbs and pair them with the plants listed above as well as with columbines (*Aquilegia* spp.), candytufts (*Iberis* spp.), and bellflowers (*Campanula* spp.)

TOP Spike speedwell (*Veronica spicata* 'Red Fox')

ABOVE Spike speedwell (*Veronica spicata* 'Icicle')

Viburnum

Viburnums

Viburnum

∎

(vie-BURR-num)

∎

Spring to early-summer bloom

∎

Sun or shade

∎

Zones 2 to 9

∎

∎ Handsome, hardworking viburnums add multiseason interest to the garden—through flowers, colorful berries that are attractive to birds and other wildlife, rich green summer leaves, and bright fall foliage. In addition, some species feature fragrant flowers or evergreen foliage. All this, plus a basically undemanding nature, places viburnums near the top of the list of outstanding shrubs for the landscape.

Viburnums are shrubs or small trees that produce clusters of small white, creamy white, or pinkish flowers in spring. There are three general types of flower clusters. Viburnums with snowball-type blooms bear round clusters of large sterile flowers. These are showy in bloom but do not bear fruit, an important consideration if autumn interest or feeding birds is high on your list. Other species bear flat-topped clusters of flowers that resemble lacecap hydrangeas. These have large sterile flowers around the edges of the cluster and smaller fertile ones at the center, which are followed by berries. The most spectacular fruit displays come from species that bear rounded clusters, up to about 5 inches across, that consist of all fertile flowers. In all cases, sterile flowers are about 1 to 2 inches wide (and don't produce berries), while individual fertile ones are considerably smaller—about 1/4 inch across.

SELECTING VIBURNUMS

Selecting viburnums can be a challenge, because each is more tempting than the last. Forewarned is forearmed: Viburnums can be habit forming. It's hard to stop with just one, and there are 150 species and lots of outstanding cultivars from which to choose. Alas, no one plant offers fragrance, attractive flowers, showy fruit, and good fall foliage color: selecting several may be the best course of action if you have the space for them. A variety of outstanding hybrid viburnums are available, and the ones mentioned here feature four-season interest. If you have space for only one viburnum, choose one of these new hybrids. Unless otherwise noted, all of the viburnums listed below grow in full sun or partial shade and rich, moist, well-drained soil.

Viburnums for Fragrance

Although viburnum flowers are fleeting in spring, the following are among the most fragrant shrubs you can grow. All add delightful fragrance to spring bouquets. After cutting, smash the stem bases or slice up through them with a sharp knife, and then condition them overnight in water.

Viburnum × burkwoodii. Burkwood viburnum. Pink buds and white flowers in rounded, 3½-inch-wide clusters in mid- to late spring; 8- to 10-foot plants that spread to about 6 to 8 feet. Flowers have a rich, spicy fragrance. The red berries ripen to black in summer but aren't particularly showy. Plants sometimes show good red fall color and are semievergreen in the South. They have a somewhat coarse branching habit, which is revealed when the leaves drop in fall. 'Mohawk' is a compact hybrid (to 7 feet) with red buds, abundant fragrant flowers, and excellent red-orange fall foliage. It is resistant to bacterial leaf spot and powdery mildew, which can be a problem on the species. Zones 4 to 8.

V. × carlcephalum. Fragrant viburnum. Rounded, 6-inch-wide clusters of fragrant white flowers in late spring to early summer; 6- to 10-foot plants with a loose, somewhat coarse habit. Red-purple fall foliage. Summer fruit is not showy. Zones 6 to 8.

Fragrant viburnum *(Viburnum × carlcephalum)*

V. carlesii. Korean spice viburnum. Pinkish buds and fragrant white, $1/2$-inch-wide flowers borne in 2- to 3-inch-wide, rounded clusters in mid- to late spring; 4- to 5-foot plants that spread to 8 feet. Some reddish fall color; insignificant red-to-black fruit in late summer. 'Cayuga' is a hybrid that blooms more abundantly and is resistant to bacterial leaf spot and powdery mildew. Zones 4 to 7.

V. × juddii. Judd viburnum. Fragrant white flowers with a pale pink tinge borne in loose, rounded, 3-inch-wide clusters from mid- to late spring; rounded, 6- to 8-foot plants. Summer fruit is not showy. Resistant to bacterial leaf spot. Zones 4 to 8.

Viburnums for Four-Season Interest

The following species offer spring flowers in 3- to 5-inch-wide clusters that are generally scentless, but they add color to the garden later in the season with their showy fruit and bright fall foliage. Branches of fruit are attractive in fall flower arrangements.

V. dentatum. Arrowwood viburnum. Small, creamy white flowers in flattened clusters from late spring to early summer; 6- to 8-foot plants that can spread to 15 feet. Dark green foliage in summer turns yellow, red, and red-purple in fall. Clusters of blue-black fruit aren't especially showy but are popular with birds. Plants spread by suckers to form broad clumps. A native North American shrub suitable for any well-drained soil. Zones 2 to 8.

V. dilatatum. Linden viburnum. Abundant clusters of small, creamy white flowers in late spring to early summer; 8- to 10-foot plants that spread as far. Dark green summer foliage with some rust-red fall color. Clusters of bright red, $1/3$-inch fruit that ripens in late summer and stays on the plants into early winter, when it is gobbled up by hungry birds. 'Erie' is a cultivar with 4- to 6-inch-wide flower clusters, abundant red fruit, and excellent red, orange, and yellow fall foliage. 'Iroquois' features handsome dark green foliage that turns orange-red in fall, abundant flowers, and especially large, showy, scarlet fruit. 'Michael Dodge' has yellow fruit and red fall foliage. Zones 5 to 8.

V. lantana. Wayfaring-tree viburnum. Flat-topped clusters of small, creamy white flowers in late spring; 10- to 15-foot plants that spread as far. Some purple-red fall foliage color; attractive berries that turn from yellow to red to black. A tough, reliable plant that tolerates alkaline soil, clay, and some drought. Coarse looking in winter. 'Mohican' is a hybrid with a compact habit (to 8 to 9 feet) and good red-orange fall color. It is resistant to bacterial leaf spot. Zones 4 to 8.

Korean spice viburnum *(Viburnum carlesii)*

Berries of linden viburnum *(Viburnum dilatatum)*, which stay on the plants into early winter

Doublefile viburnum (*Viburnum plicatum* var. *tomentosum* 'Mariesii')

V. lentago. Nannyberry viburnum. Flat-topped clusters of small, creamy white flowers in late spring; 15- to 20-foot plants that spread to 10 feet or more. Dark green summer foliage with some purple-red fall color. Fruit starts out green and turns yellowish or pinkish before ripening in fall to blue-black, remaining on the plants into early winter, when it is eaten by birds. Spreads by suckers to form broad clumps. Tolerates sun or shade, moist conditions or dry. Powdery mildew disfigures the leaves, but a site with good air circulation helps prevent it. A native North American shrub. Zones 2 to 8.

V. opulus. European cranberry-bush viburnum. Showy, flat-topped clusters of white flowers in late spring; 8- to 12-foot plants that spread to 10 to 15 feet. Showy red fruit in fall and some yellow- to purple-red fall foliage color. 'Compactum' reaches only 4 to 6 feet in height and features good flowers and foliage. 'Nanum', which grows 1½ to 2 feet tall, rarely flowers. 'Roseum', commonly called European snowball or guilder-rose, bears round clusters of sterile flowers but no fruit. Aphids are a particular problem on this cultivar, and their feeding distorts the new foliage. 'Xanthocarpum' bears yellow fruit. Zones 3 to 8.

V. plicatum var. *tomentosum*. Doublefile viburnum. Very showy, flat-topped clusters of white flowers in rows along the branches in late spring; 8- to 10-foot plants that spread to 12 feet or more. Attractive red berries that turn black in mid- to late summer but are quickly eaten by birds. (The species, *V. plicatum*, bears round clus-ters of sterile flowers in spring but no fruit.) Dark green leaves in summer with red-purple fall foliage color. 'Mariesii' is a popular 8- to 10-foot-tall cultivar featuring large clusters of flowers on tiered branches. 'Shasta' bears abundant flowers on 6-foot plants that can reach 12 feet across. 'Summer Stars' is a compact selection ranging from 4 to 6 feet tall that blooms from spring to fall and also bears showy red fruit. Zones 4 to 8.

V. prunifolium. Blackhaw viburnum. Creamy white, flat-topped clusters of small flowers in late spring; 12- to 15-foot shrubs or small trees. The edible fruit, which sometimes is used for jams and jellies, is pinkish at first and ripens to blue-black in fall. Dark green foliage turns red-purple in fall. A native North American plant that grows in sun or shade and tolerates dry soil. To train it as a small tree, select one to three or more main stems and remove the lower branches. Zones 3 to 9.

V. × rhytidophylloides. Flat-topped clusters of small, creamy white flowers in early to mid-spring; 8- to 10-foot plants that spread as far. Large, 8-inch-long, semievergreen leaves that remain on the plant into late fall. Reddish fruit in late summer that turns black, but plants are self-sterile, so more than one plant or cultivar is needed to set fruit. 'Allegheny' is a dense, rounded cultivar with abundant flowers, red fall fruit, and handsome foliage that is resistant to bacterial leaf spot. Zones 4 to 8.

V. sargentii. Sargent viburnum. White, flat-topped clusters of flowers in late spring; 12- to 15-foot plants that spread as far. Showy red fruit

from late summer to fall. Bronze-purple spring foliage that turns dark green in summer and shows good yellow to red fall color. Coarse looking in winter. Zones 3 to 7.

V. setigerum. Tea viburnum. Small, flat-topped clusters of white flowers in late spring; 8- to 12-foot plants that spread to 6 to 8 feet. Very showy, abundant red fruit in fall along with some red-purple foliage color. Zones 5 to 7.

V. trilobum. American cranberry-bush viburnum. Showy, flat-topped clusters of white flowers in late spring; 8- to 12-foot plants that spread as far. Bright red, edible fruit in fall that remains on the plant well into winter. Yellow to red-purple fall foliage. Requires well-drained soil that remains moist. 'Compactum' is a dwarf cultivar that reaches 6 feet in height. A native North American shrub. Zones 2 to 7.

Evergreen Viburnums

Use evergreen viburnums as hedges or screens, or as background plants in shrub borders. The shade-tolerating leatherleaf viburnum *(V. rhytidophyllum)* can add evergreen foliage to the edge of a woodland or at the back of a shade garden.

V. × pragense. Prague viburnum. Rounded clusters of pink buds open into slightly fragrant white flowers in late spring; 8- to 10-foot plants that spread as far. Glossy, 2- to 4-inch-long, evergreen leaves that stay on the plant to –10°F. Zones 5 to 8.

V. rhytidophyllum. Leatherleaf viburnum. Creamy to yellowish white clusters of slightly fra-

grant flowers in late spring; 10- to 15-foot plants that spread as far. Flower buds are formed in summer and add some interest over winter. Red fruit that ripens to black in fall and stays on the plants into winter. Leaves are damaged in cold winters, and plants are killed to the ground if temperatures dip between –10° and –15°F, but they will regrow from the roots. A protected site is best near the northern part of its range. Will grow in full sun or heavy shade. Zones 5 to 8.

SITE AND SOIL

Plant viburnums in full sun or partial shade; *V. lentago, V. prunifolium*, and *V. rhytidophyllum* will grow in full shade. Viburnums thrive in evenly moist, well-drained soil that is rich in organic matter but will grow in soil of average fertility provided it is moist and drains adequately. Although a slightly acid pH is best, they will grow in acid to slightly alkaline conditions.

PLANTING

Plant balled-and-burlapped or container-grown viburnums in spring or fall. Bare-root plants may be available, but they are harder to establish and are best avoided. For optimum results, loosen the soil over a wide, fairly shallow planting area. Ideally, the site should be large enough to encompass the eventual spread of the plants' branches. Do not amend the soil with compost or other organic matter unless you do it over a large planting area. Be sure to set the plants at the same depth at which they were growing in the nursery. See

"Planting" on page 274 in the **Shrubs** entry for details on getting plants off to a good start.

CARE THROUGH THE SEASON

Viburnums can be pretty much left to their own devices after they are established in the garden. It's a good idea to renew the mulch around the plants each spring to help keep the soil moist and cool. Water deeply during dry weather. They don't need regular feeding.

Pruning. Viburnums produce their flowers on old wood, so prune them if necessary in late spring or early summer, immediately after flowering. Keep in mind that heavy pruning will reduce fruit display. Generally all have attractive habits that require minimal pruning. (Chopping them into cubes or rectangles destroys their shape and reduces flowering and fruiting. Use them in informal hedges and other plantings.) Regular renewal pruning helps keep the plants vigorous — annually remove up to one-third of the oldest branches on established plants. Use heading cuts to encourage branching and denser growth on species that become rangy looking. (See "Pruning" in the Techniques Glossary for specifics on proper pruning cuts.) *V. plicatum* var. *tomentosum* produces water sprouts, which are vertical, fast-growing shoots that do not flower. Remove these shoots, as they destroy the natural, horizontal shape of the plants.

Propagation. Propagate viburnums by cuttings or by digging up the suckers that appear around the base of the plants. Take cuttings in early to midsummer, dip them in rooting hormone, and root them in a 50-50 mix of peat and perlite. Cover the cuttings with a Mason jar or plastic to ensure high humidity during rooting.

Potential Problems. For the most part, viburnums are trouble free. Plants that don't flower well may be growing in too much shade. Plants can flower but fail to set fruit for a couple of reasons. The flowers are fertilized by wind and insects, and if the weather is cold and rainy when the plants are in flower, little fruit will form. In addition, some viburnums are self-sterile and require a pollinator. Another seed-grown plant of the same species or two different cultivars can pollinate one another. (Two plants of the same cultivar won't necessarily pollinate one another, since they are genetically identical and technically are the same plant.) Aphids infest viburnums but seldom do any real damage.

LANDSCAPE USES

Plant viburnums in shrub borders, in foundation plantings, and as backdrops for plantings of perennials. Species that produce abundant fruit are ideal for wildlife or bird gardens.

Vines

Trumpet vine (*Campsis* spp.)

■ Whether they are shading an arbor, scrambling up a tree, or decorating a trellis, vines make a garden feel lush and romantic. Unruly plants by nature (and for this reason a bit intimidating to use at first), vines are an incredibly versatile and diverse group of plants that can be incorporated successfully in nearly any garden. Actually, the only thing all vines have in common is their ability to climb, and they don't all do that the same way. See "How Vines Climb" above for informa-

Japanese wisteria *(Wisteria floribunda)*

How Vines Climb

Vines attach themselves to their supports in various ways, and it pays to know how a particular vine climbs before you select a site or a support for it.

Twining Stems

Many vines climb simply by winding their stems around trellises, branches, strings, or whatever comes their way. The size of support that is appropriate will vary greatly depending on the size of the plant. Annuals that climb using this method may need no more than a lightweight wooden trellis, while the more vigorous woody vines such as wisteria need a permanent support that is very sturdy. Twining vines can be trained to grow on arbors, trellises (either mounted on a wall or freestanding), pergolas, fences and fence posts, lampposts, and even tepees made of poles. They can also be trained to grow over shrubs and up trees or on wires stretched between fence posts or mounted on a wall. Use them to cover sheds and other buildings as well. Select the vine depending on the effect you're after: one of the smaller annual twiners can decorate a shed, while a rampant vine will obliterate it. If you are planting a twining vine against a surface that must be painted or treated periodically, either set the trellis 1 to 2 feet out from the wall so the area can be reached by rollers, or mount the trellis with hinges at the bottom and a fastener at the top. That way the entire trellis can be moved out of the way when necessary.

Tendrils and Leafstalks

Anyone who has ever grown peas or grapes is familiar with how effective tendrils are at holding a vine in place. Clematis have a similar system: their leafstalks twine around branches and other supports just like tendrils do. Vines that climb by these methods need smaller supports to cling to than do twining-stem climbers. Tendrils and leafstalks can grasp strings, netting, branches, pea stakes, and small slats on a trellis, but they can't get a good hold on larger structures. Use strings or a trellis to get clematis vines started up trees. Once they've reached the lower branches, they'll be able to climb farther by gripping smaller twigs. Tendril and leafstalk climbers can be trained to grow on any of the structures twining vines can be.

Rootlets and Holdfasts

Vines use both rootlets that grow along the stems and tendrils that end in round, suckerlike disks, called holdfasts, to attach themselves firmly to any solid surface. These allow them to climb with ease—while making them very difficult to dislodge. For this reason, do not plant vines that climb by these methods next to wood surfaces that must be painted or treated with a preservative periodically. They're fine climbing up trees, stone walls, or other maintenance-free surfaces. Keep in mind that the rootlets or holdfasts can damage mortar if it is loose and will damage aluminum siding. They'll also remain on the wall for some time if you decide to remove the vine. Trumpet vine *(Campsis radicans)*, climbing hydrangea *(Hydrangea petiolaris)*, Japanese hydrangea vine *(Schizophragma hydrangeoides)*, and English ivy *(Hedera helix)* all use rootlets to climb. Boston ivy *(Parthenocissus tricuspidata)* uses tendrils that end in holdfasts.

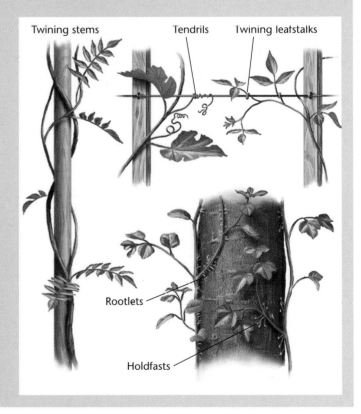

Twining stems   Tendrils   Twining leafstalks

Rootlets

Holdfasts

---

tion on how they scale structures and ideas on how to use them in your garden.

Select vines the same way you select shrubs: Start by evaluating the sun and shade your site receives, along with the type and condition of the soil. Planting vines that thrive in the conditions available in your garden gets you well on your way to success. Hardiness is another important consideration. While you may want to experiment with a marginally hardy vine in a particu-larly warm, protected site, sticking to species that are reliably hardy in your area is the best approach. Also consider size at maturity. In a small garden or a tight spot, a small- or medium-size vine is nearly always a better choice than one that needs to be hacked into submission each year to keep it in bounds.

Selecting a trellis or other support system goes hand in hand with selecting a vine. That's because the trellis should be installed before the

Vines as Ground Covers

When left without support, vines scramble along the ground, and the more rampant among them will engulf anything in their path. Several vines make dense, weed-suppressing ground covers, including fiveleaf akebia *(Akebia quinata)*, climbing hydrangea *(Hydrangea petiolaris)*, vining honeysuckles *(Lonicera* spp.), and the vigorous species clematis (including *Clematis alpina, C. montana, C. terniflora,* and *C. viticella).*

vine is planted, and the size and bulk of the trellis will help determine if a particular site is appropriate. There are annual vines that may be satisfied with a temporary lightweight trellis, as well as massive woody vines that require extremely sturdy supports to hold them. Even the way a vine climbs will affect the site and type of trellis that are appropriate. *Always* install your trellis before you plant: it's too easy to damage the vine during the installation process. (Trellis installation also generally involves walking on and compacting the soil, and it's difficult to fluff it back up if you are trying to work around an already planted vine.) See "How Vines Climb" for suggestions on support systems.

PLANTING

Vines are available as balled-and-burlapped (B&B), container-grown, or bare-root plants. Plant B&B and container-grown vines in spring or fall. Plant bare-root ones in early spring, while they are still dormant.

Plant B&B and container-grown vines as you would shrubs. Dig a shallow hole that is twice as wide as the root ball. Loosen the soil on the bottom and sides of the hole, then set the plant in place and check to make sure it is positioned at the same depth at which it was growing in the nursery. (Lay a straight board across the hole from rim to rim to gauge this.) Refill the hole without amending the soil.

Examine the roots before you set the vine in the soil, severing any that wind around the bottom of the container. If there is a solid mass of roots around the outside of the root ball, score the sides in three or four places with a sharp knife. Then tease some of the roots out to encourage them to spread into the surrounding soil before refilling the hole. (Sprinkle or mist them frequently with water so they don't dry out before you finish planting). If you are planting a B&B vine, set it in the hole and remove any staples or ties holding the burlap in place. Then cut off as much of the fabric as you can easily manage without disturbing the root ball and push the rest down into the bottom of the hole before filling over it with soil.

Form a broad saucer of soil around the plant that will collect and direct water, then flood the soil to settle it and eliminate air pockets. After the water drains away, add additional soil if necessary. Finally, mulch with shredded bark or other organic matter, keeping the mulch an inch or two away from the stems of the plant. Then water again, and continue watering regularly — providing 1 inch of water every 10 to 14 days if nature doesn't do so — for the first season to give the plant a good start and to encourage a vigorous, wide-spreading root system.

To plant a bare-root vine, soak it overnight in a bucket of water, and carry it to the garden in the bucket to make sure the roots don't dry out. Dig a hole the way you would for a B&B or container-grown plant. If the roots on your plant all radiate out from roughly the same point, build a cone of soil in the bottom of the hole, set the plant on top of the cone, and spread the roots out in all directions. If the plant has a more irregular root system, a cone of soil will just get in the way, in which case the easiest approach is to hold the plant in place and spread the roots as you fill. Refill the hole with unamended soil, stopping several times to gently firm the soil around the roots. When the hole is half full, flood it with water and let the water drain away. Then continue filling and tamping down. (The filling, tamping, and flooding process is important because it eliminates air pockets in the soil.) When the hole is full, form a wide saucer of soil around the plant and water thoroughly. Water bare-root plants deeply and thoroughly every week for the entire first season to encourage a vigorous root system.

Most vines need training to get them started up a trellis or other support. For some species, all that may be required is winding a tendril or young stem around a slat, string, or stick near the base of the trellis. Other vines may need to be tied in place with soft string until they are firmly attached.

CARE THROUGH THE SEASON

Vines need annual pruning but very little other attention to look their best once they are established. Some vines may require regular training for a couple of seasons to become established. Check on them every few weeks when they are in active growth and direct new stems onto supports. Prune them as necessary to establish a strong framework of one to three main stems or trunks and a few main branches. Remove excess growth that is spreading where you don't want it. Always make proper heading and thinning cuts when you prune — see "Pruning" in the Techniques Glossary for illustrations and explanations of these essential pruning cuts.

Propagation. Most vines can be propagated relatively easily by cuttings. Dip the stem bases in rooting hormone, and stick them in a 50-50 mix of peat moss and perlite or vermiculite and perlite. Cover the cuttings with plastic or a Mason jar to maintain high humidity.

POPULAR FLOWERING VINES

In addition to the vines listed below, clematis (*Clematis* spp., page 78) and climbing hydrangea (*Hydrangea petiolaris,* page 168) are covered in individual entries. You'll find information on annual vines on page 33 in the **Annuals & Biennials** entry. Finally, climbing roses, which aren't true vines because they can't climb unassisted, are covered on page 259 in the *Rosa* entry.

Actinidia spp. / Hardy kiwis

Large, vigorous vines that climb by twining stems, hardy kiwis bear lightly fragrant spring flowers and edible fruit in fall. *A. arguta,* hardy in Zones 3 to 8, is vigorous to rampant and reaches 25 to 30 feet. Male and female plants are required for fruit set; plant one male for up to eight females if you want fruit. The cultivar 'Issai' can pollinate its own fruit. Grow both in full sun or partial shade and any well-drained soil. Poor soil will help reduce their rampant growth. Variegated kiwi *(A. kolomikta),* hardy in Zones 5 to 8, has 5-inch-long leaves marked with white and/or pink. Male and female plants are required for fruit set. It is less vigorous than *A. arguta,* reaching 15 to 20 feet. Grow it in full sun for best fo-

liage color and average to rich, well-drained soil. Too much shade, too much fertilizer, or hot weather will reduce variegation. Grows in acid or alkaline soils. Prune both species as necessary in late winter to keep them in bounds, or cut them back after flowering in early summer. To encourage fruit production, cut plants back hard—to 8 to 10 buds per stem—at that time. They can be trained like grapes to maximize yields. Propagate by cuttings taken in early summer.

Akebia quinata / Fiveleaf akebia

A very vigorous, 20- to 40-foot vine that climbs by twining stems and produces clusters of fragrant, brownish purple flowers in spring. Handsome blue-green leaves that appear early in spring and remain on the plant until early winter; semievergreen in southern zones. Purplish, 4-inch-long fruit in fall. Makes a dense, fast-growing ground cover. Grow in sun or shade in any soil. Tolerates dry or wet conditions. Prune as necessary to keep plants in bounds in early summer after they flower. Can be very invasive. Propagate either by cuttings taken in early summer or by layering. Zones 4 to 8.

Campsis spp. / Trumpet vines

Vigorous, fast-growing trumpet vines climb by rootlets along the stems and can reach 30 to 40 feet or more. *C. radicans,* hardy in Zones 4 to 9, bears orange to red, trumpet-shaped flowers from midsummer to fall. 'Flava' has orangish yellow flowers. *C. × tagliabuana* 'Madame Galen' is a

hybrid with clusters of very showy, red-orange flowers from mid- to late summer through early fall. All grow in full sun and in any soil, from poor to rich, although they prefer moderately fertile, well-drained conditions. Plants are extremely rampant in rich soil. Tie the shoots in place until the rootlets establish a firm grip, after which these vines are self-supporting. For best flowering and to keep plants in bounds, prune them back to a few buds in late winter or early spring. Leave plants unpruned if they are growing up trees or are substantially out of reach. Propagate by cut-

tings taken in early to midsummer or by digging up suckers that appear near the base of the plants.

Lonicera spp. / Honeysuckles

Honeysuckles are moderate to vigorous growers that climb by twining stems and feature clusters of two-lipped flowers. All are popular with hummingbirds. Some honeysuckles have fragrant flowers, others do not. Goldflame honeysuckle *(L. × heckrottii)*, hardy in Zones 5 to 9, has red buds that open into red-and-yellow, moderately fragrant flowers. The plants bloom from spring to summer and intermittently to fall. They reach 10 to 20 feet in height if given support, but they can be allowed to sprawl over rocks or low walls. The blue-green leaves are evergreen in the South. Brown's honeysuckle *(L. × brownii)*, a hybrid of *L. sempervirens* and *L. hirsuta*, is hardy in Zones 4 to 9. It bears trumpet-shaped, orange or red blooms in summer on 12-foot plants. Its cultivar 'Dropmore Scarlet' produces bright red flowers over a long season. Japanese honeysuckle *(L. japonica)* bears fragrant spring flowers but is best avoided because it is a rampant vine that has escaped cultivation to become a noxious weed in many parts of North America. Woodbine honeysuckle *(L. periclymenum)*, hardy in Zones 5 to 9, bears fragrant, white to yellow flowers, which may be flushed with red, on 10- to 20-foot plants. Trumpet honeysuckle *(L. sempervirens)* produces orange-red, red, or yellow flowers that are not fragrant on 10- to 20-foot vines. The plants are hardy in Zones 4 to 9 and are semi-evergreen from Zone 8 south (despite the botanical name, which means "always green"). Grow honeysuckles in full sun in average to rich soil that is well drained. The plants will grow in partial shade but will flower less. Prune honeysuckles after they flower (they bloom on old wood) by cutting back stems to encourage branching and to control rampant growth. Propagate by cuttings taken in spring or summer.

Schizophragma hydrangeoides / **Japanese hydrangea vine**

A woody vine that climbs by rootlets and bears flat-topped, 8- to 10-inch-wide clusters of slightly fragrant white flowers in midsummer. This species resembles climbing hydrangea *(Hydrangea petiolaris)* but does not form woody branches that stick out from the wall or other surface upon which it is climbing. Grow it in partial shade or full sun in average to rich, evenly moist soil. Plants can reach 40 feet but are not invasive. Propagate by cuttings taken in late spring or early summer. Zones 5 to 7.

Wisteria spp. / **Wisterias**

These large, vigorous, woody vines climb by twining stems and are grown for their pendent clusters of fragrant, pea-shaped flowers. Japanese wisteria *(W. floribunda)*, hardy in Zones 4 to 9, is the most common. It bears violet-blue, violet-purple, or white flowers in 8- to 20-inch-long clusters in spring before or as the leaves emerge. Chinese wisteria *(W. sinensis)*, hardy in Zones 5 to 8, is not as fragrant and bears 6- to 12-inch-long flower clusters. Plant named cultivars rather than the species to ensure best bloom. Grow wisterias in full sun and rich, deeply prepared soil that is evenly moist but well drained. They need an extremely sturdy trellis and can pull gutters off houses or crush wooden trellises. Metal-pipe structures are fairly easy to erect, have adequate strength, and are permanent. Plants can also be trained on wires mounted on stone walls. Prune these vigorous vines in late winter to early spring, cutting back to about 3 or 4 buds on last year's growth. After the plants bloom, remove spent flowers and trim as necessary to keep them in bounds. Planting in soil that is too rich or overfeeding plants (especially with a high-nitrogen fertilizer) can cause plants not to flower. Hard pruning, as described above, and root pruning are the best ways to shock non-blooming plants into flowering. (Root-prune in late winter, when the plants are still dormant, by digging a semicircular trench halfway around the vine about 2 feet from the base. Use a saw or a sharp spade to cut the larger roots, but leave the small, fibrous ones unpruned. Refill the trench with soil. The following year, trench and cut roots on the other side of the plant.) Propagate by cuttings taken in early summer.

Wildflowers

Orange coneflower
(Rudbeckia fulgida)

■ The secret to growing wildflowers successfully is simple and straightforward: Learn about where they grow naturally and find a spot in your garden that matches those conditions. In the right site, wildflowers are tough, easy-to-grow plants that thrive with little care.

There are any number of ways to incorporate wildflowers in your garden. You can mix them into traditional beds and borders, set aside a bed for only wildflowers, or dedicate your entire garden to growing them. In fact, most gardens contain wildflowers—or at least cultivated forms of them. That's because many of our best-loved perennials are native plants, including asters, phlox, and coneflowers. To create an authentic-

East Coast wildflower fringed bleeding heart *(Dicentra eximia)* with nonnative lungwort *(Pulmonaria saccharata* 'Mrs. Moon')

looking wildflower garden, use the species forms of some of these popular perennials, not the showier cultivated ones. Or grow a mix of species and cultivars, depending on how authentic you want to be.

Start a wildflower garden by learning about what plants are native to your area. Consult local wildflower societies and arm yourself with a field guide before exploring natural areas nearby. Not all the flowers you'll find growing along roadsides and other wild places are actually native plants, and you may want to make a distinction between true native wildflowers and introduced ones. Queen Anne's lace *(Daucus carota)* and oxeye daisy *(Chrysanthemum leucanthemum,* now *Leucanthemum vulgare)* are naturalized, or introduced, wildflowers. In field guides, naturalized species are identified as aliens or exotics in the descriptions. Naturalized plants can be relatively harmless to native-plant communities, or they can become noxious weeds, crowding out everything in their path. Purple loosestrife *(Lythrum salicaria)* is a case in point. It spreads rampantly in wetland areas, crowding out species that provide valuable food for wildlife but offering little for them to eat in exchange.

Using plants native to your area guarantees that they will grow well in your climate and soil (provided the soil hasn't been altered substantially by construction). Southeastern natives withstand hot, humid summers without complaint, while species that grow naturally in the Upper Midwest survive bone-chilling winter cold. Sticking to plants native to your state or even county also highlights another reason wildflower gardens are so appealing: they celebrate our native and local flora. Gardeners in different parts of the country will have completely different gardens. Someone in the Great Plains may decide to re-create a piece of prairie, complete with purple prairie clover *(Dalea purpurea),* Kansas gayfeather *(Liatris pycnostachya),* and gray-headed coneflower *(Ratibida pinnata).* In the mountainous West, a wildflower planting may consist of alpine species such as Rocky Mountain columbine *(Aquilegia caerulea)* or plants that tolerate the dry summers characteristic of that region, such as penstemons *(Penstemon* spp.) and buckwheats *(Eriogonum* spp.), which are difficult to grow in areas with rainy, humid summers.

Don't start a wildflower garden by going out and digging plants from the wild. Growing plants in a backyard garden doesn't preserve them—after all, gardens come and go, and to truly preserve plants you need to move them to permanent homes. If you want to help save native plants from destruction by developers, participate in organized rescue operations: local wildflower societies, conservation organizations, and botanical gardens all sponsor rescues designed to move plants that are in the path of bulldozers to permanent locations such as parks and natural areas. (They always welcome the help of someone who knows how to wield a spade, too.) These organizations also commonly propagate wildflowers and offer an excellent, responsible source to turn to for both plants and expert advice.

In addition, buy wildflowers only from reputable nurseries that sell nursery-propagated plants, not wild-collected ones. Native orchids *(Cypripedium* spp.) and trilliums *(Trillium* spp.) are commonly collected from the wild, although collectors take other species as well. Individuals who collect wild plants decimate natural areas, and buying collected plants from them puts money in their pockets. Ask specifically for nursery-*propagated* plants; plants that are described as nursery-*grown* may have been wild collected and grown at the nursery for a year or two. Take a close look at the wildflowers in a nursery, and you'll learn to spot collected ones: nursery-propagated plants will look uniform and healthy, while wild-collected ones often have a just-potted-up look, with an off-center crown and broken leaves. Other signs of wild-collected plants include weeds in the pots and unusually cheap prices for the size of the plants offered. Unlike nursery owners who don't know where their plants come from—or don't care—owners who propagate their own plants, or who buy only from responsible sources, are proud of the fact and may advertise it. If in doubt, ask where the plants came from; shop elsewhere if you receive an unsatisfactory response.

WILDFLOWERS FOR SHADE

Wildflowers are the jewels of the shade garden, whether combined with nonnative shade plants such as hostas or grown with natives alone. The best known among them are showy, spring-blooming species that flower before the trees above leaf out, while the woodland floor is still sunny. Wildflowers called spring ephemerals go dormant after they finish blooming and need to be planted with other species that will fill in the spots they leave. It's also a good idea to mark their locations in the garden to avoid digging into them accidentally later in the season. Virginia bluebells *(Mertensia virginica)* is one popular wildflower that falls into this category.

Planting Wildflowers. Wildflowers can be planted in spring or fall, and all of the plants listed under "Popular Wildflowers for Shade" below thrive in well-drained soil that is slightly acid and very rich in organic matter. They require sun in spring, when trees haven't yet leafed out,

Queen Anne's lace
(Daucus carota)

Oxeye daisy
(Chrysanthemum leucanthemum)

but grow in partial or full shade in summer. Sites that are shaded year round by evergreens or buildings aren't suitable.

Prepare the soil by digging in compost, leaf mold, or other organic matter. When you encounter tree roots, work around them with a trowel, taking care not to damage the roots. If you need to remove any roots, cut them off cleanly with a sharp mattock or pruning shears. (Don't remove many, though, or you may damage the tree.) Pockets of prepared soil between large roots are ideal for planting wildflowers.

Plant wildflowers as you would any perennial, water them, and then mulch them to control weeds and to keep the soil moist and cool. Chopped leaves are an ideal, natural-looking mulch for a shade garden.

Care Through the Season. New wildflower plantings will need regular weeding until the plants are established. Replenish the mulch layer annually. In addition to keeping the soil moist and cool, and weeds under control, organic mulch such as compost, chopped leaves, or shredded bark adds organic matter to the soil, which shade-loving wildflowers need to thrive. Don't worry about feeding wildflowers; annual additions of organic matter will suffice. Water if the weather is dry in spring and early summer; most wildflowers will survive drier conditions in summer.

Ephemerals will disappear in early summer; the rest will die back by themselves in fall. Cut plants to the ground in fall, if you like, or leave them as they are. While a thin layer of fallen leaves from overhead trees will help protect a shade garden from fluctuating temperatures over winter, too many will smother it. In late fall or early winter, after the ground has frozen, rake off most, but not all, of the leaves that have fallen. In very early spring, rake off any excess leaves, but be sure to do this before the plants begin to emerge; otherwise they'll be damaged. You can mulch the garden at the same time: chop up the leaves in a shredder or with a bagging lawn mower and spread them back over the garden. Do not cover the crowns of the plants with leaves, however, or you may smother them.

Popular Wildflowers for Shade

In addition to the plants listed below, the individual entries for the following genera include native plants for shade: *Anemone* (anemones, page 16), *Aquilegia* (columbines, page 34), *Aster* (asters, page 37), *Coreopsis* (coreopsis, page 85), *Dicentra* (bleeding hearts, page 99), *Heuchera* (heucheras or coralbells, page 157), *Iris* (irises, page 172), *Lilium* (lilies, page 187), and *Phlox* (phlox, page 233). Don't forget to consider native ferns (see **Ferns** on page 112) for a shady wildflower garden. **Ground Covers,** page 125, features three native species that make fine ground covers or can be used in wildflower plantings—Canada wild ginger *(Asarum canadense),* wintergreen *(Gaultheria procumbens),* and Allegheny spurge *(Pachysandra procumbens).* Spiderworts *(Tradescantia* spp.) and violets *(Viola* spp.), both covered on page 226 in the **Perennials** entry, make great additions to a shady wildflower garden as well. There are native bulbs for shade, too—camassias *(Camassia* spp.) and dogtooth violets *(Erythronium* spp.) are covered on page 57 in **Bulbs.** Finally, don't forget native shrubs: see *Rhododendron* on page 246 and *Viburnum* on page 294 for some outstanding natives that tolerate shade. Flowering dogwood *(Cornus florida,* page 87) and sweet bay *(Magnolia virginiana,* page 195) also make excellent plants for shade.

Maidenhair fern (*Adiantum* spp.)

Arisaema triphyllum / Jack-in-the-pulpit
Hooded flowers in spring consisting of a leaflike bract called a spathe surrounding an erect, central column—the "jack"—called a spadix. The 1- to 3-foot plants die back in summer, and red berries follow the flowers in fall. To propagate, sow ripe seeds outdoors in pots or where the plants are to grow. Zones 3 to 9.

Cimicifuga racemosa / Black snakeroot
Fluffy, branched spikes of tiny white flowers held far above the leaves in summer. Plants range from

Black snakeroot (*Cimicifuga racemosa)*

Solomon's plume *(Smilacina racemosa)*

Virginia bluebells *(Mertensia virginica)*

4 to 7 feet in height when in bloom, with the foliage rising to about half that height. Propagate by dividing the clumps in fall. Or sow fresh seeds outdoors, although they are very slow to germinate and can take up to 2 years to do so. The plants will self-sow in a good site, and seedlings can be moved with a trowel. Zones 3 to 8.

Dodecatheon meadia / Shooting star
Clusters of downward-pointing flowers with reflexed petals in pale rose-purple and yellow tips in spring. The 1- to 2-foot plants are ephemeral, retreating to dormancy shortly after they flower. Divide the plants in summer, just before the leaves disappear (but after they have turned completely yellow). The plants have fleshy white roots and grow in crowns; separate the individual crowns and replant them immediately. Plants are very slow from seeds, which can be sown outdoors in summer, as soon as they are ripe. Zones 4 to 8.

Lobelia spp. / Lobelias
Two popular species produce erect spikes of showy flowers in late summer and fall. Cardinal flower *(L. cardinalis)* bears scarlet flowers on 2- to 4-foot plants and is hardy in Zones 2 to 9. Great blue lobelia *(L. siphilitica),* hardy in Zones 4 to 8, bears deep blue flowers on 2- to 3-foot plants. Both require rich, constantly moist soil for best growth and can be grown in marshy areas or along streams. They will grow in full sun with adequate moisture. Plants are short lived. Divide every 2 years or so in early fall and replant the new rosettes of leaves that arise around the old rootstock. Or grow from seeds sown indoors in late winter or outdoors in spring. Cool temperatures are best. Do not cover the seeds. Self sows.

Mertensia virginica / Virginia bluebells
Nodding clusters of pink buds that open into pale lilac-blue bells in spring. The 1- to 2-foot plants are ephemeral and have stout, fleshy rootstocks. To propagate them, dig the clumps after they flower but before the leaves disappear completely. Plants self-sow, and seedlings are easy to move in spring. Zones 3 to 9.

Polygonatum biflorum / Solomon's seal
Arching stems with oval leaves and small clusters of greenish white, bell-shaped flowers under each leaf in early to midsummer. Plants spread by thick, creeping rootstocks and range from 1 to 3 feet or more in height. Dig the clumps in spring or fall and cut them apart with a sharp knife to propagate them. Or clean the black, berrylike fruit to reveal the seeds, and sow them outdoors in fall. Zones 3 to 9.

Foamflower *(Tiarella cordifolia)*

Coneflowers *(Rudbeckia fulgida)* in a meadow planting

Smilacina racemosa / Solomon's plume

Arching stems with oval leaves ending in a plume of creamy white flowers in spring. Red berries follow the flowers in late summer or fall, and plants range from 1½ to 3 feet tall. Propagate by dividing the clumps in spring or fall. Plants also self-sow, and seedlings are easy to move anytime during the growing season. Zones 4 to 9.

Tiarella cordifolia / Allegheny foamflower

Spikes of bottlebrush-like white flowers in spring with attractive triangular or maplelike leaves. The plants spread vigorously by runners and make a fine ground cover. Wherry's foamflower *(T. wherryi)* is similar but does not spread as quickly. Both species are hardy in Zones 3 to 8 and range from 6 to 10 inches tall. Propagate them by division in spring or fall, or sow fresh seeds outdoors.

WILDFLOWERS FOR SUN

Gardeners with sunny sites have hundreds of native wildflowers to choose from. You'll find some of our best native wildflowers for sun in the in-

Creating a Wildflower Meadow

For a natural-looking planting of sun-loving wildflowers, consider a meadow or prairie planting. Don't expect to scatter seeds from a can and magically grow a field of wildflowers, though. These plantings take time and effort to establish successfully, but they offer low-maintenance benefits in the long run. You can start a small meadow planting with homegrown or store-bought seedlings, but for really large areas, seed is the only economical way to go. Select a mix of wildflowers and native grasses that has been developed for your region. Avoid generic mixes developed for the entire country or "instant" meadow mixes, which generally contain mostly annuals.

The best time to start a meadow planting is in midsummer, and killing existing lawn grass and weeds is the first step. Mark out the area you plan to plant, then scalp the site by cutting all vegetation as close to the ground as possible with a lawn mower or a string trimmer. Scalping alone won't kill grass and weeds, so the next step is to either till the site repeatedly or smother the existing vegetation. To prepare the site by tilling, till it once, then wait a week or two and till shallowly again to kill newly sprouted weeds and grass. Repeat the tilling process two or three more times until very few weeds emerge. To smother the site, cover the scalped vegetation with either heavy plastic or old carpeting and leave the covering until spring, or blanket the area with a thick layer of old newspapers topped with shredded bark to hold them in place. Tilled sites may be ready for fall planting; smothered ones usually are not ready until the following spring.

Plant transplants in either fall or early spring — whenever you commonly plant perennials. Use a bulb planter or a trowel to dig holes for the plants. (Don't fertilize or otherwise improve the soil before planting, because meadow and prairie species thrive in average soil, and conditions that are too rich may favor species that you don't want.) Arrange the plants in a random pattern, clumping groups of the same plants together in some areas. Water and then mulch with chopped leaves or other organic mulch — up to but not touching the stems — to control weeds.

To seed a meadow, in Zone 3 and south, sow a month before the first fall frost date or in early spring as soon as you can work the soil (after preparing the soil the previous year). Broadcast seeds over the entire area. Then top-dress with a ¼-inch layer of topsoil or finely screened compost. Water well.

Weed your new meadow by walking through it every few weeks and pulling up unwanted plants. Cut it annually in winter or very early spring with a string trimmer. (A lawn mower, even with the blade raised as high as it will go, won't be able to handle the tall stems.)

dividual entries for the following genera: *Aster* (asters, page 37), *Baptisia* (baptisias, page 43), *Coreopsis* (coreopsis, page 85), *Echinacea* (purple coneflowers, page 104), *Oenothera* (sundrops, page 204), *Phlox* (phlox, page 233), and *Rudbeckia* (coneflowers, page 267). All are suitable for a garden in full sun with average to rich, well-drained soil. You'll also find native perennials for sun on page 226 in the **Perennials** entry and on page 133 in **Ground Covers**.

Yucca

Yuccas

Yucca
∎
(YUCK-ah)
∎
Summer bloom
∎
Full sun or very light shade
∎
Zones 4 to 10
∎

Adam's needle *(Yucca filamentosa)* in flower

∎ Rugged, adaptable yuccas produce large, dense clumps of bold, evergreen leaves topped in summer by showy, erect spikes of waxy, creamy white flowers. The spikes of nodding, bell-shaped flowers rise to a height of 5 to 10 feet or more, well above the 2- to 2½-foot-tall mounds of sword-shaped leaves. Adam's needle *(Yucca filamentosa)* is a North American native with stiff, blue-green leaves. Variegated cultivars are available, and these add year-round color to the garden. 'Bright Edge' features leaves with yellow margins, while 'Golden Sword' has yellow-centered leaves. 'Variegata' has leaves edged in white. *Y. flaccida* resembles *Y. filamentosa* but has leaves that are less rigid and tend to droop at the tips. Both species are hardy in Zones 4 to 10.

SITE AND SOIL
Plant yuccas in full sun or very light shade. They grow well in a wide range of soils—including the average to rich, well-drained soil characteristic of a perennial bed or border as well as dry, sandy soil. They will also grow in clay soil provided it is well drained, but they will not survive in wet conditions.

PLANTING
Plant in spring or fall, spacing the clumps at least 2 feet apart to accommodate their spread. Since yuccas can be left for years without needing di-

vision, and are quite deep rooted and difficult to dig, give them plenty of space at planting time. Loosening the soil deeply and incorporating organic matter helps ensure good drainage.

CARE THROUGH THE SEASON
Yuccas are the ultimate in low-maintenance plants. Once established, they don't need watering, feeding, mulching, or regular division. New leaves will cover up the old ones in spring, which look tattered and drop to the ground by late winter. (If you live in a very dry climate, you may want to water occasionally, as this encourages larger, longer-lasting leaves.) Cut off the flower stalks at the base after the blooms fade. The individual crowns die after they flower, so cut them out as well when the leaves begin to fade. New plants, called pups, appear around the outside of the clumps and also fill in the spots left by the older crowns that have already flowered. Yuccas gradually spread to form broad mounds, which can be divided in spring or fall if they outgrow their space.

Propagation. The easiest way to propagate yuccas is to sever pups that appear around the outside of the clumps using a sharp spade and/or a knife. Try to get as many roots as you can (the plants are quite tough and woody). Pot up pups that come off without many roots and grow them in a sheltered spot for a month or two until they can be moved to the garden.

LANDSCAPE USES
Use yuccas as specimen plants, or combine them with other drought-tolerant perennials such as sedums, lavenders *(Lavandula* spp.), thymes *(Thymus* spp.), daylilies *(Hemerocallis* spp.), and ornamental grasses.

Variegated yucca *(Yucca filamentosa* 'Golden Sword') with orange coneflowers *(Rudbeckia triloba)* and *Sedum* 'Vera Jameson'

Appendices

USDA Hardiness Zone Map

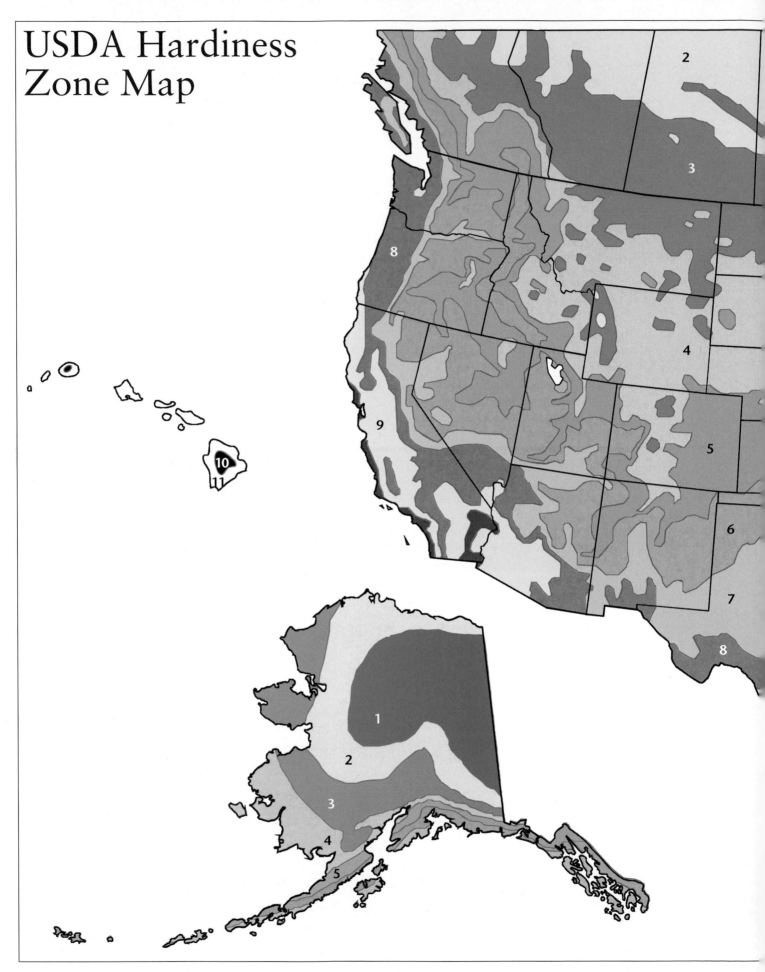

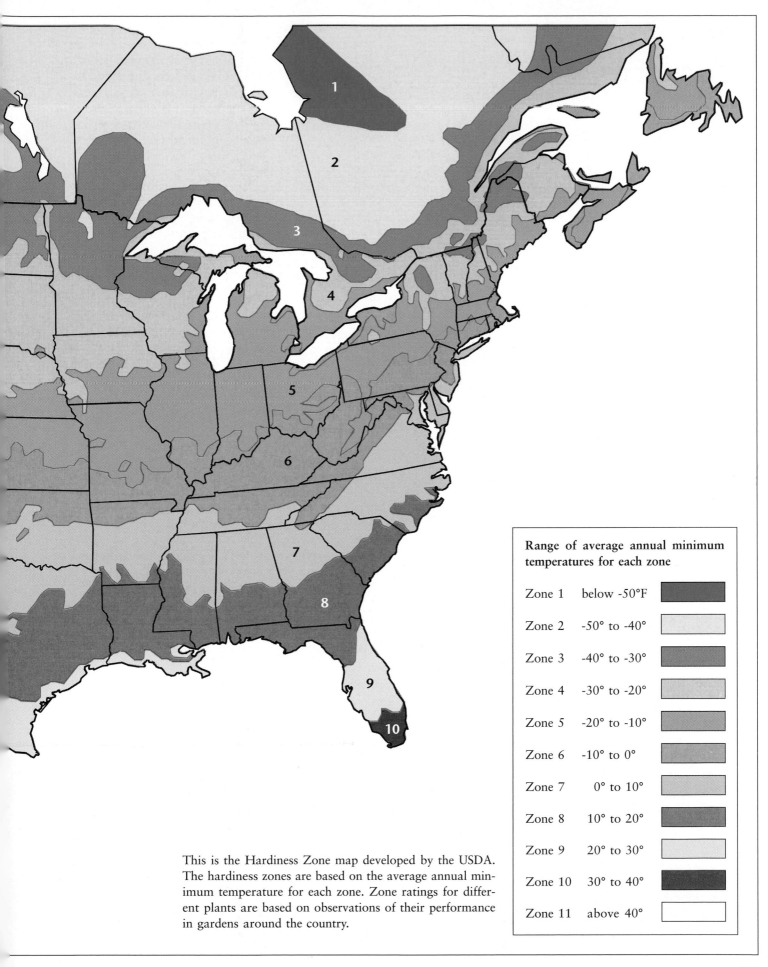

Range of average annual minimum temperatures for each zone

Zone 1	below -50°F
Zone 2	-50° to -40°
Zone 3	-40° to -30°
Zone 4	-30° to -20°
Zone 5	-20° to -10°
Zone 6	-10° to 0°
Zone 7	0° to 10°
Zone 8	10° to 20°
Zone 9	20° to 30°
Zone 10	30° to 40°
Zone 11	above 40°

This is the Hardiness Zone map developed by the USDA. The hardiness zones are based on the average annual minimum temperature for each zone. Zone ratings for different plants are based on observations of their performance in gardens around the country.

Techniques Glossary

Deadheading. Deadheading is removing flowers after they have faded either by pinching them off between thumb and forefinger or by clipping them off with pruning shears. This prevents plants from spending energy to set seed, and directs excess energy to overall growth. Deadheading keeps the garden looking neat and encourages many plants to rebloom later in the season. Plants with an abundance of small flowers can be deadheaded by shearing, in which case hedge clippers or garden shears are the tool of choice. To shear a plant, cut it back by one-third to one-half. To deadhead flowers that bloom in clusters on one main stem, you can deadhead the first few individual blooms as needed, then cut off the rest of the whole cluster when the remaining flowers are done blooming. Many gardeners don't deadhead perennials that have seed heads that feed the birds and add interest in winter, such as coneflowers (*Echinacea* spp. and *Rudbeckia* spp.). If you want a plant to self-sow, leave at least some of the flowers on the plant to set seed.

Dividing. Perennials, bulbs, and some shrubs can be propagated by division of the clumps. This technique is also used to rejuvenate plants that tend to develop old, woody growth near the centers of the clumps. In addition, division is an effective way of dealing with plants that have spread too far and are threatening to overtake their neighbors. The best time to divide varies from plant to plant — see the individual plant entries for specific recommendations. Dividing plants when the weather is cool and rainy or overcast is best, because it reduces the amount of stress on the plants. (Newly divided plants have reduced root systems and will have trouble supplying top growth with water until the roots begin growing again. Cutting the top growth back by about half can help divisions recover more quickly.)

To divide a plant, dig the clump up with a spade or a garden fork. To minimize damage to the roots, start digging about 6 inches or more from the outside edge of the clump. Dig all the way around it, then lift the plant out of the hole. (If the plant you are dividing is very large or heavy, divide it into smaller, manageable pieces while it is still in the hole.) You'll find that different plants have different types of clumps. Some form loose, easy-to-divide clumps connected by rhizomes, which are underground stems that produce shoots and roots. Rhizomes are often fleshy and thick — bearded irises are one example. Other plants form dense crowns that may or may not be woody, and these can be more difficult to divide because they are denser and it's harder to see where to cut. Most plants can be divided by the techniques described here, and exceptions are noted in the individual entries.

Separate small plants with fibrous roots into pieces with your fingers. Work apart clumps of bulbs in the same manner. Use a sharp knife or shears to cut apart plants with woody or dense crowns or rhizomes. Cut apart large clumps with a spade or force them apart with two garden forks placed back to back. Ornamental grasses are so dense and woody that a mattock or an ax is required to divide them. If you have difficulty deciding where to cut, wash the soil off the roots with a stiff stream of water from the hose so you can see the crowns clearly before dividing.

While the plants are out of the ground, make sure the roots do not dry out. Cover them with mulch, loose soil, or a piece of plastic if they are going to be out of the ground for more than a few minutes and could dry out.

Get in the habit of amending the soil with compost or other organic matter every time you divide a plant — it's your best chance for improving the soil in established beds and borders. Use a garden fork to work in the compost and to loosen the soil.

Discard old, woody growth and replant the youngest, most vigorous portions of the clumps. To create good-size clumps within a season or two, plant three to five pieces together, spaced as you would new plants. Don't overcrowd, or you'll defeat the purpose of dividing. Water new divisions deeply and thoroughly. If the weather is sunny, shade new divisions with bushel baskets, cardboard boxes propped up on sticks, or burlap for a few days, until they recover from the stress. Plant extra divisions elsewhere in the garden or

Dividing

Cut large clumps with a spade.

Pull apart small clumps with your fingers.

give them away to friends. If the individual plants are small or you don't have a spot prepared for them, pot them up (use commercial potting soil, not garden soil), water, and hold them in a shady, protected location.

Feeding. If you keep your soil well supplied with organic matter (see "Soil Building" on page 224 in the **Perennials** entry for details), most perennials and shrubs don't need to be fertilized throughout the growing season. Exceptions are noted in the individual entries. Most plants benefit from a spring feeding with very well rotted manure, compost, or a balanced organic fertilizer. Spread it on the surface of the soil around plants, but under any mulch layer, and keep it away from plant stems. If you have fresh manure available, spread it in late fall—again keeping it away from plant stems—so there is plenty of time for it to rot over winter.

Hardening Off. Hardening off is the process of gradually exposing seedlings or plants that have been grown in a greenhouse or other protected location to the outdoors. It minimizes transplanting stress by helping them withstand drying winds, sun, and fluctuating temperatures and thus eases the plants' transition into the garden. About a week before you're ready to move seedlings or other tender plants to the garden, set them outdoors for a few hours in a shaded location that is protected from wind. Leave them out for a few more hours each day, and gradually move them into a more exposed location. Be sure to keep them well watered during this process. The night before you transplant, leave them out all night. (Gardeners who work during the day should start this process on the weekend, and then leave the plants in a very protected location the first full day they'll be away.) If the weather is mild (no cooler than in the 40s at night), you can generally harden off hardy perennials that have been grown in a greenhouse by simply setting them in a protected location (such as on the north side of the house, sheltered from drying winds) for a few days before moving them to the garden.

Heeling In. This is a temporary measure for storing plants that can't yet be moved to the garden, either because their permanent site isn't prepared or because it is too cold or wet for planting. It's commonly used with bare-root plants, although container-grown plants can be heeled in as well. To heel in a perennial, simply plant it in a protected, shady location with loose, rich soil. Taller plants, such as bare-root shrubs, roses, and trees, are usually heeled in into a trench. In this case, lay the plant along the trench at an angle and

cover the roots. Water heeled-in plants thoroughly to settle the soil. To minimize stress, move them to their permanent locations in the garden as soon as possible.

Layering. This is an easy technique for propagating a wide variety of shrubs, vines, and perennials. In late winter or early spring, select a low stem that is flexible enough to bend easily to the ground, and gently bend it down to determine where it will touch the soil. (Roots appear at the leaf nodes, and leaves on a stem indicate where the nodes are located. If you select a stem that doesn't have any leaves on it, look closely for tiny buds or bumps that indicate where the leaf nodes are, and make sure that section of stem gets buried.) Mark the area where the stem will touch, then loosen the soil in that spot to a depth of 4 to 5 inches, working in organic matter such as compost.

Remove all the leaves from the stem you are planning to layer except at the tip. Then use a sharp knife to wound the stem by removing a thin sliver of bark, 1 to 2 inches long, on the bottom of the section that will be buried. Push the stem back to the ground and bury the wounded section about 3 inches deep in the center of the loosened

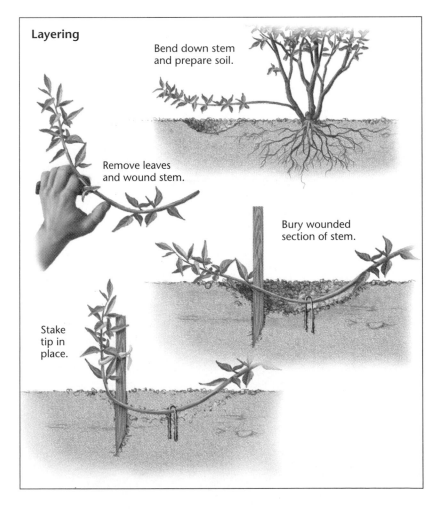

Layering

Bend down stem and prepare soil.

Remove leaves and wound stem.

Bury wounded section of stem.

Stake tip in place.

area, pinning it down with a U-shaped wire pin if needed. (You may also need to set a brick or rock on the buried section to help hold it down.) Stake the tip, which remains above ground. Keep the soil moist all summer. The following spring, check for roots along the wounded section of stem and cut apart and pot up the new plant.

Making Compost and Manure Teas. Both compost and manure can be turned into liquid fertilizer. To make a "tea" from either one, place a shovelful of finished compost or manure in a burlap sack or old pillowcase, tie the top closed, and let the sack soak in a tub or large bucket of water for several days. When the water looks dark, remove the "tea bag" and toss the sodden contents on the compost pile. Add enough water to dilute the remaining liquid to the color of weak tea. This is especially important with manure tea, which is strong enough to burn plants. Apply compost or manure tea to the soil around plants with a watering can or sprinkle it onto the leaves. Strain it through a piece of nylon stocking if you want to spray it on the foliage. A dose of compost or manure tea once or twice a summer is ideal for giving plants—especially those growing in containers—a gentle nutrient boost. As with a compost mulch, don't use compost or manure tea on perennials, shrubs, or trees after midsummer.

Mound Layering. Mound layering is a handy technique for propagating shrubby plants such as artemisias, lavenders, and thymes. Mound-layer plants in spring by piling roughly 3 to 5 inches of crumbly, sandy soil or finely shredded bark mulch—ideally mixed with a handful or two of compost—over the center of the plant. Leave 3 to 4 inches of each shoot tip exposed. Work the soil or mulch around the stems with your fingers to eliminate air pockets. Water carefully just after mounding (a strong spray of water will wash away the soil or mulch). Over the next few

months, water as needed to keep the mound from drying out. Add more soil or mulch if heavy rains wash part of the mound away.

In late summer to early fall, pull away some of the soil or mulch with your fingers to see if roots have formed along the covered parts of the stems. If there are few or no roots, leave the mound in place and check it again in spring. If the shoots look well rooted, pull away more of the mound, and snip off the rooted stems near the original soil level. Plant well-rooted stems directly into the garden or move them into individual pots. In some cases, the original plant may produce new growth from the roots after the mound-layering process. If it isn't growing in a highly visible spot, you may want to leave it in place for a season after removing the mound, to see if it sprouts again. If it is too prominent, just dig it out, work a few handfuls of compost into the site, and replant the spot with one or more of the rooted stems.

Mulching. Keeping a layer of organic mulch such as compost, shredded bark, or chopped leaves on your garden not only controls weeds, it also improves the soil by adding vital organic matter. Mulch also benefits soil by holding in moisture, keeping it cool, and protecting it from erosion by wind and rain. Your choice of mulch will depend on where you live. Shredded bark is available nearly everywhere, but pine needles are more commonly available in some regions. Most gardeners have a ready supply of chopped leaves—pick them up off the lawn in a bagging lawn mower or chop them in a shredder. Compost has the advantage of improving the soil and adding some nutrients at the same time. If you don't have enough of it to mulch the entire garden, spread a thin layer around your plants and top it with a more readily available mulch such as shredded bark. *Never* use peat moss as mulch, because it forms an impenetrable crust on the soil. Plants that demand perfect drainage are best un-mulched, but if you do choose to mulch, consider pea gravel, granite chips, or limestone chips, which are commonly used to mulch rock gardens.

The best time to mulch a garden is in late spring or early summer, when most perennials are up and the soil has had a chance to warm up a bit. Spread a 2- to 3-inch layer over the soil, but keep the mulch away from plant stems. For best results, feather out the thickness of the mulch layer as you get closer to the crown or stems of the plant, keeping the mulch 1 to 2 inches away from the stems. Many gardeners remove and compost mulch in late fall, as part of fall cleanup, and replace it each spring. Other gardeners leave mulch on their garden year round, although

Mound Layering

Mound loose soil over plant.

Check for roots and snip off new plants.

mulch can encourage rodents to spend the winter dining on the crowns of your plants. In the North, some plants benefit from a loose mulch over winter. Install winter mulches—evergreen boughs are a good choice, but weed-free straw or salt hay is also effective—after the ground has frozen completely. Don't use anything that will hold moisture around the crowns. Remove winter mulch in late winter or early spring.

Nursery Bed. A nursery bed is a holding area for plants that are still too small to be planted in the garden. Use it for seedlings or plants you propagated by division, cuttings, or layering that still need regular watering and feeding until they reach full size. Choose a sheltered but sunny spot where the soil is well drained—a corner of the vegetable garden will do. (If you're growing shade plants, such as hostas, choose a shady spot.) The bed can be any length you wish, but don't make it wider than 5 feet if you can reach in from both sides or 2½ feet if you can access the bed from only one side. Prepare the soil thoroughly to provide the best possible growing conditions. Dig deeply to loosen the top 10 to 12 inches of soil, and dig or till in a 2- to 3-inch layer of compost to loosen and enrich the soil. If your soil is rocky or hard to dig, build a raised bed and fill it with a mix of compost and topsoil. Sow seeds or plant hardwood cuttings directly in your nursery bed, and also use it for setting out all manner of plants that aren't quite ready for the garden. Plant them just as if you were planting them in the regular garden, spaced at least 8 inches apart. During the growing season, give your nursery plants good general care, paying special attention to watering during dry spells. In spring or fall, dig up the plants that are large enough for your needs, and move them to their permanent spots in the garden. Avoid leaving plants in a nursery bed for more than 2 years, or their roots will spread far and wide, making them difficult to transplant.

Pinching. Perennials and annuals are commonly pinched to encourage branching and denser, shorter growth. To pinch a plant, use your thumb and forefinger to snap off the tip of each shoot just above a set of leaves. If the growth is too hard to remove with your fingers, use pruning or garden shears. Pinching a plant often results in more, although smaller, flowers and is best used on bushy, multistemmed plants. It won't work on plants with unbranched stems (such as lilies) or basal foliage (such as daylilies).

Planting. If you've purchased plants through the mail, unpack them promptly. Water plants that are still in their pots whenever the soil surface dries out. Keep bare-root ones packed in the material in which they were shipped, moistening it if necessary. If they were shipped without anything covering their roots, soak them in lukewarm water for an hour or so and then pot them up or heel them in in a protected spot with their roots covered with damp soil or compost. Ideally, plant as soon as you can after they arrive.

A cool, cloudy or even rainy day is the best time to plant. To plant a pot-grown plant, dig a hole large enough to accommodate the roots, tip the plant out of its pot, set it in place, and firm the soil over the root ball. If the plant has roots that wind around the inside of the pot, use a knife to score them on each side. This may seem harsh, but it encourages the roots to extend out into the surrounding soil. If you are planting a bare-root plant, soak it in water for a couple of hours (shrubs are commonly soaked overnight) before planting. See the **Shrubs** entry on page 273 for complete directions for planting bare-root plants.

Set container-grown plants at the same depth at which they were growing in the pot, or position them slightly higher to allow for settling. Set bare-root plants with the crown of the plant—where the roots meet the buds or top growth—at the soil surface, unless otherwise noted in the individual entries. If bare-root plants have sprouted, cut back top growth by about one-third to give them a better chance to recover from the shock of transplanting. Water each plant thoroughly. If the weather is warm or windy, cover new plants with burlap, bushel baskets, or spun-bonded row covers for a few days to protect them while they recover.

Propagating Bulbs and Corms. The easiest way to propagate clumps of plants that grow from bulbs or corms is simply to dig the clumps and break apart and replant the individual bulbs or corms. Dig spring bulbs after the foliage has turned yellow but before it disappears completely. Alternatively, mark the location of the clump you want to divide and dig it in the fall. You can propagate bulbs with individual scales—such as lilies—by pulling off the scales and planting them one by one. After pulling off the scales, dust the base with a fungicide such as sulfur, and plant in moist vermiculite or a 50-50 mix of coarse sand and peat moss. Cover the pots with a plastic bag. When the new bulbs are large enough, plant them out in the garden. Some plants (again, lilies are a good example) also produce small bulbs along their stems, either above or below the soil, but above the bulb. These can be detached and grown on into full-size plants. Pot them up in containers or plant them in a nursery bed until they are large enough to go into the garden.

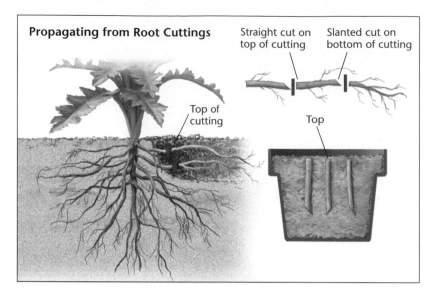

Propagating from Root Cuttings

Straight cut on top of cutting

Slanted cut on bottom of cutting

Top of cutting

Top

Gladioli, crocuses, and a number of other so-called bulbs grow from corms, which are swollen pieces of stem. Corms die each year, but a new full-size corm is produced on top of the old one each year. Like true bulbs, corms produce offsets, called cormels. These can be broken off and re-planted individually at a depth of about twice their height.

Propagating from Root Cuttings. Bear's breech *(Acanthus* spp.), purple coneflower *(Echinacea purpurea),* and a number of other perennials, shrubs, and vines are easy to propagate by root cuttings. In general, root cuttings are gathered in late winter to early spring, when the soil has thawed and dried out enough to be dug. (See the individual plant entries for exceptions to this rule.) To gather root cuttings from small plants, dig up the whole plant, rinse the soil off the roots, take your cuttings, and replant. With larger plants, dig carefully around the base of the plant to expose the roots, take your cuttings, and re-place the soil. It's best to take no more than about five roots from any plant.

For plants with relatively fine roots, cut off whole roots with clean, sharp scissors or garden shears, then snip them into 2-inch sections. Where the roots are thick or fleshy, select pencil-thick roots and gather 2- to 3-inch-long sections with a clean, sharp knife or pruning shears. Like stem cuttings, root cuttings must be planted right side up. To keep track of which is which, on each thick or fleshy cutting, make a straight cut on the end that was closest to the crown of the plant and a sloping cut at the other end. Place the cuttings you have gathered in a plastic bag to keep them from drying out until you are ready to prepare and plant them.

Plant the root cuttings in pots filled to just below the rim with a moistened mix of equal parts peat moss and perlite, and set the pots in a cold frame or a cool, bright room. (Cuttings from shrubs, vines, and trees can generally withstand planting directly outdoors in a well-drained nurs-ery bed; simply loosen the soil a bit and smooth the surface before planting.) To plant the cuttings, lay thin-rooted cuttings horizontally on the sur-face of the mix, spaced about 1 inch apart, and cover them with an additional 1/2 inch of mix. Insert thicker cuttings vertically into the mix or soil, with the flat end of the cuttings pointing up-ward. Space them about 2 inches apart, with the tops even with or just below the surface. Water thoroughly to settle the medium around the roots. Keep the medium evenly moist but not wet. Root cuttings often produce top growth before their new roots are established. Wait until you can see roots through the pots' drainage holes before transplanting to individual pots or to a nursery bed. Transplant the young plants to the garden in the fall if they are large enough, or leave them in a cold frame or nursery bed for an extra grow-ing season.

Propagating from Suckers, Runners, and Off-sets. Plants that spread by sending out these spe-cialized structures are very easy to propagate. Suckers are shoots that arise from root tissue below ground or from stem tissue at the base of the plant. They may appear close to the parent plant or as much as several feet away. Keep in mind that suckers of grafted plants may be from the rootstock, not the top growth, in which case they should be dug and destroyed, not used for propagation or left to crowd the parent plant. Runners are horizontal shoots that grow along the soil surface, with long spaces between the nodes (the points where leaves emerge from the stem). As the runners creep along, the nodes may produce roots and top growth, yielding self-sup-porting new plants. You can encourage runners to take root by pinning them to the ground with a U-shaped piece of wire or to a pot of moist grow-ing mix sitting near the parent plant. An offset is a type of side shoot or branch that develops from the base of the main stem. Offsets become inde-pendent of the parent plant by establishing their own root systems.

To propagate from any of these structures, wait until the new plants have formed their own roots, sever their connection to the parent plant, and dig them up. Either move the new plants to a nursery bed or the garden, or pot them up.

Pruning. Pruning intimidates many gardeners, but it doesn't have to. If you learn how to make proper pruning cuts and take time to step back and look at the plant you're pruning as you work, you're well on your way. There are two types of pruning cuts: heading cuts and thinning cuts. A cut made across a branch to remove the stem tip is called a heading cut. Heading cuts stimulate branching—pinching out the tip of a seedling to encourage branching is actually a form of heading cut. Use them to encourage dense, twiggy growth or to remove diseased, dead, or damaged stem tips. Since they also promote vigorous growth, don't use them in an attempt to control the size of a shrub—use thinning cuts instead.

To make a proper heading cut, always cut just above a bud or a side branch, and angle the cut at a 45° angle *away* from the bud. (This directs water away from the bud and prevents rotting.) Make flat cuts on plants with opposite leaves. Since pruning will cause the top bud remaining on the branch or stem to grow, cut just above a bud that's pointing in the direction you want the growth to go—generally toward the outside of the plant to encourage a spreading habit. (Buds are located just above where a leaf was or is attached. In early spring you won't have leaves to guide you, but buds are still easy to find. Look closely and you will see the scars left by last year's leaves. The small, swollen buds are just above each leaf scar.)

Thinning cuts remove a branch or shoot at its base, where it arose from a larger branch or the base of a shrub. When making thinning cuts, always cut just outside the branch collar, which is the swelling where a branch joins a larger branch or the trunk. Leaving the branch collar intact promotes healing of the wound. At the same time, don't leave a stub, which invites disease—if you can hang your hat on it, it's too long. To make a proper thinning cut on a large limb, always use a three-step cut: Cut partway up through the branch from the bottom, then saw off the limb 6 inches or so outside the point where you'll make the final cut. Finally, saw off the stub cleanly, just outside the branch collar. A three-step cut leaves a smooth wound that will heal much more quickly.

Use thinning cuts to remove stems from overcrowded shrubs simply by cutting the stems off at the base of the plant or as close to the ground as possible. This type of thinning cut is often used on flowering shrubs and roses to remove old wood that is no longer blooming well. Thinning out old wood generally causes the plant to produce vigorous new growth. Also use thinning cuts to remove dead and damaged growth, to open up the center of a plant to let in light and air, to eliminate rubbing or crossing branches, and to remove water sprouts (fast-growing, vertical shoots, which seldom bloom) and reverted growth (an all-green branch on an otherwise variegated plant,

Heading Cuts

Align the bottom of the cut as shown and slant it upward at a 45° angle to keep excess moisture away from the bud.

On plants with opposite leaves, cut straight across the stem just above a strong pair of buds.

Thinning Cuts

for example). They can also be used to reduce the size of a shrub without stimulating the rampant growth that repeated shearing does: simply remove large branches and leave smaller ones behind. Although thinning cuts do not cause a flush of new growth the way heading cuts do, they do tend to invigorate the growth of buds remaining on the plant, because they change the amount of top growth the roots are supporting. Try to pull up or dig out suckers, however, because then they are less likely to grow back; if this isn't possible, remove them with thinning cuts.

For more on using heading and thinning cuts, see "Pruning Shrubs" on page 275 in the **Shrubs** entry.

Rooting Cuttings. Cuttings offer a fast, easy way to propagate a wide range of plants, from perennials to vines and shrubs. You'll find recommendations for the best times to collect cuttings in the individual plant entries. Mid- to late summer is a great time to gather cuttings of many annuals and perennials. A few perennials root well from cuttings taken in mid- to late spring from newly emerging shoots that arise from the base of the plant. If you don't have luck rooting certain plants from midsummer cuttings, try gathering cuttings earlier the following year.

For best results with soft-stemmed cuttings, it's important to keep them from drying out before they can establish a new root system. Before collecting the cuttings, fill pots (4-inch ones are fine) with a moistened rooting medium such as a 50-50 mix of perlite and vermiculite or peat moss and perlite. Also set up a system for maintaining high humidity around the cuttings: consider a wooden or wire frame draped with plastic, large clear-plastic sweater boxes, or an old aquarium with a piece of glass over the top. All will accommodate several pots of cuttings.

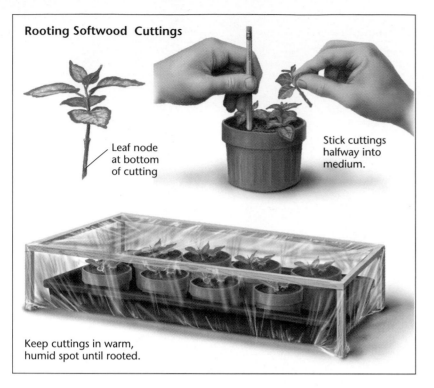

Rooting Softwood Cuttings

Leaf node at bottom of cutting

Stick cuttings halfway into medium.

Keep cuttings in warm, humid spot until rooted.

medium, then insert the cutting about halfway into the medium, to just below the lowest leaves. Push the medium back around the stem to support the cutting. Repeat with the remaining cuttings, spacing them 1 to 4 inches apart. The cuttings shouldn't touch, so if the leaves are large, either space the cuttings farther apart or trim their leaves slightly (by no more than one-half). A 4-inch pot will usually hold several cuttings. Different plants root at different rates, so it's best to use separate pots for each different species or cultivar. Label each pot with the name of the plant and the date. After planting, water all cuttings thoroughly.

Set the cuttings in a warm (65° to 75°F) spot in the sweater box or other enclosure you prepared. The growing medium should be a steady 70° to 75°F, so use a heated propagating mat if necessary. Good light, but not direct sun, is also essential. Outdoors, set covered cuttings at the base of a north-facing wall or in a spot that's lightly shaded all day by trees or shrubs. Cuttings also root well under fluorescent lights such as those used for starting seeds.

Within a day, condensation should build up on the inside of the propagation enclosure. If not, water again thoroughly. Otherwise, leave the cuttings covered and water only when the condensation thins or disappears; don't let the pots sit in water. Remove the cover for an hour or so two or three times a week to allow some air circulation around the leaves. To discourage diseases, remove any dropped leaves or obviously dead cuttings immediately. Most soft-stemmed plants start rooting in 2 to 5 weeks. Try to resist the urge to check for roots until you see the cuttings producing new growth, then tug lightly on the stems. When the cuttings feel firmly anchored in the medium, they are ready to be transplanted to individual, larger pots. Gradually remove or open the enclosure over a period of a few days to increase ventilation and to decrease humidity. This will help the new growth harden off and reduce the chance of wilting.

Move the rooted cuttings into pots filled with moistened potting soil. Lightly tap the base of each pot against a hard surface two or three times to settle the mix around the roots, then water thoroughly. Set potted cuttings in a shady spot and mist them a few times with a hand sprayer daily for 2 or 3 days. Then move them to their preferred light conditions and water and fertilize as usual.

Shrubs, vines, and trees tend to be slower to root than soft-stemmed cuttings—especially when you take them during the dormant season (while the plants aren't producing new growth). If you are taking cuttings of woody plants in mid-

Gather cuttings early in the day, while the stems are full of moisture. Cuttings from wilted or water-stressed plants are much less likely to recover and root well. In fact, if the weather has been dry, water the day before gathering cuttings. Take cuttings from strong-looking growth, with leaves that have fully expanded and growth that has hardened a bit. Avoid spindly shoots or ones that are growing very rapidly. To judge if the growth is at the best stage for cutting, try bending one of the plant's stems firmly. If it snaps off cleanly, it's a good time to collect cuttings. Growth that just bends over is too soft, while growth that crushes or partially breaks is old and may be slow to root. Snip off 2- to 6-inch shoots with a sharp, clean pair of pruning or garden shears. Make sure each shoot has at least two nodes (the joints where the leaves or leaf pairs emerge from the stem). Collect cuttings in a plastic bag to prevent them from drying out, and keep them out of direct sun. As soon as you have all the cuttings you need, take them indoors and prepare them for planting. If you can't plant them immediately, wrap them in a moist paper towel and keep them in the plastic bag in a cool, shady spot until you are ready for them.

Use a sharp, clean pair of shears or a utility knife to trim each shoot to its final cutting size — 2- to 4-inch-long cuttings are ideal. Whenever possible, trim each cutting so there are at least two nodes left, and make the bottom cut just *below* a node. Trim the leaves off the bottom half of the cutting, and remove any flowers or flower buds. Use a pencil to poke a hole in the growing

to late summer, treat them just as you would soft-stemmed plants. If you collect hardwood cuttings in late summer to midwinter, gather them with pruning shears and plant them either directly in a nursery bed or into 4-inch pots filled with the same rooting medium you would use for soft-stemmed plants. Collect cuttings at least 2 to 3 weeks after the plants have dropped their leaves. You'll usually get the best results from wood of the current year's growth (first-year shoots), although second-year or older growth may root as well. Look for healthy, moderately vigorous shoots that are about as thick as a pencil. Cut stems at least 8 inches long (you may be able to get several smaller cuttings from one long stem piece), and trim an inch or two off the tip. Trim hardwood cuttings into 4- to 8-inch lengths, with at least two buds on each length. Make a straight cut about 1/2 inch *above* a bud at the top end of each piece (the end that was closest to the shoot tip) and a sloping cut about 1/2 inch *below* the bud at the base. Since cuttings planted upside down won't root, it's important to plant them right side up; this system will help you keep track of which end is which.

If your winters are relatively mild (roughly from Zone 6 south), you can plant hardwood cuttings outdoors immediately. Dip the base of each cutting in a rooting hormone to encourage roots to form. Insert them vertically into moistened, loose soil, leaving only one or two buds above ground, and lightly firm the soil around the cuttings. Mulch the soil around the cuttings after the ground freezes to prevent rapid thawing and refreezing, which can damage the tender new roots.

In the North, store hardwood cuttings for early-spring planting. This protects them from extreme cold and promotes the growth of callus tissue at the base of each cutting, which increases the chance the cuttings will root successfully. After treating the cuttings with rooting hormone, gather them into bundles with the top ends all facing in one direction, and secure them with rubber bands. To keep them cool and moist over the winter, bury them outdoors in a well-drained spot filled with sandy soil, sand, or sawdust; place the bundles horizontally, 6 to 8 inches deep, or vertically, with their tops down and their basal ends 3 to 4 inches below the soil surface. Or store them in boxes of moist sand, sawdust, or peat moss in an unheated room or garage or in the refrigerator. In early spring, plant the stored cuttings outdoors in moist, well-prepared soil deep enough to cover all but the top one or two buds. Space them roughly 4 to 6 inches apart.

Cuttings from deciduous shrubs, vines, and trees may take several months to a year to root.

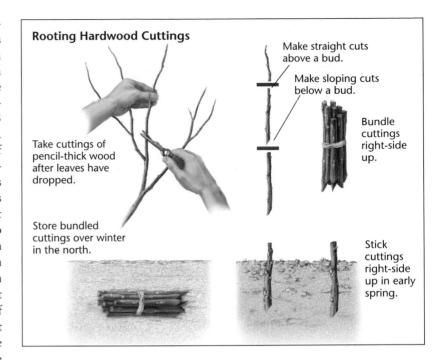

Rooting Hardwood Cuttings

Take cuttings of pencil-thick wood after leaves have dropped.

Make straight cuts above a bud.

Make sloping cuts below a bud.

Bundle cuttings right-side up.

Store bundled cuttings over winter in the north.

Stick cuttings right-side up in early spring.

Cuttings from these plants taken in summer are usually the quickest to get started. Whether you plant in spring or fall, care for woody cuttings as you would soft-stemmed ones. Once they have rooted, however, set them in a sheltered corner or a cold frame for the winter instead of transplanting them right away. Feed them after you see new growth start in spring, then transplant them to individual pots about 2 to 4 weeks later. In mid- to late summer, transplant them to a nursery bed, then move them to the garden the following spring or fall.

Many woody plants need to be treated with rooting hormone, available in powder or liquid form, in order to root. Wounding the base of the cuttings also encourages rooting. To wound a cutting, use a clean knife or razor blade to make a 1-inch-long vertical slice, through the bark and into the wood, on one or both sides of the base of the cutting. After wounding, treat the cutting with rooting hormone (make sure to get powder on the whole wounded area) and plant as usual.

Shearing. This is a type of deadheading that involves cutting off flowers en masse with hedge clippers or garden shears. It is an efficient way to deadhead perennials with many small flowers. It is also effective for cutting back plants that have grown lanky, because it encourages branching and new growth.

Soil Preparation. Deep digging, or double digging, is the tried-and-true technique for preparing soil for garden beds. It ensures good drainage, allows you to work plenty of organic matter into the soil, and encourages plants to grow deep,

Soil Preparation

1. Spread organic matter such as compost over the site, then dig a trench about 8 inches deep and 1 foot wide along one edge of the planting area. Pile the removed soil on a tarp or in a wheelbarrow.

2. Spread a 1-inch layer of compost or other organic matter over the bottom of the trench, then work it into the soil with a garden fork.

3. Dig another trench next to the first, turning the soil into the previous trench, then add more organic matter to the bottom of the new trench and fork it in. Continue this process until you reach the other end of the planting area, then fill the last trench with the soil you removed from the first one.

Drawings by Elayne Sears

wide-spreading roots. Follow the steps above to double-dig a garden. If your soil is good, and you simply don't have the time to double-dig, single digging is a good alternative. Spread compost over the site, and then turn the soil over to a shovel's depth, working in the compost as you go. Ideally, prepare the soil the season before you plant—this gives it plenty of time to settle. If you can't wait, water the site thoroughly to help it settle, then wait a day or so before planting.

Raised beds are an option for sites with poor soil or for areas that are too wet. You can build a raised bed directly on top of the ground, but tilling the site first encourages deeper roots and helps water percolate down into the soil. Till the

site as deeply as you can, and incorporate a couple of inches of compost or chopped leaves into the soil as you work. Then install landscape ties or sides consisting of rock or brick and fill the bed with topsoil mixed with compost. Water it thoroughly to settle it, and top it off. Then you're ready to plant. See "Soil Building" on page 224 in the **Perennials** entry for information on keeping your soil fertile and in topnotch condition.

Whatever method you choose, keep in mind that working the soil when it is either too wet or too dry will damage it, so always take a minute to test for moisture before you dig. Before digging or tilling, squeeze a handful of soil from the site. If it makes a ball that holds together tightly after you open your hand, it is too wet. Wait a day or so and check again. If the soil is dust-dry, give the site a good soaking, then test again the next day. Ideally, the soil should hold together when you first open your hand but crumble easily when you tap it with a finger.

Soil Testing. To have your soil tested for pH and nutrients—by the Cooperative Extension Service or a private soil lab or with a home test kit—you first need to collect a representative soil sample. Remove organic matter such as grass, roots, and leaves from a site, then dig a 3- to 4-inch-deep hole and collect a spoonful or two of soil from the side of the hole. Repeat the sampling in 10 or so spots around your garden, and mix all the soil together. To compare different parts of your yard (a new, unimproved bed against an established garden, for instance), collect samples from each area and keep them separate.

Many gardeners have their soil tested to determine its pH, which is a measure of its acidity or alkalinity. Soil pH has an important effect on the vigor and health of plants, because it determines which nutrients can dissolve in the soil water and are thus available to them. It also influences the activity of soil organisms. In general, a pH range near neutral (roughly 6.5 to 7.0) is considered ideal for most garden plants, although most will grow in a much wider pH range. Within this range, most nutrients are available in forms plants can use. As the pH becomes more acid or alkaline, some nutrients join with others to form compounds that will not dissolve in water, and therefore they are unavailable to plants. Keeping the soil rich by adding regular doses of organic matter helps neutralize pH— bringing both acid and alkaline soils closer to neutral. Good, rich soil also helps plants cope with less than ideal pH.

If the pH of your soil is outside of the ideal range for the plants you want to grow, you have two options: either add amendments such as lime

320 ■ TECHNIQUES GLOSSARY

or sulfur to adjust the pH, or revise your plant choices to include those that are adapted to your soil's natural pH. You'll find recommendations for adjusting pH in the results of your soil test. In general, it's not practical to try to adjust the soil pH more than a point in either direction — you're better off selecting plants adapted to your growing conditions. Talk to local gardeners and experts at botanical gardens or garden centers for suggestions. You'll find information in the individual entries on whether plants require a specific pH range to grow well.

Soil-test results also indicate fertility and may give specific levels of nitrogen, phosphorus, potassium, calcium, magnesium, sodium, sulfur, and trace minerals. You'll also find recommendations for adding fertilizers to meet the needs of the plants you want to grow. (Ask the laboratory for recommendations for organic fertilizers when you submit your test.)

Staking. There are several effective methods for staking plants, and the methods you choose will vary depending on the type of plant and its size. For plants with tall stems, such as delphiniums and dahlias, staking each stem individually is often the best approach. Bamboo stakes are effective and relatively unobtrusive. Wooden poles are serviceable and may be the best bet for tall, heavy plants such as dahlias. Metal stakes covered with green plastic work well, too, and aren't too noticeable in the garden. You'll need stakes at least a foot longer than the plants will be at maturity, so you can drive them solidly into the ground. Install the stakes before the flower stalks are much more than a foot high, taking care not to drive them into the crowns of the plants. If you don't want to look at a forest of stakes, you can install shorter stakes at first, then add taller ones later in the season as the plants grow. As the stems grow, tie them to the stakes with yarn, old shoelaces, strips of nylon stockings, or soft string. Don't tie them too tightly, or you'll constrict the stems. The stems should be able to move slightly. Figure-eight ties — around the stake, crossing over in the center, and around the stem — work best.

A system of stakes and string is one of the traditional methods for supporting clump-forming plants such as peonies and is best installed when the plants are still relatively short. (Installing nearly any staking system after the plants have already flopped over is generally a futile effort — the end result is an unattractive, hog-tied effect.) You'll need stakes that are slightly longer than the plants are high for this method. Pound them into the ground around each clump. Then wind string around the outside of the stakes and through the center of the clump to form a spi-

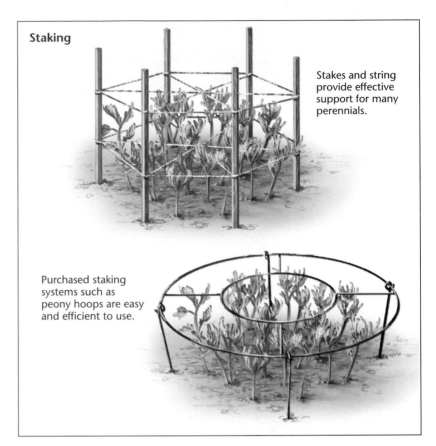

Staking

Stakes and string provide effective support for many perennials.

Purchased staking systems such as peony hoops are easy and efficient to use.

derweb-type pattern. Add another tier of string, if necessary, as the plant grows. As the plant's stems grow up through the string, the string that crosses the center will provide even support; if you'd simply supported the clump around the perimeter, all the stems would tend to flop to one side or the other, giving a lopsided look.

"Pea brush," "brushy twigs," and "pea stakes" are all terms used to describe another traditional staking method that works much the same way that stakes and string do. This method is generally better for smaller, lighter-weight plants such as catmint (*Nepeta* spp.) rather than for peonies, unless you have access to large brush. Cut well-branched twigs from shrubs, ideally with a fairly straight section at the bottom, and push them into the soil around the clumps. You can break the tips of the twigs and point them toward the center of the clump to provide added support. Keep in mind that twigs from some shrubs will root when stuck back in the garden. Try cutting them several weeks before you need them and leave them in the sun. Even then, watch for leaves or other evidence that you've accidentally added a shrub to your garden.

Several commercial staking systems are available, too — hoops, stakes that link together, and individual supports for flower stems. You may want to have a variety of options on hand — both traditional and commercial — so you can stake plants quickly and easily.

Starting Seeds. Late winter to midspring is the busiest time for most seed sowers, but you can sow seeds virtually anytime, depending on what you are growing. The benchmark most gardeners use is their last spring frost date. To find out the last frost date for your area, talk to gardening friends in your neighborhood, or ask at a local nursery or garden center. Once you know that date, mark it on your calendar, then count backward to determine your sowing dates—most sowing recommendations in this book are gauged from this date. Midsummer also is a great time to sow seeds of many perennials. In fact, for some, midsummer sowing is essential because the seeds must be sown as soon as they are ripe to ensure adequate germination. For example, spring-blooming wildflowers such as Virginia bluebells *(Mertensia virginica)* and bleeding hearts *(Dicentra* spp.) produce seeds that are quick to dry out, so you need to plant them as soon as they ripen in order to get good germination (usually the following spring). For other perennials, summer sowing gives you sturdy young plants that can stay outside through the winter and reach blooming size the following year. Some perennial, shrub, vine, and tree seeds germinate best when you sow them outdoors in fall, either in pots or in a nursery bed. If you've had poor results sowing these kinds of seed at other times of the year, try this treatment. Sowing outdoors in fall (and even into winter, if your seeds arrive late) provides the chilling period, or the periods of alternating warm and cold temperatures, that these seeds may need to start sprouting. You'll usually see seedlings emerge the following spring, although some seeds may take 2 or even 3 years to germinate.

Keep in mind that growing plants from seeds can give somewhat unpredictable results. Here's why: When you propagate a plant using a vegetative technique such as cuttings, division, or layering, you are making an exact duplicate, or clone, of the original plant. As a result, in nearly all cases the new plants will look exactly like the parent. With seeds, however, each new plant can look different, sometimes only slightly, sometimes considerably. Seed-grown plants that do resemble their parents are said to come true from seed. See the individual plant entries for indications of which cultivars will come true from seed; all species do.

To sow seeds indoors in containers, fill 2½- to 4-inch plastic pots with seed-starting mix. For best results, moisten the mix before filling the pots by pouring it into a large bucket or tub and adding warm water (start with a quart or so of water for a bucket, or a gallon for a large tub). Knead the mix with your hands to help it absorb the water. Keep adding water until the mix is evenly moist. When you squeeze a handful of mix, it should stay in a ball but then break apart easily if you tap it lightly. Fill each pot to overflowing, then press down the surface of the mix to firm it. The final surface of the mix should be ½ to ¼ inch below the top of the pot.

A few plants germinate more reliably if the seeds are scarified before they are sown—morning glories *(Ipomoea* spp.) and baptisias *(Baptisia* spp.) are examples. To scarify seeds, nick the seed coat gently with a razor blade or utility knife (don't damage the embryo inside). Another option is to rub the seeds on a piece of sandpaper or a nail file. Still another option is to soak the seeds in hot, but not boiling, water for 12 to 24 hours before sowing.

To sow, scatter the seeds evenly over the surface of the mix, or sow them in rows spaced about 1 inch apart. Large- and medium-size seeds are easy to handle with your fingers or with tweezers, or you can just snip off one corner of the seed packet and tap them out individually. Don't sow too thickly: overcrowded seedlings won't be as healthy as ones sown at the proper spacing, and thinning is a tedious task. Even properly spaced seedlings will need thinning, and adequate spacing makes this easier. As a general rule, cover seeds with a layer of mix that's about two to three times the thickness of the seed. Don't cover very small seeds; just press them into the surface of the mix.

Very small or dustlike seeds that are sown on the surface of the medium take some special handling. They are best germinated inside a plastic bag or other container to keep them constantly moist. Because high humidity encourages mold to form, sterilize the medium before sowing. To do this, just before sowing pour boiling water over the medium, and allow excess water to drain. Then let the soil cool for a few minutes before sowing your seeds. To sow, crease an index card lengthwise, pour the seeds onto the card, and tap the card lightly with your finger to scatter them over the mix. Then use your fingers to lightly press the seeds into the surface. Place the pot in the bag, and close the bag loosely. Bagged pots can sit under fluorescent lights for months without additional watering because the bag holds in moisture and keeps the humidity high around the seeds. Once seedlings have germinated, expose them gradually to the outside world. Open the top of the bag for an hour or two one day and for a few more hours the next. Then remove it and begin watering and fertilizing as usual.

Label each pot with the name of the seed and the sowing date. If you've moistened the mix well before sowing, many seeds will germinate before they need additional water. You can help keep the seeds moist by covering the containers with sheets of clear plastic suspended on a wire frame or with molded plastic "domes" sold for this purpose. Don't put covered containers in direct sunlight, as temperatures inside can quickly heat up enough to kill the seeds or emerging seedlings. Instead, set them under fluorescent lights. Remove the coverings once the seedlings emerge.

The seeds of a few perennials benefit from a brief chilling period before they're germinated — you'll find recommendations in the individual plant entries. Sow them in pots, place each pot in a plastic bag, close the bag loosely, and set it in the refrigerator for the recommended amount of time. After that, germinate them at the recommended temperature.

Check the mix in uncovered containers several times a day, and never let it dry out. When you need to water, set the pots in a pan filled with an inch or so of room-temperature or warmer water; capillary action will draw the water up through the mix. When the surface of the mix looks moist (usually within 10 to 20 minutes), remove each pot and let it drain. This system also works well for watering seedlings; just allow the top of the mix to dry slightly between soakings. Watering from below avoids washing the seeds out of the pots and also helps prevent diseases such as damping off.

Outdoor sowing in pots is a good option for many hardy perennials. Sow them just as you would pots to be germinated indoors, then top off the pots with a 1/4- to 1/2-inch layer of fine, washed gravel; the small pebbles sold for use in aquariums usually work well. This layer keeps the mix from drying out quickly, and it also helps prevent mosses from developing and smothering your seedlings. Also add a plastic label (wooden ones can rot quickly) marked with the seed name and sowing date. Set the pots in a cold frame, or sink them to their rims in a nursery bed or a protected spot in the garden. It's advisable to cover them with a piece of fine-mesh hardware cloth to keep mice and other animals from digging in the pots. Natural rainfall will take care of most of the watering, but you will need to water during dry spells. While some perennials will germinate in a few weeks, it may take months for others to appear.

Once your seedlings emerge, remove any covers to allow good air circulation, and give them plenty of light. Most seedlings will need transplanting only once before you move them out into the garden. When the first pair of true leaves have developed (after the first "seed" leaves), you can transplant indoor- or outdoor-grown

Starting Seeds

Spread seeds out over sowing medium to prevent overcrowding.

For outdoor sowing, mulch pots with fine gravel.

Outdoors, sink pots to the rim in soil or set in a protected location.

Indoors, cover pots with plastic to ensure high humidity.

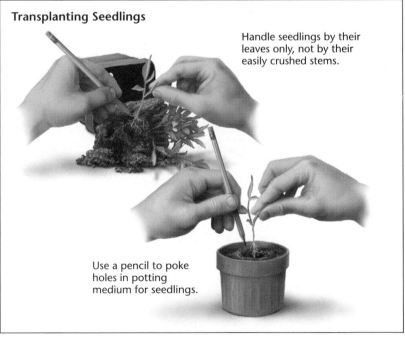

Transplanting Seedlings

Handle seedlings by their leaves only, not by their easily crushed stems.

Use a pencil to poke holes in potting medium for seedlings.

seedlings into individual 2- to 4-inch pots. Use a growing medium that's somewhat coarser — with more perlite and/or vermiculite — than the seed-starting mix. Moisten the growing mix before transplanting, as you did before sowing.

Several hours before transplanting, water the seedlings well. When you are ready to transplant, fill the new containers with moistened mix to within ¼ inch of the top. Next, carefully turn the pot of seedlings on its side, and tip the whole clump of seedlings and roots into one hand while you pull off the pot with your other hand. Lay the clump on its side on your work surface. Holding one seedling by a leaf (not the stem), use a pencil or a plant label to separate its roots from the others. Then use the pencil or plant label to make a hole in the center of the new container. The hole should be just deep enough to accommodate the roots without bending them. Lower the seedling into the hole, so the point where the roots join the stem is even with the top of the growing mix. Use the pencil or plant label to gently push the moist mix around the roots until the mix supports the seedling when you let go of its leaf. Don't press the soil down around the seedling; just lightly tap the bottom of the pot once or twice on your work surface to settle the mix around the roots. Add a little more mix, if needed, to support the seedling. Water as soon as possible after transplanting.

Continue watering indoor pots from below, but let the surface of the mix dry out a bit between waterings. Water outdoor pots from above as needed to keep the mix evenly moist.

Start fertilizing your seedlings once they have developed their first pair of true leaves. Use a liquid houseplant fertilizer, diluted to half its regular strength. Feed once a week for 3 to 4 weeks. After that, use the fertilizer full strength every 10 to 14 days until the seedlings are ready for transplanting into the garden.

Many plants—especially annuals such as spider flowers (*Cleome* spp.) and pot marigolds (*Calendula officinalis*)—do just fine if sown outdoors in the garden where the plants are to grow. Prepare the soil on or before the recommended sowing date. (You'll find germination recommendations in the individual entries.) Spread 1 to 2 inches of compost over the bed and work it into the top 8 to 10 inches of soil. Then use a garden rake to level and smooth the surface and to break up soil clumps. Broadcast the seeds thinly over the surface and cover them with the recommended amount of soil. Keep the seedbed moist—sprinkling daily if necessary—until seedlings appear. Thin seedlings to about 2 inches apart when they are an inch or so tall by snipping off unwanted seedlings with scissors at ground level. About 3 weeks later, thin them again to their final spacing.

Transplanting. Cool, cloudy or even rainy weather is the best time to transplant seedlings to the garden or to move plants from one place to another. To transplant a pot-grown plant, dig a hole large enough to accommodate the roots, tip the plant out of its pot, set it in place, and firm the soil over the root ball. If the plant has roots that wind around the inside of the pot, use a knife to score them on each side. This may seem harsh, but it encourages the roots to extend out into the surrounding soil.

If you're moving a plant from one place to another, dig the clump up with a spade or a garden fork. To minimize damage to the roots, start digging about 6 inches or so from the outside edge of the clump. Dig all the way around it and lift the plant out of the hole. Then dig another hole in its new location and plop it in place. You can transplant most plants from one place to another in the garden anytime the soil can be worked. Don't try it with plants described as difficult to divide, however.

Either way, be sure to set the plant at the same depth at which it was growing, unless the crown had pushed itself out of the soil, in which case you'll want to settle it a bit deeper. Water each new transplant with a weak solution of compost or manure tea as you set it in the soil. If the weather promises to be cloudy for a few days, you're all finished. If it's going to be sunny, shade the plants by propping burlap or bushel baskets over them for a few days.

Watering. Watering is a fairly simple, straightforward task, but you'll grow a healthier, more trouble-free garden if you observe two basic rules. The first is, when you need to water, water deeply. Moisten at least the top 6 inches of soil. This encourages plants to develop deep roots and improves drought tolerance. The second rule is to put the water directly on the soil rather than up in the air. Lawn sprinklers can cover large areas, but much of the water evaporates before it can hit the ground. Water on the foliage—especially if you water late in the day and the plants are wet overnight—can lead to foliar diseases. Soaker hoses are a very efficient way to water. You can spread them each time you need to water, or install them at the beginning of the season and cover them up with mulch. Keep the end exposed so it's easy to connect them up to the water supply when you need to.

Problems & Solutions Guide

INSECTS, ARACHNIDS, AND MOLLUSKS

Aphids

Description: Adults and nymphs are tiny green, black, brown, or reddish, pear-shaped, soft-bodied insects. Some have wings. Look for these pests in clusters on buds, shoots, and undersides of leaves.

Damage: Aphids suck plant juices, causing stunted or deformed blooms and leaves. In addition, they exude a sticky substance called honeydew, which produces a shiny coating on leaves and supports the growth of black sooty mold fungus. Aphids may also transmit plant viruses.

Control: Encourage or introduce natural predators, including lacewings and ladybugs. Pinch off and destroy infested plant parts, or knock the pests off plants with a strong spray of water. Spray serious infestations with insecticidal soap or pyrethrins.

Beetles

Description: Beetles are hard-shelled, oval to oblong insects. Some are beneficial in the garden, others are troublesome pests. Among the most common pest species are Japanese beetles and rose chafers. Adult Japanese beetles are metallic-looking green insects with coppery brown wings; the larvae are brown-headed, white grubs. Rose chafers, also known as rose bugs or rose beetles, have reddish brown bodies and long legs; the larvae are small white grubs.

Damage: Pest beetles chew holes in leaves, stems, and flowers during the growing season. The larvae of some kinds feed on roots.

Control: Handpick adult beetles early in the morning and drop them into a container of soapy water. Apply parasitic nematodes to the soil to control grubs. You can also apply spores of milky disease to lawns to control Japanese beetle grubs. Treat seriously infested plants with neem, pyrethrins, or rotenone.

Borers

Description: Borers are the wormlike larvae of moths or beetles that tunnel into leaves, stalks, branches, or trunks and feed inside the plant.

Damage: Small holes, often close to the ground, with gummy, sawdustlike material around or just below them indicate borer infestation. Plants that wilt even when the soil is moist are displaying another common symptom. Affected plants are weakened or killed. A slimy bacterial rot often follows iris borer feeding in iris rhizomes.

Control: If possible, dig out and destroy borers. On trees and shrubs, inserting a flexible wire into the entrance hole may impale and kill the borer. Injecting parasitic nematodes into borer holes may also help. Dig up iris rhizomes and destroy infested leaves and stems. Avoid damaging tree and shrub stems with lawn-care equipment; wounds provide easy access for borers.

Caterpillars

Description: Caterpillars are soft-bodied, wormlike creatures with several pairs of legs. Their bodies may be smooth, hairy, or spiny. Adults are moths or butterflies.

Damage: Caterpillars chew holes in leaves, flowers, fruit, and shoots throughout the growing season.

Control: Handpick and destroy caterpillars. (Wear gloves to prevent possible skin irritation.) Or move them to other plants—many caterpillars are the larvae of butterflies that most gardeners welcome to their gardens. The larvae of swallowtail butterflies, for example, feed on parsley, dill, and other related plants.

Cutworms

Description: Cutworms are plump, smooth, brown, gray, or green, 1-inch caterpillars. They curl up when disturbed. Adults are brown or grayish moths.

Damage: Cutworms chew through the stems of seedlings and transplants near the soil line. The larvae are active only at night and are most troublesome in spring.

Control: Prevent damage by surrounding stems with cardboard collars extending 2 inches above and below the soil line. Handpick larvae. Apply parasitic nematodes to the soil around the base of young plants.

Lace Bugs

Description: Lace bugs are small, flat, square insects with lacy, transparent wings. Larvae are tiny, wingless, and spiny.

Damage: Adults and larvae feed on the undersides of leaves through much of the growing season, sucking plant juices and producing a yellow

Aphid
(actual size)

Japanese Beetle

(actual size)

Cutworm

(actual size)

Lace Bug

(actual size)

or whitish stippling. Infested leaves turn lighter in color, then may curl, turn brown, and drop. Lace bugs are a common problem on azaleas grown in full sun. These pests also attack many other vegetables, flowers, and shrubs.

Control: Spray leaves thoroughly with insecticidal soap or neem. Treat serious infestations with pyrethrins or rotenone.

Leafhoppers

Leafhopper

(actual size)

Description: Adult leafhoppers are small, greenish, wedge-shaped, soft-bodied insects that hop quickly when disturbed. Nymphs look similar to the adults but lack wings.

Damage: Adults and nymphs feed on stems and the undersides of leaves. They suck plant juices, causing discoloration and stunted or distorted growth. The tips and sides of affected leaves may turn yellow or brown and curl upward. As they feed, leafhoppers exude a sticky honeydew on leaves and fruit. These pests may also transmit plant diseases.

Control: Use a strong spray of water to wash nymphs off plants. Spray serious infestations with insecticidal soap or pyrethrins; use rotenone or sabadilla as a last resort.

Leaf Miners

Tarnished Plant Bug

(actual size)

Description: Leaf miners are small, pale, worm-like creatures found within leaves. Adults may be tiny, black or black-and-yellow flies or black, thick-bodied wasps.

Damage: Larvae feed between the upper and lower leaf surfaces through the growing season, producing papery blotches or meandering tunnels. The damaged areas may be yellow or brown. Infested leaves may drop. This is a common pest of columbines (*Aquilegia* spp.).

Control: If you see just one or two damaged spots on a leaf, cut out the damage with scissors. Remove and destroy badly infested leaves.

Mites

Mite

(actual size)

Description: Adult mites are very tiny, golden, red, or brown spiderlike pests. Some mites spin fine webs around leaves or between leaves and stems.

Damage: Mites suck plant juices from leaves, producing a light-colored stippling on leaf surfaces. Whole leaves become pale and dry and may drop. Seriously infested plants may have webbing and exhibit stunted growth.

Control: Rinsing or spraying leaves frequently with water can suppress mite populations. Pollen- and nectar-rich plants attract natural predators, such as ladybugs and lacewings. Spray serious infestations with insecticidal soap, superior oil, neem, or pyrethrins.

Plant Bugs

Description: Adult plant bugs are fast-moving, oblong, flattened insects, $1/4$ to $1/3$ inch long. Four-lined plant bugs are greenish yellow and have four black stripes on the back. The wingless nymphs are reddish with black dots. Tarnished plant bugs are greenish to brownish and have brown or black mottling on the back. Nymphs are smaller and pale yellow with black dots; they lack wings.

Damage: Plant bugs suck plant juices, causing sunken, brown or black spots on leaves and deformed leaves, buds, and shoots. They may also feed on fruit, producing scarring, swellings or depressions, and distorted growth. Plant bugs are active through spring and summer.

Control: Handpick adults and nymphs in early morning (while they are still sluggish) and drop them in a container of soapy water. Grow pollen- and nectar-rich plants to attract natural predators. Treat serious infestations with neem, sabadilla, or rotenone. To prevent damage to future crops, clean up garden debris in fall and spring to remove overwintering sites for adults.

Slugs and Snails

Description: Adults are gray, tan, or black, slimy, soft-bodied mollusks. Snails have a hard outer shell and may be up to $1\frac{1}{2}$ inches long. Slugs lack shells; they may be $1/8$ inch to 6 inches or more in length. Both slugs and snails leave slime trails on leaves. Slugs are usually most active at night and in damp places; snails are less dependent on moisture.

Damage: Slugs and snails rasp large holes in leaves, stems, and fruit; they may completely devour seedlings.

Control: Trap slugs and snails under fruit rinds, cabbage leaves, or boards set on the soil, or in shallow pans of beer set into the soil surface; check traps daily and destroy pests. If slugs or snails are a major problem in your garden, eliminate mulches and garden debris; these materials provide ideal hiding places. Use barriers of copper screen or sheeting to repel slugs and snails. Plant ground covers to attract ground beetles and other predators.

Thrips

Description: Adults are tiny, slender, brown, yellow, or black insects with narrow fringed wings. Nymphs are similar but wingless and even smaller.

Damage: Adults and nymphs feed on leaves, flowers, buds, and stems, causing browning and white flecking and deforming flowers, buds, and leaves.

Control: Remove and destroy infested flowers

and buds. Spray with insecticidal soap or superior oil, or dust with diatomaceous earth in the evening; treat serious infestations with pyrethrins.

Weevils

Description: Adult weevils are small, hard-shelled beetles with long snouts; they are usually $1/8$ to $1/4$ inch long and tend to be most active at night. Larvae are plump, whitish, dark-headed, legless grubs.

Damage: Adult weevils chew notches in leaves, stems, and buds in summer; larvae tunnel and feed in roots or seeds in fall and spring. Notches on the edges of rhododendron leaves are a common sign that adult weevils are at work, while wilted or stunted growth is a sign of larvae feeding in roots of the plants.

Control: Drench the soil around plants with parasitic nematodes to control larvae. Handpick adults, or treat serious infestations by dusting plants with pyrethrins or rotenone in the evening.

Whiteflies

Description: Adults are tiny flies with white, powdery wings. They cluster on the undersides of leaves and fly up in great numbers when disturbed. Larvae are tiny and flattened.

Damage: Adults and nymphs suck plant juices through the season outdoors and all year indoors. Infested plants look yellow, sickly, and stunted. As they feed, whiteflies exude a sticky honeydew that supports the growth of black sooty mold.

Control: Indoors, catch whiteflies on sticky yellow cards or use a handheld vacuum to suck pests off plants. Spray serious infestations with insecticidal soap, superior oil, pyrethrins, or rotenone.

ANIMAL PESTS

Animals such as deer, rabbits, and chipmunks can be among the most damaging and frustrating pests that visit your garden. Fencing is the only surefire way to keep out pests such as deer, and an 8-foot-tall fence provides an effective barrier. Deer are less likely to jump a solid wooden fence that they can't see over. Another option is to protect individual plants—chicken-wire cages are easy to make in any size you need. Just cut a piece of chicken wire (hardware cloth also works) long enough to make a cage around the clump, and bend over and intertwine the ends of each piece to form the cage. For small plants, fasten the top edges of the cage together; for larger ones, fasten a second piece of chicken wire over the top (so the deer can't reach the plants from the top). Use bent pieces of wire or short stakes

to hold the cages in place. Gardeners report mixed results with repellents such as soap bars or bags of human hair hung at intervals. Repellent sprays, both commercial and homemade, can also be effective, but if the deer are hungry enough, they'll ignore repellents. To make a homemade repellent, mix 5 eggs in 5 quarts of water and spray it on plants that need to be protected. Reapply the spray after a rain. Hot sauce, garlic, and blood meal are other repellents you can try.

A chicken-wire fence will likewise keep out rabbits and groundhogs. For extra protection, dig a 6-inch-deep trench around the garden and line it with chicken wire as well. The repellents used for deer also work for these pests, in addition to various rodents. Use floating row covers over seedlings and new transplants to keep pests at bay until the plants are established. To discourage mice and voles from making a home in your beds and dining on plant roots and crowns over winter, avoid applying winter mulches until the ground has frozen.

DISEASES

Canker

Description: Fungal and bacterial cankers produce discolored spots and dead areas on stems of many trees and shrubs. Affected areas may be covered with small black spores or ooze a slimy or gummy material; the slime or gum may smell sour if bacteria have caused the canker. Shoot tips may turn yellow, wilt, and die.

Control: During dry weather, cut off infected parts at least 2 inches below the affected area. Disinfect pruners after each cut by dipping them in a bleach solution (one part bleach to nine parts water). Remove and destroy severely diseased plants. To prevent future cankers, avoid wounding bark with pruning or lawn-care tools.

Damping Off

Description: Damping-off fungi may attack seeds before they even sprout, causing them to turn brown and mushy. Infected seedlings rot at the soil line and fall over.

Control: Moving pots or trays to a warm, dry place may stop the spread of the disease. However, the best control is prevention. Start seeds in a disease-free medium, such as vermiculite or sterilized seed-starting mix. Sow thinly to avoid overcrowding. Sprinkle a light layer of milled sphagnum moss over sown seeds. Provide seedlings with good air circulation. Water pots from below (by setting them in trays of water until the mix is moist) to avoid wetting the surface of the medium.

Thrip damage

Black vine weevil

(actual size)

Whiteflies

(actual size)

Canker

Leaf Scorch

Leaf Spots

Mildew

Rust

Viruses

Gray Mold

Description: This fungal disease, also known as botrytis blight, produces gray-brown spots or streaks on leaves, buds, and flowers. A woolly fungal growth may be visible in the spots. Affected parts may turn brown and wither.

Control: Remove and destroy infected plant parts. Thin crowded stems and space new plants properly for good air circulation.

Leaf Scorch

Description: Plants growing in dry, hot sites, especially those exposed to heat reflected from walls and paving, may develop leaves with yellow edges that turn brown and crispy; they may also roll inward. Leaves or whole plants may wilt. Affected plants have stunted growth.

Control: This cultural problem is due to drought and excessive heat. To minimize damage, water susceptible plants regularly to maintain soil moisture. Mulches will also help to keep the soil moist and cool. When planting hot, dry sites, look for plants that are naturally adapted to those conditions. Work plenty of organic matter into the soil before planting.

Leaf Spots

Description: Fungal and bacterial leaf spots can vary widely in appearance. Anthracnose produces dark, sunken lesions, often with pinkish spore masses. Bacterial spot leads to small, circular, light green spots that later turn brown; there may be angular, purplish areas around the spots. These and other leaf-spot diseases may also produce sunken lesions on stems, stunted growth, and spotted or deformed fruit.

Control: Pinch off and destroy infected parts. Clean up dropped leaves. Applying a sulfur- or copper-based fungicide every 7 to 10 days may prevent the spread of fungal leaf spots. Destroy severely infected plants. Prevent problems by growing resistant cultivars and by spacing and pruning for good air circulation.

Mildew

Description: Powdery mildew and downy mildew are fungal diseases that produce white to gray patches on plant leaves, stems, buds, and flowers. Downy mildew also produces light green patches on upper leaf surfaces or cottony, purplish lesions on leaves and stems. Mildew-infected leaves may be distorted and drop early. Fruit may be dwarfed and russeted or distorted.

Control: Remove infected leaves. Thin crowded stems to improve air circulation. Spray with a sulfur- or copper-based fungicide every 7 to 10 days. Destroy seriously infected plants. To prevent damage, grow resistant cultivars, space plants properly, avoid overhead watering, and avoid handling wet plants. Keeping the soil evenly moist, to prevent plants from wilting, also helps prevent powdery mildew.

Rots

Description: Fungal and bacterial rots cause wilted, off-color plants. Roots of affected plants are dark and dry or mushy, rather than firm and white.

Control: Remove and destroy affected plants. Improve soil drainage. Wait until the soil is warm to set out transplants. Set plants so the crown is slightly higher than the surrounding soil. Mulch to prevent root damage from cultivation.

Rust

Description: This fungal disease produces whitish or yellowish spots on the tops of leaves. Powdery, yellow to orange spots appear on the undersides of leaves or on stems. Infected leaves turn yellow, dry up, and drop early. Roses, hollyhocks (*Alcea* spp.), and snapdragons (*Antirrhinum* spp.) are commonly attacked by rust.

Control: Remove and destroy infected leaves. Dust with sulfur every 7 to 10 days until the disease is controlled. Clean up and discard plant debris in fall. To prevent problems, grow resistant cultivars. Mulch plants and use drip irrigation to keep leaves dry.

Viruses

Description: Viruses produce crinkled, deformed leaves, often with yellow-green mottling. Plants are stunted or unusually bushy and often do not set fruit.

Control: There is no cure for viruses; remove and destroy infected plants. Rinse hands and tools with milk after handling virus-infected plants to reduce the chance of spreading viruses to your remaining plants.

Photo Credits

Karen Bussolini: 17 bottom, 30 bottom, 47 top, 59 bottom, 69 left, 95, 125, 188 top right, 194 right, 201, 242 top, 243 top, 244, 256–257, 281 top left, 281 top right, 283, 284, 290, 302 top left, 307 top, 308 bottom

David Cavagnaro: 27 top right, 28 top left, 28 bottom, 38 top left, 47 bottom, 50 top, 65 right, 66 top, 68 bottom, 86 top, 89 top, 93, 97 bottom, 111 bottom, 138, 191 top left, 204 right, 245, 256 left, 262, 273 top, 278 right, 305 left, 306 bottom

R. Todd Davis: 42 bottom left, 130–131, 163 bottom, 291 left

Barbara Ellis: 5 top, 7 bottom, 22, 27 top left, 32 top left, 32 bottom right, 43, 49 right, 53, 58 top left, 59 top, 62 right, 80 bottom, 82 right, 87, 102 right, 105 right, 108 bottom, 109, 113, 123 right, 126, 129 top, 133 bottom, 134 top, 137 top left, 139, 144 top, 144 bottom, 158 bottom, 161, 162, 163 top, 174 left, 176 top left, 202, 214 bottom, 217 bottom, 222 top, 223, 225 bottom, 226 bottom, 228 bottom, 229 left, 234 top, 271 left, 272 middle left, 272 bottom left, 296, 303 bottom, 307 bottom

Derek Fell: 7 top, 10 right, 15, 17 top right, 25 top, 33, 35, 70, 74 top, 75 right, 76, 85 bottom, 89 bottom, 90 top, 101, 102 left, 106 left, 112, 120, 122–123, 132 top, 140, 143, 148 top, 167, 171 top, 176–177, 178–179, 179 right, 191 bottom, 200, 217 top, 218 left, 218 right, 221 bottom left, 222 bottom, 225 top, 235 top right, 249 top, 273 bottom, 279 right, 280 top, 282 right, 292 right

Deborah Fillion: i, viii second from bottom, 5 bottom, 6, 13 right, 20 top, 20 bottom, 23 right, 24 top, 24 bottom, 25 bottom, 26 top, 26 bottom, 73 right, 78 top, 83 top, 85 top, 96 top, 99 top, 129 bottom, 132 bottom, 133 top, 134 bottom, 136 bottom, 141 top, 154, 155 bottom, 157 top, 198, 280 bottom, 303 top, 304 top, 304 bottom

Charles Marden Fitch: 3 bottom, 8, 12 top, 19, 21, 29 top, 32 middle left, 37 top, 37 bottom, 38 bottom left, 57, 60 bottom, 63 top, 63 bottom, 75 left, 81 right, 82 left, 83 bottom, 84, 86 bottom, 91, 92, 97 middle, 98, 104–105, 106-107, 107 right, 108 top, 111 top, 118 right, 119, 124, 130 top left, 130 bottom, 146 left, 150, 155 right, 160 left, 165, 168 left, 181 bottom, 190 top left, 190 top right, 191 top right, 195 top, 195 bottom, 210 right, 211 left, 221 top left, 228 top, 231 bottom, 233 top, 235 bottom right, 236, 238, 247, 248, 252 top, 252 bottom, 253 bottom, 258 left, 263 bottom, 267 right, 272 top left, 285, 295 top, 295 bottom, 297 right

Marge Garfield: 151, 206, 246

Harry Haralambou/Positive Images: 94

Jerry Howard/Positive Images: 188 top left, 263 top, 282 left

Dency Kane: 40 right, 96 bottom, 121 top, 121 bottom, 194 left, 241 top, 242 bottom, 255 right, 258–259, 265 second from top

Lee Lockwood/Positive Images: 237

Charles Mann: 1, 2, 9, 13 left, 22–23, 32 bottom left, 44, 49 left, 50 bottom, 51, 58 right, 62 top left, 67 top, 80–81, 90 bottom, 116, 128, 141 bottom, 142, 152, 157 bottom, 158 top, 159, 160 right, 171 bottom, 175 bottom right, 186, 187, 203, 205, 207, 220, 225 middle, 226 top, 227 top, 229 right, 231 top, 232, 235 bottom left, 270, 286, 297 left, 301 right, 302 bottom

Rick Mastelli: ii–iii, v, vi top, vi bottom, vi–vii, vii top right, vii middle right, vii bottom, viii top, viii second from top, viii bottom, ix, 4, 52, 54, 68 top, 79 right, 88 top, 88 bottom, 97 top, 100 top, 100 bottom, 110, 115, 117 left, 118 left, 135 bottom, 137 top right, 153, 170, 172, 174–175, 177 top right, 177 bottom right, 181 top, 190 bottom, 192, 197, 204 left, 214 top, 215, 216, 219 top, 219 bottom, 224 middle, 224 bottom, 227 bottom, 239 left, 259 right, 261, 264, 265 top, 265 second from bottom, 265 bottom, 266, 268, 274, 277 right, 294 top, 298 top, 298 bottom, 301 left, 305 right, 309

Nancy Ondra: 10 left, 99 bottom, 117 right, 131 top right, 180 left, 253 top

Jerry Pavia: 3 top, 11, 12 bottom, 14 top, 14 bottom, 16 left, 16–17, 17 middle right, 18 bottom, 27 middle left, 27 middle right, 27 bottom, 28 top right, 29 bottom, 30 top, 31 left, 31 right, 32 top right, 34, 36, 38 right, 39, 40 left, 41, 42 top left, 42 right, 45, 48, 55, 58 bottom left, 60 top, 61, 62 bottom left, 64, 65 left, 66 bottom, 67 bottom, 69 right, 71, 72, 73 left, 74 bottom, 77 left, 77 right, 78–79, 80 top left, 103, 131 bottom, 135 top, 136 top, 137 bottom, 146 right, 147 top, 147 bottom, 148 bottom, 149, 155 left, 156, 164, 168–169, 169 right, 175 top right, 176 bottom, 178 left, 180 right, 183 right, 184, 185, 188 bottom, 189, 193, 196, 199 left, 199 right, 208, 209 top, 209 bottom, 210 left, 211 right, 213, 221 right, 224 top, 230, 233 bottom, 234 bottom, 235 top left, 239 right, 240, 241 bottom, 243 bottom, 249 bottom, 251, 254, 255 left, 257 top right, 257 bottom, 260, 269 top, 269 bottom, 271 right, 272 right, 279 left, 281 bottom, 287 top, 287 bottom, 289 top left, 289 top right, 289 bottom, 291 right, 292 left, 293 top, 293 bottom, 294 bottom, 302 top right, 306 top

Ben Phillips/Positive Images: 277 left, 278 left, 308 top

Albert Squillace/Positive Images: 122 left, 267 left

Index

Page numbers in italics refer to illustrations.